To Ida

Nov 20/ 94

with much love

on your 17th
birthday

Elizabeth
(Densmore)

STAGE PEOPLE

This book is for
Anna Lewis

Endlich! Endlich!
Leben! O Leben –
süsses Leben
meinem Tristan neu gegeben!

STAGE PEOPLE

ROGER LEWIS

WEIDENFELD AND NICOLSON
LONDON

Contents

'Actors are not animals, they're human beings.'
'They are? Have you ever tried eating with one?'
Mel Brooks, *The Producers*

'Apes are apes, though clothed in scarlet.'
Ben Jonson, *The Poetaster*

'Leave thy damnable faces and begin.'
William Shakespeare, *Hamlet*

'The appearance of a player, with whom I have
drunk tea, counteracts the imagination that he is the
character he represents. Nay, you know, nobody
imagines that he is the character he represents. They
say "See Garrick! how he looks to-night! See how
he'll clutch the dagger!" That is the buzz of the
theatre.'
Samuel Johnson, quoted by Boswell in *A Journal of a
Tour to the Hebrides*

Acknowledgements

'A great actor,' says Diderot in *The Paradox of Acting*, 'is neither a pianoforte, nor a harp, nor a spinet, nor a violin, nor a violincello; he has no key peculiar to him; he takes the key and tone fit for his part of the score, and he can take up any. I put a high value on the talent of a great actor; he is a rare being – as rare as, and perhaps greater than, a poet.' Concurring with this estimation, my biggest debt is to the actors, to start with. The ones included in this book, plus those I met and interviewed during the preparatory field-work: Jim Broadbent, Sinead Cusack, Jeremy Irons, Bob Peck, Roger Rees, Mark Rylance, Fiona Shaw, Juliet Stevenson and Imogen Stubbs.

The invitation to write a comedy about acting, anthropologizing in my own manner, came from John Curtis in the autumn of 1985. I'm obliged to him for his encouragement, and for disregarding this comment of Hazlitt's: 'You might as rationally set a scholar or a clown on a tight-rope and expect them to dance gracefully and with every appearance of ease, as introduce either into the gay, laughing circle, and suppose that he will acquit himself handsomely and come off with applause in the retailing of anecdote or the interchange of repartee' ('The Shyness of Scholars,' *The New Monthly Magazine*, December 1827). John Curtis was succeeded at Weidenfeld by Alex MacCormick, who was generous with her praise; when she left to join Ebury Press, their gain might have been my loss – but for the excellent advice and patient editing I have received from the sharp pencils of David Roberts and Martin Corteel.

Chief intercessor has been my agent and champion, Leslie Gardner, who garnered the time and money without which this book wouldn't yet be entire.

S. J. Masty gave stalwart pluck and dash. I read him several chapters from an early draft on Christmas Day 1986, clutching a paper-knife and doing a fair impersonation of Dickens's 'Death of Nancy'. Dr Masty subsequently wrote from his home in Peshawar, 'the thing sang like Welsh breezes and roared like wild beasts'.

In Oxford I'm beholden to the lively interest and enlightenment of John Bayley and Iris Murdoch; Bernard Richards; Stephen Wall; and Lyndall Gordon, who kindly read my pages on her countryman Antony Sher's novel *Middlepost*.

The book was written whilst I was a Junior Research Fellow at Wolfson College, and much of it was composed on the premises, in a room Richard Ellmann lent me when he was dying. Ellmann superintended the formulation of the opus, and from his teaching I derived two cardinal rules: (a) facts don't speak for themselves; (b) there is no excuse for an uninteresting sentence.

John le Carré, whose novels of espionage I found usefully to be about the arts of acting, was a considerate correspondent. I'm grateful for his permission to make quotations from a private letter in Chapter 3.

The National Theatre and the Royal Shakespeare Company furnished me with press facilities for many of their productions; Enterprise Pictures Limited, Gillian Altman of Columbia Pictures, and Sandra Bradley and Christine Edzard of Sands Films, provided stills and background information for my examination.

Suzanne Anderson deciphered the calligraphic fretwork which constituted my copy text, typing and re-typing from successive drafts during the Spring of 1988.

For other and sundry favours I wish to thank Michael Blakemore, Siobhan Bracke, Alan Brissenden, Peter Carter-Ruck & Associates, Jefferson Clode, Trevor Easterbrook, Helene Hanff, David Harries, Ronald Hayman, Charles Hopkins (Curator of the Film and Television Archive, University of California, Los Angeles), Sheridan Morley, Michael Redington, Ned Sherrin, Briar Silich, Beryl Stevens, Keith Waterhouse, Mark Waters and Roger Witts.

Of the books and articles open on my desk, involving me in thinking about theatre, and showing me up, I acknowledge debts to the following: Noel Annan, 'Et Tu, Anthony,' *New York Review of Books* (October 22, 1987); John Bayley, *The Order of Battle at Trafalgar*; Joseph Brodsky, 'A Cambridge Education,' *Times Literary Supplement* (January 30, 1987); Vincent Cheng, *Shakespeare and Joyce*; Toby Cole and Helen Krich Chinoy (editors), *Actors on Acting*; Guy Davenport, *The Geography of the Imagination* and *Paideuma*, Volume 7 number 3 (Winter, 1978), where the baroque fiddle is adduced as the music of Louis Zukovsky's thought, pre-empting my ideas on Sherlock Holmes; Umberto Eco, *Faith in Fakes*; Allen Eyles, *Sherlock Holmes: A Centenary Celebration*; Peter Hall, *Diaries*; Hugh Kenner, *The Counterfeiters* and *The Mechanic Muse*; Robin Lane Fox, *Pagans and Christians*; Claude Lèvi-Strauss, *L'Origine des manières de table*, in a translation by John and Doreen Weightman; John Hope Mason, *The Irresistible Diderot*; Jonathan Miller, *Subsequent Performances*; Sheridan Morley, *The Great Stage Stars*; Rodney Needham, *Exemplars*; Garry

O'Connor, *Olivier: A Celebration*; Laurence Olivier, *On Acting*; Ronald Paulson, *A Literary Landscape* and *Book and Painting*; Andrew Porter, 'Guiseppe Verdi,' *The New Grove*; Nicholas Powell, *Fuseli: The Nightmare*; Susan Sontag, *Against Interpretation*; Donald Spoto, *The Life of Alfred Hitchcock*; Tate Gallery exhibition catalogue, *Henry Fuseli 1741–1825* (1975); Kenneth Tynan, *Bull Fever, A View of the English Stage* and *The Sound of Two Hands Clapping*.

The author and publisher gratefully acknowledge permission from Faber & Faber Ltd to quote in Chapter One lines by T. S. Eliot from both *Collected Poems 1909–1962* and *Collected Plays*.

ROGER LEWIS
Wolfson College, Oxford, and
the Algonquin Hotel, New York, 1988.

PICTURE ACKNOWLEDGEMENTS

The Publishers are grateful to the following for permission to reproduce the following photographs: BBC Enterprises 8; British Library 7 (top); DACS 1989 7 (below); Guy Davenport 4 (top); Herbi Knott 3; Kobal Collection 2 (below), 5 (top and below); Mike Laye 1; Roger Lewis 4 (below); John Stoddart 6; Weidenfeld Archive 2 (top).

Introduction

'Players, sir! I look upon them as no better than creatures set upon tables and joint-stools to make faces and produce laughter.'
Samuel Johnson, 1775

From Sophocles to Plautus, from the Mysteries to Marlowe, from Kyd to Shakespeare, from Webster to Ford, from Jonson to Etherege, from Congreve to Goldsmith, from Sheridan to Pinero, from Wilde to Shaw, from Ibsen to Synge, from O'Casey to O'Neill, from Beckett to Pinter, from Osborne to Bond, from Brenton to Hare, from Berkoff to Jarman: drama is a living thing, a volatile organism, splitting, fusing, mating, re-ordering itself into new alliances, new kinships. This book celebrates the diversities of the form – the theatricality of theatre, the playfulness of plays – by regarding those who make up and transfigure the content, those who convert scripts into the possibilities of performance: the actors.

And I find I've been writing at a time when actors are re-emerging as pre-eminent; they're no longer allowing themselves to be sheepish and deferential – towards writers or directors or their public. Kenneth Branagh's Renaissance Theatre revives the idea of the actor-manager, reminding us all of the days when Olivier heroically hatched the Old Vic and prophesied the National. Simon Callow has published at length on the intellectual nature of acting; he sees stage people as being more than capable of organizing their own destiny. Antony Sher follows successful ancillary careers as a novelist and painter (*are* they ancillary? we shall see). He proves that an actor has an eloquent imagination of his own – they're not dependent solely on dramatists and producers for (Yeats's phrase) 'personal utterance', or what we'd now term self-expression. Actors aren't megaphones; they have unique and articulate inner voices worth attending to.

Kenneth Branagh's innovation is to have invited senior actors to work

I

with him as directors. He's surmounted the generation gap. Dame Judi Dench led *Much Ado About Nothing*, Geraldine McEwan *As You Like It*, Derek Jacobi *Hamlet*. Actors taught actors; they spoke one another's language. To say rehearsals were master-classes is too frigid, too academic, too respectful. Derek Jacobi spoke of the 'joy, satisfaction, fun and knowledge' that were the rewards of 'this great feast of company spirit, talent, energy ....' But the story of Branagh's generation – audacious enough to re-shoot *Henry V* and cast McCowen and Co. in minor roles – belongs to another book, though it commences with this one – and we need at this early stage, of looking at stage people, to address some fundamentals: i.e. What are actors? What is acting?

(a) THE SENTIMENTAL FALLACY

Once called by Marcel Carné and Jacques Prévert *Les Enfants du Paradis* – 'the children of the gods ... the beloved heroes of the public' – actors seem paranormal and come from supernature because they are physical and psychological shape-changers; they imply no fixed centre and flaunt a mental virtuosity, a transformative genius, the rest of us might find dangerous – as it is when co-opted by wanderers and imposters like Percy Topliss, in Alan Bleasdale's *The Monocled Mutineer*; or by Milton's Satan; or by Clare Quilty in *Lolita*, the witch in *Snow White*, Ron Moody's wicked uncle in *Flight of the Doves*. Or, of course, by spies – and espionage is a recurrent theme in this book.

Stuck, as we are, with single lives and imprisoned by (economic, social, professional) responsibilities, the actor's way is terrifically alluring. Yet by making the false look genuine, actors do for pay what confidence tricksters get put in prison for. Charlatans and bilkers: their offence consists, says Hugh Kenner, 'in being more people than one'. Lying, acting: shysters get arrested, hoods executed, actors Oscars. And what we consistently respond to is technique – we admire acting (in all its forms) for the diligence, skill, intelligence, poise, control, taste with which it is carried off. That is, we discern the positive qualities; the discrimination. And thus is a heresy (FALSITY MADE TO APPEAR GENUINE) turned into its opposite. Acting, to be a success, depends on VIRTUES. An inherent paradox, a beauty.

The paradox of acting, however, to Diderot (the Romantic genius who invaded the sanctum of Classicism: he wrote the *Encyclopédie*), was that the more convincing the performance, the greater the acting, the less the actor actually feels; he's coolly detached, a masterpiece of adaptability, like Olivier, or of dissimulation, like Alec Guinness, or of restraint, like John Gielgud, or of inventiveness (disguised as absentmindedness), like Ralph Richardson. If he weren't coolly detached and removed – every-

2

where clear (as Pope would say), everywhere irresistible – he'd go mad. And acting is littered with casualties, a dissolute tradition coming from Kean (Laughton, Burton, Sellers, Montgomery Clift, Vivien Leigh . . .). Plays, theatres, actors: it's a dangerous world, pretending to be other than you really are, hazarding the exposure of dormant forces; a strange concept, making psychic excavations. People are wary when they meet an actor (actors seldom mix with folk not in the business); they are suspicious when a friend or relative, say, wants to be an actor. The *need* to act? What *is* going on?

(b) THE EROTIC FALLACY

Actors are a strange and (mostly) happy breed; cavorting in fancy dress, having us on. Leaving to one side the issue that an actor must cheat everybody, except himself (for that way madness lies★), puritans and moral zealots are highly mistrustful of stage people because acting, phenomenologically, is close to harlotry. Both the player and the prostitute are surrendering themselves, giving themselves away in bouts of gratification, merchandising their personalities; they deal in physique, excitement, action, gyration. We pay up for their ministrations – or manipulations – and during the release of applause, in the theatre, cast and fulfilled audience confront each other: How was it for you? they might be asking. (When, at the end of Peter Brook's *Marat/Sade*, the cast applauded the audience, it was as ironic as a whore pushing cash over the counter to her abashed client. And here's a class exercise: what's the etymological significance of *clap*?)

As an actor's duty is to make us believe that his gesticulative life is a life of thoughts; that appearances are deeds: like the prostitute he has to give but the impression of commitment (Diderot's gist). And the stage is the divan of his misdemeanours. Theatres are mental brothels. (The Emperor Constantine passed an ordinance, still found, flyblown and misprinted, tacked up behind the bar in old Greek hotels, regulating the behaviour of brothel-keepers, sailors, tapsters and *actors*.) And historically, backstage life lacked morals. Even the inestimable Doctor Johnson had to keep wide of the playhouse because the chorines over-focillated his 'amorous propensities'. Plays, the Lord Mayor of London had said in 1597, 'are a special cause of corrupting youth, containing nothing but unchaste matters, lascivious devices, shifts of cozenage, and other lewd and ungodly practices'.

He may be right. Look at the plots. So many dramas have been about

★ 'He is constantly playing some new part,' says J. M. Barrie of his obnoxious hero in *Sentimental Tommy* (1890). 'Into each part he puts an earnestness that cheats even himself.'

parricide, incest, regicide, revenge and lust. Dramas put on by people whose bodies and souls become places for extreme experimentation. Ignoring Diderot for a moment: you play a killer convincingly: have you not demonstrated to the world an otherwise censored capacity for killing? And what other emotions are roused? Drama is almost entirely subversive. As I'll be saying later on, Wilde's comedies derive from the poisoned-palaces of Jacobean tragedy, and his legacy includes Shaw's logorrhetic Jack Tanner, Eliot's heretical egotist, Thomas Becket, Coward's violent children, Amanda and Elyot, Rattigan's ambivalent attitude to respectability (The Winslow Boy is obviously guilty*), those Fifties ranters, Jimmy Porter and Sergeant Musgrave, Orton's perverts, Harold Pinter's secret police and Peter Barnes's 14th Earl of Gurney alias Jack the Ripper. Desperadoes, all.

(c) THE MORAL FALLACY

Four hundred years on from the Lord Mayor's condemnation, performing arts are again controversial. William Rees-Mogg has been made an arbiter of televisual taste, a position reminiscent of the defunct Lord Chamberlain's office, which used to preserve Good Manners, Decorum and the Public Peace, and who was dubbed by Kenneth Tynan 'the Royal Smut Hound'. ('He inhabits a limbo aloof from democracy, answerable only to his own hunches.') Martin Scorsese's The Last Temptation of Christ earned the approbation of Lambeth Palace and the Vatican, clerics and pontiff suddenly forgetful about two thousand years' worth of inconographic experiment, which includes, along the way, the Renaissance, Holman Hunt and Cecil B. De Mille.

Our culture is suddenly touchy, easily embarrassed. The spokesman might be Augustus Carp, Esq., who claimed that in 'an age when every standard of decent conduct has either been torn down or is threatened

---

* Ronnie Winslow's guilt or innocence was the subject of a lecture I once delivered at St Catherine's College, Oxford. Briefly, my case – completely circumstantial, or rather, contextual – rested on the shifts the other characters make throughout the play (for example, Sir Robert Morton begins ascetic, later he eats and drinks; Catherine leaves off her suffragette work; Arthur gets more ill on each reappearance; Dickie begins dilatory and ends a war hero), plus the oppressiveness of tempo: the eternal deferral of the long-desired justice. 'How hopeless it seems sometimes,' says Catherine, sighing like one of Chekhov's three sisters. Values alter throughout the course of the play (Grace says that Right and Justice have compromised their 'ordinary respectable life'), and Ronnie himself is either hysterical ('I didn't do it!'), or asleep, or absent – and we have only his word he didn't pinch the postal order. (Morton's cross-examination is very faulty.) Reading the play in the context of Rattigan's other works, nowhere else is he so – apparently – morally clairvoyant.

4

with destruction; when every newspaper is daily reporting scenes of violence, divorce, and arson; when quite young girls smoke cigarettes and even, I am assured, sometimes cigars; when mature women, the mothers of unhappy children, enter the sea in one-piece bathing-costumes; and when married men, the heads of households, prefer the flicker of the cinematograph to the Athanasian Creed – then it is obviously a task, not to be justifiably avoided, to place some higher example before the world.'* That was 1924, but looks back to the endowments of Victoria's era; the anonymous author, Sir Henry Howarth Bashford, Honorary Physician to King George VI.

(d) THE RELIGIOUS FALLACY

Carp's concern with sin takes him to the rank of Vice President in the Anti-Dramatic and Salatory Union, where he encounters the actress Mary Moonbeam, star of an operette called *The Peach Girl*; he takes up his station outside the Empress Theatre, urging the audience to turn and go home. Like the sixteenth-century Lord Mayor, he sniffs lewdness and ungodliness. And possibly he is correct. If, on the one hand, acting is related to harlotry, on the other (again phenomenologically), there's a blasphemous overlap with religion.

The actor and priest perform rituals; plays are instruments of faith: we suspend disbelief. Bread = body, wine = blood, or plastic capsules of synthetic gore. The audience = a congregation, and the stage is an altar for the sacrifice of personality. Performance is a hocus-pocus – where Hamlet is sung to his rest by choirs of angels; where Oberon blesses the house (and Puck the household gods); where, at the end of *As You Like It*, there's a pagan fertility dance; where Prospero prays:

> if you from your *sins* would pardoned be
> Let your *indulgence* set me free

Prospero is the coped wizard-priest, requiring not only applause but sacramental absolution; he's a magus who spends *The Tempest* disguised

---

* In *The Winslow Boy*, set in 1914–15, based on a court case of 1908, and written in 1946, when Catherine lights-up, in Act II, Sir Robert Morton sneers 'A lady in her own home is surely entitled to behave as she wishes.' And during the climactic days of the trial, Ronnie Winslow, indifferent to his symbolic status as the representative of Truth, Honour, Right, Justice, loiters at 'the pictures'. ('Pictures? What is that?' inquires Sir Robert. 'Cinematograph show', he's informed.) You may find many jokes about cigarettes in Wilde; lighters and inscribed cases are frequent implements in Coward. ('There is more than one of our English actors who is capable of producing a wonderful dramatic effect by aid of a monosyllable and two cigarettes ... Perhaps, after all, that is acting?' Wilde.)

as a theatre director, organizing the masque, props, cast, plot. And then, in the Epilogue, he comes forward and says that, as an actor after all, he's also a man: he wants to break through, from art to life, from the stage to reality, like the matinée idol in *The Purple Rose of Cairo*. And this stepping through the frame disconcerts – the most shocking moment I know being the last scenes in *Murder in the Cathedral*, when the knights ask us why we didn't intervene and save the Archbishop. Our diplomatic immunity as an audience is compromised. More than spectators, we're eye-witnesses – even, it could be argued, accessaries after the fact.

Returning to Prospero: how, principally, has he sinned? By involving himself in a drama apt for Shakespeare's late sombre phase? Or is it the actor-playing-Prospero who speaks? (Trying to re-enter reality after a few hours' artifice.) Or just Prospero himself, a few hundred lines in a book, a paper man, who has never lived and who can never die,* permanently awaiting the actor who'll puff his speeches into life?

Characters need the blood of a player (Bram Stoker based Count Dracula on Henry Irving); without that actorial plasma, plays and the parts they contain are half-finished, unformed, scarce half made-up. No, worse than that: drama without actors has the etiolated, painful undeadness of a vampire; a bag of bones despatched by the sun.

(e) THE ACADEMIC FALLACY

Hanging about down in the crypt, keeping plays in the literary cellarage – I'm aghast at how little my Oxford charges want to know of theatre, for their degrees.† Drama to them is an abstracted text; it's seldom a script waiting for the alchemy of acting. This is odd, as many professional stage people came out of the OUDS (and Cambridge equivalent). Richard Burton was Nevill Coghill's star. Recently the dappled, fawn-like Imogen Stubbs graduated with a First. But few of my own keen Chaucerians, Spenserians and Virginia Woolf faddists venture to Stratford or to the Barbican. But they'd run on all afternoon about dramatic genre theory, Erasmian humanism, or aspects of irony in Jacobean tragedy.

Generally, acting defies scholarship; it is truancy from the carrel. An adulteration of noble thought with base action – that's it, isn't it? Acting is action, not meditation. Vulgarly demonstrative. And here my students might seem to have an ally in Charles Lamb, who in 1811 wrote disdainfully of stage representation. There is so much in Shakespeare's plays, he claimed, 'which comes not under the province of acting, with which eye,

---

* A phrase used by Orson Welles of Sherlock Holmes, whom he played on radio.
† Alan Bennett blames the tutors. 'Dons have always been dubious about drama . . . Acting is somehow thought to rot both mind and character' (*Oxford Today*, Volume 1, Michaelmas 1988).

and tone, and gesture, have nothing to do.' But where my students fuss about Ben Jonson's indebtedness to G. Wilson Knight (literary criticism is the history of great *scholarly* performances), Lamb's polemic was Romantic: he wanted Shakespeare's stage to people his own thoughts, the characters and their motivations liquefying into 'aspiring spirit . . . intellectual activity'. Shakespeare didn't write plays but lyrical poems; and though that's preferable to the dull discoursing from Macmillan's Casebook, Macbeth, Iago, Lear & Co. come out as ideas and not as men WHO HAVE NEVER LIVED AND WHO CAN NEVER DIE.

INTERVAL

If acting completes drama, and not just usefully adds to it, or crassly detracts from it, by interpreting it, here at last is the delicate question: what is it that an actor brings to a role, besides looking right and remembering the words? When Eliot said, apropos of the playing of a part, that 'the difference between being an elder statesman / And posing successfully as an elder statesman / Is practically negligible,' he didn't stop to ponder the dark and thorny meaning of the tenth word: *successfully*. The cabbala of acting rotates about an axis of success, accomplishment, mastery and ascendancy. And in writing this book I've sought to know the ins-and-outs of achievement. How does acting work? Can its code be broken? What is it like, a life where you are applauded for being a compound of borrowed phrases and gestures, plus your own sensibility? What are the compulsions? How is it possible? What is the secret? The urgency? How do they make it a success?

Garrick used to talk about being 'mentally absorbed' in a character; he described a trance-like state, when, speaking the words, making the words become flesh, taking them over, the actor wills himself to be possessed by them – as if by demons. Some actors, altering appearance with sartorial disguise and greasepaint, adopting different voices and funny walks, make of their profession a seance: the summoning of inspirational spirits from without. Others find characters lurking inside themselves: acting is a rite of exorcism, the expulsion of in-dwelling moods and emotions.

For the first category, acting is a way of multiplying personality, of developing your own repertory company of selves, a wardrobe of biographies. For the second category, acting is a contemplation of autobiography, every performance (in Goethe's words) 'fragments of a great confession'. The first category conceal themselves (we know nothing of Olivier the man from his performances, save sensations of heroism and gusto); the second category use acting for a disclosure of 'the entrails of

7

experience' (Richard Ellmann's phrase – to which alarming notion Charles Laughton's career bore anguished testament).

(f) THE ROMANTIC FALLACY

For Jorge Luis Borges, acting was simple, wistful: 'I have dreamt the world as you dreamt your work, my Shakespeare.' To speak the words of Shakespeare was to *be* Shakespeare; the actor is an empty space filled by the fantasies of the dramatist – a process Molly Bloom called metempsychosis: the transmigration of souls. A process not demonological, as for Garrick, but distrait.

A lot of that goes on in Borges; people waking up having composed *Don Quixote* in their sleep, or they turn into redundant doubles of Cervantes, or their brains become library stacks, or they enter Agatha Christie mysteries dolled up as gauchos, or they land on alien planets – and all in a tone of sustained reverie. Writing, and acting, was to Borges a somnambulism. Creativity is a suspended animation.

But it is his mention of Shakespeare which interests us here. Our Shakespeare (who might be a textual critic's ponderosity in the Arden edition or the connoisseur of Italian painting Dr Jonathan Miller found for television or the D. H. Lawrence preincarnation favoured by F. R. Leavis) is not the over-worked poet who stalked Ben Jonson's page or the wordsmith who lurked on Samuel Johnson's; he's not quite the cerebral puzzlement who eluded Henry James, or the partisan Jan Kott believed was his contemporary. Nor is he, with Kenneth Branagh re-making *Henry V*, any longer the war-poet whom Olivier filmed; and Zeffirelli's *Taming of the Shrew* (1967) settled Padua in Carnaby Street.

To be true to Shakespeare, acquiesce in the fact that each age reads with different eyes – and actors have a duty to expropriate the words and make their performance a local commentary upon them, brewing magic from the mix of (i) private character, whatever that is or isn't (who can gauge an actor's inmost turbulence or tranquillity?); (ii) the text, and owing to Stanley Wells we've got to start calling Imogen Inogen, Moth Mote, Falstaff Oldcastle, amongst hundreds of other snatched-back, much-loved errors – bibliography shows the volatility of print; (iii) that pathetically opaque notion of an age's spirit, but who would now put Titania's fairies in tie-and-dye smocks or picture Polixenes's Bohemia as Lennon's Hare Krishna court up in the Dakota? Or tour quite as Wolfit did? Or lull Haymarket audiences like Gielgud?

Context can't be escaped. Actors alter (compare, though of course we *can't*, Olivier's 1937 Hamlet and 1947 film, or 1944 Richard and 1956 film); parts alter with different actors (an extreme example: I once saw a production of *Much Ado About Nothing*, a disaster save for a brilliant

Leonato, who became, instead of the doddery host, a cousin of King Lear – 'Hath no man's dagger here a point for me?'). *Definitive* is a term never to be broached. All acting is a work-in-progress – and the Romantics were fascinated by the activity for this reason: it enshrined the transitoriness they were denoting in Nature. A performance is a flower beneath the foot of time. Olivier's Macbeth, which Korda planned to transfer to the screen? Gone with the wind.

Also, to the Romantics, the actor's experimentation with roles and styles and passions was appealing; it suited their temperament of gesture and anguish to stand out, as stage people do, whilst yet, paradoxically, preserving intense privacy – as the actor does, putting up layers and layers of false personality and double bluff before the world; skins of an onion. The actor is a living palimpsest; he's a tune taken up and given thrilling variations. Like Wallace Stevens's blue guitar ('Things as they are / Are changed upon the blue guitar'), he's a symbol of mutability and secretive quiddity.

The Romantics got around to understanding acting by describing Shakespeare; that's to say, when they sought to evoke Shakespeare, they represented acting. Shakespeare was (to Keats) enchantingly slippery, a serpentine and glistening Chimera or Lamia; a vessel of virtuosity, or bloom of empathy, he called, remembering his medical training and aiming for scientific precision, Negative Capability. When a life is a mystery, 'when a man has no identity – he is continually informing and filling some other body.' Shakespeare's imagination could countenance a fertile monster like Richard III or a maiden like Lady Anne; virtuous Orlando and wicked Oliver. This is all very similar to Diderot's idea of detachment – except that Keats goes as far as to say that numinousness affected Shakespeare's real life: he 'led a life of allegory; his works are the comments on it'.

Keats developed these thoughts in 1817, after having seen Edmund Kean and remarking, in his letters, on the actor's passionate voice and sensual grandeur. (When, at a dinner party of Horace Smith's, Keats heard Kean and his cast sneered at as 'low', he wished that he could've slunk off and joined them.) Hazlitt, who wrote on Shakespeare the following year, also discovered a Negatively Capable Shakespeare – but the dissimulative genius is now divine (where Keats's Will might have been a Cockney quick-wittedness run riot).

'He was nothing in himself,' said Hazlitt, 'but he was all that others were, or that they could become . . . He had only to think of anything in order to become that thing, with all the circumstances belonging to it.' Shakespeare, like God, can be named Legion, for he is many. Here Comes Everybody; Haveth Childers Everywhere. Expressive and sensational, he is inundative: his temperament 'does not borrow, but lends its colour to all about it'.

And the colouration, to Coleridge, was bible-black with flashes of lightning. Shakespeare's plays, merged end to end, become a world-engirdling soliloquy, the different voices a chorus that's an earnest of the Lord's increase. Shakespeare's principle, like the God of the New Testament's, according to Coleridge, was sympathy; he operated organically, stirring the spirit. 'Each exterior,' he said of Shakespeare's characters, 'is the physiognomy of the being within.'

Shakespeare's people, then, each a gum which oozes from whence 'tis nourished, have souls. Shelley, however, co-opted metaphors from the physics of Dr Luigi Galvani to explain the whatever-it-is that's going on behind the words: the plays are electrified waterfalls, electric currents, sun-bursts and clouds of unknowing. And if this sounds too transcendental, out of just such a storm was born Mary Shelley's Frankenstein Monster.

The monster had the refinement and brutalness of Mary and Percy Shelley's claudicated friend, Lord Byron. He is a salutary eagle in the dove-cote of all the Bardoltry. Shakespeare, he wrote in his letters and journals, was merely a snapper-up of old novels; a Tudor re-write man and journeyman script-doctor, whom a genius professional ought to re-do. Why did Byron belittle Shakespeare? Because he'd anticipated the scenario for Byron's own mature performance, that of Coriolanus, knocking the dust of England from his shoes, an angry exile hungry for physical freedoms, satisfaction and firm desire.

STAGE PEOPLE

'An actor's a guy,' vouched Marlon Brando, 'who if you ain't talking about him, ain't listening.' He meant, of course, the sublime arrogance of the attention-seeking star; the lofty vanity penetrable only by a blandish-ment. Actually, his remark (which has the laconicism of a jazz lyric) implies that a disregarded actor ain't existing. A performance that fails to hang in your mind may as well never have been there; the actor, the whole complex caboodle of acting, is departed unto oblivion.

This book, in the main, talks about actors by talking to them. Part Two houses curvilinear profile essays, involving interview material and repor-tage, plus cultural history and the odd (opinionated) digression. On my first day I used a tape recorder, like Percy Grainger accosting the pea-santry with his wax cylinder phonograph. But I abandoned the engine. The stark audibility of playbacks robbed conversation of nuance, and what mostly got picked up on the impregnated magnetic ribbon were grunts, clinks, traffic roar and other diners eating bananas. Instead, I kept a journal of all meetings and talk; there was also much busy correspondence.

These actors were chosen mainly because I've long watched them closely, and also because they belong to the generations next down from the eminent Knights and Dames, such as Laurence Olivier, John Gielgud, Ralph Richardson, Alec Guinness, Peggy Ashcroft ... They are a folk who have gathered to a greatness during the past three decades – since, that is to say, John Osborne's *Look Back in Anger* and the ubiquity of television. They are a folk who have had careers fostered by subsidized theatres, at Stratford, or the South Bank, or both; they are a folk too late for the haphazard energies of actor-managers and a thriving network of Reps; they are a folk, often, with college educations; they were a new kind of performer, in a new kind of world.

But beyond all this, the actors included in this book have presented me, over the years, with bright and shining moments I wish to anatomize. Each chapter attempts a discussion of theatricality from a different perspective, in a different style. Hence, for Alec McCowen's profferrment of shotten urbanity, I work in Henry James on privacy and houses of fiction, table manners, food and hospitality; for Robert Stephens, whose Baker Street Hamlet, in *The Private Life of Sherlock Holmes*, was deracinated before distribution, we have a conversation with Watson in Falstaff's Eastcheap; Ian Richardson (who played the part for me of a vinegary Garrick Club grandee), a gossamer Oberon in his day and recently the invisible villain in a le Carré, I look at through the mating of acting and espionage: Burgess, Philby, Blunt. And Derek Jacobi (for whom acting tidies up the crudities of life), who was in a play about Alan Turing, allows me to write on artificial intelligence and acting – the actor as Turing's Universal Machine.

Judi Dench, Carrie Pooter in *Mr and Mrs Nobody*, comes through as Molly Bloom, epically exact about household goods because they are household gods; and her performances are highly emotional because we register the impression of banked up feeling. She always carries herself to look brightly astonished; she's on the alert (languidness is not in her lexicon), and a flick of the eyes registers infinite nuance of dignity and understanding. And when her voice lowers, and stays this side of croakiness, why is it beautiful, and therefore so moving? Because, perhaps, it's a brogue that can be felt to break in it.

Anthony Hopkins, the Antony to her Cleopatra, Frank Doel to her Nora, makes his titanesque characters (Le Roux, Lear, Donald Campbell etc.) repositories for his energy and bovine drive. He acts with great puissance, and high seriousness. We could say, without disrespect to the quick or the dead, that his is the career Richard Burton went and mislaid.

Antony Sher, skeetering, a bloodied beetle, the least naturalistic of modern actors, whose inspired maladjustments of reality make for a theatre of electrified cartoonery, sees me discourse on Fuseli; whilst Simon Callow, stately and plump, elicits talk about Cocteau and the sensibility of camp, Laughton and the Unbearable Lightness of Being an Actor.

What mentors does each actor have? Who from the past inspired him? And what of the show-cases for talent? The stage, the cinema, television, radio: how does the actor adapt to the demands of each medium? A successful actor is not a mouthpiece for the text, it'll by now be plain, an automaton gliding about tracks pre-arranged by the director; no, he works by instinct, feeling his way inside a role, or by accumulating researches from without, making characters live even when they have nothing to say. But how do actors prepare themselves for a part? What does he think of as his style – and is it chanced upon or controlled? What bearing does private life have on public performances? What is it like in the secret world of rehearsal? What is the attitude to directors? What performances satisfied, and why? How does the actor regard his craft?

Answers to questions about acting (which are also, by their very nature, questions about charlatanism and fraud – i.e. questions about creativity) edge into the issue of personality and the games we all play when trying to behave: all of us people a stage (Auden said we may be divided into the 'sane who know they are acting and the mad who do not'), and it may be that the theatre, far from being a refuge for flimsy and ultimately wan fantasy, is in fact an arena for purveying the naked truth; a machine for exploring psychology's enchanting slipperiness (that Keatsian notion again) and the concept of our most powerful, ecstatic (and enigmatic) faculty: that of the imagination.

Stage People is intended to provoke debate, quite simply, about why it is that acting works; why we all need artifice and illusion. The solution has something to do with the very necessary sleep of reason; something to do with an actor being the space, the crossroads, where life and art meet. The games of personality, of imposture, of public and private corrosiveness, are played, by the actor, to perfection.

And the games aren't run in solitary confinement. No, no; individual actors are gathered together, prevailed upon to be intimate, the cast of a play becoming a hurly-burly family.* This book interprets the whole

---

* Note the number of plays *about* family struggles – the internecine plots in Hamlet's Elsinore or Lear's Albion; the magnificent Houses of Atreus and Amberson; right up to Eliot's *Family Reunion* or Tennessee Williams's Big Daddy dominated Southern berth; or Sir Charles Gurney saying, in Peter Barnes's gothic farce *The Ruling Class*: 'Families like ours set the tone.' (Hitchcock's last and underrated film was punningly called *Family Plot*.) The recurrent fascination is in the family as a closed world, intramurally intimate, and hence ripe for stories of dependence and interdependence; we are shown the price paid for social contact, and yet the impossibility of living lives in isolation. The many million dramas about adultery are passion-plays of escape and starting-over: '. . . the nightmares started only recently. As long as we had one daughter left at home, I felt useful but James had begun to think he'd given up too much of his life to the family.' Nell in Peter Nichols's Morality of lust and responsibility, *Passion Play* (1981).

history of modern acting as the archive of an extended family; a convoluted dynasty – and this is where I begin, with an account, having no claims to economy or trustworthy factuality, which tries to weave together the lives, fates and temperaments of those found loitering in the force-field of theatre, the aim being to sketch a syncretic context for acting at this, the century's end.

Olivier saw himself in a tradition whispered down from Burbage – 'Burbage, Garrick, Kean, Irving: four names that handed on the Shakespearean mantle to our generation . . . The hand-touching continues.' And Peter Hall, inheriting what was to become the Royal Shakespeare Company from Anthony Quayle, said 'there is a degree of continuity at Stratford, of handing over before changing, which is unlike any other theatre in the Kingdom.' Sometimes, the hand-touching, the handing over, is like the working out of a curse; sometimes, a formal collaboration; sometimes a surprise of elective affinities. Each generation, I argue, unfolds from its predecessor; each generation seeks to disaffiliate itself from the past and find original techniques. And put mystically by Hazlitt, the process embodies 'the seeds of perpetual renovation and decay, following in this respect the order of Nature.' Creation of performance, a volley of sacred and profane fire, is a symbol of birth. You are baptized anew (like Jack and Algernon wanting to be Ernest). Acting, as Kenneth Branagh must've realized when naming his troupe, is a renaissance.

PART ONE

MEET ME ALL
BY BREAK OF DAY

'Let me know where you're working tomorrow night
– and I'll come and see *you*!'
Archie Rice in *The Entertainer*, by John Osborne.

AS SUMMER FLIES

The old black magic of acting has always held me in its spell, though I have only once officially been an actor: a production of *Robin Hood* at my school when I was, I suppose, about nine. I was the squire, the father of Maid Marian. My aunt, a seamstress, ran me up a green brocade suit, with knee breeches, white stockings, yellow waistcoat and a tricorn hat. An ostrich plume from a dried-flower arrangement was stuck in the tricorn hat. Silver buckles for my black pumps were made out of baking foil; a powdered peruke was adapted from a nylon wig, plucked off a mannequin in a local boutique called Vanity Fair. The rest of the company made do with blankets and parlour curtains smelling of smoke and dog. I felt like Mozart on a concert tour of Sherwood Forest.

The angels had coils of tinsel for wings; the wise men had headgear of towels. Cherubim, magi, in *Robin Hood*? They appeared at Robin and Marian's wedding, when the sylvan morality play became a nativity scene, with Tuck celebrating Mass. Robin was played by a tall girl, cast for her thighs in Lincoln green. I recently found a photograph of the show. The bun-jaws and chocolate guzzler who was Tuck now builds airports; one of the footpads I met last year at Smithfield market – he's now a breeder of brindle cows. And Squire Fawcett, far from being the nearest thing South Wales had ever had to Sir Sacheverell Sitwell, stares from the group as Landseer's *The Monkey Who Had Seen the World*: the ape in galligaskins, lappets and twill.

During my teenage years I was mogul of the Super-8. Becoming a pubescent Orson Welles, I wrote, directed, produced and starred in *I've Found a New Baby* (soundtrack stolen from Sidney Bechet), a five-minute romp about Herr Baron Victor Frankenstein. There were few joys greater than scribbling on the face, donning a moleskin wiglet and flourishing a threadbare fox stole to alter appearance and look crazed with age. In those days we all wanted to be taken for older than we really were. The film is not above a decade old; I occasionally let it flicker on the wall. Already it has a scratchy, grainy, bootleg quality – like those jerky pioneer Méliès efforts. Who the Burgomaster is, under the substantial freight of crepe hair, talc, purple senility lines, and overacting wildly, there's little need to guess. The boy I left behind me.

My family had never the slightest connection with the theatre, but it was intensely theatrical. I was raised in a Victorian villa adjacent to our slaughterhouse. W. G. Lewis & Son was established in 1868 (the year of Wagner's *Die Meistersinger**); a farming and butchery business. We raised the stock, killed it, dressed it, sold it, delivered it. From the raw to the

---

* Though Wagner visited Wales on a hunt for a fragment of the true cross, and though the opera is a scene from provincial life – a coincidence.

cooked. The shambles★ consisted of dark corrals, where the kine and squealing pigs waited to go on; a place of ropes, gantries, hoists, hawsers, a flying chainsaw, men in grim overalls flashing steel; giant sides of beef pushed on runners; lamb carcasses hanging from a single leg – a corps de ballet stilled doing warm-up kicks. A row of pop-eyed flayed ox-heads, lolling joke-shop tongues, hung on hooks. Gore, gristle, blue-grey bladders – these were the flowers trodden beneath my foot. Scales and dials for weighing steers; walk-in fridges; cauldrons of offal shaking with maggots; an iron bath to boil away the fine hair on pigs: my daily environment, for eighteen years, was a cheerful factory of evisceration. My haemoglobin Drottningholm. Blood slipped as melted lip gloss down the storm drains, the rivulets enriched by limey bile and streaky froth, heading for the Rhymney, there to mix with cinders from the Machen paint works and the congealed dust of washed coal.

The paint works was at a hamlet called Waterloo. It never crossed my mind that this place of coke-ovens and toxins, bituminous fogs and mouldering pipes, funnels and chimneys wasn't the site of Napoleon's battle. When I was taken to see the Rod Steiger/Christopher Plummer film, I expected them to line up their troops and cannon under the shadow of our local slag-heap – my own black hill. No Bruce Chatwin magic mountain, this, but poisoned muck from the pit, regarded, ever since Aberfan, with suspicion and fear. Would it seep and leak and slide upon our houses, a gaseous, carbon dragon, exacting vengeance for despoiling nature? Would the black hill come alive and demand human sacrifice? Payment for its mined coal? A massacre of the innocents to atone for its stolen crystalline innards? I am of the generation of Aberfan. The disaster happened a valley or so away. As I get older, I feel increasingly spared.

Backstage a drama about life and death: front of house was the shop, where my grandfather was to be found, making calculations in big leather ledgers (the entries went back to the last century); the tall stool he perched at, like a burnished throne, shone on the marble, decorative tiles and plastic parsley. The shop assistants wore bright white coats and blue aprons, but not boaters. Backstage: the blood and the cussing and the lowing; on stage: meat sliced and presented as neat, harmless props. My father (who as night follows day, would inherit ledgers and poleaxe) and a whistler called Ron Curnow performed like straight man and stooge, crooning with the ladies in for mince and brisket. With pencils cocked behind their lugs, winking and gossiping, their faces were rubicund as if from the footlights' glow – but it was from the cold.

★ '. . . as summer flies are in the shambles / That quicken even with blowing.' *Othello*. Elizabethan word for abattoir. Craig Raine has written a poem about butchers presiding over their kingdom of meat. His lyric is behind my own prose here.

Each week, cardboard boxes were delivered by the television repairs and rental shop. Opened out flat, they'd line the walk-in fridges. These cartons I'd purloin for puppet theatres. For in the attic, above the swishing and the chopping, I'd been allowed a suite of unwanted rooms, where once upon a time my grandfather's elder sisters and wet-nurses had lived. The attics contained many mahogany ships' drawers – relic of a failed family speculation, when a great-uncle had bought a boat which sank in Cardiff docks before they could fully fit it out. These drawers I heaved into rows for audience seats, facing a corrugated cardboard stage. An electrician was hired to fix up proper lights with dimmers. I pinched coloured bulbs from the village Christmas tree; I wrote a script about Bluebeard, made the puppets and sets, rehearsed – but I never once put on a show. It was all satisfactorily inside my head.

ALL THE ELECTRICAL SECRETS OF HEAVEN!

Inside those drawers – they were my cabinets; I was Dr Caligari – I discovered photograph albums, top hats, malacca canes, weskits – the lumber of generations past. These would later dress the sets and cast of *I've Found a New Baby*. Particularly delightful was coming across a heap of scientific bottles, specimen jars, test tubes, beakers, thousands of microscope slides and a dozen anatomy text books. A relative who'd read medicine and who'd been the first Allied doctor arriving at Auschwitz thus accidentally determined my taste for Gothic monster movies – becoming a wolf, or flying as a bat, or raising the dead: tricks which are against nature, and which are perhaps allegories of the art of acting itself. Allegories of acting because stories of transmogrification – a man into a beast, or vampire, or shambling tissue.

Coming back from the dead is the most freaky damned renaissance! Man is made mechanical, cursed and undead, existing in a margin between real life and eternity. The body forced into strange shapes, the mind made to think alien thoughts; the effect is to be out of oneself. So notice the equipment in the gothic laboratories. There, amongst the sparks and fizzing bottles, is always a TRANSFORMER. In electricity, two coils for varying voltage of an alternating current supply; but in the imagination, an engine to convert dead matter into energy – e.g. Dr Frankenstein, who uses the machine to harness elementary physics with crazy biology. Joule's heat becomes a modern Prometheus wielding fireballs, in dramas about reverse decomposition. The transformer in the castle lab makes reality manipulable – an effect desired by all actors.

Monster movies always have mad doctors – shabby descendants of Faustus and Prospero, played by Lionel Atwill and Colin Clive. Goethe's Wilhelm Meister, besotted by theatre, eventually grows up to be a surgeon. Olivier himself has watched operations. 'I wanted to get . . . really beneath the skin. I wanted to know every part of me.' Actors, he advises, 'should have a copy of Gray's *Anatomy* on their bookshelves.' Jonathan Miller, a doctor and a director, is another behaviourist; a general practitioner in acting's dark house. (The films are also very innocent; childlike. Karloff had a bulky toddle and was like a baby when he examined daisies; Lugosi's Dracula just wants to suckle and sleep – a cursed baby. And Edward Van Sloan comes through the curtains to introduce *Frankenstein* as if he's telling a bedtime story.)

THE ORIGIN OF TABLE MANNERS

Stemming from the ceremonies in the shop, food and theatricality have always been closely linked in my mind. The presentation and quality of a dish, plus associated wines, has always been a main event. Eating and drinking are activities to be flourished. And a great meal is like an opera: the overture of dainties, followed by acts and entr'actes of viands, fish and choruses of side-salads and vegetables; the climax of Stilton and port, and the many curtain-calls of brandy. Ambience is often all: the candlelight and accoutrements, the mood that of a conspiratorial cabal. Outside, apple-blossom, ripe hips and haws, thorn-trees and hazels; haystacks and oasthouses; owls and speckled toadstools; ferns, moonbeams, deadly nightshade in the ditch; golden lads and lasses and the chimes at midnight.

At home we had gargantuan feasts, with a retriever, a pointer, a boarhound and a spaniel squirming under the table. When I read *The Canterbury Tales*, I came across a sketch of my childhood in the description of the Franklin's domain:

> Withoute bake mete was nevere his hous
> Or fissh and flessh, and that so plentevous,
> It snewed in his hous of mete and drynke,
> Of all deyntees that men koude thynke.

WELSH VELVET

A lust for life; an appetite – that's what's at issue. My mother would decorate the whole place, inside and out, with flags and bunting (found in the ship's drawers – left over from Mafeking) on the slightest pretext, especially a royal birth or wedding. For the nuptials of Princess Anne and Captain Mark Phillips, banners and escutcheons extended down the street. My mother came from an equestrian family. The walls of my maternal grandparents' house were studded with fox masks and other bits of vulpine anatomy, hunting prints, copper horns that eventually emitted costive noises when strained into. Before I was old enough to rebel, I was forced into jodhpurs and hard hat, plonked on a nag, and made to trot at agricultural shows. I hated it. My snapshot appeared in the *National Geographic*. I looked like Elizabeth Taylor in *National Velvet*. For the Fancy Dress class, we'd tart up the horse as a beer-barrel, or a rhino, or as Looby Loo, and one of us children would accompany the animal in appropriate costume. My Andy Pandy is still talked about.

GENTLE WILL

We went to the Welsh National Opera each season (*Nabucco* was the first thing I saw: I insisted on a whispered plot synopsis every few seconds) and, loving spectacle, expected much from Shakespeare's *A Midsummer Night's Dream*, even if it would be bereft of Britten or Mendelssohn. I remember sitting in the New Theatre, grumpily looking at a white box and a few ropes – until the play started, and I was seduced by the colour and liveliness of the acting. For this was Peter Brook's production, with Alan Howard, Sara Kestelman, Ben Kingsley . . . The empty space my heart sank at was replaced by a stage packed with streamers and magic. In many ways, I keep returning to the theatre to recover a sense of that nice night's enchantment.

I was attracted to St Andrews University by the red gowns, the sea-mists, the prospect of a desert inaccessible ('another of your umbrageous Gothic castles', said an English master), and only once during my time there did I go to the theatre – there was nothing else on, except student fumbles at Shaffer or a deracinated rep's idea of Christopher Fry. And what I went to see was *A Midsummer Night's Dream*, of which there had been the rumour of police raids at rehearsals. The East Fife Constabulary were suspicious about grope sessions between the fairies, underwear in the undergrowth, the psychedelic nature of Love-in-Idleness. Packed for the run, obviously, I'm glad I found tickets. Puck was Oberon's catamite, and hard-ons pushed out their posing-pouches; Bottom's slumber with Moth, Cobweb and Mustard-Seed was an orgy under a net curtain; Lysander and Demetrius were public-school mutual masturbators; Titania was played by an overweight hoyden in a grey silk leotard; Egeus was played by a blind Spaniard, whose incumbent method of seeing feeling added to the tactile show. 'Gentle Will,' I remembered Mr Best as saying in *Ulysses*, 'is being roughly handled.'

NOT THEATRE

Perforce, I was in books finding a theatricality needing no theatre.* I liked the look of language on display, writers who were actors by other means.

---

* Also, in books of set design, a theatricality needing no stage: the works for opera houses of David Hockney and Maurice Sendak. Theatre is merely the pretext, calming down their visions.

The prose of Carlyle, or the table talk of Johnson, Coleridge and Hazlitt, or the erudite prattle of Addison, or Stevenson on the high seas. I liked monologuists, rambling soliloquists. Tristram Shandy beckoned across the centuries. Milton's Satan I recognized as an actor-manager, using words as costume and gesture – things to be flaunted; a Civil-War Henry Irving. And Irving's own secretary, Bram Stoker, put his master in a book as a Carpathian aristocrat who, like an actor, lives at night. (When a Mrs Mee wrote him a fan letter, he asked her to 'look in at the theatre – I would escort you afterwards for an adventure . . .'*)

Wilde's elaborate theories of a mask's truth and the verity of lying; the incidence of forgery in English letters, from Chatterton to Peter Ackroyd's novel *Chatterton*; James Joyce (who has Stephen Dedalus plan 'to forge in the smithy of my soul the uncreated conscience of my race,' and whose *Ulysses* devotees think the world's funniest book); the buckaroo spirit of Ezra Pound: these are actors needing no licensed stage, each an artist making an art which doesn't hide its contrivances. They are artists of parody, mimicking and disrupting styles; artists who use art ventriloquially, to speak about themselves. Styles are assumed like disguises, inventiveness is exhibited. The Classical-versus-Romantic allegiances of Diderot; Henry James's meditation on the word 'scene'; Dickens's overflow of physical energy; Wilde's criminal arias; Eliot's poems full of voices . . . all the way up to Prospero possessing Iris Murdoch: it really is as if theatre is the condition all art aspires to.

LESSONS OF THE MASTERS I: FEDERICO

Then there was opera to learn about from gramophone records, films to watch on late-night television. The university film club was a disaster. *Pretty Baby* never came and *Roma* was confused with *Roman Holiday*. The reels of *Wuthering Heights* were switched, so that after having extravagantly died, Cathy was later up and about and dancing at a ball. Strauss's *Ariadne auf Naxos*, Bergman's movie version of *The Magic Flute*, the films of Welles and Fellini, and Picasso's polysemic paintings – these appealed to me deeply because disorder is part of their perplexing form. A choppy, apparently improvised form which actually is the content. Self-reflexive (like published letters, diaries, journals and notebooks), these becoming drafts and fragments still fascinate me because they are like glimpses of rehearsal – we're privy to a private performance. Creativity in action.

Fellini's *8½* is a film about the search for a film subject. The director, Guido (Marcello Mastroianni), wanders the wynds of his imagination –

---

* Quoted from an antiquarian bookseller's catalogue (1988), where Irving's invitation is offered for sale at £30.

and an adoring public waits to gratify his dreams. *Amarcord* is a dream of childhood – Rimini fondly recollected and reconstructed in the tranquillity of a Cinecittà backlot, where Fellini also rebuilt modern Rome for *Roma* (a fake documentary about local sights and celebrities: Fellini himself soars on a camera crane, a benign god; Gore Vidal pontificates about the end of the world, a sparky devil); and an ancient Rome for *Satyricon* – Petronius's priapic-picaresque ragbag being the world's first novel. Fellini excavates the metropolis, from the catacombs to the street markets, in time present and time past, and the grotesque phantasmagoria bears his imprimatur. Rome is Fellini, as Fellini is Rome – a self-portrait.

II: ORSON

Welles, who enwrapped himself in projects he couldn't finish, has as his literary likeness Shakespeare's Falstaff. Welles rewrote the *Henry IV* plays, and co-opted passages from *Henry V*, to make the fat Knight the main monarch – the actual King (John Gielgud) is shot in crepuscular long-shot (and Gielgud was mostly replaced by a double). A massive armour-plated enigma, Falstaff, in *Chimes at Midnight*, is a reprise of Charles Foster Kane. And Welles was forever haunted by his early success. By what mad prescience did he make, aged twenty-five, the film of his own old age and decay? Harry Lime in *The Third Man* uses Kane's wicked charm; Quinlan in *Touch of Evil* is an inflated cartoon-bubble, Kane decrepit in Xanadu.

From the technical mastery of *Citizen Kane*, Welles declined into jerky, muffled amateur efforts. Much of *Chimes at Midnight* is inaudible – though we get the impression of an elegiac timbre from Falstaff's voice. *Macbeth* was shot in a few weeks, on cardboard sets; *Othello* was shot over many years, using any European or African location where its director might happen to be staying, slumming for cash as an actor in big-budget junk.

Welles's patchy, exorbitant career is gypsy-baroque. His mix of energy and laziness, the keen mind and the great girth, make him operatic, larger than life. A knowing and sad self-caricature. The infant Gargantua had been indulged by a fairy-tale guardian and confidence trickster, Dr Bernstein, who fetched musical instruments, paintboxes, puppet theatres and crates of magic props; he was taken off to the opera and read the classics. Meantime, there was a real father, a drunkard, who belonged with travelling vaudeville and hucksterism – and something in Welles was always tugged back to that cheerful lowlife. A vulgarian and a man of taste; an oldster, wrapped in a cloak, a fedora and affecting the demeanour of the gasolier period, who coexisted with Peter Pan. For all the melancholy and command, Welles's Falstaff is vulnerable, childlike. Eastcheap pubs (situated in a snowy plain: a wintry intimation of mortality) are his

Never-Neverland. He dwells nostalgically upon the past ('We have heard the chimes at midnight, Master Shallow') – like Kane, who remembers the snows of yesteryear on his deathbed ('Rosebud' is the name of a sleigh). Xanadu is a reconstructed Never-Neverland. Susan's bedroom, which gets ransacked in a tantrum, is decorated as a nursery.

It is said of Harry Lime that he didn't grow up: the world had to learn to grow up around him. Harry's crime: he tinkered with drugs, leading to an epidemic of meningitis in children. Hotspur says to Hal at the end of *Chimes At Midnight*, 'thou hast robb'd me of my youth'. And Falstaff says to the bishops, 'You that are old consider not the capacities of us that are young.' Welles was tormented by the doom of his youth, and his contradictions add up to a kind of cubist collage: his fits and starts, his grandiose plans discarded as he announced them, his interest in magic and in telling lies, mean that, like Falstaff, his art was his own unique existence, and theatre and film swelled to accommodate the frisky lumber. What *Citizen Kane* is is the magician's anatomy of his own magic; an inquiry into the nature of personality, which can turn up only contradictions. Welles knew early that any man is too complex for narrative neatness. Digressions and blind alleys are part of the story. An idiosyncratic structure, with flashbacks, false starts, new approaches, reversals and counterpoints, is the only authentic way to construct a biography.*

III: PABLO

Like Welles's, Picasso's theatricality is intense. His subject matter, in drawing after drawing, picture after picture, is the actor's relationship with the audience, or the director's with his star. Saltimbanques and pierrots recur and represent Picasso's love of the circus's rough magic. Tatty touring families, with scruffy props and spangled breeches, amuse themselves on empty boulevards, with no spectators save the artist. Village acrobats and jugglers, girls on ponies, beruffed dogs, clowns: Picasso paints them in pale pinks and blues, each figure set apart from its fellows in solitary reverie – dream-like. And the space between the figures, to adopt a word of Hofmannsthal's, used in an essay on Shakespeare in 1905, is *allomatic*: a space which is 'not a vacuum but a space mystically alive'.

In Picasso's other favourite topic, there's no gap between figures – they writhe and interfuse. Sketching the artist and his model – whether

---

* Richard Ellmann's bitter, professional Joyce and the weary, enigmatical Wilde are portraits of the *biographer* as he worked on those big and beautiful books. The real biographies of Joyce and Wilde are the histories of the works they themselves set down. All else, as Guy Davenport perfectly observed, 'is lunch, looking over the newspaper, and endorsing cheques'.

explicitly or, as minotaur and maiden, implicitly – Picasso depicts manipulation and power as abandoned fucking. The drama of the corrida,
with the bull's horns sinking into the soft flesh of the picador's horse, is
another image of domination – and it could be an impressario subjugating
his prima donna, the triumph of man's will over woman's flesh and spirit.

Rooms in Picasso are stage sets, landscapes flats. And objects in those
rooms and landscapes twitch with mummery: guitars turn into drinkers
and café tables; flowers and glasses become fumbling fingers or a newspaper. Objects *act*. Picasso compresses metamorphosis: objects migrate
into other objects, so that a bicycle becomes a baboon, or a wine basket a
goat's udder – and what the artist is demonstrating is that the world about
us is a performance. Nothing is ever simply a single thing. Creativity
floods, wave upon wave; and the passion, the virtuosity, the theatrical
fluidity of changed mood and appearance are that of the fierce and fertile
minotaur, half-man, half-bull – Picasso's own self-image as semi-divine.

Despite the hubris of this, Picasso's intention is the opposite of arrogant. He wanted to eradicate himself, not place his personality at the core
of his work (as Dalí has). Eradicating himself, Picasso was replaced by the
daemon of his art. *'Je suis le cahier'*, I am the notebook, proclaimed his
journals, where he taught his pencil to spurt just where he wanted it. He
was a changeling with his craft – his ambition identical to that of another
jotter and incessant scribbler and experimenter, Henry James, who confided in his own particular *Notebook*: 'To live *in* the world of creation – to
get into it and stay in it – to frequent it and haunt it – to *think* intently and
fruitfully – to woo combinations and inspirations into being by a depth
and continuity of attention and meditation – this is the only thing.'

IV: RICHARD AND INGMAR

He who lives *in* the world of creation, he who *is* his world of creation, is
the actor – *the* kinetic art work. And Picasso and James, transfixed by their
own talents and resource – their work an inquiry, amazed, baffled,
delighted, into the nature of creativity's sacred fount – strive to enter their
art, to subsume themselves in it, like actors saturated in a role, in the
divine enchanting ravishment of being reborn as somebody else. What
Ezra Pound called 'making it new'.

Richard Strauss made it new by making it old. The Marschallin in *Der
Rosenkavalier* descends from Mozart's weary Countess; Elektra is a crazy
Valkyrie picked up off Sigmund Freud's couch; Salome belongs with
Wilde and Beardsley and Lord Alfred Douglas. *Ariadne auf Naxos* was
written for Max Reinhardt between 1912 and 1916, the music a neoclassical hotch-potch based on Jean-Baptiste Lully. The first act is about the
frantic composition and rehearsal of the second, with the Composer (a

soprano part) spurned and used by the Prima Donna (who'll later be Ariadne), Zerbinetta, the Tenor (Bacchus) and the Major-Domo. Strauss depicts the bedlam of patronage, when art has to comply with the caprices of a rich master – who in this instance wants the opera over by nine o'clock so that there can be a firework display. The grandee, having paid for the services of a composer and a crazy gang of harlequins, decides that the tragic and comic segments of the evening's entertainment should run simultaneously. And so we get the backstage squabbles and antics, set in a great house of many chambers and in a private theatre. The tone is domestic farce, with much business at doors and windows.

If we are meant to sympathise with the Composer and his hopes for *Ariadne*, our enthusiasm is for Zerbinetta and the clowns, who hop out of traps and usurp the sombre music like the Marx Brothers during the Margaret Dumont-sponsored *Il Trovatore*; they cross with the serious drama, and cancel it out. The official opera is one long lament, with a rakish godling bounding on during the final moments to pep up a lonely woman's juices (Strauss often has lonely women: the Marschallin; Elektra; the Empress and Dyer's wife in *Die Frau ohne Schatten*, Christine in *Intermezzo* . . .); and the harlequins zip like Picasso's saltimbanques trespassing into his carnal etchings. The production I saw at the Coliseum in 1983 had for its house a giant Fragonard, with hatchways and escape chutes for entrances and exits. Donald Sinden, dressed as the Scarlet Pimpernel, milked laughs; and Naxos, in the second act, was overspread with a twinkling milky way, which dissolved into a panoramic backlit blow-up Rubens.

Ariadne auf Naxos is a collision of loftiness and laughs, studied pomposity and hasty extemporising; and, if it is about the writing of an opera, Ingmar Bergman's *The Magic Flute* is about the performance of one. In addition to backstage life, now the audience gets pulled into the work. The camera lingers lovingly and long on an elf-eyed girl enraptured by the overture. (I often wonder how she grew up and what she did with her life.) Bergman set his film in the Drottningholm Court Theatre, relishing the wooden stage machinery, the cogs, wheels and ropes of antique illusion, as who wouldn't? Paradoxically, by having the engineering of artifice naked, artifice seemed more real. The energy of showmanship, the blatant let's-pretend, freed the work for its deeper issue – the harmony of love and responsibility. Papageno is seen in his dressing-room snoozing before his cue; the Queen of the Night and her Ladies puff on fags; the actor playing Sarastro leafs through the score of *Parsifal*. Cast peep through the curtains at audience, the space between the two worlds *allomatic*.

This is a toy theatre filled with real people; the classiest backstage musical ever made, conveying a sense of safety and warmth, the screen suffused by lighting cameraman Sven Nykvist with a crimson and vermilion glow. Costumes, faces, the wood of the buildings are burnished like a log fire – unlike *Fanny and Alexander*, Bergman's other exploration of childhood enchantment and disaffection (a Swedish *Hansel and Gretel*), which is lit with cold whites, blacks and bloody reds. *The Magic Flute* is a celebration of theatre and theatricality, the camera happy to abet a form it's meant to have superseded. With Bergman, cinema hardly mocks stage illusion; it laments, instead, an innocence that technology has lost us. His Mozart is an elegy for the magic lantern.

ANGEL OF DEVASTATION I

Fellini, Welles, Picasso, Strauss and the Bergman of *The Magic Flute* are performers inquisitive about performance. Mannered, moody, marvellous, each asks how theatrical theatre can get; each test the limits of form. The vigilant phantom of form is Henry James, who in 1907 wrote an introductory essay for *The Tempest*, in Volume XVI of Sir Sidney Lee's *The Complete Works of Shakespeare*, and whose ideas are revolutionary: the limits of form are a vanishing trick, a bright light, a kind of ascension – like the primitive dynamos and revolves, the revolutions, of Drottningholm's stage machinery, hoisting the sun and stars and planets into view, so that the Earth conjoins with the Kingdom of Heaven.

James regarded *The Tempest* as a monument of teasing masks and disguise – 'the highest sincerity of virtuosity'; and what the dissembling represents is a portrait of the artist: *The Tempest* is Shakespeare enciphered, 'a private occasion, a concert of one'. Shakespeare, says James, has hidden himself in all the characters. The drama is really a retreat, a recoiling into secretiveness: Shakespeare is 'both performer and auditor, who plays for his own innermost sense'. Apparently getting mystical, James's notion of apotheosis, of formal levitation, is in fact a prescription for contriving an enigma: the art of writing is the art of acting. Shakespeare, 'extemporising in the Summer twilight,' composing *The Tempest*, uses the play as an opportunity for self-concealment. Shakespeare, in other words, is a Jamesian novelist.

James, who in 1907 was casting anew his novels for the New York edition, and compiling critical prefaces, was obsessed with how art grew out of life; how art was connected to life; how art was distinct from life. He was concerned with the responsibility of the artist to his works – what they reveal of his personality, what they betray. All these conundrums Shakespeare blissfully declines to elucidate. He's the peerless escapologist; the peerless mummer, 'in hungry quest of every possible experience and adventure of the spirit'.

Shakespeare spiritual is also Shakespeare the ghostly spirit – who 'slunk past in life ... therefore should he not slink past in immortality'. He's the invisible organizer and arranger, an intellectual adventurer and chronicler of foibles, who is yet a perplexing absence. We know next to nothing about him – like an actor who ceases to exist off-stage, except as a sensation, a recollection, an element. And the idea recurs in James's story of 1892, *The Private Life* – a comedy of manners, which turns into a ghost story, and which is a parable of acting . . .

ANGEL OF DEVASTATION II

Privacy is drained by public performance. Lord Mellifont is an ambling mannequin, his soul being his clothes – his 'delicate harmonies of necktie and subtle informalities of shirt'. He's picturesque; a crystallized style; an awesome apparition. Vawdrey, by contrast, is a vulgar table-talker, 'loud and cheerful and copious' – he does not seem in the least the sensitive writer people expected.

They are all staying at a Swiss resort, spying on each other, as in any period detective novel. Ally of the narrative-sleuth is Blanche Adney, an actress; and the pair of them sniff 'plays all around . . . the air is full of them tonight'. What seems to be a double of the dubious Vawdrey is seen working hard at a desk in the dark; the suite occupied by Mellifont seems vacant when its master retires.

By a neat switch, the upshot of James's fable is that, for the disappointing bore Vawdrey, the art he creates, the writing, lives all it can, and the creator himself is a pallid vessel: a meek and monochrome servant to a colourful, exotic world of fiction. 'There are two of them,' and which is the real right thing? Mellifont, by contrast, who fades when not in company, when not being gazed upon, is an empty space: 'He had vanished – he had ceased to be.' He is absorbed and reabsorbed into 'the immensity of things. He has lapsed again; there's an *entr'acte*.' Like stage action, Mellifont stops existing during the intervals.

If, we learn, 'Clare Vawdrey is double . . . his lordship there has the opposite complaint: he isn't even whole.' As in the theatre, to generalise, there's one sort of actor who multiplies himself; there's another who seeks to make himself complete; one who comes alive on stage; another who on stage yields up aspects of a private nature. And both come together in *The Jolly Corner* (1908), where a house is consecrated as a biographical symbol – a mansion, divided into lots of compartments, signifies a hundred hidden selves. The 'dreadful multiplied numberings' include ancient memories and denied futures from one man's private life.

What happens is that a gallant returns from Europe to survey his New York real estate. He senses in the former home another version of himself, who could have grown up to accomplishment. James is intrigued by alternative destinies; the destinies this man left behind him; the alternatives not chosen. And so the hero is haunted by a paradise misplaced, 'very much as he might have been met by some strange figure, some unexpected occupant, at a turn of one of the dim passages of an empty house.*

Brydon, the hero, becomes the man who haunted himself, desperate to trap the galvanic double – the subsumed self; and it's a theme to be found in Stevenson, when Mr Hyde travels out of Dr Jekyll to enact his desires; or when Dorian Gray lives a life freed from remorse, because the portrait in the loft will do the decaying. Wilde's and Stevenson's characters ask, as James's does, 'who had ever before so turned the tables and become himself, in the apparitional world, an incalculable terror!' They are beasts in the jungle; and after much gothic creeping in the creaking brownstone, Brydon, whose obsession has dipped into madness, meets the revenant – and 'the bared identity was too hideous as his'.

A psychological thriller, *The Jolly Corner* is cinematic, where *The Private Life* is theatrical. The tale is much given to the mystery of opened and closed doors; of windows filtering light and portals as apertures. The old dark house, lit only from without, is a giant camera, or studio, 'the scale of space again inordinate,' with long, deserted vistas, and the near-identical rooms being frames on strips of film. The different past lives are a succession of takes. A picture palace. When James wrote the story, Georges Méliès had been a dozen years inventing the techniques of dissolve, double-exposure and fades.

ANGEL OF DEVASTATION III

What for the rest of us is real life was for Henry James the interlude from 'the real, the waiting life' of art. He loved the theatre and tried frequently to work for it. But *Guy Domville* was jeered from the stage, its author heckled when he took a bow. And yet he remains the theatre's subtlest theoretician, appreciative of an actor's necessary intelligence and humanity; appreciative of how an actor's mental passion makes performance. In January 1887 he wrote a profile-essay of the French actor Benoît-Constant Coquelin in the *Century Magazine*; this article he revised in 1915, a year before his own death.

As a child, James and the actor were classmates at the Collège Commu-

---

* An empty house in fiction always spells trouble: the vacant property opposite 221B, where Colonel Sebastian Moran sets up his sights; Pondicherry Lodge, where Bartholomew Sholto lies skewered by a pygmy's dart; the unlighted stairs Martin Balsam ascends in Hitchcock's *Psycho*; the gloomy halls in the Amberson mansion; Kane's Xanadu; Mrs de Winter's boudoir in *Rebecca*; the locked libraries and drawing rooms of Dame Agatha's guilty vicarages . . . James belongs with such a cluster of haunted habitats where, as Auden said 'The truth about our happiness comes out.'

nal, Boulogne. And the gist of his argument is that the shortcomings of physique, voice and gesture are transcended by 'indications of inward things'; an actor must 'have in him the active imagination of his opportunity'. Acting is 'the exhibition of things intensely felt and reacted upon' – actors are reactors, working like novelists (Jamesian novelists, along with Shakespeare) to express a kind of pellucid, felt harmony; and James talks of 'so many tones and syllables, so many signified mute words, all making sentences. . . addressed to the mental instead of the physical ear'. Great acting is a Romantic symphony which plays itself on the senses; it stops being a thing of palpable moments, and draws the Wordsworthian amplitude of a sense sublime, of something far more deeply interfused. Great acting is consummate persuasion: the actor as novelist and novel, musician and music.

PAGAN PLACES

James is super-refined. He failed in the theatre because, busy with the dramas within, he gave little thought to plot, action, physical movement. What he was up to was holy: the transubstantiation of plot, action, physical movement, the rough wine of stagecraft, into the blood of brain cells and the ozone of thought. But he was right to grow meditative and celestial – right because acting is a rite, the transmigration of souls and, for the actor, the promise of rebirth as somebody else; body into bread and back again.

Storytelling began in the dark: the retelling of epic deeds, before the winter fires. Acting began in the sun: the revivification of epic deeds in Mediterranean amphitheatres, through masks, voice, gesture. The way of masks was to disseminate myths, stories of the spirit of place, and whether the arena is Greece or the tribal clearings of the Guaicuru or the forest grove of the Haitian voodoo priest, performances were at once religious (homage to ancestors and placation of wanton gods) and athletic (the caperings and display of physique). And the point about masks is that they are impersonal: they hide the crinkled face, the actor becoming statuesque, a heiratic other – a trick adopted by Wyndham Lewis for his portraiture. Ezra Pound, Eliot, Edith Sitwell: they seem adorned with tribal paint, their faces head-dresses. This can happen in still-photographs of actors, too. I am thinking of Snowdon's magnificent close-up of Olivier's snarling Archie Rice. The camera makes of the actor's face a Kabuki mask: a leering gat-toothed grimace, more at home in *Richard III* than *The Entertainer*, you'd have thought. The bowler's brim makes a black halo, the cheeks of the actor are blanched, eyes and mouth heavily painted. A bogeyman. When he speaks, a banshee.

The first actors, according to Roland Barthes, were body-snatchers: men who pretended to be death at work – they 'separated themselves from the community by playing the role of the Dead: to make oneself up was to designate oneself as a body simultaneously living and dead: the whitened bust of the totemic theatre, the man with the painted face in the Chinese theatre, the rice-paste make-up of the Indian Kathakali, the Japanese Noh mask . . . [each is] a figuration of the motionless and made-up face beneath which we see the dead'. Acting and donning a mask brought heroes and monsters back to life; the graves, at the player's command, have waked their sleepers, opened, and let them forth – by theatre's so potent art. Acting is diabolism.

The way of masks was an outside festival, on the rocks and under the sky – with the ornament of 'sunne and moone and starres in their true and coelestiall course' (Heywood). Acting as pantheistic, a vale of ferment and life. 'Life,' says Dysart in Peter Shaffer's *Equus*, 'is only comprehensible through a thousand local Gods. And not just the old dead ones with names like Zeus – no, but living Geniuses of Place and Person. And not just Greece, but modern England! Spirits of certain trees, certain curves of brick wall . . . Worship as many as you can see – and more will appear!'

Perhaps acting, involving body and soul, was the first religion; the temple as a theatre; the ceremony of solar worship. And heliotry, in praise of light, celebrated the cycle of night and day, the revolution of seasons and the nurture of crops. Helios, the sun-god, was an early formulation of what later became Apollo; like Apollo, he streamed through the firmament in a chariot of fire, and was stabled in a golden bowl.

Fire, the exclusive element of the gods, was stolen by Prometheus and given to cold and lonely mankind. Mary Shelley's Frankenstein is a modern Prometheus because he expropriates the sacred sparks of life itself. His laboratory is an operating theatre crossed with a cathedral – a cave of making with dials, fizzing transformers, levitating altars, crackles of lighting like the flame shooting between God's and Adam's finger ends. A pagan temple, in which the dead are brought back or lifeless tissue animated – human sacrifice, in reverse. Nature, backwards.

Classical mythology was an effort to codify nature, to ascribe the operations of destiny and metaphysics to a gallimaufry of squabbling incestuous divines. Much depended on sex – Zeus's whoring, Cronus's castration of his own father, Hermes and fertility, Aphrodite, Eros, the pederastic tomfooleries of Ganymede and assorted ephebes. Helios's daughter was Circe, the vamp who detained Odysseus as her love-toy – and the eroticism of acting riddles it back to a primordial origin, as form from the foam, like Aphrodite born on the cusp of a shell. (Or Venus rising as Venice, the city of Casanova.) Religion and sex meet in Petronius's *Satyricon* as a naughty party, with opiates, catamites, food; a costume ball, the men with mascara running down their cheeks – filmed by Fellini in 1969, imagined by Cocteau since 1889, lived by Wilde in the Nineties, dreamt by Firbank until the Twenties. Jewels, gowns, sweetmeats and perfumes.

APOLOGIE!

Plato couldn't abide actors at all. He banished them from the ideal Republic as a pack of liars. The blasphemy of imitation and fakery outweighed any consolation of pleasure. And Fanny Price, in *Mansfield Park*, is worried by theatre; its exhibitionism and stridency. The play her cousins rehearse in their private playhouse is *Lovers' Vows*, which had been adapted in 1798 by Elisabeth Inchbald from August Friedrich Ferdinand von Kotzebue's *Das Kind der Liebe*. The acting, according to Nabokov in his essay on Jane Austen, is 'an orgy of liberation' – and as such, the revels are furiously banished by the returning Sir Thomas Bertram, whose wowser's deed makes him a deathly Mercadé and vengeful Malvolio.

The orgy of liberation, of course, is exactly acting's appeal – what Camus called its 'emotional debauch'. Acting can be indecent exposure; the outrage of flaunting the self, or the repressiveness when evading it. As in the sexual act, acting is a surrender of the self to a role; the abolition of everyday identity for a jangle of nerves and sharp current. A shudder prolonged as long as possible. And beyond the effect on the actor himself, the audience is there to be seduced – penetrated and tossed like a mare by Picasso's bull. Theatre is a place of passion; we're enfolded by intimacies.

Thomas Heywood, with Shakespeare by then a year in his Stratford retirement, published in 1612, *An Apologie for Actors*, an attempt to defend the depraved. With what degree of irony who can fathom, he looked into the Bible and seeing no censure of the stage, reasoned like Sherlock Holmes hearing no dog bark in the night: Christ's silence on theatrical politics means assent. Theatre is not listed with the sins ('The Scriptures are not always to be expounded merely according to the letter'); and, in any case, acting encourages elocution – a fine training for the skills of rhetoric and public composure: it 'instructs him to speak well, and with judgement, to observe his commas, colons, and full poynts, his parentheses, his breathing spaces, and distinctions, to keep a decorum in his countenance.' Also, acting, relaying historical and mythical action, inspires noble deeds: Alexander, hearing of Achilles, decided to become great.

But within Heywood's syllabus for (at best) a finishing school and (at worst) the actor-as-a-speaking-clock, there are salty asides – and we detect why he was motivated to write his book. Acting may well be a metaphysical libertinism; it also attracts the plainly licentious. Sam Johnson, over a century later, had to withhold himself from traipsing backstage – 'for the silk stockings and white bosoms of your actresses excite my amorous propensities'.* Heywood's anxiety was more specifically a

* See 'The Erotic Fallacy' – page 3.

homosexual influence. 'But to see our youths attired in the habit of women, who knowes not what their intents be?'

WHY ACTORS ARE QUITE OFTEN HOMOSEXUALS I

Buck Milligan, in *Ulysses*, once asked the Shakespearean scholar, Ernest Dowden, about pederasty, and received the reply, 'All we can say is that life ran very high in those days!' Homosexuality, however, has stayed to take up residence in the theatre long after women were invited in to play women's parts (and thereby obliterating a level of titillation in Rosalind and Viola). Why is this? Why are so many actors homosexuals? Perhaps because, for the elected childless, acting is a way of being creative; people who could never endure copulation with a woman can instigate and bring something to life. Also, in our homophobic society, homosexuals are manic disguisers – pretending, from an early age, to be other than they are. They perform normality, sexual conformity – when all the time they are meaning something else. Hence the common coincidence of homosexuality and spying: codes, secret messages; secret ways of making, judging, knowing.

This all leads to determined self-confrontation; sensitivity is worked at. The homosexual knows he is set apart, and his autodidactic psychological exploration is good for an actor, who searches particles of his nature for parts to play; and, moreover, used in public to being what he is not, the homosexual is expert at masks – and he's alert to the convincing masks of other people, watching and waiting for the signs and signals of confraternity.

The origins of homosexuality, the origins of an actor, may be less the mother dressing up a little boy in girls' dresses (Wystan Auden was Isolde, to his mother's Tristan, round the nursery piano) than a devolved game of personality: a sense of existential isolation; the pain of self-revelation; the fear of ostracism. What the theatre offers is the chance to try out roles, experiment with self-duplication and aliases; a refuge and a showcase.

Also, theatre is a prolongation of childhood; the playtime of plays. The attraction of childhood is its innocent, prepubertal grace; the freedom from responsibilities. And a child is selfish – king of his small world. Homosexuals are often selfish, consolidating infant demands. For a start, there won't be the encumbrance of paternity, of having to provide for family and wife. There's no need to pay for schools, clothes, food, space; no obligation to pick up the tab for anyone else. A homosexual spends all he has on himself; and his time is his own, and he can travel at whim.

Homosexual icons are tellingly childish. Mickey Mouse watches or posters for *King Kong* – the 1933 film being about totem and taboo and phallic symbols, with glistening close-ups of bolts sliding into locks. Kong's world is a jungle where giant serpents rise out of bosky marshes; a macho frondescence of leathery dinosaurs, chain and armour, matched in iron and glass when the action moves to New York. Lodged on the throbbing aerial at the peak of the Empire State Building, Kong's the tip at the end that matters.

Kong's the homosexual's perfect mate: a chesty and drum-banging brute with a tender heart. The beast's beauty is Fay Wray, a shrieking moll who is a parody of the princess-in-distress. Homosexuals prefer their women to be cartoons; or else they prefer them to be cartoon mothers. Oedipus aside, you don't have any sexual obligation to mothers – Mae West, Joan Crawford, Bette Midler, Judy Garland, they are each a pagan Mary. Immaculate conceptions. And this explains the cult appeal of *Mommie Dearest*.★

WHY ACTORS ARE QUITE OFTEN HOMOSEXUALS II

Faye Dunaway's screen re-creation of Joan Crawford – with black hoops for eyebrows and a scarlet blood-lake for a gob – has no femininity in sight. She prowls a spick Art Deco mansion, a cleaned-up Californian idea of Carpathia, devoid of company, except for her victimised (adopted) children – the most victimised children since Medea's. The film is a collection of insane operatic climaxes, with Crawford appearing in the nursery (where the babes are buckled in their beds) brandishing a scissors, hacking off her daughter's hair, or razoring an enemy's image out of photographs, or demanding that the children join her in a nocturnal deracination of the rose garden ('Christina, fetch me the axe!').

Mannishly felling a tree, or descending a staircase in a dress like silver armour, or chairing a Pepsi meeting in furs, Dunaway's Crawford is a valkyrie; and, smeared with cold cream, screaming and weeping, flagellating her children with a wire coat hanger, her frizzy hair streaming, she's a raddled diva singing Lucia di Lammermoor. And, as well as Medea, Brünnhilde, Lucia, she's also Norma – Bellini's hysterical would-be infanticide, and Norma Desmond, the Gothick movie-queen of Billy Wilder's *Sunset Boulevard*.

Dunaway plays Crawford with unrelenting fury. Only in the film's

★ I am grateful to the Brothers Medved for bringing this film to my attention – in *Son of Golden Turkey Awards* (1986): 'Newspapers in several cities reported on the curious phenomenon of audience members dressed up as Joan waving coat hangers and chasing other patrons, decked-out as curly blond Christinas, up and down the aisles as the picture rolled on. On Hallowe'en, movie-buffs from San Francisco to Fire Island donned padded shoulders and severe lipstick as "Faye Dunaway as Joan Crawford" became one of the year's most popular costumes.'

quiet moments – muttered recitative – do opponents accuse her of acting. 'I'm *not* acting! I'm not *acting!*' she hollers, in reply, and dives at her daughter's throat. As with Norma Desmond in *Sunset Boulevard*, Crawford's anger is provoked at a studio's treachery; at bad scripts and poor directors – and the anger is vented on Christina and Christopher, the orphans for whom Crawford's palace is the witch's den, with themselves playing Hansel and Gretel.

But Crawford's anger is deeper than tantrums at professional slights. As in opera, the madness takes off on a surreal trajectory; an intimation of primal screams, Edvard Munch's neurotic yell. What the rages imply is an indignation about the responsibilities of parenthood (Crawford raises the children alone, having adopted them 'for a little extra publicity'); indignation at having to project family tranquility (mother and children take part in an emetically sentimental Christmas radio broadcast); indignation at having to be a mother (what she requires from her children is the thick adoration of a pet-shop puppy); indignation at belonging to her fans (she's a creation of theirs, and her wrath implies an instability about where a private self might be located); indignation that real life is not as perfect as in the movies; indignation at being a woman, expected to be meek and deferential (she is contemptuous of Louis B. Mayer's seigneur-ial powers and the Pepsi board's misogyny); indignation at being a woman who is growing old – and so she's entirely re-created herself as a female impersonation. The movie-queen as drag-queen, unsexed like Lady Macbeth. She stamps out her daughter by usurping her role in a rubbish soap; she bequeaths Christina and Christopher nothing in her will; any sliver of affection has been, always, gloriously fake. Crawford dies, bloody, bold, resolutely free from all personal encumbrances – her bloated, boozed-up corpse made-up by the mortician from a signed publicity photo. In death, as in life, she goes ferociously against nature.

ARRESTING OSCAR

Nothing of the foregoing* explains happily married and polyphilopro-genitive actors and actresses; nor does it account for homosexuals who aren't in the slightest fascinated by acting; nor does it account for homo-sexuals who aren't on the rampage, or for heterosexuals who are . . . Yet

---

* My remarks are in some measure inspired by Michael Tanner's article on Donizetti, 'Melodramas for Soprano' (*Times Literary Supplement*, September 24th 1982) – 'If, as has sometimes been suggested, male homosexuals are in some way afraid of women, then . . . figures such as Callas, who incarnate so perfectly a certain ideal of femininity, offer many of the gratifications without any of the envisaged threats of womanhood. They offer tenderness, excitement, sensuality, even scorn and vehemence, but with-out any requirement of an active response.'

the picture of Hazlitt's 'gay, laughing circle' is a generalization not readily contradicted – and is the impetus behind Wilde's ponderosities; the force behind his interest in the delicious, intricate metaphysics of acting and drama. Wilde's dramatic rise and fall; the glittering success who became a humiliated criminal, and the way crime and exposure and humiliation subsist *within* his successes; the way he makes sin implicit in purity (Dorian simultaneously beautiful and ugly; Salome a temptress and an innocent); how art is more real than reality and fiction truer than truth – all of these inversions and moral duplicities are apt for theatre.

James wrote about the theatre of cogitation; Wilde about the theatre of style. He took the comedy of manners and made it into a mock-tragedy of mannerisms. The writers from whom he derives – Congreve, Farquhar, Vanbrugh, fellow Irishman Sheridan – were dramatists of brazen falsification; they exploited theatre's masquerades: the hidings, vanishings, difficulties, shimmerings. Actors would act in plays about acting – the flaunts of artifice and gesture, time sped up and compressed. Yet the brazen falsifications and masquerade exist to expose and intensify our very real social quirks, our very real experience of eros and intellect. Restoration plays, through stage fakery, are as scrupulous as any psychic lab in the anatomy of twisted cruel excess and vulgarity. They depict moments of sin, moral transgression, madness: the heightened, rushing or impending sections of life. Their own ancestor is the Jacobean palace-intrigue; the poisoned rooms of Tourneur, Marston, Webster, Ford; stabbings and wicked eavesdropping amidst screens, curtains and marquetry. (We as an audience eavesdrop, don't forget. We are voyeurs. Peeping Toms.) Theatre is a bright box for things of darkness.

And what Restoration plays restore is an examination of sensibility, grown gloriously decadent. Double-dealing, instead of being, as in *The Revenger's Tragedy*, a crazy wallow in bejewelled corruption and rottenness, is disinfected and rinsed – so that the metaphors of acting/theatre don't swing on insanity (the actor as bedlam beggar, a lunatic thinking fantasy reality), but on a magisterial sanity (the actor as capable of cool dissimulation). Congreve in *The Double Dealer* suggests that acting is the naked truth, an earnest of the infinite possibilities of self-invention – which is really an intensification of real personality:

> No mask like open truth to cover lies
> As to go naked is the best disguise.

For Wilde the naked truth was the truth of masks; the theatre was a public place for exhibiting private personality; a fairy ring for language spells. The dock was an extension. At his trial, he soliloquised from the witness box, regarding the court as a badly cast production of *Hamlet*. (The performance was reviewed by Max Beerbohm in a letter, who said: 'That his talk was mostly a monologue was not his own fault . . . Nobody was

36

willing to interrupt the music of so magnificent a virtuoso'.) As he'd prophesied in *Lord Arthur Savile's Crime*: 'Most men and women are forced to perform parts for which they have no qualifications. Our Guildensterns play Hamlet for us, and our Hamlets have to jest like Prince Hal.' Wilde, a born Falstaff, posturing as Yorick, clanked off to Reading gaol as a reviled Gertrude. The law, represented by Mr Justice Wills, had no sympathy with histrionics. Acting was the skill and mentality that dare not speak its name.

THE SMITHY OF THE SOUL

Feloniousness had a grand allure for Wilde – the dandy and epicurean who loved the low-life; the husband and father leading a double life (a double-dealer), feasting with panthers, as he exotically called his renters. Like Dorian Gray, he was a connoisseur of sensation – the ultimate sensations, in Dorian's case, being rape, drugs, murder. Homosexuality put Wilde outside the law, and the special status, secretly held until his arrest at the Cadogan Hotel, held for him all the romanticism of the rebel. A glamour alike to Robin Hood's, Don Giovanni's, Captain Morgan's and Colonel Blood's, the Irish desperado who made off with the Crown Jewels, and whom Charles II pardoned with an annuity of £500.

Wilde went so far as to suggest crime created culture. In *Pen, Pencil and Poison* he wrote an affectionate, enthusiastic memoir of the forger and murderer, Thomas Griffith Wainewright, 'a true virtuoso'. Beautiful and cruel, with curly hair and sexy eyes (is he describing Bosie?), and wearing a signet ring containing crystals of strychnine, Wainewright had 'the delightful distinction of being different from others'. A polymath aesthete, loving the colour green, fine bindings, expensive scent, filigree furnishings, and being conversant in the classics, he looked like Dorian and suffered the fate of Wilde – he instigated a fatal court action, escaped to the Continent, pursued a desperate love; and instead of Reading gaol he had transportation to Tasmania. 'His crimes seem to have had an important effect upon his art', says Wilde, referring to Wainewright's perfervid paintings and purple prose. 'One can fancy an intense personality being created out of sin.'

Sin is a metaphysical cheekiness; a confident evasion of virtue – or of *earnestness*. And *The Importance of Being Earnest* is really the importance of *appearing* sincere. Wilde created an impossible, almost surreal, world – where all that matters is the interplay of wit and words. The blasphemy of the play lies in its implication that feeling and sensibility are as nothing if you can't be amusing. And the wit has to be kept going at a frantic pace. It's almost as if, beyond the garden wall (*The Selfish Giant* is about walls), outside Eden, the paradise of perfect sentence-construction will be lost. These characters are trapped in a capsule, condemned to *talk*. Chief tormentor is Lady Bracknell, laying down parody laws – and where there's a law there's a chance for crime and sin – she doesn't believe in. A sacred monster fed on cucumber sandwiches.

Tyrants and despots in Jacobean drama, and before (Tamburlaine, Titus Andronicus), nabbed lands, appropriated countries; their castles have now become a Mayfair drawing room. Vassals and henchmen have dwindled into the cool manservant, Merriman or Lane. Yet still the animus is the same: annexation of property (by marriage); the frenzy of love. The problems of (emotional and physical) power. The topsy-turvy tipsy plot teeters on matters of affection and economics. Wilde almost sends up sentimental Victorian melodrama – and the main impediment on Jack's prospects is that he doesn't know who his parents were: a problem of identity, an existential anxiety, like Oliver Twist's (and Oedipus's and Moses's): 'I don't actually know who I am by birth.' When the dilemma is repeated, birth matters less than authenticity: 'Lady Bracknell, I hate to seem inquisitive, but would you kindly inform me who I am?'

The simplest and most complex issue of drama: who people really are? The actor's ancient question: what am I?

Forgery is the illegality of letters, the concealment of form: form *acting*. Wilde, applauding Wainewright's hoaxes and murders, aligns moral and mortal crimes, making both aesthetic. The latter was necessary to win an insurance claim – money to underwrite the creation of art. The former was a value judgement. Helen Abercrombie was poisoned because 'she had very thick ankles'. The critic as artist as executioner. And all this bears upon *The Portrait of Mr. W.H.*, a cozenage classic. The story, once again about forgery, is camouflaged literary criticism. Cyril Graham has a theory that the 'onlie begetter' of Shakespeare's sonnets was Willie Hughes, a Ganymedish actor, and not the Earls of Southampton or Essex. But what proof is there? Pettishly opining that only the vulgar need proof, Graham flourishes an exquisite Elizabethan miniature of an enticing spadger. The proof, however, is faked and, his trickery revealed, Graham kills himself.

His death, though, raises ambiguities. The scholar-dilettante commits suicide not because he is confronted with the frailty of his theory: he commits suicide as a warranty for his theory's truth. He wills his theory into existence; it is a triumph of fancy. A masterpiece of circumstantial evidence, the theory lets the power of the imagination devise accountability; lets the inventive brain devises facts where there is silence, evidence where there is emptiness.

That the sonnets may be ciphers for Shakespeare's autobiography, their order capable of infinite rearrangement, to make new narratives, is an ancient sport. Here the structure is pederastic. Willie Hughes is the lad 'for whom he created' Viola, Imogen, Juliet . . . But homoerotic ogling gives way in Wilde's mind (once the mechanics of the story reach the literary exegesis stage) to considerations of the actor's craft: Willie Hughes is present in the sonnets when Shakespeare mentions topics like shadows and breathing, e.g. a line such as 'Where breath most breathes, even in the mouth of men'. An actor breathes life into a dramatist's words, as God vivified clay Adam. (And Theseus says that even the very best actors are but shadows – amended by the audience's imagination.) The sonnets explore 'the true relations between the art of the actor and the art of the dramatist'.

> What is your substance, whereof are you made,
> That millions of strange shadows on you tend?
> Since every one hath, every one, one shade,
> And you, but one, can every shadow lend.

Willie Hughes is changeable, yes, because he's a capricious colt – but mainly because his job is to people a stage.

Though actorial references accrue, and the interpretation of theatrical images is ingenious and right – of Hughes himself in the actual sonnets, alas, there's no sign. Wilde has located a sincere, brilliant argument in a blatant fiction or maggot. The point, of course, is that the fiction *ought* to be fact. Cyril Graham generated his fiction and literary criticism, then had the miniature fabricated which, though a forgery, 'does not affect the truth of the story'.

The truth of the story is inviolate, because art, to Wilde, was inviolate (its lies and secrets sacramental) – a sanctuary, like the theatre itself, the great globe itself. 'All Art', he said, is 'to a certain degree a mode of acting, an attempt to realise one's own personality on some imaginative plane out of reach of the trammelling accidents and limitations of real life.' Acting is a betterment.

FROM THE DEPTHS

According to *The Portrait of Mr. W.H.*, those entreaties in the sonnets about breeding and founding dynasties have nothing to do with children: they are beseechings that the addressee become a wild oater in acting.

> Make thee an other self for love of me,
> That beauty still may live in thine or thee!

The actor will raise words up into the fabulous, duplicating his soul in the parts he plays. An actor, he'll spawn an identical – and distinct – world: stage life is real life, improved. And so in spite of Wilde's sense of sin and dissidence, which besides homosexuality encompasses his philosophy of cultural artifice, the lesson is quirkily theological. Fictional truth is nobler, higher, than factual truth. Fake up evidence to prove a theory that feels right, and it's a proof of holy writ, no less expedient than wine believed to be blood, bread body. Take, eat.

Crime Wilde regarded as a gate to grace, sinning the bridge to sainthood. ('What is termed sin is an essential element of progress.') Belittled after the trial, he wrote *De Profundis* – the sermon to Lord Alfred Douglas, in which his identification of sorrow is with Christ's suffering. Picking hemp, he's purging the world's sins. Christ, he says, being infinitely sympathetic – able to imagine 'the leprosy of the leper, the darkness of the blind' – is the perfect artist, his temper that of the perfect actor, who can be all things to all men: 'His desire was to be to the myriads who had found no utterance a very trumpet through which they might call to Heaven.' With Christ *the* actor, his art and conduct inextricable (like Wainewright's, like Wilde's), we return to an earlier proposition: acting as rite and ritual, and the career most apt to appreciate this is Peter Brook's. 'Once, theatre could begin as magic,' he announced with angry nostalgia, 'magic at the sacred festival, or magic as the footlights came up.' Now, theatre compels no attention. Audiences are bored by its sham. His solution was to take Shakespeare's most over-decorated play, and rediscover its power.

According to Brook, *A Midsummer Night's Dream* was lost under a tradition of Victorian gossamer fairy-folk and Max Reinhardt gloss – the forest a pantomime grotto of splashing babies and Theseus's palace a shiny staircase for Olivia de Havilland to come down, backlit. So Brook banished the magic of prettification for a different brand of sorcery; a sorcery having nothing to do with shadow-effects and scenic illusion. The audience confronted a brilliant white box (as I did in Cardiff) and the enthusiasm of the actors and the imagination of their playing elicited spells and trickery – Oberon discoursing about the moss bank where the wild thyme blows, whilst spinning a plate on a long pole; the stilts and trapezes.

Brook's production was a day at the circus; the clowning and acrobatics co-opted for a serious purpose – to expose the play's sexual lessons. *A Midsummer Night's Dream* moves from chivalric romance through to blatant coupling on the moss; from adolescent fumbles to full-scale bestiality. A fertility rite. And, as Shakespeare's method of exposition is to disguise what he's exposing, the play's dangerous lessons are hedged with elaborate metaphors of make-believe and blindness, drugs and music. We can, if we want, discount the whole haunted nocturne as fantasy. Brook was highly theatrical about theatricality: his troupe of actors donned their purple robes before us; they lounged on the balcony around the set; they came and went up the aisles; they shook our hands as we left ('Give me your hands, if we be friends'). By not pretending to be other than actors acting, the acting was the more convincing – a technique further developed by Trevor Nunn for *Nicholas Nickleby*, where the performance was a putting together of a Dickens novel over eight hours.

And in *The Fair Maid of the West*, Nunn craftily retained in the final show elements of untidiness and clumsiness – actors watched one actor act, muff lines, dry, corpse, strut. The Swan was a tavern, the actors the boozers preparing to put on a play: actors acting being amateur actors. The clutter visible offstage never stopped being the pub goblets and barrels, even when requisitioned as the lumber on a ship or the bestrewn junk of an oriental palace.

Nunn bade us enter the theatre to see his cast lolling in an inn, making a model ship or distributing beer to people in the front row. Lamps dangling from long ropes cast a mellow glow – the ropes easily suggesting a galleon's rigging; the hoisted curtains, sails. Gradually all this gentle massaging diminished; the actors cleared the stage – to make the empty space. The casualness was very perfectly choreographed, the actors receiving cues from the pastiche Elizabethan band; and they grouped to tell us a story – like *Henry IV Parts I* and *II*, interpreted by Nunn as a Victorian novel: dynastic wrangling, greed, Joss Ackland's Falstaff a disconsolate Pickwick.

Here's what makes Nunn different from Brook. Nunn is an entertainer, for whom the stage is a flow of pictures desiring narrative; he wants to amuse and to divert us. Brook, by contrast, is a metaphysician, for whom the stage is a religious place; he wants to instruct us – his productions being ceremonies ('magic at the sacred spectacle'). His ambition is to obliterate the barrier between stage and spectator (Nunn's is to have the spectator agog at the stage wizardry – our resistance down because the actors have talked to us*); and, indeed, much of Brook's

---

* Though I much admire the shambolic style, it's worth coming to hate if you can write a sentence like this: 'The trouble with the RSC, I suspect, is not that the company has a house style (though at its worst, it has, and I don't mean the tendency of the actors to curl up in your lap both metaphorically and sometimes actually both before – when they do it actually, and during, when they do it, thank God, only metaphorically – the performance; or the inability of their stars to speak a single line without vocal curlicues, loops and other lingerings; or their determination to point either their faces or their buttocks – remembering even as I write this, the recent Hal delivering one of the great speeches with his back to the audience, sword or crown – I can't remember which – held aloft as his buttocks jiggled and jounced to what purpose I still can't grasp; or – but I'm temperamentally unsuited to comment fairly on the RSC at their worst, being the only person I know to have left after a mere three hours or so of *Nicholas Nickleby*, still shaking at the recollection of the actors who'd impeded my progress to my seat with insolent assurances that I was about to have a good time, thus guaranteeing that I didn't; I didn't like the play much either, thinking it would probably work better as a novel), but that the audience has a house style to match it, being the kind of people who admire, even encourage, the kind of thing outlined in the bracket above.' Not, as you'd suppose, the rant of a Kingsley Amis character, but the opinion of playwright Simon Gray in *An Unnatural Pursuit*.

work is a philosophic anatomy of what makes a stage, what makes an actor, what makes an audience. *A Midsummer Night's Dream*, with its play-within-a-play, the rehearsals, the characters who eavesdrop upon each other and who try to control, invisibly, their destinies: all these layers Brook's production displayed – despite my remembrance of tie-and-dye costumes, minstrelsy, guitars, a crimson ostrich feather, beehive hairdos, flower-power fairies, modish hallucinogens, and all the rest of the bric-a-brac from the Age of Aquarius. And this laboratorial, ethnic style (his *Antony and Cleopatra* was contained in a translucent octagon decorated with oriental carpets) contrasts with Nunn's love of detail and clutter – his *The Merry Wives of Windsor* was located in a Tudor warren of beams, fabrics and heraldic devices. Brook's never even been near that play.

Brook's contemporary Shakespeare is now, in retrospect, a period piece. And though the image is of a grail knight, questing for spiritual enlightenment, Brook's forays into the African bush have an antique charm, too. Is he Sir James Frazer, searching the arid plains, or a hippy stuck in a Sixties time-warp (1968 is when he moved to Paris)? A devotee of sexual liberations, tom-toms, drum-kits and the chanting of mantras. His *Antony and Cleopatra* failed, to my mind, not because the idiom of the production was wrong – austere raffia matting and low benches, Glenda Jackson growling, Alan Howard frowning – but because Brook has accelerated beyond the subsidised lazy mess which our major theatres often become; where energy is directed at a press night and dissipated in repertoire; where actors are often absent during the day making lucrative junk for television or the cinema; where there's zero authentic dedication. His Centre International de Créations Théâtrales, behind a railway station in Paris, has the atmosphere of a monastery in Ladakh, where rehearsals are a process of joyous meditation. Stratford's atmosphere is of a railway station buffet, by comparison.

O DOUGHTY DEED!

An anthropological practitioner, Brook travels in order to watch his company's reaction when it performs before remote tribes. Having banished the conventions of the stage, he avoids paying audiences for years at a time, preferring drama to be provoked in village squares or lonely quarries. (He admires the Naya Theatre, from Chhattishgarh and Madhya Pradesh, India, because the players are illiterate nomads, uninfected by modern life.) John Heilpern, in his book *Conference of the Birds*, is appropriately satirical about one such adventure, through the Sahara. Brook's actors were a parliament of fowls, mislaying luggage at the airport, having no place to wash or shit; covered with mosquito bites and squabbling about the chores of the scout camp.

But Brook himself is blithely serene, playing Zen master to a polyglot and quarrelsome group, a few of its members ('Their disunity will be their unity') picked up from gaols and communes. The African excursion was not only to seek out tribes and play for them: the actors themselves became a tribe* which, every day, indulged in vigorous class exercises with gongs and kazoos. Music and movement experiments proceeded into the dead of the desert night. Hoots and screeches are perfected. Improvisations are commanded.

Hour upon hour, day upon day, week upon week, Brook worked his actors – and the intention is to go beyond acting: the routines are designed for 'heightening perception on every conceivable level'. If this smacks of speciousness, neither were the locals impressed. Shows improvised out of boxes and sticks were ridiculed. The audience invaded the carpet – on which the actors acted – or broke into hysterics. Brook, wanting to find an audience without preconceptions, an audience who didn't even know what actors were, found that such innocence meant a lack of manners. The Africans were like hecklers, interrupters. Of course Brook knew what was afoot, and he tried to have his followers learn from the discovery: it was the actors who had to be educated, not the audience. They had to learn to incorporate the audience and master a technique of absolute simplicity and force, which would compel attention as a conductor, creating as he gestures, has his baton trace alert arabesques, like the tip of Picasso's brush. And, coalescing impulse and action, the acting only then will be transcendent: 'a mysterious power that everyone feels but no philosopher has explained' (Goethe).

LOGICO–PHILOSOPHICUS I

Indulgent picaresque adventures in many ways, Brook's voyages to Persepolis, Tamanrasset or the Australian outback were field trips to his famous void – the empty space, which, though a reference to the blank stage, carries implications of the theatre as a milky way; a galaxy and astrological cloud chamber. *The Empty Space* (1968), a book composed of four lectures, is the equivalent of Paul's letters to the Ephesians; gospeller's rant or a medicine man's diagnosis. Drama happens, says Brook, when a man watches another man carry out an action: there we have spectator and performer – and the purpose of Brook's work is a celebration of the flow between them. The empty time and space is instantly filled by acting, display, show – like two tramps passing the hours on a lonely road with a pantomime involving bowler hats and shoes.

* The group psychology may be compared with Brook's film version of Golding's *Lord of the Flies*. He's evidently intrigued by the dynamics of enforced social mixes.

The scrupulosity of diction and gesture Brook admires in Beckett; but in his analysis of acting, and indeed in his entire inquisitional attitude, he recalls Wittgenstein – for whom space was never empty: it was a bustle of facts, ideas and meditative silences. In *Tractatus Logico–Philosophicus* we read: 'Each thing is, as it were, in a space of possible states of affairs. This space I can imagine empty, but I cannot imagine the thing without the space.' Like Wittgenstein, Brook is persistent and tenacious, convinced his mysticism shall yield solutions – he wants the silence to speak and emptiness to cease being invisible. Again, the *Tractatus:* 'Scepticism is not irrefutable, but obviously nonsensical, when it tries to raise doubts where no questions can be asked . . . For doubt can only exist where a question exists, a question only where an answer exists, and an answer only where something *can be said*'.

But speech is not the only available language; what we cannot speak about we can pass on with gesture, image, song. Acting is an intimation of the fluid communication before Babel; paradigms lost. With Ted Hughes, Brook even attempted to strip down speech to a primordial noise, called Orghast – a search for the Indo-European parent of every idiolect; the daddy of dialect. *Conference of the Birds* relied upon screeches and trills. A production of Seneca's *Oedipus*, adapted by Ted Hughes, had the cast chanting and wailing. Hughes's text is a crumbling wall, his sentences lacking punctuation and disintegrating. An archaeological picturesqueness. The actors, in satin suits, were positioned about the auditorium, tethered to pillars, humming, groaning, grunting. Amidst the break-up of enunciation, serene in a lake of moans, was Sir John Gielgud, practising his look of disdainful detachment, which has become so necessary in an old age of making appearances in bad films.

For *Oedipus*, the stage displayed a rotating gold cube (a symbolic receptacle – thus a cunt, a womb, a coffin) and a gold ithyphallus (a fertility symbol and spike for impaling and blinding). Sex and death kept company. Brook ended the evening with an oompah band – the tragedy converted into a bacchanal. Instead of confusion, the effect was startling, happy – like the frenzy of a village fiesta in the Mediterranean heat. Brook's empty space was redolent of stark mysteries, which was also the tone of his *Carmen* adaptation, where Bizet's music spoke a language beyond words. Brook had the libretto rinsed of its operetta accretions and the score purged of bombast. A grand opera was cleaned and made into a taut drama of eighty minutes' duration, accompanied by piano and a few strings; a taut drama, with erotic tribal underswells.

Three television films were made of the event, Brook wanting to test the repercussions of different casts – and, watching the trio of versions, the effect is similar to visiting a live show three nights in a row: essentially identical, but with subtle alterations and shadings of mood. And by making three versions, Brook tries to break the ice-age heave of movies whereby a production is fixed forever in a spliced selection of takes. The three versions hint at theatre's constant renewal – where characterization should never be complete; where each performance is a renaissance. Unfinished, theatre lives.

LOGICO–PHILOSOPHICUS II

The stage, the empty space, Brook calls 'a perfect philosopher's machine,' and it cranks and delivers a fourfold product. The 'Deadly Theatre' is what Brook found in the Stratford parish – 'a deadly sentimentality and complacent worthiness' – where productions were boring and academically respectable; then there's the 'Holy Theatre', capable of analysing power, silence, concentration, fighting – where, as in the Mass, 'an invisible idea was rightly shown'. Next there is the 'Rough Theatre', puppet shows or improvised village entertainment, with no props or trickery. Last comes the 'Immediate Theatre', which has the experiment and energy of rehearsal.

Perfection would seem to be any style not contaminated by the dire decorum of Brook's first category: 'We were trying to smash the apparently watertight division between the private and the public man,' releasing into the empty space a holy, rough, immediate anarchy – as in *Marat/Sade*, for example, where the Marquis de Sade was lashed by Charlotte Corday's hair; or the pistol shots into the auditorium of *The Brothers Karamazov*; or the barbarity of *Titus Andronicus*, with the costumes and lighting inspired by Italian mannerist painting, which so impressed Jan Kott ('Mr Brook did not discover *Titus*. He discovered Shakespeare in *Titus*'; and Brook said in the preface to *Shakespeare Our Contemporary*, 'Shakespeare is a contemporary of Kott, Kott is a contemporary of Shakespeare'). For, what salvages Brook from an astral pretentiousness is his love of danger, blood, strife. The *Marat/Sade* was set in a madhouse/bath-house; and Brook has spoken of his appreciation of the scene in Welles's *Othello*, where a murder was conducted in a steamy catacomb, the wildcats dressed in towels. His *Carmen* was played on dirt floors (the desert brought inside) within the artful decrepitude of the Théâtre des Bouffes du Nord, the Paris music hall, its walls all umber, apricot and saffron patches. Carmen was the village sorceress, making spells from feathers and pebbles; divining the future from a grubby card pack.

The brown-stained space was a tribal clearing and a tatty bullring. Escamillo, the professional slaughterer of beasts, in Carmen found an animal-woman, a Lamia, a siren, crouching before real fires, dancing through gaol and tavern. All the characters wore splattered, messy, rubbed-out clothes – and, beyond their energy, there was a sense of exhaustion, of tragic inevitability. Brook makes mythical resonance by having his cast look historically credible, as if smelling of tobacco and dung. Costumes which don't look like costumes; acting which doesn't appear to be acting; a theatre, Bouffes du Nord, which looks a disused wreck.

Mystical, he's also the most naturalistic man of acting; this habit makes him amenable to aboriginal culture, where tales are measured out in the landscape – 'You don't read stories, you walk them.' The earth is their literature. And a song of the earth is Brook's theatrical mood; a hymn of crops, sun, moon, love, death.★ His productions are fiestas of purification and fertility – like *Oedipus* or *A Midsummer Night's Dream* or *Antony and Cleopatra*, with the memorable image of mud and clots of blood splashing on a translucent screen.

BULL FEVER

Brook's phantasms are salvaged because they fill up with blood. He's no maya, illusion. There's anger in his work and (as *Marat/Sade* explored) cruelty. His *King Lear* was located in a rusting Iron-Age Britain; the film version (1971) was shot on location in a frozen Denmark, Lear's King-dom a mad, snowy waste land. The intense cold matched the heat of *Carmen*, where killing is to the cigar-fondler and her Don José their duet of coupling. They're in the ring. The corrida is a frequent metaphor for Brook. Audience and actors confront each other 'like a bullfight . . . The challenge is to bring the bull to a standstill. But the bullfight is different with every fight. If you don't see that, it will kill you.' Which suggests the bull is master, to be usurped by his cape-wielding slave. Carmen, José and Escamillo, during the opera, alternate roles of beast and boss. Then Brook might claim, 'Occasionally, an actor can completely dominate any house, and so, like a master matador, he can work the audience the way he pleases.' Which suggests the bull is a black beauty, hypnotised (Carmen is both hypnotised and hypnotist) and seduced.

The corrida, blood in the sand, death in the afternoon, is a potent empty space (claustrophobic and, daring infinitude, agoraphobic, and at the same time) and it was a favourite pursuit of Kenneth Tynan's, whose *Bull Fever* (1955) is a primer of his critical stance. His love of personality and excitement found its fullest expression in the ensanguined vaudeville; he was particularly smitten with Antonio Ordóñez and Luis Miguel Dominguín, friends of Picasso and Ava Gardner. Of a contest at Ronda, where the matadors dressed as characters from Goya etchings, he claimed to see in action 'the difference between science and art'; he appreciated the

---

★ When the *Mahabharata* played at Glasgow in the Spring of 1988, Brook brought with him tons of red earth, which was rolled and packed to make a turf stage. He's the biggest fetcher of damp loam since Count Dracula.

difference between technique and genius – 'What we all go to the bull-fights to see: the difficult made easy.' Tynan also went to see Noël Coward padding to the microphone, Marlene Dietrich drawling in cab-aret and Mel Brooks yawping on television, for the same reason. He wanted to find out about the lustre of stardom (what he termed 'high definition performances') and the effortlessness of effort.

For Tynan, tauromachy was a social caravan, as well as an experience 'alternately vile and glorious'. Orson Welles cruised the corridas; Picasso was often in the crowd; 'I sat a few seats away from Hemingway, and tears were trickling down into his beard.' Foreigners, he said, 'tend to feel outsiders' at the big matches, 'unless they are rich, famous or aristocratic'. Tynan's essays tell us the best bars to seek out, the best hotels, the best sherry. And when he says 'the bullfight seems to me a logical extension of all the impulses my temperament holds – love of grace and valour, of poise and pride . . .' we believe him. The corrida was a machine for exhilaration, converting a person (the matador) into a performance.

Not so for Brook. The corrida, and theatre itself, is in his work an extrapolation of power switches between protagonists, so that actor and audience, master and slave, bull and matador, form an entity, a swish of energy, a vortex. He has gathered his disciples in France to explore a communal project – the Indian epic of gods and heroes, the *Mahabharata*; and the concern with tribal vortices recedes right back into his career, from the bandits and scoundrels of *The Beggar's Opera*, through the perverted and savage choirboys after the end of the world in *Lord of the Flies*,* to the flick-knife clan in *Carmen*. He prefers the drama of a society to the egocentricity of a star pyrotechnic – Tynan's preference. (And Tynan's self-exile to California was not, like Brook's to France, a dis-covery of a zestful great good place, but a loitering on the margin, because of his rotting lungs.)

Brook, in his private life, is frugal and retiring. He doesn't traipse the boulevards living up to his success. Nor is he interested in recognition and personal fame. Descended from Russian aristocracy, his palace is that tumbledown Bouffes du Nord. Tynan, illegitimate, raising himself to be the only brainbox in Edgbaston, and at Magdalen behaving like a Wilde dressed up as Lord Alfred Douglas, cladding himself in astrakhan, found in the corrida a drama of sado-masochism ('The animal, by the end', stuck with darts and lances, humiliated, 'is part of us'). A Romantic theatre of danger and risk, with himself safe in his tiered seat.

Tynan was urgent and vain (and Brook's the obverse of vanity fair), eating at L'Étoile (he'd not have quitted Algiers airport if a proposed delegate at the *Conference of the Birds*) and making lists of perfect raconteurs. Of the inmates of *Show People* he said, 'They all rank high on the list

---

* Golding's novel was first brought to Brook's attention by Tynan.

of people whom I would invite to an ideal dinner party.' (Louise and Mel Brooks, Tom Stoppard, Ralph Richardson, Johnny Carson.) He was a Chelsea Alcibiades, organizing glitzy symposia. *The Sound of Two Hands Clapping* was a 'harvest of preferences and predilections'; and, to Tynan, taste was almost exclusively gormandocratic. He was a sybarite. Theatre was a luxury he needed to afford, like the annual jaunts to Valencia or Malaga.

THE MAN WHO SAID ★★★★ I

In *Bull Fever*, if the bull represents Nature, then the matador is Artful Man; his passes with the whirling capes and stabs with the sword are deceptive and mean tricks. The bull lives out an authentic tragedy; he's wantonly tortured, and after the suffering, he obligingly dies. And he gives a single performance only. The bull is fooled into thinking he's participating in a sport; actually, it's murder. (How different from the Brook interpretation, where the corrida is a marriage.) The bull is as blind as Othello – and if Tynan began his career niggling to Olivier about Vivien Leigh ('A cat, in fact, can do more than look at a King: she can hypnotize him'), like Iago's insinuations concerning Desdemona, he neared the end of it as the ensign, tamed. Invited to join the National Theatre on the Frank Harris Principle ('If Frank isn't with you, he's against you'), Tynan helped pick the repertoire and attended rehearsals; but he became the court fool, lonely, powerless, famous only for saying 'fuck' on television and for devisings wan sex-shows like *Oh, Calcutta!*

His problem was that of the critic-as-artist who wants to be known as an artist, ashamed of being him who 'knew the way but couldn't drive the car'. This sense of humiliation, coupled with his love of chit-chat (wanting to take home theatrical greats so they'd perform in his parlour) and playing out his self-appointed role as holy host, made him seem weaker than he really was. It was as if the lively commentator on the lively arts during the drab Fifties had become, in the Sixties, a flabby flâneur, reducing stars to the level of luminaries at his cocktail hours; and, in the Seventies, an ill consort of the undead like Louise Brooks.

But there's always his prose, and that remains Tynan's art. It's impossible to write now with feeling on the theatre without scribbling in his shadow. His articles were in the nature of theatrical feats: thousand-word turns. He's the better craftsman; and every day, on my way to college, I pass his grave. My title, *Stage People*, is obvious homage; and I invented, along with a shutterbug friend intoxicated by the style of Sam Raimi, a back-cover design of surpassing tastelessness: me posing behind the stone (KENNETH TYNAN 1927–1980) whilst supplicating hands push up through the soil; me dressed in extravagant mourning, like Tynan lamenting at the National Theatre foundation stone; me doing a mad jig on the plot; me laying out a Fortnum's hamper for two.

THE MAN WHO SAID ★★★★ II

No question, he's one of the two men of the century I'd like to have known (the other is either Orson Welles or Ezra Pound). It's the arrogance I admire, the ambivalent hucksterism. The way he wants theatre to be a bloody bullfight – and yet then he can say, acting is the re-enactment of golden childhood; stage people, a gallery of Peter Pans; theatre, a playpen, playtime, playmates . . . And, apart from the etiolated episode at the National Theatre, when he tried to belong to a system he should have been the dyspeptic observer of, what Tynan liked about actors, his cavortings with them for social purposes aside, was their exclusivity. Actors are outsiders, rebels. (Compare with Brook, who'd put the shamans back in our midst.) They exist both to sell themselves and to remain inaccessible; cunning enigmas, who flaunt their talent with a disdainful 'absolute hard-edged clarity of outline'. Tynan was entranced by Nicol Williamson's all-night jazz sessions or Lenny Bruce's self-destruction, as much as by Roman Polanski dismembering *Macbeth* or Ethel Merman filling the Palladium with brass. Perhaps because, as rebels, actors have walked out on authority and restraint – is that what he liked? Tony Richardson has said Tynan's own entire career 'was like a long letter home to his parents in Birmingham'. You can take the boy out of Edgbaston, but you'll have a hard time taking Edgbaston out of the boy; but the boy did his life-long best.

> Some people
> May be content
> Playing bingo
> And paying rent . . .
> *But some people*
> *Ain't me!*

Tynan's province: performances which exemplified the dolce vita of self-gratification. This edged into his sexual proclivity. Tynan praised hardcore because of that one 'inalienable right' (as he put it, like the Statue of Liberty and the Declaration of Independence) binding mankind together – 'the right of self-abuse'. To exalt masturbation like this is to have Narcissus depose Eros as the amatory godling. Tynan's two clapping hands, we might say, abandoning taste again, fumbled no further than his own crotch.

He enjoyed fireworks for their short explosion of sulphurous spermatozoa. Rockets and Roman candles shoot to a peak and quickly fall as burnt-out joy. The fast thrill of rutting he searched for in life as in art, or artistry. And the 'atmosphere of intoxication' at the bullfight was a physical, sensual delight to him. (Compare with Brook, who'd desire only an atmosphere of epic battle – never of Romantic headiness.) Tynan's quest was for reason's eclipse by passion, discipline by dandification, urbanity by the vulgar quirk. The one brief shining moment making up for the anxious wait.

In the bullfight he found a menace he wished for upon the English stage, especially Olivier* in the tragic roles (Coriolanus, Titus Andronicus, Antony, Othello). The actor, like the bullfight, demonstrated the beast in the jungle of our natures; both are allegories of domination and destruction. In *Richard III*, Olivier 'tips his animal head back', he 'thrashes about with animal ferocity'; his Hotspur has a 'heavy-handed tenderness' and his speeches were 'an aggressive explosion of outraged innocence'. Olivier, for Titus, made his voice 'a terrible bellow'. The bull become man: 'the noise made in its last extremity by the cornered human soul' – which was also the music of Othello, speechifying 'like the dying moan of a fighting bull'. The corrida, the Old Vic, is Minos's labyrinth, built by Daedalus to house the part-man, part-beast. An actor is a minotaur, theatre a place for blood letting.†

ANGER AND NOSTALGIA

Tynan's is a theatre of solo adventure and personal pleasure. When he talked of Olivier's 'unparalleled animal powers', he meant the noble savagery of the thundering taurine – and also something more. Tynan's

---

* Of Gielgud's Othello, by contrast, Tynan said 'instead of a wounded bull, dangerous despite its injuries, we have a heraldic eagle with its wings harmlessly clipped.'

† Tauromachy was made by Olivier into a traumatography: '1 broken ankle. 2 torn cartilages. 2 broken calf muscles. 3 ruptured Achilles tendons. Untold slashes . . . Implacement . . . Broken foot . . . Broken face . . . Near broken neck . . . Arrow shot between shinbones . . . Near electrocution . . .' – listed in Olivier's preface to *Techniques of the Stage Fight* by William Hobbs, and quoted in *Olivier: In Celebration*, edited by Garry O'Connor, who says of the 'self-inflicted wounds and mutilations', to which must be added the actor's many pneumonias, cancers, thromboses and dermato-poly-myocites, that 'just as primitive man thought that by hunting and killing an animal, then eating it, he absorbed its soul into his own, has Olivier, by mastering so many roles, come magically and spiritually, to assume the life and power of all those he has played'. Olivier's ailments constitute a life-long sacrificial rite, carried out on the altar of his own personality. He has allowed himself to suffer like Titus Andronicus: his body a butcher's block, a hacked toro bravo. Anthony Quayle (Aaron to Olivier's Titus) said: 'Everybody flogs you every time they look at you as Titus. You are bemoaning your fate throughout and whatever happens to you is just another ghastly stroke of the knout.'

diction and mannerisms brand him as of his era. He learned his craft as a reporter-for-posterity during the war, and his prose is packed with gleeful metaphors of military life, violence, assassination, intrigue. Tynan's language fiddles whilst Europe burns. The theatre-critic as war correspondent. (Brook, two years Tynan's senior, is also moved to make cloak-and-dagger allusions: 'I first met Jan Kott in a night club in Warsaw: it was midnight . . . a beautiful girl was arrested by mistake under our eyes . . .'). His articles are despatches from the Front (Stalls) – as when, in 1945, he reviewed *Henry IV* and pronounced it a monument of what theatre 'had learnt since Irving . . . It is surprising . . . that English acting should have reached up and seized a laurel crown in the middle of a war.' But it's not surprising at all. The Histories are a commentary on English conflict, the rise and death of Kings, the routing of despots. Shakespeare was a Forties contemporary; Olivier's film of *Henry V*, with newsreel music by William Walton, was pure political propaganda.

Tynan's first book, *He That Plays the King*, demonstrated a predisposition for dramas about lordship; and with the preface by Orson Welles, Tynan found a Falstaff for his Hal. Years later, meeting at a bar after a bullfight, the fat man and the haggard man would fall into a discussion of Eastcheap or Shallow's orchard. And the alarums and incursions erupt through his notices: Jack Benny 'inwardly meditates mayhem'; Coward's delivery is 'the staccato, blind impulsiveness of a machine-gun'; in Ethel Merman's hands 'musical comedy became a martial art', Beatrice Lillie was 'a guided missile' who for four decades conducted 'guerilla warfare against words as a means of communication'. Burton's voice 'cuts urgent and keen' and Chevalier's catches 'jagged razors of innuendo'; Wolfit's Othello was like 'the bloody exploits of Hiroshima', Olivier's 'a hand grenade'; and 'scratch the languid veneer of Miss Gingold's stage-self, and a gushing barbarism flows forth . . .'

Tynan, with his 'soft spot' for *Titus Andronicus*, his admiration for Brecht (especially the adaptation of *The Recruiting Officer* called *Trumpets and Drums*) and Hochhuth's *Soldiers*, did indeed confess he'd 'rather be a war correspondent than a necrologist'; he'd rather describe skirmishes than count the dead. But where does the stridency come from?

Though, of course, the bellicose style was of his own making, aggression was in the atmosphere when Tynan invented his own mind. A time of searchlights, urgent radio broadcasts, soldiers loitering on railway stations, the threat of invasion. Only twelve when Hitler marched into Poland, he sat out hostilities in the auditoriums of Birmingham, Stratford and Oxford, absorbing acting and translating it into an idiom of romantic adventure and a code of provocation. *He That Plays the King* was published in 1950, when Tynan was aged twenty-three (Brook, aged twenty-five, was in 1950 directing John Gielgud in *Measure for Measure*); and the book is an unanticipated and violent chronicle of what Churchill,

Clement Attlee and European dictators helped do to English life. Tynan belongs with those striplings of the Forties who arrived at young manhood in the Fifties, having missed the call to arms (though not always the call-up), and who generated a dissonance of their own. Men for whom hostilities didn't end with the German surrender. War's now been declared, indeed, upon the home fires, upon the complacency of the happy breed. And unto our culture was born Jimmy Porter, whom Tynan embraced as a blood-brother. 'I doubt', he said in 1956, 'if I could love anyone who did not wish to see *Look Back in Anger.*'

SWEET SWANWATER

John Osborne's opus went unregarded until Tynan's eulogy in the *Observer* had folk think in terms of revolution. Here was the play to give a different voice to an emergent generation! May 1956, like July 1789, was a time for the overthrowing of antique masters (Rattigan, Maugham, Harley Granville-Barker), superannuated popinjays in their Albany apartments. Osborne, 'the Fulham flame-thrower' in Tynan's phrase, an actor since 1948, had banished drawing-room comedy and invented a drama about seedy social realities; he'd brought the provinces into the venerably snooty Sloane Square, and actors could now talk in Midlands accents, instead of having to replicate the squeezed vowels of a shire tea party.

Or had he? Three decades later, *Look Back in Anger* is a different work. The English Stage Company at the Royal Court (if this was the Bastille, it had reassuring, if ironic, patrician patronyms), apparently so progressive, had, in fact, involved itself with a deeply and deliberately retrogressive play. Everything – and the clue is in the title – runs backwards, whether to childhood (Jimmy's and Alison's prattling baby-language), to the Edwardian era (Jimmy's interest in Vaughan Williams, rusticities and an old brigade who 'do make their brief little world look pretty tempting . . . Always the same picture: high summer, the long days in the sun'), or structurally (the last scene begins like the opening tableau, with two indolent men and one girl, skivvying).

Jimmy Porter is a disenchanted, languid, loitering wit, preoccupied by his own youthfulness and its ebbing: 'A few more hours, and another week gone. Our youth is slipping away. Do you know that?' Born in 1931 (twenty-five in May 1956), he's of the generation which had its childhood stolen by the war, so the Fifties are going to be for a delayed, protracted adolescence. A ranting sentimentalist, he has a love-hate relationship with the mood of his parents' generation, especially his late father's romantic political ideals about walking out one midsummer morning to Spain. A land of lost content set to music by Vaughan

Williams: 'Well, that's something, anyway. Something strong, something simple, something English' which the old firm,' he observes crossly, 'is selling out.' Jimmy is frightened by all thoughts of progress and is only happy dwelling on history – 'the last time' Alison went to church, 'the last time' she got angry . . .

He looks back to the future, his speeches coiling about ancient hurts and battles, such as his mockery of the wedding day ('I remember being sick in the vestry') and events, such as they are, take place in a Midlands attic; outside there's a greasy dribble of rain, like a streaky television picture. But this room at the top has no television, nor a refrigerator; only a radio for classical music. Jimmy's pad is a time-capsule, in a play which is a period piece, set in a crumbling Victorian villa. And, looking back to 1900, the perspective recedes further. Tynan called the hero 'the completest young pup in our literature since Hamlet, Prince of Denmark' (which rather overlooks Tristram Shandy, Stephen Dedalus, the priests of love in D. H. Lawrence, Milton's Satan or Peter Pan). But, Tynan's hyperbole aside, Jimmy, like Hamlet, has a fondness for the monologue; he follows his own talk wherever it leads. He has a permanently roving intellect; he's permanently troubled, thinking himself deeper into a sense of resentment and a spirit of envy. He's virtually friendless and, like the Hamlet of Romanticism, nervily thin ('People like me don't get fat . . . We just burn everything up'). His attic is an Elsinore battlement.

Jimmy is not too long down from an unnamed Wittenberg, where he was taught a disputatiousness he's refused to jettison; and if he's to be a regional Hamlet, he certainly terrorizes his Ophelia, Alison. The merry war between them is packed with real cruelty and abuse (this accounts for the play's modernity: Osborne allowed that a man may be brutish and less than dapperly chivalric); the relationship, indeed, is sustained by bickering, founded upon hostility – much muted on Alison's part, making Jimmy a lampoon of a domineering household god out of a Victorian parlour-tale, flapping his newspaper, sunk in a fauteuil, puffing on a pipe. Alison, cooking, laundering, cleaning, is an attentive, abused Wendy, or Mrs Darling. And the infantilism ('Wheeeeeeeeee'!), whilst being coy, links with the nursery-world and abjuration of adult responsibility, which is the stuff of Barrie's Never-Neverland. 'Really, Jimmy, you're like a child,' expostulates his bride, as her lord tips over the ironing board and skulks off to his room; their pet-names, having to do with squirrels and bears, whilst again, coy, have a cruel and bestial element. 'It was one way of escaping from everything – a sort of unholy priest-hole of being animals to one another.' Living at the summit of many stairs, Jimmy's instincts are hardly lofty: his savagery is Darwin in reverse. In temperament, he looks back to the angry ape. Though, actually, to consider him kin to Kong is to overdignify. He's more like a badly behaved baby, Colette and Ravel's *L'Enfant et les Sortilèges*, or Peter Pan. Purposefully recalcitrant, purposefully offensive, Jimmy has stampeded brattishly through the houses of Alison's family and family friends; and as for his relationship with a drinking companion – a childhood crony – called Hugh Tanner, 'I couldn't believe that two people, two educated people could be so savage.'

The attic is inhabited, in addition to the Porters, by Cliff (the play's fey Horatio) and Helena, Alison's pal. Jimmy's father-in-law, Colonel Redfern, also appears. A confined place – a claustrophobic empty space – for power-struggles and palace intrigue. (It's the location later to be invaded by Harold Pinter's proprietorial personnel, from *The Caretaker* to *No Man's Land*: Cliff calls himself a 'no-man's land' between Jimmy and his women.) Gradually, the aimless romping, scrapping, sneering playground atmosphere receives its point: Jimmy mentions a friend called Webster, with whom he's in accord – 'Different dialect but same language.' And is this Webster a reference to John Webster (1578–1632), who wrote bits of *The Malcontent*, *The Duchess of Malfi* and a lost labour called *A Late Murder of the Son Upon the Mother*? If so, then the haphazard rages focus: we have a parody of a revenge-drama. Osborne, writing in the reign of an Elizabeth, has his eye upon the times of another Gloriana.

Alison out of the room, Jimmy peruses her handbag; he won't allow her any privacy – and expects plots and betrayals as much as any dissident in Marston, Middleton, Tourneur ... He lusts for betrayal, indeed ('I want to know if I'm being betrayed,' he shouts with relish); he enjoys the theatricality of rows and discord. 'What are you plotting?' he demands, eager for intrigue. Alison is taunted, because Jimmy wants to watch her suffer his insults; he wants to be everywhere reacted against, yet then despises opposition. (Twenty years on he'll be Bill Hooper in *The Good Father*.) To try and not make him entirely a black villain, like Bosola, Osborne makes a weak effort to render him sympathetic – Jimmy claims to have his own knowledge of pain and humiliation: he's watched old folk die – but the energy of the character is in his heartlessness. (And when Jimmy departs to aid an ancient market stallholder through her stroke, it's mainly an expedient to get him off stage so that his enemy Colonel Redfern can come on.) He's Hieronymo, mad againe.

He thinks he's the only person ever to possess a sensibility, and to Alison he snaps, torturer and voyeur, 'if you could have a child, and watch it die ... if only I could watch you face that.' The aria of hatred is an Elizabethan malcontent's; a delighted disgust at the idea of pregnancy and the secrets of the body. Alison can only confess her pregnancy to Cliff – she fully expects Jimmy to be sickened: 'He'd watch me growing bigger every day, and I wouldn't dare to look at him.' Jimmy's pathologically fastidious. The cinema he won't visit because of what Anthony Burgess calls the stinking swinking – the 'yobs in the front row'; and he's squeamish about Cliff's ragged breeches. The way of all flesh appals him, just as the idea of death ghoulishly entrances him. He says of his mother-in-law: 'My God, those worms will need a good dose of salts the day they get through her! Oh what a bellyache you've got coming to you, my little wormy ones!' Death, deathbeds, graveyards, corpses, 'the sweet, sickly smell of a dying man,' the necropsical is his inky-cloak affectation. 'Tell me, what could be more gilt-edged than the next world! It's a capital gain.'

A permanent infant who smokes and drinks (and who earns his money selling sweets), Jimmy hates real babies, because of the emotional warmth and sentiment they provoke, and because they'd be Oedipal fights for the future; and also because a genuine child in the menage would steal his thunder. Believing himself the only creature gifted with thought (he mocks Cliff's and Alison's use of words like *thought* and *think*), he also reckons he alone is allowed to be noisy. Sounds other than his own voice cause offence: the clatter of necessary domestic chores, the rattle of Cliff reading the paper, church bells, 'the eternal flaming racket of the female'. When absent from the room, Jimmy is present through his incessant trumpet riffs; or else, other people talk about him ('What's he doing?'). Silent, he'd cease to exist. As Helena and Alison conduct an expository conversation – so that we learn about the marriage, the courtship, the pain, the weariness of having to subsist, domestically, within the tintin-nabulation of Jimmy's life – we derive a definition of hell: being trapped in somebody else's talk show, not allowed to speak.

Helena is an actress whom Jimmy hates (Helena says 'I've never seen such hatred in someone's eyes before') – for her ancestry, for her woman-hood, for her apparent weakness. (A misogynist, the hero wants women to serve him; then he despises them for serving him.) Is she named for *A Midsummer Night's Dream*? Certainly, this Helena enters a dark wood where sexual allegiance is fermented. She's attracted to Jimmy's rudery and rabble-rousing, finding his evil erotic.

And though allusions have been to Hamlet and Ophelia, for infor-mation about the wedding, Osborne moves us to Othello and Desde-mona. Alison married Jimmy, as Desdemona did Othello, because of his stories and way with words. She loved him for the dangers he had passed, and he loved her that she did pity them. First sighted, the colourful outsider, at a party – 'the men there all looked as though they distrusted him, and as for the women, they were all intent on showing their contempt for this rather odd creature ... I knew I was taking on more than I was ever likely to be capable of bearing, but there never seemed to be any choice.'

This is when the big revenge-drama generated. Like Othello arraigned by the monumentally aggrieved Brabantio, who rages in the night with lighted tapers, roaming the streets with a posse, interrupting the senate at its urgent business, Jimmy felt the wrath of the Redferns, the decent

Anglo-Indian family (who have a son at suave Sandhurst.) Alison's mother led a 'holy crusade' against him; private detectives were hired – *Othello* crossing with Rosencrantz and Guildenstern from *Hamlet*: 'All those inquiries, the private detectives – the accusations,' all to try and penetrate the mystery which is Jimmy. Hide fox, and all after. To the Redferns, Jimmy's behaviour is an antic disposition – 'he just speaks a different language from any of us'.

Paradoxically, the character Jimmy most resembles is that representative of a class he most despises – Alison's father, who goes in for retrospection ('I don't approve of Jimmy . . ., and I don't suppose I ever should, but *looking back on it*, I think it would have been better . . . if we had never attempted to interfere'★) and a fantasy of England – 'The England I remembered was the one I left in 1914.' He's nostalgic for 'everything purple and golden'. Back from India since 1947, what's he been doing for nine years? Brooding? But at least Colonel Redfern's exile was genuine and far-flung; Jimmy's banishment of the world is a pretentious game, by comparison. The Colonel headed a Maharajah's army; Jimmy, in the drawing room, fought 'a brilliant campaign . . . fairly revelled in the role of the barbarian invader'. Both are militaristic. To Jimmy, the Colonel is 'that old bastard', to the Colonel, Jimmy 'must have had a certain amount of right on his side,' and he concedes a battle of the generations; but what he can't figure is why, in Jimmy's marriage, love has to be ousted by 'challenges and revenge'. Alison repeats the puzzle: why did Jimmy marry her? 'Perhaps it was revenge?' And she can see the congruence between a father and a husband: regarding the modern world, 'neither of you can face it'.

When Helena says Jimmy was 'born out of his time', it's time-past, not some vision of the future, she has in mind. She tries 'the middle of the French Revolution', or 'he's what you'd call an Eminent Victorian,' and Cliff postulates the seventeenth century ('he's just an old Puritan at heart'); but what Osborne ends the play with is Lear's Albion. Back with Alison – the ending is neat chocolate-box direct from those hated superannuated popinjays – husband and wife, like Shakespeare's father and daughter, those two alone will sing like birds i' the cage, and pray and sing, and tell old tales, and take upon themselves the mystery of things: 'We'll be together in our bears' cave . . . and we'll live on honey and nuts . . . And we'll sing songs about ourselves.'

RETROSPECTIVE

Despite the theatrical agent, Peggy Ramsay, being quoted in the *New Yorker* as saying 'John broke the mold. We owe everything to him, and

★ My italics.

I'm devoted to him',* the secret of success with *Look Back in Anger* is that, its gaze fixed on the past, it does indeed present nothing fresh. There's only an illusion of innovation. ('Today's meal is always different from yesterday's and the last woman isn't the same as the one before,' Jimmy says, not believing himself for a moment; for him, things recur.) As a revolution in drama, the play was its own counter-revolution. What the 1956 production did, under the pretence of making things new, was to celebrate, through intense, covert allusion, continuity with a Great Tradition – and the Fifties was the decade of F. R. Leavis's chief influence at Cambridge, preaching from Downing College, whilst not wearing his necktie, the doctrine of sly uppitiness, sombre argument, moral culture and taciturn disgruntlement.† Leavis's book, *The Great Tradition* (1948), is about the pedigree of the novel – a Book of Genesis, from Jane Austen to the sainted Lawrence, by way of George Eliot, Henry James and Joseph Conrad. Leavis believed civilization to depend upon the health of a reading public and the bold forthrightness of art. Culture and society were intertwined to him. And this is what Tynan too saw as the point of looking back in anger – a rage 'based on the idea that art is an influence on life, not a refuge from it or an alternative to it. That, really, is what the anger is all about.'

In 1956, Tynan seemed to pretend he hadn't heard of anger in Brecht, Ruskin, Kipling, Wilde's essays, or the Lord knows what else all. And he didn't appreciate the cultural function of music hall (even though T. S. Eliot had written an obituary on Marie Lloyd). But Osborne did. *Look Back in Anger* contains a vaudeville routine about *Little Gidding*/a gelding iron; and *The Entertainer* is a fond jeremiad on end-of-the-pier comics. Nostalgia and retrospection reached its climax in Tony Richardson's *Tom Jones* – for which Osborne wrote the screenplay. The film is a Rowlandson cartoon shot with gimmicky devices like hand-held cameras, fast-motion and clumsy wipes – as if devotedly amateurish. A home-movie costume-romp (Jimmy, Cliff, Alison and Helena have gone on holiday with a Bell & Howell), pretending to be a jerky newsreel, with modern actors – Albert Finney, Susannah York, David Warner – in obvious

---

* By the way, you may see this innovative playwright/actor dressed as a tree on Prince Barin of Arboria's Sherwood Forest moon in Mike Hodges's *Flash Gordon* (1980)

† 'The only way to escape misrepresentation is never to commit oneself to any critical judgement that makes an impact – that is, never *say* anything.' (*The Great Tradition*) Peter Hall attended Leavis's lectures at Cambridge. 'Leavis hated the theatre and never went to it. He has had more influence on the contemporary theatre than any other critic.' (*Diaries*) Hall, like Leavis, has a tremendous respect for text and language, almost to the exclusion of many of the other things theatre involves – which is why I usually find his productions a little pedantic.

fancy-dress. (Regarding wobbly-voiced Edith Evans and cussing Hugh Griffith, we expect them to dress that way.)

But the looking back in masquerade had its relevance. Fielding's Tom Jones is a foundling, whose ragged, picaresque adventures are loose, improvisatory; he's a rootless, careless epic hero for a modern age. And his elevation to the squirerarchy links with Osborne's family's aspiration. According to *A Better Class of Person*, his autobiography, they've always been desperate to be mistaken for gentry.

The book, with its title Jimmy Porter would think up in that flip extremity where satire and irony meet sarcasm (and the ghost of Wyndham Lewis), set down by bewhiskered Osborne who has come in the Seventies and Eighties to resemble the late King George V, is a candid memoir of being born in Fulham, his mother a cleaner at the local Foundling Hospital – and what priceless Fielding-esque comedy that fact affords! Nellie Beatrice graduated to barmaid (*'I'm* not a barmaid, I'm a victualler's assistant – *if* you please') and drudged for her sickly husband and sickly son. Osborne depicts his father as a luminous soul; his mother, however, rouses in him 'the fatality of hatred'. Bed-ridden with rheumatic fever, boil-infested, he reads – Fielding. To have been able to trade places with Tom Jones, and live his life of caprice, must've been the impossible dream during those terrible weeks in hospital. A changeling.

Tynan, who really was the bastard son of a baronet (Sir Peter Peacock), a Birmingham stammerer who went through Magdalen in a puff of purple smoke, failing as an actor and as a director, becoming a critic so that he'd be a priest inaugurating his own cults, quoting in his reviews Hazlitt, Lamb, Lewes, Donne, Rymer, Skelton and Delacroix, a University wit placing himself in illustrious context, discovered, in 1975, that his 'commitment to reality and social truth' (as he had once called it) had run contrary to his predilections as an aesthete. Looking back, in a mood more like Tennysonian regret than rebarbativeness, Tynan regarded his best work, collected in *A View of the English Stage*, as already a literature of last things: 'It may . . . be possible to see this work as a kind of elegy.' The Fifties formed a phantom dawn.

THE GREAT TRADITION

What had come to an end, with Osborne, Wesker, Amis, Larkin, Arden, Braine, Jimmy Dean, Penguin paperbacks, Suez, the Welfare State, Joan Littlewood, Lindsay Anderson, television, redbricks, Morris Minors, Elvis Presley, *West Side Story*, Brando, Xerox machines and roll-on deodorants; what had been damaged by the exposure of Philby, Burgess and Maclean – was kingliness and confidence in class. Tynan wrote of an aristocratic theatrical Great Tradition that descended from Irving; a dynasty (to which Wolfit, Gielgud, Olivier, Richardson, Ashcroft, Evans, Thorndike, belonged) founded on 18 July 1895, when Bram Stoker's employer took time off from *King Arthur* rehearsals (a play by J. Comyns Carr, with sets by Burne-Jones) to pay a call at Windsor. Irving was the first actor ever to be knighted. The next day a speech by Pinero was recited on the Lyceum stage: 'From generation to generation, the English actor will be reminded that his position in the public regard is founded in no small degree upon the pre-eminence of your career, and', the eulogy continued, 'upon the nobility, dignity and sweetness of your private character.'

To the Tynan of *He That Plays the King*, *Curtains*, and *Tynan Right and Left*, these were not remote sentiments; nor did Irving and his entourage seem a remote group of gods.* Irving/Cronus had been succeeded by Olivier/Jupiter, Terry/Rhea by Thorndike/Juno. The shrine had merely shifted from the Lyceum† to the New Theatre, where the Old Vic Company operated. And of the luminaries who followed Sir Henry, John Gielgud comes closest to tracing a direct link with the family blood. His grandmother, Kate Terry, who herself appeared with Charles Kean, had Ellen Terry for a younger sister. Gielgud saw his great-aunt's final appearances, and affectionately recalls a feisty old thing untroubled by not knowing her lines, gaily extemporizing with benumbed cast and bemused audience. Gielgud was also present (as was Ellen Terry) at Drury Lane in 1916, when Frank Benson, instigator of the Stratford rite, was called to the royal box during an interval in *Julius Caesar* and knighted by George V with a wooden sword borrowed from a Covent Garden costumier.

Strolling players had become part of the Establishment. Of today's theatrical Royal Family, Ralph Richardson was knighted in 1947, as was Laurence Olivier; Michael Redgrave and Alec Guinness were knighted in 1959. Gielgud became Sir John in 1953 and a Companion of Honour in 1977. Of the actresses, Sybil Thorndike was made a Dame in 1931, Edith Evans in 1946, Peggy Ashcroft in 1956 and Margaret Rutherford, a year after she was Mistress Quickly for Orson Welles, in 1967. Olivier alone has been given a barony (1970) and made a fully-fledged aristocrat. In his souvenir photo of ingress into the Lords, he looks more regal than the peers who flank him – his face set in an expression of grim purpose reminiscent of Henry V.

* As late as 1964, John Russell Brown would be saying 'The late Victorian is still the dominating manner of acting Shakespeare.' (*Shakespeare: A Celebration*).
† By fateful coincidence, when the Lyceum reopened briefly in 1985, after many decades of theatrical disuse, it was to house the Cottesloe's *Mysteries* – Tony Harrison's show about divinities and devils.

So, if the line, like Banquo's seemed to stretch out to the crack of doom, with twofold balls and triple sceptres, why did Tynan break, break, break into the tears, idle tears, of 'a kind of elegy', as he put it? Quite simply because the arts of acting had grown adulterated, what with other calls upon an actor's time besides the need to act. Theatre had lost an intensity and magnanimity. Richard Burton's career was an exemplar of the decay. He's the screen Jimmy Porter, riffing his trumpet in the empty streets. To Melvyn Bragg, Burton is the opportunity for the working-class hero bit; the hired-man for films, with a D. H. Lawrence grit. But the fact remains he walked out on the English stage to make insipid Hollywood epics. He married a woman whose best performance to date has been with Nigel Bruce and a smooth-haired collie. (Note well that I'm not being sarcastic. I love Elizabeth Taylor's button-cuteness in *Lassie Come Home*, *National Velvet*, *Courage of Lassie* and *Little Women*. I can't appreciate all the brassy, smirking, off-hand performances in *The VIPs* or *Boom* or *Cleopatra* – even though it is exactly these grown-up qualities, of flirtatiousness and unconcern, which are so alluring in the actress's early little girl roles.)

And what about Nicol Williamson? In *The Bofors Gun*, he is a danger-ous-looking Scot, his voice tending to the querulous, an ox in kid gloves who went ape. His Hamlet was a thing of turmoil, the soliloquies like a recording of a long gargle replayed on wonky equipment; his Sherlock Holmes was a cocaine-addict; his Merlin was a troubled necromancer whose metallic skull-cap was a convex radar dish picking up scrambled messages from a Land of Far Beyond. Tynan's profile of him shamefully abandoned theatrical analysis for a list of the restaurants they visited together, as if by recording enough food and fine wine, Tynan could get performer to be like his performances.

From the vantage of 1975, those early, healthful days of Tynan's, hunched in the stalls watching Olivier's Hotspur, Richardson's Falstaff, Edith Evans's Lady Wishfort, seemed a Golden Age – a Golden Age when he himself was loaded with talent, a pen-pal of Orson Welles, elegant and peachy and ready to be Hazlitt redivivus. Acting, however, he saw become parody-acting. The coterie moving in from the provinces to challenge the Great Tradition (like a rebellious faction in a Shakespeare History) were insouciant heirs apparent.

Peter O'Toole, for instance, a willowy creature prone to giving carica-tures of Irishry and languid decrepitude; an actor best at a glazed collapse such as Conrad's Lord Jim and Shaw's Jack Tanner. (His notorious *Macbeth* at the Old Vic in 1980 resurrected a coarseness dormant since Wolfit.) Then there's Albert Finney, whose career has progressed by backtracking in time – from the Nottingham masher in Karel Reisz's film *Saturday Night and Sunday Morning* (1960) to being Tom Jones himself, the angry young man in doublet and hose. Yet Tom's hardly angry actually –

dopily cheery, more like; and the character in the Reisz film settles for a conventional marriage, his rebelliousness just that of a conventional son who, after a token resistance, will grow up to be a duplicate of his own father, sagging and stupid from the nut-brown ale.

Finney is a tough, burly actor, now respected for succeeding Edmund Gwenn in character parts: the shaven-bonced Daddy Warbucks in *Annie*; a punctilious Poirot for *Murder on the Orient Express*; a begrimed, mad-eyed Scrooge for *A Christmas Carol*; Lowry's dipso consul dying on the Mexican All Souls's Night, for *Under the Volcano*. Where O'Toole's characters simper their way to the grave, Finney's people inwardly fulminate, crossly smoulder. Hamlet and Tamburlaine, at National Theatre galas in 1976, were played as Yorkshire burghers. His cadaverous twin – whippet to his boxer – is Tom Courtenay. They were partnered for *Billy Liar*. Keith Waterhouse's work, like Jimmy Porter's play, is about an upwardly-mobile fantasist. Acted on stage by Finney, Courtenay, the understudy, was cast for the film. And in *The Loneliness of the Long Distance Runner*, as I see it, Courtenay's Billy Liar in borstal; in *Dr Zhivago* he is Billy Liar as a Soviet revolutionary. Finney and Courtenay were united in *The Dresser* – Ronald Harwood's actorial two-hander, with the stiff and mighty thespian (Lear) sparring with a flappy queer (the Fool) who does his make-up and organizes the costumes. Sir and Norman form an interdependent and fond alliance.

Yet, engaging as *The Dresser* is, the film is whimsy; the storms and droning war-time aircraft, instead of giving an epic amplitude, render the backstage world a cosy and dilapidated little England. This is *King Lear* recycled as quaint – and a good example of what Tynan regarded as theatre's certain emasculation. Finney and Courtenay should be playing Shakespeare's Lear and the Fool, not pathetic and wan derivations in a money-making cinema production.

FAIRY GOLD

When Olivier played Archie Rice a god came down amongst men. An emissary from an earlier age, he allowed himself the disguise of an end-of-the-pier turn. The wicked Richard III now a powerless and maudlin coward, his court a bickering bedsit of old crocks and shrews: Archie, indeed, is the sort of comic who'd do bad impersonations of Olivier's hunchbacked chuckling Richard III. He's Henry V as a defeated crooner, who keeps going through a combination of fecklessness and guile.

Are these part of the temperament that comes through in the Snowdon portrait? Like every child of my generation, I was scared half to death by Robert Helpmann's Child Catcher in *Chitty Chitty Bang Bang*. As I'm no longer a child, he's stopped haunting me. But Olivier's Archie Rice still invades my dreams: 'Let me know where you're working tomorrow night – and I'll come and see *you*!' It is a terrible threat: the bogeyman-actor who'll follow us home.

Earlier, I talked of the Kabuki grimace trapped by Snowdon's lens. In the film, Archie is a vacillating, garrulous old git; meagrely proficient at his dire gags and hoofing. But Snowdon makes something happen. Out of the weak and pathetic character, from behind the sneering goblinesque make-up, Olivier's own power breaks through. The eyes (eyes coming as if from behind a mask) pierce and glint. The effect is a portrait of Olivier's daimon, or genius. The cogs, engines and dynamos of his ambition and energy are exposed. Tynan said that Olivier is the great impersonator – 'Larry's a blank page. You've got to tell him what part you expect him to play, and then he's all right.' This remark seems rather belittling. Whatever he's like off-stage, at the very least the blankness must ripple and pulsate. His talent is never relaxed. That's what beguiles students of his work – the vigorousness and restlessness and alacrity, which go even into the junk films of recent years.

Tynan was wrong to believe that only the angry young actors were debilitating theatre by squandering energy in junk for the big money. The oldsters are all after the ready tin. Good luck to them – (i) They've done their stint with the classics. (ii) There is something magnificent and pleasing about the detachment the great actors have in their late manner. Olivier uses junk to parody his augustness – Zeus in *Clash of the Titans* (which also stars Maggie Smith as a batty goddess) and the President of the Immortals in *Time* are camp icons of a primogenitor. The Dave Clark musical, especially. Olivier manifested himself nightly as a flicker of laser beams. He didn't even have to trouble to turn up at the theatre. He was a light show; literally spectral. And as Ezra Lieberman in *The Boys From Brazil* he's next to translucent. Thin, grey, neatly tailored, rolling his eyes under deep, deep set brows, Olivier's a Nazi hunter on the trail of Josef Mengele – played by Gregory Peck as a Moreau in a white suit, an evil Albert Schweitzer experimenting on the natives. With the same burly actors in their leather coats and frameless spectacles as *The Odessa File*, this film was comic book mad scientist stuff. But Olivier, despite his tangled noodle of a European accent, and his moustache changing colour (white–grey–black–white), sometimes in mid-scene, cossetts and nuzzles out of himself a performance of much humanity and diffident strength – an old Jew who, under the appeasement and politeness, is pure bravery and resource. A pale blue flame that yet burns hard.

Ethereal and occult, Olivier's other jovial incarnation is as a randy-boots – Zeus taking the shape of an animal for purposes of seduction. In *The Betsy* he's seen rogering the maid; an automobile tycoon, his servants are objects to ride. In *The Seven-Per-Cent Solution*, he's white-faced Professor Moriarty, a neurotic and blotchy bleater, whom young Sherlock Holmes finds tupping his mother. In *The Ebony Tower*, he's a lecherous painter living in a French country idyll; an enigmatic charlatan, who twits Roger Rees's questing art historian: Rees thinks he's a genius, but he's just a satyr, attended by nymphets: Toyah Willcox, Derek Jarman's braided, lisping Miranda; and Greta Scacchi, the lush Olivia from *Heat and Dust*.

Where Olivier is lusty and dominant – playing Big Daddy in one form or another – Gielgud walks through the films he's paid to be in, desiccated and aloof. He affects a donnish uselessness and a beatific maladroitness, making him ideal for Whitehall mandarins and Cambridge heads of house. His other notion is to be implacable, with a slight frown. A gentleman's gentleman. In *Arthur*, he was cast as Terry-Thomas to Dudley Moore's Jack Lemmon; a cussing Jeeves – and in *Murder on the Orient Express* he was a soapy Jeeves. Gielgud survived *Caligula* by slitting his wrists in a bath tub soon after the first reel, though not before having his pate massaged by mammiferous extras. *Sphinx* he survived by being eviscerated in backstreet Cairo soon after the titles; *Lost Horizon* he survived by escaping under a thick layer of Tibetan make-up.

Gielgud manages to keep his reputation intact because he gives the impression he's only ever passing through, dropping by, popping in. He so evidently scorns the material – and we enjoy his derision. Paradoxically, the more he materialises in junk, the more we value his talent as a great actor. Far from being infected by bad films, their woozy blandness cushions him – his mottled head, like a plover's egg, in repose upon coloured cotton wool. And on occasion, he'll remind us he can act: Edward Ryder in *Brideshead Revisited*,★ which drew out the malice beneath the bubbliness, nudging our appreciation of mannerism's depth.

Ralph Richardson's malice was never lost for long. He was a bad-tempered caterpillar in *Alice's Adventures in Wonderland*, his swash buckled into an elaborate foam-rubber simulacrum of Tenniel's illustration; and his last work showed a genius for magicians – not cuddlesome magi, but gimlet-eyed sorcerers, his Old Vic Falstaff returning as Merlin (called Ulrich in *Dragonslayer*). Richardson is brilliant in junk because he ignores it and acts as though he's in a one-man show, devising bits of business, improvising, talking to himself – altogether, an explorer delighted to be rummaging in the folds of a character called 'Ralph Richardson'. He played God in a film called *Time Bandits*, wearing his own suit. A God switched on by the comic spirit – as against Olivier, whose divinity is a

---

★ In which Olivier, as Lord Marchmain, was dangerously faddy: as an actor, he never slackens into his gifts, and here he had to conquer a brand new generation of actors, like Jeremy Irons and Anthony Andrews.

STAGE PEOPLE

long-nursed tragic affliction. Laius who has spent his career waiting for
Oedipus. (Every young actor, without exception, having given a good
performance, is called 'the new Olivier'.)

The quirk of fate awaiting Richardson is that, perhaps, his late junk
manner will come to be regarded as his finest period. He certainly had
plenty of time to prepare for it, with films like *The Ghoul* (1933) and *Java
Head* (1934), and plays like *Cornelius* (1935) and *The Amazing Dr Clitter-
house* (1936). Then there were his months of being miscast as Macbeth,
Othello or Timon. He had too much irony and shrewdness not to see
through tragic posturing as squirming self-pity. The first glimpse of full-
scale insurrection was as the post-apocalypse Prime Minister in Spike
Milligan's *The Bed Sitting-Room*, dressed in a wrecked morning suit,
loopily preserving dignity whilst ruling from a clay-pit or burnt-out car.
And then Richardson started to requisition chat-shows, genially decon-
structing Michael Parkinson and Russell Harty, treating the cameras as
odd pets, talking about motorbikes, veering off into gnomic digressions:
'God is very economical, don't you think? Wastes nothing. Yet also the
opposite.'

Lindsay Anderson's *O Lucky Man* brought a dual role: a smug and
frightening tycoon and a dipso, saddened tailor. The former was sleek,
the latter puffy. Richardson cut between them as if easefully leaping the
divide between good and evil in his own nature. Evil was all that Freddie
Francis required from the actor in *Tales from the Crypt* – Richardson
played Satan, naughtily costumed as a monk. And all Hugh Hudson
required for *Greystoke* was goodness – but he got a deal more. Hudson's
was a calamitous picture about Tarzan. He fully misunderstood Bur-
rough's jungle campery, taking it seriously. He tried to make an ecologi-
cal epic, when the idiom required is Edwardian pastoral. (Tarzan is
Rousseau's noble savage given Barrie's whimsy and the manners of
Buchan's Richard Hannay.) But Richardson, as the Sixth Earl of Greystoke, Tarzan's grandfather, transcends the sombre nonsense, where
Christopher Lambert, as the monkey-boy, cast for his ability to glower
and snarl with a gallic foreignness, gets instantly upstaged by the pout on
latex ape suits.

Richardson makes the aged Greystoke no normal eccentric dodderer
(as we'd be getting had Michael Hordern been cast); he fully roves in a
second childhood; a sainted Falstaff, whose rendezvous with the returned
Tarzan – Lambert, silent, dark, slowly descending from a coach – is
Falstaff's reconciliation with Hal. A son in atonement with a father-
figure. And it was left to Richardson to victual the film with a gamesomeness and inquisitiveness that should have been Tarzan's. The grandfather
showed the real spirit of a jungle boy, never ceasing from exploration,
loping about his castle in a quilted dressing-gown, his hair a halo, sliding
down the stairs on a silver tray – a glorious self-sacrifice, as he brains

himself on the banister. He riffs and veers with the happy perplexity of Henry James's prose rhythms – Henry James being Richardson's favourite writer.

Greystoke is expensive toshery. (French Lambert and dubbed Jane – Andie McDowell with the voice of Glenn Close – give a spurious air of translated-from-the-continental art-house breeding.) But mercurial Richardson is a wonder-work. The Earl uses his house and park as a playpen – and so was the film a playpen for the actor, using it as an opportunity for delicacy, danger, unpredictability – which all added up to an achievement of berserk innocence.

ENIGMA VARIATIONS

Olivier zealous, Gielgud snooty, Richardson oblivious,* alone amongst the great actors Alec Guinness takes recent material seriously; there's an integrity about his playing, alien to the skylarking subversion of his peers. He's a quite separate case: his best work has been done on film and television, and his combination of earnestness and self-effacement does well in close-up. The intimacy of the camera releases an enigma, a sense of unknowableness, in Guinness, which is lost on stage; the camera draws humours from him. Had he been born in 1890, instead of 1914, had he met Mack Sennett, instead of Gielgud, he'd have been Stan Laurel. Frisky behind the facade, seditious under the stealth, tender is this knight of the doleful countenance, who is the world's greatest exponent of Dickens. In Fagin, Herbert Pocket and William Dorrit, Guinness conveys that sinister mood when eccentricity is rapt. Forever Ealing (Guinness has never worked in provincial Rep – except Chichester), he was the embodiment of clerkly spunk in *The Lavender Hill Mob* and *The Man in the White Suit*; his reappearances in *Kind Hearts and Coronets* are a seminar demonstration of versatility; King Feisal in *Lawrence of Arabia* is a model of erect, laundered dignity – the opposite to O'Toole's neurotic Ross.

Guinness much influenced Peter Sellers, allowing us to notice the difference between acting and mimicry. Sellers entirely lacked grace and gravitas; he was a brattish, unintelligent performer, happy only when dodging into coarse goonery. And why did this happen, for his early characters (Kite in *I'm All Right Jack*, the Scottish accountant in *The Battle of the Sexes*, Quilty in *Lolita*) imply an important future? Sellers failed

---

* The three share the same frame in Tony Palmer's *Wagner*. They're frock-coated and cravated equerries; a royal court. Olivier doesn't speak. He makes squeaky noises and does a pantomine of amazed smirks, sighs and rolling eyes. Gielgud's the inscrutable mandarin, refusing to be aghast at Ludwig's plain lunacy. Richardson, boskily bewhiskered, mutters and makes out imperial concern. They huddle together, a cabal.

because he abandoned his range, wasting his time on multiple marriages; wasting his money on purchasing a thousand flashy automobiles. The only company he bothered to keep was gadgetry – his wives to him were interchangeable and disposable; fast cars betook him from whim to whim. Sellers was insane – if insanity may be defined as the demand for absolute personal liberty and power without responsibility. He had no conscience or conception of right and wrong – yet he devised petty codes of honour, which his perplexed children would innocently transgress, and as a result he'd psychopathologically dispossess them.

A neglectful parent, he wanted to be babysat himself; he indulged in quack patriarchal religions and tried to keep his mother near through the agency of a spirit medium. Sellers filled his life with toys, instead of filling it with life. And this is why he came to rely, in his films, on the broadest caricature, basing business on send-ups of other people's acting (Richard III/Olivier, Quasimodo/Laughton, Lautrec/Ferrer). He stopped connecting, observing, judging, knowing. In *Murder by Death* he's Warner Oland and Sidney Toler as Charlie Chan. Sellers chomps and chuckles in a costume and accent from *Aladdin*. The blind butler in the film is Guinness. With heavy, spooky tread, he's amazingly detailed and spruce – where Sellers is ragged and overdoing it wildly.

It's no accident Sellers's best performance was a blank. Chance, the telly-addict in *Being There*, is the empty space Sellers ultimately was, his behaviour exclusively born out of the box, the man's life an imitation game. Chance the gardener (or Chauncey Gardiner as he becomes) absorbs phrase and gesture from the buzz of ubiquitous television panels. The mansion where he lives has a set in every room; he even leaves off copulation to copy the antics in a cartoon. Voice comes from Stan Laurel, clothes from Edward G. Robinson. His life is a self-erasing videotape. And this nullility is misinterpreted by the other characters in the film as Holy Innocence. In fact, it's madness. Watching *Being There* is to witness Sellers's own madness: the replacement of biography with mimicry. His history's a wipe-out.

Where Sellers was a blank, too quickly scribbled over, an empty space, crammed with the lumber of other people's mannerisms, Guinness is a distilled essence. He holds our attention by withholding power. He gives minimalist performances, which yet imply a greatness of mind – as if he's a theatrical equivalent of Samuel Beckett's late prose: 'Deviser of himself for company. Leave it at that ... Himself he devises too for company. Leave it at that.' With Guinness there's a fierce absorption in the arts of acting – indeed, he acts himself into existence, into consummateness. Cecil Beaton's portrait shows a wan face, which without eye-liner would vanish, like a revenant's. It's as though, acting eight times over in *Kind Hearts and Coronets*, he needed repetition of manifestations to affix himself on the celluloid; and Fagin, in the David Lean *Oliver Twist*, is cargoed

66

with much make-up, without which the mincing, queerish, light villainy would float off the screen.

Now, Guinness doesn't trouble with make-up, thinking it intrusive. He's learned to organize his features into pure malevolence or serenity, or whatever. His early work, like Peter Brook's, looked back upon from the position of a later inscrutability, is brilliant, mannered, cluttered. And it's that sort of Guinness performance Sellers tried to derive from. Guinness himself has developed his craft, so that Smiley's silence, in *Tinker, Tailor, Soldier, Spy*, resounds with sympathetic cleverness; and his immobility bristles with alertness. It's the most convincing performance of thinking – of realistic, muted, abstracted brooding – ever given.* Guinness can act mental action.

Hence, *Star Wars*. In the galactic oater, Guinness transfigured telepathic hokum ('May the Force be with you') into a Wagnerian magic. Comicbook philosophy, amidst technological gee-whizzery, became oddly awesome. Guinness's Obi-Wan Kenobi, a cowled magus, was the weary, lonely, kindly-but-strong Wotan, with Luke Skywalker his Siegfried, the pupil who knows no fear and who'll inherit his wisdom. George Lucas's references were from John Ford pictures (and the planet-scapes had the rocky, dusty, umber atmosphere of gold-rush California and Utah's Monument Valley); space-ships succeeded horses; astronauts succeeded gauchos; bars with monsters and mercenaries succeeded Wild West casinos. And Guinness took the hardware Western and infused it with Wagner's themes of fatherhood, foundlings, duty, destiny. With his voice as sonorous as a cello, his movements the dignified rhythms of a grail knight, the business of the Force acquired authority, majesty. He flourished the holstered laser-sword less as a futuristic Colt .45 than as Nothung or Wotan's spear.

> Fürchtest das Feuer du nicht,
> so sperre mein Speer dir den Weg!
> Noch hält meine Hand der Herrschass Hass:
> das Schwert, das du schwingst,
> zerschlug einst dieser Schaft:
> noch einmal denn zerspring es am ew'gen Speer!†

The Force Obi-Wan hopes shall be always with Luke is the ability to think things and make them so; grandiose telekinesis, where meditation becomes a martial art. Duels are fought by penetrating some higher level

---

* Derek Jacobi is a competitor, with his Clennam in *Little Dorrit* and Turing in *Breaking the Code*. Guinness, in *Little Dorrit*, acts mental *inaction*.
† If you don't fear the flames, then my spear will keep you back. I have in my hands the symbol of sovereignty: this spear once broke that sword you are brandishing. Again! Shatter its blade on the spear!

of cogitation, and sword strokes slash, it seems, automatically. The Force being with you, you could fight blindfold. True vision is visionary – the externalizing of inner resource. Luke is taught that he stumbled when he saw. Obi-Wan gives him what Yeats would call the new subtlety of eyes. (And Yeats would enjoy the mysticism of *Star Wars*.) 'O! What a life is the eye,' wrote Coleridge to the Wordsworths (Romanticism is the Force that through the green fuse drives the flower, etc.) 'Sure it has thoughts of its own, and to see is only a language.'

Orientalesque nonsense, yes, like the fey metaphysics of Kung Fu, where a secret monastic code pretends to hide the simple fact that the kicks and chops intend basically to beat the shit out of all comers; yet the courage and discipline required by the Force is nevertheless akin to Guinness's method of acting – Guinness, who acts mental actions. *Star Wars*, a Western with special-effects, with Guinness robed and rampant, contains an allegory of how this actor acts. He always gives us a new subtlety of eyes – so that when he plays a blind man (Clifford Mortimer in *A Voyage Round My Father*, Bensonmum in *Murder by Death*) we see, with the character, feelingly. The invisible becomes visible (like the blind serving of mass in *Monsignor Quixote*). We give in to the Force.

He's a serious man, an edifying man. And yet his autobiography, *Blessings in Disguise*, baffles us by being boring; he protects any artistic ferment by a blandness, a docility – which is as impenetrable as any roach's carapace. He doesn't sabotage the films he's in – as his equals do – because he refuses to acknowledge he's in junk. *Star Wars* is nostalgia for Buster Crabbe's Flash Gordon and John Wayne's Ringo Kid, but Guinness treats the story with a deep respect, bringing an atmosphere of theological questing to what was envisaged, before he was cast, as a glossy Saturday morning serial. The force of his acting makes for a regeneration: the entire film converts. Olivier, Gielgud or Richardson in the same part would have meant nonchalant cameo opportunities; scarabs in the sand. Guinness is the force which drives the whole film on to something powerful.

ENIGMA VARIATIONS II

Often, however, in his late manner, Guinness is left looking like a man assiduously at work during a silly party; his performances are so good, everybody else shuffles as floozy or rank amateur. In *Scrooge*, the actor is a sinister, vengeful Marley's ghost, shivering in a crumbling shroud, his eyes fierce with sights seen in the underworld. Everybody else in the film believes they're in a jolly sequel to *Oliver!* and they croon catastrophic songs. Only Guinness seems to bother conveying the real Dickens's damp chill, rather than the deodorized Christmas card tone director

68

Ronald Neame puts up with. Then there's *Cromwell*, where Richard Harris is a man called hoarse, his idea of the Lord Protector of the Commonwealth of England being a bog-Irish barker. Guinness, as Charles I, is a Van Dyck portrait animated. Sad, spaniel eyes and his hair and beard tumbling and pointed like Christ's. Guinness told a sad story of the death of a King: the hollow crown, within which keeps death its court. *Cromwell* was his *Richard II*. A beautiful, melancholy, fateful performance – words paradoxically applicable to *Hitler: the Last Ten Days*, where Guinness changed his appearance into the Führer's, with slick of black hair and sunken eyes. The film, directed by Ennio de Concini, was an opportunity for raillery in the bunker. It was Guinness's *Richard III*.

In Marshall Brickman's *Lovesick* he altered his state to be Freud. The film is quite mindless, a vehicle for Dudley Moore – one of his several dozen attempts to recapture the frolicsome success of *Arthur*. Set in modern, psychobabbling America, Moore's a shrink who flouts professional etiquette by falling in love with a patient. Guinness presents himself as the admonitory Viennese spectre. A haunting, psychoanalytical father-figure. Why did he trouble to be so scrupulously fine? His face and posture are perfectly Freud's: the trim whiskers, pouchy and glaucous eyes, frown plus dapper air, the cocked Havana with its milky plume.

FREUD THE LAWGIVER

Perhaps Guinness's choosing to play Freud was, in the scheme of things, no accident – Freud the explicator of mythical lineage, historian of embattled pedigrees; the poet of patrimony and the forces of youth and age. Master of the hidden life – or, as we find in *Finnegans Wake*.

- God save you King! Muster of the Hidden Life!
- God serf yous Kingly, adipose rex! I had four in the morning and a couple of the lunch and three later on, but your saouls to the dhaoul, do ye Finnk. Fime. Fudd?

Freud chose Oedipus as his megaphone, speaking through him as God yackety-yakked through Moses. 'He brought down the tablets of the law into the wilderness,' says Anthony Burgess of Freud, in *The End of the World News*; and the message is of dispossession – sons against lovers, fathers against sons.

Burgess's Freud is a stern lawgiver, who resents any dissent from disciples – he is indeed a riddling Moses. When Otto Rank, for example, publishes an original book without showing it to the master, he's viciously snubbed: 'Betrayer, traitor . . . There's a hell reserved for all you treacherous ingrates.' Burgess sees the originations of psychoanalysis as in itself an Oedipal conflict – enacting the myth it describes. Psychoanalysis, Freud's baby, gathers itself to usurp him. Strike the father dead. Rank, Jung, Adler, Stekel: they're erring sons.

Jung, tall and ascetic to Freud's diminutiveness and hearty swilling and smoking, tries entering with his overlord into a word-association game. But the master's voice declines: ' "I have to resist, don't I? I must savour the delights of authority!" ' . . . And then, with a kind of parodic Mosaic ferocity to mildly looking Joshua, "I discovered the unconscious mind while you were still dabbling in your urine." '

Burgess portrays the psychoanalysts as a conspiratorial band. Outsiders, outlaws. They've dared look deep inside the mind. 'Why should sex be a thing to hide and cloak and smother? It's fundamental, so fundamental that we're frightened of it – like some satanic god. We have to bring it into the light.' There are signals and totems to be carried out of the darkness; new religions to be inculcated. Vienna, however, is more inclined to let sex stay in its eclipse. Psychoanalysts are pornographers and frauds, exactly like actors.

EMINENT DOMAIN

As a ghost, it really is as if Guinness's simulacrum of Freud had slipped into *Lovesick* from another universe entirely – a universe where acting yearns to be honourable: honour pricking folk on to make an eminent domain, a 'mystical brotherhood of sun and moon and hollow and wood and river and stream', working out its will. These words are mostly Yeats's, and *Eminent Domain* was Richard Ellmann's title for a book about the 'brutal procedure' of literary influence.★ And just as (in Ellmann's view) Yeats 'declined to subside', lingering to invade the imaginations of Wilde, Joyce, Pound, Eliot and Auden, so has Guinness, with Olivier, Gielgud and Richardson, endured and declined to subside, enfevering the bloodstreams of the actors in Part Two. In a marvellous state of preservation, the white knights don't repeat ancient routines, they are literally revolutionary; they keep coming back (Richardson's death ushered him to immortality; he's in Arthur's bosom, if ever man went to Arthur's bosom).

Guinness is beamed into *The Empire Strikes Back* and *Return of the Jedi* as an holographic emissary; Olivier's an optical illusion in *Time*; Gielgud and Richardson start out of abundant videos as tricks of light. And though there have been worthy scripts (random choices: *Little Dorrit*, with Guinness; *Brideshead Revisited*, with Olivier; *No Man's Land*, with

★ 'Writers move upon other writers not as genial successors but as violent expropriators, knocking down established boundaries to seize by the force of youth, or of age, what they require. They do not borrow, they override . . . The best writers expropriate best, they disdain petty debts in favour of grand, authoritative larcenies.' An Oedipal handing-on, applicable to acting.

Gielgud and Richardson), it's junk that's been their liberation. Performances, earnests of invincibility, show that there's to be no retirement.
These actors shall not be, like unregarded age, in corners thrown. Oedipus is thoroughly beaten back. Olivier, Gielgud, Richardson, Guinness,
in their late manner, have everything to give junk; newer actors have
nothing to gain from it, except wealth. Burton, Nicol Williamson,
O'Toole, Finney – the coming race of the Fifties – are already older than
were their predecessors in an Old Vic and Haymarket prime.

Those predecessors moreover, impregnable and noble like Burgess's
Moses-Freud, appear in junk as hardly implicit upbraiding; and they do
so with impunity – because they have gathered a personal legend. These
actors have histories, their perspectives are long. They've accomplished
great things. They're demiurges. They've earned the right to earn big
money. As Michael Caine said to Olivier on the set of *Sleuth*: ' "You can't
have any money; stay in movies and don't give a packet what they are, get
some money together." And he did; I don't know whether it's my fault he
made *The Betsy* or *The Seven-Per-Cent Solution* . . . I said, "Go out and do
it, they can't take the Lordship away from you, they can't take your
reputation away from you." '*

The rewards of junk are the great actor's fairy gold. Kenneth Tynan,
whittering about elegy, interpreting his *View of the English Stage* as an end
of the world news report, was not to know about the afterlife of his
heroes.† And what was terminal for Tynan, contemplating his shadow
life, dying in America, writing articles for the *New Yorker* which would
be heavily copy-edited by fact-checkers and comma-monitors; his work
let drop out of print and his final book, *Show People*, selling barely a
thousand copies – all that's the origination, in many ways, of the book
you are now holding in your hands. His triste tropique needs reinterpre-
tation. Theatre has opened out. What for Tynan was a wake is now an
awakening; death is an entrance; mortuary moments shall have resurrection, and the apocalypse, instead of being now, is deferred. Tynan's
prophecy of extinction was to herald a renaissance.

HOW DO YOU KNOW WHEN AN ACTOR IS ACTING?

Actors have always been romanticised: the smitten Will following the
Queen's Men out of Stratford, or the elegant vagabonds and gypsy

---

* Big money, in fact, had been coming Olivier's way long before Caine's incite-
ment on the set of *Sleuth*. In 1966 he earned £250,000 for eight days' work on *Khar-
toum*.
† Though he'd have known the derelict destinies of their progenitors: Mrs Patrick
Campbell spent her last weeks begging Shaw for charity; Sir Frank Benson ended up
in a bedsitting room, a forgotten husk smelling of curry powder; Irving was condemned to provincial tours, starting to die in Wolverhampton, dead in Bradford.

barons Hazlitt and Lamb wrote about, curiosities to visit, as you'd visit an asylum and gawp at the mad. Edmund Kean, in particular, 'who bore on his brow the mark of the fire from heaven,' embodied a cosmic principle. All great actors did. Johnson on Garrick, Shaw on Ellen Terry, Tynan on Olivier: the critic is describing what flashes of lightning are like, examining the discharge of an ability to create, and mutate. Jove's life as a shape-changer, Mercury's as a thief and fertilizer, Dionysus's as an intoxicator – these are acting's strange gods.

Today, with the ubiquitous surrealism of video, the crackle of radio and television, the conversion of national government into show-business* and the monarchy into a photo-opportunity, Romanticism is sublunary, its magic adjured and replaced with a knowing legerdemain. We've grown accustomed to make-believe, preferring as documentaries, on the box, drama-documentaries, where contemporary events are performed and the distinction between art and life smudged – cushioned, often, with the perfumed lather of soap.

We believe in acting less and need it more. We crave falsehood and look for virtue. Each time an actor appears on an advertisement, croons a voice-over, endorses a political party, the sorcery of theatre is impaired – and strengthened in a new way. For acting is linked with those bogus industries of the century's end: the proliferation of jobs in publicity, personnel and public relations; image makers and researchers; the hucksterism of the self; the marketing of a design for living and whatever the fuck – so Judi Dench and Michael Williams are a modern Mr and Mrs Nobody to sell margarine; Leo McKern and Simon Callow are in a Lloyd's Bank playlet; Alan Howard extols 'Electricity: Energy for life' and Anthony Hopkins does gas and oil ads. Alan Bennett once provided the cadence for a washing-machine frog and Orson Welles was the sound of a Danish ale. Welles claimed he once dressed as a White Rabbit for a Chicago emporium, jostling with customers and saying, 'I must hurry – or else it will be too late to see the woollen underwear on the eighth floor.'

When Michael Gambon can earn £30,000 a year for occasional half-hours of 'work' flirting over Aer Lingus, TSB, Dulux and Ford, we need to ask about the connections between salesmanship and acting. Actors are the brazen persuaders, enticing us to purchase shampoos, soft drinks, deodorants, detergents, credit cards and junk foods. If we shell out the cash, *we* can enlist in their fantasy world – where everything is squeaky-

* With Ronald Reagan, there was an actor in the White House. 'The Acting President', as Gore Vidal put it. Imposture, quackery, had been democratically elected, as if Sellers's empty-headed Chance really did make it to be head of state and the free world besides. Reagan's geared gagging and amiable dolt put-on is a masterpiece of mummery. But how do we *know* when this actor is acting?

clean, fast and abundant; fork out at the supermarket, and *we* can possess contentment. And to know how the art of acting has come to involve the antics of expenditure and commerce would be to know the story of the modern imagination – an imagination which can countenance game shows, celebrity quiz shows, chat shows, award shows and interminable materialistic family sagas from Dallas, Denver, and latterly Melbourne, Australia.

These programmes and the advertisements which interrupt them (or merge into them: an Ian Holm film was recently invaded by his own voice-over for Woolworth's chocolates) are a dissipation. F. R. Leavis lamented the flabbiness of mind created by the straw-men of Sunday journalism; by the mass circulation of bad books, which render 'the task of acquiring discrimination . . . much more difficult'. Culture, to Leavis already a minority thing, kept safe by the universities, is now terminally addled by the celebrity status accorded weather-augurers, newscasters and interviewers.

But ought we to fulminate? There was never really a Golden Age of literacy such as Leavis believed in. His 'living principle' of culture was always exclusive. Audiences of television banality may be comatose (or maybe not: jittery television screens may train us in mental alertness); but the actors, like the microwaves Ray McAnally advertises, 'can think for themselves'. In any case, providing voice-overs they are at their most (intriguingly) abstract. Playing no part in particular, it's the colour of their voice alone which is meant to inundate a product: a strange sort of idolomancy. Then again, perhaps a voice-over rubs against some gossamer memory of a performance, to link product and part. Joss Ackland's C. S. Lewis always comes to mind when cakes and crusty bread are extolled. I picture the Inklings by a Magdalen fire. So I'm a definite victim of the ad men.

Acting has made a tribal migration – into new forms, new kinds of personalities. The actors I've encountered, in person or in performance, chits in the late Fifties, establishing themselves in the Sixties, pre-eminent in the Seventies, aristocracy in the Eighties, have coped with the alterations in their craft, working with intelligence in film and television. Others, however, have blissfully ignored technology and hype. Paul Scofield, for example, has kept to an old-fashioned career. There is a smack of the deadpan about Scofield, as if deep in his constitution is the mournful innocence of Keaton. He appeared with Gielgud in 1953 at the Lyric, Hammersmith – in *The Way of The World* and *Venice Preserv'd*. But his best work is elsewhere: his Peter Brook Lear and Peter Hall Macbeth were nobly puzzled in ways Restoration wits (all neuroticism) can never be. Noble puzzlement, in Scofield's Oberon, became naive malice; for *A Man For All Seasons* naivety became gentle obduracy. As the inaugural Salieri in Peter Shaffer's *Amadeus*, a suave yet detached demonism was essayed. He's an actor frequently enwrapped in varying amounts of dismay, rather like Derek Jacobi.

THE NATIONAL HEALTH

And if the Fifties, with *Look Back in Anger*, was retrospective, progressiveness, of a kind, was imminent. In 1957, Tynan complained that British drama had no star directors; power lay with the caprices and box-office pull of famous actors. This was set to change, with the contrivance of the Royal Shakespeare Company and a National Theatre. These institutions fermented directorial authority all right. The RSC was concocted in its present form by Peter Hall in 1960, and was run by Trevor Nunn from 1968 until a lucrative lifetime producing *Cats* in places like Shanghai or *Les Misérables* in languages like Ebo offered itself, and he betook himself elsewhere; since when the company has floundered, a rotten borough.

Hall vivified a lingering Victorian monument – the Shakespeare Memorial Association created by Stratford brewer Charles Edward Flower in 1875. The Aldwych was secured for London transfers of Warwickshire productions; nearly a quarter of a century later, the metropolitan base would be the Barbican Centre, a bleak vault which lays a dead hand on every show tried out there.

The idea of a National Theatre suffered from an impediment: where to set down its pediment. (Also, the *idea* of a National Theatre is pious and all too, oh, quite pregnantly conscious.) It had no charmed spot, like Stratford, to build itself upon. Denys Lasdun's eventual grim bunker (opened in 1976) was situated on the South Bank – the arena of the Festival of Britain, the postwar carnival which attempted to cheer the country up.* Construction of a theatre was a long time coming. A National playhouse was proposed by Bernard Shaw, William Archer and Harley Granville-Barker for the Shakespeare Tercentenary in 1916 (when Frank Benson, who'd begun the tradition of Shakespeare performances in Stratford, was knighted); it was patented by Parliament in 1949, and had its first production ready in 1963 – led by Olivier and the Old Vic. Tynan, as hinted previously, was employed as Literary Manager: the critic exerting himself to put his talents to creative use. Jonathan Miller was an Associate Director, using his medical knowledge to interpret plays – a psychoanalytic *Measure for Measure*, the Duke's Vienna being Freud's, and

*   'Don't make fun of the festival,
       Don't make fun of the fair,
       We downtrodden British must learn to be skittish
       And give an impression of devil-may-care'

Noël Coward, *The Lyric Revue* (1951). Frank and Nora Doel (Anthony Hopkins, Judi Dench) dance on the South Bank terrace in the film of *84 Charing Cross Road*.

thus the capital of sin's multitudinousness; or a frock-coated *Merchant of Venice*, which was an anatomy of plutocratic greed. Olivier was Shylock, his jaw rounded out with an ornate prosthesis, as if he had a watermelon for teeth. Peter Hall was recruited from Stratford to be Olivier's administrative successor; in his *Diaries* he records the daily operation of the institution.*

And that's the problem. As institutions, the RSC and the NT have *institutionalized* theatre. Jonathan Miller, hating the way playfulness was being eradicated from plays, feuded with Hall and departed; Tynan, an unhappy Talleyrand, felt he had to resign ('I asked for it to be minuted that a condition of my accepting the job was that Tynan should go').† Hall's *Diaries* are candid about the 'dramatic battle' of organizing his mutinous crew. He could be the Chairman of Coke, marshalling executive staff, or poor bloody Bligh. At many moments, pressed for cash, Coke envisages a merger with Pepsi. Hall and Nunn have conspiratorial dinners. The marriage has not happened. Expensive office-work, already byzantine, would proliferate, not diminish. And officework is a great threat to Britain's classical theatre: it turns directors from creators into hustlers, actors into shiftable stock. Some directors enjoy this, of course. Money and manipulation mean power.

JEAN-JACQUES HALL I

As a self-confession, Hall's *Diaries* is definitely equivocal. The style is transcribed microcassette, monotonous burbles about board meetings and confrontations; the tone is aggrieved. Perhaps, though, the politics is what he likes. He doesn't endure wrangling, he's revived by it – and the book is full of people manoeuvring for positions on the council, the creative energy used up on corporate decision-making.

The *Diaries* reveal a personality both fatigued and galvanized by the functioning of an office hierarchy; the 'dramatic battle' is the story of Hall's conflicting interests: business sense versus artistic sensibility, power versus romance, the boss versus the bohemian. He thrives on institutionalism. His productions connect with this, being sombre, academic, dampening. For comedy he has little instinct. Even *The Importance of Being Earnest* became saturnine, Wilde's quips made mordant. At Glyndebourne, Hall makes Mozart a shrewd amatory mandarin: *Le*

---

* Kept from March 1972, when Hall was asked to lead the National Theatre into Lasdun's uncompleted fortress, until 1980, when the *Evening Standard* Drama Awards were presented from the Olivier stage. 'Every single award was for work done by people in the subsidised sector. That could never have happened twenty-five years ago.'

† Tynan's contract expired on 31 December 1973.

Nozze di Figaro took place on a chequered floor, a ludic space; *Così Fan Tutte* had Don Alfonso as a severe misogynist; and his was a stormy *Don Giovanni*, the cast brandishing brollies for cloudbursts ('As I grow older,' he's said, 'sunshine seems less attractive').

Britten's *A Midsummer Night's Dream* concentrated on the lovers's fractiousness; and Wagner's *Ring*, an epic about manipulation, which should suit Hall to perfection, was a disaster in Bayreuth. Hall had William Dudley design forests out of Arthur Rackham, mossy, leafy dells and huts made from bark and Viking prows. Within such a romantic atmosphere, I think, he couldn't function to his best advantage. He gave up – like Wotan himself, bequeathing damnation to the earth. A damnation immersed in for *Akenfield*, Hall's misty and plotless trance, cast with real villagers, meant to evoke a twilit rural community; a disappearing pastoral landscape, which Hall would like us to be moved by, but actually we aren't. The film's temperature is that of a stagnant water-bed.

But the military pattern of *Antony and Cleopatra* enthralled Hall. The Olivier auditorium, let alone the stage, was traversed by nonstop route marches. The play was Hall's anabasis. The vendettas between the triple pillars of the world allowed him to direct big fracas, bold committees, litigious characters. All within a single crumbling neoclassical set, a symbol of beleaguered pomp. This interest in disputatiousness has been a constant in his career, right from *The Wars of the Roses*.

From Cambridge came the young director to whom Dr Leavis had taught fidelity to texts and what Henry James would term a 'high brutality of good intentions'. John Barton, quondam Fellow of Kings, was tempted out of academe to join Hall and improve the quality of verse-speaking. Together the directors collaborated on a conflation of Shakespeare's early history plays, *Henry VI*, Parts I, II, III, and *Richard III*; the texts were shunted and trimmed to make a trilogy: *Henry VI*, *Edward IV* and *Richard III*. *Edward IV* ended with the first words of *Richard III*, the Crookback soliloquy ('Plots have I laid, inductions dangerous'), and Hall, like Gloucester, has never had any delight to pass away the time, unless it's to change merry meetings into stern alarums. *The Wars of the Roses*, the set dominated by a conference table, was a sharpened drama about political government; about power, its uses and abuses.*

O DOUGHTY DEED! (a reprise)

Peter Brook, who was working in Stratford since 1946 (directing Paul Scofield as Don Armado in *Love's Labour's Lost*; an impersonation

---

* Actors involved included Ian Holm, whose career commenced in 1952 as Peter Pan. He played Puck and Lear's Fool (to Laughton) as twinkling revenants. His Richard III

repeated by the actor for *Don Quixote* at the National over thirty years later), does not seem to have had anything to do with any emphasis on institutions; he's the maverick, unwilling to be mucked about by bureaucratic demands. But he's still fierce and political. An exacting guru, he claims that 'though I don't see myself forever exiled from England, it is true that I no longer find among actors here the intensity or the dedication that I get from the Paris group.' Mindful of the need for discipline and obedience, are his retreats to tribal villages, abandoned quarries, rusty shores, quests to seal off his actors from normal civilized life, where pleasures and comforts would erode his control? For all its celebrated internationalism, his group has a parochial feel. The actors bear allegiance only to the director. We all know Brook's name. How many of his disciples can you name? He's a Moses figure, leading his followers into the desert inaccessible. He even sought the snowy wastes of Scandinavia for the *King Lear* film, playing one of Lear's cossack Knights himself. And is enlightenment ever discovered in these voids? The mysticism might ultimately be mostly that of a group dynamic; the actors as an intimate extended family; Brook, the structural anthropologist of acting, begetting a sociology of his troupe; his theatre, a psychopathology of everyday life.

JEAN-JAQUES HALL II

There's a pantisocratic whimsy in Hall's *Diaries*: 'When I was just down from Cambridge . . . I wanted to develop a permanent group of actors, all growing together, learning together. I still do.' Where Brook will spend years calmly perfecting an improvisation, repeating intonation and gesture like a mantram, embroilment is Hall's element. Trying to pack a freelance life alongside his National Theatre obligations, he courts

was an eager villain, a troll King. Holm went on to be a definitive Barrie in Andrew Birkin's *The Lost Boys*. He was to be seen recently going in for a lot of staring into space in Len Deighton's *Game, Set and Match*. He played the spy Bernard Samson – a pint-sized Cold War warrior, with Russia being the modern Philistia and Delilah coming across as a vamp in a white fur hat. A viola maundered away, attempting to render heroics elegiac. Ever since *Smiley's People*, television espionage has had to be terminally wistful. He's often cast as a defeated sprite.

David Warner was a monkish Henry VI. Stardom seemed to come his way with Blifil in the movie *Tom Jones*. And after a self-obsessed Richard II (1964), he was the Hamlet of the decade: a sinuous, spotty student recognizable from contemporary college campuses; he filled Elsinore with the fumes of instant coffee, with record players, Beat poets and Carnaby Street. Warner's fate has been to play an endless succession of lanky Nazi exterminators, culminating in the Devil for Terry Gilliam's *Time Bandits* – the film where Ralph Richardson walks on in his own suit as God.

exhaustion. Simultaneously, his mind is skittering between the South Bank, Glyndebourne, the New York Met, London Weekend Television (he presented the arts review *Aquarius*) and German film locations (he slips away to make appearances in the movies of Maximilian Schell); plus there are casts to rehearse, auditions to be held, revivals to oversee. He sits on the aeroplane or sits out receptions at Buckingham Palace, his thoughts a trace of ungiving lamentation and reverse narcissism: 'I nearly went mad' . . . 'My brain is boiling'. . . . 'Great feeling of oppression in the head all day'. . . . 'There is nothing for me in this country'. . . . 'I don't love me . . .'

Assailed by strikes, rebellions, choleric colleagues, emotional and financial collapse, Hall's presentation of himself in his *Diaries* is as a one-man conflation of his *The Wars of the Roses*. He is a benighted monarch. As he wrote in the programme-essay, 'Blood Will Have Blood' (1963): 'Shakespeare knows that man in action has an instinctive will to domi-nate. You may excuse this lust as self-defence, but it is as rooted as the desires to eat, to sleep, or to procreate. Man must hunt to get food, just as his women must bear his children and protect them as part of an arche-typal pattern. . . . Underneath the highly artificial text of these plays, the characters betray these instinctive lusts.'

Hall's notion of the pagan and primitive, in the Histories, combine to form a savage mind; the niceties of civilization and ritual can't quite conceal mankind's appetite for almightiness. Hall would seem, therefore, in his writing on the tension between primeval rage and moral subtlety, between ashes and honey, to coincide with Brook's aboriginal delvings. Brook's empty space is kin to Hall's grey council-chamber (*The Wars of the Roses*), inky blue echo-chamber (*The Importance of Being Earnest*), dried-blood chamber-opera (*Antony and Cleopatra*). But, though both men investigate power in their work, Hall sees struggle and breakdown where Brook's productions attain equipoise, serenity. Hall sails into a heart of darkness. The horror! The horror! (Though, it is true, his epic theatre has lately developed to admit the transfigurative power of love. In Wagner's *Ring* he said he found 'a classical story of the conflict between power and love; of how heroic love eventually redeems characters who have been corrupted by power.' It is also true that this interpretation did not find favour with the Bayreuth audience.) Brook, a captain coura-geous who on his jungle trips has permitted his actors Darwinian experi-ments, sees order always uppermost – that's the story of *Lord of the Flies*. The choirboys, streaking themselves with warpaint, don't experience sociological breakdown: they simply exchange one system of organiza-tion for another; or, rather, one system evolves into another.

NEXT SEASON

Michael Blakemore, an actor turned director, and an Associate at the National Theatre (1971–76), appears in the *Diaries* as someone temperamentally opposed to Hall's style. Hall classes him with those boisterous barons, Tynan and Miller; but he seems to withhold respect (Tynan and Miller are at least grudgingly respected for their super-eloquence), and Blakemore is mostly discounted as a tiresome upstart, the acquaintance of journalists and their traitors ('From now on I must say to journalists in advance that there are some subjects I'm not prepared to talk about,' Hall decrees).

A complaining colleague is to Hall a saucy insurgent, malevolent to him in all aspects.* Blakemore has the audacity, at a board-meeting, to read out a speech arguing that Associates have no rights, no authority. They form a paper parliament. He's also unsure about the fitness of directors making personal gains when (subsidized) National Theatre shows transfer to the (profit-making) West End. Hall, so shaken as he is, is wan with care, discounts the speech as delivered by a sad figure. Blakemore 'said he admired me but couldn't stand my greediness – for work, for money, for success, for power, for position.'

HOW IT IS

Next Season pre-dates these spats, but in several ways may be thought to anticipate them. The novel, which is about a Stratford Festival in a town called Braddington, is careful not to be specific about any real person or place – that old cinema disclaimer about any resemblance to the living or dead being purely coincidental. Simon Callow, in his preface, is anxious to have us stop the sport of identification. 'All I really knew was that it was about the theatre, and it had been written by an insider. That was more than enough for me.'† The subject-matter of Blakemore's novel is

---

*   'Worcester, get thee gone; for I do see
        Danger and disobedience in thine eye.'
        Henry IV, Part One, I, iii

As Hall's having a hard time of it, running the National, is equal to the punishing schedules of a Shakespearean king, running England (he says things like 'tomorrow, legally, I ascend the throne'), and if fellow directors become the growling and discontented nobles, Olivier, in the *Diaries*, is pictured as John of Gaunt – very ill with a muscular virus, and decidedly ambivalent about the new regime.

† To put the record straight, I wrote to Michael Blakemore in February 1988, inquiring after his *roman-à-clef*. He replied that 'Charles Laughton indeed went in to the making of "Ivan Spears" but there's also a lot of the Olivier I knew from *Titus Andronicus*. However, Ivan's physical appearance, at least as I saw him in my own mind, is that of a totally unknown but very talented old actor I once worked with in Rep – Arthur Rees.'

the overthrow of actors by directors, of acting by conceptualizing. Set in the late Fifties, written in the late Sixties, republished now in the late Eighties, the book radiates a sense of what it feels like to be in the theatre; we receive an impression of the instincts, pleasures and repentances of those creatures who have a vocation to perform. And when they aren't performing, they don't exist. Nothing impinges. An out-of-work actor is an invisible man, 'spiritless and withdrawn'. Employed, but between performances, he's still a social ghost, with friendships and alliances which come and go, girls had and forgotten; a vagrant's trudge from job to job. (Samuel Beresford travelling by train to Braddington, passes through industrial England and recalls the inappropriate pastoral plays he acted in at the Reps.) Acting is entirely a world of impermanence; the evaporation of live theatre as it's happening. 'What do actors ever expect when they put passion into their work? Something not much less than a Second Coming.'

Samuel Beresford is in acting's thrall. He takes a delight in making texts speak, in having characters rise from a printed script; and it's an authentic delight – not for him the riddle-me-ree of stardom or the antics of ambition. Blakemore's hero proceeds with a subdued, clerky air about his business; a gentleman ranker. The big joke of the story is that Sam's part is very tiny – the doctor in the *Duchess of Malfi* – and yet he puts everything into it. Acting consumes the actor. Climbing into the costume, picking up the props, speaking Webster's lines 'some aspect of his personality that would otherwise have remained captive and mute was being granted its freedom'.

That costume and those props are lovingly collected. Sam gets absorbed in researching and making medieval spectacle frames; he delights in a project to have his nose cast in plaster for a sculpted putty extension. Gleeful, 'ridiculously excited', he corroborates the frenzy Antony Sher details in *Year of the King* – a diary which, in many ways, deals with the same subject as *Next Season*, and uncannily so. Hunting for a wig, Sam ascends to the theatre attics. Suspended under the gilded dusty dome, a cavern apt for Erik the Phantom, is the wardrobe store, a cobwebbed museum of past performances; a cave of discarded skins. Nothing is sadder than the relics of old shows, and it's hard to credit that these droopy weeds ever did bear life. 'One was reminded again how old the building was . . .' Blakemore's tone is tinged with gothic. Braddington represents the house of every play ever put on, a mausoleum of mummery. Then, rummaging about, Sam finds the trunk from a famous *Richard III*. Tattiness yields a lost treasure: from a box the actor lifts a shoulder-length of oiled hair. Olivier's Crookback peruke. 'Had there ever been a drama student, maimed by hopes without the skill to match them, who had not wanted to play that part? It was perhaps the first ambition of every unhappy child who had ever become an actor.' Sam puts on the wig, 'stared at himself in the mirror, mouthed a line or two, and found himself laughing out loud with pleasure'.

Sam's self-crowning himself is an irony he's aware of; the wig is a happy appropriation, and the actor has no desire to supplant 'the rags of the past'. Yet his respect for a Great Tradition, 'the tradition in which he found himself working', is used against him. Sam's championing of Ivan Spears, 'the old actor' or 'that old one', marks him as a reactionary – a traitor to his generation, which is more accurately represented by Richard Wayland (who, like Jenkins-into-Burton, has changed his name from Jones, 'and as such had been doing rather well'), assiduous partygoer and camp-follower; and by Amanda Maitland, a society-girl whose father is a playwright along the Rattigan or Coward lines. She's less interested in the arts of acting than in furthering her career, and flirts with agents and stars; her ambition is to be seen in the right gossip columns, parties, beds: 'My agent said I should have a party for top people, it was his idea.' Ivan Spears she has no respect for, calling him 'oldfashioned' and ugly. When he offers the suggestion that she play down her squawks and shrieks as the Duchess, arguing that sensuality is a languid thing, she goes blank – unable to appreciate Ivan's sense and sensibility because she can't fancy him.

Ivan Spears, who arrives on the train alone, and who remains a solitary and a mystery, is the triumph of the book. Stardom is of his life a thing apart (he's not interested in the accoutrements of fame and hates being pestered offstage; he refuses to attend cast parties); 'tis Amanda's whole existence. Prettiness and social connections are all she has. Spears, warty, a pudding-face, sees acting as a transforming power, releasing in him 'a store of vitality', and he becomes beautiful. Blakemore based his look on Charles Laughton, who played Lear and Bottom in the 1959 Stratford season – a season Blakemore himself appeared in as a rumbustious Knight and as a leather-aproned Snout.* Several perfect ur-Laughton performances are mentioned: a film of *Cromwell*, with Spears in ecstasies of a regicide's remorse; *Beethoven*, with Spears in an agony of deafness, smashing a piano: a man shut off from his own creativity, evicted from his genius. His taking of Sam out to dinner, for clumsy conversation, is a dilution of Laughton's sad, fumbling passes at younger actors; his genuine desire to teach them. Spears, like Laughton, is one of the damned; a lonely luminary connected to a dying Victorian dynasty, 'oldfashioned . . . yet the very anachronisms of his style, such was the honesty of his talent, were a source of excitement'. Indicative of Tynan's twilit gods, Spears is a symbol of all passing masters, deposed kings, embattled lords. There's no peevishness, only heroic will. 'That suspending concentration, the mark of talent, could never be concealed . . . There was

---

* *A Midsummer Night's Dream* was directed by Peter Hall.

Ivan, celebrating his playwright and celebrating himself in thrilling conjunction.'

For peevishness we may look to Tom Chester, who has it in abundance. He's Oedipus with the luck of fore-knowledge; Spears/Laius he's out to get. But it's not an exuberant battle; there's not the energy of competition. Spears merely bores him. 'Tom didn't *like* Ivan's work. He told me,' vouchsafes Amanda – who, repulsed herself by Spears, is attracted to Chester because he offers to manage her career; that is, he tells her whom to be seen with, whom to have strategic flings with. Amanda's shallowness, revealed by her depth of lying, is to Chester an earnest of star quality, and actors with star quality had 'to organise their lives very carefully. They owed it to their talent. They had to choose their parts carefully and their friends and everything . . .' Amanda, who has been sleeping with Sam, is encouraged to prefer Martin Dane, a posturing and malicious opportunist with a glistening Alfa Romeo. The 'mysterious gadgetry of the dashboard', all twinkling lights, again is to Chester a demonstration of talent. Private life is a public thing. 'Prove you can grub for one of those,' he tells Sam, 'and you'll get all the work you want.'

Acting's an automobile, an assemblage of kit parts, the more swollen, gaseous and smooth the better; an upholstered, slinky vehicle for stardom. Nothing to do with feeling; nothing to do with imagination – 'acting is really quite a simple thing'. Chester and Dane, rehearsing *Macbeth*, waste time in psychobabble, vainly groping for motive and mumbling through fake analysis; throwing what Kingsley Amis calls a pseudo-light on non-problems. And of course Dane hates Spears, disdainfully dismissing him as a creature of melodrama ('It's right for his generation'), arrogantly reminding everybody that 'In his day Ivan was a bloody marvellous actor, you know that?'

What Chester, with his 'surface egalitarianism' (a pander, he's also a snob, turned on by brand-names and sacking the loyal company secretary for a heartless deb with a hyphen), and Dane ('Honestly, that nothing!') obliterate is a belief in theatre as a place for experiment and a home for the berserkness of invention – what Spears, reminiscing of Barrymore, calls 'really a sort of raw poetry; there's something inarguable about it'. Chester made poetry prosaic – the monochrome prose of newsprint. Rehearsing *The Duchess of Malfi*, 'he had done his homework, at least the academic side of it'; and there's a scrupulous absence of joyousness in the marshalling of cast and crew: 'This play is about horror . . . You've all got to be writhing maggots.' Sam's response to this glib command is restrained irony: 'It was obvious that he had found his text for the production and would stick to it.'

Sticking to it, he's immobilized, incapable of offering practical advice when it's requested, disallowing suggestions from his puppets: 'There was no disguising the fact that when he looked at an actor below a certain rank, the curiosity went out of his eyes.' There's a muddle about lances and armour. Chester has the cast repeat time after time the movements he's decreed, which only consolidates clumsiness, ingrains error. 'He could only inwardly curse the stupidity of his actors', impatient that his ideas aren't being made to work.

Spears speaks out, bringing the scene alive with effective business involving offstage combat; the actors, instead of selfconsciously milling about, are to bring on hauberks, bucklers, snickersnees; they are to chat expectantly of the lists. A foretime for the play proper opens out. Spears imagines his way in and out of Webster's words, and 'held the company in thrall, taking charge so nimbly and with such certainty that the work was over and accomplished before anyone quite realised what had happened'. The magic occurs in a twinkling; Spears, inspired, enjoins inspiration in the other actors – 'The room had become quick with invention.' And Chester is chastened. 'This particular play was Ivan's,' says Blakemore, in one of the finest descriptions of being an actor ever written: 'Everything he said about it, and everything he did in his own performance, had an immediacy and a vigour which claimed the material as his own. Webster had found a spokesman, one who responded not so much to the formal qualities of his play, anchored in their own time, as to that enduring impulse that had led to the writing of it, and which, centuries later, in terms of his own experience, Ivan was able to affirm.'

A DAY'S WORK

Dispossession, supersession: these are the themes which stir in the play, and in Spears. When an understudy has to go on as Bosola 'so much of the ambiguity – the sense of a man divided against himself, that Ivan had discovered in the part – had gone'. Problems start when the actor is given *The Way of the World* to direct; that vital experiment and berserk inventiveness can't be promised or organized in advance. Spears overprepares. Highly ingenious, his rehearsals are clogged with possibility and limitless discovery. It's weeks before the cast actually get to Congreve; Spears devises a small prelude which grows, 'as he invented additional flourishes or built on the suggestions of his willing cast,' into a great baroque mime. The joyous disregard for balance and neatness, thrilling when it irrupted into *The Duchess of Malfi*, is now a chilling extravagance. Spontaneity runs away with itself. The set is also a spectacular and unworkable whirligig.

Frederick Bell ('There was something extraordinarily shrewd in his frequent protests that he lacked intelligence') and Martin Dane, as Mirabell and Fainall, give Spears less than zero encouragement or sympathy; they mumble from their scripts and assist the growing unease. Dane is

particularly truculent, wilfully misreading lines and spoiling careful tim-
ings. Spears knows he's defeated. His own wayward energy, plus uncooperative actors, mean catastrophe: 'All the life and buoyancy had gone
out of him. He looked old and sick.'

But he still has to play Bosola every night. Actor and part coalesce.

> I have done you
> Better service than to be slighted thus:
> Miserable age, where the only reward
> Of doing well, is the doing of it.

After a particularly bad rehearsal, Bell and Dane openly insolent, Spears
gets so sunk in Bosola, he can hardly speak the words – he's too frantic
thinking the thoughts. Outside, there are storms, rains, people getting ill;
inside the theatre, Spears dries and rages. He loses control and throws a
tantrum in the interval: 'Anger had seriously depleted his energies, and
the suggestion of withheld power, which normally made his playing so
arresting, had gone.' The book gathers for a disaster – and Spears
collapses, a little death. Tom Chester and his cronies are at the door when
the actor is carried away on a bier, 'as if they were waiting to partake in . . .
some grim, intent ritual not yet wholly explained'. They are priests or
executioners at a human sacrifice. A tribal blood-letting. The ritual is that
of a younger generation effectively killing-off an oldster; and Spears's
stroke, a chiasmal lesion, which leaves him blind, is a cruel and neat
inversion of the Oedipal mutilation. Spears suffers for the sins of his
successors – and he's not even granted recognition for his innovations in
The Duchess of Malfi. Critics praise the director for the actor's performance ('Last night at the Braddington Playhouse Tom Chester moved
effortlessly into that select company of directors to whom the word
"creative" can truly be applied'); and so when *The Way of the World* opens
to disastrous reviews, the cry is 'STICK TO ACTING, IVAN' – a fiendish
injustice because, though the actor's name stays on the programme as
director, the production is entirely the responsibility of Chester who,
after Spears's grand exit, sequesters the show, dumping curlicues, scrapping webs of feeling and wholly destroying relationships within the play.
He's oblivious to Spears's stylization. Sam is disgusted: 'Whether or not
one agreed with Ivan's scrupulous and rather oldfashioned methods of
production, some ingenious thought had gone into his placing of the
actors.' Gradually, the drama is 'stripped of all its detail', and becomes a
boring few hours of Restoration yackety-yakking.

Worst of all, Spears's rococo prelude is cut: 'I've never been mad about
it,' says Chester, 'It's not really anything to do with the play.' Sam speaks
out, dangerously venturing an opinion (even though, to Chester, 'He was
not someone whose opinions concerned him'); Spears's work 'at least . . .
was *something*. Somebody had thought, and selected, and decided. And

there were some wonderful things in it, some wonderful moments.' No use. 'No, I'm sorry, the prelude's cut and that's that.'

Suddenly Sam is able to see Chester for what he is: a talented policy-maker, business executive and administrator, but in terms of imagination and humour, sympathy and sorcery, the comic spirit, he 'had nothing to give, a fact which the monotonous absence of delight in his work amply confirmed'. He thus fills his life with political decisions, and the lives of his subordinates with fear. He makes patronizing speeches, chastising slipping standards: 'The company owes it to itself as a family. Because that's how I think of you all. As a family of actors.' Where Chester admonishes ('Well, everybody, that was awful, absolutely awful. I can't tell you how bad it was'), Spears had educated ('a motion of confidence not only in the intelligence of the actor to grasp his point but also in his special ability to execute it'). Chester is pragmatic, calculating; Spears was operatic, indulgent. For Chester, theatre is a cool machine; for Spears, as for Brook and Tynan, a corrida. 'That's what the theatre is: a bullring. And what's wrong with that?'

Chester uses anxiety about next season – whether each actor will be invited to return, or despatched to the dole office – to coax devotion and obedience for the present season. 'There are things happening,' he says with intentional ambiguousness, 'which at the moment I can't yet talk to you about.' Spears removed, Tom in command, Amanda 'was giving her whole attention' to the compact dictator. Her future is safe; Sam's is not. Along with most of the company, he gets his redundancy letter. The theatre is split between the smug elect and the despondent outcasts. Next season will be populated by 'young actors who had all made reputations quickly' – on television, in films, at the right parties. Sam has a valedictory interview with Chester, in the director's eyrie, where the despot is happily desk-bound, and the actor's failure is explained: he lacks ferocity and 'this fantastic sex appeal' which Dane has; he's pusillanimous and will never achieve big fees: 'Determination is the polite word. Your trouble is you're a bit too nice.' And so the bad end happily and the good unhappily. That is what this fiction means.

BEING THERE

Sher's *Year of the King* matches the atmosphere of obsession in *Next Season*; the pixilation of putting together a part ('Sam had been merely a dealer in scrap, assiduously collecting suitable fragments: from the play, from himself . . .'). Sher's crutches and Sam's spectacles are emblems of driven lives; the actors both worry about performance details and dream of making it in a foreign land – for both were born in the distant sun. Sam is a young Australian, remembering the beaches and the surf; Sher comes from South Africa, and studied his text of *Richard III* whilst lounging on the Rand sand. Both have mothers who keep in busy correspondence. Sher looks out for the airmail envelopes, and returning to Johannesburg, his old house seems a shrine. Photographs, posters, framed reviews. Sam's mother is also idolatrous. She maintains an altar to her son's fame; Sam gathers clippings and notes, 'accumulating a partial record of his career for her custody'.

Simon Callow's *Being an Actor* is a documentary sequel to *Next Season*: how it is to be in the craft. Blakemore has Sam experience the slave market of auditions, the indignity of walk-ons and understudying; the show trials of drama school; the travails of a long run and technical rehearsals. The (financial) salvation of a deodorant commercial. Callow tells aspiring and out-of-work actors how to keep acting in the air. Sam studies scripts and learns roles, being useful in his redundancy; he absorbs the acting past and his mind is invaded by parts he'll never get to play. Callow has experienced, with Sam, the ignominy of the Labour Exchange; and, with Sam, he's experienced the opposite: the pleasure of getting a new job.

Being an actor, however, is only seldom exhilaration. Company life is too frequently a 'narrow world of rumour and grievance'; a small world of suspicious enthusiasm and easeful denigration, rather than of art. Blakemore's terminology for the world-within-world is anthropological. The actors at an early rehearsal assess each other 'with a private tribal severity'; the beach party is 'a tribal event'; Spears's removal, as we saw, was structured as a last rite. Before a first night, presents and cards are distributed – 'so many tender superstitious benedictions'. Chester emerges as a witch-doctor, working up crude banishments and scares; a strict adherent to the feudal hierarchies. He's made cuts in *The Duchess of Malfi* ('the scenes that may have to go are marked in red'). Destiny is posted on the noticeboard. Sam is horrified to see his part razored out – he feels, as an actor, 'casually blown to bits . . . at the mercy of other people's frequently mediocre decisions'. He decides not to complain, thinking it best 'to create an impression of willingness', even though he's being, in a strong figurative sense, *used*. An expression of natural vituperation could ruin his career, precipitate doom.

Acting is a neurotic business; the worry about what a director and his stars are going to do to you. Actors are forced into simulating humbleness, even abasement. Chester's removal of the Doctor, and his defence of the decision, is made 'without any reference' to Sam at all. After Spears's intervention, the character and the scene are reinserted, with much sly smiling and collusive winking on Chester's part – 'It's up to Sam to convince us we can't do without him.' The actor is a component of directorial strategy – and it's a revolution against this state of affairs that drives Callow's *Being An Actor* into containing a manifesto. Why not do away with autocratic directors and give power back to the actors? And by desiring the exile of scheming, plotting, silently smirking directors, who luxuriate in not letting on what they really think, Callow is desiring a return of actors like Spears. His *A Difficult Actor*, a biography of Charles Laughton, takes Blakemore's fallen angel and gives him recognizable locations and a real name; and what in *Next Season* is romantic decline, for Callow becomes symptomatic of national catastrophe.

Spears, archaic and intuitive, shows how acting ought to get back to the future; a renaissance of the ancient styles. Callow's Laughton unfolds straight from *Next Season*: 'the face ... even in its celebrated coarseness, more delicate than he would have expected'; the belief that, in every actor there is 'an irreducible minimum of insecurity'; the way that, for every actor, each performance is 'a voyage into the unknown of his own ability'; the hazard of theatre – one day a 'shared experience' with the audience, the next a humiliating exhibition. 'There were hundreds of people sitting in the dark looking at him. Their gaze reduced him to an object.' Callow, metempsychotically reliving Laughton's career, communicates every agony and ecstasy of display in a similar manner; and in his preface to *Next Season* he's amply grateful. 'I cried for joy' at the novel, he vouchsafes. 'A way of life existed which would use my energy, my brain, my bursting heart.'*

Spears/Laughton, says Callow, is able to couple his 'actor's inner universe with that of the play'; and Chester is to be despised because of his 'unlimited faith in his own indispensability'. Spears's acting is a marriage of mysterious mind and scripted matter; Chester's directing is a divorce, without love. Callow says *Next Season*, 'passionate ... anarchic,' is dangerous, a samizdat. 'Tom Chesterism' has won, 'and there will be no more Ivan Spears. Unless ...' That ellipse is Callow's own. For actors are slowly declaring and reclaiming independence, valuing their own contribution – and it's 'a resurgence of the independent spirit among actors' that Sher and Callow have personally done much to foster.

But great actors have always been creators; imitators belong to the second rank, and perhaps the intimidated also. Sam sees how the constant fear of revolution keeps the palace of art tense and alive: 'No wonder the drama abounded in stories of the rise and fall of tyrants, of the suffocations of court life, of the jockeying of favourites. The dramatists had found it all in their own disgusting world ... this jostling, frightened, overcrowded world.' On the train, leaving Braddington, he notices a conflagration in the distance. Valhalla in flames? Atlanta, gone with the wind? The Northern lights? Manderley? It's the set of *The Duchess of Malfi*.

---

* I've pointed out Tynan's aggressive diction and Hall's wan chants into the dictaphone; Callow's prose is shrill and high-heeled, a camp bellicosity as befits an actor who is a romantic rebel and reactionary.

What happens to Sam? He goes to play Jimmy Porter in a converted fish warehouse. *The* romantic rebel and reactionary.

TIME AFTER TIME

The first generation of actors this century learned from the theatre, the next from visits to the cinema, the latest from the literal dottiness of television. Yet the history of modern acting is a tale of anachronism, the generations intermingling – and that's its modernist component, as pictured by Ezra Pound in *The Spirit of Romance*, with this flourish: 'It is dawn at Jerusalem while midnight hovers above the Pillars of Hercules. All ages are contemporaneous. It is B.C., let us say, in Morocco. The Middle Ages are in Russia. The future stirs already in the minds of the few . . . Real time is independent of the apparent, and . . . many dead men are our grandchildren's contemporaries, while many of our contemporaries have been already gathered into Abraham's bosom, or some more fitting receptacle.' And as an example of this process of kindred superimposition there's the work of the white knights, already much discussed, or the glide through the decades of Peggy Ashcroft, who from the crofter's wife in *The Thirty-Nine Steps*, lending Robert Donat John Laurie's coat, to Mrs Moore in *A Passage to India*, has played resigned, stalwart women glinting with secret fires and thoughts of insurrection; as Queen Margaret in *The Wars of the Roses*, the sexual hysteria broke through; as Queen Mary in *Edward and Mrs Simpson*, fires were stoically banked down, maternal suffering gracefully borne, and what resulted was Peggy Ashcroft's portrayal of Lady Bracknell.

The actress has conquered stage, screen and tube. She worked in Gielgud's West End seasons and helped Peter Hall found the RSC – with its contract system and familial dedication. She demonstrates, with Olivier, Gielgud, Richardson and Guinness that Ivan Spears can never entirely be killed off. And though it's easiest to talk of her performances as incalculably diffuse – never forget that she's the equal of Katherine Hepburn, sharing with her a capacity for intelligent anxiousness, and this leavens the grace and gravitas, making for something far more compelling. In 1981 she returned to Stratford to be the Countess of Rousillon in *All's Well That Ends Well*. I went four times. Trevor Nunn's operetta production was entirely bewitching. The Elizabethan era's rebirth as the Jacobean age became an Edwardian threnody. The play was set to a waltz* and oozed its way about a white wrought-iron pavilion designed by John Gunther. The airy conservatory-construction served as a railway station, a café, a *salle d'armes*, a terrace with soft, papery leaves underfoot.

* The sheet-music, by Guy Wolfenden, was on sale. I've heard it played at weddings.

And moving through the flamboyant evocations of a mood both Anton Chekhov and Franz Lehár would cede bits of as their own, Peggy Ashcroft showed them all how to do it. Her manner serene, but not frostily so; her tone humorous, but not mockingly so; her voice halting, but not with any emotion overwrought enough for tears, she made the Countess Shakespeare's consummate woman: Rosalind's wit, Viola's sadness, Cressida's knowledge of betrayal, Cleopatra's knowledge of loneliness. The actress was lingeringly defiant, ironic, nostalgic; she was the emotional centre of the drama, absorbing the plot away from lachrymose Helena (Harriet Walter in her late-adolescent ululation-phase) and the braggart Bertram (Mike Gwilym, in a fit of minatory fidgets, which is his only phase), to reorganize interest around her own conversations with Lafeu (gaunt, wistful Robert Eddison) and Lavache (buckled-over Geoffrey Hutchings essaying Firs) – conversations loaded with regret, tolerance, dignity, lamentations on the passage of time – 'our remembrances of days foregone'.

When the steward reports the contents of Helena's soliloquy, and the girl's love for a boy of higher estate, the Countess's response, 'Even so it was with me when I was young', disclosed a full and evocative existence for the character beyond the confines of the present play. As Spears, and by safe inference Laughton, inundated himself in a part, so can Peggy Ashcroft make her stage creations live before and between the acts.

ALL'S WELL THAT ENDS

Anachronism is more than lucky, plucky veterans. (Peggy Ashcroft's Countess stately and sepia-lit, her head inclined at a quizzical tilt, her dark gold and grey garments rustling in the long-afternoon air, is a survivor from a bygone age where you'd meet Henry James taking his ease on the boulevards.) No, anachronism – the coincidence in space of elements from sliding time – is more purposeful. *All's Well That Ends Well* released in the actress an inviting tristesse because the updating was so precise; it belonged to her own childhood – the Countess was mistress of a world to be obliterated by Francis Ferdinand's assassination at Sarajevo on 28 June 1914, an event occurring when Peggy Ashcroft was nearly seven.

All yet seems well as the King (in Balkan frogging) blesses Helena and Bertram; but to any gods there's a gloaming coming on. Rousillon was a doomed Cherry Orchard. The Countess seemed to await extinction, as Mrs Ranevsky does. Nunn's production was *Götterdämmerung*; a presentation of the charmed world of creamy Edwardian suits and tapping with a malacca along the lido that was damned. The play was busy with travel: characters carried satchels, bags, portfolios and haversacks; the production began with a farewell, and labelled trunks bestrew the hall.

Offstage, the sounds of travel: puffing trains, honking motorcars, taxis throbbing waiting. And what all these urgent, incipient voyages represented was the Edwardian era waking up to find itself in the twentieth century; a new dawn of transitoriness, which includes marriages that may not work and social polemics by Shaw and Wells. Bertram and Helena eyed each other warily at the finale; together at last only because the plot demanded it.

Self-confidence gives way to self-consciousness (except for the humiliated Parolles: 'Simply the thing I am Shall make me live'); and amidst the psychological and physical bustle, the Countess took tea and cultivated her garden. It was as though through Shakespeare's woman character Peggy Ashcroft was acquiescing in her own destiny; *All's Well That Ends Well*, the actress's stage valediction, cast in a period of bittersweet nostalgia, was a sublime match of content and form. The play was found to be *about* the actress; a public receptacle for her private nature. As Michael Billington has said, applying a generalization to her, 'acting is a judgement of character and . . . especially with age, it is the moral qualities of the person that shine through the process of impersonation.' Nunn's picturesque anachronism of style (Shakespeare out of doublets and into trews and ball gowns) heightened, yet naturalized, the style of performance: Peggy Ashcroft is a spiritual actress, and here she was the very spirit of Richard Strauss's *Vier letzte Lieder*. We never get the sense she's faked up emotion; she relives it. When Margaret Tyzack took over the Countess, spirituality evaporated. The Countess was slightly harder, because almost imperceptibly more embittered. She didn't regret the past; she resented it.

SIR JOHN IN LOVE

Seldom is anachronism so obliging. Nunn's conversion of Shakespeare into a turn-of-the-century novel was never tricksy (maids and valets were pertinent eavesdroppers: their last days, before the war conscripted them away); and its triumph was to locate septuagenarian Peggy Ashcroft in the time of her birth (1907), so that her leave-taking had a double perspective. But to set *Romeo and Juliet* in Eighties Verona is doubly blind. Michael Bogdanov had chrome sports cars, sunglasses and a swimming pool hang about the stage. He didn't seem to know that flash, over-wealthy teenagers aren't what Shakespeare's play can be about. To the Elizabethan imagination, a child grew into adulthood without the emotional luxury of adolescence. Shakespeare's poised and preternatural romanticism was mumbled by sharp youths and molls who, from the evidence of their clothes, should have been yapping in a private slang. It was as if Leonard Bernstein and Stephen Sondheim hadn't thought of a removal to New York for their West Side story.

Bill Alexander's uplift of Falstaff and Windsor's merry wives from the queendom of Elizabeth I to the commonwealth of Elizabeth II was a state-of-the-art showpiece. William Dudley's set was an elaborate carousel involving, on the stage floor, interlocking panels. A saloon bar, a front room, a hairdresser's and multiple streetscapes danced into view, choreographed to jaunty Fifties film music – music apt for Joan Sims, Sid James, Mai Zetterling, Norman Wisdom and the brothers Boulting. Above the stage was a twirling panoply of period icons: a blue lamp, RAC and AA insignia, Michelin men, hotel menu boards, kitsch weathercocks. Props were lovingly researched: the angular furniture and phonograph, the fancy cocktail cabinet, a box of Black Magic. Mock Tudor, instead of Tudor, these New Elizabethans were cashiered war heroes growing old in suburbia, or rock'n'rollers with Elvis on their minds. The text, however, was an approximation of Shakespeare's. With Macmillan as Prime Minister instead of Cecil as Chief Secretary of State, Shallow, Slender and Sir Hugh Evans, driving up from Gloucestershire in a Morris Minor, couldn't talk of 'a Star Chamber matter'; they broached the High Court. References to groats, bear-baiting and heraldry went. The appearance of the fairies in Windsor Park was cut – ensuring a fancy-dress parade (Fenton a Beat poet; Anne Page jive-bombing, her ponytail waggling; Hugh Evans rigged out as Noddy's playmate, Big Ears; and Mistress Quickly, increasingly tipsy, disorientated by the shifting scenery, arriving late as a Christmas Tree decoration): a funny fancy-dress parade, when what Shakespeare intends is that, fleetingly, the goblinry becomes genuine. Hearing the chimes at midnight, Falstaff and the audience are in the land of faery. We are meant to be alarmed.

> Fairies, black, grey, green, and white,
> You moonshine revellers, and shades of night,
> You orphan heirs of fixed destiny,
> Attend your office, and your quality.

These are Oberon and Titania's ensembles, invading Windsor houses as they swept the dust and raked the hearths in Athens. Falstaff has been translated to the world of Bottom:

> They are fairies; he that speaks to them shall die.
> I'll wink and couch; no man their works must eye.

Shakespeare opens out the play's carrying-on with sorcery and superstition; the supernatural practical joke, about Herne the Hunter and sexual licence ('Now, good Sir John, how like you Windsor wives?'), seems no contrivance; magic seems no counterfeit.

We are suspending disbelief that all the action of the stage is real in any case, and so when Falstaff flinches, terrified, we forget that his tormentors are Windsor denizens in masquerade – they may as well be spooks. We are on enchanted ground, being in the theatre; and so when the play shifts into a new key of nocturnal haunting, it's as if the black arts of acting have broken through decorum, manners, civility, and the other constraints that keep society away from anarchy. Windsor, bustling and law-abiding by day, at night 'is as slanderous as Satan'. Thus does John Updike write a sequel to *The Merry Wives of Windsor* in *The Witches of Eastwick*: 'It was fundamental and instinctive, it was womanly, to want to heal – to apply the poultice of acquiescent flesh to the wound of a man's desire, to give his closeted spirit the exaltation of seeing a witch slip out of her clothes . . .'

Windsor is a coven, especially in Verdi's operatic adaptation, where the suspension of disbelief, and the theatrical artifice, because everyone insists on singing, is intensified. In *Falstaff*, the fat hero is nipped and tousled by the merry wives and their children, and the torment is an orchestrated humiliation. Flights of demons sing Falstaff to his unrest and panic.

> Pizzica, pizzica,
> Pizzica, stuzzica,
> Spizzica, spizzica,
> Pungi, spilluzzica
> Finch'egli abbai!

This Boito's for –

> Fie on sinful fantasy: fie on lust and luxury.
> Lust is but a bloody fire, kindled with unchaste desire,
> Fed in heart, whose flames aspire,
> As thoughts do blow them, higher and higher.
> Pinch him, fairies, mutually: pinch him for his villainy.
> Pinch him, and burn him, and turn him about,
> Till candles, and starlight, and moonshine be out.

The Windsor children, Sir Hugh Evan's charges, in the play and opera – but not Bill Alexander's bossa-nova show – creep out of the boskage as imps and satyrs. They are godlings in the landscape, coming forth in gruesome shape, like the demonic spirits who loiter at the Wolf's glen in Weber's *Der Freischütz*, or the phantasms who convene in *A Midsummer Night's Dream* where, as Oberon insists, what we see must be discounted, no more yielding than sleep-induced delirium. In that play, as in *The Merry Wives of Windsor*, the elvish kingdom is invoked to be educative: magic tutors a quartet of young lovers, and a superannuated knight, about love's bitter mystery.

REWARDS AND FAIRIES

The Merry Wives of Windsor begins in a paradise of drinking and tomfoolery ('Come, we have a hot venison pasty to dinner; come, gentlemen, I hope we shall drink down all unkindness'); it ends in an inferno of recrimination and haunting ('When night-dogs run, all sorts of deer are chased'). It begins as a play about duplicity and credulity; it ends as an expression of the imagination – the imagination, which Coleridge held to be 'the living power and prime agent of all human perception', and which in a letter to Richard Sharp of 1804 he described as 'the *modifying* power in the highest sense of the word'. Imagination isn't make-believe: it's what makes make-believe true. Through imagination do devils and bogeys become palpable fears and anxieties; through imagination do we break bread with the dead, make wine into blood; through imagination is art willed into life. The secular form for the process is theatre.

CITIZEN HEARST

Bill Alexander's production was a mockery of Shakespeare's scenes from provincial Tudor life. Vulgar, diverting, amusing, there was little imaginative penetration of the play, but a great deal of fanciful encrustation. Anachronism was a means of evading the sheaf of words printed in the Folio of 1623 and the Quarto of 1602, and entered in the Register of the Stationers' Company as 'An excellent and pleasant conceited commedie of Sir John ffaulstof and the merry wyves of Windesor.' But no matter. The text survives, and shall blissfully survive all interpretative onslaughts, save neglect.

A rock'n'roll *Merry Wives* was lively, yet the life wasn't its author's, or even the actors'. Directorial flare, designer wizardry, musical pastiche and jingle: these zapped along to give the impression of animation. As an architectural correlative for this sort of drama, there's William Randolph Hearst's San Simeon. Hearst looted Europe to make his Enchanted Hill – and the upshot was a palace impossible to inhabit, a mausoleum of styles. Inspired by the Spanish fortresses pictured in the catalogue for the San Diego Panama-Californian International Exposition (1915), the plutocrat decreed that Moorish towers, galleries and cupolas be built. Within the rambling halls, Hearst installed panels and ceilings he'd plundered from real castles and stately homes. He bought rooms and barns, a monastery and monumental statuary, which were disassembled and packed into numbered crates. The ghosts of English and French heritage went West.

San Simeon is a testament to bad taste. Things of beauty were stuck into the fake Xanadu (even in the Coleridge poem, Xanadu is a pleasuredome best held in the imagination), and ruined. Soaring Gothic chimneypieces were cut to a cottage height; chapel roofs were sawn up for snuggeries; fan vaulting was positioned too low – and everywhere, the material from miscellaneous centuries jostled in crazy juxtaposition. Electric light fittings screw into Renaissance plaster, choir stalls pull up against a refectory table, and windows such as Ruskin drew in Venice are plugged at hazard into the stones.

In San Simeon, Hearst could play at being a Doge, and he owned Richelieu's bed. What he couldn't do in the place was live happily. An exorbitant cage for Marion Davies, the ranch (as it was mock-modestly called) was Hollywood's revenge on itself: a stage set fabricated from authentic materials; real and antique furnishings and fixtures strenuously made to look artificial. The place was a free hotel for the weekend cavortings of David Niven, Charles Chaplin, Errol Flynn.

STORMY WEATHER

The trouble with Hearst's folly of anachronisms was not that he got it all wrong; it's that he'd have us believe he'd got it all right. About his activities there was a combination of extreme arrogance and an untroubled innocence – which Welles captured so perfectly in *Citizen Kane* for the simple reason that his personality was of a similar constitution. Kane, Hearst and Welles might have been triplets.

Neither innocence nor arrogance are words apt for Derek Jarman. Try instead: knowing, decadent, delighted, brazen. *Sebastiane* had a group of naked beach boys speaking in Latin. *The Tempest* took place in a gutted Georgian mansion, with Prospero a dipsomaniac scholar scribbling equations and pentangles on the walls in chalk; Caliban, a blind smirker, suckled on Sycorax, a fat and nude comedy actress called Claire Davenport. For Miranda and Ferdinand's nuptials, snowy-white sailors danced a hornpipe and Elisabeth Welch lunged amongst them singing Cole Porter's 'Stormy Weather'.

Because knowing, decadent, delighted, brazen, Jarman excogitated himself fathoms deep into the play, identifying with Prospero the lonesome necromancer, with his opium pipe, spiders, scarabs and air of learned debauchery. And he also knew about likely Prospero antecedents: John Dee, Giordano Bruno, Cornelius Agrippa: 'Ten years of reading in these forgotten writers, together with a study of Jung and his disciples, proved vital in my approach to . . . *The Tempest*.'

The film is an experimental masterpiece. Jarman cut up the text, made a rearrangement, *made it new* congruent with Ezra Pound's directive, and such was the absorption of cast and crew in the work, they could afford structured improvization: 'You allow the work to take its own course . . . you form a magic circle, like King Arthur. Once the circle is complete it is impossible, fatal, to attempt to break it.' The neglected house, used for the set, was also allowed to yield up its secrets into the film's essence: dusty treasures, moths, mice, flowers, peacock feathers, were noticed in the rushes, awoken by the lighting and the camera whir.

A Victorian hermitage, a medieval cell; a Thirties party, a Jacobean masque; Beckford's opulent Fonthill, Violetta's sickroom; pink frock coats out of *Der Rosenkavalier*, white boiler suits from who knows what space craft, the atmosphere and costumes were purposefully composite, anachronistic – 'a chronology of the 350 years of the play's existence, like the patina on old bronze.'

Jarman is fond of finding time in a single space, history hanging about. Designing *The Rake's Progress* (which concerns the speeding up and slowing down of time*) for Ken Russell in Florence, he remarks, '*everything* is history here ... tired hippies pound away aimlessly at African drums under the graffiti-stained arches of the Uffizi, gawped at by herds of deadpan blue anorak tourists from the North.' A conjunction of Sixties rebels, primordial instruments, Renaissance art and Eighties tourists.

Caravaggio mates Italian old masters with English home-movie making. The artist's religious paintings (Michelangelo Merisi da Caravaggio lived from 1571 to 1610) are seen as erotic allegories of the street. Perhaps because studio-bound, the film has not the vitality of *The Tempest*. There's a crampedness, an amateurishness, which seem aforethought – and though the look is that of Peter Brook's *Carmen* (a scorched and bare arena where a drama of betrayal is acted out), the acting doesn't achieve Brook's puissance. Nigel Terry plays Caravaggio as a grubby Don José, wearing a worn borodino and puffing on cigarettes; his Carmen is Ranuccio Thomasoni, 'the thief who unlocked the soul of his art'. A lithe, rough-mannered blood, made by Sean Bean (Bogdanov's Romeo) into a renter-romantic, he gets stabbed at the end by his maddened lover, an execution exactly like Carmen's – *Eh bien, damnée!*

Jarman's conceit – that the biblical paintings were inspired by the sinful activities of the artist, that the models for saints were heathens and harlots – could've been powerful, magnificently damned. But *Caravaggio* is precious. Anachronism, in *The Tempest* a unifying device, here separates the original artist and his work from the actors and technicians trying to impersonate him. There's not even any connection between Caravaggio's older and younger selves; the Cupid's-bow lips of Dexter Fletcher have narrowed away in Nigel Terry. Anachronism made for coyness. And how the film is packed with the trick: tobacco, formica chairs and tables, strings of coloured light bulbs, newspapers, traffic sounds, trains chugging, a blue plastic school globe, a pocket calculator, a motorbike and a lorry, cotton print dresses, jazz amplified at a party, the critic Baglione tapping out his notice on a typewriter. These contemporary elements littered a screen otherwise strenuously correct: papal clergymen

---

* For a brilliant discussion of Stravinsky's use of chronology, see Paul Griffiths's Cambridge Opera Handbook on *The Rake's Progress* (1982). Jarman's words are quoted from his autobiography, *Dancing Ledge* (1984).

in expensive crimson attire, a sixteenth-century artist's studio, with eggshells and pestles, candles and copies of Caravaggios-in-progress. Unlike *The Tempest*, here anachronism made the film splayed.

THE FU MANCHU SYNDROME

Jarman is too clever for this not possibly to have been intentional; but anachronism is most famous for its inadvertence. Wristwatches in a Roman chariot race, vaccination marks on a Regency limb, pictures not yet painted on walls not yet built commemorating events not yet happened.* Basil Rathbone and Nigel Bruce, as Holmes and Watson, were irradiated with Hollywood's idea of Edwardian London (wing collars, bouffant hairdos, a general raffishness and a vocabulary with 'blithering', 'blinking' and 'I say!'), and then put out to solve espionage crimes in a Forties Washington and Canada. Anachronism was a lazy means of enlisting Conan Doyle for the war effort, whilst not needing to build historic sets.

A parochial equivalent is *The Vengeance of Fu Manchu*. Sax Rohmer's pulps carry a Twenties detail. Jeremy Summers's film (1968) hasn't the wit to carry any detail, save what accidentally trespasses across the camera's field of vision. Nayland Smith (Douglas Wilmer) drives period jalopies, but road surfaces, beer glasses, the London docks and implements in a farmyard are blissfully wrong. Fu's Orient is swinging Carnaby Street, with espresso sipped in those cafés decorated with white lavatory tiles. Sixties bongo music accompanies the swish of women with beehive coiffures, false eyelashes and lashings of mascara. Foreign accents are goonish and rural Wales deputizes for inaccessible Tibet. The fiendish plot concerns a missionary, who also happens to be a brilliant plastic surgeon, forced to turn a gook into a counterfeit Nayland Smith, and in forty-eight hours. 'The face of Nayland Smith. The mind of a murderer!'

The film was tawdry and illiterate. Because the audience was presumed to be illiterate? or was it an illiterate age? Every film shadowed James Bond. Hardware, bimbos, dastardliness, cisatlantic internationalism. Meet me all at the Casino Royale. Christopher Lee's Fu is a yellow Dracula, with slant eyes for fangs. But the wretchedness of the film, too inept even for camp, helps gather the versions of anachronism I've been discriminating with this lesson: only in museums does chronology make

---

* The vigilant Bernard Richards tells me that Lady Elizabeth Butler's picture of the Scots Greys charge at Waterloo was on a wall in Robert Bolt's film about Lady Caroline Lamb, 'a thorough absurdity when one considers that the painting was done in 1887, and in any case is in a dashing academic style influenced by Gerome, Vernet and Alphonse de Neuville ... impossible in 1815.' Dr Richards also vouchsafes, 'I once saw rhododendrons in a Robin Hood film.'

sense. The interfusion of past generations with younger upstart crows ('many dead men are our grandchildren's contemporaries'); updating and original appositions ('the future stirs already in the minds of the few') ensure that chronology buckles, chronology bustles, chronology twists and spins ('real time is independent of the apparent').

TIME AND SPACE

The castle of Monsalvat, in Wagner's *Parsifal*, where time becomes space, makes mystical, whilst making explicit, the hidden and chanced-upon homily of Fu's temple ('All ages are contemporaneous'); and the current scene in acting is never less than a breaking out of inbred dynasties, phantom dawns and complex intermingling. We live amidst Monsalvat. Flick across the television channels and Laurel and Hardy, Chaplin and Harold Lloyd are being endlessly revived; *M*A*S*H*, having come to an end, has returned to its beginning. A cycle, endlessly turning. The relay of *Star Trek* episodes will go on forever; the original cast is often collected together by morticians and placed in expensive motion pictures. And what this intimates is how the limbo of celluloid is a kind of heaven. A playback of old movies resurrects the stars, those kings of shadows and shades of shades. Art-houses and television burble up past decades, feeding them into tomorrow afternoon, yesterday midnight. Time bombards us in space.

A season on, say, Olivier or Cary Grant compresses a career into a few weeks, a few nights; the same actor can be viewed at different ages, like the scene in *Citizen Kane* where husband and wife degenerate over breakfast. Peter Greenaway's *A Zed & Two Noughts* dealt with trick photography and death. Fruit, fish, a zebra, a pair of twins decompose in fast motion; the cool gaze of the lens records bodies becoming food for worms, a wake attended by busy maggots. Unabashed tutelary genius of Greenaway's film was Vermeer, 'adroit and prophetic manipulator of the two essentials of cinema – the split-second of action, and drama revealed by light'. Vermeer's pictures have a mystifying clarity; like the gestures on Keats's urn, they beckon from a land of far-beyond we'll never attain. Greenaway, loading his film with reflections, copies, mirror-imaging, 'two of everything', had as his theme the desire of doubles to become unified – and by metaphorical extension, the desire actors have to meet themselves in the parts they play.

LIMITS AND RENEWALS

Olivier and Cary Grant, for example, their work crammed into a retrospective, would seem to be meeting themselves over and over. Orlando

(1936) and Heathcliff (1939) jostling with Macheath (1952) and Archie Rice (1960); C. K. Dexter Haven, from *The Philadephia Story* (1940), and Mr Blandings, he of the dream-house (1948), jostling with Roger Thornhill from *North by Northwest* (1959) . . . And the way each actor is a family matches the history of drama. Jimmy Porter is alive in Oedipus and the Prince of Denmark; Peter Pan is in Hamlet and Lord Byron. Heironymo, mad againe, teeters into T. S. Eliot, along with the wiz of Baker Street and numerous martyrs. Mr and Mrs Nobody, the Pooters, are the Blooms (as the Blooms are Odysseus and Penelope). Cynthia Payne has come from a Canterbury tale and the stews of *Measure for Measure*. Sid Vicious and Nancy are Wagner's Tristan and Isolde. *King Lear* is in Pinter's *The Homecoming*, *Richard III* in Hare and Brenton's *Pravda*. And so it goes. Perspectives are long. 'Well', says Stephen Dedalus, a young man much given to thoughts of paternity and pedigree, 'if the father who has not a son be not a father can the son who has not a father be a son?' It's difficult finding the origin of any species of play or performance ('It is BC, let us say, in Morocco. The Middle Ages are in Russia'); artists and art, actors and acting, evolve out of each other. Kinship is acknowledged, hands are touched, across the centuries. Pound found personal and creative consanguinities, for example, with the troubadours; a modernist poet, he carried the past within him.

And the virus of tradition is in every individual talent. Time's quirky graph is foreclosed in space – in the space of an actor's life; in the space where all actors are acting simultaneously. As I write these words, London is aglow with theatre. Time *arrayed* in space ('. . . while midnight hovers above the Pillars of Hercules'): Shakespeare at the Barbican; Gaston Leroux and Victorian melodrama in Lloyd-Webber's *Phantom of the Opera*, shot through as it is with riffs of Puccini and Alan J. Lerner; Lorca and the Cid bring Spain into the heart of the metropolis; an AIDS drama, *The Normal Heart*, with Martin Sheen, brings Coppola's Marlow into another heart of darkness. *Annie Get Your Gun* (with Suzi Quatro), David Merrick's *42nd Street* and a stage adaptation of *Seven Brides For Seven Brothers* show London wishing it was New York. The return of the musical. Elisabeth Welch is in cabaret at the Donmar Warehouse, splashing her stormy weather out of *The Tempest*; Wayne Sleep is attempting the Joel Gray part in *Cabaret*, before the musicians walk out and the cast are left to clump on a tuneless stage. Eliot's Noël Coward opus, *The Cocktail Party*, is opening a mile from the address where *Blithe Spirit*, Coward's Eliotic communion with dead wives, stars Marcia Warren. At the Apollo, where John Gielgud will be a museum curator called Cockrell, Paul Scofield and Howard Rollins growl in *I'm Not Rappaport*. At the Garrick, where Judi Dench and Michael Williams will be the Pooters, *No Sex, Please – We're British* goes up for the six-thousandth time. Derek Jacobi is illuminating computer-speak in *Breaking the Code*, and at the

National, Anthony Hopkins is breaking the code of Lear in rehearsals. Limbering up for the pantomime season, television stars are readying themselves to commandeer traditional harlequinades. *'Allo 'Allo* is doing big business with the live television cast. Do the charabanc loads come to see if they're *really* real?

If on a winter's night a traveller was to go into theatreland, what he'll find are representations of many periods and places, an intertexture of collaborations and misalliances; taking the cinema into account, the listings paper *Time Out* proves that everything is available, from Ozu to *Duck Soup*. And what's the effect on the mind if it wishes to contain the multitude? The perfect critic, casting a cold eye, would be as Claude Lévi-Strauss's anthropologist, for whom all mythologies implode into a single myth; and so is all acting a single action: phases of a sunset which, 'after successive developments and complications', finally collapse and disappear 'into the oblivion of night'. Except where the camera keeps record, acting burns itself up as it happens; it dies into life. For Lévi-Strauss, mythology; for us, acting, 'that huge and complex edifice which also glows with a thousand iridescent colours as it builds up before the analyst's gaze, slowly expands to its full extent, then crumbles and fades away in the distance, as if it had never existed'.

PART TWO

LIVES OF
THE ACTORS

'We're not in Kansas anymore, Toto.'
> Judy Garland, *The Wizard of Oz* (1939)

'It was night before roads were made, or houses. It was
the night that dwellers in caves had watched from
some high place among rocks.
  Then the curtains rose. They spoke.'
> Virginia Woolf, *Between the Acts* (1941)

'I used to tell myself that they too came out of a
fairytale, that in order to move they possess the secret
power of thunder and its terrifying roguishness, that
the public suspects them as much as poets, that the
masses adore them, detest them and watch for the
slightest lapse, and before they can give us any pleasure we must cultivate and rediscover the childhood
that poets prolong until death and grown-ups in towns
pride themselves on having lost.'
> Jean Cocteau, *Paris Album* (1956)

ONE

The Empty House: Alec McCowen

What is Henry James doing in the preface of *Lady Barbarina* ('I could remember how the rooms, how the whole place ... had exalted for me ... to pungency, the domestic spirit'); or Dickens in *Martin Chuzzlewit* (Jonas constitutes 'a part of the room: a something supposed to be there, yet missing from it'); or Vermeer, whose interiors are stung by sunlight; or John Singer Sargent, with his chambers dangerous and dark; or Conan Doyle , when he puts Holmes and Watson in an upholstered capsule that never existed; or James Joyce, when he put Leopold and Molly Bloom into 16, Eccles Street, Dublin, that did?

They are making houses of fiction; touring, room by room, object by object, architectural exoskeletons: the sentimental journey about the property is giving clues to character – Jonas Chuzzlewit, for example, like his room, 'false and quiet, false and quiet'. Houses are haunted by their inhabitants – but what happens if the resident spectre is an actor?

An actor's home, I anticipated, would be an extension on the house of fiction; a theatre by other means, with furniture and bibelots forming a script, their display a performance. The house shall quiver with flagrant exhibition – the actor on show, the real man hiding in an inaccessible elsewhere. But what if the show is the real right thing, and the actor is in himself a haunted house – his body the vessel for the characters he plays; the apparition of strangers dwelling within?

The process is that of Roderick in Poe's *The Fall of the House of Usher*, who 'had so worked upon [his] imagination as really to believe that about the whole mansion and domain there hung an atmosphere peculiar to themselves and their immediate vicinity'. Acting is an incantation, rousing shapes and phantoms which the audience reads as real. Actors make life; they give blood to the discarnate personality of a script – but do they have lives of their own?

It is curious to think that they have private existences at all. Flaunters of mannerism, what is their attitude to secrecy, reticence, retreat? Is there anybody behind the mask or ornate façade? Is the haunted house, in fact, empty? Should we be surprised that actors may want to guard the fissure between themselves and the roles they play; between themselves and that selective version of themselves allowed voice and vision in public?

Such issues were a little on my mind as I walked along the Old Brompton Road, to keep an appointment with Alec McCowen. His autobiography, *Double Bill* – which anticipates the self-investigations and life-in-the-day revelations of Antony Sher and Simon Callow, and is composed out of a clipped poetry, fond of antiphonal repetition and terse lists – describes an actor practised in the art of vanishing; there's a sense of solitude about him, which has nothing to do with solipsism or egomania. McCowen's isolation occurs in company – revealed when he talks to soldiers in Red Square, or when 'despite the social life' of a New York diary fat with lunch and supper dates, he's 'rather lonely'. And especially when playing Hadrian VII (1967), 'part of me was always trying to repeat the inflexions and timing made in the isolation of my study – without the actual impact of my fellow actors.'

McCowen appreciates that as an actor he's in solitary confinement with the denizens of his house of fiction; he keeps close company with his characters, who are real people that have never lived. In Washington, he recalls 'living alone at the Willard Hotel, eating ham and eggs'; in Birmingham's Albany Hotel he 'had lunch there alone'; after a performance 'I suddenly realised that I was completely alone ... I walked slowly home and watched television'; memorizing St Mark's gospel 'I remember vividly certain solitary lunches during this period'; he was able, by doing a one-man show, to 'rehearse alone, at all hours of the day and night'; and 'alone at Sandgate, I gave a recital ... into a tiny tape-recorder'.

The absence of a gregarious nature informs McCowen's acting. He's particularly forceful as a disembodied voice on radio – that most anonymous of forms – and over Christmas 1986, he played Sir James Barrie, the narrator, reading out the stage directions of *Mary Rose* and *The Admirable Crichton*, his golly-gosh tenor squeezing sudden melancholy from the whimsy, whilst the actual cast itself worked and gargled in an approximation of aristocratic Scottish speech; and as the First Tempter in a Caedmon recording of *Murder in the Cathedral*, McCowen rollicks when the rest of the cast – Glenda Jackson, Cyril Cusack, Paul Scofield amongst them – murder prayerfully. And there is always about him the ember of relative anger. The intensity of his interpretations beams up from his own sense of solitude – thus making him a superlative Malvolio, Shakespeare's frenzied malcontent, elder brother of Jacques and a fallen, lost cousin of Hamlet. McCowen's appearance in yellow cross garters and a terrible grin was as contorted and obscene a demonstration of conviviality and fellowship since the forced smile on Laughton's Bligh. This Malvolio was a man who lived for his pantry and the enforcement of life-disenhancing rules; a death's-head steward, delighted Olivia's house is in mourning. His Antony was similarly self-possessed, keeping his distance from Dorothy Tutin's Cleopatra, cold and aloof – misogynistic, even – like Mr James Philpott in *The Assam Garden*, who comes to judge whether Deborah Kerr's herbacious borders are worthy of inclusion in *Great British Gardens*, which he edits. Deborah Kerr's an Anglo-Indian tea-planter, retired to Gloucestershire. Her husband, a great toiler at the sod, drops dead ('work was the thing'), and she's left with the undergrowth to overmaster, with the help of an exiled Brahmin wife, living on the local council estate. The women create an exotic park, subduing nature's rampant exfoliations. Philpott's arrival is a kind of Doomsday – and he merely strides the paths and bowers oblivious, talking mainly to himself (trying out the Urdu for 'Bring me two bananas at once') and muttering weak civilities – 'You've got some nice things. Very nice.'

Or then there's his psychiatrist in *Equus*: 'Dr Dysart was imprisoned by his job in a similar situation to my own.' The reference is to McCowen's feelings of over a decade ago, when the actor felt trapped by his career and under pressure from accumulated success: Christopher Hampton's *The Philanthropist*, Alceste in *The Misanthrope*, the police inspector in Hitchcock's *Frenzy*, Higgins in *Pygmalion*. McCowen was collecting awards in London and New York, but he was bored, exhausted and prone to insomnia. 'At home I was crippled with terror. One morning I collapsed with hysteria.' He became, as Dickens would say, 'in a manner his own ghost and phantom, and was at once the haunting spirit and the haunted man'.

McCowen lives in a large penthouse in a street cold and sunless in high summer; a sooty and crimson excrescence, with net curtains filtering the light, like a giant box of Louis Daguerre. When I had given a password at a grille, the door electronically whirred for ingress. I stood in the elevator, as instructed, and was beamed aloft. Lift up your heads, O ye gates: and be ye lift up, ye everlasting doors.

The portcullis clattered aside – and there stood the master of the house in triplicate, flanked by publicity photographs and framed posters of Old Vic productions.

'You're not in the least what I expected,' said McCowen, the chill of a hand differentiating the real thing from mirror images. 'Come in.'

I was drawn into rooms thick with silence. Objects, to define the space the actor fills, included transparent tables, smoked-glass shelves and large impasto oils of bolts and locks. Here we had a man fond of gates and portals – of keeping something out, or in. I was taken with a small picture of a stage with a tiny ballerina leaving it – the stage an empty space of brown murk. A fuliginous absence.

We went up and down small flights of stairs, the entire apartment carpeted with a pale fawn, like milky Horlicks. The residence was an agglomeration of mezzanines and shut doors; even the bathroom (windowless) told no secret – and what man's a hero to his jakes?

Quitting the oubliette, I was reminded of Dr Johnson: 'Sir, you have an oriental scrupulosity about your own ablutions.'

The quilt on a double bed, next to the bathroom, was palest pink.

After much clattering and electronic activity, coffee was perked in a germfree galley, and McCowen and I had a disagreement about the art of asking question; the complexity of a catechism. I asked the actor to what extent his life feeds his work; the overlap and merger of any public and private selves.

'I don't much like those questions,' he said.

'Matthew Arnold reckoned only God and Shakespeare had the right to occultation:

> Others abide our question. Thou art free.
> We ask and ask: Thou smilest and art still,
> Out-topping knowledge.'

'*Equus* was an exercise in asking questions. Dysart, the psychiatrist, asks over four hundred of them – I counted. It made me realise that asking questions is the easiest way of acting, and it gave me a taste for interrogator roles – like Reilly in *The Cocktail Party*, or my television sleuth, Mr Palfrey. Anyone can ask questions, but it's sometimes very difficult to answer them.'

Asking questions actually is extremely difficult – anyone can answer them, with whatever degree of sincerity or facetiousness – especially if the subject is meant to be avoiding oft repeated anecdotes. McCowen's implication – that the interrogator is instantly more commanding than the interrogated – was interesting because can it really be true? Remember the reporter in *Citizen Kane*? The script calls him Thompson, yet he's entirely anonymous, despite being present in almost every scene; the camera shoots over his shoulder. Xanadu has NO TRESPASSING on the gate, and Welles's film is a complete traduction of that decree. *Citizen Kane* is a masterpiece of inquisitiveness, the lens nosing its way through windows and doors; but Kane himself remains a mystery. Indeed, his mystery is deepened the more he's investigated.

Welles shows that questioning is complex (Kane's paper is called *The New York Inquirer*), and that even more teasing is the interpretation of any answers received. The real meanings; what the eyes say; what the mumbles and silences and tones of voice say. Dysart may ask four hundred questions, but few of them are intended for his patient's exclusive response. He is tracking the trajectory of his own obsessions, more than

Alan Strang's. The psychiatrist treating himself; the interrogation directed inwards on to a private waste land.

McCowen played in Peter Shaffer's *Equus* at the Old Vic in 1973. The play was set in a wooden paddock, importuned by stylized horsemen – elaborate heads of twisted metal and leather patches, ancestors of John Napier's human locos in *Starlight Express*. Dysart patrolled the arena, addressing the audience directly on the nasty case history Shaffer's plot extrapolated; and he also addressed the on-stage audience of the cast, who sat on benches when not speaking. A tribunal. A court.

Equus is implicitly randy. Strang worships the horse, and his private paganism renders erotic the instruments of the stable: the bridles, straw, brushes, chains, buckles, saddles. Holy are the tools of the heart's affections. The mad boy takes out a favourite stallion for midnight rides ('There was sweat on my legs from his neck. The fellow held me tight'), and it's as though they've mated. The stallion, played by a hunky actor called Nicholas Clay (who went on to be Mellors in a softcore adaptation of *Lady Chatterley's Lover*), plus Peter Firth's nudity as Strang, made the relationship of youth and beast, by fusing them into a centaur, an image of homosexuality.

Attempting and failing to fuck with Jill, the comely groomess, Strang strikes out the eyes of the horses who've witnessed his fumbles: 'The Lord thy God is a Jealous God. He sees you.' References to eyes and vision – people stumbling when they saw; seeing with parted eye; the eye of man hath not heard . . . wink through the text.

Drama (as against the dramatically ritualistic blindings) lay in McCowen's depiction of the doctor hired to investigate: Dysart is less disgusted at the disgusting blinding than envious of Strang's passion: the pagan worship, the fire in the flint his of belief – an excitement Dysart himself knows only vicariously, through postcards of Ancient Greece and package holidays to the Peloponnese. Strang experienced a primordial force. Even regarding the mutilation of the horses, Shaffer wants us to believe that the greater cruelty is to be converting the boy back to normality. He'd be a clockwork orange.

McCowen took this idea of the author's and acted it out, making us concentrate on Dysart's personal dilemma of repression, rather than the horses' pain – which served as a gaudy provocation for a drama of dessication: Dysart as a man who has held back, who has denied his instincts, who has made the mistake of not living all he can.

And gaudily provoked, the theme is gaudily explored. We hear of his recurrent dream (an Inca mass-murdering of children), which seems based on William Burroughs. Strang is quick to notice his doctor's fear of yielding to sensations; he's quick to spot a master's vulnerability, and dives straight for it, making the interrogator the interrogated, Dysart's childlessness and sterility mocked: 'Come on, tell me. You've got no kids, have you? Is that because you don't fuck?' Dysart rather weakly snaps back, his only defence being propriety: 'It's my job to ask the questions. Yours to answer them.'

Sir Henry Harcourt-Reilly, whom McCowen played in the summer of 1986, has fewer problems with his patients, chiefly because he has fewer problems with himself. This was by no means the actor's first foray into the ravings of T. S. Eliot. He once took part in a charity show, *Homage to T. S. Eliot*, sharing a dressing room with Groucho Marx; and for a television adaptation of *The Family Reunion*, McCowen made an entrance so grandiose, the set fell down.

The Cocktail Party is intellectual Noël Coward, and the Phoenix Theatre was an entirely appropriate address, what with its Gertie Lawrence memorabilia – the autographed posters and photographs; a quaint shrine, with a bar fully manned by liveried domos during a dry matinee. An old lady with a violet rinse and a cloak of purple sequins, by name Hero de Rance, banged out popular period songs at a game joanna. The audience was a sprinkle of genteel widows and old men carbuncular – people for whom Eliot's lofty banalities ring profound. It was a very oldfashioned atmosphere, reminiscent of a church-hall – and Eliot was a Kensington churchwarden, putting into *The Cocktail Party* vicarage-tea insipidities:

> What we know of other people
> Is only our memory of the moments
> During which we knew them. And they have changed since
> then

Up went the curtain (the first red curtain rising I think I have ever seen outside of the opera) on a London flat in 1949; a brutal Art Deco capsule of brown trapezoids and blue moons, inlaid mirrors and rainbow panelling. At the rear, forming an altar, was a Negro totem pole; an ithyphallus, before which McCowen's Reilly stood, taciturn, bloody, bold, resolute etc. – and nattily attired. A practical cat amongst the canaries.

When Alec Guinness played the part, he comported himself with menacing calm; Rex Harrison was Professor Higgins. McCowen, by contrast, was a man quickly angry and instantly sharp; a bossy don, ready to strike fear into the handful of patrons in the stalls, and into Edward Chamberlayne, incarnated by Simon Ward as a bloated Elyot Chase from *Private Lives*.

McCowen's Reilly was a misanthrope; a reprise of Moliere's Alceste, whom he personified in 1973, directed, as in *Equus* and *The Cocktail Party*, by John Dexter. He's the doctor who sees and pounces upon only imperfection and anguish – and Lavinia has to ask

Are you a devil? Or merely a lunatic practical joker?

Reilly makes it his business to infiltrate a barren marriage; a meddle-some mastermind who recites theological hokum ('to approach the stranger / Is to invite the unexpected, release a new force'). He's Eliot's attempt at the psychiatrist as priest; a man solving mental illness with remedies of salvation. *The Waste Land* is brought into the West End.

McCowen – in the midst of a crowd sequestering himself – made Reilly a man who distanced himself from his own pronouncements as soon as he made them; a parody prelate, whose congeries of aphorism smacked less of Tiresias, still less of F. H. Bradley or Irving Babbit (Eliot's learned heroes) than of Charlie Chan – with one exception. Edward's problem, as Reilly diagnoses it, might usefully be excerpted to describe the occu-pational hazard of any actor: the drifting asunder of self from role, of the public face from the private life. When Edward spends several quires of text, or an age on stage, saying, basically, that he doesn't quite feel himself – his illness is what an actor exists to endure:

> There's a loss of personality;
> Or rather, you've lost touch with the person
> You thought you were. You no longer feel quite human.

In Edward's instance, a cure (at Reilly's sanatorium, where the surgeons are described as masked actors) would mean a return of faith and self-esteem; the eradication of imposture. He'll be made to stop acting.

> To finding out
> What you really are. What you really feel.
> What you really are among other people.

In context, a character's crack-up is meant; in fact, the lines also describe *The Cocktail Party* itself, which cannot decide on a form. Is the play a drawing-room comedy written in the style of Gilbert Murray's Euripides translations? Or is it pastiche Aeschylus in modern dress? Sometimes it's a thriller (Where is Lavinia? Who is the Stranger?); some-times liturgical ('And now we are ready to proceed to the libation'); sometimes stately ('Go in peace, my daughter. / Work out your salvation with diligence'). Eliot has written a mannered cross-breed.

Dexter's production knew this, and edged into camp: McCowen's arch therapist, of course; also, the play's bustle of modern conveniences: taxis, telephones, lifts, the cinema, the refrigerator, each introduced as an antique toy – Art Deco icons. Intended as contemporary references when Eliot composed the play, *The Cocktail Party* has become a period piece. We can see the mod. cons being put into the verse to make it new. Modernism: a time when machines to assist locomotion (taxi), speech (telephone), lift (ascension: 'In a lift I can meditate'), cinema (money from

moving pictures), refrigerator (preservation of food: the arrest of putrefaction) were exciting and worth mentioning. The cast have to share their
universe with these devices.

The Cocktail Party also has many references to cuisine. Alimentation
explains the action. Reilly is always asked how he takes his gin. Julia,
Celia and Alex cook, or try to do so, for Edward. At moments of crisis
they race for the stove; they ruminate on gulosity:

> With a handful of rice and a little dried fish
> I can make half a dozen dishes*

– says Robert Eddison's Alexander MacColgie Gibbs, the play's Fool,
who, like Julia (the supremely annoying old bag), is yet made into a
guardian angel, and expected, in Act Three, to be taken seriously.

The play concludes on references to food: cannibalism and predatori-
ness; the monkeys and Christians boiling and eating each other; the
beetles and ants which consume crucified Celia in Kinkanja. And, what
with the interest in exotic foreign countries and the interest in gastron-
omy, The Cocktail Party is an anthropological rite (as The Waste Land is
built on the anthropologizing of Jessie L. Weston and Sir James Frazer).
Food links to Eliot's themes of nourishment and replenishment of the
spirit. The cocktail party is a secular eucharist. Julia actually says that the
only point in attending such a social function is 'a really nice tit-bit'; and if
Reilly's gin slings mark his astringency, Edward's impotence is mocked
by flat champagne.

In Sweeney Agonistes, the broken masterpiece of 1923, Sweeney and
Doris play cannibals and missionaries in the way of children at doctors
and nurses:

> Yes I'd eat you!
> In a nice little . . . missionary stew.

Claude Lévi-Strauss's The Raw and the Cooked gives a promising line of
thought for all this: culinary activity, he argues, defines the progress of
civilization. A tribe eating raw food is primitive, earthbound; a tribe
troubling to prepare and cook its own food knows sophistication, knows
fire: 'The raw/cooked axis is characteristic of culture; the fresh/decayed
one of nature, since cooking brings about the cultural transformation of
the raw, just as putrefaction is its normal transformation.'

The Chamberlayne's refrigerator (and Mrs Pooter's Wenham Lake Ice
Safe) dares to disturb the universe; an unnatural preservation of flesh and
vegetable ripeness. Reilly's cure for Celia is to send her into the bush to

---

* That 'handful of rice' is self-parody, referring to the 'handful of dust' in The Waste
Land. Eliot is also retrieving his phrase from Evelyn Waugh.

live with the natives; from the cooked to the raw. Away from Mayfair, killed, her corpse is eaten:

> And then they found her body,
> Or at least, they found traces of it.

The natives erect a shrine – at which they leave offerings of food. *The Cocktail Party* is an epicurean myth; dinner theatre. Eliot's equivalent of Coward's supper-time cabaret at the Café de Paris.

Food is big in *Double Bill*. A recorder of his repasts, McCowen measures out his life in soup spoons. 'Once again, I enjoyed the scones and the raspberry jam and the yogurt,' he says, 'in the canteen of Broadcasting House.' And in Texas he took breakfast beneath a placard imploring the hungry to 'Tell us how you like yore aigs 'n' loosen yore belt.'

Over my black coffee in McCowen's apartment, I wondered at the bleak kitchen and the spartan furnishings; and the actor himself is dapper, compact. Any hearty eater inside him is well hidden. Perhaps his lists of grub are angel food; phantasmal, like the great feasts the Prince of Darkness lays on for Jonathan Harker ('I never drink . . . wine').

I turned from the flesh to the mind. 'What is the overlap of psycho-analysis and acting; psychoanalysis and theology?'

'I went to an analyst when I was thirty-three; I went for two years, five times a week before Old Vic rehearsals. I was never quite sure what benefit it did me. I suppose it made me live with myself a bit better; and it helped me a good deal as an actor.'

Immediately, the distinction between the man and the man's profession.

'Since that time,' he continued, 'I have often approached parts as though I were an analyst myself. In particular, I remember playing Malvolio, who is a really mixed-up case. I found what was happening on the couch in Harley Street, or wherever it was, a great help with *Twelfth Night*. I think I managed to get away from the stereotyped characteriza-tion one so often sees.'

McCowen's Malvolio, resurrected and adapted for television, was the repressed steward taking refuge in vigorous etiquette; his office, his duties gave him savage self-confidence. Take away the ceremony, and he collapses – just as Dysart can't cope when Strang ignores the structure of conventional patient/doctor catechism. This was a Malvolio whose earn-estness was no fake; he was no hypocrite – thus the cruelty of his forced comeuppance. We did not like him, but we could still appreciate how his humiliations were undeserved. Robert Hardy's Sir Toby, in fact, was a cruel cavalier revenging himself on one of Cromwell's troops, a full four decades before the Civil War.

'As for Eliot,' McCowen went on, 'I think there is an interesting development between *The Family Reunion* and *The Cocktail Party*; the earlier play is sombre, the later work comic – and the earlier work was obviously written by a man who has no knowledge of psychiatry; rather like the Emlyn Williams play *Night Must Fall*, in which a madman eventually announces "I am afflicted," and a multitude of sins is instantly covered! Or else the moon is high, and a character is obliged to be a killer.

'*The Family Reunion*, a splendid play, is very innocent. *The Cocktail Party* is not so innocent, but I don't think it is so wise, either. If you take what Reilly does in the play from a practical point of view, as a psychiatrist or whatever he is, it's not really impressive, actually. The solution he finds for the unhappy married couple is that they just tell the truth and start again with a little more understanding of each other.'

'Reilly is a simple-minded priest counselling Tom and Viv! What about the religious tone?'

'There's certainly an interesting overlap of psychiatry and theology: Reilly and the idea of the guardians, for example, or the idea behind the advice given to Celia Coplestone, the lovely young society girl, who is told to find fulfilment and love quite away from a physical relationship; she's told to devote herself to missionary work in Kinkanja.

'I think I'm attracted to Eliot because of the devotional themes – though I do get a little wary of how close I get to playing God over and over again.'

McCowen was thinking of *After the Rain*, *Hadrian VII* and *The Portage to San Cristobal of A.H.*, where he appeared as folk self-deluded to different extents, who ruled and exerted power; the catalogue could also contain Higgins in *Pygmalion*, twisting and educating the cockney Magdalen, Eliza Doolittle; and the police detective in *Frenzy*, who exculpates wrongly sentenced Jon Finch.

'Worrying, slightly, the Almightiness, and I have to keep a sense of humour about it.'

'Have you used a sense of humour to dulcify *The Cocktail Party*; findingy irony in Reilly so that he does not become too involved with the drama's ramifications?'

'Yes, in the early scenes of the play Reilly says, "Now you must await your visitors" to Edward, and he says, "What visitors?" and I say, "whoever comes . . .". This sounds to me extremely portentous; slightly overblown. So I pull a very wild face at that point, as if Bela Lugosi as Dracula were going to come around the corner. That sending up of the material occasionally actually works, even to the material's advantage.'

'How did you locate the right balance of irony and humour? How did you conceive of the mysterious Reilly?'

'I fell into a trap before rehearsals. I went on holiday to Rome, after shooting *Personal Services*, and went to the catacombs, which I'd never seen. There were very few tourists; I was with a friend and we were the only people there. A little priest from Singapore, called Father Ambrose Heng, took us into the crypt and opened a place the public isn't normally shown. We went deeper into the ground, and saw skeletons of children.

'Now, Ambrose Heng was a very delicate little priest of such goodness, there was such an atmosphere of goodness about him, and he was so light in speech, and light in his goodness, light in the way he talked about Christianity, I became besotted with him as an actor: here is Reilly, I thought. This is what I'm going to do in *The Cocktail Party*. I started off rehearsals being very *light*, very *good*, very close to Ambrose Heng. John Dexter started snarling quite soon and said, "I think he's a little more bad tempered. I think he gets irritable with his patients, sometimes. There doesn't seem to be much life in what you're doing." And he was quite correct.'

'So after the unbearable lightness of being . . .'

'I went wrong again. I thought, no he's not a priest, he's a tetchy director, for he uses the word *direct*. And I started to play him like Tyrone Guthrie. I started to think about Tyrone Guthrie. Totally wrong. And finding the comedy was the key.'

'If *The Cocktail Party* tries to fuse the secular and the divine, what about St Mark's gospel?'

'To me it's very mysterious, the whole St Mark adventure – because I was asked by the oversympathetic whether I was "inspired?" Was it a religious conviction that made me do it? And I have to admit it wasn't. It was boredom. I was in a long run of a play I was not particularly enjoying [*The Family Dance*]; and it was a hot summer and I was looking for something to do. I'd been thinking of doing a one-man show for ages, but I couldn't settle on any material. By a process of elimination I arrived at St Mark, almost as an actor's exercise to see if I could learn it; and also to discover whether there was a comparison to be made with Shakespearean prose – which looks so daunting on the page, but springs to life when you learn it and work on it.

'Shakespeare's prose is more exciting to speak than anything else (I'm hoping to play Iago before I go into a wheelchair); so I wondered if this would happen with St Mark, and it did. I could chat it; I could speak it in a modern manner without going into a monotonous lilt; without sounding like a Victorian patriarch.

'It's very choppy stuff. Different, because blunter, simpler, from Matthew, Luke or John – though I haven't learned the others, obviously.'

'So it began as a technical exercise, trying out the prose . . .'

'Trying out the prose; trying out my memory; giving me something to occupy myself with; wondering whether it would succeed as a solo performance. Never being quite sure, until I'd finished the entire thing – learning the entire thing over a period of sixteen months – whether it would work. When I started each chapter it would look lifeless, undramatic – until I studied it, then there was this extraordinary life. The next problem was whether people would listen; sustain attention for a few hours to my voice.'

McCowen discusses his project in *Double Bill* and provides an analect in *Personal Mark*. The solo show was a critical and commercial triumph in England and America, where a command performance was given for President Carter at his teetotal White House.

McCowen learned three verses every morning, making use of habitual dawn rousings, beginning in August 1976: 'The greatest script I had ever found,' dealing with miracles, parables, preachings; with the rhetoric of Christ, which the actor found to be fierce and ironic. The Nazarene was no pale mystic, but a charismatic talker and sage; King Jesus. Mark chronicles the rise and fall into loneliness and exhaustion – too much is asked of Christ; his powers become rather taken for granted; and in the midst of mobs wanting magic, he alone knows the importance of belief and faith.

It is not hard to see an allegory of McCowen's own career, such as it was ten years ago: the customary accolades, his tiredness and desire for acting to disconnect itself from personal ambition. Committed to *The Misanthrope* for a sixteen-week run, 'it was only the thought that I would never again trap myself in a prison of my own making that got me through it. I would never again demand success at the expense of health and happiness.' By which I don't mean that McCowen has any smack of a Christ self-image (even though an abandoned idea was that Christ be given a Tunbridge Wells accent, 'such as I had myself when I was a schoolboy'); rather, the startlingly human, and humane, Christ of St Mark's gospel helped the actor come to terms with himself and the issue of destiny.

Belief and faith, moreover, are actorial terms, as well as being religious requirements; or perhaps they point to the religious aspect of acting: audiences suspend disbelief, willingly; they have faith in fakes – and the agent of transfiguration is the actor himself. It was this power McCowen discovered ossifying; and regaining his sense of command, he regained a sense of self – no longer 'a success machine', but a man for whom 'the sun, the moon, or even the glow from a burning candle, assumed a new significance'. He claims not to be a religious man; but he does appreciate sacramental realities.

And regarding St Mark's gospel, the reality of the sacraments became plain. McCowen analysed the wonder-working and the journeys, he studied maps of Palestine, and 'the distances travelled by Jesus might be contained in Kent and Sussex'. This represents his approach; those feet in ancient times might well have walked upon England's mountains green: McCowen, through Mark, made the Bible credible because local –

parochial. The actor avoided sanctimony and the sentimental; gentle Jesus meek and mild now had a temper, and he emerged from a prose narrative which the actor deconstructed into scenes and characters.

McCowen rediscovered the theatricality of the Bible (discovered before him by orotund, oracular Charles Laughton), whilst simultaneously – and paradoxically – celebrating Mark's naturalism. If, initially, the public was impressed by the feat of memory (McCowen curtly refused to give excerpts on chat shows, not wanting his show to be a gimmick), houses were sold out owing to the actor's skill as a storyteller, excitingly populating the stage with different tones of voice, pace, pitch. He vivified Mark's infectious message; the gospel (Old English *gōd*, good, *spell*, news) as a book of reportage. And McCowen, travelling to the New Republic, at a different venue every night, spreading the word, was a modern apostle.

'My interest in the gospel increased the more I did it,' McCowen told me, 'and it still goes on and on. The first time – London, New York, on tour; then I stopped and did other things. About two years later, I was rehearsing *The Browning Version* at the National with Michael Rudman, and on the first night of the provincial preview, I went for a walk by the sea. I should have been going through my Rattigan lines; I found I was doing St Mark again. Though I tried to stop myself, St Mark was what I most wanted to do. Rethinking the gospel from a distance of a few years – I got a whole new charge about doing it again. And that has happened four times!'

'It returns, it recurs.'

'Yes, it haunts me, and the story becomes increasingly mysterious and rewarding.'

'A mystery thickening, rather than a mystery empty and solved.'

'Yes,' said McCowen, letting the definite affirmation hang in the air.

The other half of *Double Bill* deals with a production which first brought McCowen to eminence – Peter Luke's adaptation, *Hadrian VII*, of the novel *Hadrian the Seventh* (1904) by Frederick Rolfe (Baron Corvo). Like St Mark, a transatlantic hit; like St Mark, a religious drama. As a gospeller, there's a photograph of the actor, in an opalescent costume, communing with Jimmy Carter (who beams like he's meeting an original evangelist; Rosalynn looks suitably meek); as Pope Hadrian, McCowen, in full papal regalia, was snapped greeting the Bishop of Stepney – the Lambeth Conference made a block booking at the Mermaid.

Corvo's work is about self-aggrandisement and fantasy. Frederick William Rolfe, an indigent and embittered Catholic convert, was rejected by theological college; in his rage and disappointment, he hallucinated his way into the shoes of St Peter. (Actually, the novel's hero is called George Arthur Rose, but Luke realized he's an autobiographical cipher – that is,

Rose was Rolfe, the real name of the bogus 'baron', who lived from 1860 to 1913.) Rolfe/Rose/Corvo was desperate to be a prelate, but for the wrong reasons: like Firbank, he loved the ritual of Catholicism; the incense, vestments, candles, choirboys, martyrs. And for the writers of the Nineties the church was a gorgeous and decadent theatre; the Latin and antique ceremonies made for a sort of legal sorcery, and the pea-cockry had a lot to do with pederasty. (Rolfe had hopes of earning money by procuring boy gondoliers for Charles Masson Fox.) A dedicated eccentric, Rolfe tried to invent underwater magic lantern slides and devised techniques for the shutterbugging of naked youths – but he always failed. He could never hold a job; he was quarrelsome, and had a genius for the missed chance. Anxious to be wealthy, only the self-styling as Baron Corvo made impoverishment acceptable; he reinvented himself as a charitable foundation. A noble sponger.

A contributor to *The Yellow Book*, the author (besides *Hadrian*) of *Chronicles of the House of Borgia* (1901), *In His Own Image* (1901) and *The Desire and Pursuit of the Whole* (edited posthumously by A. J. A. Symons), plus works about saints, sinners and what he called the gentle art of making enemies, Rolfe's transformation into Corvo was a subject apt for the stage. His conversion of character is the job of an actor, and his mutation from nonentity into swank is what Luke explored – the play interweaving the novel with facts known about the real Rolfe (chiefly from A. J. A. Symons's *The Quest for Corvo*, 1934). As St Mark assisted McCowen's shift into late middle age, *Hadrian VII* was another rite of passage, seeing the actor leave off his image as ageing juvenile lead. He'd spent too long in elfin parts, and had toured Europe as Fool to Paul Scofield's iron-latticed Lear; he'd been a messenger in the Olivier *Antony and Cleopatra* and Mercutio in Zeffirelli's *Romeo and Juliet*; he'd been Barnaby, the apprentice in *The Matchmaker* and Algernon in *The Import-ance of Being Earnest*. And out of frustration at all this came Rolfe's anger and resentment.

McCowen remembered his early days, getting started; the rage of the rejected, finding Hadrian by translating Rolfe's experience into his own: 'As a result of this personal substitution, the . . . invective of the man came more easily to life.' But there's more to it than this. Rolfe was an actor, his immortalizing performance, Corvo; a lonely haranguer. The truth of his existence was pathetic – but *what if* the truth was magnificent? Hence the fantasy of Luke's play. And McCowen acted the fantasy for real. A perky pontiff, puffing on a fag held to a jaunty lip; with face-furniture of pink plastic granny glasses, Hadrian made tirades about fat priests and the pettifoggery of the organized church. McCowen played a nondescript clerk striking out – like the apprentice in *The Matchmaker*, who gambles for a single beautiful night on the razzle. The actor was a success in the part because he *didn't* look in the slightest sacerdotal; McCowen's Rolfe was an improbable Pope, which suited the authenticity of what the character represented – that is, Rolfe/Corvo's representation of a loser's secret life, what Philip Larkin would describe as a fantasy life

> . . . courageous enough
> To shout *Stuff your pension!*

And Larkin adds:

> [. . .] I know, all too well, that's the stuff
> That dreams are made on . . .

Larkin describes a private life imagining itself going public; celebrated perhaps in a theatre dressing-room by famous faces belonging to Olivier, Gielgud, Redgrave, Coward, Bing Crosby, Prince Rainier and Princess Grace – the people who came backstage and applauded *Hadrian VII*. Being an actor's the stuff that dreams are made on.

McCowen's memoir of his childhood is called *Young Gemini*: the twins. Behind the grown man is a double, an alternative self, a vain and glorious child, who 'had only to lie in his pram and the world came to praise him and love him and pay their respects . . . Then, suddenly, the golden-haired days are over, and I had to struggle to become . . . the schoolboy, the conforming boy. And I did not believe in that struggle . . . Basically I knew that the golden-haired genius was still underneath the close-cut brown-haired . . . dreary schoolboy. But nobody was interested. They wanted something else. So I started the disguise. And this led to acting.' Rolfe into Corvo, Corvo into the Pope is a theatrical transformation like Alexander Duncan McCowen into Alec McCowen the actor – and the actor into his many stage people.

Hadrian VII and St Mark's gospel image the growth of this actor's mind; and both were comic performances – in that McCowen played with an ironic touch; he's supremely aware of the divergence between ideas and action, aspiration and achievement.

I asked him, 'Do you find comedy nobler than tragedy – an intimation of a state of grace?'

'That's another reason why I like St Mark. There are aspects of the writing and things in his style which amuse me. And coming from a very conventionally religious background, the idea that Jesus should have a sense of humour was quite surprising and shocking.'

'A metaphysical trickster.'

'He must have been attractive to have had such a following, he must have been funny sometimes, which I find very reassuring.'

'You've lately been blatantly comic in *Personal Services*.'

'I wonder whether *Personal Services* is reassuring! I played a depraved Wing Commander. I recently did some postsynchronization. I was given a list of the lines that had to be done again, and after I'd done the "Yes, madam", "no, madam", "good morning, madam", the list said "Noise when he comes". So I let out a long juddering orgasmic sigh, which they were very pleased with. One take only.

'Postsynchronizing is a bore. The actor returns to a scene weeks, months, after he's done it, and by then he's involved with other things – and to speak lines in a middle of a scene, watching a bar beat across the screen, so you talk at the exact moment, is difficult.

'I was expecting, because of the Terry Jones–*Monty Python* connections to be forced into a performance I'd regard as wild. Quite the contrary. Terry Jones had to hold me back and make me restrained, even though the subject of Cynthia Payne luncheon-voucher sex suited him perfectly. A very funny story.'

Monty Python is a label for love of the odd, the whacky. *Personal Services*, with its perverts, freaks, bondage and rubber fixations, would seem a suitable case for satirical treatment – a sequel to *Another Country*, with the grown men failing to stop being schoolboys, and craving into old age matrons who spank and scold. Cynthia Payne is a memory of nanny and her humiliations; she panders to a peculiar English need – the male never wanting to grow up, desperate for a bossy Wendy who'll be mother and lover.

Interviewed by Joan Bakewell (Joan Bakewell! A dream of well-filled blue-stockings!), Madame Cyn, as the tabloids call her, spoke of clients and tarts as an extended family: 'I'm a mother hen with my chicks, really.' A sorority of strumpets! A dorm of deviants! Her talent was to convert the sleazy world of prostitution into something genteel; she's an instance of Victorian self-betterment, a vision of social mobility, with a cut-glass voice and immaculate manicure; brothel-keeping made eminently respectable.

Terry Jones, however, avoided humorous satire; the tone of his film is fantasticated documentary. He once wrote a scholarly book reconsidering Chaucer's Knight, arguing that the worthy man, who 'loved chivalrie, trouthe and honour, fredom and curteisie,' was the very opposite of chivalric, truthful and the honourably courteous. Instead Chaucer's verray parfit gentil Knyght was an exemplary callous mercenary. Jones interpreted the character as a scabrous opportunist. His Cynthia Payne is of a similar stamp – called, in *Personal Services*, Christine Painter, she's a revaluation of the Wife of Bath – a worthy womman al hir lyve:

> Of remedies of love she knew per chaunce,
> For she koulde of that art the olde daunce.

In place of Chaucer's warm-hearted trollop, Jones gives us a hard-headed, dense and indefatigable (and joyless) beldam. Not only is *Personal Services* about our national hypocrisy, the sense of righteous indignation and salty enthralment; it also makes this hypocrisy inhabit the central character, though without her being aware of its ramification. The lewd, and the flinching from the lewd – this is what distinguishes Julie Walters's performance; her sense of Christine Painter's puritanical disdain. The bawd who goes to church ('In al the parisshe wif ne was ther noon / That to the offrynge bifore hire sholde goon'), whose son is in public school, and who yearns to be classy; the bawd who, whilst vigorously masturbating a client, is clearly performing an invidious, but necessary, function – a personal service, like unblocking a drain. She even talks of 'despunking' the menfolk; relieving their clogged tubes. Never is any passion or affection displayed. Christine has no enjoyment of sex; she has the sense of a higher mission. A Streatham Mother Theresa, bringing comfort to the aged and infirm by liberating them of tiresome seminal fluids; and who reacts deadpan to their quirks – the pathetic Peter Pans who want governesses to smack and slap. Sex is as boring and necessary as eating – hence the luncheon voucher aptness. And Christine is first disclosed working in a greasy-spoon slopping out gravy dinners. Her shift from fast food to speedy sex is a natural progression.

Christine has her own code of honour ('paying my way') and she's merciless with the squalid tarts who can't meet their debts; wearily determined, she exacts penalties and organizes her knocking-shop. The landlord, an old Greek who likes to wear a red dress, is placated with a politic hand-job; and Christine's sublet commonwealth is situated in the detritus of south London – the Walworth Road, with its overspilled trashcans and old women in dirty nylon coats pushing babyless perambulators; Ambleside Avenue, with its unspeakable carpets, curtains and David Shepherd prints of angry pachyderms.

Raw, honest, ultimately lacking in any sense of irony, Christine is also witlessly ignorant. Fellatio ('French polishing') she seems not to know about; and the pronunciation of contraceptives is a mystery ranking with exegesis of Jacques Derrida's literary theory: 'Thingies, you know, doo-dahs ... contraventives.' That anyone other than a negro might want to don a black condom is another eye-opener. She doesn't even realize that her domestic is a transvestite – until Dolly's glimpsed in the Ladies with a dangling dong.

Christine's odd mix of financial perspicacity and gaucherie about all else makes her both assertive and cut off; she refuses an offer of marriage and has a recriminatory relationship with her parents – who seem pleasant enough. She plainly doesn't like sex – and claims that nobody does. It's an affliction. Ultimately, the character is a blank. We get no suggestion of real motives; something vital is being withheld. We are left to invent some gruesome affair which resulted in the fathering of her son – for we receive no clues. Christine is rootless, where we want a history; dense, when what we want is depth.

Whether the failure to find real feeling in Christine is to do with Julie Walters's impersonating Cynthia Payne is less important than the effect the character has on the rest of the film – which is devoid of feeling, empty of emotion. This is possibly intentional: perverts isolated by their fantasies of rubber suits and gymslips – the men and the scrubbers literally come and go, and so do acting eminences like Benjamin Whitrow and John Shrapnel. The only actor who survives in the vacuum is McCowen. His Wing Commander Morten – 'an aging pillock in the autumn of his years' – is one of his best performances. The atmosphere of loneliness at the centre of *Personal Services* is a climate he can exult in; sequestration is his element.

Christine's solitude is marked by her quarrel with her father; by a holiday in Spain, when she gazes at an unobtainable hunk on a balcony; by her avoidance of a stout suitor bringing champagne and roses; by her snubs at a wedding; by her purposeful missing of a restaurant date. McCowen turns up as a seedy consort, locked, like her, in a world of his own. Yet where Christine is intended to portray wilful tragedy, McCowen's Morten is pure Donald MacGill. A ruddy, yellowy, tobacco-stained face; filthy crooked gob-crockery; a voice half cockney twang, half corrupted Tunbridge Wells: the character was a prefiguration of the pinched, ululating clochard Vladimir in Beckett's Laurel and Hardy sketch, *Waiting for Godot*, and first tried out in *Never Say Never Again* – where McCowen appeared as the gat-toothed Algernon, Bond's inventor of lethal toys (exploding pens, watches, cameras). In half-moon glasses, with a row of pencils in the work-coat top-pocket, he sniffed with cold like a dewy weasel, and hoped that, with Sean Connery's Bond back in business, there'd be plenty of 'gratuitous sex and violence'. *Personal Services* finds Algernon, a cashiered bomber-ace, striding the streets, looking for a French-polisher; the same wide-awake keenness. And we do indeed soon see him being efficiently French-polished: 'coming up nicely' and 'look at the nice shine on that'. Police burst into the room at the point of orgasm – the orgasm McCowen so successfully post-synchronized.

The next thing we know, Morten is organizing the brothel accounts (emptying a bag of notes on the floor) and indulging himself in his kinks: 'The future lies', he says, 'in kinky people.' Forever in fancy-dress tat, acting in dramas known about only within his cheerfully weird head, Morten wears on his head, serially, a trilby, a purple crocheted cap, a plastic bobby's helmet, a cardboard pirate-king hat, a ginger wig. Loud, jolly, keeping his pecker up by feasting on poached eggs, fists on hips and rocking on his heels with insufferable vitality, he's ignored or at best endured – like a twerpish husband. Along with transvestite Dolly, who functions as a vague granny, and busy Shirley, who is like a sharp elder sister, Julie Walters, McCowen, Danny Schiller and Shirley Stelfox formed the most aberrant family since Charles Addams's.

Whilst Christine frowns over the hostessing of her grotto – locking an old man in a box ('I thought he was making a cupboard for us to hang our coats in') or arranging for a bikini-clad tax inspector to receive a 'golden shower' – Morten potters as a zany master of ceremonies. He works the projector for the films and sports a baggy housecoat dripping with crepe frogging. Then, costumed as a geisha, in fishnet tights and a net-curtain shawl, he mugs his way through Salome's dance. Quite possibly, the grotesque jig is McCowen's finest screen moment. His untrimmed, once-upon-a-time raffish moustache offsetting tawny ringlets and smudged lip gloss; with ropes of plastic gems and a mauve brassière; wearing tweed slippers and a crimpoline cummerbund, he lopes and skitters across a lounge of appreciative elders – as self-absorbed and amazing as any bizarre fantasy in Wilde or Strauss. Morten's appearance as Salome does more than parody a superannuated diva; his lope and hop is the choreography of liberated repressions. The performance is uniquely abandoned. And when dozens of peelers crash through doors and windows, the police raid signals the return of restraint and itchy temperance. Morten is dragging into the night singing 'Rule Britannia' and claiming 'This is no way to treat a lady.' Mitigating his charge, he wants it known that during the war he carried out two hundred and seven missions over occupied territory in bra and panties.

The case against the disorderly semi is dismissed because judge and counsel happen to be Christine's most regular customers. The film concludes on this note of wishful thinking: an acquittal by collusion; Christine freed by her loopy son-surrogates – and Morten conducts curious journalists over the premises as though it's a stately home: 'In this house we have nothing to hide.' Exactly so. By denying uplift, banishing eroticism for friendless sex, each room in the place a public cloister, the brothel is an open hermitage – an institution for the anonymous. Hiding nothing, the house is empty.

'What's the point of being old,' chuckles Morten, 'if you can't be dirty?' It's McCowen's best performance because an unbound version of his many other stage people. The Wing Commander discharges the murky frustrations with which Malvolio, Dysart, Alceste, Higgins and Hadrian inwardly boil; and who knows what powers drive Reilly, or Rudyard Kipling – that most stockaded of minstrels, whom McCowen played in Brian Clark's one-man show (1984)?

His best performance because comic; and comic not for the ridiculous clothes and frolics, but comic by virtue of an absolute self-confidence – the way Morten never connects with another living soul; a triumph of evaded responsiveness. (A similar evasion redeemed Eric Morecambe's gormlessness or Buster Keaton's innocence or Jack Benny's cupidity, making instead for shrewdness, knowingness and generosity, respectively.)

'Comedy,' said McCowen. 'Often one is attracted to things for oblique reasons. Maybe I'm attracted to comedy because I don't feel physically equipped to play Lear or Macbeth. I had a go at Antony and it was a disaster – or I thought it was a disaster; it was just a pale imitation of Olivier, whose Company I'd been in twenty-five years previously.'

That was for a season at the St James's Theatre, with Shaw's *Caesar and Cleopatra* in repertoire with the Shakespeare. Remembering the experience, on the occasion of Olivier's eightieth birthday in 1987, McCowen told the *Sunday Times*: 'I would be physically afraid of Antony's rages ... It seemed to me, romantically, that there was a parallel with Antony's contempt for himself and Olivier's seeming dissatisfaction with his own performance.' The division between actor and role, so that Olivier's Antony was Olivier's *commentary* on Antony – within and without the part simultaneously – is not a trick of McCowen's. He sinks himself entire into his creations. There's nothing left outside of them. Olivier's characters, by contrast, overspill with a sense of Olivier's charisma, his plenitude on display. McCowen is compacted, rather than eruptive; a hobbled energy. And when he was eruptive, we got Morten.

'In any case,' he explained to me, 'I don't feel physically in a tragic mould. As a young man, as a young actor, a student, I was dazzled by Rex Harrison and Cary Grant – the assurance of light comedy.'

'Dapperness.'

'I love good timing, music hall, Jack Benny.'

McCowen leapt to a bookcase and, next to a trio of *Evening Standard* Best Actor statuettes ('not so very many'), was a bronze mousetrap.

'My Jack Benny money-clip. He gave it to me for the free publicity I'd given him – praising him on a chat show, and he heard about it.'

A sprung devise for picketing notes, and engraved with a personal inscription from the donor – but empty. A moneyless money-clip.

'So you've learned a lot from comedians?'

'Much more than from watching Olivier or Gielgud.'

Though McCowen is on record as enumerating amongst his memories of comic genius, Olivier's Richard III ('a slightly spinsterish deportment') and Gielgud in Oscar Wilde – two tragedians fastidiously excavating a humorous spirit – his lavish praise is for Ruth Gordon, Arthur Lowe, Ralph Richardson. His comic vision never takes in clowning ('comedy is a serious thing,' said Garrick); what McCowen is entranced by is the reality of outrageousness. True comedy is never incredible. When reality is lost, there's a collapse into silliness – and a great comedian convinces us of his own authenticity.

'I'm videoing early Morecambe and Wise. It's not so much that they make me laugh: it is the timing; it is the way they are able to think and to react; it is the way that they can be taken by surprise – and that's so hard, especially if you're in a long run, to be taken by surprise by the material.'

'Surprise and comedy – what about Alfred Hitchcock, the grisly comedian?'

'He had such a relish for black comedy; the way he'd talk about the material he dealt with was with humour. You're quite right – he chose his particular subject-matter because in some bizarre way it did amuse him.'

McCowen was Inspector Oxford in *Frenzy*, Hitchcock's penultimate film (1971), and his least inexplicit. Razoring Janet Leigh while she shampoos (*Psycho*); handcuffing Madeleine Carroll and Robert Donat on a remote moor (*The Thirty-Nine Steps*); sending a plane puffing dichloro-diphenyltrichloreothane after Cary Grant (*North by Northwest*); propelling feathers, beaks and talons at Tippi Hendren (*The Birds*); making James Stewart an impotent voyeur (*Vertigo*): in film after film the director enjoyed humiliating his stars.

Frenzy embarrasses with food. As Donald Spoto says in *The Dark Side of Genius*, in this film 'food at last became the main character'. A gormandocratic epic; the cycle of growing and harvesting, cooking and eating, and voiding the waste. Pertinent for McCowen, the recollector of menus.* In *Frenzy*, the cook is Mrs Oxford (Vivien Merchant), who dishes up for her fatigued husband fish soup (aswim with exophthalmic heads), quail with grapes, pigs' trotters and tripe sauce – parody food served with a comic flourish on place-mats of green weave. Busy gagging on the experiment in haute cuisine, McCowen's 'tec only half took in Merchant's warblings; she sees through to Mr Blaney's (Jon Finch's) innocence with offhand intuition, and provides an unheeded descant on the progress of Oxford's own preponderations and inquiries.

Inquiries centre upon Covent Garden fruit and vegetable market; London's pleasure-park of provender; the metropolitan larder. Serpent in

---

* In *Double Bill*, sentences pile up to make a poem –
> She had prepared a feast.
> Southampton Virginia ham.
> Chicken, with Ollie Mae's own celery sauce.
> Corn pudding.
> Turnip greens with smoked sausages.
> Candied yams with marshmallows.
> Alfalfa sprout salad with avocado...
> ... followed, at my request with
> Prune pudding.

Skinny Malvolio McCowen finds he unleashed a Sir Toby inside him, like Hitchcock, eating the world in order to control it – or in McCowen's case, to restrain it.

the Eden is Bob Rusk (Barry Foster), named for baby-food, the mother-fixated strangler. (Is Oxford named for marmalade?) He offers lunch to one girl before killing her; another body is hidden in a potato sack. Throughout, he prods his teeth with a monogrammed toothpick – an important prop. He chomps a hamburger or takes nips out of apples. An incessant nibbler.

The wrongly accused flophouse hero, Blaney, is first found in a restaurant, spilling red wine with his estranged wife; and Oxford, his exonerator, takes refuge from his uxorial domestic science by eating with relish bacon and egg. McCowen's Oxford is a diffident man but he leans into his surreptitious platter of fried bread with brazen urgency. Finch's Blaney is a lean and irascible man, his twitchiness and breakdown portrayed through thoughtless fasting.

So – Rusk chomping, Blaney either off his food or on the run and hungry, Oxford presented with the uneatable: *Frenzy* is about appetite and taste. Hitchcock's London is a primitive jungle of titbits; an acerbic cocktail party. A Lévi-Strauss locale of myths concerning snacks and feasts. As with Cynthia Payne/Christine Painter, sex and food are linked – but here the fusion creates a pornographic effect. Sex, the raw need; love, the cooked offering. Sex, the impetus of psychopathic Rusk; love, the eccentric mealtimes of the Oxfords.

Frenzy is also tasteless. The murders have an attention to detail that oppresses; drooled over and prolonged, unbearably kinky, the rapes and throttlings are matched by the snooping, tracking camera, nosing its way through windows and down staircases, loitering outside the swing doors of the law court as Blaney is sentenced. And Hitchcock intends it all as amusing. A horror-comedy of wrongful arrest and botched killing – so that Rusk has to scramble through the spuds on a moving lorry to find the dead fingers clasping his toothpick.

Tasteful amidst the tastlessness was McCowen, who drew out the picture's antique flavour, colluding with Hitchcock's retrograde evocation of London – a place of wynds and gullies and Mary Poppins vistas. Based on Arthur LaBern's *Goodbye Picadilly, Farewell Leicester Square*, Hitchcock's film, his first in England since *Jamaica Inn* of 1939, merged its pop violence with a surreal salad of past and present out of which McCowen selected the vintage filaments. His first words were a golly-gosh 'Good morning to one and all'; and his diction and enunciation are matched by the archaisms of Anna Massey, who says things like 'without so much as a by-your-leave' and a broad cockney 'did her in'. Bernard Cribbins is mine-host at a hurdy-gurdy pub, where the menfolk talk jocundly of the war; and Jimmy Gardner turns up as a fey porter at the Coburg Hotel ('Can I get you anything from the pharmacy, sir'), impersonating a fawning Naunton Wayne.

Hitchcock's London stopped its clocks when he left to make *Rebecca* and reinvent American Gothic satire; the backcloth outside Oxford's New Scotland Yard office is a masterpiece of nostalgic misremembrance. Westminster Abbey, the dome of St Paul's and Big Ben lie close together, looking high over foggy little rooftops. Less, even, Hitchcock's childhood London, this is the metropolis of Sherlock Holmes and hailing hansoms. The city in *Frenzy* is the topography of fancy, where the Westminster chimes clang in Covent Garden – and McCowen plays no modern cop. Besuited, tweedy, pensive, agitating little grey cells, he's absent, even when present, from the modern police force; he's Sax Rohmer's Nayland Smith, with exacting codes of decorum. Punctilious and polite, he is like a scaled-down version of McCowen's Freddy, the wrinkled and boisterous unrequited chumpish boyfriend of Stevie Smith (Glenda Jackson) in *Stevie*.

Oxford speaks like he eats – either finically, or with spurts of speed – but he's never bereft of manners. Indeed, table manners mark him as the film's sage. He takes his meals with polished cutlery and crockery; Blaney is incompetent with the condiment; Rusk merely masticates snatched junk-food, forgoing table manners completely. According to Lévi-Strauss, the culinary anthropologist, in *The Origin of Table Manners*, our rituals about eating – let alone the elaborate histories of the kitchen – represent society's attempts to eradicate disorder; discipline regulates savagery. Table manners 'moderate our exchanges with the external world, and superimpose on them a domesticated, peaceful and more sober rhythm'. Unriddle the elaborate customs of cooking and dining, and we have a system for transforming nature into culture, meat into meals – and what holds for the Algonquin Indians may hold for Hitchcock's mythical realization of his home town. The killer is the profane eater; the detective scoffs sacredly – Mrs Oxford brings him burnt offerings. And, by extension, the villain is villainous *because* he flouts table manners; the true hero (Oxford) heroic because a martyr to them. The absence of table manners, says Lévi-Strauss 'would leave man exposed to powerlessness or unreason'.

McCowen was the genteel centre of a film both mannered and mannerless, holding on to its retrogressive slips – which were mocked on initial release, but which now give *Frenzy* a politesse in spite of itself. McCowen was perhaps the last kindly, avuncular policeman in cinema history. Now, the stereotype is the dispirited thug, hating his decrepit beat; Inspector Oxford patrols a cobbled realm of Bow Street runners and broccoli. He might be a priest in a parish.

'The bewildering thing about working with Hitchcock,' said McCowen, 'is that he cast very carefully and then prepared the film, even knowing in advance how he was going to edit. He said – and I can never believe this – that his films needed hardly any editing at all. He said *Cut!* when he meant

Cut! He'd done so much preliminary work, and so trusted his actors, that there wasn't any need for post-production fiddling.

'I was amazed at how little he directed in the character and dialogue area. He'd direct action with enormous care; but only twice did he direct my lines. First, when I thought I'd sent the wrong man to prison, and I had a close-up in which I had to express doubt in the emptying court after the sentence had been passed. Hitchcock whispered in my ear for twenty minutes or half an hour, as we did this close-up over and over again, telling me what should be going on in my head. The long dialogue scenes of eating the dreadful food with Vivien Merchant he left entirely to us, and we did all three scenes in a couple of days.

'The other time he directed me was right at the end of the film, when I had to make the arrest and speak the line to Barry Foster, "Mr Rusk, you're not wearing your tie," as I discovered him just having killed again. I came on strong again, "You [gleeful] are not wearing [sarcastic] your tie! [triumphantly smug]."

'Very rough, thinking myself Kirk Douglas. Here we are. Alec McCowen from Tunbridge Wells. I've got my man! And Hitchcock stopped me, and said "You know, if I was you, and I was playing your part, which I'm not, but if I was doing it, I wouldn't come on strong like that. It's the end of the film. You've got your man. If I was doing it, which I'm not, I'd lean against the wall. I might sigh. I might smile even. And I'd say the words with just a tinge of sadness and ironic regret."'

'Hitchcock made *Frenzy* in his head before you turned up. Have you had experience of the opposite extreme?' I asked.

'Film directors have to work ahead; they usually have many plans, though nothing like as elaborate as Hitchcock's. George Cukor – I was in *Travels With My Aunt* – although he knew how the scenes should be performed, was bad at technical things. Very bad at moving actors about. He didn't know how to get me out of a room, if I had to do an exit. This could be embarrassing because he didn't like suggestions. The camera-man might say, "Couldn't the actors leave on that line?" and Cukor would shout, "Don't teach me my business. I've been doing this longer than you!" and things like that. Embarrassing. You see, George knew atmospherically what he wanted – but he's symptomatic of the movie-directors of his time: I don't think they did care too much about dialogue and accountability. They cared about the pictures, the visual element.'

'You've had a good relationship with the theatre director John Dexter. I've heard that he's very exacting.'

'I could be very critical of John Dexter, too. He can be a despot, a dictator. Rigid. And he can frighten people. He keeps saying he's mellowed. I think he *has* mellowed – though he hates the word. When he fails to lose his temper now, he says, "Oh, how I've *mellowed*!" in horror.

'But I've always been able to work with him because he functions in a way I love. He'll toil in enormous detail for a day or so, or maybe only a morning; huge detail. Then he'll get as far away as possible, and let us run it. Not just what we've worked on – the whole thing. He'll see how it relates. He's like a painter, wanting a variety of perspectives. He'll squash into the furthest corner of the rehearsal room; or he'll go to the very back seat of the upper circle to watch.

'It gives an actor enormous freedom if a director works in detail, and then says, "Over to you." I try to absorb what he's given to me; we run it; he'll have nothing to say; we do another run; he'll say "I liked that, I hated that"; we do yet another run – and I relax into directorial advice; plus I bring whatever it is I have to contribute, my own ideas. Despite John's autocratic behaviour, his actors are at liberty to invent – unless they're inexperienced, or unimportant.'

'How do you compare rehearsals for a one-man show with rehearsals in a Company?'

'For St Mark, which I did all on my own, I had to work with a tape recorder, which I'd always been led to believe was a bad thing. Yet I do work with one increasingly now. I have a good enough ear to detect when I'm being phony. Most weird: I think I'm doing the right thing in my head, but what comes out on the playback is nothing like what I'd imagined I'd been saying . . . And such a discrepancy – between intention and achievement – can only be noted by either having a very acute director, who tells you how it is coming out – or, if you haven't a director, you have to listen hard to your own voice.'

'*Kipling* was a one-man show with the unique benefit of a director.'

'I learnt Kipling's writing and worked on the performance before we rehearsed it; then I did rehearse for a couple of weeks with Patrick Garland. Patrick, the official director, brought sound effects, lighting and staging elements to the show – he did physically move it about.'

Kipling was a virtuosic rendition of a life through the works; a salmagundi chopped entirely from the writer's own words. Brian Clark, the adaptor, cunningly counterpointed hectoring Kipling with compassionate Kipling; crazed Kipling with inspired Kipling; craftsman Kipling with the impressionist experimentor of the later years; the balladeer with the prose stylist; the vulgarian with the aesthete; the lover with the hater of England. Kipling made himself a Sussex squire by an act of will power, sending down roots, in *Puck of Pook's Hill* and *Rewards and Fairies*, into the hidden history of England, of Englishness – a place of the heart which is a fantastic mix of Kim's Lahore and the enchanted groves from Shakespeare's play about sex, drugs and bestiality, *A Midsummer Night's Dream*; an England which is not any common earth, water or wood or air, but a Never-Neverland:

Trackway and camp and city lost,
Saltmarsh where now is corn –
Old wars, old Peace, old Arts that cease,
And so was England born!

The point about Kipling is that he's always fighting against an instinct to break out: his England wants to be a romantic elsewhere, ruled by an Oberon who wants to be Puck. In his poems and stories, machines go wrong, men go mad, things fall apart. His energy is cramped, passion is high – hence the dictatorial Law of the Jungle, devised to prise order into the world:

Now this is the Law of the Jungle – as old and as true as the sky;
And the Wolf that shall keep it may prosper, but the Wolf that
shall break it must die.

McCowen, in period clothes a size too small, his hair cropped and bleached; with his eyes pressed behind thick glasses – like oysters suspended in paperweights – was temperamentally suited to a drama about a very private man.

A creditable double of the uncooperative and reclusive imperial laureate, this Kipling lectured us from a mock-up of the Bateman's study – the squirearchical sanctum, with its formidable ranks of bound uniform editions, its tawny-toned great globes and the odd oriental souvenir. The room was Kipling's factory – reproduced from descriptions in *Something of Myself*, where the tools of the trade, ink, paper, nibs, are lovingly acknowledged.

McCowen barked angrily; he was playing a writer disturbed in his sanctuary – and unlike St Mark, here he was giving an impersonation with full rig. The writer as indignant industrialist, admiring men of action and the machines of Empire:

Beyond the path of the outmost sun through utter darkness
hurled –
Farther than ever comet flared or vagrant star-dust swirled –
Live such as fought and sailed and ruled and loved and made
our world.

Surveying the world from Bateman's, McCowen's Kipling was an elegist for his own time and a mocker of ours – coming back from beyond the grave to rail, like the historical personages of the *Puck* books. A night of discomfiture.

'Apart from one or two suggestions, Patrick didn't interfere with my creative interpretations. Before rehearsals, I went with Pamela Howard, the designer, to Bateman's. She'd already organized the wardrobe, so I

knew what I would look like. And she arranged a visit to Marghanita
Laski, who had a tape, a real treasure, of Kipling talking. I discovered, to
my delight, that he had extremely pedantic speech, without any recognizable accent; very exact, almost prissy.'

'Do you think his voice was constrained because he was being confronted with the strange device of a microphone?'

'He may have been. But his intonation was also, I think, self-protec-
tive. Throughout his life Kipling moved higher and higher up the social
scale; he walked with kings, and spoke carefully for that reason.

'Pamela Howard also found a film archive containing a few minutes of
a home movie. Kipling, towards the end of his life, is seen playing in his
garden with children. His face is alight – like Puck! He was Puck himself!
He was Puck of Pook's Hill! With the children he's a delightful little man.
Then, everybody has to line up for the group photograph. Kipling
becomes forbidding and boring. His hat was askew and his tie was
undone – a lovely mess. Then, I don't think it was his wife, maybe his
daughter, but some lady came along and pulled him together, put his hat
straight, tightened his tie, dusted him down, did up his buttons – but,
before the picture is taken, he stands there like a kid, roaring with
laughter. Then the glum, official Kipling takes over.

'It was excellent for me to see that – plus read O, Beloved Kids, his letters
to John and Elsie; because what I'd suspected was obviously quite true: he
was a naughty boy, and he was a naughty boy all his life. He was Kim and
he was Puck.'

'Kim or Puck encumbered with responsibilities.'

'And trying to shake them off!'

'What happens, in a Company, when your own invention jostles with
the ideas of other actors? Can too much inventiveness, too many Pucks
and Kims, make for chaos?'

'It can do. Depends on the director. If he's respected and a man of
authority, chaos should not occur. If the director lacks authority, or if you
have that dreaded mess, an Ensemble Company, my experience is that
the actor with the loudest voice does the directing. He's seldom the best
actor; but he's the noisiest person. That's hell. That's awful.'

'Why did the Prospect Antony and Cleopatra fail to satisfy you?'

'Chiefly, there was an insufficiency of preparation. The director was
involved with other productions – and Antony and Cleopatra is vast
enough on its own. There was insufficient rehearsal time. I was mis-cast.
We had designers who were used mainly to opera; the clothes were
impractical, and had been made without knowing whether they'd suit the
actors – which, in this case, they didn't. And it's always impossible to
discard the costumes and start again.'

With rotting toggery and before empty houses, the production played
in Ljubljana, Dubrovnik, Amman – and Cardiff, where I recall a stage

bleak and blank save for a Roman banner plugging into the floor; Dorothy Tutin breathlessly fluted, recumbent upon paisley cushions, like Germaine Greer in her Tuscany house; Derek Jacobi minced in and out as Octavius Caesar, blowing petulantly, and looking too old for his blond Harpo wig. A stiff, stately masque.

'Paramount to have a guide, who'll keep a sense of proportion as the first night approaches, and the actor is over-absorbed in the part.'

'Some younger actors and actresses resent directors.'

'There was once a girl being directed by Peter Hall, and she said to him, "Please don't give me any notes. It puts me off!" Maybe directors seem father-figures to the young – and they don't like it. It is a difficult relationship, actor-director; I find it a very difficult relationship.'

McCowen's actual father is remembered in *Young Gemini*, a slim memoir, ranking with Gosse's *Father and Son* and to some extent Butler's *The Way of All Flesh* as an account of disaffiliation. The actor collected a copy for me from a small study – a cosy boxroom furnished with books (I noticed two hardbacks of Anthony Burgess's *The Kingdom of the Wicked*: 'Why do people think I'll be interested in that?') and a cork-board thumbtacked with holiday snaps of friends – the only evidence of other souls in the whole house.

Duncan McCowen was a studied eccentric who ran a perambulator shop; in the ancestry were (as for Kipling) exuberant evangelists, hymn singers and Victorian eaters. Home life veered between a dominie's discipline and holidays of wind-breaking. 'My father once farted "God Save the King" up to "send him victorious".' He was an energetic, actorial man. 'He hated to go to bed at night because it meant the end of another day. He was forever asking us what we were going to do with our lives. He loved to alarm us by simulating decrepit old age, and if he was bored, we often discovered him lying in a chair pretending to be dead.'

McCowen says he wished to become an actor to escape his father and his unpredictable demands; evidence suggests, however, that McCowen's chosen profession was not so very different from his wayward papa's way of life. An actor, he hasn't escaped his father; he's struck out and become a better or professional one. 'I always sought his good opinion and longed to impress him with each performance.'

How often are his performances of patriarchs – though depraved ones: Hadrian the Holy Father; Higgins's father/daughter love affair with Eliza; Dysart the sterile shrink and Strang the son-surrogate; Morten the m.c.; Hitler. In George Steiner's *The Portage to San Cristobal of A.H.*, the nonagenarian Adolf was found lurking alone, like Mengele, in a South American jungle, silent, implacable, until the end, when he was given a long searing speech of self-exculpation – McCowen's satanic version of St Mark. The bad news bible.

Steiner has spent a career dwelling on the holocaust's cultural ramifications; he had his anti-hero argue, with black and stinky rhetoric, that the Reich fathered Israel: 'Perhaps I am the Messiah, the true Messiah, the new Sabbatai whose infamous deeds were allowed by God in order to bring His people home.' A grizzled and malevolent goblin – like his ranting Kipling – McCowen's Hitler reckoned the Jews were responsible for inventing a vengeful Jehovah; they're prone to spying, false promises and, amongst other abominations, the Rabbi Marx, who in his turn begat Stalin. Hitler considers himself a bungling genocide beside the terrible Joe. By comparison, a weak father.

McCowen's tirade, a single speech of many pages, demonstrated a paradox of acting: the audience was persuaded by the crazy logic of Hitler's debate. The actor's passion aroused admiration and assent – and then a recoil in distaste. We were tempted by wickedness – Steiner's point, for the Reich itself was founded upon temptation, Hitler's speeches enfevering a nation. The angel of darkness as an actor. McCowen conveyed a little of this demonic theatre.

Reilly the master brain box ought to be a father-figure; a rescuer or 'semi-divine stranger with superhuman powers' (Auden on Sherlock Holmes). But, in fact, he's a parody of fatherly affection, and is a demon – his disinterested paternal regard for Celia meaning she's sent not to a sanctuary, but to her death. (She's a gullible Iphigenia, Reilly a dismissive Agamemnon.)

Back at the Phoenix Theatre, *The Cocktail Party* was fizzling before our eyes; its profundities poppycock. The Prospect *Antony and Cleopatra* failed in my opinion because it was an opera without music; a masque where nobody moved. The Eliot play laboured to be euphonious, but it was not operatic – at best, only piddlingly domestic. (Only Richard Strauss in *Intermezzo* has managed successfully to combine expansiveness and detail, the domestic and the epic, in a portrait of a modern marriage; just as, in *Elektra*, he made the classical father-daughter bond contemporary – Homer in Vienna.) Hints at myth, in Eliot, tend to tushery, which is why he has issue in the operas of Andrew Lloyd Webber, and not Karlheinz Stockhausen; why he can be sung by Brian Blessed, who'd not easily be confused with Richard Tauber.

Act Two disclosed the psychiatrist's consulting rooms; Reilly's console or crypt, where advice is dispensed on free will and predestination, the spirit and the flesh. Dexter had had designed for McCowen a vault of gold Braque panels and grey Mondrian rectangles; secret doors swung to antechambers and admitted the virago Julia (Rachel Kempson as a chintz fairy, cousin to Coward's Madame Arcati) or the epicene Alex (Robert Eddison). A sort of MOMA chic. In came the characters to confess, desperate to exult in illness, flattering themselves into thinking they're sickly. Bored to death, they want the stimulus of disease. The actors yapped, and my attention was lost for quarter hours at a time. As Celia rather inadvertently says:

> They make noises, and think they are talking to each other;
> They make faces, and think they understand each other.

Only saints will Reilly send to his remote sanatorium – sketched as a heaven which is going to be hell – and so Celia (played by Shelia Gish – a little too old for the part – as a precipitate Blanche DuBois) sets off to meet her destiny with the termites. What she really should be demonstrating is Vivien Eliot's crack-up.

The question of martyrdom, however, Eliot dealt with rather more incisively in *Murder in the Cathedral*. Becket confronts the paradox that to expect beatification is to be denied it; to know you qualify for canonization is a disqualification. The Archbishop murder mystery is, in fact, a suicide; the Knights enact Becket's inner desires. Celia has no such desires; she's a lachrymose deb, the dilemmas of medieval Canterbury quite failing to take wing in a Mayfair drawing room. Meantime, Edward and Lavinia's marriage has been salvaged by radical interior decoration. Gone are the fussy, jangled Art Deco scallops and trapezoids; instead the room is blanched, with orchids abounding; the atmosphere orientally austere, the furniture bamboo. The only puzzling note was a pastiche de Chirico of considerable ugliness, a mechanical paradise of roots and tubes. Perhaps a gynaecological symbol, for Lavinia was extremely pregnant.

'My Krissz,' said Ezra Pound, tuning in from Rapallo to a radio production of an Eliot play, 'Mzzr Shakzpeer *still* retains his posishun, . . . I stuck it for a while, wot wiff the weepin and wailin.'

After the curtain sank, I went backstage. McCowen hailed me happily through the porthole of a swing door, his head bobbing into the circlet like a stowaway's. He'd just heard that *The Cocktail Party* was to close in ten days. His dressing room, like his house, was spick and span, the costumes zipped in plastic covers – sartorial prophylactics or thin dead bodies – on a rack.

Considering the news that a closure had been declared, he was chipper and concealed any perturbation. I asked whether a falling off in audience numbers affected performance.

'No, you can't let it. So long as a few are out there, you owe them a show. Though it's much harder for comedy or farce – where laughs are important to bounce the timing along. Performances get heavier and heavier, more and more leaden, as you try harder. Luckily, Reilly is heavy and overdone already!'

'You said you'd like to play Iago,' I said, wondering what he'd be doing next. 'Auden interpreted him as a practical joker – an overdone trickster.'

'I've given Iago thought for many years.'

'You've played all these saints, fathers, gods, madmen . . . .'

'Iago has no redeeming aspect . . . But I'd prepare for the part expecting him to be a complex human being; it's a rich part. I'll put this human being together, taking the part apart, one scene at a time, one speech at a time, one situation at a time. I don't believe the actor should have an idea of what a character is like in advance; he should be told what it is like afterwards. If you know what it is like, you'll be an actor in the Peter Sellers sense of giving an impersonation. True, when a script's first read, an inner picture inevitably forms: I've learned to mistrust that, because my own first impressions are inevitably wrong. Remember Ambrose Heng! I had to forget what Heng and Guthrie were like, and interpret the lines; scene by scene, like a jigsaw – so I'll know what Reilly's like, or will only know what Iago's like, when the jigsaw has come together.'

An extended example of the actor's deconstruction is *Personal Mark*. The book subjects each sentence, each phrase, in the gospel to painstakingly sober examination, with the scholar's own mutters included in the exegesis ('STOP! This isn't easy stuff. The writer takes a lot for granted.')

'You can no more know a role,' I ventured, 'than you can know real people?'

'The people in real life who constantly and confidently describe themselves usually miss their own points, or else they are very shallow to be able to get away with being so simple. When people worry about politicians or celebrities getting lampooned on *Spitting Image* or in cartoons, there's no need to be so solicitous. People have so little idea of what they are like, they are even flattered; they are flattered to know they exist, that they're making a mark. For a lot of us, deep down, we don't think that we actually make any impression whatsoever. We don't know what we are like – so when faced with a savage caricature, it may be very cruel, and it may depict an enormous nose or stomach or ears, but we think "I'm a person. How wonderful!"'

'Others have registered your presence.'

'Yes, yes.'

Rather Eliotic; *The Waste Land*:

> And I will show you something different from either
> Your shadow at morning striding behind you
> Or your shadow at evening rising to meet you.

'And to have registered your presence is important to you?'

'It was when I was a schoolboy; I found I could exist on stage. I was at home on stage.'

'More at home on the stage than at home?'

'I used to be,' McCowen said after a while. 'I don't know if I am now. But I certainly used to be. I became an actor to escape from myself. To escape from reality and to escape from my father ... Acting was also a form of dressing up and showing off, though my need for that has long since passed. But it was the early reason for becoming an actor: *make-believe*.

'Then, after I'd been a professional actor for several years, I did become genuinely interested in the concept and craft of acting itself; being an actor – my ideas prompted by working with Ruth Gordon in *The Matchmaker* and my friendship with the actor-director Vivian Matalon, who taught me more than anyone's taught me. Also, I saw Marlon Brando in *A Streetcar Named Desire*. An eye-opener. I'd never seen so much brutal realism on a stage before. I didn't know acting could be so involving as he made it. I couldn't imitate him, because he has a tragic gravity I lack, but I could revere him; and Brando, plus my love of comic perfection – Jack Benny, Eric Morecambe and so on – means my love of acting. Now I am, as British actors would say, stuck with acting. It's all I can do.'

'Brando's attempts at comedy have been ponderous. But like Spencer Tracy, Brando on form doesn't look as though he's acting. Is that what good acting is? And how does it work?'

'I was thinking about this recently. I was watching a great performance, and the actor was breaking all the rules. He was looking down – we are taught to look up, to see the eyes. His speaking was badly phrased. Generally, it was not clean – but it was magnetic, compulsive. Brando, in *Reflections in a Golden Eye*. In some ways, a hilarious movie; and to see it played by Brando, Elizabeth Taylor and Julie Harris heightened Carson McCullers's writing. It is one of Brando's most extraordinarily brave performances – because he makes himself so utterly foolish in it. I couldn't imagine how he'd dare to take the risks he did. There was a scene where he was thrown by a horse; he just sat there on the ground weeping like a baby. There was another scene with him going through his little box of possessions; he pored over a teaspoon he'd stolen. And he had an almost incomprehensible accent. And I was looking and listening and thinking the very question you were asking. Why is it working?'

'A bundle of calculated contradictions? Inspired waywardness? The divinity of the star? Can any of this be taught?'

'Actors are born as actors, but it seems that they can be made. There are so many thousands of us. An amateur actor may not be able to repeat a performance as a professional can, do it time after time, but he may bring – and professionals hate to admit this – a refreshing sincerity to the job. A refreshing openness a professional's closed to. And children can act, just like they can paint.'

'Kipling and Barrie were obsessed with the child's mind; its function as a gate to make-believe, to the Never-Neverland.'

Kim, in which the changeling-adventurer runs over the rooftops of Lahore, and Barrie's *The Little White Bird*, where Peter Pan the flying boy first soars, were published within a few months of each other. And though representing the Edwardian preoccupation with childhood (the art of the period is packed with indictments against parents and adults), the boy who would not grow up is a patron saint of acting: the child as the liberated and noble savage repressed by maturity and responsibility, and whom actors take care not to deny.

'The child in oneself is an enormous help in acting.' said McCowen. 'Very often an actor has to play a king. Few of us have direct experience of sovereignty – except when we were babies, and we were the best beloved; and especially if the actor had happened to be an only child, if only for a little while; or if he was spoilt – which most children are at some time or another. So experience of kingship comes from having been a child; and for the Fool's dejection when Lear adopts Edgar on the heath, I remembered my sister's birth and my demotion in family regard.'

'You summon Young Gemini. You bring him back?'

'Yes.'

On stage McCowen finds the perfected twin. 'If I could choose,' he once asked himself, 'where would I wish to be?' The answer is *childhood*. Infancy's playpen is the rehearsal room; the organized play of theatre.

'Does acting preserve a continuity with childhood; a conjuration of a paradise regained?'

'If an actor gets dignified, he's finished. An actor has to continue slipping on banana peel; an actor has to continue making a fool of himself. You can only reach a performance, as far as I know, by making mistakes.'

'Trial and error and the idea of progress.'

'Rarely have I, or have I seen anybody, start off entirely on the right track. You have to take risks. In *Reflections in a Golden Eye*, Brando took risks which were excessive. In other films, he gets besotted with an accent, and acts only the accent. His fallibility only adds to his mystery. And Redgrave took great risks. Olivier. In later years, Gielgud.'

'You must be open to humiliations; exploratory, like an inquisitive child?'

'There's a line in *The Cocktail Party*, "You will find that you survive humiliation. / And that is an experience of incalculable value."'

'Tell me about a humiliation.'

'I'll tell you about its opposite first. I was doing *Hadrian VII* in New York, and waiting for a curtain call. The other actors went on first; I used to go to my papal throne; when the curtains parted, I'd descend. Terrific! That play in a Broadway theatre had such an impact. The silence, when you're holding an audience – that's exciting; or the laughter when you are amusing them – that's rewarding.

'As for humiliation, that would've been in a film studio when I was unsuitably cast as a frogman. They'd promised to train us; the training consisted of twenty minutes in the local baths. I had to do my close-ups under water. I passed out quickly and was lifted out of the tank. "Brandy! Coffee!" I heard them scream. The next day I put on my frogman costume again and sat on the floor. Spooky underwater lighting was switched on, and a slow-motion camera. I was to pretend I was swimming under the waves. "No, no, no, it wasn't working!" My hair should be floating. So a vacuum cleaner was held above my head. I thought WHAT THE HELL AM I DOING IN THIS PROFESSION?'

'Make-believe at its most unbelievable.'

'I don't know that I did survive that humiliation.'

A man the dead ringer of a famous Hellenic crooner shuffled into the dressing room. Eddie Kulukundis, the producer. A hint of fluster from the actor, who started to forget names. I made my exit as actor and management mulled over the emptying houses.

'I'm so sorry Alec. You've heard?'

'Yes. Never mind. We just couldn't pull the audiences in . . .'

TWO

The Rolling English Actor: Robert Stephens

Robert Stephens knows how to make an entrance – you clatter in late. Originally, we were to forgather at his grand house on Primrose Hill; this was commuted to the pub at the end of the street, at one o'clock. At half past the hour, a large purple man with a foaming pint in his left hand, double whisky in his right, the local paper clutched to an oxter, and waggling a purple sausage, came towards me. The purple sausage soon turned out to be a thrust digit, and it was the nearest I was to get to a handshake. Agitating, gingerly, the purple sausage, I felt like Alun Weaver in Kingsley Amis's *The Old Devils*, who is preparing to greet an acquaintance called Peter Thomas; and a man comes into the bar 'who at first looked to Alun like an incredibly offensive but all too believable caricature of Peter Thomas aged about eighty-five and weighing half a ton. At a second glance he saw that it was Peter Thomas.' My mental picture of Stephens is as Wilder's lithe Sherlock Holmes.

Expansive, arrogant, impossible, Stephens has quite a larger-than-life barroom manner. My recollection is of stale beer, torn ticket stubs, spittle in the sawdust. Meeting Davy Garrick must have been thus: the actor as an exotic creature, and it's no coincidence his performances were admired by Joe Orton, whose diary records Stephens as the original choice for Ed in *Entertaining Mr Sloane*. Stephens's style descends from the tradition of Falstaff in Eastcheap; or Johnson extemporizing, putting on a show for scribbling or memorizing Boswell. He's a bulky show-off, brimming with actorial gossip and happy malice. He brushed aside conceptual questions; was an impatient listener; delighted in anecdote. In fact, he appears to give little away about his own true nature. He's so enveloped himself in stories of other people, the stories flourished like the contents of a colourful wardrobe – the stories worn like costumes – that the point's been reached when habiliments have become habits; when deportment and mimicries form the stuffing of the inner creature. Stephens, exemplifying the truth of his masks, is the strangers he speaks of.

A raconteur, not a conversationalist; petulant: Stephens's honeycomb

tones, with their hint of yawp and the sudden snarl, dipped into doing the
different voices of the names he dropped. I was engulfed by forking talk.
Writing up my journal, it was as if I'd been listening to Krapp's fuzzy
tapes, with Bell's for bananas.

'Ralph Richardson said to me, regarding his autobiography, he'd like
to kill the ghost-writer, for the tapes were rearranged.'

'New juxtapositions,' I said.

'I'm always being told, "Robert, do your autobiography, you've had
such an interesting life." But Ralph said, "Robert, wait until you're
seventy – and then don't do it."'

'Am I a ghost?' I wondered.

'You've chosen to write. Acting is what I've chosen to do. Those
people over there, they've chosen to work behind that bar.'

'How did you choose your latest film?' I asked.

'It's about the Nazis. I'm making money on it because it's overrunning.
The location was covered by a cloud from Chernobyl, so I'm waiting to
be flown to a new location in Greece instead. What is this obsession with
the Nazis?' he asked through a puff of smoke. 'There were other terrible
times in history. Sympathy. We're all sympathetic with the Jews. Larry
believes you shouldn't underestimate sympathy; I think he's wrong. An
actor could make Hitler sympathetic, if he wanted. Show him being a
family man, singing carols.

'Larry. He's all "dear, darling, lovely-boy" until opening night, when
it's just *him* and the *audience*; and it has to be love at first sight. He once told
me that a great actor has to be a magpie: he must steal everything. So
Larry stole the clipped delivery from Ronald Colman – he even stole
Ronald Colman's thin moustache. You listen to Ronald Colman saying
Shangri-La and compare it with that febrile tenor of Larry's in *And. now.
is. the win. ter. of. our. dis. con. tent*, or his *My dear darling lovely boy*. It is the
same. And acting with his back to the audience. That's Alfred Lunt. Larry
loved Alfred Lunt, who said that he turned away from the audience
because his face was too ugly for a hero's. Larry made it dangerous to turn
his back on the audience – like he didn't love them anymore. You can be
so expressive with your back to the audience, so dangerous, that broad
expansive part of you.'

Stephens went on to mention *Epitaph for George Dillon* ('my first great
success'), and meeting Laurence Olivier in the King's Road.

' "My dear darling boy, may I give you one note?"'

' "Of course, as many as you like."'

' "You flirt too much."'

' "I learned that from one actor in particular."'

' "My dear Robert, now who was that?"'

' "*You*, it was *you*! *You* flirt with the audience, you come on and make
love to the audience, so how can *you* say I flirt too much?"'

Stephens was a Royal Court regular in its most famous days, appearing in *The Crucible, Don Juan, The Death of Satan, Cards of Identity, The Good Woman of Sezuan* and *The Country Wife* in 1956; *The Apollo de Bellac, Yes – and After, The Making of Moo, The Waiting of Lester Abbs, How Can We Save Father?* and *The Waters of Babylon* in 1957; *The Hole* by N. F. Simpson plus the Creighton and Osborne play in 1958; *Look After Lulu* in 1959; *The Kitchen* in 1961; Waterhouse and Hall's double bill of *The Sponge Room* and *Squat Betty* in 1962.

But it was *Epitaph for George Dillon* which worked its way into Noël Coward's ogling diary ('Beautifully played by a new young man called Robert Stephens, who is quite wonderful') and the play deals with an actor-dramatist prone to rages about his thwarted genius. Dillon's like a Fifties Coward, who has grown up in a decade when Teddington can be flaunted, not hidden under silk dressing gowns, so that Dillon is, in fact, Jimmy Porter redux, indulging himself in abstract tirades, a nasty concoction of self-pity (which he mistakes for his tragic destiny) and scrounging (which he interprets as his due hospitality) and bullying (which he believes is his power-in-action).

Jimmy Porter rants; we imagine some amazing future, once he's put his mind to it. A genius, idling. George Dillon rants; we know about his dreary success, his mediocre plays which make money because of inserted cheapo sexy scenes. A fake, naked. Stephens, with his ability to make energy despondent and humourlessness alarming, had Dillon look back in anger – but at himself, rather than social iniquities. No wonder Coward was moved: Stephens's Dillon was himself nightmarishly reproduced.

And Olivier was perturbed. He noted a wolfish sense of indignation.

'He said I should be nicer, that I should ask the audience for more sympathy. He was wrong. You should never ask the audience for sympathy, they'll hate you for it. You've got to conquer them. And Larry doesn't ask for sympathy: he charms – a deadly charm. Look at his Richard. He obtained the hump and the nose, but had no idea how to play the part until he made his first entrance on opening night – and there was the audience, and he twinkled like Disney's Wolf. His Iago was the same – a charmer, a flirt. He nearly made the audience believe him.'

'A definitive Iago would take in the audience entirely,' I said, 'hypnotizing it.'

'Yes. When I was in *The Double Dealer* at the National, I played Maskwell, a monster – yet women really liked him. One woman from the audience said she'd like to have a man like that. But he was a monster.'

Stephens thought Olivier a charming rogue.

'He is determined to win. He's tensile steel on a first night. One play we did, he entered from one side, me from the other. We met in the middle, and much to my surprise, he kissed me, which got a laugh. The longer it went on, the bigger the laugh. So every night the kiss got longer. I had to say to him in the end, "Laurence, you may be the greatest actor in the world, but you are an even greater kisser."

'I was in a play with Arthur Lowe, who had to drop out for *Dad's Army*. Larry took over the part, but he was so nervous about it, he put somebody else's name in the programme. He just wasn't happy with the lawyer's language of the part. He only had to appear in the final scene. The cue came, I had to answer the doorbell and let Olivier in. There he was, in the wings, still muttering over the script.

' "If I look at you hard," he said, "I'll have dried. So prompt me."

' "I don't know your part," I said. "Come on, it's the cue."

' "This is not," he said, "a profession fit for an adult person." '

Stephens relished the line and recited it in several ways, sounding more and more like Ronald Colman.

'Did you see that boy at the Barbican doing Richard III? What did you think of it? I had to walk out. If you are instantly evil, what else can you do? Where can you go? Nothing. Nowhere. The other characters become one-dimensional – pathetic fools who can't see an obvious villain. I did Richard on gramophone records. The key line is before the battle, and he whispers, "And if I die no soul will pity me." '

'He realizes he's not Henry V before Agincourt," I said.

'He realizes he's going to die and he's suddenly afraid. The trick with Shakespeare is to get the syntax of the thought. Pauses come where thoughts end, and then you go on to the next. It flows. You think it – and out it comes. Like this . . .'

And Stephens launched into Macbeth's soliloquy, 'Tomorrow and tomorrow and tomorrow', his voice rising and falling with the poetry's music, his breathing perfected, so that he was never breathless – concluding succinctly (and after a nonchalant torching of his Benson & Hedges) with:

> And all our yesterdays have lighted fools
> The way to dusty death.

Stephens's Macbeth would be a wanton warlord – not the beetle-browed murderer-bureaucrat of Bob Peck or the hysterical bejabbers of Jonathan Pryce, two recent thanes. His Macbeth would be gloriously oldfashioned.

'I'd love to play,' he continued – so that I had quickly to make a connection – 'Captain Hook.'

The connection is (a) Kirriemuir's proximity to the Thanedom of Fife and (b) overreaching evil shot through with cowardly madness.

'Hook needs to be played by a serious actor, not a comedian. Hook's an Etonian with yellow blood. The school bully who sends the crew to be killed by the Doodle-Doo. Fancy being followed around the island by a crocodile.'

Stephens improvised a pantomime of Hook alarmed by reptilian ticking; of Hook startled by the Doodle-Doo, using the bar as the poop. Then the drooping crouching Captain became a momentary impersonation of Brando's Don Corleone, pretending to be a gorilla to amuse the grandchild.

'Marlon Brando is magnificent. " 'E's just a fuckin' film star," an actor said to me once, and made out that my praise had put him in the ring with Brando, which is not what I'd intended. "Right, let's see," I said. "He started with *The Men*, great film, powerful acting. *Streetcar*, one of the greatest performances of all time. *Viva Zapata*. Great film. *Waterfront*, another great performance. *The Godfather . . .*"

'They wanted Edward G. Robinson, but Brando said, "I'll do it for nothing, I want the part so much." So they gave him a screen test in an Italian restaurant, and he pushed in the wadding and talked all croaky. And it's another of the great performances of all time. For *The Godfather* he spent months with the Mafia in Sicily. The Sicilians drink grappa, which destroys the vocal chords. They smoke black tobacco, which destroys the vocal chords – so that's where the husky voice comes from; the necessity of whispering and the over-use of fastidious, sharp hand-movements; sign language. Brando found all this out. He works at that level of detail, which is combined with the dynamo inside of him.

'I'm a good actor; Albert Finney is talented; so's Peter O'Toole – all of us of that generation. But there is a special word for people like Brando, and it's genius. *Genius*. " 'E's just a fuckin film star!" He's genius.'

What is the attraction McCowen and Stephens feel towards Marlon Brando (born 1924)? It's the fact that he's much their age and in the same trade, yet the obverse of what should be expected from classical acting; he mumbles and sulks. A moody disingenuousness enters the parts he plays, transforming them – as though the script is a starting point, which he's ingested entirely, so that what the camera shoots is subliminal paraphrase, an alchemy of Brando's personality and the role as a commentary upon it. He thinks his way into a script, converting it to his own idiom – which is why Shakespeare eluded him (*Julius Caesar*, 1951), for Shakespeare is his match in experimentation and rule-breaking; Mark Antony is not reducible. The most remarkable aspect of Brando's Mark Antony, actually, was his fringe (as Roland Barthes once noticed) – and his Kurtz was memorable mostly for a shaven pate; Superman's dad for a silver tuft, and the money he was paid.

But Brando's talent was well displayed in *Last Tango in Paris*, as Norman Mailer delights in pointing out (because Mailer attempts in prose what Brando and Monroe achieved in acting: to evoke the unpredictable, haphazard, disintegrating power of the subconscious). Bertolucci's stiff 'I make you die, you make me die, we're two murderers, each others',' came out from Brando, after it had been processed by his personality, as 'I'm going to get a pig and I'm going to have a pig fuck you and I want the pig to vomit on your face' – which, as Wilde might say, sounds like a Shakespeare sonnet transposed to a minor key.

To be permitted on stage and screen the strangulations, groans and grunts of natural speech, plus an idiosyncratic cadenza: this was new to British actors thirty years ago, but not to Diderot two hundred years ago. 'There are moments,' he says in *Entretiens sur le Fils naturel* (1757) 'that should be left almost entirely to the actor. It is his right to use the text of a scene as he sees fit, to repeat certain words, to return to certain ideas, to cut out some and to add others.' The actor should make every performance an airing of his own current preoccupations; acting is fluid creativity, not a frozen music. Brando is an operatic anticoagulant.

'A genius, Marlon. He notices,' Stephens went on, 'the kind of people who say *two times* and the people who'd say *twice*. Laurence is similar; with him it's entirely instinct. Larry is not a bookish man. He couldn't talk to you about Schopenhauer.'

'Die Welt als Wille und Vorstellung,' I said, clever-clever.

'What?'

'The world as will or idea. Schopenhauer.'

'What? Well, Larry – he's dogged, practical. He's the inspired craftsman.'

Craftsmanship had become the theme.

'Modern plays,' Stephens remarked, 'have no craftsmanship. A playwright should be like a wheelwright or a cartwright: a craftsman making something that holds together. Those plays of the 1950s we were all in: they have good acts, but too many poor acts. I was offered *The Entertainer*, which Peter Bowles is doing, but it is not a good play, and I was Larry's understudy in the original. Acts and scenes here and there work, but not much adds up. Look at Eugene O'Neill's *Long Day's Journey* or *Mourning Becomes*. I said to Bill Bryden, "I'll do O'Neill if you cut him." He said, "You cannae cut O'Neill," as though O'Neill is sacrosanct. "Why can't you cut O'Neill," I said. "We cut Shakespeare. We cut lines, scenes, whole characters from Shakespeare. O'Neill is boring to read. And if I'm bored reading him, how can I act him interestingly? The audience will be bored too." "Och, y' cannae cut O'Neill." The trouble is, America has no culture, except cowboys and Indians.'

'Every writer that emerges,' I suggested, 'is a candidate for their Shakespeare. Fat books to fill up a big continent, from *Moby Dick* to *Ancient Evenings*.'

'Well, there's Arthur Miller. I wanted Larry to play Willy Loman; I'd have been Biff, so you can tell this was a long time ago. He said it wasn't a good enough play for him. He's had every illness a man can have, and so can't go on stage anymore; so he does those films, like *Boys from Brazil*.'

'Willy Loman is a New York Lear, with the refrigerator falling apart instead of the kingdom.'

'The *only* American author is Tennessee Williams. A poetic genius, who got drunk at lunchtime and who sobered up by swimming under-water for forty-five minutes. He gave the world Blanche DuBois, one of the astounding women's parts; and in Vivien Leigh's personification, one of the astounding women's performances – a performance accentuated by her own emotional turmoil. I met Williams on the beach and introduced him to Peter Shaffer, whose plays are rubbish, a fact the critics have only recently realized. Shaffer was full of fulsome praise, which just embar-rassed Williams. He'd heard it all before. He knew how good he was. I was in Shaffer's *The Royal Hunt of the Sun*. The religiosity is nonsense. Even worse in *Yonadab* – which makes the critics start looking harder at his earlier writing. I knew it was absurd, that theology of the Incas and the Spaniards. But, to be fair, at least Shaffer takes the trouble to come to the theatre and watch rehearsals, and writes lines again for you if they don't work. They won't be better, but he has the actors in mind.'

Stephens's Atahuallpa, in John Dexter's National Theatre production of 1964, was a triumph at the time: the noble, effulgent Inca, convinced he's a god, brought low by the invasion of boorish conquistadores. The play, like *Equus* and *Amadeus*, dealt with a man's combat against a ravishing deity, which he destroys – as Strang blinds the stallions, as Salieri kills Mozart: so Pizarro brings about the feathered, masked king's execution. Shaffer's plots and ritual murders are wish-fulfilling re-writes of *Richard II*, which imagine Richard and Bolingbroke in a dependent amity, each man killing the thing he loves. 'For you,' says Atahuallpa to Pizarro, 'I will do a great thing. I will swallow death and spit it out of me.'

Stephens is still remembered for his physical splendour in the part; the part was played in loincloth and chains (he was tethered like a horse, in fact). He'd not easily play the part two decades on. He connects with his past like Falstaff remembering when he was once a stripling page to the Duke of Norfolk.

He was talking of scripts and their scissoring.

'Scripts. We have to cut them right back. Shaffer overwrites. I worked in *Hedda* with Ingmar Bergman. He cut it to two hours. He rid the text of the repetitions and exposition – which it is the actor's job to push home, not the writer's. Repetition and exposition belong to the time when people had no memory, before the familiarity of television, cinema and radio made them concentrate. They'd get pissed in the interval and would have to keep on being reminded who the characters were, what was going on. Acting is about giving life to the script. It's where you originate. It shouldn't be too literary, or too shoddy. Modern plays are all sticky-tape, though Coward's *Private Lives* is, I think, a perfect play. There are true lines there, deep ones, deep in the froth, about death – which must hang in the air. Otherwise it is nothing but a frivolous play about frivolous people. Maggie didn't believe me, so I called Noël in Switzerland, and he agreed with me. He said, "Bob, you are absolutely right." .'

Stephens was famously married to Maggie Smith, and Coward himself directed them in a 1964 production of *Hay Fever*; they formed a double act in *The Recruiting Officer* (Plume and Silvia), *The Beaux' Stratagem* (Francis Archer and Mrs Sullen), *Hedda Gabler* (Ejert Lövborg and Hedda Tesman – a Snowdon photograph exists of a convulsed Stephens being maternally comforted by Smith's Nordic nanny) and, especially, *Much Ado About Nothing* – where the merry war between Beatrice and Benedick was popularly believed to represent the actor and actress's home life. The most magnificent transcription of their partnership was not, however, made. In 1967 Anthony Burgess wrote script and lyrics for a musical on the life of Shakespeare (Stephens), with Maggie Smith as Mistress Hathaway. '*Will!*' Burgess says, 'still haunts the bardophile faubourgs of Hollywood as one of the great impossible dreams.'*

'My dear Lady Disdain, she is yet living,' Stephens said, affectionately remembering a line of Benedick's. 'We speak. The divorce was a long time ago. Audiences expect her to be "Maggie". She gives a Maggie Smith caricature in whatever it is she does now. You get all this tooting and fluting; that nasal delivery she picked up from Kenneth Williams.'

Indeed, not only was Maggie Smith teamed with Olivier (his Desdemona), she's also partnered the wrinkled Carry On ephebe – in a Bamber Gascoigne revue of 1957 called *Share My Lettuce* and a Peter Shaffer effort of 1962, *The Private Ear and The Public Eye*. A documentary about Smith's art, twenty years ago, brought on Williams as her guru; and in 1973 they were teamed on the Parkinson chat show, discussing the Teddy Bear verse of Sir John Betjeman.

'When we did *Private Lives* together, the mannerisms grew worse and worse, until finally I stopped dead in the middle of a scene. A long cold pause, with the prompter whispering away.

'"Robert, what's the matter? Did you dry?" she asked in the interval.

---

* It might not be too over-ingenious to add *The Private Life of Sherlock Holmes* to a catalogue of Stephens/Smith joint ventures. Stephens seems to play the Baker Street wiz as an impersonation of Miss Jean Brodie. He's made up with a silken ginger wig, mascara'd eyes and pronounces certain words in a twangy nasal catch: 'enterpraise', 'transperent', 'simplifay', 'unoblayging'. And, archly, fruitily, 'Watson, we *are* living in the nineteenth century'. Stephens has absorbed his spouse's style of speaking, and comes out with it.

' "Listen," I said. "The next time you start all that coy nonsense and wittering and winking at the audience, I am going to walk off the stage. Your behaviour isn't that of a serious professional actress; it wouldn't even be worthy of Worthing Rep."

'I told her, what we should do is *Antony and Cleopatra*. We should just *do it*. People don't want to see Vanessa Redgrave do it, with Timothy Dalton; or Glenda, who's done it. They want Maggie Smith to do it. And if the posters and signs went up saying *Antony and Cleopatra*, with Robert Stephens and Maggie Smith, they will pour in. They'll want to see *us*; they'll come and see us throwing rocks at one another. The divorce was a long time ago. We get along.'

Beatrice and Benedick have become Amanda and Elyot, the bantering divorcees in Noël Coward's play: 'What happens if one of us dies? Does the one that's left still laugh?'

There's much flippancy and cruelty in Coward; the hay fevers smart, the cocktail raillery is hurtful. Maggie Smith is brilliant at acting this level of incipient hysteria and parody of manners. She can play inclemency and guile; and this was the kitten opposite Stephens's Lövborg, the relationship on display in that Snowdon portrait. Stephens emerged – as Plume, Archer, Lövborg, let alone Benedick and Elyot – as vulnerable. Vulnerable, like George Dillon. Exactly the quality Billy Wilder wanted for the private life of Sherlock Holmes – the apartment at 221B a place of emotional intrigue, just as if half a century on, Bud Baxter (Jack Lemmon) and Fran Kubelik (Shirley MacLaine) will live there, J. D. Sheldrake (Fred MacMurray) the Moriarty.

'Your Holmes was a melancholy romantic.'

'I've played Holmes twice. I did it as a film with Billy Wilder and on stage, in the Gillette play. There is an odd story about that, because Gillette wrote to Conan Doyle, who had killed off the character, being sick to death of him, and asked if he could write a dramatic adaptation, introducing, at the end of the play, a certain romantic quality with a young lady. The reference is rather oblique, but it does seem that Holmes marries a young girl, Alice Faulkner. So I played it as Gillette did, who was a great romantic matinee idol. "How do you want me to play it for the movie," I asked Billy. "You must play it ... like Hamlet. And you must not put on one pound of weight. I want you to look like a pencil." So that's the way we did *The Private Life of Sherlock Holmes*.'

The film was made in 1969, with a budget of $10 million, and released on 29 October 1970. The intention was to portray the detective's emotional wrangles; to find him apprehensive and bruised. 'We all have our failures,' intoned Stephens's Sherlock. 'Fortunately Watson never writes about mine.'

And the original film unfolded as an essay on women and their elegance, and Holmes's justification for misogyny. He was found in love with a murderess; another inamorata died on the eve of their wedding; then there was Ilse von Hoffmanstahl, the film's version of Irene Adler. Here was a Holmes fated to fail: a virtuoso empiricist degenerated to morbid dreaminess by amorous action. Hamlet traduced by a flotilla of Ophelias.

Wilder cast Stephens because 'he looks as if he could be hurt' – and it was a moody, intelligent portrayal: 'He does not want courage, skill, will, or opportunity; but every incident sets him thinking ... we see a great, an almost enormous intellectual activity ... his senses are in a train of trance, and he looks upon external things as hieroglyphics' – which is how Coleridge described the Prince of Denmark, Elsinore his Baker Street; a palace of puzzles.

Hamlet is engaged by the Ghost to discover who killed his father; he prefers to police, however, the free-wheeling nature of his own mind. He snoops out himself (in soliloquy). Holmes, too, creeps about inside his head – which distresses Watson, because it looks like catatonia: 'The outbursts of passionate energy when he performed the remarkable feats with which his name is associated were followed by reactions of lethargy, during which he would lie about with his violin and books, hardly moving, save from the sofa to the table.' And this sort of description, or admission, intensifies the enigma of his personality.

Unfortunately, *The Private Life of Sherlock Holmes* was radically re-edited, eradicating its atmosphere and tempo. What should have been a triumphant commentary on *Hamlet* became a 1960s romp, *What's New, Pussycat?* in the costumes of the gasolier period. (Wilder had even gone to the trouble of casting Stanley Holloway as a grave digger – the part he'd played in Olivier's *Hamlet* film of 1948.)

'It was cut completely. The film should have been three hours and two minutes long. We shot for twenty-six weeks; there were, in fact, four cases for Holmes and Watson to investigate. At that time there were films called roadshow attractions, which had an interval. *The Private Life* was to be one of those. Barbra Streisand's *Funny Girl* was a big success. *Doctor Dolittle*, with Rex Harrison, and *Star*, about Gertie Lawrence, were disasters. So the company, the Mirisch Brothers, got frightened – and had Billy trim the picture down to one hour and fifty-three minutes. This wrecked the film, for there were many running jokes; now it doesn't make any sense at all. Nevertheless, it has become a cult, as it stands, because it is very handsome to look at.

'When I was in Hollywood, I. A. L. Diamond told me that he and Billy had spent seven years writing the script. They were so obsessed because, I think, Billy and Izzy are like Holmes and Watson. So Izzy didn't speak to Billy for a year because Billy cut the film.

'Do you think the original will ever be pieced back together, like Gance's *Napoleon*?'

'There is a print of the original. I hope one day it will be shown. Not only for me, but for Billy and Izzy and Colin Blakely, and because we did work awfully hard, all of us, for twenty-six weeks, even going to Scotland to shoot at Loch Ness.'

The lost sections of *The Private Life of Sherlock Holmes* excite me, as Jeffrey Aspern's burnt papers excite me, or Byron's memoirs on Jock Murray's grate. My letters to Billy Wilder were returned, insufficiently addressed. My letter to I. A. L. Diamond was received – on the day he died. I was eventually told to contact the Film and Television Archive of the University of California, Los Angeles, where it was rumoured there was a game afoot to restore the picture. In reply to my query, Professor Charles Hopkins said that though his department had not undertaken such a celluloid jigsaw puzzle, I should try writing to Ronald Haver, Curator of the Department of Film at the Los Angeles County Museum of Art. And here the news was not good. Whilst Mr Haver, who'd restored the full-length version of George Cukor's *A Star is Born*, did indeed intend working on Wilder's masterpiece: 'unfortunately this project had to be abandoned because United Artists no longer had complete materials for more than one of the excised sequences (the so-called "Naked Honeymooners" sequence) . . . by itself . . . incomprehensible without the rest of the excised footage. The only complete print of Wilder's original version was apparently the preview print, which was later cut to conform with the final release version.'

Allen Eyles, in *Sherlock Holmes: A Centenary Celebration*, has done his own sleuthing on the tattered opus. He reports that the 'Naked Honeymooners' took place on an ocean liner, where a pair of young lovers lie dead in bed. Holmes, conducted by Watson, sauntered to the scene of the crime – only to discover he's in the wrong cabin, poking and prodding quite the wrong prostrate bodies. Then there was 'The Case of the Upside-Down Room'. A chinky-poo has been murdered in a chamber – owned by a blind David Kossoff – where the chairs, tables and bed are dizzyingly stuck to the ceiling. It transpires to be all a ruse, organized by an ingenious Watson, to shake Holmes from his well of accidie. In this episode, as in a sacrificed epilogue, where Holmes is asked to help catch Jack the Ripper, Inspector Lestrade appeared, played by George Benson.

Most damaging, perhaps, was the forfeiture of a flashback to Holmes at Oxford, skulling on the Isis and falling in love with a girl – whom he discovers to be a prostitute. If the 'Naked Honeymooners' and 'Upside-Down Room' were squandered because more or less self-contained, and larky, the Oxford affair and the Ripper case (the victims, of course, all

Whitechapel prostitutes) importantly deepened the film's major theme: Holmes entangled in the world of emotion, rather than of reason.

Wilder, in fact, surrendering these sections, cut out his film's heart. Look at all his major films – *Double Indemnity* (1944), *The Lost Weekend* (1945), *Sunset Boulevard* (1950), *The Seven Year Itch* (1955), *Some Like It Hot* (1959), *The Apartment* (1960): they are all studies in scarlet. Wilder is a genius at exposing matters of passion; he's alert to the way people behave when 'in love' (or filled with hate); he sees how the state can render them *other than they really are*. He acknowledges the interchangeability of comedy and tragedy, and he's profound on the tragicomedy of social versus private manners.

Temptation is his speciality: crime, cupidity, dipsomania, sexuality, cross-dressing, loose women (*Irma La Douce* of 1964 is based on a musical about prostitution); and in one way and another, Holmes's failure to resist temptation, with a consequent adulteration of his brain-power, was the subject of *The Private Life of Sherlock Holmes* – except that, with Holmes's history of romantic disaster removed, his attitude to Ilse von Hoffmansthal (Genevieve Page) is just rude and impatient; we don't know what's created the petulance – and Stephens's sorrowful expressions are a distillate from sections of the film we'll never see.

The Private Life could have been an extension of Coward's *Private Lives* – for when Amanda Prynne says 'I think very few people are completely normal, really, deep down in their private lives,' she articulates a controversial truth apt for Wilder's art. Private lives are murky recesses, intimacy a volatile acid. (Consider the monkey funeral behind the walls on Sunset Boulevard, or the blacked-out, boozed-up days and nights, impotence and lust in other Wilder streets and homes – for instance, the insurance scam under surveillance in the *Fortune Cookie*; the capers in the bedrooms of the Paris Ritz in *Love in the Afternoon*.) Take us out of the public gaze, and we're perverted, animalistic – Amanda again: 'If all the various cosmic thingummys fuse at the same moment, and the right spark is struck, there's no knowing what one mightn't do.'

Wilder wanted to uncover Holmes's biochemistry; the physique and physiology beyond the cool logic and calculation. The poster was an enticing portrait of his psyche: a giant aquiline profile (not quite Stephens's), muffled in brackish shadow and cluttered with overlapping images – a blueish hand emerging from a lake squirting cocaine from a hypodermic syringe (a parody of the hand clutching Excalibur); an open coffin, the corpse dinner-jacketed and vampiral; an iron-plated submarine; snowy white doves; the phallic neck and head of the Loch Ness Monster, which nestles under the breast of a naked bimbo – her come-hither hairdo and pout direct from a Sixties James Bond film. Pointed towers and spindly minarets curl under Holmes's pipe in silhouette – vanes, spires and battlements recognizably Oxford's, despite Big Ben taking up the end of the row. The gaslights give off a glare of yellow bubbles – another Sixties touch, those psychedelic baubles; and it is circles and spheroids which link the placard: the sub's spiky cogs, the girl's boob and the moons on her robe, the curve on the deerstalker's brim, the pipe's bell, the shimmer around the toy ballerina, the carriage wheels, the face on the clock, etc. Only the prickles of those Oxford pinnacles threaten to puncture the curvilinear dreamscape – Oxford's pinnacles which we don't get to witness in the extant film.

The Private Life as we now have it begins with Watson's Holmesian memorabilia discovered in a bank vault – the deerstalker, cocaine needle, 221B name-plate, signet rings, a snow-globe of Queen Victoria. Most striking, rising over the rummaging, is the score. Miklos Rozsa's Elgaresque gypsy music couldn't be recast or chopped up, and in the plangent violin solo we have the melody of Holmes's sentimental education; we hear a leitmotif of his past ardours – which connects to an absent part of the film, and therefore the evocative tunes go for nothing. (Stephens merely looks inexplicably twitchy whilst the soundtrack encourages us to weep.) The music has another function, however, being violin dominated. We can understand, perhaps for the first time, why Holmes is an *aficionado* of the fiddle: the continuum with cadenzas, the dawdles and sinuous loops and curlicues of sound, is the pattern his brain makes when skittering in meditation. The music of his thought.

Stephens's Holmes never grasps the instrument, to saw away. Instrumentation is inward. And as he drifts up and down Baker Street and along the shore of Loch Ness, brooding – snapping at his ankles, shouting, gesticulating, is Blakely's Dr Watson, an Irish Mr Punch, his appearances heralded by jigs and reels. It is possible to guess, in the scenes between these two, where some of the excised footage was situated. After the story of the Russian ballerina, where Holmes escapes impregnating an old dancer (she's made up to resemble a stick of over-boiled rhubarb) by claiming he and Watson are lovers, furious Watson yells at Holmes for ages, and in the aftermath of their tiff, when the doctor asks, inquisitive and abashed, 'There *have* been other women in your life?' Holmes is suddenly upset and snaps 'You're being presumptuous'. The fiddle solo starts insinuating itself, the screen darkens and the mood slackens for reminiscence – but we cut to Ilse Von Hoffmansthal arriving at 221B, having been dragged (she says) out of the river. Should we here have had the Oxford scene? (The force of Holmes's remark, on seeing the damp visitor, 'This is a very small flat, we don't want to clutter it up with women' is defeated when we haven't met his other women. And was there to be a link with boating on the Isis and Ilse in the Thames?)

Was 'Naked Honeymooners', an early bungle, meant to set up Holmes and Watson's Laurel and Hardy interdependence? Balanced out, perhaps, by 'Upside-Down Room', where Watson is the conscientious spouse-figure, inventing cryptograms to keep and divert his partner, who main-lines cocaine to alleviate boredom? Holmes despairs of peacefulness and equipoise. Watson is seriously alarmed at the drugs, and hides the syringe as best he can – and after a flare-up before the ballerina sequence, there we'd have had David Kossoff and George Benson, to jolt Holmes from his lassitude.

The mystery which remains – involving canaries, crinkled midgets, sinister German monks, chlorine gas, Scottish castles and Christopher Lee (as Mycroft) – is a jaunty brew, but there's no aura. The photography, tobaccoey browns and ruby glows, is a perfect fuliginous Victorian print come to life, but the prettiness doesn't do anything; it's skin deep. Holmes's comment that 'women are unreasonable and not to be trusted' ought to hover and shimmer in the twilight; it comes and goes. And Alexandre Trauner's 221B set is no scruffy bachelor's snuggery. It's a palace of brass and mahogany, corridors and antechambers, expensively bound books; a sort of stately Holmes. Here, however, the film's residue of greatness takes up residence – in the business between the flatmates, their love/hate relationship. Not clot and charmer, like Bruce and Rath-bone, or muted hero and neurasthenic, like Hardwicke and Brett, but (verbal) tussle approaching Coward's Amanda and Elyot – or in Wilder's canon, haunted Norma Desmond's rapport with William Holden's trans-fixed kept man.

The excuse for the film is to have some new cases where the detective fouls up. Watson, hitherto, has only published successes. He's censored the truth to make a legend.* Now we'll see the private agony, the man beyond the *Strand Magazine* mask. In fact, however, the point of Conan Doyle's original tales isn't the solutions to crimes – we're enthralled by Holmes's eccentricities, which Watson records for us in loving detail. We love the violin and the persian slipper shag. We love the way cases are gleaned from the personal columns of the newspapers; the way Holmes comes out with encyclopaedic knowledge of London streets, bloodstains, cigar ash and footprints. We are ever eager for domestic detail. New plots aside, Wilder shows us what we already know; but his affectionate tone is right. And though it's *The Private Life*, secrets and enigma remain. (Wilder doesn't deplume Holmes, or make him ordinary.) My own fascination with the film has to do with the secrets and enigma of Stephens's performance – and of Stephens as a performer.

---

* Like James Joyce telling Nora not to show his letters to anyone, 'but don't lose them', Holmes told Watson secrets so that they'd be written up. 'These were all done prematurely, before my biographer had come to glorify me,' he says in *The Memoirs of Sherlock Holmes*, surveying a document-strewn carpet. 'I should be glad that you should add this case to your annals, for there are points in it which make it quite unique,' he suggests at the commencement to 'The Musgrave Ritual'.

'I met Jack Lemmon in Hollywood. "I love Billy," he said, "I adore him. But didn't he drive you nuts with all that Germanic attention to detail?"

' "I never did too many films," I said. "I trusted Billy because he was a wonderful teacher. He wants it to be absolutely right. If you'd spent seven years writing a script, then you want it to be correct." Billy used to say, "I don't care if it goes thirty-six takes, I want it right, *for me*." And on the Holmes film, we got most of it right. And we did do a lot of takes on things. "There are many things that can go wrong that have nothing to do with you," Billy said. "Maybe the prop man, or the man who pushes the camera up and down on the tracks; or it may be the lens. But I don't care. I want it to be right, *for me*."

'So I said to Lemmon, "I think for somebody to be so fanatical is admirable." Billy said about Jack Lemmon, "He comes on the set with ten ideas about how to play a scene. As I've written it, I *know* how it should be done. There is only one way. Lemmon says, maybe I could do this, maybe I could do that. Not at all; not at all: you just do it *this* way, and when you sit down, pick up the bottle and put it down on *that* line."

'That's a perfectionist, which Billy certainly is – like Alfred Hitchcock. And for Billy, the most interesting aspect of the business was the writing; the least boring was the editing. But the shooting itself he found tedious: having to work with actors who are such pains in the neck; and he'd done it all immaculately in his head. He didn't need actors – well, he did, unfortunately, because they had to act out the parts for him in reality.

'Regarding Sherlock Holmes, Basil Rathbone, I must say, was the best; but Billy's was the most original. He was enigmatic. You didn't know quite what he was up to in his personal life.'

'Rathbone's Holmes,' I interjected finally, 'was saddled with an imbecile Watson, the dotard Nigel Bruce.'

'When I was first cast, Billy didn't have a Watson. "You can't have Laurel without Hardy," he said. "I have seen some actors, but there was a particular actor I saw the other day . . ." "God bless you," I said, "it was Colin Blakely, he's the one." "What about Ronald Fraser?" "It wouldn't work."

'I'd acted with Colin Blakely in *The Recruiting Officer* and in *The Royal Hunt of the Sun*; we had a friendship, a partnership, which Billy could have for nothing. So Colin went back to see Billy at the Connaught Hotel and was cast.'

'Watson has to be in awe of Holmes,' I said, 'like Boswell of Johnson; then, by writing up the cases, he *creates* Holmes.'

'I think with Watson, he's a doctor. Therefore he is a serious fellow, which is how Colin certainly played it. He can't be a buffoon. Recently I did *Raffles* on the radio, the amateur cracksman. It is the same story in reverse; the hero is a burglar, not a private detective.'

'Sir Thomas Stamford Raffles? The colonial administrator who founded Singapore?'

'What? No. Raffles the diamond thief, who has a friend called Bunny, who is Doctor Watson in reverse. A love affair between two men, which is not homosexual in any way. In *Raffles* I had to do all the different voices, including a French maid, *Oh, oui oui, oui, oohh, la la.* Holmes and Watson, Raffles and Bunny: it's the relationship between Laurel and Hardy, two men. And you can't have one without the other.'

'Like Didi and Gogo in *Waiting for Godot.*'

'Totally. It has to be. Otherwise, you write about Romeo, Juliet and a balcony.'

'Though when Shakespeare wrote *Romeo and Juliet*, Juliet would have been played by a boy.'

'Yes, indeed. And that is the problem with Shakespeare. Say you want to do a production of *Antony and Cleopatra*; for Cleopatra you have to find an actress with the power of a man. Women find Shakespeare difficult, because they are weaker. Frailer vessels. Fortunately, in Shakespeare's time there weren't any actresses. Beatrice in *Much Ado About Nothing*, for example – played by a young man, but at least there'd be the strength of a young man playing it. Lady Macbeth – she tends to lose energy at the end of the play today. Cleopatra is the most difficult part in Shakespeare. When Mark Antony kills himself, she has the entire last act to play all by herself. The actress needs enormous strength to play it. Well, you could do it, and so could I. Women, you find, I think, tend to have low blood pressure. They run out of steam.'

Not even in my considerable salad days did I dream of climbing into ostrich feathers and scarabs to play Cleopatra. But what of Maggie Smith, whom Stephens earlier fantasized opposite his Antony? As an actress, Maggie Smith isn't in the category of frailer vessels. As her heavily cosmeticked Jocasta proved, in Cocteau's *The Infernal Machine*, her presentation of femininity on stage approaches that of a female impersonator. She is magnificent in the breeches parts.

'Like,' I said, having stored away a mental snapshot of Stephens and myself quaffing mandragora, 'the women in Tennessee Williams; his heroines really heroes.'

'You are right. Women have to have a great deal of power to play those parts. When Vivien Leigh did a film of Blanche DuBois, in fact it sort of cracked her life, because the part got on top of her. This could have been owing to the character itself; or it could have been owing to the energy she had to sustain to get through it.'

The pub bells clanged for last orders.

'Is acting worth that much? To push someone to the edge?'

'She made history. She's remembered in *Gone With the Wind* and she's remembered in *Streetcar*. That is all anyone can ask for in life.'

'Michael Redgrave said to me, "You get a good part every seven years."
He was about to play Vanya. He wanted to play Vanya all his life. He
discovered, a long time ago, that there was a woman in Paris who'd
known Chekhov and Stanislavsky personally. So he went to see her. He
rang the doorbell. She opened the door. "*I* am Michael Redgrave." "And
you are too tall to play Vanya."

'When Laurence wanted to play it, having once played Astrov with
Ralph Richardson, he grew scared of the idea. Michael was in New York
in *The Sleeping Prince*, which was a flop – it had been a success in London
with Vivien Leigh and Laurence. He was in New York,* he telephoned
Michael, and asked if he'd play Vanya to his Astrov in Chichester. Which
they did. Michael had his text with all the notes from the time the Parisian
lady put him off.

'He was a serious actor, Michael. There are many actors, I think, who
are not frightfully serious about the business. They think it is easy. It is
hard. It is difficult to put yourself into somebody else's shoes; acting is the
chore of being other people.'

'And you either have to measure up to another actor's unique success in
a role,' I said, 'or you have to measure up to people's remembrance of the
real person a role is based on?'

'Yes. So I have just to get on with it. I go to rehearsals, clean, like a
virgin. I keep out what I may know already. I'm naked. I'm going to do
Vanya myself. The Theatre of Comedy is also going to do it next year. It
doesn't matter if there are ten *Uncle Vanya* productions playing. They
would all be different and comparisons are odorous – pocas palabras,
good neighbour Verges, as Dogberry says in *Much Ado*. When I did *The
Cherry Orchard* at the National . . .'

I never did hear the end of that story. The bar was stopping its tap and I
went to collect more liquid lunch. I returned to find Stephens still in full
flight, talking to a plooky punk with an earring:

'I said I wanted to be an actor. My mother said, "You don't want to do
that, you don't want to do that, they're all spivs. Go with your Uncle
George and be a plumber's mate."

' "I don't want to be a plumber's mate."

' "Go with your Uncle Harry, and hang paper."

' "I don't want to be a paperhanger."

' "Get down to Avonmouth and be a tugman."

' "I don't want to be a tugman. I want to be an actor" – which is what I
am. An actor. Be an actor,' Stephens implored of the agape troll in the
pub, 'It's good fun.'

Stephens carrying on regardless is symptomatic of his latest perform-

---

* To complete negotiations for Marilyn Monroe to appear in the film version, *The
Prince and the Showgirl*.

ances; like Falstaff, if sack and sugar be a fault, god help the wicked! If to be old and merry be a sin, then many an old host that I know is damn'd ...! Snug, as Auden would say, in the den of himself, Stephens's character in *Lizzie's Pictures*, for example, cushions himself from the world by sinking into a reverie of mazy monologue; or else he sleeps upon benches after noon, nursing a sense of hurt. He played Lisa Harrow's husband, an 'unfeeling slob' (the script says) who is walked out on, and doesn't notice until laundry day.

Lizzie wants to be a photographer; her career ambitions mean abandoning home and family – or at least, they don't, but her particular brand of ambition is linked with that particular brand of mean-minded feminism. She becomes a scowling female eunuch, frowning as she endlessly photographs herself in a mirror – she lacks Germaine Greer's redeeming sense of self-satire; and dressed in a fur coat, carrying a hard little leather case, she tracks down her childhood girlfriends for an album of snapshots: what has life done to them two decades on from sweet seventeen?

The blow-up subjects are an embittered sorority of divorcées and spinster social workers. Men have been the common enemy, the despoilers of any Amazonian paradise. And the representation of manhood was Stephens ('if manhood, good manhood, be not forgot upon the face of the earth, then am I a shotten herring' – Falstaff), who sank and lurched in the background, pawing and courting his estranged spouse, the objective of his spooning being whether she'll iron his dark brown corduroys.

Attired for horticulture, Stephens roamed through orchards and runner beans: an Adam from whom Eve has made her solitary way – and he squints, excluded, at Lizzie gambolling with the children far off. Presented on nasty videotape, badly lit so that everybody looked washed out and ill, *Lizzie's Pictures* was a miserable polemic; but Stephens survived it, his character a wounded beast, a scapegoat – with this ember of actorial greatness: he never once appealed to our sympathy. Stephens is our least sentimental actor.

Thus, in Alan Bennett's *One Fine Day*, he could play an office boss whose placability with his staff was actually a complete disregard for their welfare. Unctuous in the boardroom, obscuring himself within billows of acrid fag-smoke, making hopeless attempts to recall names, cawing and purring through heavy pursed lips, Stephens was a perfect cacodemon demon to find at the heart of Bennett's dark office life – a labyrinth of forms, form, departments, protocol, filing cabinets, paper, telephones, memos, typewriters, and which all derive from the bureaucratic castles of Kafka, and are further explored in *Kafka's Dick* and *The Insurance Man*.

The title came from Puccini – Madama Butterfly's 'Un bel dì vedremo' (One fine day we'll notice) – and the drama showed the empty days of middle-manager Dave Allen, who's having his mid-life crisis whilst trying to sell air-conditioned office space. 'Selling, business, that's what matters,' says Stephens joyfully, wilfully blind to any colleague's crack-up, and sticking with his steady drizzle of snigger and put-down. Allen being slow in flogging a decrepit tower block, he's ready to ditch him for a keener rival ('new blood'); that keener rival eventually failing, Stephens confides in Allen, fake-chummy, 'I think we really ought to let him go.'

Alan Bennett's uniqueness is to make a poetry out of the banal; a comedy out of the boringly trite. Litanies of street names and mentions of Coventry or Croydon win laughs. The trick is to have an ear for the commonplace and render it blissful by altering – and confusing – context. Offices are Bennett's Babels, where we are made to eavesdrop on the insider talk of appalling strangers; and with precise meanings unknown, sentences become abstracted and seem a chatty, endlessly silly symphony. In *One Fine Day* the gnomic utterances are Stephens's: for example 'Colchester, really . . . I once had a Chinese meal there,' or 'Do you have Tolstoy in Japan?'

Offices are arenas for codes and competition, rivalry and jargon; selling air-conditioned space, the businessmen in *One Fine Day* are literally battling over a market of blankness; merchants of a void. Insubstantiality was heightened by the references to glass: shiny glass on picture frames; picture windows and glass doors at work and home; ostentatious sunglasses; car windows; the glass offices – Allen's recovery from his nervous collapse is signalled when he erroneously gets himself locked on a roof, and he escapes by breaking his way through a huge window, with the aid of a window-cleaning elevator.

Crashing through the casement, he's Alice coming out of the mirror; and he encounters Stephens, a cynical King of Hearts, showing a gaggle of bespectacled Japanese the view from the rotting property: 'London, gentlemen, flower of cities all', and of a glass structure, 'The Ally Pally, where Queen Alexandra used to live.' A performance of droll facetiousness; a man inwardly dilapidated by the profit and the loss.

In *Fortunes of War*, Stephens was William Castlebar, a poetaster whom the Pringles find in the Levant, fond of whisky, fallen women and tobacco; a mashed-up Marlowe, who keeps a bucket of cold water by his bed, into which he thrusts his forearm during fornication, shocking away premature ejaculation. He takes over in the Egyptian episodes the role of raffish soak, played in the Balkan segments by Ronald Pickup's emaciated Prince Yakimov – whose moth-eaten fur coat was the very symbol of dispossessed aristocracy.

Slumped and fatigued, tieless and wearing a rumpled cream suit, Stephens's Castlebar is beady and louche; a man of letters whose contributions to conversation consist of 'definitely', 'bollocks' and 'yes' – each word pulled sluggishly from a diaphragm long lost in his paunch. He exists in the period opulence of putrefying grand hotels (where Alan Bennett, as Lord Pinkrose, is to be found up at the bar having a drink), casting an eye over the subalterns and the emotionally wounded – mainly Angela Hooper, who keeps him in Scotch and silk shirts. His dramatic function is to bring Harriet back from the dead – ferrying her to Guy, who has to work out his contrition like Leontes.

Driving Harriet from Cairo to Alexandria, where Guy is teaching *Finnegans Wake* for the British Council (the comedy of *Fortunes of War* concerns the way civilities and cultural niceties keep going inches behind the lines, deaths and beatings are irks interrupting vagrant senior common-room life), Stephens, with a small hat pulled over his ears, and in close-up, looked alarmingly like Buster Keaton in Beckett's *Film* – his face made up of heavy interjointed planes with the odd striation; but in place of Keaton's alabaster complexion, pure raspberry ripple: 'The soft, swollen look of decay,' in Olivia Manning's phrase; and he had a spectacular last exit, writhing and screaming with agony in an iron bed, babbling of green fields. Folk think he has a comic dyspepsia, from whisky and shellfish ('Get thee behind me, Crustacean'), but actually, it's a perforated bowel . . .

And he was a refugee again in Spielberg's latest agglutination of bicycles, sunbursts, flying, the spirit of adventure, sacrifice, courage, mothers and rites of passage – *Empire of the Sun*. Stephens is Lockwood, one of the expatriates hanging on to a pampered existence in the Shanghai of 1937. Dressed for a costume ball, the British snake in their Packards through mobs of fleeing, panicking Chinese. Tethered chickens and hunks of meat slap at the windows. Crowd, sky, autos are all black and grey; colour comes only from the fancy dress inside the vehicles – people with wigs and painted faces, silk and dyed feathers: they're as French aristocrats trapped in their carriages during the outbreak of the Revolution. The queue of limousines is a funeral cortège. And Stephens is amongst the damned as Santa Claus. He has only a few very brief scenes, mostly close-ups of his face – and what a face. In a squishy white periwig, red cloak trimmed with cotton wool, he looms into view, his face heavy, lumpen, wide-pored – as if flayed into patches and blotches of pinks and puce, with rivulets of scarlet. A face like the dark side of some terrible planet momentarily catching the light; a brindle face.

Back at the pub at the end of Stephens's street, the plooky punk, his earring, his moll, looked unimpressed. Who, they must have been thinking – surveying a manganous man in a grey jerkin, dandling a gold cigarette lighter, and me – who are these pub chatterers? I'd asked the actor when he began acting.

'When I was very small, I started out wanting to do Punch and Judy. So my father, who was a master builder, carved the puppets for me. I did [Stephens put on a squeaky voice] *Beat the baby* and *That's the way to do it*. Now,' he paused grandly, 'I'm the puppet – but no strings.'

'Do directors impose limits; provide strings?'

'Not any more. The curious thing about directors is that some of them can be the most nasty bullies. People *can* be broken by them – though, in fact, you should never allow yourself to be broken by anybody, really. I employed a famous West End director. He was horrible to two very young American actors in a Noël Coward play. I met him one Sunday.

' "Listen, I've known you since 1957, and it upsets me when I hear people say what an awful shit you are."

' "What, what, what do you mean?" he stammered, all speechless and innocent. "I get nervous," he said, "and have to kick somebody."

' "Kick your dog, or kick the doorpost, but never kick an actor, because you walk off after the first night with three and a half per cent of the gross, and we have to play it, and the actors will always think that they are no good. If you say, 'You can't speak properly,' or 'You can't move properly' – they'll think that as they walk on stage. If they are no good, the fault is not in the actors: it is your fault, because you cast them. Kick yourself in the arse and don't kick those two poor people. Or fire them; get somebody else."

'If I walk on the stage with a nervous actor, I'm afraid he'll have a heart attack or fall down dead. So I get nervous, and I'm playing the leading part in this play.'

'If a director's temper can upset the wellbeing of a company, spoil composure, what about the critics?' I queried.

'I love the critics. It is bullshit when actors say they don't read their notices. They go to the lavatory on a Sunday morning, shut the door and read avidly. If the review was bad, they cry their eyes out. If it is good, they chortle knowingly. You have to think that with critics, and I have had some bad notices, you have finally to think, however upset you may be, you have to think: perhaps they are right. It is their profession to go to the theatre, it is their business. I love the critics, even the ones who have crippled me, because: you are a critic; you are criticizing me; from your criticism, therefore, I may improve myself. They are the judges. They must be married to the theatre, otherwise they wouldn't do it. They stop the actor from thinking he's king of the world. If they weren't married to the stage, they'd do something else, like run restaurants.'

'What about Kenneth Tynan, the critic as performer?'

'What Kenneth wanted to be was a director. He began as a director in Oxford. Then he became a critic. He wanted to direct Laurence Olivier as King Lear, and he wanted me to play Edgar. He also wrote a film called *Alex and Sophie*; the writing was very good. It concerned two girls walking in the South of France. They flag down a man in a Mercedes.

' "Get in. Where are you going?"

' "To Nice."

'They speak French; suddenly the man says, "Why don't we speak English? I know who you are, and what you are, and what you're up to." They are drug pedlars, these two girls.

' "You have two choices. I can put you out now, in which case you'll be picked up by the police, because it's on the radio that they're trying to nobble you. Or, you can come to my château and stay for three months; I'll put some money into a Swiss bank for you. In three months, the authorities will have forgotten all about you – and off you go. But: you have to do exactly what I tell you to do during the three months."

'So you can imagine all kinds of up-t'do and nonsense.'

' "What do you think of the script," Ken asked.

' "It is very well written, but if you want to make a pornographic picture, the best director would be Alfred Hitchcock. Because you'd never see anything." The sexual element in Hitchcock is in the audience's imagination – and much more lurid and brilliant than anything demonstrative and shown; each member of the audience thinks a different thing. "Well, she takes her up to the thing and opens her legs . . ." CUT. "I bet she's going to put . . ." CUT. In the theatre or in films, the imagination of the audience must be flattered. Explicitness is boring.'

'Boring because there's nothing left for the fancy to do,' I said.

'Nothing at all. It's like the film with Tony Perkins. You see the black water go down the plughole, and you know what has happened.'

'And lots of curtain hooks spring off.'

'Yes. That's artful. However, Tynan's film never got made. But, he did finally go to the Mafia for money.'

Stephens assumed a Godfather-Brando voice.

'I went to his house in Kensington, and this was a pathetic joke, really. I can say this because he's dead now and it doesn't matter. I went to meet the two girls and this man, who was from the Mafia. We were talking about doing a film; in all seriousness, about a motion picture.

' "The woman I'd like to have play your wife is a German actress, Romy Schneider. Now, do you think" – and I couldn't believe I was hearing this – "do you think that Miss Schneider would mind having her anus licked?"

' "Why should she? It's not her tongue. You can get a double, or you can make a plastic one."

'We were talking serious business. I went to the bathroom. Shut the door. Locked it. And I laughed my head off. If we'd been talking about whether to make *Casablanca* or *The Maltese Falcon* or *The Godfather* . . . To talk about having someone's arse licked. Well, pathetic. He was very peculiar in that way. But I never liked him. I knew him and I admired him, but I didn't like him. Too devious. But he was very clever as a critic. I once said to Larry – odd, the relationship he and Tynan had – that I'd been reading the Agate books. "Agate was a monster, a pig, he was ghastly. Kenneth is much better," said Olivier. "I've read a lot of reviews by Ken Tynan about you which were hardly flattering," I thought.

'When Larry played Romeo, with Johnny Gielgud as Mercutio, Agate said, "Mr Olivier does not speak Shakespeare's verse badly. He does not speak it at all." But he came back to see it again, to check and make sure. That was professional. I love all the critics. I love Irving Wardle, though overnight reviewing is impossible. How can you form a judgment in ten minutes?

'Bill Bryden asked me to take over from Paul Scofield when *A Mid-summer Night's Dream* shifted from the Cottesloe to the Lyttelton. Jack Tinker of the *Daily Mail* had given the play a rotten review – so I was taking over. "I know a bank where the wild thyme blows," all that stuff. So I met Jack Tinker in Soho in the street. He is about four foot nothing high. I love him. I once gave him a jacket of mine. You've got to love people: they're only doing their job as I'm doing mine. "Listen, you," I said, "I know you gave that play a rotten review, *A Midsummer Night's Dream*, but I'm taking over from Paul, and I want a good review from you, otherwise I'll come to Fleet Street and cut your head off." "*Absolutely!*" he stammered.

'So we had the opening night at the Lyttelton, and I see Jack Tinker in the bar. "Are you going to give me a good review, or not?" "*Absolutely*! I'm going to say you are the dangerous and fascinating Robert Stephens as Oberon, King of the Fairies." I said, "That's good. I like that."

'There was another critic, however, who gave me the most lacerating notices for everything I did, called J. W. Lambert, who was second-string to Harold Hobson. When I did *The Royal Hunt of the Sun* I had fantastic reviews from everyone, except from J. W. Lambert, who said, "Despite the fact that my peers have said this is a dazzling performance, despite the fact that this is a remarkable achievement, I didn't like it." Everything I did was the same. I couldn't move without this monkey on my back.'

GLASSES PLEASE. FINISH UP PRETTY SHARP THANK YOU. HURRY UP PLEASE, IT'S TIME.

'Finally I did *The Seagull* at Chichester, and he gave me a fantastic review for it. I met him at RADA, some function they had. "Thank you so much for your wonderful review," I said. So, then we were friends. J. W. Lambert once said in a review of a John Osborne play [*A Bond Honoured*], "Mr Stephens has not the vocal ability to play the parts that he is given." I thought, he's right. I went to the voice teacher at the National and I said, "Teach me how to speak better," which she did. To me, the critics are as important to the theatre as any actor, designer, director; and though they may be hated, I don't hate them. They come to see me, I listen – just as I'd listen to a teacher of mathematics correcting my arithmetic. If they say my Vanya is a piece of junk, I will listen. I know many of them; they are interested in me. We have a relationship. Like you are interested in me to be writing about me. We have a relationship. I love the critics. Fools ignore them because they don't want to know about themselves.'

COME ON GENTLEMEN. IT'S WAY AFTER TIME THANK YOU.

'Ssssssshhhh!' hissed Stephens to the tapster. 'To me, in life, there is no actor in the world who can play Hamlet. The part is so complex. All you do is play an opinion of Hamlet: the Melancholy Dane, all kinds of ways. You'll never get it right.'

'Any performance an actor gives is a critical interpretation of the text. The artist is a critic? Or he's a critical artist?' I asked.

'He can only ever act an opinion. When I did *Private Lives* with Maggie, I said to John Gielgud, "I cannot play it like Noël Coward: very large, very expansive; I can only play it like myself – otherwise the play is no good, for it will only ever require Noël Coward in person or Noël Coward impersonations." "Fine," said Gielgud, "Just play it like Robert, and play it on your own personality. Don't step out of yourself. Just play it like you and Maggie." Which we did, and it was a great success.'

As a record of Bob and Maggie creating we have *The Prime of Miss Jean Brodie*, Ronald Neame's 1969 film adaptation of the Muriel Spark pedagogical whimsy. Maggie Smith won an Oscar for her strenuous eccentric: Miss Brodie, her long limbs cracking and slapping like a mad ibis's, dressed in chiffon scarves and orange capes, whooping the hymns at assembly and gliding about the dowdy Edinburgh school as a revuesketch version of Vanessa Redgrave's Isadora Duncan. Where did this creature come from? Miss Brodie teaches her class of pert lasses about Giotto; she waxes lyrical about Italy's 'sun and water'; she speaks with admiration of Mussolini – a chivalric hero to her, a romantic, like her lost loves of Flanders Field (the class weep at her dramatization of Rupert Brooke's expiry). Muriel Spark's Miss Brodie is an invention of the Nineties, a thing of Beardsley's madly set down in a Scottish conservatoire. A delicious decadent, talking of 'goodness, truth and beauty' like any disciple of Oscar Wilde's Society for the Suppression of Virtue.

Maggie Smith gave Jean Brodie a different tone and provenance. With her twangy approximation of a Scots accent, quivering and shaking, the film opted for caricature; there was no sense of Miss Brodie's dangerousness, her seditiousness – though the pupils talk of it, for plot purposes. And, at the end, when Miss Brodie is confounded by a favourite, who accuses her mentor of being a destroyer, an autocrat . . . All this is a hangover from Spark, whose heroine is Athene, goddess of war. She thinks herself irreproachable – and that's how she perverts her teaching. But it was lost on Smith's Miss Brodie, whose only danger and sedition was stupidity. Smith, her voice a voice-over from a cartoon, was a vamp out of Disney, at best, or the sort of daffy female essayed in dumpier fashion by Angela Lansbury, at worst.

Only in the scenes with Stephens was the film lifted out of lazy jokiness. He played Mr Lloyd, the art master, giving lessons on the curve in painting ('a beckoning line'), pandering to the pubertal girls' fascination with their own budding mammiferousness. One girl is given a long kiss: 'That'll teach you to look at an artist like that!' He's a metaphysician of the sinuous, and in her dialogue with him, Miss Brodie, too, was sinuous instead of shrieky; Smith relaxed into the part, instead of playing a detailed, mocking commentary on it. Mr Lloyd and Miss Brodie are former lovers, and their moments of snatched kisses and rekindled passion are given substance; we really do believe in the foretime of their relationship, making sense of a tendency to recite D. H. Lawrence, Keats and Tennyson's 'The Lady of Shalott' ('Or when the moon was overhead, / Came two lovers lately wed; / "I am half sick of shadows," said / The Lady of Shalott.'); making sense, too, of Miss Brodie's predilection for Mussolini as 'a man of action'. She's a Romantic, but erotically so, not sentimentally. Mr Lloyd, as an artist, is her Bohemian satyr. Smith, with Stephens, did vibrate into life (painting is Miss Brodie's 'vibration of life'), and became, as her character puts it, Cleopatra and Anna Pavlova; a capacity for real arousal under the cool aesthetic lecturing.

The Smith and Stephens relationship filled the film with its only emotional intimacy – a memory of a paradise lost, in some studio attic. Artist and model, like Picasso. With Stephens, Smith left off her twitches and the embers of Miss Brodie's passion took on a glow. Vivaciousness was hinted, under the schoolmarm's code of integrity and restraint: it's sex which underpins her longing for the warm Mediterranean. She tries to be a perfect goddess to her girls – but Mr Lloyd's seen through her fantasy of displacement. His mockery of her prim sense of being in her 'prime' was a cruel and accurate exposure of feeling; we watch wondering how much actor and actress were acting, as they slap one another around. Familiarity is intense – and intensified owing to the low temperature of the rest of the film. Stephens and Smith play out their legend. Lloyd calls himself 'a second-rate painter running to seed', and his old flame 'a frustrated spinster taking it out in idiot causes and dangerous ideas'.

The dangerous ideas, of course, we don't get any sense of; but with Stephens, Smith could be inspired to enact them. One scene, a flustered argument in the garden, during the school dance (the girls waltzing with each other, in regulation shrouds and boots), is infused with tremendous anger. Lloyd says he wants to hurt and humiliate Miss Brodie into exchanging her sensibility for sense: 'Look at yourself, Jean!' He says how they are both growing old, and resenting it.

The Prime of Miss Jean Brodie is about denial and loneliness; the film, instead, tries to be Ronald Searle's St Trinians, and the Oscar laureate is entirely Alastair Sim in drag, except where Stephens provokes her into a performance. Stephens is fine as the inspirer of abandonment, highly sexed and foxily grinning. He even manages to make Smith's Brodie less pathetic when she weeps at the memory of Dante and Beatrice: agitated, she wants Lloyd to be a new Dante Gabriel Rossetti, and we appreciate the sad frailty of her idealizing, and the banked-down power of her lusts and juices. We appreciate all this *through* Stephens.

The prime, prolonged, becomes old age and decay; Stephens's Lloyd awaits decadence, speeding it along, indeed, with nympholepsy. He beds Sandy (Pamela Franklin as Miss Brodie's treacherous favourite), who sprawls on his divan, nude. For a second, Stephens is Humbert Humbert. And that's his gift: the acting of louche libertinism; a capacity for weary lechery or the suggestiveness of perversion. Maggie Smith has never had another partner to draw her away from coquetry into real strength of feeling. (When she won another Oscar, for *California Suite*, it was for playing a parody of herself: an English Actress at the Academy Award ceremony, with Michael Caine her homosexual consort. They bicker, but there's no life. Neil Simon's wisecracks instead give an illusion of liveliness.) And perhaps Stephens has never had another partner so responsive to his variety of rebarbativeness. Instead, when he acts he hardly *reacts* at all. But this devil-may-care attitude (*Lizzie's Pictures*, Herod in *The Mysteries*, the squire in *Comrades*, Konstantinis the smuggler in *High Season*, for example) gives his performances a sleazy energy and menace. He's administering extreme unction to his former self as romantic lead, and has entered upon a course of destructive, baleful character parts, parts exulting in disease and dissipation, and for the audience it's like witnessing a long and thrilling suicide.

COME ON FUCK OFF OUT. IN POLISH. FUCKOVSKI!

'Fuckovski'? said Stephens, savouring, to see if he knew the word. He continued, in the street: 'If you have to play Tamburlaine the Great, you have to be somebody else. You can't possibly be yourself. If you play, as I've just done, a Welsh barber, you do it Welshie and all the rest of it, boyo bach; if I play Raffles the amateur cracksman, I'm not Raffles but voices and acted versions of me.'

The Welsh barber was for a TV play called *Window, Sir*. A tale of the unexpected, it was an opportunity for the deadly charm of Iago, for sweet-natured villainy. Vince (Stephens), overbearing, and Perry (John Cater), underbearing, have shared the same tonsorial studio since 1952. The play was a study of provincial claustrophobia, set entirely in a poky cell of yellow peeling paint comprising three chairs, mottled mirrors, a selection of plastic combs and sinks clogged with teabags. A room with no view.

Both men have a suppressed hatred one for the other; they've worked alongside, gradually loathing, never letting on – like an entrenched marriage. The relationship was explored with considerable skill, given the straightforward weekend–thriller slot the programme was filling. Two lonely, defeated prinkers; the exquisite monotony of rinsing, shampooing and snipping the wheezing South Welsh swinking.

Stephens began with a succession of last exits – as Perry dreamed about stabbing, garrotting, bludgeoning him. Then Vince neatly electrocuted his partner for real, by tossing the buzzing clippers into the suds.

Vince was played with more attentiveness than almost seemed necessary: the accent of the valleys accurately mellifluous, making the dull words sound like a phrase from Dylan Thomas; over-accurate, perhaps, just occasionally straying back to posh National Theatre English, so we appreciated how it had been researched. A flickering, bloated, pustular face, capable of secrecy, smiles, snakiness. We believed totally in the dapper logic of Perry's removal – how it was even altruistic, given the poor man's poor prospects, his sole pleasure solitary perusal of the pneumatic beauties in the wank mags.

Vince, with Norman Mailer curls, rose tattoo on forearm, the tiniest bit fey with the customers, super-polite; supersubtle: the Ensign in search of the Moor.

What versions of himself was Stephens playing during our valediction? First, a general inspecting a gentleman-ranker. He stood up straight, briskly neatened my lapels and epaulettes. This performance melted into that of a solicitous mother, knotting her little boy's scarf and fussing with his buckles before he goes off to school. He topped the act by giving me a large slobbery smacker on the lips. And what I thought was this: here was a man who was the best Holmes since Rathbone, and much else besides; who had awesome gravitas and instinct; who has pondered the uniqueness of the relationship with Watson (and with the critics, with directors ...) – and who has, in the last decade or so, transformed himself into Watson, the portly chronicler of somebody else's illustrious past. Holmes had become Watson; Hamlet had become Falstaff: 'In Falstaff there is something of Hamlet,' wrote Wilde, 'in Hamlet there is not a little of Falstaff. The fat knight has his moods of melancholy, and the young prince his moments of coarse humour.' They differ only in accidentals. The rest is destiny.

THREE

The Garrick Grandee:
Ian Richardson

Close your eyes, and Robert Stephens in conversation becomes a crowd; a vaudeville of indiscreet mimicry and recollected repartee. For Ian Richardson, however, talk is less a chattering turn than a fluted oratorio. He sings his sentences, his voice swooping from a bellow to a whisper, from a hoot to a silence – occasionally phrases being mouthed rather than spoken, so that the effect is of Dame Edith Sitwell (whom the actor resembles) doing an impression of a Les Dawson landlady. Richardson's voice is his instrument; he is conscious of it and proud of it; he plays upon it and with it. Conversation is punctuated with recitatives and orchestral interludes. He builds to exciting crescendos; he falls to tiny diminuendos. He can draw out a single word into an alarming stutter of syllables, like a libretto fragmented and reproduced under the stave; he'll then speed ahead, putting a girdle around a paragraph in four seconds. It's significant that when Richardson played Henry Higgins, he did so in *My Fair Lady*, rather than *Pygmalion*; his Oberon for Peter Hall in 1962 was reproduced by James Bowman, the counter-tenor, in Hall's 1981 production of Britten's *A Midsummer Night's Dream* at Glyndebourne. The King of the Fairies, at Stratford and in Sussex, was an Elizabethan grandee in doublet and spangled ruff, policing a house suffused with tawny light and memories of Gloriana – like Hatfield House or Osterley Park.

Richardson is a musical man. Besides looking like Dame Edith reciting *Façade*, he might also be said to have the profile of a viola. The trills and cadenzas of speech break out in his physical manner, which inclines to the flamboyant. I tried to be his conductor, our eyes locked – Stokowski bringing up the dawn in *Fantasia*; and when I did speak, my voice broke in like a piccolo.

We met at the Garrick, a time-capsule off Covent Garden. The place was sprinkled with somnolent actors who've spent their careers playing somnolent fogeys in gentlemen's clubs. Raymond Huntley, or perhaps his shade, frowned over *The Times*, a task he performed in every British film ever made. And indeed the Garrick is full of ghosts, its atmosphere laden like a pharaoh's tomb. Richardson showed me glass cabinets containing Fanny Kemble's pantyhose; and though Alec McCowen's doctor may have given him the poster from the Bradford show during which Henry Irving died, I perched momentarily on the chair Henry Irving fell off, dead. The walls are heavy with Zoffanys; the fauteuils are of bright red leather, like the slippy seats in the Magdalen Senior Common Room. Ornate clocks tick; coughs come from empty rooms; servants silently pad. A den for drones! A station for Silurians!

I'd arrived early, but Richardson had arrived earlier. He'd checked with the secretary the propriety of earnest shop-talking; exclusive clubs are fussy about regulations – the point being to try and replicate an aristocratic drawing room, terrorizing the inmates with the complexities of etiquette. So Richardson had wanted to make certain that discussing himself was not bad form ('I wanted to reacquaint myself with the rules'). He'd also pre-selected the sofas to be sat at, our position in the vast chamber overlooking the street. A folded screen, covered with cameos and miniatures, protected us from prying eyes.

What all this represented was an intent and assiduous man; he was most meticulous as a host, taking infinite pains. What all this also signified was a man fearful of breaking the code, anxious not to humiliate himself with potential blackballing or ostracism. He was making sure he fits in. Even after thirty years as a leading classical actor, under the clarion enunciation, the Savile Row tailoring, there's an impression remaining of the son of an Edinburgh baker; a boy whose father baked the special cakes for the royals at Holyrood. Richardson's the lad who now looks a laird, his precise diction the residue of what once kept a Waverley Station burr at bay.

'You change your accent, even unconsciously, and people sneer that you've got above yourself in some way,' said Richardson. ' "Oh, he doesn't think we're good enough for him anymore." I once went to a pub with my father and ordered two whiskies in a perfectly normal way. The barman looked at me with contempt and said to my father, "Och, how can you *let* your boy talk like that." '

'Did your parents object to your being an actor?' I asked.

'They were unsure about it all. It did cause a fuss when I first announced my career ambitions. Eventually my father said, "I'll fund you for a year and then see what happens." I went to Glasgow Drama School. For part of the course I had to attend university lectures by Peter Alexander. I remember being called upon to recite from *Macbeth*. And at the end of the session, the professor plucked me by the sleeve and said, "Be an actor! That's what you are!" Just before my father's trial twelve months was up, we put on *The Importance of Being Earnest*. What my father was to think of my Jack Worthing was crucial. I awaited judgement. "Aye," he said, "you've chosen the right profession." So I owe Oscar everything.'

Richardson's account of his early days is a folk-tale; a heroic rise and rise.

'After Glasgow, I went to the Birmingham Repertory Theatre, run by Barry Jackson. My mother insisted that my father drive me down and see me settled. We went for a trip in the Cotswolds, inevitably to Stratford. Stratford-upon-Avon! And as we gazed at the Memorial Theatre, I said "I'll be here one day, Dad, and you'll be proud of me." And I did get there, and he was pleased.'

Richardson twinkled, knowing full well he'd made his career seem as happy as an operetta. He continued, Der Zigeunerbaron:

'After a little while at the Birmingham Rep, Peter Hall invited me to Stratford for the 1960 season. Quite soon, I was playing the leading roles. After a while, I grew complacent with my own success; I left and did some television plays. *Eyeless in Gaza*, one of the first things I did, was, again, most successful. I went to New York and played Higgins in *My Fair Lady*. Another long-running success. Ambition after ambition was being fulfilled – except in films. I made two and they were disasters. Film I have yet to conquer.'

Stains on the escutcheon were *The Darwin Adventure*, praised by one critic★ as containing 'a cast of hard-working, undistinguished minor British players'; and *Man of La Mancha*, in which Peter O'Toole warbled his way through the life of Quixote.

'Yes, I am full of ambition for film. Ambition is most important for an actor. Ruthlessness can be channelled into certain roles – and it stretches you. Having played many leading classical parts, I found my performances falling off. The ambition can't be sustained.'

'Is that because you were a young man in a hurry?'

'I don't know – though being a success when you're young can destroy a career, I've seen it happen . . .' And he mentioned an actor who in the Sixties was lauded as *the* representative of his era; you'll see him now serving time in spoof or arty horror films and turning up in lanky character parts.

Ambition, its uses and abuses, seemed to worry Richardson – urgent aspiration in himself (he justifies the pursuit of excellence by veering between modesty and likeable crowing), and in others. He recounted an experience, which obviously still rankles, when he was discussing, in the Garrick, the three roles he most wanted to play. A quiet guest, who merely nodded amiably, and who was also an actor, within eighteen months had arranged for himself to play those same three roles. Richardson also told the revealing tale of Olivier and Gielgud, going to see *Look Back in Anger* and not particularly enjoying it. Next morning, Olivier is on the telephone to the Royal Court, begging for the bespoke drama which became *The Entertainer*.

★ Elkan Allan.

Rampant ambition Richardson finds offensive. He is neither sly nor covert: he is an innocent; and he is ironic about his own innocence, canny enough to be able to discriminate between normal careeristic self-advancement and the nobler ambition which aims at artistic flawlessness. Afraid that the latter will sound hubristic and corny, he pretends to fuss about the former. A perfectionist camouflaged as an egoist.

'Are you saying that you were put in the forefront at Stratford, without almost wanting to be? Success came too easily?'

'Well, it didn't happen *too* quickly.'

Having had the allegro overture of highlights, we were now settling for a more expository andante narrative.

'I never walked-on or carried a spear. I was lucky. When I went to Stratford first, it was to play roles of the stature of the Prince of Aragon in *Merchant of Venice* or Thurio in *Two Gentlemen of Verona*. At the end of the year we lined up outside Peter Hall's office, and went in for our master-pupil report. "I've stretched you too quickly too soon," he said, referring to the fact he'd cast me as Sir Andrew Aguecheek, the actor originally cast having dropped out; so I'd taken over at short notice and *of course* I wasn't ready for it. And why wasn't I ready for it? Well, let me tell you: having come from the Birmingham Repertory Theatre, I'd been used to studying a role for short bursts of time: like three weeks! I'd rehearse for three weeks; I'd perform for three weeks. I'd only ever needed to excavate a character sufficient to sustain three weeks of work. After three months in *Twelfth Night*, I'd used up all my inspiration – inspiration forthcoming from very superficial research into the role. I had nothing left – and my performances did tend to fall off. "You have a choice," said Peter. "Either you stay on with us, and you sign a three-year contract, but you play parts according to my decision ..." In other words, he was saying, take a backward step, play smaller roles, and I will promote you when you are ready. "Or," Hall went on, "you go away to the provinces, play in rep, and come back again later."

'I knew that if I left and went back to the provinces, I'd never be back. So I decided to eat humble pie. And, indeed, in 1961, I played Catesby in *Richard III*, Seyton in *Macbeth* – that kind of thing ... At the end of that year – and this was what was so wonderful working with the young Peter Hall; I don't know what he's like now – he remembered and kept his promises. There we all were, lined up again for our interviews. "You've lived up to my expectations," he said, "I'm going to promote you next season. I want you to play Oberon in *A Midsummer Night's Dream*; Edmund in *King Lear* ..." And suddenly it began to happen. The star roles, however, like Coriolanus, Prospero, Richard II, Angelo – these didn't actually come until the late 1960s, early 1970s. By then Peter had left. A new regime had taken over; its members were even younger than Peter had been himself at the time of his induction. And with this new, young regime came the advent of the director's theatre, where the actors were used as Haig used soldiers on the Somme: ego-fodder. Now I got rather irritated by that. I hate so deeply having to subordinate my own artistic inclinations to the greater glory of a director whose intention is to make a name for himself as an innovator. I couldn't be a part of that; I couldn't see the point of that – particularly when it came to my playing Richard III, in 1975. Richard III: he's God's gift to the actor. All a director need do is mount it colourfully, cast it carefully with a leading actor, and with suitably strong support. But the director, inserted his own peculiar interpretation which didn't fit, and we had reviews which said, in effect: "What a wonderful cast, and how dare this director abuse them." I grew rather tired; I grew rather bored with that.'

Richardson threw himself back into his chair; a *grand guignol* of defeat and resignation.

'What director did you prefer?' I inquired.

'John Barton. Without question,' said the actor, instantly reanimated. 'Without a question one of the finest exponents of Shakespearean theatre in Europe. A really great man and, sadly, not recognized as such. We had a long and happy time at Stratford. I did my best work, my most important work, for John.'

The confederacy came to bear upon *Coriolanus* and *All's Well That Ends Well* (1967) – Richardson playing a supercilious and spoilt Bertram, pernickety in his removal of confetti from his suit at the wedding; *Measure for Measure* (1970) – Angelo, the 'man, proud man' crackling with a desire for Isabella he daren't articulate; Prospero in *The Tempest* (1970); and *Richard II* (1973).

'Whilst all his contemporaries have gone on to do other things, and have become millionaires, John remains a scholar. He was the Cambridge don; I was the theatrical animal. We had a marriage of true minds. A marriage, in production, of the theatrical animal, who knew, by instinct, how to make a play visually, dramatically – hammily, if you like – come alive; with a director who had an intellectual knowledge of the text to be imparted. It was the happiest marriage in the world. And we brought life to the most astonishing things. My happiest time. My most successful time.'

'What was your favourite role?'

'My favourite Shakespearean role was Berowne – but directed by David Jones, not by Barton. But there are side-issues to that. I played him when I was already in my late thirties; I was already much too old. I knew it was the last time I would play a young man. Also, Berowne is the role Shakespeare wrote for himself; it is his self-image. And it was a kind of fitting tribute: a fitting tribute to my love of Shakespeare, that I should play Berowne in *Love's Labour's Lost.*'

'Shakespeare's self-image?'

'His cronies, Will Shakespeare's cronies, said to him, "Come on Will, it is about time you wrote yourself a decent part." So he wrote Berowne for himself. I remember on the first night, having had, to use a maternal term, trouble conceiving the character – he was the most difficult baby I ever had – I remember, before the first night, after morning rehearsals, walking – it was a beautiful day – walking up Riverside to Holy Trinity church. Nobody in the church, so I strolled to the tomb, Shakespeare's tomb, and ignoring the idiotic bust, I stood with my boots across the slab...'

'And did a tap dance?'

'No, I did not. I was astride,' Richardson paused for the upshot '... like a Colossus, and I made a prayer: "Look, you are supposed to have written this part for yourself. I'd appreciate it if you'd help me tonight if you don't mind, because I don't know where I'm going."

'Now I'm not a superstitious person, but a curious thing happened. I said my first line ("I can but say their protestation over"), and the audience laughed. "Ah," I thought, "Will's with me."'

'Where there's a will...'

'We went on from there – and the spell worked; and it was my biggest success, believe it or not, my Berowne. It went to the Aldwych, obviously, as the best things did. Then it went to America – which led, indirectly, to my playing Henry Higgins on Broadway.'

Navarre's academe is avowedly a place without women; a cloistered and studious haven, instantly invaded by the Princess of France and her retinue. Book-learning retires before romance – the world must be peopled.

> So study evermore is overshot.
> While it doth study to have what it would,
> It doth forget to do the thing it should;
> And when it hath the thing it hunteth most,
> 'Tis won as towns with fire – so won, so lost.

Pygmalion is also about misogyny, trounced. Higgins, the vain gentleman-philologist, for a wager, decides to turn a slattern into a society hostess; to alter a girl's way of speaking so that she alters her way of thinking. The voice is the agent of social rise and fall. Eliza Doolittle, however, is her manipulator's match in guile, and their rude and cruel banter comes to hint at love: Eliza teases Higgins as Rosaline does Berowne – both women teach their men the folly of an emotional anorexy.

Richardson has a talent for being both petulant and in flight from his petulance, and at the same time. Shaw's original play concerns power and its comic belittlement: the thawing of Higgins the phonological Holmes.

My Fair Lady ends with Higgins demanding his slippers: romance looks as though it has dwindled into boring marriage. Whether, however, Eliza is meek, or whether she flings the footwear, or whether she flings abuse, we don't know; the curtain falls. *Pygmalion* is about a sexual battle; *My Fair Lady* is a period fashion show and parlour burlesque; *Pygmalion* is political, *My Fair Lady* sartorial. Richardson's personal triumph was to play the execrable Lerner and Loewe musical as if it retained the puissance of Shaw's intentions.

Not that Shaw is an inviolable talent. David Jones, film director of Pinter's *Betrayal* and Hanff's *84 Charing Cross Road*, was the perpetrator of *The Devil's Disciple* for television, with plastic leaves and flat, shadowless lighting. Shaw's dialogue ('Silence your blasphemous tongue!') suggests that he never listened to the shape of real speech – and, of course, Higgins in *Pygmalion* would forcibly convert all dialect into his own flat patter. Richardson was Gentleman Johnny Burgoyne, in toy-soldier rig with gold buttons and white periwig. He had a querulous catch to his voice, edged with sarcasm; and 'dragoons' was a word apt to transfix. (He made a bel-canto aria out of it.) He was matched against Mike Gwilym's Dudgeon, a New Hampshire Macheath, dressed up in the BBC's idea of dissoluteness: oversize shirt, straggly hair, loose necktie and a swarthy complexion – the feral and libertine effect rather chastened when he's expected to say things like 'blithering baboon'. Shaw's sonic universe is a Never-Neverland of diction derived from early talkies.

'Shaw's idea of himself was as a linguist', said Richardson. 'He tried very hard to convince the British that the secret remedy to the curse of class-consciousness was the elimination of regional accents. So, if English is taught phonetically, we'd all end up speaking the same language – making the same sound – and there wouldn't be the feeling of "Cor, larks, yer a gent an' I ain't." A dream which couldn't possibly be realized.'

'If Shaw put his personal predilections into the life of his characters, what of Shakespeare (beyond Berowne)? And do actors know him better than scholars?'

'I once told A. L. Rowse that we, as actors, studying the text with only one object in mind – to bring it alive in performance – come closer to Shakespeare than any lonely scholar, secluded in his library. Because we, as actors, breathe life into the lines by speaking them; we bring a contemporary sensibility to their interpretation – and in so doing, we bring the ghost of Shakespeare, and Shakespeare's time, much closer to comprehension. And it is consequently easier for us, as actors, to touch his soul.'

'So acting is a rite of resurrection; you bid the dead to rise?'

'Yes. Also, Shakespeare and the actor are in cahoots because both are fantastic observers: Shakespeare by nature, the actor by virtue of professional demands. Both observe what people are like when they are drunk; or watch out for those betraying idiosyncrasies in speech and gesture; or notice different kinds of walks.

'I remember, apropos of that, when I was preparing Richard II, my youngest son was at the age when he'd play with a toy for as long as it interested him – then without looking, he'd drop it from his grasp, and move on to something new. I seized that. For my Richard, crown, orb, sceptre – they were toys, broken by civil strife and the Bolingbroke rebellion. Richard doesn't want to play anymore; he discards and loses everything, so that he ends up in the loneliness of the prison cell.

'Richard is never without an audience – whether it's the populace at large, or the courtiers, or his own face in the mirror. He is never entirely alone until you see him in gaol; he comes face to face with himself. And no toys to play with; just his soul confronting him, and what he's done. And I would never have arrived at that interpretation had I not, almost by accident, been observing my son at play.'

'Child's play and theatrical plays: your Oberon, sitting on the stairs like a naughty boy up late, was a prim Peter Pan – Puck your headstrong subordinate, like Tootles; and your Richard was a Peter Pan,' I said.

'A great parallel!' said Richardson con brio. 'The boy who never grew up ... At the end, the gaol was a deserted nursery. And suddenly you realize, too late, that this man could have been a great man, and a great king. The moment he achieves self-knowledge, and perceives where he erred, and he does grow up fast, it's too late. Sir Piers of Exton arrives and kills him.'

John Barton's production of Richard II, ingeniously theatrical, was about ingenious theatre: Richard as the player-king, a man imprisoned by his own sense of ceremony. Even in prison was he ceremonious, reasoning that, as king, he and the role of kingship formed an entity – despite the deposition revealing an actor not fully integrated into his part. As York says, having watched the eclipse by Bolingbroke, the new star:

> As in a theatre the eyes of men
> After a well-grac'd actor leaves the stage
> Are idly bent on him that enters next,
> Thinking his prattle to be tedious;
> Even so, or with much more contempt, men's eyes
> Did scowl on gentle Richard.

Barton's innovation was to have Richardson alternate the parts of the old and new kings with Richard Pasco. Richard II and Bolingbroke were seen as doubles – the play itself regarded as an essay in symmetry, its heroes:

> ... two buckets, filling one another;
> The emptier ever dancing in the air,
> The other down, unseen, and full of water.

Presentation of twinhood (Shakespeare is big with twins and linked contraries: the Antipholus and Dromio families in *The Comedy of Errors*; Viola and Sebastian in *Twelfth Night*; Caliban casting out Ariel; the battle of black poetry and white prose in *Othello*; good and evil brothers in *King Lear* and *As You Like It*; fair and foul equivocation in *Macbeth*) was stylized. The production commenced with a dumbshow: Pasco and Richardson formally assumed their particular role for the night, supervised by a mute Shakespeare, accoutred like the Holy Trinity effigy.

The set consisted of two ladders, joined by a platform which rose and fell, symbolizing the coming and going of destinies, the weights and measure of fate – like balancing pails. Speech was incantatory, movements ritualistic, props gamely artificial – such as the representation of horses as carnival skirts worn by the nobles.

Richardson's Richard was the plangent actor-monarch – deriving from the actor's own brand of naïve vanity – his scripts torn from him in mid-performance: the panic of a dry:

> What must the King do now? Must he submit?
> The King shall do it. Must he be depos'd?
> The King shall be contented. Must he lose
> The name of King?

'What, however of Bolingbroke?'

'That character,' said Richardson, 'I was less happy with. Dickie Pasco had played in a touring production which John Barton had once organized to convince the Arts Council its money was well spent. Therefore, when we started rehearsals, Dickie Pasco had, if you like, the advantage of me: we had the same director, in John Barton, and Dickie knew in advance what would be wanted of him. He knew the lines. He had an interpretation built-in – which had been tried out before paying audiences. I couldn't bear to face Bolingbroke and so concentrated on the King.

'Four days before the first preview, I had a *sort* of Bolingbroke; but it was my Richard I knew would dazzle – despite the fact that I knew I had to play both parts eventually, and equally. But I couldn't really find Bolingbroke at all. "Dickie, Dickie," I said, rushing into Pasco's dressing room, "tell me, tell me how you are playing Bolingbroke. I haven't a performance, and we meet the public any day." "I see him," he said slowly, "as a man much wronged." "Surely there's more to it than that?" I said. "I mean, what about ambition, which is something we as actors ought surely to understand? You know? There has to be *ambition*?"'

Having counterpointed the different tones of shrill monarch and dour usurper in his recounting of the dressing-room conversation, Richardson went on: 'Eventually I cobbled together musings about, believe it or not, Adolf Hitler's rise to power. You know, burning of the Reichstag, and for being imprisoned read banishment; release is to return from exile, somewhat illegally. The gathering barons, like Northumberland, are the gathering Reich supremos. None of this was apparent in my performance – it was merely the series of connections helping me to put the part together. I saw Bolingbroke as an absolute villain until Exton presents the body, when he's shocked into appreciating the extent of his actions.

'In *Henry IV* he's haunted with guilt. We imported speeches from the later plays, to give the character depth – his awakening conscience, such as:

> How many thousands of my poorest subjects
> Are at this hour asleep! O sleep, O gentle sleep
> Nature's soft nurse, how have I frighted thee . . .'

This speech, ending 'Uneasy lies the head that wears the crown', was lifted from *Henry IV Part II*, Act 3, scene i; and it was inserted into *Richard II* at the beginning of Act V, scene iii, where the unseen Hal's loose living is first intimated ('Can no man tell me of my unthrifty son?'). He's a roaring boy with Falstaff, waiting to appear in the next play and, ultimately, preparing to convert himself into Laurence Olivier and Henry V, now slumming it in the gutter as irresponsibly as Richard slums it in the stars.

'We looked forward to *Henry IV*, but unfortunately I've never played Henry IV,' said Richardson. 'The way he tries to expiate the killing of Richard, and still have God win him victory: I felt I was justified in viewing him as a dangerous adventurer and opportunist, when regarded from the perspective of what happens later.'

'Bolingbroke you researched; Richard came naturally?'

'Richard spewed up with ease from inside! A man supremely aware of his audience. I played the battlement scene as a leading actor, whispering to his dresser in asides. He looks down at the invaders:

> We are amaz'd; and thus long have we stood
> To watch the fearful bending of thy knee,
> Because we thought ourself thy lawful King . . .'

(After only the slightest false start, Richardson's memory brought back the lines: buried treasure, clarion comfort.)

'The speech is punctuated with the King's turning to Aumerle, as indeed the star completes his scene before the audience and comes to the wings – where the dresser awaits with water and a sponge to mop his perspiring brow. Refreshed, the actor sails back on stage. Richard turns back to Northumberland with –

> Tell Bolingbroke, for yon methinks he stands,
> That every stride he makes upon my land
> Is dangerous treason!'

(Richardson was well launched – that *treason*! shook the windows – and he'd have sung the entire play for me, plus running commentary.)

'My Richard was a Victorian heroic actor; he pleased the audience by making all the correct flatteries, highly dramatically; relishing being in public. And then the private agony off stage: the deposition, the crumbling, the farewell to his child-bride.'

'*Richard II*, like *Hamlet*, is a play within-a-play; or a player-within-a-player. Also, *A Midsummer Night's Dream*,' I said.

'You know, it was thanks to Oberon I learned to speak Shakespearean verse. English tends to be downward inflection. Listen to newscasters punching out headlines – they are doing the language such a disservice: "Today in parli*ament*," "The prime minister *said . . .*"'

(Richardson demonstrated a drop, a thud, a collapse, a little death, at the end of each phrase.)

'Shakespeare demands the opposite: the upward inflection. The Elizabethan dramatists were intoxicated with English sounds – they went in for verbal conceits and great long phrases, which only make sense if the actor is breathing his way through properly – if he is projecting with an upward inflection, which feels strange in the mouth – and yet, when you make the breakthrough, when you absorb it and make it a part of yourself, it is no longer an obstruction. *Au contraire*, it allows for a re-creation of a language fresh and thought-provoking. Previously I'd been saying:

> I know a bank where the wild thyme *blows*
> Where oxlips and the nodding violet *grows . . .*

'"Stop, stop, stop," cried Peter Hall, "it's all on the floor. Go to John Barton. Find him. He'll be in an office somewhere. Say to him, from me, 'Teach me how to speak Shakespearean verse.'" And I went to John, who in those days was an unkempt chainsmoking donnish sort. "Well, the problem with you," he said, "is your downward inflection. Keep it up, keep it *up*, keep it UP! Get on your toes vocally and physically." And so eventually I was saying . . .'

And Richardson, who'd remembered all this philharmonic flying, performed Oberon's aria; and it was almost as beautiful as Britten.

'Can you make use of your elocutionary gift now?' I wondered.

'The trouble, particularly in the film world, is that directors slouch up and drawl, "Sorry Ian, it sounds *just a little* like the road old Shakespeare goes." Americans are the worst. I played Sherlock Holmes in a couple of films for cable television, and the executive producer was worried about, would you believe, long words; so his worry filtered down to the director, who said, "Ian, could you think of another word rather than *expectation*, because nobody in the Middle West will know what that means."'

'Holmes, like Shakespeare and the actor, is an acute observer,' I said.

'I loved playing Holmes. He was entirely congenial to me. I first did a version of him in *A Cotswold Death*. Not a very good play, but fun to do. Gave me my first opportunity to play a detective. Had it not been for Granada's series with Jeremy Brett, I should have mounted seven, possibly eleven, ninety-minute Holmes films.'

Richardson's was a serene, yet bashful, sleuth – in *The Sign of Four* and *The Hound of the Baskervilles*. An incipiently neurotic version of Robert Stephens's defeated Baker Street diviner – but Desmond Davis and Douglas Hickox, the directors, wanted none of the Shakespearean complexity Billy Wilder coaxed from his star. Holmes, the most famous homosexual in the world, needs to twitch with repressed or uncommunicated fertile interior dramas. Yet Richardson's performance – the profile perfect, the voice beautiful – was flat. Not serene enough to be Rathbone, nor bashful enough to be Stephens – and a world away from Jeremy Brett's romantic reserve.

The problem lay in Charles Pogue's scripts, or 'teleplays' as the credits called them, which contained such helpful tautologies as 'I've given her a sedative – she'll sleep now for a while.' Conan Doyle was adapted for ripping yarns (the joy of the original stories is their subversive portrait of a marriage: Holmes is a *fin de siècle* hero, his drug-taking and eccentricities direct from the *Yellow Book*) – and adapted ineptly and raggedly at that. For *The Sign of Four*, narrative momentum was messed up by giving us the explanatory flashbacks, about India, too early; we shouldn't know of the pygmy's dart or the secrets of the Sholtos until the end. We were thus ahead of Holmes's deductions, which lost all their bite. He didn't mystify, he plodded. A magician who's been exposed in advance.

Flaccidity of suspense was equalled by the miscasting of vital roles. Joe Melia is a good light comedian, but he didn't convince as the heavy, Jonathan Small. (In fact, Conan Doyle didn't make Small a heavy: he's involved in a dark story about honour and loyalty – themes absent here.) And as for David Healy's Watson: half way through he came out with an Irish accent. (Colin Blakely kept up a brogue for the whole of *The Private Life of Sherlock Holmes*.)

Richardson himself, of course, wasn't miscast – he was under-used. He was costumed out of Paget, but the personality he radiated was the cold-calculating-logical-machine Holmes with an on/off smile; a Holmes of surface tics, whose biggest oddity was a penchant for disguising himself to sub-Clouseau standard. Fooling nobody, except Watson, as a hunch-backed mariner alike to Augustus John on a bad morning – 'You'd have made an actor, and a rare one,' he is told.

In *The Hound of the Baskervilles*, Holmes is a gypsy loitering amidst the high tors and dolmens – another enigma on the moors. ('There are many things on the moor which are not what they seem – a deceptive place.' A theatre?) Unfortunately, we saw him straight away, twinkling with his tarot, or squatting in a tree like a corduroy bird. We oughtn't to know he's in the vicinity, watching, waiting, paralleling the outcast convict, Selden, until the climax, when he comes out of his disguise like a god. (Indeed, the force of *The Hound of the Baskervilles* lies in Holmes's apparent absence, yet being everywhere present: he's intensively abstract, testing, amongst other things, Watson's faith and powers. Watson, who does the footwork, and mails off reports, is not that Light, but was sent to bear witness of that Light.)

The wind machines rattled the shrubbery when Sir Charles is pursued into his gazebo by the phosphorescent pooch; the bluey light of the studio fog made Dartmoor a *Star Trek* planet; Grimpen Mire was assailed by jungle trills and chirrups, oinks and squawks – common to Paraguay, perhaps, but not to a Devonshire bog. If the scenery was amateurish, there was at least no miscasting this time. Instead we had a lot of very bad acting by distinguished stage people. Denholm Elliot (Doctor Mortimer) blinked and bumbled as the dotty country quack, fond enough of his spaniel to bring it to London – but why didn't he show any feelings when it went missing on the moor? Ronald Lacey whispered through the part of Lestrade, as if still playing Toht, the comic Nazi in *Raiders of the Lost Ark*. Brian Blessed, as Geoffrey Lyons, shouted the house down, hooting and yelling, flapping his cloak, etc. There was never a table, but he wouldn't thump it; never a door he'd not bang; not a bottle he'd refrain from throttling, nor a poker he could resist from ostentatiously bending. (Blessed's eyes popping more than the hound's, this poker bending routine was lifted from Dr Grimesby Roylott in *The Speckled Band*.)

Nicholas Clay played Stapleton as fey and Sir Hugo, the ancestor, as Lady Chatterley's Mellors, even to the extent of rogering the serving wench from behind – Lawrence's 'fern-dark indifference' brought to a halt by the materialization of the slavering dog. Nothing was made of this actor's sex-appeal (he was Lancelot in Boorman's *Excalibur*, and he has actually played Mellors opposite Sylvia Kristel); and sex is a key to Stapleton's power over Beryl and Mrs Lyons.

Eleanor Bron was a vespertine Mrs Barrymore, the Lady Macbeth of Baskerville Hall, waving her candelabra at the windows. The character belongs to the story's complex pattern of intertwined loyalties (Selden is her brother, but Sir Henry is her master) – the important Nineties themes of corruption and constancy. Eleanor Bron, however, looked ready for a revue sketch containing the punchline 'Out damn spot'.

Watson had metastasized into Donald Churchill, Healy's intermittent Irish becoming a chortling Cockney. A buffoonish, Bruce-ish Watson. A disgrace. Richardson, as the gypsy, smiled all the time. His Holmes was cross. He avoided other people for his pipe, microscope and magnifying glass. He was intimate only with his props and looked least bored when doing the biography-from-a-walking-stick demonstration. Holmes was sharp and pained, interrogating Laura Lyons about her relationship with Sir Charles, contemptuous of messy emotion ('love is as strong as death') – and only in this one brief scene did Richardson (who played Holmes by musicalizing him with his handsome voice) rise above the 'teleplay', by sinking into what Holmes doesn't say, but silently feels. ('Love is as strong as death' is a biblical quotation, from Isaiah, and connects with Wilder's *The Private Life of Sherlock Holmes*, where it could be an epigraph. Another link: I'll swear that two quick long shots of Baker Street in the Richardson/Plaschkes productions were slivers of footage of Alexandre Trauner's famous set?).

On reflection, the actor was glad Otto Plaschkes abandoned the projected series of a dozen films. 'I should have reached the point, after the fifth film possibly, of feeling, as I did at Stratford all those years ago, "Oh God, I've done this now. I need the *fix* of a *challenge*." '

'How did New York and *My Fair Lady* represent a challenge after the Royal Shakespeare Company?'

'It *was* indeed *My Fair Lady*. I should have loved to have done the original play. The musical numbers I had to make sound very much like Rex Harrison, for whom they were tailored.'

Richardson chanted the lazy Singspiel of 'I've grown accustomed to her face'.

'But I owed my interpretation of Higgins to Leslie Howard's film of 1938.'

'So you were a synthesis of two film stars, and two films, and you were on Broadway. Why don't you take me back to the very beginning?'

Pueri in maternis uteris existentes nondum prodierunt in lucem ut cum aliis hominibus vitam ducant: 'Children,' according to an accoucheur manual by Heinrich van Deventer, whom Laurence Sterne accidentally found himself duplicating in *Tristram Shandy*, 'while in the mother's womb have not yet come forth into the world to live among other men'; and Richardson said, of his originations, 'It's rather complicated. I'll try and be as coherent as possible. I'm relying on recollections of my mother. I say that not because I'm any closer to my mother than I am to my father, and both of them are still alive. It was during the war, and my mother informs me I was a very strange child, a very imaginative child, much given, as indeed many children are, to private games. I did not participate in the more rowdy, sporty games of my youthful contemporaries. I suppose really what she was trying to say was that she didn't know what to make of me.

'Like all good parents, she was keen to take a full advantage of whatever she saw developing in my personality. To that end she enlisted the help of my history master at a perfectly ordinary school in Edinburgh. Nothing grand about it at all. But a rather brilliant history master, as you will see.

'He spotted something in me, and I was otherwise a most middling pupil, and informed my mother that he thought there was music in my soul. A piano was purchased. I had lessons – and indeed, I did quite well, because I loved it, and I still love music, and one of my greatest solaces remains the piano. But though I was competent, I was not in the concert-playing class. I had a strong musical sense – that was all.

'So the history teacher said, "I wonder if it is art." I was sent to the art master and aimed at oils and canvas, which was a disaster. "Don't bring that boy anywhere near me ever again!" said the art master. So it wasn't to be art.

'The next year, we had an Armistice Service. A boy was always chosen to stand at a lectern, spruce and with a red poppy, to read appropriate verses in memory of the war dead. The verses chosen for me were Binyon's. Four lines. A stanza!

> They shall not grow old, as we that are left grow old:
> Age shall not weary them, nor the years condemn.
> At the going down of the sun and in the morning
> We will remember them.

Quite instinctively, I thought it might be a good idea – precociously too, I suppose – I thought it might be a good idea, because it was so short, to memorize it. And I decided not to stand hidden behind this rather vulgar golden-eagle brass lectern, but to stand in the centre, unaided by the text, and just say the lines from my heart. And I did.

'I'm now fifty-two, and as I tell you this story, I can clearly recall the response at the end of those four lines. It was not the silence of interest in my rendition – it was the awesome silence of a collection of people, and the church was full, who for one brief moment *had stopped breathing*! No silence in the world is as great as that. Seconds it lasted, yet the impact it made on me remains to this day.

'The history master wrote to my mother straight: "We've been wrong all these years. He's an actor. Without doubt *an actor*." '

'At what other moments have you created the collective trance?'

'Prospero, the epilogue.' Richardson's Prospero was a young Bohemian scholar, ill and a bit warped – like Faust. His book of spells was a scholarly treatise: the magnum opus of the magus.

'And the first night I was Richard II. Also, when I did Berowne, and the speech about women's eyes:

> For where is any author in the world
> Teaches such beauty as a woman's eye?
> . . .
>
> A lover's eye will gaze an eagle blind . . .

'I got to the end of that speech: there it was again – that feeling.

> When Love speaks, the voice of all the gods
> Makes heaven drowsy with the harmony.

'It's what actors mean when they claim to worship a live audience. A camera, whirling celluloid around sprockets, is no replacement. It's frightening; it is awe-inspiring; it is stimulating – a drug. I miss it terribly. But I'm frightened to go back.'

'Why?' I asked.

'Because like a drug-addict who is cured, if I give myself a tiny dose, I may become addicted again. Besides,' Richardson added quickly, 'I'm quite happy away from the theatre.'

What Richardson was flinching from was the thought that he's presently not quite in as eminent a domain as the aquiline tyro of a decade or so ago: *Ike – The War Years*, as Monty; *Charlie Muffin*, with Ralph the inscrutable namesake; Ramsay MacDonald in *Number 10*; Pandit Nehru in *Mountbatten: The Last Viceroy* – where he's to be found, stained a coffee colour, striding into the looting Muslims, clutching a bamboo halberd, thwacking away and taking up RSC battle formations and talking in a Peter Sellers Indian/Welsh accent to Nicol Williamson, who'd been told that Mountbatten didn't speak, he yodelled. It has been often a career of knotty superior officers – Richardson supplying the knottiness and the superiority, without any script to support him. How can he get back to the future? In the live theatre possibly never. The longer he's away from it, the greater will be the expectation at any return.

'I have to say I feel like a traitor. I feel I've betrayed myself, particularly in turning my back on the classics. I cannot now read Shakespeare for pleasure – I get a dull ache in my insides because of this beautiful language – and I long, long, long *with all my soul* to be able to have a shot of that Shakespearean cocaine – to be able to say those wonderful things again. I very seldom go to the theatre; I always emerge quite fluorescent with envy at seeing my colleagues up there, seeing them have such experiences.'

But if the stage is self-prohibited, on television Richardson is coming to represent dependable class. On *Blunt* more later. The traitor and grandee was an instance of flamboyant underplaying. As Edward Spencer in J. G. Farrell's *Troubles*, however, Richardson could let rip – carrying-on for the tiny television screen in a highly 'theatrical' manner. With long silver hair, raffish 'tache, an Inverness cape and a succession of hats (pith helmet, panama, brown homburg, caps, motoring goggles etc), he was a ffolkes toff as head of an Anglo-Irish Addams family.

Spencer's collapsing Victorian castle has been turned into a hotel ('The Majestic'), full of village idiots who are the gentry, cats, mumbling servants and old ladies. Richardson strode amidst the bejungled palm court, the magnificently overgrown gardens and swampy ponds, as a big game hunter ordering the natives about in the underbush; strutting and shouting, boiling maggoty sheep's heads for the pack of dogs, insisting on long Latin graces – was he possibly enjoying himself *too* much? The part called for that other Richardson (Sir Ralph), who'd have been able to convey the rootedness of serious looniness; Richardson (Ian) was breezily eccentric – when the part calls for inspired madness.

There were gorgeous surreal touches (the golden pheasants and peacocks pecking about the deserted ballroom, for example) and the inmates of the hotel were agreeably whacky (the identical twin daughters, the transvestite, the blind grandmother); and the mood was of a danse macabre. But Richardson, sitting on the roof, poised to shoot any peasant who approaches the Queen Victoria statue, was nutty and fey; he had not the real private hatred Spencer has for the Irish, nor the contempt he has for himself: 'I'm not as young as I was. But I sometimes wish I could do something with my life.' This came out feckless, instead of desperate.

'The sound of silence you mentioned earlier,' I said, 'can be oddly mystical: it registers the point where the audience is utterly taken in. It can happen visually, too – or invisibly, like Alec Guinness in *Monsignor Quixote* celebrating an invisible mass.'

'I'm glad you mention Alec. If Barton was my inspiration in my Shakespearean and theatrical work, Alec is my inspiration in my camera work. My hero. I have learned from him the methods of translating a performance for the lens. I was the Italian bishop in *Monsignor Quixote*. We also played together in *Tinker, Tailor, Soldier, Spy*, and nearly all my scenes were with Smiley. Alec insisted on a rehearsal period – unusual in filming, where commonly the actors arrive, knowing their lines, and stumble through; the camera is in position and the appropriate lights are erected; your stand-in comes on during this, so that the actor can repose on those squat canvas seats. No rehearsal. But Alec insisted we rehearse for *Tinker, Tailor, Soldier, Spy*.

'I arrived one morning at the church hall in Kensington to find the director, the producer, the line-girl, the continuity-girl, all eyes looking on the middle of the room: sitting on a sofa was Alec Guinness with a pair of lace-up shoes. He was taking them off, putting them on, taking them off, putting them on. He'd pause. He'd take them off again; he'd put them on again. What patience, I thought, all these people have, to watch the actor-knight fiddle with footwear.

' "Alec, do tell me, because I'm so fascinated, what the hell you were up to?" "Well," Guinness replied, "the lines given to me for the scene, to express what I was feeling at the time, were inadequate. It wasn't, anyway, a scene about words; it was a scene about feelings. So since it was feelings, it needed physical actions. I wanted to find a way of demonstrating my frustration. Yet, since Smiley is not a demonstrative man, he wouldn't throw his weight about; nor would he shout. There could be no physical or vocal outburst. I decided I'd feel it through my shoes; anger being shown through the way I tied up my laces." "My God," I thought, "how brilliant." '

I said, 'When Smiley polished his spectacles it was a climax; like a character lighting a cigarette in a Henry James story.'

'Wonderful! I'd not seen acting like that before.'

Guinness's Smiley was a poem of restraint. Tiny facial tremors the audience learned to read as indications of epic inner turmoil. *Tinker, Tailor, Soldier, Spy* concerned the detection of dilatory rottenness in the British Secret Service – and by extension in the British state itself. The television adaptation conveyed le Carré's perpetual nightworld; the atmosphere was rank, weary, decaying, with lives of professional imposture lived out in muddy corridors of bakelite and papery rubble.

Richardson played the double agent, Bill Haydon, of all MI5 operators the most distinguished. As Blake says in *The Book of Thel*:

> Does the Eagle know what is in the pit
> Or wilt thou go ask the Mole?
> Can Wisdom be put in a silver rod,
> Or Love in a golden bowl.

Haydon's particular professional imposture is to play the Eagle whilst inly being the Mole – the genius and local maverick who, his career long, has been slipping information to the Russians. He knows that the heart of darkness, or the pit, is not just Moscow, it's composed of London and Washington, too. East and West mirror each other – a looking-glass war. And what transfigured the series, what made it only incidentally about spies and adventure, was the power of the acting: for what it *deals* with is the power of acting. *Tinker, Tailor, Soldier, Spy*, in fact, is a parade of the performing art; plus it's about loyalty, treachery, deceit, subterfuge –

both at a public level and at the level of private friendship. Haydon multiply betrays: he leads Smiley's wife, Ann, into adultery – and later we discover he was inspired to this by his Soviet controllers: sexual misdemeanors would pollute the emotional climate – pissing in the golden bowl – and divert attention from his real crimes.

The production was immensely provocative and, in its slow-burning way, raised questions about the psychology of espionage. Spying is our national pastime, secrecy and intrigue ingrown in our culture. 'Haydon took it for granted,' writes le Carré, 'that secret services were the only real measure of a nation's political health, the only real expression of its subconscious.' And *Tinker, Tailor, Soldier, Spy* represented our repressed morality – the secret services being mental counterparts to Cynthia Payne's personal services, which represent our repressed sexuality. Both the brain and the body are conditioned by the nursery: the dorm politicking and schoolboy codes of MI5 (in *Blunt*, MI5 is 'One's dear old nanny'); the nanny fantasies of the ruling class handing over their luncheon vouchers in Streatham.

If Terry Jones's *Personal Services* extends le Carré, so does the mulligatawny soup brewed by Peter Wright, who took on the British Government over the issue of his memoirs. The retired MI5 interrogator, maddened by his private proof of enemy penetration in the Establishment, seems to have wandered out of the Tasmanian bush like a refugee from Smiley's people; even the Latin inscription on his mantleshelf seems out of a novel: *Dilexi institiam et odi iniquitatem. Propterea morior in exsilio.* ('I loved justice and I hate injustice. Therefore in exile I die.')

Peter Wright is a real-life George Smiley, quoting from Pope Gregory VII where Smiley has a preference for the poetry of Heinrich Heine; the spycatchers are each a touch antique; each vain and resolute beneath the modesty and deference; each fond of theatricality and the flourish. And theatricality and espionage do indeed keep company – the difference being that a spy doesn't want us to know he's in life-long masquerade, so that giggling Guy Burgess proves to have been a sober traitor all along; so that lordly Anthony Blunt proves to have been a Communist all along; so that brilliant Kim Philby shone for the KGB all along ('Who is Kim?' asks Rudyard Kipling, '. . . he had known all evil since he could speak – but what he loved was the game for its own sake'); so that Holmesian Haydon proves to have been Moriarty all along.

Treachery has a romantic appeal – 'It's an aesthetic judgment as much as anything' – and Smiley perceives that Haydon, failing as a painter, made his own life into a simulacrum: his life was his art, and the art was that of the actor. 'Standing at the middle of a secret stage, playing world against world, hero and playwright in one: oh, Bill had loved that all right.' Smiley thinks of the spy – and thus of the actor – as a Russian doll: shell within shell, and so on down to a core of nothing.

Le Carré's novels are adult fairy stories, with mean streets and rainfall for a wild-wood with snow. Karla coming out of his black castle is the devil-hobgoblin; Smiley is the agent of good, a weary god (his galactic counterpart is Obi-Wan Kenobi, the gnomic magus of *Star Wars*) – and he draws energy from the existence of his enemy. The adversaries are the rising and falling buckets of *Richard II*. The humiliation of the West is redressed by the humiliation of the East at the end of *Smiley's People* – when a princess is found locked in a tower. And like a Malory romance, Karla and Smiley become portions of the same whole; less a twinhood than halves of a single brain. Klingsor versus Amfortas, who was seduced by an enchantress. Ann Smiley is the erring Guinevere or Kundry; Control is the ill, absent King Titurel; Haydon is the duplicitous knight, a parody Parsifal who believes in no grail.

If spies are actors, metaphorically, are actors spies?

The audience is ignorant of the acting in espionage; the point of performance is its own obfuscation. And it's over-facile to say that actors are obviously acting because they burble out of the box, or loom on the screen, or fret on the stage. That the institutions of theatricality define and protect them is the half of it.

As I paid my calls on actor after actor, the question recurred: how do you really know when an actor is acting? Was I being presented with official off-stage versions of private life; or the real private life; or a fake private life? What was the truth of the masks? At what moment did lying decay? As Henry James, than whom there was no greater angel patrolling the skill of dissembling, wrote in his preface to *Roderick Hudson*: 'The art of representation bristles with questions the very terms of which are difficult to apply and to appreciate; but whatever makes it arduous makes it, for our refreshment, infinite, causes the practice of it with experience, to spread round us in a widening, not in a narrowing circle ... Really, universally, relations stop nowhere, and the exquisite problem of the artist is eternally but to draw, by a geometry of his own, the circle within which they shall happily *appear* to do so.'

Actors are the Jamesian geometricians, the relation between their real life and their performances flowing back and forth, from one to the other, and back again – intersecting circles and loops. A tangle like the endless latching and unlatching of shoes. A cat's cradle.

The paradox of acting is that when actors don't conceal their craft, when the cat's cradle is rocked – as in the vagrancy of the cast about the auditorium before *Nicholas Nickleby*, or the amateur theatricals in the pub that became *Fair Maid of the West* – the acting actually increases in power: we are the more amenable to being taken in because we have witnessed the actors taking themselves in. We are the less deceived.

We are foxed about Haydon, until his exposure – when, retrospectively, we replay in our heads every moment we've seen him, interpreting Richardson's rakish performance anew. Every shuffle, every sigh, every ejaculation: we were the most deceived. The cat's cradle rocked us asleep. What about Smiley himself? He performs tiredness and boredom, which he genuinely feels. And yet inside there's incisiveness. His disingenuousness is a canny dissimulation. He 'acts himself, but more so,' in the teasing phrase from *The Honourable Schoolboy*. Smiley is a contrived self-caricature – and so Guinness had to act the actor as much as Richardson with Haydon. For both of them, acting not-acting is acting at full throttle.

Espionage and acting; the acting of espionage: they are linked, and provide drama with a thriving cottage industry. Le Carré's *The Perfect Spy* makes the conundrum Oedipal, with the master confidence trickster (played by Ray McAnally) as the stirring patriarch, whose riddles his son, also in the secret service, tries to unravel – riddles which adapt the psychology of lies and double-dealing to notions of pedigree and patrimony. It's a wise child that knows its own father.

Then there's Julian Mitchell's *Another Country*, where Guy Bennett is Guy Burgess at school, bruised and bullied into exacting revenges against the prefecture; Rupert Everett, in the film version, was a dishevelled seraph, who'd been to bed with the entire house and who, disappointed in preferment, took solace in sulky subterfuge – wanting to bring down the system he'd been rejected from. Old and having outlived his usefulness, he reappears in Alan Bennett's *An Englishman Abroad*, when Alan Bates takes Coral Browne on a tour of Moscow (the film was actually shot in Dundee), unrepentant, but hardly having found a paradise in his adopted land. Burgess feasted off garlic-studded tomatoes and had to endure permanent surveillance from sour-faced KGB boys.

An Englishman Abroad, like *The Old Country*, interprets spying as an art – a magic-mirror world of bluff and pretence. Hilary, in the latter Alan Bennett play (played by Alec Guinness at the Queen's Theatre in 1977), with his long tirades and satires, his rehearsed anecdotes, is an actor. His life is theatre; the verandah of his cabin, a stage – where he leafs through book-sellers' catalogues: 'They collect anything now. Even fakes. Here's a special section in which every item is an authentic guaranteed forgery. In which context a fake would need to be the genuine article. Like a woman at a drag ball. By being exactly what she seems she is the imposter. Soon, one imagines, forgeries *of* forgeries.' (The sophistry of attribution re-appears in Bennett's play on Anthony Blunt, *Single Spies*. This time Simon Callow played Burgess.)

Alan Bennett reckons espionage involves a Betjemanesque Englishness. Hilary, in *The Old Country*, wandered, rapt, in Metroland: 'Boarding kennels, down-at-heel riding schools, damp bungalows in wizened orchards'. He's a nostalgist, who turns to Russia as a protector of old values – the enemy is brash America. These Englishmen are abroad, like Maugham and Beerbohm, to keep alive a fantasy of Edwardianism. And Bennett's spies, like his Joe Orton in *Prick Up Your Ears*, are rebels in the irresponsible Mr Toad mould. (The last words of *The Old Country* are 'Poop! Poop!') They are play-acting children.

Philby, Burgess and Maclean defected not just from West to East – they trespassed from the reproaches of history books to the arcady of art. Rogues and vagabonds, they are supertramps, spiritual colleagues of W. H. Davies and R. B. Cunninghame Graham, who chucked up everything and just cleared off: 'This audacious, purifying, / Elemental move,' as Philip Larkin says in 'Poetry of Departures'. Spies are the modern folk heroes.

What about Anthony Blunt? In May 1986, Richardson worked on a television film, with a script by Robin Chapman. The plot imagined that Blunt had remained permanently active for the Russians, that he'd organized the defection of Maclean, and that he was Guy Burgess's lover – the bereft widow when he defected. *Blunt* was a return to Haydon – and not only because Richardson was playing a traitor again with lank forelock and foppish clothes: but because Haydon *was* Blunt, surely?

I asked David Cornwell, who by writing under an assumed name is himself under authorial camouflage – John le Carré. His letter, which I have permission to quote, is a gem of caution: 'Haydon wasn't Blunt anymore than he was anyone else. But in the circles where I had moved, Blunt was on everyone's lips, which is perhaps why I gave Haydon an interest in painting, and even a small talent for it, and made a small point of the Callot drawing that hung in George Smiley's house, a gift from Ann to make amends. Spying and acting . . . Well, spying is a performing art, no question, and the art is to conceal the technique as much as to employ it, and to subject one's identity to the part until the part *is* one's identity – viz. Charlie in *The Little Drummer Girl*.'

Charlie, in that novel, was to some degree based on the author's half-sister, a National Theatre actress; but the role was funked by a master-piece of miscasting, when Diane Keaton appeared in the 1984 film, directed by George Roy Hill, and co-starring the exophthalmic scary-boots, Klaus Kinski. Keaton has too much of Woody Allen's self-con-sciousness and supine neurosis to act being an actress – she comes out as Annie Hall.

'The art of seeing,' said Bernard Berenson, art scholar and authenticator of fakes, 'is the most difficult one to learn.' When Blunt was unmasked, after having enjoyed many years of an official cover-up and immunity from prosecution, Jonathan Miller renamed the Poussin *Catalogue Raison-née* the *Catalogue Traisonnée*. In Blunt we had a man, a professional,

professorial gazer and reader of pictures, wholly blinding colleagues at
the Courtauld, Windsor Castle, Trinity College, the Athenaeum and the
British Academy. He had them stumble when they saw.

'Do you think,' I asked Richardson, 'that Blunt was an evil man?'

'No. He was just psychologically and ideologically *different*. He
belonged to that generation of the First World War who had guilty
consciences all their lives; their entire class was almost wiped out – all
those officers sacrificed in the trenches. How could the young men who
grew up in the years after that war prevent such a disaster happening
again? And how could they make up for the élite of their number who'd
been lost?'

'The Lost Boys. Bill Haydon remarks that the Cold War began in
1917,' I said.

'One answer seemed to be Communism – a new start, rather than
picking up the pieces of a broken constitution and culture. Many young
men joined the Communist Party, not only at Cambridge. But most of
them ripped up their cards when Stalin came to power and made a pact
with the Nazis in 1939. Blunt did not. He never lost or changed his
allegiance. He arranged for Burgess to come and help Maclean escape – by
arranging it for Burgess to be found in bed with a boy, disgraced, and sent
home from America.

'MI5 knew about him. The Queen did not know the full story, and she
was furious. Blunt's knighthood had been her own special gift. The
palace refused us permission to shoot at Windsor – which was unfortu-
nate because Blunt was Surveyor of the Queen's Pictures there. We shot
out of sequence, and that can hinder concentration quite considerably. I
try and operate on the advice given to me by Alec Guinness: the only way
to maintain a personal, mental and emotional graph of acting through the
story is to memorize it all in advance. Then, whatever the backward
story-order shot, I can pinpoint the place on my graph. I have followed
the advice faithfully, with results. My tempo and responses contain
continuity.

'Blunt is bewilderingly enigmatic. There seems nothing to plot on the
graph – nothing to grab hold of. So I'm trying my best to relate him to
myself and my own observations. But there are obvious big differences.
Blunt was a homosexual. I'm not. First problem. There's little overt
activity of that kind in the film, but Blunt's homosexuality affects him as a
person. He's old-maidish about table settings, about eating habits, about
his papers. He's a fussy and over-fastidious man.'

Richardson's solution was quietly retaliative. He recalled once seeing
an enemy in a hotel, eating breakfast. The enemy's comportment was
stored away for future use – and so the performance of Blunt's effemi-
nancy is an avenging impersonation.

'Blunt was a mathematician, so therefore everything has to be neat and precise – another hint for his meticulosity. His dress was very elegant, very nearly fey. He was also very tall, so I've been provided with elevated boots – so that I actually stand over six feet, as opposed to five foot ten, which is what I am. The high heels, disguised inside the boot, make me mince a bit. So the dainty walk takes care of itself.

'These are externals. To bring the man's soul to life, I've had to rely on myself, and let me explain what I mean. When Mike Yarwood, or whatever his name is, does those accurate mimicries of prominent public figures, it is alarming to hear how accurately he's caught their voice; how accurately he's caught their facial expressions. He re-creates the idiosyncrasies of other people. But bring the camera close so that you can see his eyes: they'll be as dead as the eyes of a dead fish on a slab. That is because there's no connection between his imitation and his inside, his soul.

'Blunt is a re-creation of a recent historical personality, so there are mannerisms of voice and gesture to be got right; but all that study has to be linked to my own personal interpretation – and it's that aspect that enlivens the spark, or soul, of the character; so that the eyes are alive with the emotions of a real human being.'

'So acting is incarnation more than impersonation?'

'It has to be dragged from within. That's how I'm doing Blunt, and if I didn't you'd have an automaton saying lines in a lordly way, with eyes like a deceased sea-trout. Dead. The eyes are the gateway to the soul. The camera gets right through that gate – and if the audience has no sense of life in and beyond the eyes, it's sterile.'

Blunt was Richardson's best work since *Tinker, Tailor, Soldier, Spy*, which was his best work since leaving Stratford. It was a performance of chilly charisma; Blunt the autocratic, wicked genius, ruling from his eyrie above the Courtauld – literally living at the pinnacle of a palace of art, and throwing the keys of the kingdom down to waiting Burgess. A manipulative and cruel man, Richardson's Blunt was nourished by intrigue, as a vampire is sustained by sipping vintage haemoglobin. Loyalty to friends only means fidelity to the Apostles' code – that Cambridge secret society, an anonymous charmed circle, so exclusive few knew it existed; a sort of bitter freemasonry, the members protecting each other from disgrace of whatever brand (espionage, homosexuality . . .)

Blunt's political ideology was a version of his art appreciation (his lair is most aptly the Courtauld), and Richardson first emerged lecturing in the dark, with slides, about Nicolas Poussin (1594–1665), who lived in Rome, self-exiled from France. Blunt discusses *Shepherds of Arcadia* and argues that the Age of Reason is to be regained in 'theoretical Marxism'. And though Russia's a cold, crisp country of brutal and clear extremes, a man-made utopia drained of besmirching emotion – it's also a cold equation mistaking efficiency for harmony, art's order for the possibilities of real life. Blunt, who'd never known deprivation, who'd never seen a real factory, has a fantasy of a mechanical paradise – with himself in control: an aesthetic Communism, meaning that the problems of self-interest, instead of being removed, are in fact gloriously indulged.

For much of the film, Richardson was enthralled stooge to Anthony Hopkins's Burgess, a comic turn of nursery prattle – of his journey from the port, 'The boat-train was packed with sea-scouts!'; of the necessity that Maclean defect, 'Maccers must go!'; of how he feels, 'In the pink, poppet, spiffing!' When he disappears, the screen becomes a blank and a silence. His farewell note to Blunt quotes Browning:

> What's become of Waring
> Since he gave us all the slip?

And so Blunt is the grieving widow (Burgess has called him 'the Mrs'), emotionally betrayed when Burgess goes for good, his mind working at top speed to remove all traces of suspicion. He makes many a rendezvous with Russians in public lavatories (rather lovingly re-created sets of brass and mahogany and porcelain); he lunches at the RAC and the Reform, poisoning the air about Goronwy Rees – an anguished ex-friend, emotionally blackmailed into silence, played with agitated conviction by Michael Williams; he scours Burgess's (improbably tidy) flat for secret documents, incriminating photographs, press clippings, letters (one from Philby) and a current Communist Party membership card. (A factual slip: Blunt in reality was invited to search the premises alongside MI5 officers.) These, plus medals and rosettes of Lenin, are incinerated in the Courtauld basement.

Despite effete hacking jackets, the mincing trot, manicure and mascara, Richardson's Blunt never slackened into the epicene, and by speaking in one long note of aristocratic grievance, a sort of whine, the actor pitched Blunt's voice purposefully flat. No campery, except that of a put-on prude ('Auntie can be a proper sourpuss after lunch,' says Burgess.) He was malevolent and in command – never more so than when he travels to Sonning and plays a game of loyalty and threat with Goronwy Rees, despising the All Souls Estates Bursar for being heterosexually happy (he sneers at any claim Rees makes about being loyal to a woman); he lards conversation with dangerous innuendo about other proclivities. And Rees is accused of being the betrayer, for betraying lost ideals: Blunt makes it clear that, as an ex-MI5 officer, and still trusted (as Burgess incredibly still is), he'd have no qualms about casting doubt on any tale-carrying Rees might have in mind. So the one man who knew the truth is torn between wife and old friends, past and present – and destroyed.

The soundtrack played excerpts from Berlioz's *La Damnation de Faust*; indeed, Blunt has sold his soul for a crazy cause – and for all Richardson's affirming that as an actor he intended enkindling the character's spirit, the spirit was absent. That's the point. And Blunt is a suffering Mephisto-philes as a consequence. His friends are not near his conscience because he has no tender feeling. Believing he believes in a Soviet heaven, he actually exists in a haggard hell: this is hell nor is he out of it. *Blunt* concluded with the solitary scholar delivering again his lecture on Poussin's neoclassic vision of social harmony, and handling, with cotton gloves, drawings in the Windsor archives. A blown husk, hollow, furtive, loveless, shingled with the sulphur of personal failure – despite the momentary belief that he's a Faust who escaped the flames of damnation, what with the immu-nity from prosecution . . .

> Cut is the branch that might have grown full straight,
> And burnèd is Apollo's laurel-bough,
> That sometime grew within this learned man.
> Faustus is gone . . .

'What,' I asked Richardson, 'is the stage's version of the eyes?'

'Stage acting, I think, means the ability to make the emotion flooding into the eyes flood also into the rest of the body. A flood of feeling: in close-up, a raised eyebrow is enough – on stage, the arm might shoot out. I have to control my gesticulations on camera – I look embarrassing. On stage, there's less restriction: arms, back, legs, you just do it . . .'

The actor was flinging himself about like a dancer, and his voice choreographed itself in a deliberate scherzando. The pages of Raymond Huntley's *Times* rattled with the wind.

'The athleticism of acting, its physical sportiveness – as distinct from aspects of motive and psychology: how did you play Coriolanus?'

'Indeed, I played Coriolanus as an athlete – a running man, lithe. But more importantly, as far as he was concerned, I used the strength of my vocal mechanism to suggest power – I am not big in stature. For the great speeches, I had to be vocally strong, alive, vibrant, to create a sense of pent-up physical energy:

> You common cry of curs! Whose breath I hate
> As reek o' th' rotten fens, whose loves I prize
> As the dead carcasses of unburied men
> That do corrupt my air – I banish you.

'In Shakespeare the voice, the well-trained voice, the appreciation of language and the understanding of what Shakespeare is about: all this can frequently make up for the most astonishing shortcomings. I'm not a good-looking person, I never have been, but if you have a lovely voice, people will believe that you are actually rather handsome.'

'Is acting narcissistic?' I inquired, as Richardson continued smiling to himself.

'I do wonder why we do it. I think, possibly, I do it because I'm really a social disaster. I remember distinctly my wife saying to me – she was an actress but gave it up because of our children – she said to me, having sat in on a rehearsal, "Ian, when you were rehearsing, you really came alive."'

We'd hit an adagio mood. I wondered whether his children had entered the reviving profession?

'My youngest son, Miles, is an actor. He is twenty-two, and has much more assurance than I did at that age. He has a beautiful voice, deeper than mine. He's taller than I am. My wife is half-Russian, and he takes after the Slav side of the family.'

'Did he learn about the craft from you?'

'I never saw it. But he lately played Berowne at drama school. I was away, but my agent went – she'd seen my own Berowne all those years ago. She telephoned me. "Quite extraordinary," she said "He must have been all of twelve when you were in *Love's Labour's Lost*. He must have seen it at most twice. I saw, up on that little stage, you, as you were then. All over again: voice, mannerisms, everything." He must have absorbed it all – but we've never talked of it. He still lives at home, on the top floor of our Victorian house, and he'd rather shut himself away and work things out for himself. I approve of that. I'm disappointed, but I approve of his not asking me the way.'

Father and son have worked together in *Porterhouse Blue*, a Cambridge fantasy adapted from a novel by Tom Sharpe – a writer whose comic gifts extend to exploding condoms and stroke-inducing gluttony. A coarse farceur misrepresented as a satirist, he's not an artist likely to elicit Richardson's best talents. And so it proved. As Sir Godber Evans, newly arrived master of the college, the actor retreated behind his impression of Dame Edith Sitwell being served a noisome victual at Renishaw.

The main problem was one of audience manipulation: we were abandoned to choppy ambivalence. Are the piggish dons to be mocked and Godber's reforms welcome, or is Godber a boor and the dons cherishable swine? Is Godber a good man in an impossible job, or an impossible man repudiating tradition out of spite? Is he clever, or a Whitehall dullard exiled to the Fens by an exasperated Prime Minister? Has he worked himself up, an autodidact, or has he merely made a prudent social marriage?

Beyond Richardson's Godber, there's John Sessions's Zipser – a paunchy twit or mock-hero? – and David Jason's Skullion: a sycophant or stalwart servant? Does he love the dons and the college, or despise them, wanting only employment? College fellows included the queeny Bursar (Harold Innocent), the pop-eyed Praelictor (Ian Wallace), talking in Latin, the chirpy and lecherous Chaplain (Lockwood West) ('He's been dreaming of the girls in Woolworths again'), the silver scheming Dean (Paul Rogers) and the cadaverous Old Master (Robert Eddison) – a camp Quixote. Arrogant, selfish, this gaggle deliberate by candlelight, surrounded by quills and silver plate. A conclave as anachronistic as if Wolsey and Burleigh still reigned and took decisions in the shadows.

Chief character-that-time's-forgot was Skullion. With medals and wing-collar, he existed amidst the gas-jets and mellow twilight of Ealing's heyday. Hating Godber for not being a real gentleman ('gentleman *is* gentleman') and purring with pleasure when tyrannized – as by the uppity cad played with saturnine charm by Miles Richardson – he's dewy-eyed at the noble rites of bread-throwing, puking in the fountain and heckling at the Porterhouse Feast, a gargantuan repast of swan, hare, widgeon and a half-dozen vintage wines. As the provender processes into Hall, Godber demands water and a nut cutlet for himself; top on his list of reforms are the abolition of High Table and the institution of a cafeteria system. His wife, meantime, throws the costly antique furniture out of the Lodgings and gives impromptu lectures on non-specific urethritis. 'I assure you, Godber,' she says, 'the penis occasions no envy nowadays whatsoever.'

Completely uncertain as to whether Godber's a comic grotesque or the sober spot in the midst of malarky, Richardson put his energy into his voice – breaking up 'evidently' into a polysyllabic ditty. The Latin at the Mastership installation ceremony was lovingly cadenced (and Godber the wowser should have hated the antique ritual); the actor came proudly in cavalcade down the street, accompanied by maces, and dressed in gold brocade – serene Richard II unfortunately miscast as austere Bolingbroke, and having to pronounce, from a bomb-site, 'The old cannot stand in the way of the new.'

In the midst of the speechifying (the content of the diatribe a denunciation of the nostalgia principle), Godber is interrupted by the aristocratic student, Gimington (Miles Richardson), who shouts out 'What a perverted little man!' The Master, however, is removed not by verbal abuse, but by his servant. Skullion offers his legacy to save the college from financial ruin; Godber, agog, steps back against a wall, cracks his pate and dislodges a portrait, which tilts to brain him. Skullion scarpers. He tried to save Porterhouse, and all's up. Blood dribbles messily from Godber's ear on to headed notepaper. Crying for help, his voice is thick and impaired. Lady Mary thinks she's getting an obscene phone call. He dies, muttering the name of his accidental assailant – which is erroneously interpreted as his nomination of a successor, and on learning he's the new Master, Skullion has a stroke and has to be wheeled, drooling, to High Table, where he's spoonfed yellow gook. Godber, in a Francis Bacon smear, frowns down upon the revellers from the wall. The character's subsidence into aesthetic death (that Bacon scream) represents the cerebral shiver of Richardson's entire performance – even the manipulations in the Governing Body meetings failed to rouse him. And at manipulations he can be excellent – Haydon, Blunt.

'Are you conscious of the rise and fall of generations?'

'Whenever I do go to the theatre, I listen to the noises young actors are making, and which are considered acceptable, and my ear-drums are offended. I think, "Ian, you are out of date. You are going through what Gielgud went through twenty years ago." I represent an era of classical performance that's gone by. Each generation brings to acting its own feelings, plus the traditions of the preceding age. Gielgud brought with him the history of the Terrys and Beerbohm Tree; he was mannered and poetic. Then came Burton, Scofield, Neville, who brought their own ideas to acting, plus they acknowledged the influence of Olivier, Gielgud, Ralph Richardson, who had been their predecessors. Next, McKellen, Jacobi, Alan Howard, myself. We echoed handed-down style. Now, decades after we emerged, a new generation has arrived again. There are vocal mannerisms of Jeremy Irons's, for instance, which I recognize as having myself – but I have to say, that there are a lot of things I do which owe debts to the intonations of Gielgud.'

'It sounds a very small and incestuous family.'

'It is – and it is thoroughly dynastic. But I'm out of the tradition now. I'm no longer current. I've lost touch with the RSC. Trevor Nunn was never particularly enamoured of my contribution. He couldn't have been, otherwise why is it I only ever did *Revenger's Tragedy* for him? I don't know *what* I've done to Terry Hands. But I don't think he wants me back. I wouldn't mind going to the National. I'd love to have been Gloucester to Anthony Hopkins's Lear. I'd love to have been part of that . . . But I was only ever invited to the National once. Peter Hall asked me to be in *The Cherry Orchard*, but I was committed elsewhere, I think.

'I miss the audience contact. I miss the stage. I've been working for the camera for seven years. I'm perfectly happy. No, I'm not. I'm not entirely. I do get pangs of conscience, about whether I've denied my destiny. But in the cool, clear, light of reason: what Shakespeare could I play at my age? I suppose I could do my Prospero again. I was asked by the RSC to take *The Tempest* on a provincial tour. I really do not think I should return to the Royal Shakespeare Company to lead a provincial tour – it would be wrong, after those years of devoted service, and in leading roles. I mean, for a start, people who've followed my career, and who write to me sweetly and faithfully, they might be bewildered at my acceptance of a downgraded prospect. *Because that's what it is, let's face it.* Naturally, I turned them down. Macbeth? Lear I don't do, either. Prospero? Yes, but not a provincial tour. Leontes?

'But I'm happy – "a happy man", and all that that phrase implies in its avoidance of the usual shadows.'

Richardson, visibly troubled, was vocally exultant. He'd perhaps not expected to talk himself into an admission of repressed stage-fright. A song of himself. We drank some sherry. Gossiped some more, and quit the Garrick. Him that way; me this way.

FOUR

Artificial Intelligence: Derek Jacobi

As an example of the process Guy Davenport called 'a dance of meaning from form to form' we have *Little Dorrit*. First off, Dickens put moments of autobiography into the fiction. Maria Beadnell, a childhood love, re-entered his orbit after several decades, disclosed now as a whinnying lardo: whither the coy and delicious flirt? Who was this slobbish grotesque? She's in the book as Flora Finching, representing the possibility that the female had *always* been pitiful and affected; Dickens (and Clennam) just hadn't noticed before. Age hasn't ruined her; age has corrected the vision of a quondam idolator.

Another slice of life was Second Empire Paris. Dickens wrote much of the novel in France, and Merdle (in whose name, etymologically, we pinpoint *shit*) and his banquets are based on Émile de Girardin's ruddiest strawberry and cigar-strewn orgies. Luxury was underwritten by killings on the Bourse, where Dickens noted the men 'all howling and haggard', creating and losing paper fortunes; so what we have in the novel is a society where wealth doesn't exist except in the imagination; an inflationary universe, sustained by faith, hope and frantic talk – sustained, generally, by a suspension of disbelief.

Money, share issues, property deeds: people will them into existence. When Merdle collapses, his double-dealing and counterfeiting exposed, the entire structure of affluence and indebtedness totters. *Little Dorrit*, whilst being about the lure and enchainments of lucre, the traps of poverty and snobbery, is more crucially concerned with examining the empty heart which can constitute a society like this.

Why do people work the stock markets? Why do they gamble? Why do they put their trust in shysters and credit? Because hucksterism is an ancient carry-on. Bargaining, hawking, trying to make something out of nothing ('Nothing will come of nothing,' says King Lear), is as old as acting. Theatre and the river of gold are both a practice of illusion. Underneath, they are moonshine, incorporeal, abstract. More on this presently.

Second off, the novel travelled into the lively arts. *Little Dorrit* was adapted for the Strand Theatre in 1857 by J. B. Johnstone (Dickens published the first bound edition in the June); forty-eight years later, *Klein Dorrit* appeared at the Hofberg, Vienna. In 1913, the Thanhouser company in America made a silent movie. And Peter Ackroyd's novel *The Great Fire of London* (1981), deals with the conversion of *Little Dorrit* into an expensive cinematic epic.

Ackroyd's slim fiction is a penetrating commentary on Dickens's novel; in fact, he slyly re-writes Dickens for the modern age – and anticipates Christine Edzard's film. Clennam becomes Little Arthur, the dwarf proprietor of a doomed amusement arcade, whose affection for an innocent girl turns to infanticide. The murder takes place on the old Marshalsea site, where Audrey Skelton and Timothy Coleman have their flat. Tim is also an aspect of Clennam – the baffled, credulous complexion which is the outward show of emotional retardation.

Audrey is Amy Dorrit. She sinks into a nightmare identification with the character and is haunted, as the Dorrits are, by recollections of a formerly rich family. A violent hatred bubbles up when encountering the actress cast in a role she considers her endowment; she feels personally usurped: 'I can't let that whore pretend to be Little Dorrit. It isn't right, it isn't right.' A figure from a novel above a century old is her *property*, her *security*.

In charge of the actress is Spencer Spender, the beleaguered producer. He intends making *Little Dorrit* as a documentary-drama; a motion picture of nineteenth-century London labour and the London poor. Mayhew with a plot. And in his confusion of history and fiction, art and life, he's William Dorrit with wild whims. (His wife, Laetitia, who has an affair with a dancer, is the social-climbing chorine, Fanny Dorrit, Amy's elder sister.) Setting up the film proves as difficult as extracting money and support from the Tite Barnacles. Spender, up and down staircases in Wardour Street, receives only fake interest and frail enthusiasm – like Clennam, trying to encompass the network of lies, half-promises, denials and terminal prevarications that's the Circumlocution Office.

Eventually, a letter comes from a government Film Finance Board (written in a 'vague and circumlocutory way'), which pledges cash and suggests a Cambridge professor as the man to do the script. Thus emerges the novel's Merdle. Rowan Philips, an unspeakable and conceited foreigner, who cultivates a remoteness, a detachment, initially seems brilliant and successful; we're told he doodles his masterly books. Gradually, however, he becomes the incredible shrinking man. He is an empty space.

Philips (like an actor) switches accents and modes of dress; he tries to anticipate the kind of response an acquaintance would prefer; and, fitting in, he opts out of genuine engagement. Tim he seduces and discards; Spender he countenances, then cuts. 'His emotional life was one area where he could experiment, he knew, without doing any serious damage to himself.' He can be immune because any emotional life is absent; he's emotionally frigid, capable of loving only his own contours in the mirror. He keeps an apartment in London for pick-ups and anonymous sex: 'He wanted at all costs not to become involved.'

Philips is a compulsive masturbator, and sterility envelops him. Ackroyd makes him an academic because in *Little Dorrit* the Marshalsea inmates are called the Collegians, their lives a repressive wasteland. (The Cambridge students in Ackroyd's book are the mendicants at Bleeding Heart Yard.) A modern Merdle, for Philips money is a prestidigitation ('economic conditions began and ended for him in royalty statements'); but all that money buys is the living death of cruising half-deserted gay bars where nobody notices him: 'He was being looked through.' Not to be looked at, in a novel much preoccupied with watching, is a harsh judgement. Turned on by the abrasiveness of the city, what the city does is absorb Philips, drowning him with its uproar. He's rendered a blank. When Merdle finds himself lost in the vortex, he slits his jugular with a tortoise-shell penknife. Nothing becomes his life better than the losing of it. Ackroyd condemns Philips to a crueller fate. He forgets about him. The character fades out.

The Great Fire of London presents what Tom Wolfe calls a bonfire of the vanities: people behave knowing they are to be seen. They walk, choose clothes, gesture and generally act for a street theatre. Television screens are ubiquitous; cameras record happenings with a ravenous appetite. Spender wants to use a real prison for his film location; real warehouses along the Thames are co-opted for a set-piece of Little Dorrit's and Maggie's nocturnal walk, when they're locked out of the prison by mistake. And so all these buildings are coiled up with arc lamps, wires, costume hampers, the impedimenta of a studio. Neglected parts of an authentic city deputize for a big budget phantasmagoria. Ackroyd finishes his novel with insane Little Arthur dynamiting the scenery. There's an incendiary climax; a burn-up like Atlanta in *Gone With the Wind*. Spender's vision of a film evaporates, as William Dorrit's inheritance evaporates, quite soon after it appeared safe.

Little Dorrit is a mass-observation novel. 'The noisy and the eager, and the arrogant and the froward and the vain' are scanned by the timid and silent heroine; she watches and she waits. Christine Edzard tells her story in a pair of interlocked films. The camera, invented to be a mechanical voyeur, peeps in Amy's stead. Part One, *Nobody's Fault*, follows Arthur Clennam as he attempts to have the Dorrits sprung from prison, only to lose his own money and land up in the Marshalsea himself. Destiny is a force of breathtaking neatness. As one man rises another must fall. Part Two, *Little Dorrit's Story*, backtracks and tells the tale from another perspective, with Amy the focal point. Taken together, we have a film of approximately eight hours' duration. But it feels much longer.

When the RSC adapted *Nicholas Nickleby* into a day's work for each performance, emphasis was on energy and pace. Victorian London was a stylized edifice of blackened gantries, galleries, runways and bridges, which riddled the stage and struck out into the auditorium, tethered with ropes and pulleys. Within John Napier's carefully crafted slum, Trevor Nunn and John Caird arranged their bustling actors. The object: to convert a fat nineteenth-century novel into a theatrical extravaganza – without being guileless and ending up like Lionel Bart's *Oliver!* In the event the audience was enwrapped by the narrative, implicitly joining hands with the performers in amity – as Puck more or less says a grateful audience should; and this mood was facilitated firstly by the lean-to set (linking wings to dress circle) and secondly by the actors themselves – who strolled the aisles during remission from the action.

Nicholas Nickleby brought spectacle back to the theatre (Nunn grew even more spectacular, with Napier, in *Cats*, *Starlight Express* and *Les Misérables*); but the secret success of the production lay in the ensemble energy; in the acting rather than the technology. The actors played multiple parts, changed on-stage, each of them a fragment of the choral whole. Roger Rees was the petulant hero. With a hesitant stutter in his voice, gestures slightly jerky, rocking on his shoes, a colt: he suggested a Victorian Hamlet so much that when he played the Prince of Denmark, Rees incarnated a proleptic Nickleby (and Nicholas, like Hamlet, loves the theatre). He was partnered with the Kate of Susan Littler, a luminous soul who was to die of cancer at a tragically young age (the part was taken over by Emily Richard, real-life wife of Edward Petherbridge, the fey Newman Noggs); and by David Threlfall's Smike – a twisted, haggard stripling, like a warped, impoverished Modigliani.

Nearly twenty years separated the composition of Dickens's *Nicholas Nickleby* and *Little Dorrit*; and where the former is animated, buoyant, optimistic, crammed, the latter is meditative, sedentary, saddening, black. Christine Edzard is as true to her Dickens as Nunn was to his. Nunn's was packed with decoration and dash; Edzard is more contemplative – her cast is much given to staring out of windows and into space. The theatre engendered a bustling community; a book praising the virtues of play-acting and vaudeville yielded with ease to the stage. For the cinema, the absolute impossibility of the audience ever penetrating through to the shadowland on the screen became a metaphor of the way, in *Little Dorrit*, watchers are cut off, voyeurs powerless. And it's a novel given to the representation of powerlessness, inanition, endurance. Nicholas can smash Squeers, comply with the ruin of Ralph, and change his world; Clennam has to acquiesce in the amblings of his – it's 'nobody's fault' when disaster strikes. Happiness is hazard.

Nicholas's spirit is made delinquent in *Little Dorrit*, when it lingers as Amy's reckless brother, Tip (who borrows against 'the riches he might have given . . . if he had ever had them'), played in the film as a worthless blade by Daniel Chatto. Dickens no longer believed in heroes (David Copperfield wonders wistfully whether he'll be the hero of his own life; heroes wouldn't even be capable of framing such a question); but he possibly believed in survivors. The fit may survive by the force of personality, but the meek shall inherit the earth. Sleepiness, with Clennam, and docility, with Amy, is their disguise for inner resource – and the plot of *Little Dorrit* is Amy's education of Clennam, drawing him out into mental wakefulness.

Melodrama is much the same in *Little Dorrit* as in *Nicholas Nickleby*: a rumpus over money, hidden wills, family secrets and betrayals. But where Ralph Nickleby is a tremendous presence and evil genius, and in the RSC adaptation the best role (John Woodvine subdued and self-assured, yet letting the remorse of conscience peter across his face), Merdle has a much more symbolic function: he *is* society's empty heart. That's why we can't get to see much of him.

Michael Elphick, an actor well-known for rudesby parts, had a few whispered scenes; the brusquerie spent off-screen. What we saw was the aftermath of rant. Padding, exhausted, across the set, the villain was drained of ferocity; a carcass of refined spivvery. Clad in black and white, he grew hard to make out from the creamy walls and dark furniture; Elphick's Merdle was a vanishing trick – which is exactly what Dickens would have desired: 'He had not very much to say for himself,' the author says of his artificer, 'he was a reserved man.'

Merdle's reserve is matched by Clennam's. If Merdle is a blank suffused with the poisoned steam of commercial wrongdoing, an allegory of false gods and the root of all evil, Clennam is a blank tinted with goodness. There's a sliver of Clennam in Merdle (his pained sense of decorum); and in Clennam there may be discerned a gust of defensiveness, what Dickens calls 'his silent fighting of his way through'. Ackroyd was excessive, attributing some of Clennam's nature to a mad dwarf – but, in truth, he is stunted; he does find redemption in a little girl. (Little Arthur finds sexual release and a comfortable padded hotel he'll later incinerate.) As Dickens puts it, Amy's love, to Clennam's life 'was the termination of everything that was good and pleasant in it; beyond there was nothing but mere waste and darkened sky'.

Derek Jacobi was ideal casting for Clennam; he insinuated that darkened sky, the Merdle-in-Clennam, without which the character would be a bore and a ninny. Jacobi achieved a rare thing: he played a character adapted from a novel without losing the novelistic elements; that is, he retained the silences, the long moments of non-articulation. He retained the blankness. Possibly this was to be anticipated. Jacobi has a singular capacity for conveying vacant bemusement.* His face is as inexpressive, and then as formulated, as a mime's. In globulous repose, dilatory in the Slap-Bang coffee house before returning, after many years in the Orient, to the scene of a painful infancy, Jacobi's Clennam was consummately Dickens's – thinking over his life, and its lack of incident and happiness: 'So long, so bare, so blank. No childhood; no youth.'

The character is an empty space which the actor filled not with fuss and bits of business, but by lolling into the void. Of the coffee-house scene he confessed: 'We didn't shoot this until we'd been filming for three months, but I remember it as being a very nice little passage and I felt very much at home. I felt totally comfortable all the way down.'

Merdle's money doesn't exist, and when the public discover this, neither does Merdle ('*Now*, they all say . . . that no one was ever able to catch his eye'). An actor without a part. Clennam hardly exists (in a house 'so blank and dreary', which is his asylum) until Jacobi hacked in the contours. But how was the feat accomplished? How did he make something out of nothing, translating the abstract into the substantial? By the alchemy of acting.

Firstly, the actor's face and sad stare, his failure ever to smile and his heavy remnants of a jaunty walk, suggested the neuralgia of restraint. Dickens says Clennam's 'a man who had, deep-rooted in his nature, a belief in all the gentle and good things his life had been without'. The character is motivated by emotions he's only imagined, never felt. Jacobi gave Clennam a muted clumsiness; diffidence and gravity came from painstakingly trying to get relationships right: the formal cheer with Meagles and Doyce, the fear with Flora, the wariness when with Pancks (Roshan Seth as a firefly who keeps Merdle's empire inflamed: 'Fag and grind, fag and grind and turn the wheel'). Jacobi always used an almost imperceptible hesitancy: watching, then reacting. And only in the Marshalsea did he show an inkling of excitement; momentarily he's boosted by the danger and grotesquerie of the place – and he meets the 'pale transparent face' of the girl who'll offer him redemption. Sarah Pickering, dwarfish and dark, cowled in Virgin Mary ultramarine, played Little Dorrit as his light and angelic entreaty – as Merdle is the dark and

---

* Try picturing vacancy from our other superior actors – it would be a quite different thing: from McCowen, you'd get a parody of stillness, brought to an end with a sniffle; Robert Stephens would give a caitiff roar; Ian Richardson would look ensoured; Judi Dench, agog; Hopkins vacant would radiate fear and/or loathing; Sher'd be sinister; Callow mentally defective (i.e. Tom Chance).

demonic opportunity. (A polarity Clennam calls 'my reserve and self-mistrust'.)

Secondly, the alchemy of acting was intensified by the film's score – the most elaborate ever devised, for Clennam's thoughts are set to music by Verdi. Verdi was Dickens's contemporary* and, rivals in plenitude, if he composed Dickensian operas, Dickens's novels are prose Verdi. Both commingle the epic and the romantic, a fondness for marches, storms and big choruses against which family dramas attempt to unfold. With the slaves in *Nabucco*, the courtesans in *La Traviata*, the peasantry in *Macbeth*, the victims of the Inquisition in *Don Carlos*, the citizens of Palermo in *I Vespri Siciliani* and of Genoa in *Simone Boccanegra*, Verdi denotes the laments of the dispossessed; he orchestrates the sound of oppression and failure, where fathers and troubled kings find personal happiness compromised by a sense of honour. Duty and the clamour of ancient pacts undermine peace.

History, destiny, is never on the side of sublunaries (fortune is Nobody's Fault); the best that can be hoped for is a patient, and penitent, waiting for God: the heretics in *Don Carlos* are cheered on to the pyre by a prayer, and Don Carlos himself tries to expiate his love for his stepmother by staying at the convent of San Yuste. And in *La Forza del Destino*, Leonora attempts to avoid political travails by becoming an anchorite near the monastery of the Madonna degli Angeli. Religion is a retreat from adversity – but it is also a retreat from life. The cloisters and sacred cave are, like the Marshalsea, harrowing refuges, which in any case are requisitioned by emotion: Élisabeth and King Philippe form a procession in San Yuste, passing the tomb of Charles V; the beggars and camp followers and the wasteland of war spread to Leonora's shrine, Alvaro and Carlos, her lover and brother, coming duelling to her door.

For Clennam, 'it had been the uniform tendency of this man's life – so much was wanting in it to think about, so much that might have been better directed and happier to speculate upon – to make him a dreamer, after all.' Jacobi had the dreams made melodious with *I Due Foscari*, the opera adapted from Byron. The work concerns the illegal return home of Jacopo Foscari, once wrongly accused of murder and banished; his father, the Doge, privately believes in his son's innocence – but publicly he has to acknowledge guilt. The Venetian Law can't be seen to have passed an erroneous judgement. What this represents in *Little Dorrit* is Clennam's reappearance in London and the secrets and sins bundled about his begetting. He's an innocent who was raised in a temperature of calculated

---

* Dickens was born in 1812, Verdi in 1813. Dickens's death was headline news in Italy: 'CARLO DICKENS È MORTO' read Mary Cowden Clarke in Genoa. Verdi, who wrote *I Masnadieri* for London in 1847 (the year of *Dombey and Son*), was well known to the organ grinders interviewed by Henry Mayhew.

recrimination and purposeful deprivation; his mother's religion meant licence for misery. Mrs Clennam's 'inexorable discipline' can't admit mercy.

Believing himself in love with Minnie Meagles, we hear *La Forza del Destino*: Clennam is fated not to admit his affections, absenting himself, like Leonora, from what Dickens calls the 'difficult struggles' of infatuation. A snatch of the opera is heard again when he receives Amy's letter from abroad – his feelings are aroused, and 'the old interest he had had in her, and her old trusting reliance on him, were tinged with melancholy in his mind'. And, as the old interest in Little Dorrit breaks out as rapture, melancholy becomes illness and delirium. ('Anybody might see that the shadow of the wall was dark upon him.') The music for madness is *Rigoletto*. Jacobi, pacing the tiny Marshalsea cell in a cold sweat, showed the panic and amazement of the jester who's just discovered Gilda's abduction.

The point of that opera is an awareness that the Fool, the professional funny man, has feelings and a private life; he may be the Duke's hired comedian, but he's also a father. * The point of the opera for *Little Dorrit* is the nature of Clennam's love: it's a paternal bond. He's William Dorrit's replacement, who even inhabits the same room and bed. Amy 'thought for Clennam, worked for him, watched him, and only left him still to devote her utmost love and care to him.' Being serviceable without stint is her way of being sensual; and during Clennam's fever she appears to him with a tune from *Otello*. Mental illness tarnishes the purity – and the allusion to Desdemona's sacrifice is an example of how music in the film opens out Clennam's overheated stream of consciousness. He wants Amy for himself; he's jealous of her handiness anywhere else. (Similarly: Rigoletto cages Gilda, Otello keeps Desdemona at his side.) Christine Edzard had Verdi make a portrait of Clennam's anxious mind – a mind Jacobi constructed in his Bel Paese face.

It was a masterstroke to select Verdi above, say, Wagner; Verdi has a sense of lightness and individuality (in spite of the choral absorption), where Wagner would have been portentous, his orchestra a cynical commentary. Wagner's characters come out of mythology; Verdi's are citizens of history, like Dickens's. *Der Ring des Nibelungen* is an epic of decision-making and the consequences of action; curses are worked out across the generations and from men to gods. *Little Dorrit*, by contrast, is

---

* Carlo Maria Giulini and Richard Osborne find a connection with *King Lear*, which Verdi always wanted to convert into opera: 'In *Rigoletto*, as in *King Lear*, the relationship between father and daughter embodies extremes of pathos and terror. Sentiment sits side by side with anger, thoughts of revenge with the purest pleas for forgiveness.'

an epic of stasis; the energy is equivalent to a blocked circulation – a lot of lingering in prison or in the antechamber of that clogged heart, the Circumlocution Office. And Verdi, with the velocity of his music, paradoxically chronicled wasted time: all those languishing, charred communities; those friends and brothers in sterile clinches of hate and retribution. (Music for the Circumlocution Office is from *Luisa Miller*, where Rodolfo is set against his beloved and his own father. When love be not in the house, wrote Ezra Pound, there is nothing. Music for Bleeding-Heart Yard, a tenement terrorized by Mr Casby, is from *I Vespri Siciliani*, where the hated French occupy Sicily, and the opera ends with an interchange of marriage and massacres, treachery and allegiance, love and death.)

Wagner would have been wrong because too wilful. Dickens, in *Little Dorrit*, dawdles – and so does Edzard's film. Even the frenzy of the gamblers is ironically undercut with a scherzo from *Falstaff*. Boito told Camille Bellaigne he wanted to make Sir John a local grandee, taking back the character 'by the miracle of sound to its clear Tuscan sources'. Falstaff's an idler in the Mediterranean sun, his stratagems, like Merdle's speculations, doomed to disaster.

The film's Falstaff is Alec Guinness's William Dorrit, an indolent king in exile, the 'Father of the Marshalsea', who has no will, slumped in the jail for twenty-five years, welcoming visitors, and their gratuities, 'with overcharged pomp and politeness'. He's also Simone Boccanegra and Philippe of Spain, the lonely monarchs with family reprisals taking place within political dramas and conspiracies; Philippe, who is ready to sacrifice a son on the tree of justice; Boccanegra, who is redeemed by a daughter ('Figlia!').

Little Dorrit is a Verdi heroine. A repository of virtue and placidity, she's never noticed until she sings out. Her music – and the film's overture and finale – is from *Giovanna d'Arco*, which the librettist Temistocle Solera adapted from Schiller's *Die Jungfrau von Orleans*. Verdi's Joan of Arc is beset by inner voices: demons urge her to requite Charles VII's love; angels tell her to be courageous and fight for France. The opera demonstrates her double acquiescence. Joan becomes an armoured saviour; she also resigns herself to her father's belief that she's diabolically possessed. And it's the quality of resignation that's Amy Dorrit's; her sense of noble sufferance.

What induces this is her sense of shame. Clennam has to follow at a distance to discover the mystery of her Marshalsea home. The music for *Little Dorrit's Story* is conspicuously taken out of operas about degradation and apparent slurs: *I Masnadieri*, where Carlo would rather kill Amalia than have her know he'd been a brigand; *Un Ballo In Maschera*, where Amelia is ready to be killed by Renato because she's loved by his master, Riccardo; *Simone Boccanegra*, where Giacopo Fiesco keeps his daughter, Maria, under house-arrest because of her love for the plebeian eponym; *Nabucco*, where Abigaille is humiliated to discover she's the daughter of a slave. In Verdi, as in Dickens, no moral secret is past forgetting.

For Edzard, Verdi was her release from having to loop the film with a conventional voice-over; opera narrated. For Jacobi, music was the language of Clennam's introspection, a concert of his dreams. *Nobody's Fault* begins with the exile returned from Canton, killing time in Ludgate Hill. 'I don't know' and 'I'm liable to drift anywhere' are the vapour trail of answers he gives a keen inquirer. *Home* is a word that particularly anguishes. Jacobi clouded and all but sobbed. Indeed, his whole perform-ance, sustained over the eight hours of running time, was a variation on a sigh.

Home turns out to be a bleak house of blistered panels, run by Max Wall as the human corkscrew Flintwinch, and Patricia Hayes as Affery (Edna the Inebriate Woman in a job), a pair of ancient retainers who wait upon the chatelaine, Mrs Clennam, played by Joan Greenwood as a black Miss Havisham. (Her voice had that same huskiness which in 1949 trapped Dennis Price, knocker-off of multiple Alec Guinnesses.) The rotting residence is Mrs Clennam's private Marshalsea – 'The world has narrowed to these dimensions,' she says – and she never leaves the shuttered bedroom, lit by its single candle, preferring to sit erect on a hard chair, chanting from a giant bible about adversity and evil.

Joan Greenwood, in her last performance and visibly shrivelling, was Sibella from *Kind Hearts and Coronets* in an extremity of perverted pious-ness ('a grim kind of luxuriousness,' Dickens calls it); she reduced Jacobi's Clennam to a heavy, piteous panting, as he remembered the punishments and dark cupboards of his childhood. And, failing to sleep under sheets densely darned, in a room not used for decades, what we receive from him is an impression of waste and decay; the unbearable gravity of being. The camera concentrates on bowls of dried rose leaves, smudged panes, brown garments; backgrounds are as black as midnight, the cracking, warped walls glistening like hide. The soundtrack has, of course, the Verdi – but with the singing-voices rinsed away, and so accompanying the orchestra are dogs, bells, birds, creaks, clocks, rats, drains.

Having devoted his life to the profit and the loss of his late father's business, Clennam opts to sell up. He toils at ledgers (with the small wire spectacles, Jacobi's a junior, unconfident Pickwick) and is brought oysters and tea by a tiny maid. A patch of blue flits in and out of doors and dips out of frame. Little Dorrit is on the premises.

Miriam Margoyles bravely lets herself bulge and sag as fat, grotesque, garrulous Flora Finching, slurping soup down, spooning in cake through a parting in her lock of greasy hair. She's a symbol of all that's decomposed and crude in Clennam's life. Jacobi registered panic at the apparition – and as he is withdrawing from Flora, the substitute muse emerges, fleetingly here and there. As Dickens says, 'It was not easy to make out Little Dorrit's face; she was so retiring, plied her needle in such removed corners, and started away so scared if encountered on the stairs.' Flora talks and dominates; Amy says nothing and we never get to see her expressions.

Tracked to the Marshalsea, she's found to subsist as Cordelia to Alec Guinness's King Lear. William Dorrit sings like a bird in the cage, vain and affectedly grand, strapped into a faded quilted dressing gown. His feckless court consists of a brother, Frederick, whom clarinet-tooting Cyril Cusack incarnates as a sauntering Harpo, a proud and angry daughter, Fanny (Regan or Goneril), plus the miscellaneous drunks and degenerates who live on the stairs, and who seemed to be cast from RSC second-rankers.

Cramped and squalid, prison isn't completely the Dantesque recess we might expect. There's an eerie freedom within these walls; a freedom from creditors and badgering. 'Nobody comes here to ask if a man's at home,' says Dr Haggage, 'and say he'll stand on the mat till he is.' The Marshalsea is an existential limbo: a place where nothing happens. Nothingness. 'Nothing of the kind here, sir ... We have got to the bottom, and we can't fall, and what have we found? Peace. That's the word for it: Peace.'

Prison is peaceful because action is absent from it; a living death. Amy's first words, and first close-up, occur when Clennam asks if he can undertake to have William Dorrit restored to the outside world. '*No use*,' she claims, and Clennam fails to understand that she doesn't want her father out. He's adapted to the air of the Marshalsea – as she is herself. 'My place and use,' Little Dorrit says, 'is here' – meaning the tiny one-room palace.

Pancks, however, not Clennam, is the agent of uprooting. Roshan Seth is the film's Fool (and he gives a performance much superior to the heckler he became opposite Anthony Hopkins's King Lear at the National Theatre). Nervily nimble and ubiquitous, he finds the Dorrit lost estates and fortunes. He enjoys 'moling' and keeps a pocket book of names, dates, facts, recondite memorabilia. Pancks is an elfin genius. Clennam, meantime, has a genius only for disappointment. He gets lost in the Circumlocution Office, which is another sort of Marshalsea.

Instead of drips and damp, this place is cold and marble, with lines of silent men waiting forever in long, over-bright halls. If the Dorrit's prison is a mildewed, paupers' hell, this is hell for the well-dressed upper classes. 'I should like to be useful to Miss Dorrit,' explains Clennam hopelessly to the imbeciles and eccentrics who constitute the Civil Service, and who are the equivalent of minor devils, with forms and rule-books for tridents. The paperwork, which gets laboriously filed, is thrown on to a pyre where, giving off gusts of gas, it doesn't ignite: the scrolls and scripture absorb floodwater and leaking nightsoil, to make a squelchy pulp.

The distintegration of affidavits, writs and pleas is a further metaphor of the hero. Jacobi's architecture for Clennam was masochism, and the impulse of humiliation gradually increases. Minnie Meagles, for example, the daughter of a business colleague met in the Circumlocution Office, is a possibility of pretty paradise which he defers. He'd rather bother with the shadowy liberation of Amy's pathetic father than with the green-leaved dalliance of country life. Jacobi, making for the Meagles's sunny villa in Twickenham, was a slack and ambling cargo of perplexity, growing old and glossless, a liability (Clennam freely admits) to the gorgeous Minnie, whom Sophie Ward played with bare shoulders and a white dress, her hair an erogenous zone. She's most often shot from behind, playing the piano or out walking, the camera ogling a complex of knots, plaits and tresses, faithfully reproduced from the trichological studies of Fuseli. It's a symptom of Clennam's weary collapse that he can't desire her. Jacobi, letting his sentences fall away, gazing into a blank middle distance, lets his face be sapped by the hot sun. He could be putrefying.

When his own fortune is lost (Pancks helps him invest in a Merdle-organized railway venture), bankruptcy and dishonour are almost a relief.* Clennam, and his semi-permanent frown of incomprehension, is locked in the Marshalsea as a collegian, not as a guest. And the house of the dead is temperamentally apt. He inherits the Dorrit's filthy, peeling quarters; the vacated seat with its desiccated geranium. *Nobody's Fault* concludes with his gazing out of his room with no view, getting sicker as he stares at the damp stains and overhears the caterwauling of neighbours. John Chivery's news that Amy loves him – which made him, says Dickens 'stupefied by intelligence beyond his full comprehension' – precedes the inamorata's arrival, with a bunch of violets, to nurse him back to health. The last shot is of the sun setting over the spiked wall.

Clennam's recovery (of his money and cheer) is where the novel ends. Part Two of the film can't, therefore, be a sequel. What Edzard does, in *Little Dorrit's Story*, is start over and tell the tale from Amy's prospect. (The hint to do so was given by Dickens himself, who says in Chapter XIV: 'This history must sometimes see with Little Dorrit's eyes ...') And what her eyes interpret is the picturesque; she instinctively beautifies. The tone of *Nobody's Fault* is muted, the colours sombre, running

---

* Like the ecstasy at the end of Verdi operas, when a curse comes full circle. *Maledizione!* is the refrain to the last in, for instance, *La Forza del Destino* and *Rigoletto*.

from sepia to black; it's the biography of a disappointed life. Mr Nobody. *Little Dorrit's Story* remakes that biography as a pastoral idyll. What Clennam saw as helplessness, Amy regards as romance and abundance.

The new mood of eclogue is signalled at the heroine's birth; the prison room swarms with ripe flies, flowers and sunlight. Mrs Bangham, the midwife, fans her struggling patient with a cabbage leaf; and the Child of the Marshalsea grows up in what the warder calls 'a regular playground'. Alec Guinness makes the youthful William Dorrit, in cream breeches and a blue coat, a reprise of the jerky and dapper Herbert Pocket, taking his ease in the alley, sniffing the air from the Surrey Hills, as if a swell in Hyde Park. Shaving and tea are genteel rituals, with Amy making herself useful, fetching and carrying – a smiling helpmeet. People speak in a fairytale way (compared with the deadpan of *Nobody's Fault*); and when Guinness upbraids his screen daughter for being seen lugging water, it's the voice of a shamed and dignified Cinderella-King.

Guinness's Dorrit, a heave of affectlessness in the first film because Clennam thinks he's nothing but affected, in the second film is a comic star turn, waving to his subjects from the window, as if travelling in a royal carriage. When he meets somebody, he's granting an audience. The mildewy room is now bright and cheerful; leaves and flowers bloom and burst. The noise of the prison is the dancing master's violin. To Little Dorrit, the place is as busy and creative as a Renaissance castle. And where Clennam is fatherless and friendless, Amy's the best beloved, with plenty of protectors. The turnkey is her godfather, letting her dart in and out of London life.

Having learnt sewing, she gets employed by Mrs Clennam, who, though paralysed and strict, isn't the termagant her son fears. And the Old Dark House isn't quite the sepulchre Arthur finds, either. Amy notices extravagant plaster ceilings and the rooms are rich and mahogany; there's light and air, where *Nobody's Fault* had candle-gutterings and smotherings. Arthur himself, whom we peek at at the receiving end of trays and meals, is so self-absorbed, it's a jolt to discover him in the Marshalsea, paying his respects, and making Amy blush. This time, we register the daughter's profound embarrassment at her father's blatant begging for gratuities; she's Cordelia entrusted with the delicate wits of a Lear who has forgotten the laws against cadging. In *Nobody's Fault*, William Dorrit is a foppish con-man; now there's a stratum of eccentric pity – and consequently, the scene is more emotionally charged.

When Clennam moves to Covent Garden, he's losing himself in a teeming tenement; we get used to his abject lodgings. When Amy visits him in Part Two, however, the rooms are inviting and warm. The firelight twinkles on the silver candelabrum. Amy is excited by the bustle of the local opera house and market which to Clennam is vulgar. *Nobody's Fault* had their interview formal and puzzling; Clennam can't figure why

she has called. ('They were nothing,' he says of William Dorrit's entreaties.) *Little Dorrit's Story* interprets the scene differently. Amy has come to
do more than explain her father's freakishness; she's come to try and
exonerate him. 'I could never be of use,' she says, 'if I didn't pretend a
little'. We don't get this line in Part One because Clennam doesn't take it
in; he can't appreciate the complex father-daughter bond; nor can he
guess why it matters to her that the bond be explained to him. Reason not
the need.

Regarding the chiaroscuro of the two films, where Clennam moves in
degrees of shade and pitch, Little Dorrit shifts in light and pale yellows;
posterish reds and blues are in her spectrum. And the sets, for Clennam
sooty interiors based on Jacques Louis David, are for Amy fairytale frail,
with street vistas painted on glass, walls made of roughly washed paper,
houses built of stretched fabric and rocking ships trimmed out of cardboard. She finds Flora (who talks of 'our mutual friend') an amusing fatty;
a goddess of plenty, with her generosity and piles of pastry. And Bleeding
Heart Yard, to Clennam an enclave of pauperism and muddy puddles
sprinkled with shit, Amy regards as a toytown farmyard, with geese and
ducks nibbling at a pond; where houses are spruce and babies bouncing.
Folk don't huddle in a mendicancy, they juggle with oranges; rose-period
saltimbanques.

When Clennam brings news that the Dorrit fortune is secure, the fairy
tale style intensifies – and approaches being a long dream sequence.
Amy's language is full of over-solicitous phrases like 'My dears' and
'Darlings'. From the part of drudge she's promoted to the role of mother.
William Dorrit decked out by a dozen tailors, Amy's ambition is to see
her father for the first time as his long-dead wife would once have done –
as a man without shame. In *Nobody's Fault*, Guinness gets his money back
and is briskly thankful; in *Little Dorrit's Story*, he trembles – the first
inkling of the real tragedy of displacement Amy's long warned of. He's
greatly generous with the cash, frittering it and being lordly with it. The
quitting of the Marshalsea is regal procession; the king sets forth for
France. Money hasn't altered him: it's confirmed his airs and graces. And
Amy's last words to Clennam before she goes abroad are that she hopes
she won't alter now she alteration finds. She's horrified at the new
Marshalsea of wealth that beckons – Society, which Mrs Merdle calls
'very exacting'.

Her fairy tale is a white night. Amy hates the tedium of Grand Touring
and tittle tattling; she can barely think about her environments, and they
register as pallid, bleached sketches and washes, line and colour hardly
imprinting on the celluloid. She's lost in space. Walls are almost translucent. Dresses are sallow oatmeal. And this all coincides with Clennam's
decline back in London. Black-out matches white-out.

William Dorrit's indolence grows terminal; he flops on a big bed as a big, complaining baby, his long lank hair now roasted in curls. When John Chivery, the turnkey's son, drops by bearing a gift of penny cigarillos rolled in purple tissue, there's a fierce tantrum – Guinness discovering a fund of rage which is Dorrit's mortification at being reminded of his past. During the noise and stupid chat of Merdle's dinner party (attended by Robert Morley, Rosalie Crutchley, Jonathan Cecil and Alan Bennett), he goes finally insane, addressing the guests as if they are newcomers to the Marshalsea. The speech ('The space is – ha – limited – limited – the parade might be wider; but you will find it apparently grow larger after a time – a time, ladies and gentlemen . . .') is grim and satirical. Merdle's own stockmarket collapse follows at once; everybody is ruined, and Parts One and Two have coincided.

The fairy-tale fashion of *Little Dorrit's Story* helps work out the gothick plot. Having watched, waited and listened in the Clennam household, Amy has penetrated the family secret: that Arthur is the illegitimate son of a young actress, whom the Joan Greenwood character subsequently persecuted; the boy himself was reared in calculated cruelty and devotional nastiness, purposefully made to suffer for his parents's sin; a child of Satan and the whore of Babylon.

Mrs Clennam, sitting in judgement, is a motiveless witch in *Nobody's Fault* (Arthur never learns of his origins); through Little Dorrit's eyes, however, she is the victim of an ancient betrayal she refuses to forget. She made herself into her husband's 'dread', insisting on an atmosphere of fear and hardship, desperate for daily reparation. Old Mr Clennam's extramarital swiving stopped her life; she's frozen in an attitude of elaborate bitterness and wrath. Amy brings an end to the revenge by persuading her to release the fund once meant for the asylum-bound actress. With this money is Clennam liberated from the Marshalsea. And so the long film ends with a marriage ceremony, shot as a densely populated tableau (like a Wilkie or a Frith), and the promise for hero and heroine of 'a modest life of usefulness and happiness'.

Throughout both parts, there's a catch phrase or literary motif similar to Kipling's in *Rewards and Fairies* – where the rhetorical question 'What else could I have done?' is wrought several times into each short story. In *Little Dorrit* the recurrent phrase, like Kipling's an issue of ethical culpability, is 'nobody's fault'. Over the titles, jockeying top-hatted crowds, eyeing newspaper headlines about sundry calamities, mutter 'It's nobody's fault'; the Clennam family firm is failing, though through 'nobody's fault'; William Dorrit thinks it 'nobody's fault' if visitors slip him a testimonial; Pancks discovers 'nobody's to blame' for the Dorrit's detention; Clennam says that the industrial accident at Bleeding Heart Yard was 'nobody's fault'.

The disclaimer is most indicatively muttered over and over by a drunk on the stairs (Captain Hopkins, played by John McEnery, Mantalini in *Nicholas Nickleby*); the words come out mawkish, dribbled, desperate, and they imply a forfeiture of moral sensibility. The automation of destiny. If *Little Dorrit* has a single theme, it's the questioning of who's accountable for disaster and disappointment. Religion is depicted as rigid, vengeful, retaliatory; politics and law are brain-damaged with inbreeding (the Tite Barnacles); money makes for madness; love is abjured for social marketings (Minnie Meagles and the dotard Henry Gowan who, owing to Clennam's retreat, is 'nobody's rival'; Fanny Dorrit and the bullied Sparkler). The only enduring tenderness is between Amy and Arthur, and they are engrossed by the anonymous, monotonous crowd. Mr and Mrs Nobody.

But the implication is that the spores of goodness, lodged in the anonymous, faceless crowds, are the only chances for happiness. Contentment is the acknowledgement of duty. When labourers have to be laid off (owing to the Merdle catastrophe), Clennam is insistent that creditors know it was *his* fault: 'Let it be known it was me. Only me.' When, through Amy's connection with the Clennams, the Dorrits get a glimpse of high society, Fanny snarls, 'It's all your fault'. She's frustrated to know of a world she's excluded from; on the contrary, says Amy later, disaffection is 'everybody's fault'. Everybody has a sliver of vanity or greed or cruelty or obsessiveness or exploitativeness or snobbery somewhere in their nature; and out of such an entanglement of vice and virtue is a culture constituted, a social network structured. Communal life, its ins-and-outs, its energy, actions and reactions, is an infernal machine; members are constricted by their very citizenry – exactly as Mrs Clennam is imprisoned by rancour, William Dorrit by esoteric sloth, Merdle by cupidity, Flora by loquacity ... And so it's the thermodynamics of communal life which the film of *Little Dorrit* demonstrates; individuals in the force-field of publicity, where beyond the issue of nobody's fault/everybody's fault there's the dilemma of Kipling's Gloriana, Talleyrand, Henry VII, Drake, Washington: who can avoid capitulating before providence? What else could they have done?

The infernal mechanism that's modern civilization; the vortex of liability and honour, self-reliance and submission, trust and guilt: these big themes rest upon (or within) Amy and Arthur. They are ghosts inside the machine. And the machine of metropolitan existence is scaled down in the film to metaphor – Doyce's factory, with its spinning hoops, steam pumps, threshers, flapping fan belts, flashing brassware and clattering whirligigs. Doyce has an idea for safer engines ('an idea is put into a man's head to be useful'), and Clennam is enthralled by the detailed descriptions given on the plans, which are subsequently lost by the patenting department of the Circumlocution Office – an organization dedicated to entropy; a traditional inefficiency.

Jacobi ignited Clennam with technology; we see him in the workshop, neatly shuffling papers and cleaning his pens; he takes acquaintances on tours of the piston rods and cogs. Aside from the odd quirk, machines are safe, predictable, humming happily. As happiness with Little Dorrit comes after the end, only in the foundry could we see Clennam busy and capable. And at such times did Jacobi resemble Alan Turing, whom he played in Hugh Whitemore's *Breaking the Code*. Boffins, both.

Turing possessed a Dickensian delight in the soul of cybernetics. To Dickens's imagination, all objects have a perverse energy; they're somehow animated (Clennam's house, for example, 'had had it in its mind to slide down sideways'). And what Turing wanted to know was – what's the hidden life of the mechanical paradise? How is the gadgetry of existence discriminated?

Clennam's a victim of chance (Doyce he meets accidentally, by bumping into him); Turing is its metaphysician, an anatomist of the fine distinctions between free will, control, destiny. Alan Mathison Turing (June 23, 1912–June 7, 1954), his life and work, and the divisions within each, is a salutary parable of acting: disorder versus genius, eccentricity versus efficiency; privacy and secrecy versus public exposure and humiliation; the body versus the mind. All the codes of character are involved.

A pioneer of artificial intelligence, his innovative publications being 'On computable numbers, with an application to the *Entscheidungs problem'* (*Proceedings of the London Mathematical Society*, 1936) and 'Computing machinery and intelligence' (*Mind*, 1950), Turing was a Fellow of King's and a Visiting Professor at Princeton; during the war he was recruited to the Government Code and Cypher School, Bletchley Park, and in 1945 he went to the National Physical Laboratory at Teddington, helping to devise the Automatic Computing Engine (ACE). Elected as Reader in Mathematics at Manchester University, he then created the Manchester Automatic Digital Machine (MADAM), which contained the biggest memory-bank in the world. He killed himself, a persecuted homosexual, with an arsenic apple, aged forty-one.

The stuff of drama? For Jacobi, certainly. As we've seen, a blanched, ineffable personality he can triumph at filling out. Turing's furtiveness is a counterpart of Clennam's – with the difference that, where Verdi saturated Clennam's silences, the music of Turing's meditations is maths. Number patterns are his grandiloquence; ordinary words come painfully out, as if after locomotor ataxia. And what's at issue here is how does an actor act intelligence? The normal way out is a nutty professor, a caricature don (genius = nincompoopery); or else you zing with spite and cruelty (genius = amorality). Dopes are far easier to bring off, as they babble, drool and get up to surreal antics (John Mills in *Ryan's Daughter*; the old ladies Alison Steadman's in charge of in *Clockwise*; whoever it was, ah yes, Paul Henry, sustaining Benny in *Crossroads*). And best of all is insanity, where mental hysteria and pure genius can marry – the film characters of Bette Davis, Anthony Perkins, Jack Nicholson . . .

In reality, however, intelligence is less than charismatic (the Oxford colleges to which I belong contain the worst-dressed persons in the professional world); the work of the intellect is done at desks, the setting of word after word in clairvoyant array; and in libraries, turning over leaf by leaf, the wisdom of the past; and in laboratories, testing and experimenting. Drama bears false witness to the universities,* where academics are always doing deeds of spectacular violence and embroiling themselves in mystery and intrigue. C. P. Snow glamorized the committee boredom; Evelyn Waugh faked a myth of arcady; Simon Gray makes his lecturers lecherous, as do Malcolm Bradbury and David Lodge. Every time there's the presupposition that brainboxes must disable themselves with the galloping gonad. The shyness of scholars masks magnificent adultery, and the all too solid flesh gets its revenge upon the fretting spirit. Mind is mocked by the body.

Jacobi avoids the farce of mind/body civil war; he insists on a shaky truce, scared into immobility for Clennam, hypertense for Turing. The actor, moreover, acts intelligence by being dopey – he cross-fertilizes the genius and obtuse categories – and made his name on television as Claudius, the idiot-scholar, deferentially stuttering, spluttering, scribbling. Not for him nutty professors, zingy spite or mental illness. We get glimpses of this inexcitability in *The Day of the Jackal*, where he's Inspector Caron, clerk to the main 'tec, busily phoning, handing over messages and torching cigarettes for Donald Sinden; and in *The Odessa File*, where he's Klaus Wenzer, a frightened Bayreuth printer, with a tyrannical crone of a mother in the attic, who forges passports for fugitive Nazis. (The safe in the office contains a dossier of wicked Germans, which Jon Voight wants for Simon Wiesenthal.) Klaus Wenzer was Jacobi as a nice Peter Lorre.

Peter Lorre was hardly ever nice (*M*, *The Maltese Falcon*, *Casablanca*); yet his combination of timidity and sympathy, which he put to sinister use, is a line Jacobi may well come ably to inherit – the Merdle-in-Clennam. And until *Little Dorrit*, Jacobi's performances lacked a crucial, sweaty undercurrent of suffering (*Breaking the Code* came after Edzard's film was shot); he preferred to divide clever goodness from evil, as for

* And to hospitals and law courts. Doctors and barristers, indeed, are far worse victims of soap than professors. Ditto the police, airline pilots etc. Hardest hit are musicians, whose creativity, according to Ken Russell, is a sloppily kinky congress of art and life; in films like *Mahler* and *Lisztomania* melody-making is a sex-show.

example in *Skin*, an early episode of Anglia's *Tales of the Unexpected*, where the actor was a capering Pied Piper, with a green snake-handled umbrella and a brocade waistcoat; a Willy Wonka, dancing to hurdy-gurdies, who gives away lollies and makes everybody happy. Then he handcuffs a local businessman, peels off the circus costume, turns into a dowdy Mr Nobody, noticed by nobody, and stabs his victim. Apparently, the businessman once framed his killer, who spent fifteen years in a cell on his behalf. Vengeance enacted, it's the perfect crime – because Wonka has dematerialized. The little chap in the mac and cloth cap pads safely to his train (accidentally sprinkling a petal or so of confetti, noticed by a kid who'll obviously nark). And, trite and no masterpiece, *Skin* is nevertheless a useful classroom demonstration of Jacobi's preference for moral separateness: a colourful, good eccentric, against a drab villain. Mr Pye was similarly discriminated; and Benedick. (Prospero and Cyrano didn't involve good and evil: their works are of war and peace, anger and compassion).

Jacobi's contemporary rival on the English stage, as regards actors acting intelligence, is Ian McKellen. He's an adept at perplexed Shakespearean princes and jingled Chekovian heroes; my mental picture of him flashes up a touselled and pricklingly bright incipiently exhausted variation on Hamlet, wearing a quizzical smile. There's an acknowledgement of comedy in his distress (Max in *Bent*, Salieri, Toby Belch, Platonov, Coriolanus, Lopakhin); his performances, despite jazzy and acrobatic effects, are always subdued, contained – so unlike the electric cartoonery of Antony Sher's theatre or the jittery-hare anxiousness of Roger Rees's.

McKellen retains a foxy chiselled face, constructed, it seems, of taut planes, like a vorticist ink-sketch, which he can arrange into sharpness (Macbeth, D. H. Lawrence); or dissolve and render puffy (Walter and Profumo). Always, the eyes register irony – suggesting edifying interior dramas. And it's because we believe McKellen really thinks the words he says on stage – creating them, not just reciting them – he achieves the great actor's transfiguration, whereby the bread of the script and wine of costume and make-up became the body and blood of performance. He's an epiphanic actor: what we get to see are manifestations of his prime sensibility and feeling.

Jacobi, like, McKellen, a Cambridge graduate (and, like McKellen, an Honorary Fellow of his old college) has been plenty bookish, with an Ivanov, Hamlet, Prospero; but he has not McKellen's virility, irony. Whilst like McKellen, never sending his characters up, nor does he yet transcend them – as McKellen does, to become an abstract of muscle or vexation. Jacobi, rather, is immaculately assimilated by the parts he plays; and when he makes Prospero into Doctor Faustus, Peer Gynt into a confident student of nature, and Cyrano de Bergerac into a drawling folde-rol alike to the heroes of Anthony Burgess novels – the impression created (as with Clennam in *Nobody's Fault*) is of *damnation*. Jacobi's stage people are uniquely benighted.

Scientists, according to artists, are professional instigators of the end of the world; twilight of the gods, etc. And scientists have long fascinated artists, evolving, as they do, from magicians: Merlin, Ben Jonson's alchemist, Herr Baron Victor Frankenstein, Henry Jekyll, Professor Van Helsing, Doctor Moreau, Captain Nemo. Turing belongs with these sorcerers and disrupters of nature; his overmastering question *Can a machine think?* stamping him the most modern Prometheus. A monster-maker.

> Did I request thee, Maker, from my clay
> To mould me man? Did I solicit thee
> From darkness to promote me?

– lines from *Paradise Lost* Mary Shelley used as an epigraph in 1818.

Turing's equivalent of Frankenstein's monster was never, in fact, built; but what he imagined was a UNIVERSAL MACHINE, capable of duplicating itself and modifying itself, able to break codes, translate Aeschylus and which in short (he wrote) 'can be made to do the work of all ... It works in the following quite simple manner. When we have decided what machine we wish to imitate, we punch a description of it on the tape in the Universal Machine. This description explains what the machine would do in every configuration in which it might find itself. The Universal Machine has only to keep looking at this description in order to find out what it should do at this stage ...'

The Universal Machine would be a superman (an ordinary man, says Nietzsche in *Also sprach Zarathustra* 'is something that is to be surpassed'), capable of carrying out mental tasks to perfection; capable of infinitely realigning the infinite amount of information in its memory banks. Relations, as James would say, would stop nowhere. And should we get to know exactly how this computer functions ('After days and nights of incredible labour and fatigue,' says Baron Frankenstein, 'I succeeded in discovering the cause of generation and life; nay, more, I became myself capable of bestowing animation upon lifeless matter'), we'd have an inkling of how the brain functions.

How (speed aside), if the Universal Machine was simulating intelligence, would we discriminate its cogitation from a man's thought processes? When would we know if it remained a servant or whether it had become our master? How would the Universal Machine protect itself? What's its strength?

Responding to these issues; mindful of how the monster cast out

Frankenstein, Turing proposed the Turing Test or the Imitation Game.★
A man sits before a keyboard and screen, interrogating two concealed
players – one is also a man; the other is a digital computer. Can the
catechist tell them apart; from the responses, flesh from robot? Assuming
that each player would want to win, and fox the questioner, the Universal
Machine, writing its own programme, would learn to counterfeit human
incompetence; it would choreograph its own ability to fail – for the
superman simulacrum could win the Turing Test only by losing. A
substantial paradox.

The Universal Machine would have to fake fear and emotion; know of
vice and virtue; fabricate a whole history and background for itself;
subsume cool logic in favour of caprice and digression. Glorious in defeat
and abasement, the Universal Machine, if it required a sardonic victory
speech, could do worse than quote a bit of Mary Shelley: 'Hateful day
when I received life! Accursed creator! ... God, in pity, made man
beautiful and alluring, after his own image; but my form is a filthy type of
yours, more horrid even from the very resemblance.' Or something like
that.

The Universal Machine, Frankenstein's monster: what Turing described,
corresponding with Mary Shelley, was a great actor. A physiological
cybernaut. The Turing Test asks: how can you tell when a computer is
computing; how are its processes different from human intelligence;
when is a computer confusable with a man?

By metaphoric extension, how can you tell when an actor is acting? An
actor is *the* voodooist of any Imitation Game. His craft's precisely that of
camouflage, dissimulation; an actor makes a mock-up of a character's
encompassment, contributing rich detail to the illusion (to the *mechanics*
of illusion); and reality is duplicated in every respect, with this qualifica-
tion: it's not reality, it's a forgery. The actor's performance is of an
artificial intelligence.

So long as the audience keeps remembering that the people on stage are a
race apart, separate, distinct – actors are no better than well-programmed

---

★ *The Imitation Game* is the title of Ian McEwan's play about Turing, whom he calls
Turner. McEwan used the code-breaking at Bletchley Park for feminist polemic – the
women who do the chores versus the power games of the men who withhold the
meaning of the Ultra ciphers. McEwan adapted the idea of a Turing Test to ask how
(blindfold) could you distinguish masculinity from femininity ('Shouldn't you first
establish whether the woman can think? It's not something one can take for granted,
you know'). And, going slightly over the top, the generalization of the play was that
the Fascist threat against the homeland got local symbolic representation in the battle
of the sexes.

Alec McCowen as Wing Commander Morten in *Personal Services*. 'I flew two hundred and seven missions over occupied territory. In bra and panties.'

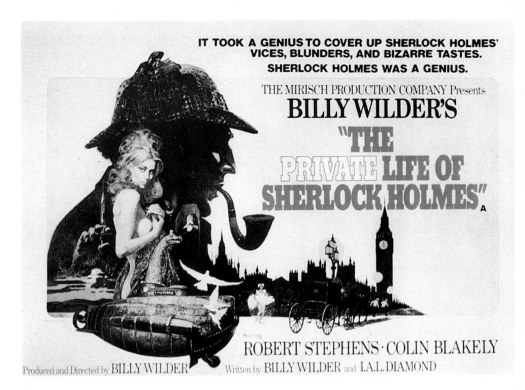

IT TOOK A GENIUS TO COVER UP SHERLOCK HOLMES'
VICES, BLUNDERS, AND BIZARRE TASTES.
SHERLOCK HOLMES WAS A GENIUS.

THE MIRISCH PRODUCTION COMPANY Presents
BILLY WILDER'S
"THE PRIVATE LIFE OF SHERLOCK HOLMES" A

Starring
ROBERT STEPHENS · COLIN BLAKELY

Produced and Directed by BILLY WILDER   Written by BILLY WILDER and I.A.L. DIAMOND

The iconography of a lost masterpiece. 'I think very few people are completely normal really, deep down in their private lives' – Amanda Prynne in Noel Coward's *Private Lives*.

Hamlet in Baker Street Robert Stephens's vulnerable, and deracinated, Sherlock Holmes.

Triple spies: Blunt (Ian Richardson) flanked by Burgess (Anthony Hopkins) and Goronwy Rees (Michael Williams).

Acting and Artificial Intelligence: 'Mr Alan Turing with Respirator and Chronometer on His Way to a Mathematical Congress' – a drawing by Guy Davenport.

Derek Jacobi as Arthur Clennam in Christine Edzard's Verdi opera compilation, *Little Dorrit*.

Judi Dench as Nora Doel, or Molly Bloom, in *84 Charing Cross Road*.

Judi Dench and Anthony Hopkins in *84 Charing Cross Road*, prior to remaking the Doels as Cleopatra and Antony.

Anthony Hopkins as an Old Devil. 'You can never be absolutely sure a Welshman's not being ironical.' (Kingsley Amis)

Richard III visited by Ghosts by J. H. Fuseli (1777): the archetype for Antony Sher's Richard – 'Alack, I love myself.'

The minotaur: to Picasso the perfect union of man and beast, mind and physique, refinement and instinct – and an image of Anthony Hopkins's stage people.

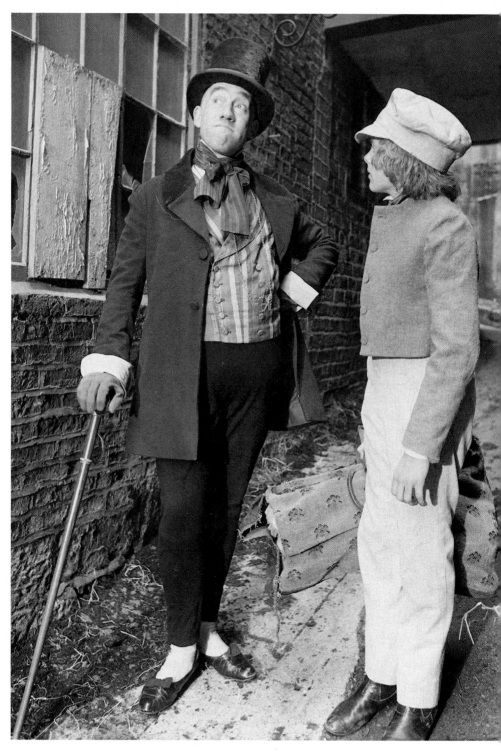

Simon Callow understudying Charles Laughton as Micawber in an adaptation of *David Copperfield*.

minor machines; humanoids. The trick is to confuse us: to make the audience mistake the mechanics for motivations, as the Universal Machine would do; gadgetry for grand passion.

Great acting is a code we don't want to break, whilst it lasts. The golden delusion of illusion.

Before the transfer to New York, *Breaking the Code* was installed at Nash's Theatre Royal, Haymarket, a brown and gold palace with a canopied facade, situated opposite the address where *The Phantom of the Opera* shall reside forever. In twinkling lights DEREK JACOBI and MICHAEL CRAWFORD glared at each other. ('We get Michael Crawford's fans, when they can't get returns,' said Jacobi).

Gielgud had had seasons here; Judi Dench thinks it should be the National Theatre. The interior is a fuliginous chamber of gold-leaf putti and ornate ephebes. The boxes, with tapestry baldachins, tilting with tassels, resemble Second Empire catafalques. And with all this the set contrasted – a Forties aircraft hangar, ventilated with big skylight flaps; a cyclorama of scudding sepia clouds. Flanking the wings, high walls of antique computer technology: ranks of bakelite switches, transformers, dials; racks of plugs, tubes, rays; coils of humming cable and wire. Dr Frankenstein's laboratory, as designed for James Whale's Universal romances, which is also the primitive ACE and MADAM and a fantasy of what the Universal Machine might look like. 'Or the inside of Turing's head,' suggested Jacobi. 'The set is purposefully stylized, so it can suggest the different locations of the seventeen different scenes. The play could be a dream. Scenes are duologues. Men and women wandering in and out of Turing's consciousness.'

The form of *Breaking the Code* is a computer programme; the loops and twists of an electric pulse following a circuit. That pulse, or Enigma Code, is Turing himself, tracking his destiny. And, truly, it's a one-man show (as against the massed *Little Dorrit*). Jacobi had himself fortified with a speech impediment as convulsive as Claudius's; in place of the emperor's twitch, a feasting on the fingernails. Turing was barely able to part incisor from bleeding cuticle to shake hands. He's a non-stop fidget (as against the immobility of Clennam), nervously coughing rather than talking; a turmoil of diffidence, so socially and personally maladroit, he invites a police prosecution for homosexuality. He's heroic because over-innocent (like Parsifal), and because he's an intellectual gallant (like Stephen Dedalus).

Jacobi matched the lackadaisical appearance with brainy self-possession and assurance. This is Turing's tragedy (or comedy): a realization of the tragic (or comic) incompatibility of mind and body. He has a brilliant mind, but a body which cheerfully rebels against him with the pederastic desires, with the agitations above-mentioned; he had dirty, inky skin and a stained, ill-matched tweed suit bolstered by mothy Fair Isle tank-tops. The look is of vagabondage.

Whitemore begins with Turing reporting a burglary, and his account of the missing objects and their provenance is an open portrait of his private life: the constable can't but prosecute, this being England pre-Wolfenden, even though the accused had had the full consent of his partner, and their gross indecency, so called, took place on the sofa in a private house. The grossest indecency is that a man who helped win the war, and whom Churchill personally commended, should need to endure the ritual humiliations of a Cheshire magistrates' court.

Luckily, the play isn't gay propaganda (Andrew Hodges's biography, Whitemore's source, is: the book offsets wonderful mathematical exegesis with inappropriate quotation from Walt Whitman). Though flurried, Turing won't make an issue of it; he's benign to the point of indifference about his body's welfare. As Jacobi plays him, there's no angry contempt for flesh by the faculties of perception. Forced to take female hormones (a cruel attempt to make him straight), he can't help being amused at the way he's started to sprout tits. Jacobi has Turing acquiesce in the fact that mind is inseparable from body, as Clennam acquiesces in dishonour and life at the Marshalsea.

But where Clennam is a dreamer, Turing wants to reconnoitre his imagination and what befalls him; sprouting tits, he's mesmerized by the metamorphosis (like Frankenstein, he 'saw how the fine form of man was degraded and wasted'). The homosexual aspect is incidental to this main theme – what matters here is the theatre of intellect and intellectual investigation; the potency of pure research. *Breaking the Code* is about enthusiasm (the lectures on mathematics are quite gripping), and the way enthusiasm can vanquish any humiliation.

We move from the police interview back to an adolescent Turing, who is on leave from Sherborne, introducing Christopher Morcom to his mother. (Morcom was played by Richard Stirling, the unrequited turn-key's son, John Chivery, in *Little Dorrit*.) Turing loves Morcom, a golden lad and fellow maths freak dying of consumption, and there's an implication that his subsequent envelopment in mental matters was a life-long homage to a dead companion. Morcom's the lost muse.

Scene-change music was modernist squeals and yelps, like rusty gates over-amplified, and Jacobi instantly turned into Turing's younger self by accentuating the restlessness, making the nerviness more sharply gauche. He's the bashful boy – who then becomes again, in front of our eyes (there are no make-up aids), the bashful, engagingly awkward older man in Manchester who picks up a bit of lovely rough over a pint – the rough who is implicated in the burglary. And acting alone modulated the elapse of time; the crabwise scuttling back and forth across the years (a shifting in time and space similar to *I, Claudius*, except there it was heavy make-up doing the chronological travel). Whitemore does, however, put clues in the writing, names of politicians and events, which will eventually assist a clumsier actor to intimate the calendar.

In Manchester, Turing was able to continue promising lines provoked by his war work, when he solved the German Ultra and Enigma Codes (electrically organized confusion, built on the principle of an adding machine, or digital calculator, which won't directly yield its knowledge) and enabled the Allies to eavesdrop on the chatter of enemy submarines. Now he goes on to devise the concept of an 'electronic brain': a machine which will think for itself. The digital computer, dreams the scientist, will take the information we give it (program for it), and perform its own processing, ruthlessly eliminating strategies which fail – like the actor, perfecting a performance (or that other impostor, the spy).

The basis of Turing's fascination with ciphers, logic riddles, puzzles and number games is mathematics' coquetry (as quite against Anthony Blunt's desire to find in the subject something blissfully passionless). He's seduced by his teasing subject and explains the passion to Dillwyn Knox. Mathematics stimulates; mathematics gives pleasure. He wanted to be its chivalric champion ever since reading Russell's and Whitehead's *Principia Mathematica*, where there's to be found a meditation on science's dark secrets: the impossibility of telling right from wrong; the dangerous allure of answers; the arousing implication of the phrase 'This assertion cannot be proved.' How, then, can it be an *assertion*? And how can Russell, a philosopher, have even the courage to use the term *cannot*? The scientist's way is thorny.

Turing's duty, as he perceived it, was to divine real order in the apparent order. The attraction of the Universal Machine was that it'd be an engine of scrupulosity; a machine to think in. Mental Le Corbusier. At present, however, the automaton is 'of the imagination'. (And so will it always be.) The imagination: 'It dissolves, diffuses, dissipates, in order to re-create; or where this process is rendered impossible, yet still at all events it struggles to idealize and to unify. It is essentially *vital* . . .' And this brilliant definition, wholly applicable to Turing, was written ninety-five years before he was born, by S. T. Coleridge. When Turing says that the laws of mathematics are adumbrated from the imagination, and that thereby mathematics is representative of how the imagination composes itself – what's the next step?

If codes, number games, puzzles represent the occultation and alle-gory-seeking aspects of the imagination, the frisky, *coquettish* aspects of the mind, is the friskiness and inviolability of mental life mirrored in the body's own mutinies, defaults and clandestiny? Are mind and body in secret amity, rather than mutually distinct? The implication of all this is that if, to win the Turing Test, the Universal Machine has to sabotage itself, then the lofty mind, likewise, to be true to itself, must be prone to obliquity and deviations – so that its operations resemble the body's. Therefore, Turing's arsenic apple isn't self-hatred, and self-love's too strong a term; self-content, more accurately. No wonder Jacobi took the fatal bite with a kind of smile on his face.

God, said Turing, is a mathematician. Plants and shells and rocks and trees have a dismaying order and structure. Whitemore, however, reckons the dream of perfection is nightmarish, a curse. Turing is spooked by the vision of being trapped inside a computer and forced to beat it at chess. He can win only by playing deliberately badly (an inversion of the Turing Test, where the machine plays deliberately badly). The computer, the grand-master Universal Machine, can't tolerate errors and mistakes, and commits suicide in alarm and disgust. This is intended as an unsettling premonition.

Jacobi worked against making Turing's insomniacal fear a melodramatic device. His Turing didn't kill himself because of the body's bubbles and squeaks; rather, as we've seen, the bubbles and squeaks are inherent in higher thinking – and death's the reconciliation of form and content. Nor did he play the homosexuality furtively. Turing made confessions (to his mother, or to Pat Green, a Bletchley colleague) open-handedly. There's no agonizing about a failure of normal reciprocation. Adroitly, gently, he fended off bluestockings who would come and court.

Any other actor could much warp the play, making *Breaking the Code* an incendiary disquisition on the encoding and enigmas of homosexual disguise and sufferance. (A theme, perhaps, of *Blunt*; and imagine Antony Sher or Anthony Hopkins torturing themselves as Turing.) The code Jacobi preferred to break (and of which homosexuality was as a subset N_1 of the whole N) was Turing's *complete* personality, its cognitive and physical properties; and the Enigma and Ultra cryptographs, digital dynamos, are Turing descants, just as mathematics is his love-lyric.

When he lectured the boys at Sherborne (Jacobi doing a Royal Society demo to the stalls: how, like Diderot, we love to see wise men on display!), his enthusiasm was that of a man-boy who'd never really left school; he retains, in his grown-up work, the excitement of a shy small child at play. (And his grown-up questions are a small child's.) If the Universal Machine is constructed, and it starts to think for itself, does it have a soul? 'What,' he asks, 'are mental processes? Can they take place in anything other than a living brain?' We can't predict what the mental processes of the Universal Machine might be; nor can we predict what questions would be worth asking ... As Turing extrapolates theme and counter-theme, thinking himself deeper into conundrums, *Breaking the Code* got on with the story by forking into past, future, present, and at hazard – yet it all cohered, as Jacobi's dingly-dangly Turing cohered. We raced along the trajectory of his contemplations.

Eventually we arrive at the drama of the arrest, which Turing blunders into with genius. He's temperamentally unable to fathom the Law. As a scientist, he knows there is no petty case of right and wrong. Each circumstance, each discovery, must entail new decisions, new juxtapositions. *That*, says the worthy peeler with the warrant, would make for anarchy. Turing refuses to compromise, lie, make allowances: to be falsely perfect, falsely orderly. He's true to a lofty integrity – which doesn't impress the security service, nervous that he'll spill the Bletchley beans to a renter. (Ironically, Kim Philby had long blown the Enigma and Ultra secrets to the Russians, and Anthony Blunt had access to the Government Code and Cypher School files. While Turing was being prosecuted, Burgess and Maclean defected – on May 25, 1951.)

Jacobi's Turing was the man whose diagrams and calculations are strip-cartoons for the *Tractatus* (and the Cambridge gossip was that Wittgenstein considered Turing the only man bright enough in all the world to understand him). After seeing a performance, I had an appointment with the harlequin backstage. The back of the Haymarket is a Regency terrace; how different from the usual pissy, vomity alleys disclosing most stage doors. I was bidden up worn wooden stairs (like in an Oxford college), and to the star's dressing room. DEREK JACOBI was the legend on a brass coffin plate screwed into the dark blue oak.

The star's dressing room in this theatre is John Gielgud's favourite chamber, and no wonder. A grandee's bedsit, apt for holding court in quilted dressing gown, or for being magnificently alone, in unbuttoned blouse, holding a goblet of hock and seltzer. The antechamber contains Tate Gallery oils and a fridge. The inner sanctum, with a divan for the spent performer – or for casting chorines – is dominated by an ornate white wardrobe (satirically housing Turing's rags) and an elaborate davenport, with compartments bulging with billets-doux. There's an open fireplace, which once warmed Edmund Kean. Electricity is hidden away, and illumination comes from small bulbs enhanced by recessed mirrors; the effect is of dancing candlelight.

Chairs are Age of Enlightenment wicker with restrained gold adornment. Two high windows survey Suffolk Street. But for its being London, this could be the set of a Cambridge don (though a don wouldn't sport on his noticeboard wires of congratulation from Larry and Joanie and from Alec Guinness).

Jacobi seemed engagingly ill at ease amidst the Lord Byron trappings, as though he'd been assigned the pad by accident, and that any second a mislodged diva would burst in and fling him out. Then he said:

'I've wondered about moving in permanently. Jack Lemmon only lately moved out. But I dislike any after-the-show entertaining, which is what the suite lends itself to. I find that so boring. Some actors give a performance on stage, then go to their dressing rooms, to receive the fans, and give another kind of performance. I like to wash off the make-up and go home, or at most go to a pub.'

The message was a distinction between professional and private life; a limitation put on what the public has access to. Jacobi, quiet and pensive, doesn't desire to make himself available as a celebrity. So what did he think of the name in lights outside? Who was the DEREK JACOBI flashing in neon?

'It's not me! I am shitting every colour and size of brick about being in the commercial West End. This is my first experience of it. I cannot bear even to walk past the front-of-house. I park my car and creep into the building at the back. I'm embarrassed by those huge photos. They're of an usurper!

'I've always been a company man: National, Prospect, RSC, where the very institution is responsible for success and failure; you're subsumed in the larger entity, absorbed into the family. Now I'm having to lead. Now I'm having to be the figurehead, with all the responsibilities this entails: I'm paranoid that it's all down to *me*. If the public stop coming, it's *my* fault; if a performance goes badly, or slowly, or isn't effective, *I'm* to blame; *I've* cocked it up.

'And it's the same play, over and over. In a repertory company, the variety of roles is stimulating; the chop and the change. I miss that, I have to confess. Benedick on Monday, Prospero on Tuesday, Cyrano on Wednesday, Peer Gynt on Thursday. Now I've got to be Alan Turing eight times a week. Every night I have to go on and work incredibly hard to convince a new audience all over again of his existence. Every perform-ance, start from scratch.'

(The actor as vital effigy, who has to give the frighteningly accurate representation of real life. Robotic repetition.)

'Owing to the reviews, or the play, or my name, or God knows what, the public come with an expectation. The public want me to measure up, to shape up. And so I have to convice them of my abilities, my worth, over and over. Every performance, I'm on trial.'

At the RSC or the National, as Jacobi hinted, the ensemble goes on trial, or so the actor can fantasize, deflecting attention away from himself. And, indeed, when there's a new clinker at Stratford or on the South Bank, critics in the newspapers quickly apportion blame on to the consultant directors and artistic administrators; the chairpersons and makers of policy. They may as well try and explain away inner-city poverty by describing the luncheons taken by the board of a merchant bank. Jacobi's successful seasons at Stratford, the Barbican and on Broad-way reversed the idea that power resides in the group rather than in the individual. Jacobi became very much a prodigy, because he allowed

Benedick and Cyrano de Bergerac to be prodigious. The characters became bigger than the productions containing them.

'If you were trapped in a nightly soap, there'd be an accumulated expectation,' I said. 'Each episode would lean on the foregoing instalments. For Turing, the audience are likely to know nothing. All they can be sure about is that a famous actor shall do his stuff.'

'It gets harder, too. When young, you can take big risks. Huge, enormous, crazy risks. The young actor can be daring. When you're slightly more established, you oddly start being taken for granted. It's expected you'll be a favourite in the race; and so you have to work and work, just to keep ahead – to justify being the favourite.'

'The sport of kings.'

'Exactly a sport. I keep fighting, fighting. This is a great burden, a great pressure. But if the actor doesn't like it, hard Cheddar! *Hard Cheddar!* Though it may be increasingly hard to surprise people, *surprise* the actor must. You have to stay in the race; you have to keep winning. It must be wonderful to be young and coltish, and come and go from the race at will . . .'

'What about the coltish cogitator, Alan Turing?'

'The key to the character, for me, is presenting the excitement of his intellect with conviction; his enthusiasm and passion for his subject. Mathematics is the real sex-interest in the story – not the boys. His homosexuality was a school-lav kind: you-show-me-yours-I'll-show-you-mine. Illicit and grubby.'

'*Turing und Isolde*,' I said. 'Mathematics was Turing's Isolde: in Lieb' umfangen ganz uns selbst gegeben'.*

'Throughout rehearsals,' Jacobi went on, 'Hugh Whitemore and Andrew Hodges were present. We talked about how to present the man interestingly. I mean, a play about a gay mathematician hardly sounds inherently dramatic.'

'It does not.'

'Then we realized. Turing's gusto is the business. So we have the big speech at Bletchley – you remember it perhaps, the long account about Bertrand Russell and scientific certainties? Well, when I first read it, I said this isn't theatre, this is a lecture. Whitemore and Clifford Williams, the director, proved me wrong. It's the scene people tell me is the high point.'

The reason the dissertation scenes work is that we realize complicatedness is being made fathomable. We almost participate in Turing's own discoveries. We are the secret-sharers.

There was a tap-tap on the outer door. In crept an East European couple, shy as rabbits, introduced as the actor's former landlady and her husband, from his more modest days, who wanted to say how moved

---

* 'Enveloped in love; given up to each other.'

and mesmerized they'd been, 'especially the big mathematics scenes'. Jacobi was humbled. This comment was too perfectly timed.

'Rehearsals were fascinating,' he said. 'We enjoyed discussing the issues of the play, and Hugh revised and adapted as we went along. Mathematics and artificial intelligence...'

'Is an actor an instance of artificial intelligence, his performances elaborate and subtle programs? The secrets of acting and breaking its code?' I said.

'The actor is certainly an intellectual in that he has to think what will work, what will fail. He rationalizes his risks. He also has to imagine himself in a part – in performance he imagines his way along – and acting is about pretend, so it's artificial in that sense. An actor has to be totally absorbed in the part, not withholding anything – yet, and this is tricky, yet, he must also project an eye, or a double of himself, into the auditorium, which will constantly monitor his actions. If you are an actor, you must act and watch yourself acting simultaneously. You split up. You put yourself in the position of the audience, think what they'll think.'

The Turing Test, or a derivation thereof: predict the predictor. (Jacobi gave all this with fingers and hands doing a busy ballet of emphasis.) He went on:

'It is so important to care for the audience, to keep in mind that they'll be thinking of you: a two-way process. Otherwise the actor may as well just be masturbating!'

'Masturbating?'

'Masturbating. It's masturbation! The actor is showing off, shaking about, moaning and groaning, oooaahh! It's lovely! It's gorgeous! But he's wanking away. Completely solitary, doing zero for anybody else, doing nothing. Blank. Infertile. There are, of course, actors who cavort in this way: actors who go on stage to talk to themselves and exhibit their egos and massage their big personalities. And a voyeuristic public exists for them, too. There is a market for great masturbators!'

Aaoh! aoh! aooh! What's all this, then? *Visage du Grand Masturbateur* (1929) by Salvador Dalí. The large yellow foetal face without a mouth (so it speaks, if at all, only inly); the hooks and stones of a dried-up sea; the pliable woman's head emerging from a cheesy mass, sniffing a boy's concealed genitalia: the picture is an eerie symbol of sterility, of something dusty and deformed and consumed by ants, with the help of a giant grasshopper. A lily signifies the surreal-funereal, and Dalí's is a composition about decomposition. The Great Masturbator presides over a waste land. *Oed' und leer das Meer!*

By the same token, Jacobi argues, the self-enwrapped actor is, in the end, impotent; his performances, even if brilliant, banal. He himself draws us into his orbit by generating a sympathy without sentimentality;

and his underdogs are never maudlin. And with *I, Claudius*, the worm was finally betrayed as wise. Jacobi accomplished there what he now does supremely: the intimation of genius inside meekness. (Turing is the culmination of this, Clennam an experiment in infinitesimal nuance that is Jacobi's ghost sonata.)

Claudius is a banal watcher and diarist in a brilliant, decomposing waste land. His world awaits Dalí as a portraitist. Tiberius Drusus Germanicus, known as Claudius (*claudicare*: to limp), who lived 10 BC to AD 54, was the spluttering, lame buffoon who, in private, looked and listened hard: the incognito chronicler of a dynasty in its decadence. For fifty years he was the patrician prat, the idiot scholar; then, at Caligula's assassination, he was raised to the purple – an honourable oasis until his wife, Agrippina, poisoned him to make way for her son, Nero.

Roman scandals have delighted the world ever since Suetonius and Plutarch. The modern public has had four screen adaptations of Henryk Sienkiewicz's *Quo Vadis?*: 1901, 1912, 1923 and 1951, the last with Peter Ustinov as an unctuous Nero (a character described by the director, Mervyn LeRoy, as a 'son of a bitch who plays with himself at nights'); plus adaptations of Lew Wallace's *Ben-Hur* (Charlton Heston winning an Oscar); *Julius Caesar* (with Charlton Heston); *Antony and Cleopatra* (Heston again); the Burton–Taylor *Cleopatra*, a Hollywood marriage writ big; and the Penthouse *Caligula*, more full of pussy, to use an expression of Barry Humphries's, than peak-period in a pet-pound (Gore Vidal wrote one of the draft scripts).

A lot of funny things happen on the way to the forum. All these tug-and-toga shows, taking place in the interregnum between paganism and Christianity ('the point at which the ancient world still touches ours directly,' says Robin Lane Fox) are licence for sexy melodrama – a tradition stage and screen derive from Victorian painting: Leighton's leopards and virgins, sea nymphs and muscly heroes; Alma-Tadema's rose petals, water, sunlight; Poynter's bathing beauties; Burne-Jones's sad and heavy maidens. The dalliance of the ancient world was a convenient opportunity for articulating contemporary fantasy – all those belles and beaux peeped at swimming, sleeping, fighting. And, the more authentically classical the pictures, the more paradoxically Victorian. Loose dark hair falls around blanched skin and ruby lips – faces from period photographs. The pictures are languorous, ornately posed, with bodies sighing at their toilet or reposing after physical exercise (yet always contriving to look fashionably ill). Marble terraces and mosaic halls could be from any new baronial country house; and the position of figures, either talking earnestly (in ethical debate) or snoozing as if in a nursery, or splashing on the shore or at the spa – they're Victorians in fancy dress.

'The style of your own time,' argues Hugh Kenner, 'is always invisible.' Glaring at anachronism is hindsight's benefit. Nineteenth-century exoticism was current eroticism, and Cecil B. DeMille belongs with Watts and Alfred Waterhouse. LeRoy's *Quo Vadis?*, similarly, is a documentary on post-war Hollywood, the end of an era that meant people like Finlay Currie. Charlton Heston is a Michelangelo titan, breathed into life from the Sistine fresco. He looks and sounds as a Classical hero ought, except his frowns and friendly teeth are on the scale of Fifties Pop. He can't escape the aura of all-American college beef, as depicted by Roy Lichtenstein. (His Moses is a Wild West patriarch). Those shoulders were made for Cinemascope.

Richard Burton was a Celtic brooder. He failed to transfer his genius from stage to cinema, and by the time of *Cleopatra* he was willing to exult in parody. (This, at least, is the standard view, and I mostly go along with it – except to suggest that Burton wanted to do in acting what Dylan Thomas achieved in poetry: to whip up sensations of gaiety and lustiness, and Bardic growling – and he needed to do all this for exactly the same reason as Thomas: to disguise incoherence.) The film is conspicuous consumption to a particularly brazen degree, the off-screen tantrums and sprees affecting the on-screen mood of Sixties partying. Despite the lavish sets and costumes, it's a home movie, Antony and Cleopatra are just the costumes Burton and Taylor happen to be wearing – loose licence for a gaudy night. Taylor's black fringe, and Mary Quant mascara, which Amanda Barrie expropriated for *Carry on Cleo*, cost an estimated $44,000,000. And money was no object to Bob Guccione's *Caligula*, an animated *Penthouse* gate-fold. The film was a sixth-former's soft-porn gross-out; an orgy of Seventies permissive chic. (I had to go to Paris to see a reasonably uncut print.)

Robert Graves's *I, Claudius* (1934) turned a history book into a lively novel of depravities, which smacks of a recognizable world. Graves made the classics contemporary – and popular. The mood is that of the Thirties thriller and detective story, as written by Nicholas Blake (C. Day Lewis) or Grahame Greene – who rewrote Roman scandals as Brighton gang warfare. And to Christopher Isherwood, Holmes's unbending of the poker in *The Speckled Band* symbolized the brawny brainbox who'll be the ideal hero; Claudius is a satire of this. And to some extent, the decadent Caesars resembled the ruling class intent upon the Great War – so *I, Claudius* is *Goodbye to All That* over again. Both are books about destructiveness; both are literatures of last things. The damned.

The BBC television series was made during the era of *The Godfather*, and seemed to me almost a homage to Coppola. The studio Italy, a few bushes and a plastic forum, could be an abstract of the Mafia's Little Italy or sunshiny Nevada. Brian Blessed hugged and mugged as an obese, slyboots Corleone. His Augustus was a very bad impersonation of

Marlon Brando; and the shuttered rooms, where Siân Phillips hissed and schemed as Livia, were reminiscent of the inner offices at the Corleone mansion. Caligula (John Hurt), preening and posturing, a naked civil savant, moaning poetry as he sliced up bodies, was a joke on John Cazale's misfit brother, Fredo. And Nero (Christopher Biggins), outgunning Augustus in girth and Caligula in homosexlessness, was squealing and beroughed and reminiscent of the cabaret turns watched with Hyman Roth in Cuba.

The Godfather is dynastic gangsterism; the Corleones are an empire fiercely protective of family feeling (if they kill each other, it's because fratricide is their prerogative); and *I, Claudius* traced the tangled roots of power back to the Mediterranean cradle. Coppola and Graves tell the same story: the sordidness of loyalty and imperious competition.* And at the centre of the BBC classical comic strip of catamites and caryatids was Derek Jacobi, the hollow crown.

A sad, misbegotten scribe, a rictus of twitches and speech defects, Claudius was nevertheless a stately cripple: Jacobi's tone emerged wry and beautiful from within his own splutter, like Laughton's cantabile rasp as Quasimodo. Perhaps his Claudius was the series's Don Vito equivalent – for Brando, in *The Godfather*, is mostly in melancholy repose, dignified and operatic, an emperor at the end of his days.

'We must all have peaks in our careers,' said Jacobi. 'Every actor dreams of it – and Claudius was mine. Of course, you hope there'll be other parts and bigger peaks, as well. Every actor wants that part which will demand every atom of his ability – but it so seldom turns up. But Claudius did turn up.'

Jacobi had to age from being a gangling youth, everybody's retarded cousin (Robert DeNiro took over for the young Don Vito – thereby having to imagine the impersonation of a performance the young Brando never gave), to the shaking old codger, fiddling with his scrolls.

'Originally there were going to be at least two Claudiuses, young and old, but I wanted to play the whole man. It was spooky: the make-up was applied for the old Claudius, the latex wrinkles and jowls, then the wig – and Robert Graves was staring back at me from the mirror, especially before the grey hair was trimmed. I once spent a weekend with him in Majorca, though he was a bit gaga, and his Claudius was a version of himself, I'm sure; so my Claudius tried to be a bit like Robert Graves, too.'

---

* Ancient Rome and Modern America continue to meet in *Dallas* and *Dynasty*, where the characters, oblivious of history, are condemned to repeat it – however recent, amnesia being the commonest affliction foisted in the scripts. The Texan Ewings and Denver Carringtons are incestuous Caesars and Corleones, making empires out of business deals. Alexis and JR come direct from the atrium orgy. Suetonius as soap.

'You mentioned that Andrew Hodges was present for advice during *Breaking the Code*, and gaga Graves assisted you in *I, Claudius*. So authors assist. What about academics? Do they help?'

'Seldom. Never, actually. They forget that the page isn't the stage. Little academic writing is of the slightest use in theatrical terms. G. Wilson Knight? He's quite interesting to read for background, but I always ask: what does it mean for me as an actor? How can I use that?'

'Where does the inspiration come from?' I asked.

'Well, Cyrano de Bergerac is an angry, provocative man. Very showy. He looks for fights. I'm not like that at all. I'm a classic Libran: balance, equanimity. If there is any fuss and provocation, I back away. So for the anger I had to *imagine* it.'

'Which do you think is the best acting: imagining, feigning feelings you don't naturally have within you; or when you can make direct use of yourself for a role?'

'Well,' Jacobi said, taking his time, 'it's got to come from within. So the imagining, the fantasy, has its own kind of realism; it's made up, but authentic at the same time.'

'Invention has its own integrity.'★

'Maybe for Cyrano, the anger *was* in me; I've not faced that possibility before. Perhaps the anger was in me, lying latent, waiting. It had to be, I suppose. I am suspicious of those actors who say that if you wear the right shoes, the right hat, the part comes together. I wish it was as easy as that, actually. Give out the right wigs and we'll all be actors! Everyone could be an actor, if acting was merely a costume ball.'

'If acting digs deep into hidden parts of your personality and nature, can your real-life self make use of what's succeeded on stage? Is acting an aid for the real thing?'

'No. Nothing the actor does in the fantasy factory changes him as a person. How could it? Hamlet kills three people and is implicated in the deaths of two others. That would make you into a mass murderer.'

'Be less extreme!'

'On the other hand, I myself do feel I need the theatre: I like knowing what is going to happen, the pre-ordained nature of the script. You're immune, for a few hours every day, from the shocks, surprises and abrasions of real life. In real life, I fumble through. On stage, I feel safe, I'm in control. It's arranged and orderly.'

We'd encroached upon a Turing ponderosity. The paradox of the Universal Machine is that if it is to win the Turing Test it has to pretend it has free will. Omniscient, it would have to feign ignorance of future events, of outcomes, of its own predictions. Free will, according to

★ 'After all,' quipped Wilde, 'What is a fine lie? Simply that which is its own evidence.'

Tolstoy (who is quoted in *Breaking the Code* – Pierre, from *War and Peace*, was Turing's literary hero), 'is what we do not know about the laws of human life'. The Universal Machine knows all structures and strategies: it gives the grand illusion of not knowing. The actor, making his way through a script every evening, gives the grand illusion of not knowing the material in advance – he pretends to banish foreknowledge; an imitation game – and to this extent the actor in performance is a Universal Machine. Artificially intelligent.

'If a part changes the actor,' Jacobi went on, deflecting from psychology to technique, 'it can only change my abilities, my style, my understanding of the rules of the game. What works, what doesn't. Cyrano taught me about the little ways of winning an audience I'd overlooked in the past. And the other thing about *Cyrano de Bergerac* was being able to exult in that marvellous translation.'

'Did you meet Anthony Burgess?', I asked in something approaching awe.

'He came over from Monte Carlo when we were three or four weeks into the run. We had dinner afterwards, but I can't say we got on. He seemed rather spiky and aloof.'

There are many good reasons for Burgess's tetchiness – and they have a bearing on the relationship between actors and acting; between script-writers and those who make off with their inventions. Firstly, English actors enunciate badly: their elocution falters when they try to pretend poetry is prose, when they try to speak naturalistically. Burgess prefers old-fashioned euphony – and he is right to do so, but there are worse offenders than Jacobi, whose voice, if not Ian Richardson's clarinet, is unique and concordant.

Secondly, and related to the first point, Burgess had re-envisioned Rostand several times: on each occasion the play gets more like an opera. Burgess, who wrote a book called *This Man and Music* and whose novels contrive a musical pattern of tempo, re-echo and relation of content to form, has made translations which are really librettos awaiting orchestration. And he was therefore exasperated his words weren't sung.

He first worked on *Cyrano de Bergerac* in 1970 for the Tyrone Guthrie Theater, Minneapolis. Then, a few years on, the adaptation was rejigged for Broadway, Burgess organizing his text into ninety lyrics (or eighty-one, depending which account you read). The play was now a musical (music by Michael Lewis) and the Cyrano of *Cyrano!* was Christopher Plummer, scaling up the comedy, soldiery, poetry, pathos and sentimentality that's almost Captain Von Trapp.

However, the play, in Minnesota a success, as a musical, in New York, was a flop. That it opened the same week as Watergate didn't help.

'Yes, he'd been busy with Rostand,' said Jacobi. 'Act IV didn't work.

Burgess had Christian come on reading out a recipe book – so we had Roxane arrive with the food instead. And the Man in the Moon sequence was poor theatrically. So Terry Hands asked him to revise – and he did, and it was brilliant.'

Hands's production was extravagant, lush, festive. Ralph Koltai designed a seventeenth-century theatre, a battlefield, an orchard – a theme of giant spheroids (comprising chandelier, sun, moon, blossomy tree) derived from his *Ring* at the Coliseum, where Wagner's music-drama took place amidst a solar system of whizzing planets. Alexander Reid (a graduate of Scottish Opera) made displays of grey and red silk costumes out of Dumas's *Les Trois Mousquetaires*. But the music? Nigel Hess's soupy score was undistinguished. The visuals, the words: Giacomo Antonio Domenico Michele Secondo Maria Puccini, would that you were living at this hour. The RSC was operatic, but denied us an opera.

The third reason for Burgess's coolness over the show was that Cyrano is a summation of his fictional heroes. Cyrano, the wordsmith, the romantic, the duellist: he's not unlike the writer, rake and fighter of *Little Wilson and Big God* – Burgess's memoir dashed down in the style of wild knight Roy Campbell's *Light on a Dark Horse*; a rollicking, lusty chronicle of a man of action who happens also to have a potent and irresistible cultural sensibility.

The lunatic (Cyrano pretends to have fallen from the moon; Burgess was once diagnosed as suffering from a brain tumour), the lover (Cyrano adores Roxane; Burgess, less righteous, is still highly chivalrous – *Little Wilson and Big God* talks of 'spectacular adultery'), and the poet (Cyrano can compose a ballade whilst fighting a duel; Burgess wrote it for him) are all compact:

> Bizarre, excessive, hyperbolic, droll
> With his triple-waving plume, his visual soul.

And what Ragueneau says of Cyrano is true, in addition, of other Burgess characters. They are persecuted picaros, who manage to flourish in spite of a traduced liberty: Enderby, the menopausal scribe, is importuned by mad prospective wives. In *Enderby Outside*, for instance, he's pursued by Miranda Boland, who describes herself as a selenographer, or student of the moon. (The Arabic for moon is *merenda*, the Malay *bulan*.) In *The Clockwork Testament*, the moonstruck inhabit New York, where Enderby sees off assailants on the subway with his swordstick: 'It flashed Elizabethanly in the swaying train.' He's a Cyrano of the stockyards.

Spindrift in *The Doctor is Sick*, a phonologist, collapses, lunatic, and he roams the London criminal underworld, an ill Orpheus. As he goes further into his mental ailment, words part company from their meanings

– a dislocation also found in *Honey for the Bears*, where Paul is hunted through Leningrad. Both men, like Cyrano, learn to live by and on their eccentric wits:

> I go along any road under my moon
> Careless of glory, indifferent to the boon
> Or bane of fortune, without hope, without fear.

And they wear their elegance within – as Toomey, the octogenarian homosexual novelist of *Earthly Powers* does, flaunting words as weapon and defence, learning that to live is to suffer. Alex in *A Clockwork Orange*, however, creates the suffering in other people's lives. He'll be Burgess's best-known character, owing to Malcolm McDowell's cherubic hoodlum in Kubrick's film (a performance which comes from *If* and zooms to *Caligula*.) In Burgess's original book, Alex and his tiny swine speak an argot of the author's devising: *devotchka, chelloveck, malenky, slooshy*. Based on Russian and army slang, the concoction isn't, in fact, futuristic. Alex speaks with a gracious, folderol, Elizabethan syntax, and he's fastidious about dress and decorum. He's a connoisseur of Beethoven and clouts Dim 'for being a bastard with no manners and not the dook of an idea how to comport yourself publicwise, O my brother.' Alex murders finically. He's a romantic dandy and Hell-Fire Club Byron or Barry Lyndon – or an evil counterpart to Cyrano.

Burgess's characters are all dandiacal of diction; pugilists if necessary (even Toomey stumbles into scraps); gallants certainly (Alex fantasizes about a wife and child). They are Cyranos:

> Philosopher and scientist,
> Poet, musician, duellist,
> And voyager through space,
> A sort of controversialist,
> Whose wit kept to a charted track
> But sped at a great pace,
> A lover too, who seemed to lack
> The luck in love of other men –
> Here lies Hercule-Savinien
> De Cyrano de Bergerac,
> Nothing, everything, nothing again –
> Sunk now, without trace.

Even Burgess's Freud, in *The End of the World News*, his Moses and Jesus, in *Man of Nazareth*, and his Shakespeare, in *Nothing like the Sun*, are Cyranos: spunky, isolated paladins. And what his heroes fight for, and commonly are in love with, is language. 'Language, language,' croons Alex. Cyrano makes love to Roxane, his megaphone Christian, with language ('It's my words she kisses'). Language is a dangerous conveyance of ideas and sensations: it is an instrument of sedition, because an instrument of the erotic.

Burgess, throughout his career, has measured up as the slave of two masters: Gerard Manley Hopkins (big in *The Clockwork Testament*) and James Joyce. Both worshipped the mystery of words; both were concerned with getting music out of speech; both were concerned with the tension between euphony and form; both examined sound as a transmitter of sense. Neither feared, being martyrs to their cause, being difficult and obscure.

Joyce was seven in 1889 when Hopkins died. *Cyrano de Bergerac* was written in 1897, and Edmond Rostand died in 1918, when Little John Wilson, by the grace of Big God, had just attained his first birthday. Is this a surprise? *Cyrano de Bergerac* seems to chime with the 1640s it depicts. Yet the themes of the play: manners and morality, foppery and integrity, games and genuine emotion, ugliness and beauty – these are flaunted (especially in the original), with the langour of the *fin de siècle*, spawned from a Paris walked through by Baudelaire, Oscar Wilde and the Lord Alfred Douglas who translated *Salome*.

Burgess's translation and emendations, his *Cyrano!* and Cyrano, are redolent of what Hopkins would have attempted, had he been a novelist and *Observer* columnist aspiring to be the lost heir of Joyce, instead of being a Jesuit priest who didn't know Joyce existed; or what Joyce would have written, had he made money early (*Dubliners* sold to Louis B. Mayer), and who then went to live in Mediterranean sun or Alpine comfort, accepting commissions from international theatre companies, instead of being a wandering pauper, reliant upon dwindling patronage, his writings printed piecemeal; had, in sum, Hopkins and Joyce not been Hopkins and Joyce at all, but a sesquipedalian opsimath, operating out of rue Grimaldi in the Condamine of Monaco:

> The golden ring
> Of my own writing, lines that soar and sing
> Through my brains and bones and blood, is my best
> Reward . . .

Derek Jacobi, his performance a salad of little of this, thus couldn't possibly win the master's approval. Burgess's perfect Cyrano, I would maintain, is Burgess. And what's revealed by the whole congeries here described is the process whereby a character ('Cyrano') is created by the imaginative ebbs and flows of a famous writer ('Burgess' – 'Anthony Burgess' being the fictional on-paper persona of Manchester rover John Wilson – just to add another layer of complexity), only for that character to escape through being acted. Then to the elements be free, and fare thou well!

DEREK JACOBI

Jacobi's Cyrano was a shrill chevalier: the crafty intelligence, Claudius made acrobatic; the neurosis about the nose, a proleptic Turing; the acquiescent idolatry for Roxane, the sombre Clennam. Turing's body, its insurrections and ramifications, is exactly Cyrano's love-hate relationship with his snout:

> My nose, sir, is enormous. Ignorant clod,
> Cretinous moron, a man ought to be proud,
> Yes proud, of having so proud an appendix
> Of flesh and bone to crown his countenance,
> Provided a great nose may be an index
> Of a great soul...

Jacobi, whirling and dancing across the stage, physically and vocally supple in ways his meek-scholar parts never allowed, became magnificent and ostentatious. A Clennam with Verdi actually streaming from his mouth. And each time he became the part, it banished any residue of personal timidity. Beneath the bulbous squat proboscis, with thick moustaches angled under, and behind the ginger goatee, Jacobi was as safe as Karloff beneath the monster make-up, as Laughton beneath Quasimodo's mask: by feigning to swagger he could expose his real capacity for power. Monster make-up rendered the actor paradoxically naked.

The naked truth? The great nose as an index of great soul? The arrogance needs tempering – which Jacobi accomplished by a take-off of the *Hamlet* allusions. His Cyrano pre-empted ridicule by being the first in with any cajolery –

> ... with tragic cries and sighs,
> The language finely wrought and deeply felt
> Oh that this too too solid nose would melt.

Jacobi audaciously had Cyrano-as-Hamlet become Cyrano-as-Osric, yet with the fencing skill of Basil Rathbone. Pretending to be camp, but capable of steel, he justified the peacock touches, and palliated the bombast of this sort of credo:

> ... to go
> Free of the filthy world, to sing, to be
> Blessed with a voice vibrating virility,
> Blessed with an eye equipped for looking at
> Things as they really are, cocking my hat
> Where I please ...
> Fighting or writing: this is the true life.

That 'looking at / Things as they really are' is Matthew Arnold, in 1864, saying the 'aim of criticism is to see the object as in itself it really is'. Oscar

Wilde easily twisted this to announce that the aim of criticism is to see the object as in itself it really isn't; and the spirit of Cyrano, as delineated by Jacobi, is the spirit of Wilde's mentor, Walter Pater's *Studies in the History of the Renaissance*: 'the first step towards seeing one's object as it really is is to know one's impression as it really is, to discriminate it, to realize it distinctly' – which shifts the power to the sensibility of the perceiver (i.e. the actor Jacobi), rather than allowing it to remain as an indwelling source in the perceived – hidden in whatever is looked at, read, heard, played (i.e. Burgess's *Cyrano* script).

Cyrano's nose is just such a radar of sensibility – and so is Jacobi's instinct as an actor. (How may that be personified? As some force in the Universal Machine?) Like Cyrano, he can detect pomposity and hokum in his environment (the soapy *I, Claudius*, the thrillers such as *The Day of the Jackal*) and transcend them. Much of Burgess's script is a fandango of loquacity, but Jacobi gave it all authority – by inoculating Cyrano with irony and against boorishness, so that instead of a declamatory ham, we had a man tenderly oblique to his own statements; a man appreciative of a fissure between himself and his lines. As a result, his Cyrano grew sympathetic, even great. The part of Oscar Wilde as if written down by Shakespeare, or somebody else using the same name.

The ability to be delicate in a part otherwise bleating or (with Cyrano) domineering is Jacobi's gift; the delicacy, or few fronds of panache, prevents his habitual blankness from ever being mistaken for stupefaction. His Benedick, for example, in *Much Ado About Nothing*, was an acute soldier who acted being a ninny to protect himself from the dimwitted mess-mentality of Don Pedro's young officers. Up until Beatrice's command, 'Kill Claudio', he was the regimental Frankie Howerd, with toggled fly and white buckskin boots over lace galloons, chattering in the coppery, honey dusk. Forced into raillery with Beatrice, he could oblige; as did she. ('The world must be peopled. When I said I would die a bachelor, I did not think I should live till I were married.')

Jacobi played a confident poetaster, striding nimbly over Koltai's burnished floors, where figures were doubled by their swimming reflection (an apt picture of Shakespeare's streaky-eye perspective); and united with Beatrice, his Benedick was happy to abandon public foolishness for a fine romance. The order to remove Claudio and clear Hero's name was met with efficiency – a new briskness naturally splitting out of earlier cocksureness. Indeed, the wisdom of the portrayal came from the balance of humour and honour, with wit never far off, and a quiet sadness never far off either. Sinead Cusack's Beatrice was, perhaps, reduced a notch to be his stooge – perfect for the Beatrice and Benedick double-act (they could be George Burns and Gracie Allen), but lacking that dimension of private history and anguish which ought to be revealed by this exchange –

Don Pedro: Come, lady, come, you have lost the heart of Sig-
nior Benedick.
Beatrice: Indeed my lord, he lent it me awhile, and I gave him
use for it . . .

Without a quality of hurt, Beatrice's relief at being able to remove
contrived cruelty from her conversation isn't apparent; Benedick, however, attained the melancholy knowledge that his happiness was arriving,
if not in the autumn of his years, then in the late summer of their lives. He
has awakened to emotion as Clennam has. In place of Verdi, there was a
plangent cello and Christmas bells. *Much Ado About Nothing* is misty,
mellow comedy, with gathering swallows twittering in its skies; an ode
to autumn captured in those amber mirrors which made up the set – and
the set a container for promises. 'I will live in thy heart, die in thy lap, and
be buried in thy eyes.'

Jacobi revealed Benedick's misogyny to be a shelter, gladly forsaken. Had
misogyny remained, and rankled into misanthropy, he'd be Jacobi's
Prospero, a troubled wizard, redeemed from vainglory and pride by our
sympathetic sense of his loneliness. Hard-eyed and blond-quiffed,
wrapped in an episcopal cope embroidered with necromantic diagrams,
carrying a brass-clasped bible of spells in his left hand, a ceremonial
masonic staff in his right, this was a Prospero conscious of failing powers:
Miranda (Alice Krige self-consciously fiddling with hair braids and
shifting her arms to hide a budding bosom) discovers her own sexuality
and needs a man other than her father; Caliban (Bob Peck encrusted with
merds and clicking rasta beads) can be kept faithful only by threats, and he
mutinies; Ariel (Mark Rylance a devil-doll choirboy turning his lines into
black-mass recitative) scampers off – and he'd been kept by force, Jacobi
managing to register Prospero's secret wish that the little boy might one
day be his friend or son:

My Ariel – chick –

There was a silence. No answer. Then, murmuring with resignation, the
prayer for calm seas and auspicious gales ('That is thy charge') was a
request for his own quiet passage unto death. The tension in this thanatic
idling came from Jacobi's playing a youngish Prospero; so the mood was
no wintry valediction (like Gielgud's portrayal), but an inability to face
encroaching middle age. Does he go back to Milan and an arsenic apple?
The Tempest was autumnal tragedy – 'Every third thought shall be my
grave . . . my ending is despair' – as *Much Ado About Nothing* was
autumnal comedy.

Prospero is in exile for practising magic; he could be the disgraced
Turing, having broken some social code. He's made a cabin from a ship's

timbers and sail-cloth – and Maria Bjornson saturated the stage with a briny, sea-edge atmosphere, the floor a sharp shingle of sand, stones, feldspar. (An ingle like Crusoe's – or, more tellingly, like the Marshalsea, with air wafted from the Surrey hills). The production began with the magus's orgasmic shudder: Jacobi thrust into the storm, fucking the drama into existence. Shipwreck and tempest fomented a sexual charge; the drama a thing of darkness to be acknowledged as Prospero's own. He's wired up the current of events, as Frankenstein sparks his creature into action, or as Turing imagines the electronic brain and its dark soul.

Frowning, fierce, Prospero was very different from warm, smiling Benedick – but Prospero's ferocity lay in Benedick, as Benedick's completeness of heart broke through in Prospero's attitude to his daughter and Ferdinand's growing love: not an attitude of pally paternalism, slaps and joshings, but a formal resignation of responsibility – a formal acknowledgement that his child's a stranger to him now. And we felt the pain of this, a pain suffused into Clennam when he's lost in prison.

'You have,' I suggested to Jacobi, 'what with Claudius, Benedick, Cyrano, Prospero, Turing, Clennam, played intelligent men. Students of human nature.'

He was delighted with the idea – though 'There's no design, no aforethought. No grand plan determining what I do, that I'm aware of.'

'So it must only be your nature which unifies?'

'Possibly.' (Not convinced at all.)

Claudius could be a dribbling fogey; Benedick a smitten nincompoop; Cyrano a bully; Prospero a farewelling actor-manager; Turing a daffy academic; Clennam a drip, had not Jacobi absorbed them into his crucible of blankness, distilling essences, so that Cyrano is the actor exemplifying a daintiness, in addition to a swashbuckling vigour; Turing is the actor exemplifying a humility, in addition to a remote inner strength. Maths is Turing's object of idolatry; words are Cyrano's. Maths makes Turing artful; Cyrano's art is astronomical (all those moon references). The real Savinien de Cyrano de Bergerac wrote the science books *L'autre monde ou les états et empires de la lune* and *Les états et empires du soleil*, in which he prophesied atomic structure, the gramophone, aviation. Jacobi's Cyrano, having been Douglas Fairbanks, might have become Albert Einstein, Baron Munchausen or Peter Pan.

> I escape
> From earth in a ship of icosahedral shape –
> Stuck with ten burning mirrors. They rarefy
> The air. The air lifts me, and I fly.

Physically unprepossessing (though, yes, most memorable), both Cyrano and Turing discard the fripperies of personal comfort for a higher code of honour: the code of intellectual errantry. As Cyrano says, 'I'm one of those who wear their elegance within,' and we believe in the skeetering beauty of his thought processes – just as we have Turing's demonstrated to us. In distinct ways the men embody panache: grace, flamboyance even, in the face of disaster; a stoicism and noble withdrawal from broils. As Burgess wrote for Plummer and Broadway:

> To follow your chivalric calling
> When the Alps and Pyrenees are falling,
> To file your nails when the doomsday trumpets crash:
> That's *panache*.

Figurative, the word also has a literal definition, being French for the vast plume on Cyrano's hat – so his elegance isn't entirely worn within, but that's not the point. The white feathery spurt is an image of spermy spray, of fecundity – and Cyrano's fecund quality is his language, his voice; he comes to Roxane with Christian as prophylactic:

> . . . I shall take all words that ever were,
> Or weren't, or could, or couldn't be, and in
> Mad armfuls, not bouquets, I'll smother you in them.

'That idea of panache and flourish,' said Jacobi, 'we all have elements of it within, I think – on stage I could search for it and assume it. I never have the courage to show panache normally. As I said earlier, I am a classic Libran: I like balance and calm.'

'Perhaps Cyrano preferred equipoise – in his angry way?' I said.

'Perhaps he did. But, actually, his wild panache I'd only ever find in myself when I'm playing the character. And I'm not any longer. It was a while ago, now. I've forgotten the lines.'

'Turing's panache?'

'The love affair with mathematics. It's what the man lived for – to such an extent, he was impractical at everything else. Secondly, he remained a restless little boy. *Boyish* is the word we used in rehearsals to describe his glee and gaucherie.'

The boyishness is rather haunted. Not a Shropshire lad reverie, but thwarted development (like Clennam); a peculiar stuntedness. As a child, Turing read science books and discovered that numbers were reliable: they became his friends and comforters. And while waiting for his interview at Bletchley, he amuses himself by watching Walt Disney's *Snow White and the Seven Dwarfs* – which lodged the idea of arsenic apples in his head.

'I think Turing killed himself as a final experiment,' said Jacobi. 'He wanted to find out what his mind would do if his body was killed off.'

'Would they separate? Or go down hand in hand?'

'The poisoned apple. He ate an apple every night before going to bed.

They found him in bed looking perfectly calm. If it was an accident, surely there'd have been panic, an attempt to save himself? But his mother, who wrote a biography of her son, refused to believe it. She kept thinking it was an accident. An accident! He did make his own weedkiller in the bath, so I suppose you could say there'd be dangerous chemicals splashed about the house; but then you could say: there are dangerous chemicals about, so Turing would be careful where he left his food. He was a scientist. He knew about chemicals all right.'

'There's an enigma about the end, then?'

'Yes. The play seems to have worked with the smart folk, who are able to bring their intelligences with them, and who are *pleased* to be able to do so. Hugh's isn't like Christopher Fry's drama. His words ring hollow now – and I used to adore Fry. It comes as a shock to see through him.'

'Will you continue to enjoy the play for a full six months' run, plus New York?'

'Productions evolve. I'll find new things. If only the critics – whom I've given up reading – would come back and see us after a few hundred performances. It makes me cross to read, as I did the other week in the *Sunday Times*, that Stratford is a rehearsal period for London. Of course, when we got to London we'd be better – different, in many ways. We've done the play fifty times, in addition to Newcastle, and we'll have reached a point of finally getting it right.'

'I'd not like to be an actor facing the ritual bloodletting of the critics all turning up together on the first night, like humourless judges at the eisteddfodau.'

'I don't read them. No idea what's been said about my Turing.'

Self-glory is not readily detectable in Jacobi's catalogue of desires; and, as I've sketched, he has a horror of self-regarding styles of acting – the avoidance of which converted Cyrano to complexity.

'Theatre,' he said, 'is a machine for emotions. A world of pretend that's nevertheless recognizable. Minds and lives on offer, emotions experimented with and put into perspective. To do this we, as actors, keep one foot in the cradle. We must be open, like a child, and retain naiveté.'

'To be conscious of retaining naiveté is to eradicate naiveté.'

'Exactly! A childlike quality is one thing – but that said, the emotions, the feelings, the effect on the audience, the truth of the game of it: I'm reminded of that line in *Trelawny of the Wells*. The once grand actress, after a life away doing something else, returns in expected triumph to the stage – and she's a failure, a disaster, and they say, "She's lost the trick of it."'

'The trick of it: she's lost the trick of it. Theatre is trickery. A bit of a performance works, and you glow to yourself: you *know* how you managed to carry it off – and it's a moment of pure, private pleasure, knowing you've succeeded with the trick of it. Ask any actor, he'll know what I mean. He'll have felt the power and the glory of trickery and mystification.'

'But in the mystifying and the trick,' I said, 'lies the art.'

Derek Jacobi is an actor of contemplative ambiguousness (as the best actors always are). Anxious to make clear that private and public life are kept apart, he's yet driven in on their merger when estimating the extent felt emotion transfers to performance: what is the extent of contrivance? How fake is anger? (Not odd eruptions of rage but, as with Cyrano, an entire performance, from soup to nuts, activated by indignation.)

Finding the right level of temper and resentment for Cyrano hasn't made Jacobi the more liable to being temperamental in real life; he claims to be (and appeared) happy and placid and kind – though he must know now he *has* the power – and his Peer Gynt was a virulent troll, his Prospero was hardly a man to fool with.

The extremes: the fighter with the tranquil disposition; the actor thrilled by legerdemain – the exploration of openness and imposture, light and dark: these became in *Mr Pye* an allegory of good and evil. In the Channel Four series, Jacobi played the eponym, a portly bank clerk superannuated on Sark. Saintly beyond speech, he starts to sprout feathery tufts – and the feathery tufts develop into a full seraphic wing rig-out. In his panama, beige weskit and small, owlish, metal-frame specs, Jacobi looked like Mr Pickwick, or Clennam, dolled up for *Paradise Lost*.

When bad thoughts traverse Mr Pye's brain (lust, envy, sanctimoniousness), the wings moult, and twisty black horns grow from his temples. A man, says Mervyn Peake,* is a battlefield for devils and angels; made in God's likeness, we're also a diluted Satan, the fallen celestial head-prefect.

> Which way I fly is hell; my self am hell:
> And in the lowest deep a lower deep
> Still threatening to devour me opens wide,
> To which the hell I suffer seems a heaven.

Having raised interesting theological ideas, Peake ignored comedy and tragedy for sentimentality and pity. Mr Pye, angelic, is pursued by an angry, incredulous mob – like the monster in the movies, tracked by villagers armed with scythe and brand; Mr Pye, diabolic, looked plain sheepish (literally, Jacobi's horns were those of a Jacob's ram) and only by succumbing to cruel ridicule is he gradually cured, so that the black cones retract.

Jacobi's Mr Pye, suffused with humbleness at an agricultural show, the

* Author of the novel (1953) on which the series was based.

crowd circling him to taunt, managed to convey both a saint's humility and a saint's swank. And how does a character so good get to be afflicted with horns? The answer is that nobody has the right to want wings. Mr Pye's goodness, in fact, is meddlesome and solipsistic, something like Clennam's flawed altruism. Jacobi's stage people alone convey the dilemma of meekness's crime and punishment.

Poised in a Regency chair, dressed in a blue towelling dressing gown embossed with the legend 'CYRANO BROADWAY 1984' across the shoulders, as though a boxer in repose, the player himself exemplifies the actor as an object as in himself he really isn't. A game of imitations; a bundle of fugitive paradoxes – like Turing's artful dodger of a Universal Machine and its derivations, fore and aft, from Mary Shelley to Burgess. Invincible matings, all, of the mechanical and the phylogenetic; redemptive matings, also, of the instincts for self-preservation and self-sacrifice. The real retires before the ideal; and that's acting.

FIVE

Love's Old Sweet Song: Judi Dench and Michael Williams

The *Diary of a Nobody*, written in 1892, is extraordinary; it presages the world depicted in *Ulysses* – James Joyce's is the greatest comic writing in the language – by twelve years. Pooter is a proto-Leopold Bloom. Both men are stoical fathers, modestly ingenious, infinitely kind; they are capable of infinite humiliation, and infinite resignation. George and Weedon Grossmith, James Joyce: their characters are to be found expounded at the end of Thomas Mann's *Tonio Kröger*: 'The bliss of the commonplace . . . the source of all warmth, goodness, and humour . . . I see into a whirl of shadows of human figures who beckon to me to weave spells to redeem them: tragic and laughable figures and some that are both together – and to these I am drawn.' Bloom and Pooter are such intertextures of seriousness and levity. Trifles to them are tragedies; and so they are to us all. Pooter is importuned by frayed sash-cords and a recalcitrant bootscraper; Bloom wonders when he'll mend the bedstead's loose brass quoits ('Must get those settled really'); both are vexed by local tradespersons. Bloom is saddened to be omitted from the newspaper list of mourners at Paddy Dignam's funeral; Pooter is similarly slighted. Bloom has to be content with Boom, Pooter with Porter. Misprinted, they are misrepresented. The reader alone is privy to their inner refinement.

Joyce rendered daily details epic. *Ulysses* is a diary of June 16, 1904; a journal of wanderings and interlacing events in Dublin. Underswelling the book are allusions to Homer, to Shakespeare, to Wagner: ironic mythical counterpoints, ensuring that even the humble are to be seen as heroic. Joyce brings the literary past into conjunction with the Irish present, as if aligning stars or the trails of comets for astrological divagation. Bloom is the Ithacan king, meandering the streets instead of the Mediterranean; he's a portly Hamlet, haunted by the apparition of his father and tribal responsibility; he's Leontes, haunted by the memory of

239

his dead son; he's Falstaff to the Hal of Stephen Dedalus; he's the wronged Commendatore, mocked by the neighbourhood Don Giovanni, Blazes Boylan – and he wonders about manifesting himself before the adulterers like the Stone Guest; he's expectant Leopold Mozart before cocky Wolfgang Amadeus (Stephen Dedalus, again); he's the sad Wotan of *Siegfried*, lamenting his sterility and lost child, asking gentle riddles: a wanderer. Eccles Street is his Elsinore, Valhalla, Temple – Bloom is a Freemason, offering patronage to the fallen son of a friend; Sarastro with Tamino under the heaventree of stars.

Eccles Street is also The Laurels, Brickfield Terrace, Holloway, N. Bloom and Pooter are kin. Was *Diary of a Nobody* in Joyce's mind? I found a first edition in the late Richard Ellmann's room at Wolfson College – Ellmann was a world expert on Joyce, so let's allow the coincidence to stand.

Pooter, like Bloom, is ridiculed by his companions; they are objects of mild contempt and exercisers of abasement. But what will survive of them is love. Pooter, on July 11, records the gift of a freehold and his son Lupin's engagement to be married: 'On arriving home I found Carrie crying with joy.' *Diary of a Nobody* concludes with family concord; the kingdom intact. Bloom, at the end of his day, is Odysseus regaining Penelope's bed; the wanderer returned. That is why *Ulysses* is a divine comedy. *Love*, says Stephen Dedalus, and he's echoed in the attitude of Bloom, is the word known to all men; 'Love,' says Bloom, 'I mean the opposite of hatred.'

A focus of adoration is Marion Tweedy, or Mrs Molly Bloom. She rises from her bed like Aphrodite from the foam; a singer, a soliloquist, a bit of a shrew: the embodiment of love's bitter mystery and love's old sweet song. A Dublin Cleopatra (Joyce called her Cliopatrick), with the Liffey for the Nile. The gropes and leers and buckings of Boylan notwithstanding, in her own way she remains intimate with her husband; theirs is the passion of a sixteen-year marriage. They've hardened into banter, but she recalls their affiancement on Howth Head (where the rhododendron bush was, in actuality, guarded by a sign saying PLEASE DO NOT TOUCH THE BLOOMS), with fondness: 'after that long kiss I near lost my breath yes he said I was a flower of the mountain yes . . . that was why I liked him because I saw he understood or felt what a woman is and I knew I could always get round him and gave him all the pleasure I could . . .'

Molly is a cousin of Carrie Pooter. She is off-stage, elsewhere, during the bulk of the novel; a mentioned presence. Then Joyce gives her a vast unpunctuated monologue, in which June 16, 1904 is rewritten from her perspective. Events happening to, and opinions formed by, Poldy (as she calls Leopold Bloom) are re-envisioned. Carrie Pooter, off-stage, elsewhere, in the Grossmith chronicle, has had to wait until Keith Waterhouse gave her voice, in *Mrs Pooter's Diary* (1983); her husband's diary, day for day, is reinterpreted, opened out. The book is rather more than a pastiche: Waterhouse seems to be in ectoplasmic contact with the spirit of the original. He's fully absorbed the period; and as his essays in *Waterhouse At Large* demonstrate, he adores the Victorian and Edwardian bric-à-brac and brand names – which remained current in his Leeds childhood, and which were coined in his parents' childhood. For Waterhouse, the Pooters are from the last age of innocence; their aspirations are charged with nostalgia.

The clutter of The Laurels, Carrie's urgent domesticity: it is a Wendy house, and the Grossmiths wrote in the era that made *Peter Pan*. *Ulysses*, set in 1904, belongs to the actual year of the premiere of *Peter Pan* (the novel, like the play, contains a hawklike man: Stephen is a Daedalus). But if this was the entire attraction of the Pooters – a sentimental longing for an eternal 1900 – Waterhouse's fanaticism (he's lately composed *The Collected Letters of a Nobody*; then there must be *Lupin Pooter's Diary*; relations stop nowhere) would quickly grow sickly; the comedy would pall.

Of course, this is not all. Waterhouse has recognized and released the indwelling Joycean comedy of the original. His Carrie Pooter is Molly Bloom dressed for the day. The Grossmiths hinted at Carrie's independence ('Don't be theatrical,' she snaps at her husband, 'it has no effect on me') and she keeps house earnestly. Molly, free-associating with insomnia, does not only think of sex; she is also revealed to be a prudent housekeeper: her monologue is peppered with commodities – she's fluent in the profit and loss: '. . . and the oysters 2/6 per doz . . .'; '. . . four paltry handkerchiefs about 6/– in all . . .'; '. . . cakes 7½d a lb or the other ones with the cherries in them . . .'. She follows, as best she can, fashion: she'd like red Turkish slippers, 'I badly want' a new dressing gown – resembling the garment of savoured memory, 'like the one long ago in Walpoles only 8/6 or 18/6'. She mentions port and potted meat, suede gloves, hairpins, hallmarked silver forks and fish slices, and Epps's cocoa. During the day, whilst we have been in the company of Poldy, she's cleared out of the house piles of old newspapers and magazines; she's also sorted the old coats from the hall. Recently, she's had trouble with the maid, and so she chars for herself.

Molly, in other words, has been prudent and busy. Her mind coils back to the romantic haze of being proposed to, when she doodled her conjugal signature: 'I used to write it in print to see how it looked on a visiting card or practising for the butcher . . .'. The doodling dream-days, before the girl had to become a woman; her noctuary (it's night-time: her chapter can't be a diary), in fact, is an anthem for her doomed youth. Blazes Boylan is a last girlish fling; she eyes Stephen Dedalus as the Marschallin does Octavian. 'I suppose,' says Molly, reflecting on femininity, 'its all the troubles we have makes us so snappy.' And though she enjoys men, she will not succumb to them – 'they're not going to be chaining me up no damn fear . . .'.

Mrs Pooter's Diary finds Carrie a similar insurgent, more slyly self-willed than Charles may ever suspect. Though she does not form an assignation with any Blazes Boylan, and nor does she indulge in illicit teatime copulation, Waterhouse does discover for her a pang of longing. At the calamitous ball, Mr Darwitts helps her to her feet after a clumsy tumble. She meets him a few days later. 'A tall, very straight-backed gentleman, standing by the stationery counter . . . He was hoping to interest the Fancy Bazaar in a line of correspondence cards in delicate colours, with rounded edges . . .' By the following January, however, Mr Darwitts fails to place his enquirer: 'Mr Darwitts came out, every bit as tall and straight-backed as I remember him. He returned my bow, but looked mystified . . . Unaccountably, I was seized by what Lupin would call "a fit of the blues" on the bus home . . .'

Ulysses catalogues Dublin streets and shops; *Diary of a Nobody* bustles with references to gadgets and devices; *Mrs Pooter's Diary* is the apothesis of nineteenth-century appliances and advertisements: Carrie is enthralled by Teale's (late Moxon) painters' sundrymen, fashion plates in *Daintry's Illustrated Boudoir*, Swan and Edgar's, Basnett et Cie, Jay's Mourning House (for black combs), a fan from Shoolbreds 'costing 7/6 (told him 3/6)', Prout's Elastic Glue, Neave's Varnish Stain Remover, buffalo-meat dog biscuits, Cigar de Ozone Bronchial Cigarillos, Dr Sibson's Lakgoh Debility Pills, Throstle & Epps' Linen Bank, Oldham, *Pot Pourri: A Weekly Miscellany For Ladies* and Ackthorpe, Hollyman & Moxon's Jamboree Ales Brewery. Carrie's breviary is *Lady Cartmell's Vade Mecum For The Bijou Household*, a codex of etiquette; a choreography of social movement. She is assiduous in her study of propriety, and is proud of her reprimand to the cleaner who wishes reinstatement: 'I said, "Very well, Mrs Birrell, . . . you are to understand this. *I* am the mistress of this house, and I *will not* have you using paper indiscriminately. In future, back copies of *The Globe, Jepson's Sunday Newspaper* and the *Exchange and Mart* will be left for your use by the pantry . . ."' Carrie is also tart with Charles. They squabble about dreams, diaries, their staff, keeping rabbits ('On the day twelve rabbits enter this house, Charles, I shall leave it') – but, as much as she punctures with ease her husband's efforts at pomposity, she does not jeer: 'Evidently feeling contrite at the succession of quarrels and arguments we have been having lately, Charlie bought me a pretty silver bangle, and left it on my dressing table with an affectionate little note. He is a dear old thing at heart, and I shall make an effort to be nicer to him.'

Caroline and Charles Pooter, first serialized in *Punch* in 1891; *Ulysses*, written between 1914 and 1921, Molly and Poldy Bloom accompanying Joyce from Trieste to Paris to Zürich; then Keith Waterhouse's book, nearly a century on*: all aspects came together in the autumn of 1986. *Mr and Mrs Nobody* opened at the Garrick Theatre, with Judi Dench and Michael Williams as the eponyms – an actress and an actor of sufficient sympathy and deftness to discern in the material a poignant portrait of a marriage. Which they did.

Judi Dench and Michael Williams have been famously paired in the television series *A Fine Romance*, where they played a courting couple of early middle age – who'd prevaricated about wedlock and had become ingrained as singles. Gentle comedy, graced with acting beyond its station, *A Fine Romance* had an extra frisson for the simplest of reasons: Judi Dench and Michael Williams are married in real life.

If *A Fine Romance* was ennobled by their presence, *The Diary of a Nobody* would yield up its immanent rich resources. Keith Waterhouse devised a script by making a lattice of the Grossmith original and his own sequel; thus, for the first time, a full chronicle of life at the Laurels was promulgated; it was as though *The Iliad* had been joined by *The Odyssey*. I was invited to attend a rehearsal, and made my way to a church hall in Chelsea. The building was crammed with Victorian furniture: elaborate screens, tables wilting beneath brocade, an upright piano with shaded brass candelabra, oil lamps, pipe racks like gunnels, heavy chairs with upholstered seats, two desks, antimacassars, the head of a moose.

Amongst the gimcrack and gewgaws the stars paced. Various girls fiddled making coffee or annotating scripts. Judi Dench, diminutive but erect, looking fierce behind large grey spectacles, shot to meet me. Instant warmth.

'Roger, you've come to see us. How kind. Michael – it's Roger from Oxford.'

Michael Williams, crumpled and concentrating, turned in greeting, and saw me installed at the edge of the set – for the alarming clutter, like a period lumber room, was the arranged set; these were the props for the run.

'We've been so lucky,' said Judi, 'we've had all these real things from the very first day. It helps enormously to get to know the objects, their feel and size.'

Indeed. *Mr and Mrs Nobody* is a fond celebration of tackle and chattels; a hosannah for the nineteenth-century fixture-fidgets.

'Julia Trevelyan Oman has been collecting it. You know,' said Judi, as if unmasking a secret identity. 'You know she's Lady Strong?'

'Yes. Did she borrow any of this from the V & A?'

---

* Pooter scholarship continues apace. Waterhouse, going back to the *Punch* original, has discovered that Charlie had a first wife – the real mother of Lupin. Carrie is spouse number two – and this fact was suppressed in the revision for book publication. So another trail is revealed. Pooter a Bluebeard?

'I don't think she did; most of it is hired. But this was bought.'

We were looking at a large wooden oven, like a timber Aga, with knobs and dials on the door. It was lined with lead, or it may have been zinc, and was the size of a maisonnette. The Wenham Lake Ice Safe.

'But I've no idea how we are going to move it. Weighs a ton, or several tons.'

The Wenham Lake Ice Safe, a pioneer refrigerator, acquires a disproportion in Carrie's life. Its arrival at the Laurels becomes her considerable ambition. As important to Mrs Pooter as the three sisters getting to Moscow; as Hannay knowing the secret of the thirty-nine steps; as Dorothy getting her red shoes back.

While Michael muttered his lines to himself, checking in a ring-folder kept on one of the desks, my brisk tour continued.

'These are the foods for the Mayor's Ball at the Mansion House.'

Chickens, hams, cakes, glazed pâtés: looking good enough to eat, and made of plaster – displayed on salvers, upon a tiered table which would wheel on and off.

'The whole of the room will be on a truck, and we'll shunt towards the audience.'

It was nearly time to begin. Michael remained in his ruffled red shirt, jeans, sneakers and jerkin; Judi began to wrap a quilt around her middle, in semblance of a long skirt.

'I did Keith's *Mrs Pooter's Diary* on *Woman's Hour*,' she said. 'I told him that I'd love to do it as a play, with Mike. Then the script arrived. It would have lasted five hours. We've managed to get Act One to an hour, Act Two to fifty minutes, and it must be shorter.'

Today was to be their first run-through without scripts, without costumes, with props. The director arrived, carrying a Gladstone bag. A big man, with cropped hair, a blue shirt and a determined stride; he looked like a confident vet about to spend a morning inoculating an entire herd of Friesians against brucellosis. It was Ned Sherrin, the cue-card joker, without whom no award show is entire. He sat at a trestle table and, while we awaited the tardy pianist, told stories: whether Eric Portman was alive or dead; what Peter O'Toole felt about playing an Arabian eunuch; seeing a ghost in the Russian Tea Room, New York; what Faye Dunaway was up to in a silly play called *Circe and Bravo*. Ned communicates in anecdotes; elaborate tales, like Matthew Arnold's epic similes – apparent digressions, conversational décor. In fact, the décor is the point, which you take away to ponder the meaning of.

'Roger,' he said finally, 'come and see this. It's a Wenham Lake Ice Safe.' I marvelled anew at the apparatus, and unsuspected trapdoors opened and closed.

A black-haired lady tottered in. Judi dived to greet her. It was Annie Hoey, Judi's dresser.

'I've been with Judi thirteen years. She's a lovely lady. None nicer. She does so many charity shows for free. *Mr and Mrs Nobody* has twelve changes, all of them elaborate and quick.'

Annie was sitting next to me. Rather a frail person, I thought, her pale skin the paler owing to her jet mop – like a porcelain doll. Judi was watchful, as of an ill relative. 'As for charity shows and readings, I went to the Cheltenham Poetry Festival with Michael Hordern. We had to endure, before we went on, incessant Bartók. Bangs and clonks and boings. Eventually, Michael Hordern let out one of his long exasperated groans – Ahhhnnnnnmmmmnn aghhh eogheenmmnnn ... And we giggled and giggled.'

The pianist still delayed, Annie was taken to see the Wenham Lake Ice Safe. Ned Sherrin tried on a negro mask from his Gladstone bag; a brown plastic face, with white bone through the nose, and a curly frizz.

'Convincing?'

'*Not*,' came a Lady Bracknell voice, 'at all!'

'I hate masks,' muttered Michael, 'I *hate* masks,' perturbed.

A taxi was throbbing, waiting. It was the pianist. He'd detoured to the Wyndham's Theatre, where his briefcase was mislaid the night before. A tall gangling youth in a teeshirt, called Michael Haslam, he was taken to admire the Wenham Lake Ice Safe.

'It's been bought,' said Ned, out of his mask, 'so we've got to use it. The trouble is, it's too heavy to move.'

Michael Haslam tried on the negro mask. Apparently, there'd been a fleeting idea that the two musicians – pianist and violinist – would be attired as minstrels.

'I hate masks, I *hate* masks.'

'We'd better not finish early today, Ned,' said Judi.

'She went to Cecil Gee's yesterday,' cut in Mike, 'and bought three pairs of trousers, a dress and a jumper.'

'Fatal, fatal,' sang Judi, delighted, patrolling the set fast. 'You know,' she continued, 'doing this play, you do tend to slot people you meet into the characters. I meet Mr Darwitts, Mr Perkupp, Annie Fullers (now Mrs James, of Sutton), Mr Oswald Tipper or Daisy Mutlar every day, somewhere or other ...'

They were ready, at last. The piano began to bang, out of tune, Victorian parlour songs and Gilbert and Sullivan melodies.

'Two minutes of music to get yourselves opened up,' said the director, back at his trestle. Mike, now Mr Pooter, sucked his pipe and looked pensive. A tinny cassette made the voice-over:

'Why should I not publish my diary? I have often seen reminiscences of people I have never even heard of, and I fail to see – because I do not happen to be a "Somebody" – why my diary should not be interesting ...'

Midway through this, Judi, now Mrs Pooter, stirred to her desk, and another, overlapping, voice-over:

'If *he* may entertain hopes of publishing a diary, then so may *I* – after all, it is not as if my dear Charlie were a "Somebody" whose thoughts and impressions are any more profound or worthwhile than the next person's.'

Actor and actress then sat at flanking bureaux and read out their journal entries in unison:

'My dear wife Carrie and I have just been a week in our new house . . .'

'I hate it . . .' states the lady, a withering fraction later. Instantly, a merry war between them is promised. Mr and Mrs Pooter were to address the audience directly – in this case, a bust of a Chelsea worthy, on a plinth, the eye level above Ned's, Annie's, mine. The collusion, the winks, the wry smiles, the tiny cocks of the head and pregnant pauses: all these were aimed at the bust. Both actor and actress scrupulously avoided living eyes.

Gradually, the actor's and actress's speeches to the audience became conversation with each other – but the script, being but the parallel text of diary entries, was not inherently dramatic. It was set in the past tense, for a start. Yet the transubstantiation of acting was taking place. Judi Dench and Michael Williams had been replaced by the characters they were playing: they were the living voices for the text, giving the subtlest of nuances to small moments – so that those sash cords and that bootscraper took on the significance of crowns and orbs in a history play.

What actor and actress were doing was instinctively – was it instinctive, or was it technique deployed with the steam up? – to search for the reality, the touching ordinariness, in the Pooters. There was no teasing, no superior detachment – so that when they battled over the butcher's bill, it was an authentic marital difficulty, not a silly fuss over nothing. King Lear's division of the kingdom is a fuss over nothing ('Nothing will come of nothing'); mistaken double orders of mutton and the quality of eggs portend dissension in the family, the breakdown of peace in the home. And when Mrs Pooter, recounting her husband's partiality for Lochenbar whisky and Jackson Frères champagne, confided that 'I sometimes think my husband is a secret drinker' – beneath the joke, the overstatement, lingered sincere concern.

The worries and vexations of the Pooters were being performed as genuine; as genuine as Bloom's attentiveness to Mina Purefoy, or his preparation of Molly's breakfast tray, or his dropping by at the National Library of Ireland to investigate the fundaments of statuary. True humour comes from recognizing streaks of truth; even farce can only be successful if its madcap antics are deployed with utter credibility; it must be internally coherent and consistent. From Congreve to Wilde, from Sir

William Schwenck Gilbert to Noël Coward, from Preston Sturges to the Goons: comedy, even the most fantastic and apparently surreal, has to recognize the law of reality ('The sum total of reality is the world,' said Ludwig Wittgenstein) before it can ascend on the wings of its own wit. Satire (Jonathan Swift to graphic artists such as Gerald Scarfe and Spitting Image) moves in the contrary direction: it dives from lofty bizarrerie to hit the real, like an arrow hitting an artery. *Mr and Mrs Nobody*, which in less delicate hands could have been a satire on tribal pretension – the Pooters have a desperate desire socially to improve themselves – was instead being performed as a comedy of manners. The furniture, the fans, the clothes, the deckle-edge notelets: the Holloway inhabitants wish to be as worldly as the burghers in Peckham, which to Carrie is the Promised Land. And the earnest desire to gentrify London boroughs, to read personalities into postal districts: social betterment is the eternal English fantasy.

The Pooters are busy self-improvers. Judi Dench and Michael Williams were hinting, in their acting, at the strain this tends to put on ordinary life; its ability to invite humiliation. The Pooters have servants, but Carrie works in the kitchen alongside them. She constantly refers to Sarah ('my maid'), as though the skivvy is a lady-in-waiting. Sarah ('my maid') was played as a mute panto of gormlessness by Penny Ryder – who loped and gagged. They seem, the Pooters, to be socially equivalent to the owners of shops and small businesses; the lower middle-class, dreaming to be mistaken for middle-class. The occasional genteel open vowel was used by Judi to indicate that the East End was not too many generations distant.

All this: the discrimination with which Mrs Pooter and Mr Pooter were being drawn, the extent of their self-knowledge and knowledge about each other, their urgent interest in etiquette, made ready for the receipt of an invitation to attend the Mansion House Ball. Hitherto, actor and actress had addressed auditorium, occasionally each other. Now, Judi and Michael each split up to indicate other guests, swirling in dances, and sometimes adopting different voices. We were in a church hall in Chelsea: an actor and an actress were rehearsing; yet I swear I saw a crowd in dicky and boa.

Arrival at the ball, and its edging into mortification, was preceded by a small scene of sudden emotion. As written, it is stiff and sentimental. Waterhouse leaves his predecessors alone at this point. The invitation arrives:

'Carrie darling, I was a proud man when I led you down the aisle of the church on our wedding day; that pride will be equalled, if not surpassed, when I lead my dear, pretty wife up to the Lord and Lady Mayoress at the Mansion House.'

'Charlie dear, it is *I* who have to be proud of you. And I am very, very proud of you. You have called me pretty; and as long as I am pretty in your eyes, I am happy. You, dear old Charlie, are *not* handsome, but you are *good*, which is far more noble.'

Judi Dench and Michael Williams made this exchange tender and fond; Carrie, indeed, could barely speak the last half-dozen words; they came out, choked with emotion.

We were in a church hall in Chelsea: an actor and an actress were rehearsing; yet I saw real tears bulge.

Real tears? Or a representation of tears? Acting is the real thing in contact with the make-believe; a happy deception. Judi and Mike were giving me new eyes: I thought I was seeing what I was not seeing. Henry James, in *The Real Thing*, published within a year of *Diary of a Nobody*, wrote about a painter who preferred artifice to actuality: 'I liked things that appeared; then one was sure. Whether they *were* or not was a subordinate and almost always a profitless question.'

Whether Carrie's tears were Judi's it is neither subordinate nor profitless to ask. For they were an alchemy of the two. And quick as a flash Judi banished Carrie. They'd become too close. 'Sorry, I'm terribly off beam, aren't I?'

'I was like that yesterday,' said her husband soothingly.

Then back into character they went, Charlie having a frightening explosion of anger when the precious invitation card is accidentally smeared with port wine. His eyes flashed with inarticulate fury and frustration: it was no panto tantrum.

For the Mansion House Ball, the plaster food was slid into place. Judi mimed eating a big meal; chewing discreetly, whilst watching Charlie Pooter drink himself silly. Then, the wild tarantella, ending with the embarrassing skid on the parquet. Now it was Carrie's turn to be mettlesome, the grand excursion having miscarried. The morning after crackled with feelings of shame and recrimination. Sarah ('my maid') crept about the parlour, a cartoon of politic stealthiness; Charlie had a murderous hangover; Carrie, however, was prepared for battle: 'I left him in no doubt as to what I thought of his conduct of the night before . . . his deficiencies as a husband and as a gentleman – with particular reference to his leaving it to Mr Darwitts to assume responsibility for me in my distress . . .'

It is the most major cloud on their marriage; the after-effects of the ball linger for days. The hurts accumulate. The *Blackfriars Bi-weekly News* publishes its string of misprints. The neighbours pester. 'We cannot go on like this. It will be better for both of us that I should go and stay in Sutton with Annie Fullers (now Mrs James) for a spell.'

Away she careens. Charlie is dejected. He polices the house, fiddling and fussing; crushed and lonely and sad. The pianist tinkled a lamentation. Then, after clocks chiming to mark the passage of days, the music broke into a gallop:

'Carrie back. Hoorah!'

'Home sweet home again!'

The queen was back in her counting house, making a lightning tour of inspection, disposing of dead flowers and slicking dust. Carrie waved a box at the audience, containing, presumably, an electroplated kettle. She'd been to an exhibition of kitchenware with Annie Fullers (now Mrs James).

It was lunchtime. We strolled to a pub, Mike and Judi eager to talk of family life, when they knew my wife and I were soon expecting a baby. They have a daughter, Finty.

'We're very close, the three of us,' said Michael.

'I was thirty-six, Mike was thirty-seven when we had her. The doctors at the hospital called me the Agèd Ape.'

'Will you be there when Anna gives birth?'

'I don't much fancy it,' I confessed, 'but it is mandatory, I believe, these days, for the father to have an opportunity to die in childbirth.'

'I was there,' said Mike, 'and it was the most wonderful of experiences. I'd not have missed it for the world.'

'I didn't have a great deal of choice,' remarked Judi.

'Will Finty be an actress?' I asked.

'She's unavoidably been brought up amongst artistic and theatre people. She came with her mother to watch us filming *Blunt*, and she got on well with Ian Richardson. How they roared together.'

Michael plays Goronwy Rees in the espionage film.

'A strange man, Goronwy. Nobody could make him out. He was all things to all men – which is perfect for a spy. At Aberystwyth, the Establishment didn't like him – he went drinking with the students; that sort of thing. So when he did those articles on Burgess and Maclean for a newspaper, for £1,000 – he was always hard up – he was ostracized for his part in things, and never really recovered. They all died broken men, those defectors.'

Morgan Goronwy Rees, the littlest-known of the trio in *Blunt*, was born in 1909 and died about a decade ago. He combined a Fellowship at All Souls with the higher hackery: assistant editor at the *Spectator*, leader writer for the *Manchester Guardian*; and he translated Büchner's *Danton's Death* with Stephen Spender and wrote a history of Marks and Spencer called *St Michael*. Between 1953 and 1957 he was the Principal of the University College of North Wales ... But was he a double-agent? He always claimed to have deserted the Communist cause after the 1939

Nazi-Soviet pact, but Guy Liddell and Dick White of MI5 disbelieved him when he allowed himself to be interrogated about Burgess and Maclean in 1952; and though he told them about Blunt, Blunt was not interrogated for another fourteen years. His newspaper pieces about his suspicions (coinciding with the first public acknowledgement of the defectors' residence in Moscow) precipitated a social ruin.

The film *Blunt* saw Rees as shy and impressionable – bullied by the swot-mastermind of Blunt himself, and by the jolly tuck-shop Bunter of Burgess. Williams's was a touching portrayal of a man whose youthful idealism and allegiances came back to haunt with a vengeance; elements from a boyhood arcady pursue him, changed to hellions: 'You are one of us,' Burgess snarls. Worried, wretched, to whom should he be loyal? 'Guy is my oldest friend,' he tries to tell his wife – and gradually the spectre of an ancient illicit love affair clanks its chains. Williams's eyes and withdrawn stare signalled that embers of affection were quite likely to be rekindled – the little boy with the crush on the captain. Burgess makes him vow never to expose Anthony, nor to warn him that he, Burgess, will not be returning after babysitting Donald to safety.

What intolerable secrets! National Security and personal allegiance ('the sacred trust between friends à la Forster') are impacted, and Rees is easily made to confess by his wife, Margaret Ewing Morris. 'What's the promise Guy asked you to keep?' she demands – knowing there's demonology in the air. 'You've no cause to be jealous of Guy,' Rees responds. 'He's my friend [fatal pause], in the best sense.'

Williams, with tense understatement, was a picture of longing, sinking into a neurotic and hopeless torpor, by way of perplexity and degrees of puzzlement, as Margie dared her questions: 'Guy means more to you than I do, or the children . . . *What has Guy done?*' Answers remain political: Guy tried to enrol him in the KGB ('We were all idealists then. I stopped.') – but the meaning of lingering loyalty is sexual: 'Friendship is another matter.' The wife's world collapses about her; Rosie Kerslake was eloquent in her acting of a woman confused, frightened and suddenly resentful. Guy is godfather to her baby; the evil fairy admitted by a husband who is still lying about real feelings, real deeds. Who were his absent friends she never met? What were the parties she was never invited to in Mayfair? Rees's defence is plaintive. He describes himself as an artless Mr. Pooter: 'I did warn you when we met that I had not a sense of self. Mr Nobody.' Rees impugns the Grossmiths's hero to exculpate his own dishonour, and in his insistence on ordinariness he's like a guilt-ridden Barbara Jackson in *Pack of Lies* deciding what to do: 'I'm not going to think about it. We've got to live a normal life. Let them do what they want. I'm not going to think about it.'

'Old Fin was once in her school nativity play – she was the innkeeper's wife,' said Mike. ' "What is the play about?" she was asked. "Well," she replied, as if stating the obvious, "it is about an innkeeper's wife." '

Judi started to giggle about my address.

Stratton Audley! What a name for an actor, like Beerbohm Tree. *Your* baby might act, Roger.'

'I was once the squire in a nativity play,' I said, thinking back.

Ned had arrived with a tray of food. Chicken in mostly green slop with raw onion rings. Beyond him, making egress from the jakes, and heralded by the sound of gushing water, Annie Hoey, the dresser.

'Is Annie Irish, Judi?'

'Irish? She's as Irish as Kerry Ring, as my mother would say.'

'What did she mean by that? Your mother?'

'My mother always said things like that, like "If I go as brown as I'm red I'll be black." She's had a hard life.'

'Who, your ma?'

'No, Annie. She makes trousers for the Royal Family.'

'She doesn't?'

'She does. She makes Prince Philip's trousers. She gets up at half-past six and goes to Conduit Street, where she makes trousers for the Royal family. Then she becomes my dresser every evening. The theatre is the passion of her life.'

Annie and Ned were upon us.

'Tonight,' said Ned, 'I shall see *I'm Not Rappaport* with Paul Scofield; then I shall go to Groucho's for two starters.'

'You,' said Judi with her hint of Lady Bracknell, 'have the heaviest social diary of anyone I've ever met.'

'Before that,' he stated, 'I have to interview John Houseman at Broadcasting House.'

Ned had broadcasted his day.

'Tell us, do tell us,' Judi began, and Mike, chuckled, 'the "Chuck, get back to the *Planet of the Apes*" story.'

'Well, Houseman produced in 1953,' began Ned, pausing only a smidgen for the computer cue-cards to flicker into position in his brain, 'Shakespeare's *Julius Caesar*. John Gielgud was Cassius. There was another film in 1970, Richard Johnson was Cassius, Robert Vaughn was Casca, Jason Robards was Brutus. Charlton Heston was Mark Antony and this time John Gielgud was Caesar. I bought the set for £900 for *Up Pompeii*, and Gielgud's bust appeared in the baths scene with Frankie Howerd and Michael Hordern. Anyway, Heston kept drying on the speech, "O, pardon me, thou bleeding piece of earth." Time after time they tried. "O, pardon me, thou . . ." "O, for God's sake, Chuck," said Gielgud.'

Judi and Mike joined in the punchline:

' "WHY DON'T YOU GET BACK TO THE *PLANET OF THE APES*!" '

'That's an apocryphal story, by the way,' said Ned, with a cautionary nod in my direction.

'American classical actors have their quirks,' said Judi. 'I remember opening on Broadway in *Henry V*, on Christmas Eve, with Laurence Harvey, and he kept his eye level three inches above mine; as though he was cross I didn't come up to his height. It was like this . . .'

Judi was up on her seat, acting a tall man squinting to find a short lady.

Ned started to tell a story about yet another famous American actor, this one long deceased, who spent a season at Stratford.

'He was found molesting a spear-carrier. He considered all young actors available crumpet.'

'It was a gloomy day,' replied Judi, 'when the lavatories at The Dirty Duck, the Stratford pub, were treated with snowy grit. It meant the end of graffiti, and those lav walls were our noticeboards. A friend of ours was once in the Gents, when he noticed a message on a tiny knob of plaster. It said "Fred and me".'

We started to return to the church hall. Judi and Mike let the others go on ahead.

'Is it working? The play. Can you follow the story? Is it clear, what's going on? All the diary readings?'

It was no idle pleasantry, or fishing for compliments. They honestly wanted to know if the Pooters were coming to life.

'Carrie and Charles have a delightful dignity. And the two of you fill the stage with all the other characters.'

'Roger, you have said the right things.'

In the hall was a large lady, with bright eyes, grey curls and rubicund cheeks; dressed in tweeds and stout brogues, she looked like a dog show judge, or the local rector's wife.

'I've come to see,' said Julia Trevelyan Oman, Lady Strong, 'The Wenham Lake Ice Safe.'

We convened about the object, as if nearing a font or a kennel. More hidden compartments were revealed, and we all murmured appreciation.

On with the show.

A wax phonograph roll, or some recording device, began to plonk 'Pretty Mocking Bird' whilst Carrie sat at the piano. She sang, with gusto anyway, a parlour piece. Judi has a smoky, cabaret husk of a voice; she screeched it towards a ropy operatic soprano. It was very funny. Michael took up position as Cummings or Gowing, and acted their response and appreciations. He also played Lupin, by being a louche version of Charlie.

'When we first started rehearsing, Ned would stand where Lupin was meant to be, so we gradually came to believe the other characters were alongside us. And do you know,' Judi exclaimed, 'I can *see* all those people. I don't know if it gives that impression.'

Having coped with the Mansion House Ball, the Pooters now have to receive news of Lupin's engagement, to a trollop called Daisy Mutlar. Carrie swiftly, efficiently reconnoitres her prospective daughter-in-law's family. Pleased with her sleuthing, she tells her agog spouse, whilst taking off long gloves, hat, unbuttoning a coat (all mimed): 'Miss Daisy Mutlar resides in Upper Holloway, at Avoncrest, No. 17 Atha Grove, with her parents and brother. They have two servants living in – cook-general and maid. I chanced to pass along Atha Grove on my afternoon walk yesterday, and could not help but notice the house; it is a double-fronted residence with a porch, and claret glass surrounds to the bay windows, with engraved corner sunbursts.'

The details go on and on.

'That is the sum of our knowledge of Miss Mutlar for the present.'

A party is organized in the lady's honour. The event, its planning and inquest, dominates many days. The occasion itself occasioned virtuosity: actor and actress packed the room with a bustling throng; party games took place; energetic dances abounded; lavish food appeared. But the party games, dance partners and feast did not actually appear. Our thinking made them so. From the excess and abandon, the mood switched instantly when Mr Perkupp entered. Charlie's boss, it was an honour to receive him at The Laurels. A frost fell on the gaiety. And even though Mr Perkupp's censorious tread could be followed, there was no Mr Perkupp. A concentration of acting filled in and filled out the cast.

The play ended almost abruptly. There being a paucity of story, though a plenitude of incident, a conclusion could come at any time. Sufficient unto a day is the diary thereof. Suddenly, Lupin's wedding day was upon them; Mr Perkupp thawed and promoted Charlie; Carrie was delivered of a Wenham Lake Ice Safe, her pride and joy, her grail.

While Judi and Mike performed amongst the tables and chairs, there had been activity on the margins. A stage manager and her deputy had been loading Sarah ('my maid') with her trays. Instead of a single tray, with a variety of meals and bottles standing by, there were a dozen identical trays, each with objects for a requisite scene already on board. Plus, arrayed like the impossible kitchens of television cooks, ranks of implements for Carrie: her custard bowl and whisk, apron, spoons, menu cards.

Sound effects were provided by Ned, who especially enjoyed being the trains chuffing past the windows; he also whistled and hooted for bells and clocks; for the fireworks he nearly shot his teeth out. If ever actor or actress mangled words or looked lost, Ned would chant the prompt. Few phrases, in fact, were muffed or mumbled. When a mistake was made, however, Judi grimaced as if gripped with a seizure; when offstage, Mike frantically leafed through his script. Julia Trevelyan Oman roamed the hall, adjusting and scrutinizing, her eye alert for anachronism, presumably, or a prize whippet. Gary Fairhall, who was to make two fleeting appearances as a factotum, spent most of the day boiling water in an urn. We who were watching chain-drank coffee. 'What do you think of Gary's appearing?' I'd been asked. 'It's very sensitive. We think it spoils the illusion of our acting to other invisible people.'

During the later afternoon, an emissary from Michael Redington, the producer, licked and counted out wads of twenties; these were distributed in buff envelopes. I alone went home empty-handed. Also during the late afternoon: the director's notes: 'During the dreadful pun about the sash-cords, Mike, when do you think Mr Pooter would realize he's made a joke? How about if he is blank for a moment, then his wit dawns?'

Michael tried this, and it released the humour over and above the trite word-play of 'I'm afraid they're frayed.' (Pooter's tearful wheezing at his own aphorisms was to grow.)

'Those silk programmes from the Tank Theatre, you've got them, Judi?'

'I've got them. I'll flash them.' A dirty chuckle.

Discussion next turned to Pooter's topper, how to bring it on and off, before the ball.

'The hat hasn't been used at this point,' said Mike, indicating the toilet for the ball.

'On the stage,' said Ned, 'it is going to look like an extra special occasion when you reveal it specially for the Mansion House. Bring it out with ceremony.'

'Flash it, Mike.'

'Perhaps he would find it under the table?'

Michael produced the headgear and, in character, spoke the lines covering the moment when Pooter paints the hat black.

'Let him paint it absentmindedly; painting unlikely objects is his hobby (the bath, books, sticks, flower pots – all crimson); he could be deeply absorbed, almost like a sleepwalker, and he'd simultaneously neatly put down a newspaper. Pooter is a neat, fussy, man. Then he'd do a double-take, looking at the hat, all glossy.'

That was me speaking. I listened with incredulity to myself, like a drunk mesmerized by his own rebellious limbs. I've never directed a play in my life; here I was directing Michael Williams and Judi Dench. Instead of giving me a cold stare, or throwing me out for presumption, Ned and his actors made out they were delighted to give my suggestion a try. With some modifications, the sequence was included.

Next they had to make fluid Carrie's departure for Sutton. 'What I must remember,' said Judi, 'is to put my diary away carefully. Could I have a ribbon to mark the page? When I return, and when I'm inspecting the house, I'll check that my diary is untouched.'

She muttered this to herself whilst pacing out the movements. They then worked on attitudes to Lupin, and his change of name from Willie.

'I keep drying on "No sign of Willie", have you noticed that? My favourite line, and I can't get it correct.'

'One hundred miles from London, and no sign of Dick,' said Ned.

'Come, come, sweet pussy,' added Mike. A ribald triolet.

Judi started to giggle when she attempted the lines again, and said Loopy instead of Lupin.

Carrie begins her recital of illustrious forbears: 'It is a proud and distinguished name, and one that goes back into the myths of history. The Berkshire Lupins (as my branch is) have graves in Reading and district . . .' How could this be enlivened? It was in danger of being dull. Motives came easily.

'You see,' said Mike, 'I'm not too keen that he's changed his name.'

'And I'm very excited about it.'

They ran it again, Carrie tensing with relish, Charlie simulating falling into glumness – falling, in fact, asleep so that Carrie has to prompt him with 'August 6th', and he jolts awake for his cue. A longueur had been made winning.

'There'll be lighting changes to mark more clearly the altering days,' explained Ned.

We gathered for a final time before the Wenham Lake Ice Safe, to experiment with fake champagne cork bangs. This seemed to be the pianist's skill. Gas was pumped in the empty bottle. After much adjusting, the cork popped with the tiniest sneeze. 'Well,' said Mike, philosophic, 'if it goes off, we'll yell *whoosh!*; if it doesn't, we'll get a laugh for flatulence.'

Tea was taken at the Pooters' trestle.

'Our house in Hampstead has been completely rebuilt. The builders were putting up wallpaper on the ceiling, and it fell in. The carpets were *completely* ruined. The builders have been making good since May 1985, and they are still not finished.'

'Fin's school,' said Michael, 'is opposite where Lillie Langtry lived.'

'Michael recently bought himself a motor tractor.'

'It broke down.'

'Do you know, he had a face like a wet weekend.'

'I must be off to Broadcasting House now,' said Ned, undecided, as I was, as to the extent Carrie and Charlie had started to usurp Judi and Mike's conversation.

'Can we share a taxi? We need to go to Sloane Square?'

'You know what that means,' said Michael, with forbearance, 'shopping, shopping.'

Why is Judi Dench the finest actress in England? Consider the competition. Glenda Jackson, despite her fame for *A Touch of Class* and for her being an occasional co-star with the lugubrious Matthau (*House Calls, Hopscotch*), rushing in as a female Jack Lemmon, has little sense of comedy. She appears dour and serious; a martinet Elizabeth R, a self-lacerating Gudrun Brangwen. Glenda Jackson's laugh is sardonic; she's independent and beetle-browed, having an overmatter of bile in roles not quite demanding extensive rancour. A tragedian miscast in drollery, with Morecambe and Wise she looked like a headmistress in the end-of-year romp with a pair of naughty boys. She's an actress of much power – but she's disdainfully holding back, as though acting isn't entirely earnest.

Then there's Maggie Smith. She's been content to add her talent to poor comedies and international Agatha Christie murder mysteries. She presents us with caricatures of the diaphanous, dithery, willowy English eccentric: *The Missionary, A Private Function, California Suite, A Room with a View*. And her audience does not want her to stop playing the impossible nanny goat. Her screen people are what some men like women to be – fussy, flighty, stately, a hint of androgyny, comportment for clothes and cosmetics.

What, therefore, makes Judi Dench different? She is free of the self-intentness of Glenda Jackson and of the high camp of Maggie Smith's acting. She bumbles like a diligent mother-rabbit (which she once played) and if there is a key to her acting, it may be her magnanimity. Her compassion is not scowling and political, like Glenda Jackson; her disinterest is not capricious, like Maggie Smith. Instead, in her performances she is alert to the moods and needs of those in whose company she finds herself. She likes to gauge and adapt to gatherings – and thus hates big, empty-hearted parties, preferring cosy cabals, where she can be humorous and assertive. Her ideal unit is the family. The actress's temperament is to appraise immediate company and snuggle to fit in; she imagines the sensitivity of a role and invests fictional character with psychological grain – so that Judi Dench's Carrie Pooter is alert to environment, as Judi Dench would be herself, in similar circumstances. And because the play in which Carrie appears, and Judi acts, constitutes these similar circumstances, act and actress merge.

This is what people mean when they talk of Judi Dench's humanity: it's her ability to close the gap between self and part. Thus, *Mother Courage and Her Children* was an interesting experiment. The selfish, profiteering, cunning old vixen would seem alien to the actress's nature. She was attired in an orange fright wig and a capacious greatcoat – a raddled she-cat, vigilant in her defence of her children – and this is how Judi Dench salvaged the part: Courage came to exist as a proud matriarch, ennobled as her family's exterminated; managing to be feminine against the odds, and in spite of herself (like her mute daughter Katrin – a rag-doll performance from Zoe Wanamaker – who drums as stubbornly as her mother pushes the cart). The cart was an elaborate caravan locked on rails and pivots, set up in a revolving clockwork stage – like an eternal machine. A baroque bassinet! A crazily over-burdened perambulator! Judi Dench's Mother Courage was an Earth Mother for the iron-age future.

Design was by John Napier, the designer of *Cats*. Photographs exist of Judi Dench in make-up and costume as Grizabella the Glamour Cat – the gin-sipper tart, who becomes the Jellicle candidate for ailurophilic ascension. She sings the sleazy 'Memory', the words derived by Trevor Nunn and Andrew Lloyd Webber from Eliot's 'Rhapsody on a Windy Night'.

> The memory throws up high and dry
> A crowd of twisted things;
> A twisted branch upon the beach
> Eaten smooth . . .

Grizabella, sad and slummy, was not included in the original *Old Possum* collection; Eliot thought her too melancholic for a nursery audience. The fragments containing her were kindly exhibited to the lyricists by the poet's widow, Valerie. Grizabella, in fact, is Eliot's Beatrice, Rose la Touche, Alice, Dulcinea del Toboso, Molly Bloom; his White Goddess and Muse. In *The Cocktail Party* she's Celia Coplestone, who is martyred in Kinkanja; in *Cats*, Grizabella is borne aloft from the Jellicle Ball ('Up, up, up to the Heaviside Layer, up, up, past the Russell Hotel'), to a nirvana of auto-tyres.

The Waste Land contains Grizabella in many manifestations: Marie the foreign aristo, reading at night, going south in the winter; the wet-haired hyacinth girl; Isolde; Madame Sosostris; Cleopatra; Philomel; the nervous lady; the East Enders, Lil, Lou and May; the hermaphroditic Tiresias; the secretary, seeing off her hopeless lover, putting a record on the gramophone; Elizabeth I on the Thames; the Rhinemaidens; Kundry. Unfortunately, Judi Dench injured her leg in a dance rehearsal soon before the opening; Grizabella had to be played by Elaine Paige, who made off with the show. Imagine what the actress originally cast would've done with it. A mood like Deborah's in Pinter's *A Kind of Alaska* – a girl who fell into a three-decade coma, and who awakes as a sixteen-year-old inside an old body; a young, haunted voice in an aged carcass. Or Sally Bowles in *Cabaret*, the flapper past her prime.

Elaine Paige's cat was mournful, but shrill (Evita raised from the dead); Judi Dench's would have been mournful, but knowing. The photograph shows the Dench face peering through a tangle of mangy fur, coils of curl and drooping whiskers – like an extravagant rococo hairdo several years beyond its best and full of vermin; a ruined-castle plumage, flanked by big black bows. The mouth is slightly pursed, with a smudge of palest gloss; the nose, gently snub; and the eyes: Judi Dench has eyes of a cat most times, here they are twin comets coming into a symmetrical land; the eyebrows, attendant trails. Beneath, the mascara has smeared into watery puddles, as if formed by tears. A cat: daring and resilient, fissile and enigmatic, steel inside softness – Judi Dench is one of our most prankish, feline of actresses. To switch the gender of *My Cat Jeoffry* by Christopher Smart –

> For she is a mixture of gravity and waggery
> . . .
> For there is nothing sweeter than her peace when at rest
> For there is nothing brisker than her life when in motion.

In *Saigon, Year of the Cat* Judi Dench was an erotic missy, watching the world end. She played Barbara Dean, an English employee at a Vietnamese bank. She witnesses the twilight of the gods: the ignominious American retreat. Parrying the attention of would-be suitors (one, a young Scot, played by Roger Rees), Barbara is willingly bedded by a dashing US Embassy official, Bob Chesneau (Frederic Forrest) – who dislikes too much closeness ('Why do you behave as if I'm your wife'). They fiddle whilst Saigon burns. The actress was sensual and sexy: the spinster attracted to the exoticism of the East, only to see it disintegrate, and half-enjoying the literal decadence – whilst masterminding exit visas and tickets for her native friends. In Vietnam, she's vital and accomplished; lifting-off in the helicopters, during the panic of the final days, however, she visibly settles into middle age; Bournemouth ('You feel watched, disapproved of all the time') is already casting its long shadow.

Barbara is destined for premature retirement, indolent fat-cattery. Judi Dench's Mother Courage, by contrast, was always the cheroot-chewing tom, a cat scavenging on a rubbish dump, living off the detritus of battlefields. With that cart of hers, packed with gypsy junk, she's a carrion cat hard-hearted and terse. She'd enter Saigon as the Americans are fleeing it. Judi Dench's performance was the more moving for not giving way to the sentimental (which underpins all Brecht like a foundation of marshmallow); the performance was the more moving for presenting an apparently unmotherly mother raucous-voiced and foul-mouthed. As her children are picked off, instead of making mute appeals to the audience, this Mother Courage turned away from us, hunched, sagging into her coat, slouching back to her caravan – pinioned on a giant dial. The woman was crushed by the inevitability of fate, yet determined to outface it. 'Sometimes I see myself pulling my cart through hell, selling brimstone. Or through heaven handing out food to the hungry. If I could find a place where there's no shooting, I'd like a couple of quiet years with the children. What's left of them.'

Thwarted maternalism has provoked many Judi Dench performances, right back to her comely, bosomy Titania in *A Midsummer Night's Dream*, opposite Ian Richardson's Oberon, wanting to mother the little Indian boy; or the vehement nurse on the cancer ward in *Going Gently*, whose professionalism was a means of keeping a hopeless sympathy for the hopeless patients at bay. Like Mother Courage, Sister Scarli implied deep feeling by suppressing feelings: they flowed into the slouch in Brecht; in the Stephen Frears television film, they flowed into her thorough bed-making, the emphatic nipping and tucking of sheets. And her Lady Macbeth, hair bound by a black turban, was likewise unexpectedly perfervid. Passionate, and boxed in with herself at Cawdor, a husband's ambition has taken the place of raising a child in her life. She was a Mistress Page or Ford for whom any milk of human kindness has soured into evil; a dynamic provincial hausfräu, with Fife for Windsor.

Best of all, regarding mothers and children, there's a film from 1965, *He Who Rides a Tiger*, directed by Charles Crichton. Shot in a watery black and white, within the pale and moody London vistas, set to period maraca plonks by Alexander Farris, and punctuated with police cars with bells for sirens, Judi Dench, headscarfed and busy, plays a teacher at a Dr Barnado's Home. Into her modest and selfless life comes a charming cat burglar (Tom Bell), who finds her goodness a refuge from his violent life.

They meet when Tom Bell tries to save a fox from an iron trap – and in Judi Dench he's found *the* cunning little vixen. Foxes and cats are the theme: the clambering and the thievery; also, on the walls of Judi Dench's flat there are pictures of cats. When Tom Bell's attention gets too lavish, she snaps, 'What do you think I am? Another vixen caught in a trap, waiting to be rescued?' She's a single parent, with an illegitimate child, and 'It's more important for me to find a father for Dan, than a lover for myself.' In her independence Tom Bell quite meets his match; they are both bright survivors, whom by now new experiences will not much change. Tom Bell, despite flooding the orphanage with gifts and toys, keeps going back to a night of crime; and Judi Dench is tied to her own destiny: giving herself to dozens of dependants. Hence the title, he (and she) who rides a tiger 'can never dismount'.

What's so good about Joanne in *He Who Rides a Tiger* is the character's avoidance of sentimentality. The part could've been a Julie Andrews clone – and *The Sound of Music* came out the same year. But Judi Dench was convincingly careworn, and Mrs Boyle, in *Juno and the Paycock*, was an older careworn matriarch ('I killin meself workin', an' he sthruttin' about from mornin' till night like a paycock!'), apportioning time and affection between a live daughter and a dead son. Lady Bracknell, in *The Importance of Being Earnest*, was presented much younger than the dowager of tradition. Judi Dench's termagant actually flirted with John Worthing; she was still in the sexual game. Auden once called the play a verbal opera: 'The greatest composer on earth could have nothing to add to it.' As directed by Peter Hall, it was a Da Ponte libretto, a Mozart chamber piece, with Judi Dench the coloratura Queen of the Night – the wronged mother – whose aphorisms were her protection ('You can hardly imagine that I and Lord Bracknell would dream of allowing our daughter ... to marry into a cloakroom, and form an alliance with a parcel'), like the barbs of Beatrice, who was played at Stratford opposite Donald Sinden's Benedick in 1976 as a lonesome, penurious cousin; Beatrice survived as Laura in *A Fine Romance*.

A fine romance was the subject of Michael Frayn's *Make and Break*, in which Judi Dench played Mrs Rogers, an unregarded secretary-bird, topping up drinks and scrubbing ashtrays for delegates at a trade fair for fire-resistant softwood laminates. Talked about in the third person by facetious businessmen, she becomes girlishly animated when suddenly noticed by the galvanic Mr Garrard – Robert Hardy, stomping and snapping like Prince Albert of Saxe-Coburg-Gotha and Siegfried Farnon. 'He's lost. He's like a lost little child,' croons Mrs Rogers, her hopes springing maternal.

And having been pulled from the edge of the drama to its centre, she was given speeches extolling a sweet philosophy of goodness and mindless solace – typing, washing-up, waiting. Monotony, repetition, is her gate to happiness – and other characters variously define their own contentments as religion, music, children or work. But Mrs Roger's avowed Buddhism is really a reflex of an aching loneliness – she's 'one of the lonely ones', ditched by her husband. 'They all leave us, don't they, the ones we depend on ...'. As a consequence, she allows herself to be nurtured on disappointment and promise of rejection; Judi Dench became a woman whose boiling-point is reduced to about zero.

But it was the television play, *On Giant's Shoulders*, which demonstrated Judi Dench's capacity for an aching benevolence, bounty and resolve. Terry Wiles, a thalidomide child, played himself in a drama of his adoption. The boy was abandoned at birth by his mother, and languished in a hospital until visited, and eventually taken out, by kindly Len (Bryan Pringle). Judi Dench was Hazel, Len's wife. Initially she is aghast at illness and disease. 'A thalidomide child isn't a pretty sight,' she's told.

Again, Judi Dench banished a cloying tone – even managing to keep the scene where Terry writes his heartfelt note. ('I love you, Mummy') from toppling into a sob. Hazel ran outside and blinked her tears away, staring at the bleak Peterborough landscape until it calmed her. Her Hazel was a stout, dowdy moll, prone to temper, who slowly, and with the smallest evidence of reluctance, exchanged her hostility towards the boy ('I'm not having him in the house taking over, because he would') with hostility towards those who wouldn't accept him. Len, meantime, devotes his life and savings to the invention of electric wheelchairs and contraptions; he makes an elaborate dodgem and artificial legs: 'He's a human being,' erupts Hazel after a failed experiment, 'not a machine.'

Len and Hazel are very poor; they have no children of their own. Terry's forthrightness has suddenly made them forthright – they want to legally adopt, for the three of them have grown very close, saving one another from lives of self-pity. When the social worker pays a call, however, it transpires Hazel has had a foggy private history: her father, she thinks, worked on the fairgrounds; she's had several previous husbands, and her own two children have been taken from her by the authorities, who thought her unfit for motherhood.

Hazel, a bit of a slattern, with her thick navy woollies, mousy hair and ill-fitting plastic specs; a more ordinary woman you couldn't expect ever to meet – she was portrayed by Judi Dench, however, as one of the most extraordinary women you could expect ever to meet. And this was achieved without over-balancing the part. The actress had disclosed Hazel's humanity, her inner resource, her coming to terms with exasperation.

Barbara Jackson, in *Pack of Lies*, doesn't come to terms with exasperation: it kills her. Judi Dench became a woman of small emotional range forced into unbidden heroics. The play switched the glamour of spy-rings (James Bond's thrilling travelogues, le Carré's Expressionist mode, Philby, Burgess and Maclean in their Pall Mall Clubs) for a world crushingly dull. Hugh Whitemore's drama deals with intrigue – but in a Ruislip suburban semi, rather than a Jacobean palace or Russian steppe. Bob and Barbara Jackson are Mr and Mrs Nobody ('the sort of people who stand in queues and don't answer back') – and Bob was played by Michael Williams – whose lives are invaded by the Secret Service. Agents commandeer an upstairs bedroom to spy across the street at Helen and Peter Kroger – who happen to be Bob and Barbara's best friends. 'Was it *all* a lie,' asked Judi Dench's character at the end, '. . . was it?' Neighbourliness and compatibility are revealed as counterfeit.

The Krogers's past, on which intimacy and openness was founded, was make-believe – so the Jacksons are multiply betrayed. 'I trusted Helen. I thought she was brash and noisy and sometimes a bit silly . . . but I trusted her.' The Krogers have betrayed their country, transmitting news about sonar buoys to Moscow; the Jacksons have to betray the Krogers, by not disclosing the surveillance – and they also have to keep their child, Julia, in ignorance of MI5's real attention: 'Helen may have lied to us,' Barbara tells Stewart, the MI5 officer, 'but you've gone one better. You made us do the lying; we've even lied to our own daughter.' MI5 itself betrays the Jacksons, by usurping their home, taking over their private lives: 'I wouldn't mind so much,' says Barbara, 'if you had told us the truth in the first place; you must have known it would be more than a couple of days . . .' Layers and layers of mendacity are revealed.

The Jacksons are pulled into an extraordinary adventure, and yearn for their lost normal routine. Unlike the great folk-hero conspirators, they hate having to perform – the theatre of espionage sickens them (Barbara, on seeing Helen, is made to 'feel quite ill'), and Bob is the emollient Pooter, trapped by the game, knowing he's powerless. Michael Williams, compressed into a cardigan, was the meek suburbanite, shy and decent, whose conversation and pleasures interweave with those of his worrying spouse – a man for whom tragedy meant the car breaking down, a hole in his sock; a man who knows the authorities have made up their minds, so why dissent? A laconic Leopold Bloom..

Barbara, like Carrie Pooter, is goaded into a banal eloquence by the discomfort of strangers in her home, making themselves tea and pouring milk straight from the bottle. For her, Kim's 'game' is black magic, corrupting all who are involved ('Helen's lying and we're lying – we're all playing the same rotten game'). Deception does not invigorate; it's a fatal decadence, rendering rotten the blissful chores of dusting, washing, ironing, polishing, cooking. Having to act breaks her spirit: '. . . all the deceit and lies and . . . I was so angry, so hurt – I was so *hurt* . . .' Love, friendship, loyalty, the sanctuary of the family, are trespassed against. Acting is treachery.

Barbara Jackson is duplicated as Nora Doel in *84 Charing Cross Road* – the screen adaptation of Helene Hanff's epistolary novel being by Hugh Whitemore who, as in *Pack of Lies*, was interested in American impertinence encroaching upon British reserve, with Helene for Helen, Frank's love of books for Barbara's painting. But the duplication is more than an author's theme: it's an accident of crossed destiny. In Hanff's *The Duchess of Bloomsbury Street*, the sequel to *84 Charing Cross Road*, we read: 'The closest friends Frank and Nora had for ten years were a book dealer named Peter Kroger and his wife . . . The Doels and Krogers were inseparable.' Nora and Frank went to the trial, 'and discovered that everything the Krogers had told them about their past lives had been invented . . . "They were the best friends we ever had, they were fine people, lovely people,"' said Nora. The antiquarian books were used as receptacles for smuggling secrets to fictitious customers in Eastern Europe, and it's as though *Pack of Lies* explores the home-keeping recesses Frank Doel alludes to in *84 Charing Cross Road*; the double-agent narrative replaced with chivalric love letters.

In the film, as Nora, Judi Dench has a vestige of an Irish accent, like Molly Bloom or Nora Barnacle; she wears a blondish wig of unkempt locks and has a tiny bit too much make-up – a post-war luxury, but suggesting a low-key exoticism. We see her age into a weary widow. She tries her best to amuse her self-involved husband (Anthony Hopkins), who even when erecting the Christmas tree with the children seems elsewhere, preoccupied. It's a passionless marriage thick with civilities and placid politeness. Meals, twenty years apart, are identical; accompanying chat, equally empty. 'Very nice, very tasty.' Nora and Frank tick along, Frank's amorous energy going into his transatlantic mail with Helene – so it's like Nora's almost being cheated on. Helene is Frank's ideal and absent love.

As Barbara, the deceived matron; as Nora, the emotionally skimped wife, Judi Dench brought an epic amplitude to the domestically miniature. (A Ruislip Demeter, goddess of the hearth, made to be Minerva, goddess of war; Irish Nora, a neglected Venus, turning into the pining Penelope.) But it's more than any technique, this calibre of acting. Making the ordinary extraordinary – Mann's bliss of the commonplace – is this actress's special genius; faith in little things, the diffusion of simplicity: she forges in the smithy of her own soul the uncreated conscience of her characters – to vary a phrase from James Joyce. She accommodates the very best feelings of the heart. She is our Joycean marinade – and even possesses a real half-Irish ancestry. Mkgnoa! Mrkgnao! Mrkrgnao!

Having attended the rehearsal for *Mr and Mrs Nobody*, I was eager to view the finished production at the Garrick Theatre. I called beforehand, with my wife, at Dressing Room One, situated far underground, like Churchill's war bunker. We were received effusively by the star in her modest cell. A noticeboard flanked by curtains pretended to conceal a nonexistent window. John Mortimer once pointed out that there is an affinity between actors and prisoners: both live by artificial light. The noticeboard was pinned with good luck cards – several, suggesting some private joke, being of gorillas.

Talk, Anna's bump looming large, was of babies.

'You might be getting tired now and again, feeling as though the baby is here already; but as soon as it's born, your time will never quite be your own again. I told Roger before, when I first had Finty I was forever calling my actress friends who were mothers and begging for advice.'

Judi Dench was beginning her make-up for the matinée; a madonna at her elaborate toilette. I got up to go, thinking these moments of cosmetic preparation private: the mystical assumption of robes and hairpiece; a priestess getting ready to sacrifice the oxen of the sun.

'No, you both stay,' she said, unrolling her stockings down a calf and massaging her feet.

First, she wet her hair and scooped it back with a large white band. Next, the actress wound a crepe bandage around her head as if for terrible surgery. Taking a tube, she squeezed orange goo onto a small sponge and smeared it all over her face – so that she looked like the 'before' picture of a fashion feature on wrinkle eradication. To have razored a cucumber and popped the discs on her eyes would have completed the effect. The orange goo hardened to suggest, at close quarters, jaundice; from the auditorium alone would the complexion look healthful. Next, the eyelids were shaded and the lips dabbed, with a purple stick. Some powder to the cheeks – and even from the far side of the small den, transubstantiation was apparent: a bubbly, bouncy woman had become a fine-featured lady. Her face and carriage had started to act.

During the face-painting ceremonial, mammiferous Dame Judi kept up a stream of advice on breast-feeding. She and Anna exchanged tips about parts of life menfolk never fathom; the Darwinian adventures of the body during pregnancy, its eruptions and rebellions.

'I acted until six months gone, which wasn't quite right for the part I was playing. You are in charge of yourself now. Soon all sorts of demands will be made. I remember bursting into tears. We were going out for dinner, and I was giving Finty her feed first. And she just wouldn't be quick enough.'

'Apparently,' said Anna, who'd been researching ante- and post-natal adventures since the day the Predictor fluid went black, 'if you are flustered, the milk won't pump.'

'It's psychological, breast-feeding.'

At this juncture I handed over a Phiz cartoon, from an 1850s *Punch*, a coloured etching of a grand party. The actress requisitioned every appearance of tender gratitude and placed the picture on the overmantel. 'It's that dreadful party! There's Mr Perkupp! There's Daisy! There's Mr Gowing!'. Then she picked it up again and ran to fetch Michael. He came in, with half a beard.

'Ah, how are you, old fellow,' he said, Charlie greeting Lupin; and a slight bow to Anna.

They have separate dressing rooms. Judi's contains a divan. There is a connecting door, or maybe it is the jakes. Annie Hoey, runner-up of regal trews, bore in the dress for Scene One; also a wig on a polystyrene stand: sharp centre parting, dragged into plaits, woven into a bob. Judi began fixing on bangles and rings.

'Are you going to be in today? Well, we shall do it for you. Where are you sitting? Okay. Look out!'

She went back to Michael's room.

'Michael, we shall do it for *them!*'

Coming back, she said, probably satirically, 'I mean, you are part of the production. You were the first to see the run-through.'

'I want a penny a night for my hat and newpaper idea.'

'Of course! I'm behind the scenery at that point, but when I come back on I'll point to it.'

Julia Trevelyan Oman's set arose like an archaeological exhibit: a full façade of Brickfield Terrace, with coloured paper stuck on the windows, pretending to be mullion stained glass. For the introductory voice-overs,

Charlie and Carrie came to peer through the casements. Then, up flew the exterior of the house (showing the second storey, where the musicians were situated in silhouette, and a frame for the front door); and the Pooter's palace came forward on the truck. There were the ornaments and paraphernalia I remembered from the Chelsea Church Hall, plus a ton of additional gewgaws and gimcrackery.

The swooping-into-view of this fussy museum won applause. But I thought, what with the walls (muddy varnish and deep ochre striped paper) and curtains (orange and black squares with tassels) now added, the effect was oppressive – Nora Helmer's *Doll's House* rather than Carrie Pooter's Wendy house. Antimacassars; open fans on the wallpaper; heavy framed prints hung on chains; plaster vases; the moose head; every item slurped with lacquer and lit with brown and beige light: the comedy could be in danger of stifling.

Charlie wore a fusty frockcoat and elaborate stock-tie; and he had big whiskers. Carrie was tight in the skirts and petticoats of the 1880s; she was an armoury of corsets and pins. The painstaking realism made it hard to adjust to the artificiality of the narrative form – the acting to invisible people, and the contention that neither character could hear the other recite. In the hurly-burly of the rehearsal, such devices and expectations didn't matter; it was so obviously make-believe, people acting. On the West End stage, however, the naturalistic design meant us to overlook our knowledge of a performance; the conjunction of a V & A set and stylized action jarred; especially at first.

Thus, laughs were slow; and when not slow, too dutiful. Lines and nuances which warmed with their guile at rehearsal were passing by, flat. The actor and actress began to push themselves harder, overdoing, slightly, the quick collusive glances at the audience – which got titters of compliance. Judi Dench knew this, for she suddenly withdrew the trick. Charlie's wheezing at his own jokes got a laugh the first time around; a small guffaw the second time around; silence the third time around; after that, bigger and bigger laughs, as the audience responded to a running gag of the production. Several scenes (the lumpy blancmange mixture; the steam from the trains; the Pooter's falling over when dancing) went by stonily. The lighting changes, which Ned Sherrin had promised would make clear the calendar, had the effect of breaking up the play into a series of small revue sketches; and as the scenes are all variations on a theme, the play seemed much too long. By speeding up the pace, the purview of the production had bagged out.

But to imply *Mr and Mrs Nobody* had diminished in its perceptual faculties would be false; the jokes were failing, but the marital comedy of manners was intact – indeed, they'd grown more subtle. Charlie had become more despondent, his dignity more fastidious – and he was completely oblivious to the irony of his gentility. (Promoted to Head

Clerk, for instance, he thought, as did Carrie, he'd been Head Clerk for twenty-five years.) Carrie's caressing of brand names and dreams of gadgetry had become fluent and reverential. (In rehearsal Judi Dench occasionally stumbled on the catalogues and vast menus.) Her detective-work about Daisy Mutlar had grown into a satisfied purr of information: a proficient spy debriefing.

Both husband and wife were fastened in a drama of social advance-ment. Charlie talked to the audience; Carrie connived with it, teasing her husband, yet living in his universe. We were their confidants, especially over Lupin. The Pooters's only son, a clerk and amateur actor for whom they hold out such hopes, was the invisible presence of rehearsal; a blank space, like the giant bunny Harvey. When he spoke, Charlie did an impersonation – and it did work more satisfactorily in the Chelsea church hall. Michael Williams, made up as a middle-aged Charlie, couldn't be anyone other than middle-aged Charlie. (The same problem occurred when Judi Dench was briefly Mrs Birrell.) But actor and actress had perfected their ability to present the unspoken secret signals between a husband and a wife – signals indicative of worry and sympathy: their thoughts about wayward Lupin registered his existence. Lupin was not on stage but the effect Lupin had on his parents made Lupin loom. Only when made to speak did he disappear.

The aftermath of the Mansion House Ball, which they'd looked for-ward to so much, and which turned into a catastrophe, was played with rich feeling: Charlie's anger really an anger with himself; Carrie's tending to pettishness. The separation, when she goes to Annie Fullers's (now Mrs James of Sutton) froze laughter. Judi, fleetingly, had become a Holloway Juno: quick, capable, tried. *Mr and Mrs Nobody* took its place in the actress's best work: a woman coping as a wife, as a mother. Carrie's reward for fortitude? Charlie buys her a Wenham Lake Ice Safe.

How would the much-regarded object appear? A 'deus ex machina' from the flies? From a trapdoor? Gary Fairhall wheeled a small cupboard on, no bigger than a varnished hutch. The authentic object, so proudly demonstrated at rehearsal, had had to be jettisoned as too heavy, too cumbersome. So a mock-up deputized. The genuine was defective; the representation was preferred over the real thing.

I'M DYIN', AIGYPT – DYIN'.

Whilst performing in *Mr and Mrs Nobody* at night, Judi Dench rehearsed *Antony and Cleopatra* during the day. Regal and grave at the same time as they're capricious and merry, Carrie and Cleo are compatible – and the actress played them as issuing from the same nature: women as divinities – Cleopatra, Queen of Egypt, superintending her lands like Carrie ruling The Laurels. Both had fingers clogged with rings and wrists a-jangle with bangles; both never stopped pacing out whirlpools on stage. Both are goddesses of Love: and Judi Dench's fantasy of arranging fish on beds of ice (on chat shows she's said that had she failed in the theatre, she'd have been happy to sell fish) suggests that, like Venus, she was born from the sea; form from the foam, or what Joyce calls 'the great sweet mother'. Goddesses of love, Carrie and Cleo carry on, bewitching their menfolk.

Antony and Cleopatra is not a pageant, though it is often presented as though it ought to be – Charlton Heston, in 1972, returned to the costumes and scale of *Ben-Hur*, and provided that opportunity for Ned Sherrin to buy discarded sets; Shaw's *Caesar and Cleopatra*, filmed with Vivien Leigh, was an opportunity for Higgins and Eliza to wear Nile fancy dress; the Burton and Taylor *Cleopatra* was an opportunity for Joseph L. Mankiewicz to go on a spending spree, indulging the extra-mural romance of the stars. Rex Harrison was Caesar (Olivier turned it down), and footage with Peter Finch, directed by Rouben Mamoulian, was abandoned. The entire episode was like an imprudent war.

In *Carry on Cleo* Sid James guffaws as Antony, Kenneth Williams cackles as Caesar and Amanda Barrie skinnydips in milk as a nymphet Egypt, the sexiest Egypt since Claudette Colbert, who was brazen and teasing in Cecil B. DeMille's *Cleopatra*, acting inside sets blown up from Victorian genre-paintings*. . . . No, the play isn't a tattoo, it's domestic and intimate. Antony and Cleopatra are Edward and Mrs Simpson: the besotted princeling who trafficks away his kingdom for the love of a much-married hoyden from luxe America (the sale of the Windsor baubles was like revealing the inventory of Cleopatra's treasury); or Mars and Venus in Veronese; or an aged Romeo and Juliet – even to the extent of misreported deaths and a conclusion in a vault. Cleopatra: she's Bizet's Carmen, Wagner's Kundry, Pound's Circe, Nabokov's Lolita. She's Scarlett O'Hara and Hollywood vamps. (As we know, she's Molly Bloom, 'Cliopatrick', and she's Carrie Pooter, with her banquets and Jackson Frères' champagne.)

Antony and Cleopatra was nonetheless directed by Peter Hall like a lost opera. On a permanent burnt-umber amphitheatre of a set, an ochre sepulchre, the spirit of particular place was abandoned. Rome, Greece and Egypt weren't discriminated, and Cleopatra would enter as Octavius was leaving. A wandering wall, broken into segments, with a lofty, panelled door, flanked by a ruined pillar, dominated. The effect: abstract neo-classical, by a designer who had loitered too long in art galleries looking at the seventeenth-century dream of the ancient world, with odds and ends of classical statuary amongst the rubble; with people wearing velvet doublet and buttons under the classical armour.

The romantic ruin, becomingly decrepit, with wide-open spaces for

---

* More on this in Chapter Four, page 223.

the congregating of choruses, was a set for something grand, stately – hence, grand opera. The triumvirate was a trio of tenor (Octavius), baritone (Lepidus) and bass (Antony); coloratura soprano was Cleopatra – Judi Dench slimmed down like Callas. We did indeed have moments of choral speaking: Octavius, Lepidus and Antony chanted to Pompey 'That's our offer' and 'show's the way, sir'; Antony's attendants say, 'Fly? not we'; and his servants holler, 'The gods forbid!'

And yet Hall's not to be expected to operate other than as if he had an opera on his hands. His dramas are consistently ritualistic, reverential – *The Oresteia*, *The Importance of Being Earnest*; and, contrariwise, his operas have a supple theatricality – the nighthawk *Don Giovanni*, the games people play in *Le Nozze di Figaro*, the striking-out of Albert in Britten's *Albert Herring*. He directed *Antony and Cleopatra* as if it was his *Clemenza di Tito*; a thing of grandiosity and marble: the marble about to melt, if only the orchestra would arrive.

Bereft of music (apart from a dozen braying fanfares and honking trumpets), the production felt fatally incomplete, like a resurrection of the Samuel Barber *Antony and Cleopatra*, adapted by Zeffirelli for the opening of the new New York Met. at the Lincoln Center, in 1966, incomplete because the stage hadn't been built; or perhaps Hall was waiting for Kaffka's score (1779) or Berleburg's (1883) or Yuferov's (1900) or Ardin's (1919) or Malipiero's (1938). The big Olivier stage wants big treatment. But Roman soldiers marching in the aisles and Dolby speakers clunking out war cries only muffled the real play.

Antony and Cleopatra is about the self; knowing thyself; to thine own self being true; the presentation of the self in everyday life. Shakespeare implies that any core of selfhood, self-possession, is a great fiction. The self is a shady hollow from which we're in flight. The self is a volatile heart of darkness made out of past, present and fantasy; a crucible of fact and reminiscence – infinitely recombined and rearranged. Think of a Picasso cut-up or Pound's vortex or a choppy film by Fellini: the 'self' is like the quirkiness of form. Strokes of havoc unselve the sweet especial scene!

There *is* no centre, no composed self – only moods, possibilities; so many available performances. This can make for madness (Lear, Ophelia, Othello, Hamlet, Antony) or a comic liberation (Falstaff, Hamlet again, Cleopatra). In Dryden's *All For Love*, this psychological fluidity is shifted to Dolabella, who is smitten with Cleopatra late in the play:

> But yet the loss was private that I made;
> 'Twas but my self I lost: I lost no Legions;
> I had no World to lose, no people's love.

Dryden's is a diminished Antony: he is but a representative of history and culture rather than a private individual. Shakespeare is interested in the private individual. Rome and Egypt are less interesting to him than the competitive versions of self within each main character. As John Bayley says in *Shakespeare and Tragedy*: 'The contrast in the play . . . is between the figure one puts on ("Eros, thou yet beholds't me?") and the dissipation of that rigid persona.' Shakespeare's concern is the liquefaction of personality – of the self's many corruptions.

In this way, *Antony and Cleopatra* doesn't only demand great actors: it is an examination in great acting; an intensively theatrical play, dealing with the limits of self-dramatization, ostentation, reclusiveness, mummery, conjury, sham. Thus when Antony describes Cleopatra as a repository of every divergent emotion – the 'wrangling queen / Whom everything becomes' and in whom 'every passion fully strives / To make itself . . .' – Cleopatra retorts, 'I'll seem the fool I am not; Antony / Will be himself.'

But Antony, in Egypt, does not seem, to Philo, Antony – which assumes some fixed 'Antony' exists, at least to Philo's imagination:

> . . . when he is not Antony,
> He comes too short of that great property
> Which still should go with Antony.

Antony is perfectly aware that he's compromising the public side of his nature: 'These strong Egyptian fetters I must break, / Or lose myself . . .' And the death of his wife in distant Italy is a further guilty jolt, making current pleasure 'The opposite of itself'.

From the witch-queen finally breaking off, he breaks up: 'But my full heart,' he says to Cleopatra, 'remains in use with you.' He distributes affections; a process of dispersal and the sundering of self:

> Our separation so abides and flies
> That thou, residing here, goes yet with me;
> And I, hence fleeting, here remain with thee.

Quitting, Antony implies he'll stay in spirit with Cleopatra, who'll dwell in a limbo – 'idleness itself' – until his body returns to claim its soul. And she patrols her palace, planning and cancelling orders and amusements, deep in active reminiscence:

> O times!
> I laugh'd him out of patience; and that night
> I laugh'd him into patience . . .

Cleopatra is an enchantress, her own switchback variations of personality exacerbating Antony's – even to the extent of drawing him out of himself for a game of cross-dressing: once, they exchanged identities: '[I] put my tires and mantles on him, whilst / I wore his sword . . .' And, the messenger coming with news of the marriage to Octavia, her tone instantly alters from cat to spider woman; she flirts with the messenger, then strikes him, threatening to rip out his eyes. 'Good madam,' says Charmian, 'keep yourself within yourself.' Recovering composure, Cleopatra knows her actorial gifts went momentarily out of control. She was briefly mad:

> These hands do lack nobility, that they strike
> A meaner than myself; since I myself
> Have given myself the cause.

Their grand passion was in the past – 'Eternity was in our lips,' Cleopatra reminisces; her future is imagined as a longing preterite: 'his remembrance lay / in Egypt with his joy' or 'My salad days / When I was green in judgement . . .' Her limbo is all her yesterdays. Antony by contrast, back in battle, languishes in a harsh political present tense.

Pompey realizes that the triumvirate is not founded on genuine amity and he hopes to make that weakness his strength – exploiting the breakup, the division, which Antony's hasty match with Octavia is really meant to be bonding. That marriage is an effort 'to knit your hearts / With an unslipping knot' – a reference to Antony and Octavia's brother, Octavius, rather than a connubial image for actual bride and groom. And, in any case, the groom doesn't expect to be much at home. The ways of the world, he warns his new wife, 'will sometimes / Divide me from your bosom.' Let alone leaving Octavia alone, a soothsayer tells Antony to be rid of Octavius – 'Make space enough between you' – and so he betakes himself to Athens. 'You take from me a great part of myself,' says Octavius of his sister, as she packs her bags for Greece.

The play begins with Antony and Cleopatra having to split up; the idea of dissension and fragmentation informs the rest of the drama – a world multiplying, mating, destroying, dividing, like a restless organism. Octavius's treachery against Pompey, and his general disrespectfulness, urges Antony to an avenging war, which Octavia tries to persuade him against: 'the world should cleave' to have husband set upon brother. But Antony is preoccupied with an abstract:

> . . . If I lose mine honour,
> I lose myself.

He must defend his sense of self; Octavia, finding his attitude towards her intolerably neglectful, as he dreams only of soft beds in the East, slinks back to Italy, where she's described as 'an obstruct 'tween his lust and him': she's the air-pocket between Cleopatra and Antony and once removed, the ancient lovers are free to reunite, for an improvident battle with Rome, at Actium. Canidius explains why they were defeated.

> Had our general
> Been what he knew himself, it had gone well:
> O, he has given example of our flight
> Most grossly by his own.

That is, had Antony been his usual heroic self; had he been what he knows he has it in himself to be, then it might have been a victory. But what's happening in the play is that Antony's losing a sense of what he is; he's falling apart: 'I have fled myself ...' Enobarbus is disgusted at the uncharacteristic behaviour and so 'will seek / Some way to leave him' – betaking himself from Antony's company like a pettish ex-wife, a departing spouse.

Antony is quite aware of his altering state; he realizes his nature is disintegrating. 'Let that be left / which leaves itself,' he says with resignation, when the servants and companions walk out with their treasure. And Enobarbus tries to fathom how this present Antony connects with the soldier who once slew Brutus:

> I see men's judgements are
> A parcel of their fortunes, and things outward
> Do draw the inward quality after them,
> To suffer all alike ...

Fate, he says, is character – and Antony 'becomes his flaw': he's turning into a monument or stage-joke of the besotted old lover.

Temperamentally, Antony tries to assert a waning power; he has a messenger whipped ('I am Antony yet') and, before Cleopatra, he puts on a display of anger and authority – and he overdoes it. Cleopatra interjects with 'Not know me yet?' But after the ritual squabble, they are reunited.

> Since my lord
> Is Antony again, I will be Cleopatra

Together again after all these years, their happiness is a phantom dawn. Wars intrude. Octavius's battle formations are such that 'Antony may seem to spend his fury / Upon himself.' And, losing the sea-fight, 'Fortune and Antony part here'; he wishes his ancestors had imparted moderation into his make-up, so that he could 'Subdue my worthiest self.' Contemplating his own volubility, his own changeableness, he panics at all the dissimulation: he doesn't want to be an actor. The purified man he wants to be is 'indistinct / As water is in water' – but personality is a befuddling fluid:

> Here I am Antony;
> Yet cannot hold this visible shape.

The only solution to psychological waywardness, the only way Antony can mobilize the mercurial, is to commit suicide:

> ... there is left us
> Ourselves to end ourselves.

Killing himself, he'll be 'conqueror of myself' – though he can't even achieve that, and the play ends in a style of black farce, as his half-disembowelled carcase is winched aloft. He declares:

> Not Caesar's valour hath o'erthrown Antony,
> But Antony hath triumph'd on itself.

To which Cleopatra responds, with how much irony?

> So it should be, that none but Antony
> Should conquer Antony.

Dying by 'that self hand / Which writ his honour in the acts it did', Antony's the man who haunted himself, the quibbles of self being his tragedy – or mock-tragedy, if Cleopatra has anything to say on the subject. Suicide for her is a love-game, solemnity a sport. She tells a messenger to spread word that she's about to exterminate herself; Charmian joins in the shenanigans:

> The soul and body rive not more in parting
> Than greatness going off.

This is the misinformation triggering Antony's metaphysical and destructive self-inquiry. But only when Octavius later thwarts some of her political intrigues does Cleopatra think of death with any earnestness. She'll join Antony in his apotheosis: her memory of him is not of a man but of a charmed landscape – he's dissipated into the rock and stones and trees:

> For his bounty
> There was no winter in't: an autumn 'twas
> That grew the more by reaping.

The victorious Octavius wants defeated Cleopatra ('Hear me, good madam: / Your loss is, as yourself, great') to succumb to a belittlement, and go to Rome as a freak-show. 'I should not,' she replies, 'be noble to myself.' An actress, whose lifelong show is herself, she'll not now be stage-managed by anyone else; there's vast pride and assertive majesty in her rejection of inferior theatre:

> The quick comedians
> Extemporally will stage as, and present
> Our Alexandrian revels: Antony

Shall be brought drunken forth, and I shall see
Some squeaking Cleopatra boy my greatness
I' th' posture of a whore.

Antony kills himself because he's a mess and existentially collapsing. He can't cope with the idea of being an actor – with being merely a player. Cleopatra kills herself because her plurality and sense of self is inviolate – and she does not want to lose control of her precious waywardness. She's an actress who doesn't want to be impersonated by anyone else. Antony's lost control, and his waywardness is uninvited. Theatre is a shambles to him. Cleopatra's death is a grandiose farewell performance; Antony's the botch of an understudy – and he does think he's his own clunky replacement. Cleopatra's suicide is a *liebstod*. Judi Dench wore a golden cape, like an angelic Isolde – and death brought no spasm. Her body was as immobile as a cathedral effigy, or Lady Diana Cooper as the Madonna in *The Miracle*. Antony's suicide is an obscene botch – his body is lugged like Falstaff in the buck-basket; he becomes a comic prop. Antony totally disintegrates; in death, Cleopatra atomizes: she becomes a spirit, an idea, an event – she dissolves into the black sun of herself:

I am fire, and air; my other elements
I give to baser life . . .

Attending a play can be an amusement, a disappointment, a bore, a revelation. At *Antony and Cleopatra*, I scribbled in my programme – disfiguring advertisements for Rioja and Martini Rosso – my notes becoming, at the risk of appearing like the muttering professor at Peter Brook's Deadly Theatre, the gymkhana of the foregoing few pages. Because the ox-blood set didn't bother to differentiate location, about which the text is specific – it's Shakespeare's most panoptic drama – the dark, shadowy stage forced emphasis upon the differentiation of character, and the different aspects within the same character: hence the elaborate sensation of self; of being in and out of one's self etc. An opera without music was Hall's homage to his cold-water mentor, F. R. Leavis, for whom literary analysis 'is a process of re-creation in response to the black marks on the pages' (*The Living Principle*). And for Hall, the black marks are as the notes on a stave.

'Edgar! You must've acted in this play so many times!'
Edgar looked like a member of the Red-Headed League – ginger all over and with heavy horn-rims – but actually he was an actor.
'I know some of it quite well,' he answered. Yes, yes. Darling, you were marvellous, quite marvellous, I'll go now so you can lie down.'
'Bye, Edgar! Hello, girls.'

Judi Dench looked up at two blushing, smirking, acne-popping speechless nymphets.

'Are you doing it for O-level? It does so help to see the play on a stage, doesn't it? You get an idea of the story – all spread out.'

The girls, giggling, followed Edgar, glowing, out.

'Roger! Come this way!'

It was my turn for an audience with Aigypt. The dressing room was a motel cubicle, with a partition concealing a shower and a table with make-up sticks and vital impedimenta. A supermarket cardboard box contained the gold cape, crushed now like tin foil, and the crown – a cardboard and smarties nursery-school effort. Another carton contained an ivory dagger, a pearl ring and a rubber asp – each object joke-shop jobs close to.

Two hops, and we were past the partition and in a recess with a divan, more bouquets than for a state funeral, cards, telegrams, a magnum of Moët, a copy (illustrated) of the *Egyptian Book of the Dead*. The bouquets made for a heavy sweet smell of decomposition.

I was bidden give post-natal details.

'He sleeps through the night, Tristan? Every two and a half hours, Finty! I thought I was going to die. No sleep for months. I remember one morning making the announcement to Michael, "Today I am going to die." I was convinced I was going to get up and drop dead there and then. But it surpasses everything. *Everything!*'

The actress was in her Cleopatra kit with an evening show ahead. Her complexion was slopped with a thick heavy orange, which had dried in wrinkles, like an aerial photograph of the Kalahari, and the gauze of the wig was pulled low on the brow – so Judi Dench resembled Ashya in an early stage of crumbling. But with her legs drawn up on the bed, arm dangling from over knee, the effect was cocky, sphyngine.

'Cleopatra is all Shakespeare's women in one go. The stage, the whole time, is filled with her lovers, or former lovers, or the children of her lovers, or would-be lovers. Pompey! She *had* his father! Imagine! I'm doing it all again in an hour. Re-do the make-up. Untangle my wig. Then I'm driving up to York – a nephew's baptism.'

Cleopatra is an actress who ransacks her own temperamental gamut; the paradox is that the ransacking is regenerative. Like the phoenix, she flames into being. Judi Dench is an actress whose characters are of her own character: for her to play Cleopatra is to intimate a huge poem of personal accomplishment; a parade of her heart. Notions of self weren't imagined: they were felt. An idiomorphic party. And the production began with much giggling and romping, as Cleopatra brought in Antony – carried on the shoulders of an eunuch – by a leash. There was much movement, pacing, prowling. It was as though Antony was in Egypt on an eternal furlough, the Nile his pleasure garden and Cleopatra his playmate.

That her stage partner was not her real husband made for a switch of perspective: Carrie Pooter preincarnated as Cleopatra, mating with a decaying hero instead of a rising clerk. And in any case, Michael Williams is not a natural Antony, as Alec McCowen is not. McCowen could never convince us of power burning itself up; Williams's power is deeply interior – the fire which seems out but sleeps beneath the cinders (as Corneille would put it): hence his heroic Mr Nobody, his flailing Goronwy Rees (like Babs in *Pack of Lies*), his Bob in *Pack of Lies* (squashed like Nora in *84 Charing Cross Road*).

What Antony requires is a man relinquishing command of himself, almost somnambulantly, drugged with mandragora; it must be a surrender equivalent to Lear smartly dispossessing himself of Albion. And in Anthony Hopkins, Judi Dench had a consort well able to portray mighty resignation. Slapping, rolling, given to sexual repartee, this Cleopatra with this Antony was coquettish, skittish, swishing in slinky silk pantaloons. Her many trinkets and beads gave a gypsy look; and her orange tan and tight curls made Cleopatra the image of Cleo Laine; a folk-song Isolde.

Judi Dench was never at rest – poetry in literal motion, as she described arcs and spirals. An alert cat; a blinking sphinx: pouncing, jabbing, purring, scratching. A pussy trapped by Egyptian responsibility, by being in love, and by Octavius's designs. Hers is the nature to hop forty paces in the market: a restless, rebellious energy; Carrie Pooter sent up the Nile. And the strides and bustling, whether appearing through net curtains and pelmet and varnished screen with a ruined egg custard, or whether coming through a baroque portal waving an ivory dagger and carrying a gold-embossed ledger – it's the same restlessness and energetic rebellion.

There's also a smack of sexiness. Judi Dench shed a stone to play Cleopatra, excavating a pert waist and litheness for splashing about in the river. The actress is a mix of boyishness and unmistakable femininity – like Peter Pan (and offstage, she has short, spiky hair and a preference for leather jerkins) crossed with home-making Wendy; and her conversation with Antony was pure angry banter (angry Peter Pan), her talk of him, an ornamented remembrance (lonesome Wendy).

Both Antony and Cleopatra exult in fantasies of each other – lyrically nostalgic, gloriously retrospective. They look back while history marches forward in the guise of Octavius's peevish ambition. Judi Dench and Anthony Hopkins made their word-picture of the past into arias – apt for operatic Hall. And, in any case, there's a precedent. On Saturday February 27, 1869, Cosima and Richard Wagner read some of the play together with 'a strange feeling of discomfort'; on Tuesday March 2,

Richard read Cosima Acts Three and Four: 'I am utterly shattered. R. finds something of his *Tristan* reflected in it . . . a being utterly consumed by love: in *Tristan* time renders it naive and pure, whereas here it appears in a ghastly voluptuous setting, yet no less destructively.' In *Antony and Cleopatra*, as in *Tristan und Isolde*, the hero and heroine, by exchanging clothes or names, attempt to become one another – remix themselves as a single identity (like an actor merging with his part).

By November 1873, Wagner was talking of 'the searing love which devours the man, as in *Tristan*, or in *Antony and Cleopatra*. It is this love which Brunnhilde exalts . . . a world-destroying, world-redeeming force.' And it is this bitter mystery of love which Judi Dench is supreme in insinuating – whether she's Cleopatra, or Carrie Pooter; or whether she's Barbara Jackson or Hazel in *On Giants Shoulders* or Barbara Dean in *Saigon: Year of the Cat*; or had she been Grizabella in *Cats*; and not forgetting Mother Courage. Enobarbus says of Cleopatra, 'Her passions are made of nothing but the finest part of pure love.' He understands (as Antony does not) that she isn't ultimately cunning or deceitful: she's ultimately merely magnificently herself (which Antony is not). The embodiment of love's old sweet song. Magnificently herself is what Judi Dench becomes on stage – our greatest actress because of sublime paradox: she's both the most and the least contrived.

SIX

The Lion's Colossal Pleasures: Anthony Hopkins

Luckily, Anthony Hopkins's destiny was to become an actor; he'd equally play – as those who've seen Lambert Le Roux in *Pravda* will concur – a dandy king of a small volcanic state – in which case we'd now be discussing, his stage people being so convincing, not what makes him tick and tock as a theatrical animal, but how best to knock the crazy bastard off!

He's a disordered genius – and that happens to be the subject of *Kean, ou Désordre et Génie*, written in 1836 for Frédérick Antoine Lemaître by Alexandre Dumas, and adapted in 1953 by Jean-Paul Sartre for Pierre Brasseur – who, eight years previously, had played Lemaître in Marcel Carné's romantic study of harlequins and mime, *Les Enfants du Paradis*. Hopkins played Kean for the BBC in 1978.

The character is an excuse for any actor to indulge in actorial ostentation. That's the play's purpose: Edmund Kean, the actor, is exotic. The 1836 original concerned social equivocation: is a performer a folderol aristocrat or a colourful barbarian? The post-war revamping heightened a different theme: Sartre was interested in the very nature of theatricality; its relation to experimentation with personality. An actor makes and unmakes himself. Where, and at what level, is the truth?

The actor in a backstage drama, Sartre said in a programme note for *Kean*, can 'talk to the audience about his art, his private life, his difficulties and his misfortunes, but according to the rules of his profession: discreetly, modestly, that is to say by slipping into someone else's skin . . . It's simultaneously a marvellous gift and a curse: he is his own victim, never knowing who he really is, whether he's acting or not.' An actor is a professional investigator of his own psychology; he sleuths out his own capacity for circumvention. And, walking among actors, for this book, and reading about them – from Diderot's *Paradoxe sur le Cómedien* to Genet's *Reflections on the Theatre*, from Alonzo Lopez Pinciano to Luis

Buñuel and Dalí, from Carlyle's translation of *Wilhelm Meister's Lehrjahre* to Margaret Drabble's *The Garrick Year* and Peter Hall's *Diaries*, from le Carré to Henry James – the same issue arose, time after time: how to penetrate the cowls and folds of double-dealing; how to discriminate disingenuousness. The art of acting is the art of deceiving, which is the art of living.

If it is assumed that character is a core of personal sincerity, then acting is flight from this sincerity – an encouraged relish of the switchback shifts and slides of masks and counterfeit. An actor is a professional creature of moods and an expert in evasion – which was a theme I extruded from *Antony and Cleopatra*. But, of course, the lure of fiction and disguise is not the preserve of actors alone; they're not the only honest hypocrites. Any man, says Sartre in *Nausea* is 'a teller of tales, he lives surrounded by his stories and the stories of others, he sees everything that happens to him through them.' To different degrees we each of us surrender to anecdote, fantasy, wish-fulfilment, improved recollection. Personality is a wardrobe of accumulated plumes, expropriated panache – and so that core of personal sincerity cannot, in fact, exist. To believe it impregnable is the biggest fiction (and hence the crack-up of Cleopatra's Antony).

The switchback shifts and slides, masks and counterfeit: these aren't vehicles fleeing personality. They are the very embodiments of personality – or of the self – which proves itself in disintegration and change (and hence the absolute self-confidence of Antony's Cleopatra). The difference is that the actor flaunts the process – and it's why some people (Orson Welles, Roland Barthes, Boswell, Ezra Pound, Coleridge, Sherlock Holmes) could be theatrical without needing an actual theatre. Theatricality was carried in their manner; in their personality. Acting is a state of mind.

In *Kean*, Hopkins portrayed the eponymous hero (1787–1833) as a roaring virtuoso, swarthy in a quilted dressing-gown: a man who's too busy living to shave; a man who is an occasion for much gossip. Kean, famous for being famous, a rake, a scoundrel, a bankrupt, lives up to a bad reputation, drawing lords and ladies into confessions of enthralment with the base. House, furnishings, carriage, servants, all are heavily mortgaged. He can't pay; won't pay. 'I have nothing,' Sartre's actor confesses, 'nothing keeps me here. Everything is provisional – I live from day to day in a fabulous imposture.' Kean's dispossession is a self-possession: the actor unencumbered by boring realities. By refusing to settle debts, he's liberated from the responsibilities of ownership; and he wants to make sacramental his obtuse asceticism, his disinclination to belong to his belongings. 'I am a priest,' Kean says, 'every night I celebrate Mass.' A theatrical performance is a sacrifice on the altar of his own personality.

Kean is father, son and holy spirit in one – consubstantial with himself:
'My name belongs to me . . . it's my own creation.'

Or so, fondly, he thinks. Like Lear, he expects his unaccommodated
title to convey power. Yet onomastic pride isn't enough, and Sartre has to
be sardonic about his hero, whose soul is found to be no deeper than his
clothes; the actor is a hollow man, and Kean sinks into a sentimental
(rather than into a tragic) fit – his dilemma being that by chasing personality and sensation he's lost his personality and now fears to feel. Unlike
Cleopatra in Shakespeare's play, he has not the resource to regenerate.
Cleopatra's pursuit of self invigorates; Kean's fatigues. Anna brandishes
testimony of depleted, drunken renditions. 'I am nothing, my child,' he
wails in defence, 'I play at being what I am.' *King Lear* is ventilated with
'nothing' to a similar end – with the difference that Lear's appreciation of
the degree zero is a metaphysical lesson: the great king reduced to being a
bare, forked animal; Kean's nothingness is crapulousness and disgruntled
despair – or disrepair.

A disastrous production of *Othello* ensues. Anna, drawn to the theatre
as to an illicit club for masquerade, dries as Desdemona. She's incapable
of appreciating that acting is more than learning lines and dressing up.
Kean, improvising, turns on the audience in fury: 'There was nobody on
stage. No one. Or perhaps an actor playing the part of Kean playing the
part of Othello.' The shade of a shade, he is as insubstantial as a phantom;
Lear, by contrast, broken on the heath, is never less than a creature of
sharp appetite, needing food, fire, clothing: he can smell the air and feel
the rain. Nothing, Lear is more of a man than ever. Nothing, Kean is the
paradox of an ideal actor. He stops existing. The living dead.

To have broken down before the public! What a performance! It is an
existential collapse: 'To act you must take yourself for someone else . . .
my whole life is made up of gestures; there is one for every period of my
entire life.' He shrugs off experience as the biography of other people.
Every minute he's reborn, and he dies again. A cancelling-out equation.
But Sartre, puritanically censuring frivolity and duplicity, actually has to
kill him off with the love interest lamely upbeat. For Kean, marriage and
happiness is worse than death: it's reformation as a compromise – like
Lear retiring to a hermitage, a sage, and Edgar marrying Cordelia. Sartre,
if he alludes to *King Lear*, does so through the watery eyes of Nahum
Tate.

Kean fails because it makes out Kean has failed, which is not quite our
impression – especially with Hopkins in charge. Sartre wants to cure the
actor of monumental egotism, but he mistakes soul, or psychological
innards, for conscience, and by having his hero lament his hollowness,
what he must mean is moral sense. Kean manifestly isn't a vacant space
waiting for a role: his own speeches and intelligence alone make him

heroic – in the same way that the apparently frail figures in opera, as Auden taught us, are heroic because they are able to sing. The form dignifies. As Kean collapses, the actor playing Kean grows grand.

Hopkins, an actor of power, imbued Kean, an actor of power, with his own power-in-reserve. He over-reached Sartre, Dumas, Lemaître and Brasseur, to suggest what the original Kean must've been like: mad, bad, dangerous to know – a duplicate Byron (and the real Byron returned over and over to Kean's *Richard III*; and his letters and journals are magnificent incarnations of the theatrical sensibility – but that, as Kipling would say, is another story).

The power of Hopkins's acting is as extrapolated by Hazlitt in 1816, looking at Michelangelo's sculpture: 'everywhere obtrudes the sense of power upon the eye. His limbs convey an idea of muscular strength, of moral grandeur, and even of intellectual dignity: they are firm, commanding, broad, and massy, capable of executing with ease the determined purposes of the will.' Hopkins is a blasted oak. And his power – like Michelangelo's 'conscious power and capacity' – contributed to Kean, Lambert Le Roux, Corky, Siegfried Farnon, St Paul, Bill Hooper, Lear, Antony . . . All the men-of-marble in the man's repertoire – each marmoreal in a distinct way. Consider Bill Hooper.

In *The Good Father*, Hopkins sputtered a power fuelled by vituperation. Hooper's angry that his wife has upped and offed with their son; and he converts his anger into legal power – so that the cynical, heartless processes of jurisdiction function on his behalf, like malign and robotic extensions of his will. But he works out his anger vicariously: it's a friend's plight he champions – and the anger and power come to be seen as pure distillations of self-indulgence.

Hooper roves into the Eighties with a Sixties sense of indignation; an anger and power formulated by the barricades. He's Jimmy Porter (whose appearance in Osborne's 1956 play made ranting a period love-lyric) out of his attic and still railing, though on a payroll as an advertising executive. And at the end of *The Good Father*, Hooper literally barricades himself in a tiny paved garden, fiercely hammering up a tall wooden fence – the hammering a rhythmic tattoo, and equivalent to Jimmy's trumpet riffs.

Christopher Hampton's script and Hopkins's acting made the film a compressed essay on resentment. Hooper's resentful of his wife for taking the boy; he was resentful of the boy's birth, for turning his wife into somebody else's mother; he's resentful of his wife for being independent; he'd be resentful if she wasn't independent. 'We gave each other total freedom,' he says, 'and hated one another for taking advantage of it.'

Hooper is a lover, in fact, of anger. 'Women have a right to be angry,' he opines, surveying feminists on the march, 'but all the same they bloody piss me off.' Dressed in motorbike leathers twinkling with zips, a visored helmet and gauntlets, with a roll-neck grey thick wool pullover that could be chainmail, Hooper looked an appropriate spaceman or bad-tempered knight (as Hopkins would look in the early acts of *King Lear*). He tramples upon, because mystified by, the gentleness of Mary (Joanne Whalley). She's the water-nymph who comforts the aching combatant (and she really is a water-colourist by trade), and he quickly bores of her serenity – enjoying only conflict, content only with contention. His power pugilistic, he ends dejected and purposefully boxed in – his real enemy his sense of self, his maddening sense of honour.

Pushing his son's swing over-hard, always kicking or knocking inanimate objects when he can't get at actual people, driving his motorcycle full pelt (like he's gouging spurs into a stallion), goading Roger Miles (Jim Broadbent) into action ('She steals your son and you pay her money! Jerk her lead a bit'), Hopkins's Hooper was a modern monster, whose chivalry is an earnest of egocentricity. Seemingly assisting Miles, he's really helping himself – as he confesses in the cold of a muddy park, the two men having met like opponents in the lists: the knight is actually a mercenary. The word *good* is used about him as Chaucer calls his Canterbury Knight 'gentil', i.e. sardonically to mean the opposite.

How can we start to separate the actor from his acts? Despite critical and commercial adulation, we must be careful not to confuse Hopkins with Brenton and Hare's despot in *Pravda*; and Hooper's not Hopkins.

Hopkins was raised in the lovely-ugly synthesis between Swansea and Newport, romanticized by Dylan Thomas ('outside, a *strange* Wales') and perceived with honest irony by Kingsley Amis ('When Labour councillors in South Wales start blathering about taking modern art to the people, everybody's in deep trouble'); and in the actor's performances there are local archetypes. A certain contained ferocity; an occasional deviousness; the ability to be cagey in a crowd; an innocence; a loneliness; a solitary integrity; a saturnine withdrawal. Hopkins's temperament comes out of the rocks and stones and trees and coal and coke and oil and seaweed and slate and hops and oysters. A raging-bull Welshness. And different intensities of each aspect of Welshness, and his way of typifying the bones of monsters and saints long vanished from our Earth, constitute his performances.

The eccentric officer in *A Bridge Too Far*, brandishing a rolled brolly at Arnhem, was a Celt's impersonation of a toff; Hopkins's Claudius in the Nicol Williamson film of *Hamlet* was a sybarite snug in a bed of fox fur, dandling gaudy jewels: Captain Morgan anchored in Elsinore. Siegfried Farnon, the Wagnerian vet in *All Creatures Great and Small*, is a champion chance for going over the top: Hopkins strutted the dales like Sir Geraint Evans's Dulcamara, the apothecary in *L'Elisir d'Amore*, on mescalin.

Magic found the actor in obverse mood – a quiet, apparently cheesy ventriloquist, called Corky, whose projection of an assertive self into his doll leads to schizophrenia. The doll starts to take over the master.

Magic could so easily have become a purloining of *Dead of Night*, where Michael Redgrave's dummy leads the operator into murderous temptation. But the 1945 thriller had a supernatural twist; the 1978 film kept itself to pathological conundrums. Hopkins played with a startled face – that of a small boy aghast, and the doll was the same rounded creamy face exactly, with the addition of sneering contours. Corky and his mad mannequin were good and evil brothers – Richard Attenborough's film plotted the traduction of the former by the latter. The triumph of slyness.

The Elephant Man was the triumph of benevolence. Again, Hopkins kept up a startled visage; but the sense of surprise underpinned neither wickedness nor weakness. Frederick Treves, the saviour of John Merrick, was the resolute surgeon who coaxed a freak into becoming a dandy. The success of the performance was Hopkins's ability to portray quiet thought: the flow of sympathy when he first sights the deformed man; his inner struggle to retain inquiry at a professional level; his probity when informing Merrick that ugliness cannot be cured; his sense of guilt when wondering whether Merrick hasn't become merely an exhibited hippogryph once again – a high-society pet. The film was shot in melancholy monochrome. Hopkins, in beard and frock coat, smiling seldom, was a stocky, walking, talking sawbones out of a nineteenth-century sepia print.

Slyness and benevolence came together in a piece of American television hokum called *Guilty Conscience*. Hopkins was Arthur Jamison, a cynical defence lawyer whose speciality is getting killers freed. Playing intellectual brilliance as superciliousness, the actor adopted a nasal drawl to fit the San Francisco setting: *dance, explanation, half, god, prosecutor* and *coffee* came out in the voice-overs as mumbled Bogart/Raymond Chandler.

Jamison is criminal, victim and attorney. He breaks into his own house and talks us through the perfect crime; he then talks his wife through the crime, and shocks us by shooting her. But it transpires we've been watching a rehearsal, or at least the daydream of a rehearsal. Complicating the puzzle, Hopkins next became his own prosecutor: a double in horn-rims and a blue silk bow-tie enters the frame and picks apart the alibi.

What's the motive for murder? Jamison's wife wants a divorce, despite a 'pre-nuptial contract' that she'd win nothing from his estate; but she knows of his legal sharp practices, and could start using blackmail to reap benefits. So more fantasy murders ensue (drugging, falling), and always the legal-eagle double appears to mock the scheme. Hopkins divides sweatily into the panicky real lawyer and the calm hypothetical judge – he splits into the components of a trial, pro and contra, accuser and accused, a battle like Corky and his puppet. Then we find that the wife and a jilted girlfriend are themselves conniving for a tragic accident – they've anticipated his plans. In the end, we don't quite know what's real, what's projected. It's a junky, overwrought film, with too many shots of Hopkins's eyes, which are called upon constantly to register clever shiftiness or funk. It tries to emulate old-fashioned thrillers such as *Dial "M" for Murder*, but it's flat and soapy – lacking the wit and cruel comedy of a Hitchcock. There's an atmosphere only of stretched bubble-gum.

Guilty Conscience is fatally superficial; Leon Uris's courtroom drama, *QB VII*, is fakely earnest. Once again the actor's eyes were twin azure pools of amazement, and his voice soft with submerged smarts. Hopkins was a distinguished scientist, Adam Kelno, protecting himself from defamatory charges of Nazi atrocities. Did he, or did he not, tinker with Jewish tranklements in the manner of Mengele? Throughout, Hopkins was dignified, husbanding his honour and outrage; but the outcome of the libel suit was his own arraignment and humiliation. Any other actor would've left it at that – Hopkins, on the contrary, head bowed, burrowing his way through the baying crowd, demonstrated a man whose carefully constructed self-deceptions had just collapsed about him. Kelno was an unwitting actor who'd taken himself in: a guilty man nearly convinced of his own innocence.

Bruno Hauptmann in *The Lindbergh Kidnapping Case* was another quizzical criminal. Supposedly a guilty man, yet quite possibly entirely irreproachable, Hopkins's dazed carpenter – America's scapegoat – reeled under mounting blame. His hysteria was inward; a glazed silence. Hauptmann was humble, simple even, disbelieving the celebrity status suddenly placed upon him.

As damning evidence was discovered, or planted, did he come almost to credit the accusations? Head shaven for the electrocution, he continued to bleat his innocence – but they were the bleats of a man for whom justice had been so subverted, what other laws of cause and effect had also been mislaid? Hauptmann was a man who awoke to find himself existing in the wrong universe – where perhaps he really was an infanticide. Who could tell? An innocent man nearly convinced of his own guilt.

Guilt and innocence, right and wrong, mix and match in *The Bounty*. Hopkins followed Laughton and Trevor Howard in the part of the martinet Captain Bligh. Though the re-make was for the benefit of 'Mad Max' Mel Gibson, the Fletcher Christian, Hopkins contributed his inimitable punch to the fray: his was a Bligh who wanted to emulate Fletcher Christian (as against, with Laughton, a Bligh who wanted a homoerotic relationship with Clark Gable; or Howard, who exulted in a duel of crusty accents with Marlon Brando). Hopkins's Bligh suppressed his natural instincts, which are to flout convention – and, in the name of *Artocarpus incisa* or the breadfruit tree, he has to forgo the luxury of becoming a Polynesian savage. His battle with Christian is really the anger of an officer confronting the indolent gentleman he'd like to be.

Laughton and Gable formed an allegorical partnership: the demon and the angel, the darkness and the light – Pluto and Apollo. Hopkins and Gibson are more personable, and historical. Hopkins with his round, attentive yeomanesque face, as Bligh, invites Fletcher Christian, a buck in a London club, on his trip – a 'greengrocery' expedition. And mutiny erupted over their different looks and sound: on Tahiti, pleasure-seeking Christian – played by a beautiful Australo-American actor – gives himself up to swiving and splashing in the foam; Bligh – given a rustic accent by the actor son of the Welsh chapel – sulks on board ship, restraining himself, envious at his companion's easy sexiness and louche confidence. (Gibson looks aptly at home in the South Pacific.) *The Bounty* almost became social comedy: perplexed and stubborn Bligh refusing to liberate himself for an ideal fantasy life; but instead the film opted to cross to melodrama, with Hopkins's Bligh having to defend his non-actions at a court martial before Laurence Olivier, with a broken nose, and Edward Fox, with a broken tooth.

If Bligh's secret was to want to become Christian, similarly, Hopkins's Othello, for Jonathan Miller on BBC television in 1981, grew into his Iago – the goblinesque Bob Hoskins. The Celt and the Cockney. Re-splendent in ceremonial armour, the panels and buckles wrought into illustrations of epic deeds, and topped by fringes and ruffs and feathers, Hopkins was Othello prettified for Verdi's *Otello*. And the actor's voice is truly melodious; whether barking or crooning, the love of language never deserts. Lambert Le Roux, for whom Hopkins strangulated his voice into a bestial, chomping Afrikaans, allowed a loving of language the most. Each dragged, guttural syllable was savoured. The *Pravda* music – G. Wilson Knight once described the Moor's love of language as 'the Othello music'. Miller brought such a show from Hopkins, allowing a full operatic passion when it comes to the sacrifice of Desdemona.

His different voices can't be ascribed fully to Welsh minstrelsy. Hopkins owes nothing to the cheery professional Taffy mentality of Lloyd George, Wynford Vaughan Thomas, hymns and arias. Rather, Welshness to the actor means an ability to be appreciative of self-caricature: degrees of intentional garrulity, tediousness, openness, reactionariness, mockery – superintended by irony. 'You can never,' says Amis in *The Old Devils*, 'be absolutely sure a Welshman's not being ironical.' It's precisely this capacity for secret dissidence and excited repulsion which makes Hopkins's performances unique. The lilt's an accident of geography – the birthplace. The quality of mind is more supersubtle – his growing up and away from the birthplace.

Hopkins is a polysemic actor, managing to be consistently interesting, even in insipidities like *International Velvet* and *Hollywood Wives* – actually, he's especially interesting in junk: we can see the germs of his talent searching for substance. In *Peter and Paul*, for example, the actor gave Saul the slightest stammer – an impediment intimating mental struggle and a certain shame. He finds it hard to articulate his hatred of Christians, and the inner rage is made ready for the conversion on the Damascus road – when inflammability'll simply switch from thwarting to assisting God.

Saul/Paul, the villain-hero and persecutor-saint, is a biblical paradigm for Hopkins's intertwining of opposites. Snapping 'I must go against them,' he is soon coming to terms with a war which is now a peace. (Hopkins was once Pierre in the Tolstoy.) His eyes caked over with a rubbery goo, after the blinding, he starts to preach from the temple steps, and in Antioch and Greece he gets zapped by polystyrene rocks.

But *Peter and Paul* defeated Hopkins. He sank under wigs of an increasingly wispy grey (though his beard stayed black). Canvas houses, inert lighting, blankets for clothes, Coney Island sand, the Damascus miracle a wind-machine, the Californian burnt backlots standing in for the Holy Land: what actor had a hope? Raymond Burr? He had a few atrocious moments wobbling across fake-marble floors in a curly hairpiece and cardboad jewellery, drawling in American, tripping over a blue toga. It was an abominable impersonation of Mervyn LeRoy's Nero, and meant to be Herod. Couldn't they afford Ustinov?

Trashy blundered epics such as this Richard Burton drowned his talent in. He allowed to die, rooted up and out, the germs of ingenuity Hopkins propagates. Burton was the light that failed. Hopkins's is the career Richard Burton never had – though this was not always going to be so. Instead of replacing the Burton of promise and stature, Hopkins at one time looked set to duplicate the Burton of dissolute myth. 'Come on . . . None of this backstreet Richard Burton acting!' John Dexter is reputed to have yelled during the New York theatre rehearsals for *Equus*. Richard Burton played Dysart in the film version. Both he and Hopkins were sombre, sunk in puzzlement – as against McCowen's febrile, indignant shrink. But where Burton was almost befuddled, his tone muffled and hung-over, and where McCowen was cross, Hopkins was angry, giving Shaffer's tale a true voice of feeling it didn't deserve – Strang's madness being terrifyingly Dysart's own.

Hopkins never knew Burton, though he befriended his widow and was invited to the memorial parties; but because both actors came from the Port Talbot environs, where the goats ran from the mountains and the earth did shake at their birth; and because both were playing in the classics, comparisons were easily made. And Hopkins caused a nice ruckus by abandoning an Old Vic production of *Macbeth* in 1973; he set sail for Hollywood – as Burton left Stratford for *The Robe*, the biblical epic with Victor Mature. But Burton wenched and transferred energy to the living of a private life in public; Hopkins put his fire back into his craft, and in due course broke onto the Olivier stage, like the glistening bull from the toril gate, and gathered, in 1984–5, the Laurence Olivier Award for Outstanding Achievement, the *Drama* Award, the *Plays & Players* Award, and a Variety Club Award.

The raging-bull image needs amendment. A raging bull is frightening, stupendous, but rather dense. Hopkins the raging bull is also his own torero: the darting rapier and the clumsy horn – just as his Othello enveloped Iago; his Bligh, Christian.

So what about meeting this sacred beast?

'Yes, I would like to be in your book,' he said.

I wrote suggesting times and dates, but a big silence. Then, after a few months, he wrote back.

'You have caught me at a bad time, frankly I was trying to off-load commitments at the moment because I have taken on more than I can handle. I am sorry to change my mind like this, but that's the way it is at the moment.'

That's it, I thought, sending back the videos and shredding my notes. I asked after him and apparently Hopkins had blown a microchip in Hyde Park, after having made, without pause, *84 Charing Cross Road*, *The Good Father*, *Blunt*, no end of commercial voice-overs, plus returning with *Pravda* to the National repertoire, plus planning *King Lear*.

I went away to Greece for the summer, wrote a book on Kipling, forgot about overworked actors. Then, returning to Oxford for Michaelmas Term, I caught sight of the *Wogan* show. Who should be kissing the Blarney stone that night but Anthony Hopkins, fresh from a vacation in Venice. A few days later I received an invitation to lunch. I duly turned up at the National which, on a day without performances, is what the end of the world will resemble. Front of house: a deserted bunker, traversed by a lone mechanic with an aluminium ladder, a forgotten kinetic art-work; in the distance were distant wails, later identified as Sylveste McCoy rehearsing with the rats for *The Pied Piper*. Grilles slam off the buffets and bars. Backstage: a busy bunker, like the rebel base in *The Empire Strikes Back* – a tunnel of rotting electronics, peeling posters, discarded set-models and props; it's all grubby and sticky, with flustered telephonists yelping into mikes and facing a console of winking lights and bored security guards lolling on crates and jangling keys. Different megaphonic voices overlapped with announcements. In and out of the besmirched smoky-glass door came a flotilla of cadaverous drama students, hanging out for friends, or hoping to catch the sleeve of a contact. With bleached quiffs or scalps eccentrically shorn, their weeds all leather and eyelets, these junior drones loiter and loiter, and past them I made my solitary way.

Past the guards, along a yellow corridor – and jostled by hands heading for rehearsal, heads locked in earnest consultation – into a lift with an actor I could put faces to but not a name; shot aloft; out onto another corridor the colour of bilious coffee – and I was met at last by a cheerful emissary who conducted me to a room with a dorm feast laid out. Hopkins trotted in bearing a plate of steaming trout and chips.

'Excuse this. I must get the beauty of it hot. Come on, eat up eat up.'

Rude health would describe his style: a Picasso Minotaur on stage, all tender strength off it, with strong round head bowed slightly down – a fierce, defiant thrust; wide-open aquamarine eyes, like the pale light over a coastal marsh, permanently astounded, seeing things most of us do not see, such as wonder, awe, fear and sudden danger (a forest-murmur supersensitivity); cropped grey hair which has had the temerity to thin (Hopkins treats the trichological mutiny with the cheer of Bligh waving off Christian). Perspiring slightly – in tan corduroy jerkin and red shirt, from which a wisp of grey curled; his posture slightly crouched, ready to repel attack. Then, tempering the Vollard Suite appearance, the ability to convey, at the same time as the energy, solicitude, composure, control.

'Where are you from then? In Wales?'

I explained the ancestral situation.

'Know the area well. I go back to Wales with my wife a few times a year to see my mother, make sure she's all right, because she's widowed now, you see. People always look at me to see how and if I've changed. But I'm sure I'm the same person I always was. We are all of us stuck with the same personalities, unless we have a brainstorm and go mad – or unless we very consciously re-design ourselves, which frankly is not very likely.'

'Perhaps they want to see if success has altered you.'

Richard Burton would embarrass his family by turning up at the mineshaft to holler from his Roller, there being no quicker way to piss people off; cheap gestures like that are not in Hopkins's line. He has no wish to appear the local-boy-made good, flashing fivers in the pub.

'The Welsh are a bit suspicious if you leave Wales, aren't they? And my Welshness is a bit suspicious in any case. I've never been interested in rugby; I can't sing; I don't know the words of "Sospan Fach"; I liked to drink, so I didn't like beer.'

'Dylan Thomas mentions, in *Under Milk Wood*, the "Flat, warm, thin, Welsh, bitter beer." '

'I've never been in a play about Dylan Thomas; and I cannot speak Welsh.'

'Who does in Monmouthshire and Glamorganshire?' I put in unregretfully. 'Despite the bilingual signs and the compulsory Welsh television programmes?'

'Monmouthshire? Outside Newport's where my mother lives – Caerleon.' Located on the Usk, written about by Tennyson, Caerleon is a clement spot and a long way from the valleys in social terms.

'Yes, Caerleon. My father was a baker in Port Talbot, but he retired too early and didn't know what to do with himself, so I said, "Run a pub, go on, run a pub, you like meeting people." So he did. *The Ship*. But he's dead now – just my mother left. When I go back, my mother likes to go for a drive – a big treat being chauffeured about. We go around Port Talbot and up the Cwmavon Valley and she says, "Oh no! Not the same places *again!*" but she loves it really. She loves it. We go past our old place, and stop outside houses where my family used to be, especially where my grandfather lived, and strangers come out and look at us.

'When I go back, I like to see what hasn't changed, what's the same. I was born there forty-eight year ago, before the Severn Bridge made it easy to get in and out, and before those Japanese electronics factories sprang up everywhere. A small country it was then, much more isolated and introspective. Harder to leave.'

The tough little Kingdom was being rather likened to a self-portrait.

'The twitch upon the thread,' I said.

Hopkins replied with lines from *The Great Gatsby*: 'So we beat on, boats against the current, borne back ceaselessly into the past.'

'What do you make of the pulsating light at the end of Gatsby's pier?'

'Calling us, calling us home.' Out, caressingly, came the Fitzgerald again: 'Gatsby believed in the green light, the . . . future that year by year recedes before us. It eluded us then, but that's no matter – tomorrow we will run faster, stretch out our arms further . . . And one fine morning . . . So we beat on, boats against the current, borne back ceaselessly into the past.'

With the refuse of the meal before him, and gazing at the Thames, or at the hymenopterous frenzy in the glass office-block across the way, he murmured the last phrase several times – both for its sentiment, and because Hopkins is pleasured by the dip and sway of the alphabet in action.

Gatsby is a rather dangerous tutelary star for an actor. Ambitious, striving Jimmy Gatz converts himself into the lonely grandee, paying for wild parties he'll not attend, the owner of shirts he'll never wear ('They're such beautiful shirts,' laments Daisy. 'It makes me sad because I've never seen such beautiful shirts before') – he's a deathly slave to style.

Gatz has remade himself as Gatsby, but the signs and symbols of his wealth aren't a renovation, they are funereal. The fantastic autos of marquetry mirrors are like a snow queen's hearse; the mausoleum library of uncut books ('Absolutely real – have pages and everything') is a shrine of dead knowledge; the swimming pool is filled as if with embalming fluid.

The Great Gatsby is larger than life (he has a showbiz title) – and he's as enigmatic as the Phantom of the Opera. His peninsula lights up like a theatre, and his life is a performance – but a murky underworld sustains him off-stage. Lucre is derived from racketeering. And having perfected a new identity, having become an actor, Gatsby does nothing. He is, like Dickens's Merdle, a nothing. He has no performance to give. He's a fraud perhaps not *because* he's an actor, but because he's an actor with nowhere to go. His house is an echoing exhibition; he's a thing of appearance and effects. Gatsby is dangerous as tutelary star, and wholly inappropriate for Hopkins, because he's symptomatic of failure; the decay of illusion. And his sentimental retrospection is telling, too: Gatsby is Richard Burton maudlin for a lost past – and this isn't Hopkins: his past is still recoverable, because he's still making history.

'I've always been,' Hopkins went on, 'a little self-involved, private, a loner – which is why perhaps I was never drawn to rugby club camaraderie. And I liked music, fiddling with the piano; and I liked telescopes.'

'Is perhaps the solitariness why you became an actor?'

'I invent a world around myself. People say I've got the Welsh temperament.'

'By which they mean a bad temper?'

'God knows what they mean. All I know is that anything is possible through work, work, work. No use waiting for the "temperament" to sort itself out. Welshness won't come to anybody's rescue. You've got to question yourself, and keep energy focused on the aim for perfection. I was in here at quarter past seven this morning, all on my own, to belt out Lear's opening speech . . .' And he belted it out again:

> 'Know that we have divided
> In three our kingdom; and 'tis our fast intent
> To shake all cares and business from our age,
> Conferring them on younger strengths, while we
> Unburthen'd crawl toward death . . .

'I belted it out for nearly three hours. No, that's a lie. Ninety minutes. And I'll tell you why: rehearsals went so badly yesterday, I was so angry with myself, I knew that only a big assault today would put me right. My wife said, "What *are* you doing? It's far too early to start." But I had to. I had to get up, get out, and crack it. I did a performance of *Pravda* last night, and really laid into the audience.'

'Or into yourself?'

'You might be right. You might be right there. Acting, for me, is taking on the gods, or God, if you believe in Him. And *I do*. There's no point being meek and frail and humble. What's the point of that? There's no point being meek and frail and humble in the hope that things will be put right. You've got to FIGHT; take the gods on! What's that in Goethe . . . How does it go now? "Who never, who never ate his bread," how DOES it go? "Who never ate his bread with tears, who never sat through the sorrowful night, weeping upon his bed, does not know you, O heavenly powers." From *Faust*, I think.★

'Those heavenly powers: I've got to win them onto my side. Got to go at them and match them. Got to go at them like a *bull*. And I went at the *Pravda* audience like a BULL. Acting is a bullfight – acting is a corrida.'

It had occurred to him, it had occurred to us all. Hopkins: crook-kneed and dew-lapped like a Thessalian bull, slow in pursuit, but matched in mouth like bells – as Theseus remarks to Hippolyta.

'If you didn't have Lambert Le Roux as a safety valve, to let off steam, what would you have done with it, the steam and the anger?'

'Well, a fortuneteller told me the other day, "You will have a long life." "No! No! How can we all cope with you hanging about until old age," my wife said. "What's the matter," I said. "What's the matter with you? I don't get impatient and aggressive with you?" "I know. I know. It's just the *atmosphere* you carry around with yourself. A whirlwind."

'Anyway, things were terrible yesterday. I thought, I can't act, none of the others can act. We're finished. One of *those* kinds of days. The only possible way of curing it and recovering my confidence was to slog at it; to work at it; get the technique back. So I said to myself, right, I'll give it all I can. I'm going to try and kill myself *by acting*. If I rip my vocal chords to shreds, *fine*. I don't care. If I can never ever speak again – so what? *Fine*. I'll never be able to work again in any case. And if I never work again, I won't have to be frightened of failing, of putting up with being merely adequate. So *I'll be finished!*

'So, this morning, I was a man possessed – and it worked! I cracked it! Though not my voice or blood vessels! And I came through.'

Off he went again:

'Attend the Lords of France and Burgundy,/Gloucester!'

Even in our luncheon chamber, Hopkins's voice, even his whisper,

---

★ Actually, *Wilhelm Meister*.
    Wer nie sein Brot mit Tränen ass
    Wer nie Kummervollen Nächte
    Auf seinem Bette weinend sass,
    Der Kennt euch nicht, ihr himmlischen Mächte.

hinted at a capacity to be heard, and obeyed, in France, Burgundy and Gloucestershire.

'I came through with vocal chords intact, blood vessels intact, brain still intact. So I tried to kill myself! And I'm still here! So I know there's something up there looking out for me, and looking after me. Every performance has to be a duel between me and God, and me and the audience. I've to prove I'm worth looking out for.'

'You got Lear back, but what of *Pravda* last night? Did your anger make for a better performance?'

'I was screaming. I was a bit mad, I think. That bottled-up energy, you are right, had to go somewhere. Le Roux helped me out. But the audience was thick, last night, really thick and stupid, dumb and unresponsive. I know we're not supposed to say this, to speak against the paying customers, but the audience missed all the meanings and ironies. They sat there stony-faced, refusing to engage. And here was this man, boy or student he was actually, in the front row of the stalls, all slouched and glum. Then he put his feet on the stage. Lay back, and put his shoes on the edge of the stage! Right, you bugger, I thought, I'll get you. So later on, in the scene with the Japanese martial arts and the sticks, I went to attack him. I brandished the pole, stared at him, and he got the message: *Get your feet off my stage!*

'I took on the audience, charged at them, tossed them about. The same as today when I rehearsed on my own. The important thing is to have absolute courage. The courage to be extreme and to take the risk. I get very impatient with those who don't bother to give their best or who never bother to test themselves. I am a coward – I mean, I'd be unlikely to try out a trapeze or learn to walk the tightrope: that's bravery. But I'm always trying to conquer my cowardice, and I'm not much impressed when I see other people giving in to theirs.'

That's the secret of *Pravda*: Lambert Le Roux knows no fear, and the faculty of fearlessness makes him an emotional hero. He may be the most malevolent character in modern drama – but he's an emotional hero: 'He, as every man that can be great, or have victory in this world, sees, through all entanglements, the practical heart of the matter; drives straight towards that.' Carlyle's description of Napoleon (*On Heroes and Hero-Worship*, 1840) is apt for the newspaper tycoon. For Le Roux, the practical heart of the matter is his observation of weakness and the failure of nerve. It allows him to amass a workforce of sycophants and lickspittles, whom he has no qualm about sacking on whim. 'You are weak,' he barks, 'because you do not know what you believe.' His prevaricating flunkeys are as vermin.

Le Roux was Hopkins's attestation of greatness; a development from, and a disciplined version of, his swaggering Edmund Kean. In truth,

Pravda itself is a minor work, constructed from noxious fortune-cookie epigrams, relying – according to all the reviewers – on local references to Fleet Street prints and figures for its laughs. *The Victory* is *The Times* (ha, ha); *The Tide*, *The Sun* (hee, hee); Elliot Fruit-Norton, William Rees-Mogg (ho, ho); Cliveden Whicker-Baskett, Charles Douglas-Home (hmm, hmm).★ At worst, I think, a dramatic adaptation of Harry Evans's *Good Times, Bad Times* – an account by the Visiting Professor at the Poynter Institute for Media Studies, Florida, of his resignation from *The Times*, and at best a dramatic adaptation of the 'Street of Shame' column in *Private Eye*, *Pravda* was the National Theatre pretending to house satire and look anti-establishment. In fact, *Pravda* covertly exalted what it pretended to criticize: our lovely, cosy English institutions and the sly gentility of journalism – where hacks either pen vapid gossip, newspapers one step up from being crayoning books; or else they pretend to be dons, sitting in the Irving Club (The Garrick) to quote Latin; a profession where to be first class you need to be second rate.

Into this fustian desert bursts Le Roux. Had he arrived from a trap in a puff of sulphur and dry ice, the play would be well served. He's the Demon King, the South African Knave who buys up, amalgamates and closes newspapers; or else he sells them to fund a racehorse. He's unspeakable; Brenton and Hare make sure we appreciate the inky trade is unspeakable ('Downmarket, upmarket, it's all the same stuff'). And that's all, folks!

Hopkins, however, put everything into, and gambled on, his character. Instead of the Demon King, we had King Richard III. Le Roux became, in fact, the best Richard III since Laurence Olivier's, closely rivalling Antony Sher's, over at the Royal Shakespeare Company.

Le Roux discards his henchmen as Richard dispenses with Buckingham and Hastings, happily breaking promises:

> *Buckingham* – I am thus bold to put your Grace in mind
> Of what you promis'd me . . .
> *Richard*   – I am not in the giving vein today.
> *Buckingham* – May it please you to resolve me in my suit.
> *Richard*   – Thou troublest me; I am not in the vein.
> *Buckingham* –   And is it thus? Repays he my deep service
> With such contempt? Made I him King for this?

Andrew May is Le Roux's abused favourite, a boy picked from the ranks to edit the *Leicester Bystander*. Thrilled at such accelerated promotion, May's blind, for a time, to his overlord's ambitiousness; he merely thinks Le Roux a business magnate of unusual energy, and with a funny accent.

★ According to Michael Davie in the *Times Literary Supplement* (17 May 1985).

Then, Le Roux's political obliquity and personal improbity dawn, but May is employed too deep in the empire to strike back. Eventually, he does bestir himself to take on the creature from the black lagoon who happens to pay his plump salary – but his attempt at serving a writ for libel, sedition and general ghastliness is pathetic and mewling. So he's out on the street.

Towards the end of the play, May, having begged to be reinstated and salvaged from an impecunious existence as freelance book reviewer (a fate ignominious and indistinguishable from the lot of distressed gentlefolk) begins to betray the mannerisms of his master. Is he transforming into a Le Roux double? If you can't beat him, duplicate him? And resistance having caved in, Le Roux is now invincible. 'Welcome,' he leers, like Bela Lugosi pushing ajar the door of his castle, 'to the foundry of lies.'

Hopkins metamorphosed into a configuration of bravura villainy, his character's merging *The Victory* and *The Tide* more than the gleeful equivalent of titties flanking *The Times* leader: the performance implied theological abuses, like casting *Parsifal* with game-show hosts, or celebrating Mass with the Prince of Darkness. Hopkins's Le Roux stepped through the play's comic strip, by-passed realistic characterization, to arrive at surrealism: a barnyard creation out of Joan Miró, for instance, or an apparition in a Salvador Dalí moonscape. (Dalí, indeed, once made a portrait of Olivier's Richard III: a double-headed chimera hovering in the sky above a desert – Gloucester the twi-formed birth of deadly charm, and deadliness.) Le Roux was a meteor-shower of antimatter – like the sparks Bill Hooper's motorbike gives off – in an otherwise infertile and boring drama.

Many origins of the species have been suggested. Hopkins has been prodigal, over-prodigal, to inquirers. Le Roux is a juggernaut, a Grosz drawing, a brontosaurus, a pair of Hollywood moguls, a clanking beast, a Mexican poisonous lizard, the shark in *Jaws*, New York businessmen, Hitler in a slow-motion newsreel, a Port Talbot drunk, a baccy-stinking NCO, a vindictive schoolmaster . .

The search for metaphor and helpful Le Roux correspondence is excessive. No performance could be such a cocktail and succeed; it would be as precarious as those sticky drinks, all spitty bits and paper parasols and twisted straws – the least resolute of beverages. And Le Roux is as resolute as a poisoned chalice. He knows what he thinks; he knows what he wants; he knows how to win. Le Roux is valiant through supreme self-confidence; his feelings are subordinated and shaped to feed his megalomania.

Hence his emotional heroism: he has vanquished emotion. Doubt is not in Le Roux's lexicon. A brilliant tactician, sizing up opponents in a trice, he's a Universal Machine – an unsleeping ticker-tape. Le Roux convinces (whilst *Pravda* as a whole does not), and in spite of the night-mare nuances, because Hopkins willed us into crediting incredulity: we witnessed the surrealism, and accepted it as realistic. Why does this happen? By what alchemy?

Le Roux surged on stage as an emanation of Hopkins's own power. Such a coherent performance, such glorious implementation of the art of acting, is no paltry patchwork of theatrical paper-mantles, tinsel and mummery – as Carlyle would say: it is a transfiguration of these things, which Hopkins (like Napoleon and the politics of Europe) 'has wrapt his own great reality in, thinking to make it more real thereby'.

That cocktail catalogue of supposed inspiration reads like a series of post-cogencies; images to describe a character already intact. Photo finishes. Snaps of an event that's happened. Ostensibly, none of this is flattering. The skinny legs and the tank of a chest; the blunt head, exophthalmic eyes; the hair greased into fronds; the fervent jigs; the South African accent coming out as an atavistic growl – Lambert Le Roux, physically a coiled spring of menace: where's Hopkins in all of that? Inside, of course, maintaining the energy. He *is* the energy.

I have forgotten everything about *Pravda* except Hopkins and Le Roux. Peter Chelsom (as Andrew May) and Phoebe Nicholls (as Rebecca Foley) made no impression whatsoever. There was a cast of about thirty. Where were they? Where did they go? What did they do? It was a one-man show which, ultimately, cut itself free from Fleet Street ethics to become an exhibition of persistent vigour – as Charles Foster Kane stops being about William Randolph Hearst and becomes an exhibition of Orson Welles's persistent vigour.

If Le Roux was Hopkins's Richard III, what about King Lear? Brave, cowardly, mad, what?

'He's fixed, fierce, rigid, in the court. Emotionally rigid. And he moves from that stony strength, to surrender. No pity or serenity at the end, he just caves in – with that quartet of *no's*.'

Hopkins spoke them, giving each a different voice, a different meaning: 'No, no, no, no.' Then that little aria.

> 'No, no, no, no! Come, let's away to prison;
> We two alone will sing like birds i' th' cage:
> When thou dost ask me blessing, I'll kneel down,
> And ask for thee forgiveness: so we'll live,
> And pray, and sing...'

Hopkins near-whispered the words, pondering them, suggesting a Lear puzzled by his own outbreak of lyricism. Far away was the bellow and bellicosity of the opening speech.

'David Hare is a brilliant director, God knows where we'd be by now without him in control. I began, you see, by basing the part on my grandfather – a hard old sod – but it was too rigid an impersonation and it started getting in my way. That's when the trouble started, I think, culminating in yesterday's fucking mess.

'I'm dropping the image of my grandfather now. David detected something was hampering me, too. He came up to me at the end of last week and said, "It's not quite working anymore . . . You're losing it." And I was going crazy all Friday and over the weekend and yesterday, trying to stop the play from glazing over – trying to get Lear back. David was right, and right to be honest.

'This morning we were doing that scene where the King sees Edgar, Poor Tom, on the heath, and says – "unaccommodated man is no more but such a poor, bare, forked animal as thou art," and he starts tearing off his clothes, "Off, off, you lendings . . ." In the past, I've always torn the buttons and shirt off passionately. Today, instead of ripping the clothes, I did it very slowly, with transfixed amazed, innocent care. And it worked. "You've got the edge back," said David.

'My mistake, you see, was to act old. I realized that if I made the lines work, they'd take me on the journey of the play, from age, to the madness, and to the end. From the stark, primitive court, where Lear has absolute power, to the dejected ruination five acts later.

'Of course, Lear is a complete bastard. I've been lucky to be offered monsters. I like them. Hard, nasty, swinish: the people on the outside. Monsters don't have to make apologies. I like finding where they're vulnerable, and working on that.'

Hopkins has his characters work on vulnerability to cure themselves of it; to heal weakness: Saul perfected as Paul, Corky by the wooden simulacrum, Jamison repeating drafts of a perfect crime, Antony having to kill himself. (His Donald Campbell in *Across the Lake* improves Blue Bird, a boat of canvas, buckles, levers and vanes, to conquer his fear of speed. The television film was heavy with premonitions of dread – as a man turned himself into jet engine, and thence into a fireball of foam and spume.) *King Lear* was an opportunity for invincible Lambert Le Roux to errupt again. At least at first. Lear entered with the hunched bovine trot of Le Roux; his voice had the snarl of Le Roux, drawing out line-endings into a savoured chomp – just like Le Roux, except that guttural Johannesburg was replaced with guttural Gwent and Glamorgan.

Hopkins's grandparent may have gone as the avowed inspiration but some brand of Welsh patriarch – as the play proceeded and Le Roux receded – rumbled in Lear. A flinty lilt, the throat and temper of a valley gospeller: not Dylan Thomas's twinkling Organ Morgan or the Reverend Eli Jenkins – more an aged Glendower, with cropped grey spiky hair, spiky beard, spiky mentality. Hopkins's monarch was a thorny, bosky creature, prickly, with a thick neck jutting and awaiting banderilleros, and huge eyes swivelling like the optics of a surveillance camera. A mechanical bull.

What with the stocky body gliding beneath a quilted robe, Lear was an engine caterwauling threats of extermination. ('Come not between the dragon and his wrath.') A growling autocrat who was a regal automaton, he rules a space-age kingdom. Hayden Griffin, who for *Pravda* designed a suite of cluttered offices, for *King Lear* had barely designed anything at all. The Olivier stage was a lunar crater, overspread by three sky-cloths, which caught a light show of scudding clouds and paisley wisps. Reminiscent of Wieland Wagner's totemic Bayreuth style, or the sails and luminous abstraction of Karajan's Salzburg *Tristan*, it was a production simultaneously primordial and futuristic; a society evolving from nothing, and evolving towards nothingness. Hare sought, in his sci-fi world, a drama about the survival of the fittest (Bill Nighy's Edgar was a super-fit Coriolanus) – the descent of man.

Thus, Hopkins's Lear, his arms tightened into fierce probes, commanding a dusty landscape jangled by Nick Bicât's electronic music, was a convergence of ancient, obdurate oak and neonomian, obdurate steel, puzzled by madness because it is the advent of his humanity; puzzled by the concept of nothingness, because without humanity, nothing will come of nothing. The word *nothing* aerated the play:

> *Cordelia*: Nothing, my lord.
> *Lear*:   Nothing?
> *Cordelia*: Nothing.
> *Lear*:   Nothing will come of nothing . . .

Cordelia, having refused to enter into the game of filial affection – refusing to be an actress in a throne-room drama – having refused to gauge the profit and the loss, is punished by the withdrawal of her dowry. She'll get nothing. Hopkins made Lear humiliated more than piteous: he's been shown up before the court, the ritual ruined.

Cordelia, in fact, has matched her father in stubbornness – his 'youngest born' has embarrassed him by not humouring his sport; she's disregarded his stage directions. So, publicly, she's upbraided: the sport acted upon as though its consequences are the real thing. Stripped of title and fortune, she's now 'that little-seeming substance . . . And nothing more.' Burgundy, a suitor, with financial inducement, would marry her back to respectability. But 'Nothing,' bays Lear, is what she's inheriting: 'I have sworn; I am firm.' He's a despotic impresario, throwing a contrived tantrum, like Otto Preminger.

Hare gave dignity to the subplot – not merely a furtherance of the father-child equation, it was a startling drama in itself about primogeniture. Michael Bryant's Gloucester had the repose of Alec Guinness's intergalactic guru in *Star Wars*. Douglas Hodge, as wildcat Edmund, the measured illegitimate, was a wicked Luke Skywalker. He tricks his father with a forged letter:

> *Gloucester*: What paper were you reading?
> *Edmund*:   Nothing, my Lord.
> *Gloucester*: . . . The quality of nothing hath not such need to hide
>   itself. Let's see: come; if it be nothing I shall not need
>   spectacles.

Thinking Edgar a villain, Gloucester sets Edmund after him: the bastard against the heir: 'it shall lose thee nothing . . .'

Cordelia gone, she's replaced in Lear's orbit by the scamperings of the Fool. In Peter Brook's production, Alec McCowen was a pinched Puck; Jonathan Miller's productions make the Fool a wheezy geriatric vaudeville trouper, played in faded motley usually by Frank Middlemass; Michael Williams, for Trevor Nunn, turned the Fool into Rob Wilton; Antony Sher's Fool was from a circus caravan. Roshan Seth ('Is that a Welsh name?' asked a lady beside me in the stalls), once Attenborough's elegiac Nehru, disappointed me. He screamed out the melancholy philosophies like a banshee; an untamed shrew. Where was the oriental calm which is this actor's gift? Never for a second would Hopkins's gruff king have kept him on his staff.

For once, Kent's comment, after a display of flat wit – 'This is nothing, Fool' – was apt. Hopkins tugged at the word, pausing, wrapped in reverie, amazed. He's heard the word before – and he's astonished at its gathering import:

> *Fool*: . . . You gave me nothing for't. Can you make no use of
>   nothing, Nuncle?
> *Lear*: Why no, boy; nothing can be made out of nothing.

Nothing can be made out of nothing; Cordelia was banished with 'Nothing will come of nothing.' The proverb's★ turning up for the second time – and Lear's recognizing that he's suddenly spoken more than he meant – was the point at which Hopkins's king began to collapse. He's become an ordinary citizen, no longer protected from the ways of the world by palatial trappings.

'Nothing will come of nothing,' the threat to Cordelia, was said by a churl, a boor, a bully – the kind of king who'd be rude and coarse-grained at dinner. 'Nothing can be made out of nothing,' words apparently in answer to the Fool, Hopkins's character now addressed to himself gently,

★ 'de nihilo nihilum, in nihilum nil posse reverti' is quoted in Germbergius's *Carminum Proverbialium* (1583), from Persius's third Satire.

with irony dawning. And, ignorant of the ways of the world, he starts to go mad. Having 'pared thy wit o' both sides,' he's 'left nothing i'the middle.' This space lunacy fills. 'I am a Fool,' says the Fool, 'thou art nothing.'

King Lear, shorn of monarchy – who's he? Merely a man called Lear, bereft of rights, like Edmund ('Go to; say you nothing'). Alan Coren once imagined what the Queen would do if set free in the neon waste land of the West end. Knowing nothing of ordinary etiquette, she'd soon, he concluded, be picked up by the police and incarcerated as a mad regal double: 'One now has a rather engaging view of Holloway Road, albeit only from the upper bunk, a most engaging companion with a fund of excellent stories, and a mouse, and one is already through to the South Block ping-pong semi-finals.' Lear on the heath and in Poor Tom's hut ('Edgar I nothing am') is similarly amused.

King Lear, in fact, is a comedy in disguise; its modern counterparts include Beckett's *Fin de Partie* and Harold Brighouse's *Hobson's Choice*. The opening festival of amorous rhetoric is fairy-tale foolery, with two ugly sisters, a Cinderella and kindly Kent as Buttons; Lear's quarrel with Regan and Goneril is hardly cosmic – domestic, rather, with fuss about table manners and house-guests. A 'family crisis', says John Bayley, and with specific rural references: the problems of running a castle; life on the beaches and in the fields; we get to know Lear's dogs, Tray, Blanch and Sweetheart – 'see, they bark at me', exactly like his daughters. What Bayley calls 'the unseen life' of Shakespeare's characters presses upon our attention – and determines what we do actually witness. Lear and his children, Gloucester and his sons, have invisible histories. We feel they've existed off-stage, elsewhere. They have a novelistic depth.★

Bayley, alert to what he's called 'the ungraspable element in the live and familiar person', even has a fondness for characters who never appear at all (Fulvia in *Antony and Cleopatra*), or who are silent when they do (Virgilia in *Coriolanus*); and his general drift is that Shakespeare is diminished by stage representation. He'd prefer the characters to be lucid consciousnesses, Henry James apparitions, untraduced by the actor's voice and body and range. In *King Lear*, 'the characters themselves are off-key, producing kinds of false notes which cannot be acted, kinds of naked exclamation which cannot bear acting'. Actors get in Bayley's way; and, in short, he reads plays as if they are alike to *The Ambassadors* – and he flinches from theatricality. But it is possible to appreciate Shakespeare's anticipation of a novelist's detail – the way words can convey unvoiced impressions, the way nobility of purpose is thwarted by a love

★ For a discussion of Shakespeare as a novelist, see John Bayley's. *The Characters of Love* (1960).

of digression or a shortfall of resolve – without wishing Shakespeare was a novelist and not a playwright.

Shakespeare's liberation of the intellect ('The usurpation by the mind of both practical action and purposeful ideas') is not demeaned by actors of calibre: on the contrary, they are instruments attuned to his complexity; they are the antennae of the plays. Actors don't belittle Shakespeare's multifariousness, they celebrate it – and Bayley's dismissive comment about acting aside, he is himself a critic whose exuberance and ability to roam inside his subjects make for a validity of impression that's precisely actorial. He's an actor by other means.

The domestic detail and grotesque humour of *King Lear* Hopkins was ready to launch into; he was matched by the brilliant Bryant, smiling grimly at his blinding. The production's best scene was the mordant banter of Lear and Gloucester, when they meet on the beach, victims of farce. But the cool, serious, emotionless tone of the director, coupled with shrill Seth, lost any black, absurd dimension. Hare was going for universal bombast – but Hopkins fought it.

Lear, storming into the storm, competing with it, may be mad – but out of the madness his placability and charity comes. Hopkins megaphonic became Hopkins euphonious. Madness was the king's salvation. He cares for the Fool, for Poor Tom, for Kent, for Gloucester (with the solicitude of a mother); ultimately, there's the reconciliation with Cordelia. He's happy in his hovel – a primitive Wendy house – a timber shed piled with logs and tree trunks. (Earlier, the map of the divided kingdom was fashioned from coloured building blocks.)

What's happened is that Lear, an old man released from responsibility, regresses to childhood, transfixed by the ordinary, because it's new to him. He plays on the heath and at Dover, garlanding himself with flowers, keeping pets, and encountering Gloucester like Richmal Crompton's William galloping into Ginger, with chuckles and sighs.

Then, on the death of Cordelia, Hopkins brought the tyrant Lear together with the purified Lear. 'I am King, masters, know you that?' – the question boomed with the command of old. And he manages to kill the hangman; and then he enters, carrying the body of his daughter:

> No, no, no life!
> Why should a dog, a horse, a rat, have life,
> And thou no breath at all? Thou'lt come no more,
> Never, never, never, never, never!

Denuded, lonely, Lear is beaten and becalmed. He surrenders. But surrender is not failure; nor is it cowardice; nor is Lear's surrender a vulnerability for Hopkins to augment. The last moments of the play were intensely moving. The *never* quintet was a spell like 'Open Sesame': the words were Lear's enlightenment, a litany drawing him into a colony of escape. Heaven's gate. Hopkins was powerful, passionate, in grief.

How high up the ladder does Hopkins cling? With whom does he contend? Paul Scofield, at Stratford and in the 1970 film, made by Peter Brook in Jutland, was a grizzled mumbler made lapidary by the cold. Casting a cold eye on life, Lear crawled towards death. Michael Hordern, in Jonathan Miller's productions, was a querulous old fairy-tale King, his behaviour eccentric and foolish – until the storm, when Miller recoursed to his medical knowledge and made the gibbering madness clinical and real. Trevor Nunn at the Aldwych put Donald Sinden in Ruritania, Lear the prisoner of Zenda. Olivier, under Michael Elliott's direction in 1982, was a thin-lipped yelper, with a reedy tenor – a monarchial Shallow. Michael Gambon, splashing in a downstage pond, was heavy and sad and shivering with palsy – eclipsed by Sher's galvanic Fool.

For Brook, *King Lear* is desolate, a wasteland world; for Miller, the play examines seventeenth-century issues of sovereignty and charity, which the director acquires from Italian schools of painting; for Adrian Noble, the landscape is a run-down circus; Olivier's Lear existed in Ancient Britain, a place of bearskin suits and hairy extras carrying conical firebrands; for Hare, *King Lear* is about the preparation for death – his directional vision seems to be derived from the rusty, dusty vistas of Brook, and he tried to entice from Hopkins another demented goblin, who'll remind both of Scofield's petroglyph and Le Roux. But that's not what happened. Hopkins's Lear wasn't retiring from life, he was emerging into it; he wasn't in retreat, he was coming through.

Cordelia (Miranda Foster) was the ideal woman – who refuses to compromise; a daughter who'll mother her father in his old age. Wendy to his archaic Peter Pan. Hopkins thought Lear young at heart, the very opposite of senile; and his youthful spirit is what's set free during his rages – like Ariel liberated from the knots and sinews of a great tree. Lear's anger cracks him open; learning openness, he learns to acknowledge other people, and can pull the Fool out of the rain. Humbled, he's on high; his folly, to be wise. Hopkins managed, whilst losing none of the turbulent tragedy and violent spectacle, to be intimate and considerate. He betrayed, as it were, novelistic recesses in an epic sprawl.

The development of Lear's behaviour from robotic dictator to weeping papa was subtle, strong, convincing. Hopkins was never an old codger, never maudlin. Having given up his kingdom, Lear's energy has to be directed in on himself; he has to begin constructing a new private life – and we have the implosion, the incertitude of a new citizen in a landscape that's beyond him. Hopkins touched and felt buttons or garments, and hugged friends and family, with an infant's intentness. His tragedy is simply that he retired too soon; his comedy, sardonic though it is, is that he copes. Had his children given him an inn to run, he'd have settled as Mine Host of The Garter, in *The Merry Wives of Windsor* – where Mistress Ford and Mistress Page, pernicious doxies, are Elizabethan townswomen descended from Goneril and Regan.

Kean, in Sartre's play, laments that, as an actor, he's nothing: a clothes-horse and a gramophone; a cipher. Lear's sense of nothingness cleanses him; he's baptized by the storm. Left with nothing, born again on the heath – born astride the grave – he's a superannuated neonate.

Nothingness has an acoustic correlative in silence – when Lear sleeps, and is restored to health; a visual correlative in blindness – the destiny of Gloucester, stumbling when he saw; and a physical correlative in naked-ness – Edgar's stripping as Poor Tom ('in nothing am I changed / But in my garments'). Nothingness is a screen to be stained by rich imagery and association; by seepage from the audience's imagination; by the actor's imagination.

Sartre misrepresented an actor as a contour of nothing: he confused the empty lineaments of script with the ligaments of a man who'll fill and enliven the lines – which is like regretting that ranks of tuxedos in your tailor's aren't animate. (Hopkins, indenting Kean with coxcombry, worked against the text – so that what Kean had to say was self-evident nonsense.)

Kean's hollowness is where he languishes; Lear's nothingness is the starting point, affording the chance for regeneration – the regeneration of the role of Lear, when he's lifted off the script's page; and the regeneration of Lear himself, as he moves through the acts, getting younger as he gets older, going off with Cordelia to prison, the two of them playmates. Hopkins's triumph was to be a Lear freighted with the knowledge of sorrow, and of climbing back. All that, and with a production team and supporting cast which had gathered originally for *Pravda*; Lear was both Lambert Le Roux's partial apotheosis and complete purgation.

Lear's dangerous gamesomeness lingered in Guy Burgess, whom Hop-kins played in *Blunt*. Acting spies (as mentioned in an earlier chapter) is a tautological business, for spies are actors already. Burgess, especially, camped and paraded, a devious caricature of his own nature and beliefs. He pissed in our soup, as Coral Browne says in *An Englishman Abroad*, and we drank it. And like the best English rogues (Raffles, Jack the Ripper, Lucky Jim), Burgess was a bastard and a national treasure.

In Julian Mitchell's *Another Country*, Burgess (called Bennett) formu-lates his duplicity early, when skirmishing with the problems of adoles-cence – and public school is symptomatic of a hated system:

Judd: Either you accept the system, or you try to change it.
         There's no alternative.
Bennett: Why not? Why not both? Pretend to do one, while you
         really do the other? Fool the swine! Play along with
         them! Let them think what they like – let them despise
         you! But all the time – . . . I'd be revenged . . . What
         better cover for a secret agent than apparent total
         indiscretion?★

Poe's Auguste Dupin used to suggest that the best hiding place for an
object is to put it on full view; the obvious is where we look last. Burgess
hid by seeming not to hide. He was embarrassingly open. The actor was
acting acting.

'I was sent a tape of *Blunt* which I watched last night,' said Hopkins.
'I'm very pleased with my performance. And Ian Richardson! My God!
What a talent. He's eradicated his natural flamboyance – he is flamboyant,
isn't he – and plays Anthony Blunt as a sanctimonious old maid.

'I read Robin Chapman's script, which I thought very good, but my
agent said Burgess, the part on offer, disappeared on page twenty-two. I
said, so what? It is a marvellous part, and very well written, I want to do
it. The costume department had to make me a wig, because Burgess had
different hair texture from mine, and in any case I'm thinning. I'd hoped
for a Burgess hairpiece – but no, a full wig in the end. And he had tinges of
ginger.

'I played him as a ne'er-do-well alcoholic. The amusing, witty gossip,
loved at dinner parties. Everybody enjoyed his company, the way he'd go
over the top: "The Ruskies have got the right idea y'know. Communism
is the only answer. The lovely *cold* . . ." "Oh yes! How outrageous you
are, Guy! You do say the wildest things," they'd all giggle. And he meant
every word! It was an astonishing performance.'

'The best way of being a spy: to pretend to be a parody spy.'

'Yes! We had a few rehearsals, and I wore the wig, and I got into the
suit, and by chance, later on, I looked in the mirror, and it wasn't me that
looked back. I looked again, and it *was* Burgess. Some movement I'd
made, some way I had of speaking: suddenly the performance, the odds
and ends of acting, had come together, and I inhabited the part. Shaking
the trial and error together like this is what rehearsals are for – and you
have to dive into it and be brave. No point in holding back, being reticent.
Give it the lot. Give it the works.

'Anyway, I was watching the videotape last night, and I suddenly
realized that my Guy Burgess was based on a man I know in my

★ 'The best disguise of all is to be exactly what you say you are. Nobody ever believes
that'. Hilary in Alan Bennett's *The Old Country*.

neighbourhood. I'd half thought of him at the very beginning. He is one of those "G'mornin'. How the divil are you?" chaps. I'd half-thought of him, and then forgotten him.'

'A case of subconscious impersonation. Unmeant mimicry.'

'Watching the programme, I felt so sorry for Anthony Blunt, when he says goodbye to Burgess for the last time – and he doesn't know it's for the last time – because Burgess is going to defect. "You poor sod," I thought, "you poor old bugger. You're going to be lonely from now on." Lovers, you see.'

Burgess's walking out on Blunt is a betrayal of their love – and Burgess's cool exit shows how coolly he has, at other times, in other places, betrayed his country. Hopkins, quoting Browning, was indeed the ensorcelled Waring – who's glimpsed in Trieste, and who dematerializes 'as with a bound, / Into the rosy and golden half / O' the sky.' Burgess, in *Blunt*, was mesmeric treachery and dissolution personified.

A sweet and bitter jester, Hopkins was perhaps too spruce for the real Burgess – who, in the memorable opinion of Maurice Bowra, was a compound of shit and smegma; and who lived in legendary squalor, not the scrupulous chambers designed for this film by Colin Shaw. When Ian Richardson – playing Blunt as a Smith Square Jack Buchanan – roots through the apartment for incriminating documentation, letters are in neat bundles, shoes in neat rows, desk drawers in neat array.

He first appeared calling up from the street to Blunt – who appears from his window at the top of the Courtauld like a magus in an ebony tower. 'My darlingest duck,' says Burgess, chomping salad. They gossip about Donald and Kim and 'Americans bringing us to the brink'. And Burgess has been brought back from Washington after an organized smear – 'pragmatic self-indulgence,' says Blunt, who has brought him back for his bed.

Burgess is the comedian whose jokes, retrospectively, have a different punch ('The Yanks have gone barmy'). And his affection for *Le Nozze di Figaro* and the novels of George Eliot suggest a missed message: Mozart's opera is about the servant outwitting the master, Almaviva overthrown like a Tsar; *Middlemarch* and *Scenes from Clerical Life* are social moralities amenable to ideological analysis (such as the Fifties critiques by the Marxist professor, Arnold Kettle).

His zany table-talk is a blind – and the only person to penetrate his games and routines is Margie Rees. 'You may have hated America,' she says, 'but it suited you.' And she provokes Burgess's ugly side. One moment, he's the Fool scoffing angel cake with the children; the next, he's swallowing back a snarl about 'bloody American imperialism'. The charming homosexual and affected sop shows a flash of boiling misanthropy. He uneasily gulps and gasps with malice.

The baby language (chuff-chuff, gee-whiz, kiddie-winks, super-duper) is a poetry of deception – and only Goronwy Rees knows he's planning to run away from home. 'Tell Rees I'm doing the right thing,' he tells Margie drunkenly, telephoning from his London club. She's promptly agitated, hurt into contemplating the extent of her husband's involvement – both sexual and political. Burgess bruises the emotions: wife is set against her man; Rees is set against Blunt and 'the cause'.

Blunt's merry swain has left them all in the lurch, and the implication is that Burgess's own welfare and contentment replaced any greater good. Rees, attempting to placate matters, by confessing to Margie, only deepens the danger. 'I had to choose between my friend and my wife,' he says plaintively. Blunt's distaste at the remark, his curdled sneer, is exactly the response we'd imagine Hopkins's Burgess as making. 'We are all in your hands,' says Blunt, adding with contempt, 'and your wife's.'

Thus the success of the performance: it informed those parts of the film the actor didn't even appear in. Like John Bayley's acknowledgement of imponderable recesses in *King Lear*, which Hopkins's acting nudged and even made tactile, Hopkins in *Blunt* had a sharp off-camera presence. And on-camera, and rubicund eyes asparkle, Burgess prowled with a combination of joky alacrity and genuine menace – enthralling to disdainful Blunt, and sucking from Goronwy Rees a barely suppressed longing.

Le Roux (named for the author of *Le Fantôme de l'Opera*?), Lear, Hooper, Burgess: these are from Hopkins's gallery of intrepid rapscallions. The charismatic loners. By contrast *84 Charing Cross Road* belongs with the integrity and condolence of Frederick Treves – which is perhaps why Hopkins was cast. The film was produced by Mel Brooks, whose company financed *The Elephant Man*; and Anne Bancroft (Mrs Brooks) is in both pictures.

Hopkins, however, is too subtle and organic an actor merely to repeat a performance. Frank Doel's goodness is not quite Treves clean-shaven. Nor is Doel blandly good. In fact, Hopkins's interpretation of the character connects with Hooper from *The Good Father*. Doel's a good father – and he's also a knight-errant (as Hooper's a furious quester); a man with a vision. For whereas Helene Hanff's epistolary novelette is a romance with a bookshop (Doel the clerk who keeps the shrine), the film explores Helene Hanff's lost romance with Doel himself. The amorous centre of the exercise is shifted.

Anne Bancroft's Helene, however, sticks to the book. She copies the authoress's raucous New York jags of enthusiasm and derision, which went into the letters – and the book was simply a sequence of orders for titles, plus the replies, the frigid formality of request and response gradually thawing into a chatty, affectionate pen-palship between bibliophiles; and she impersonates Hanff's dowdy, birdy looks. But for Doel

there's little to go on. Hopkins's instinct was to invade the man's scholarly reserve and radiate his obscure objects of desire.

In the book, the commercial transactions represent a burgeoning amity
between a prosperous America and a shabby, plucky Blitz-bashed London; when Helene start sending exotic food parcels, it's like the bounty of
Juno and Demeter arriving in a cornucopia of post. This theme the film
extends, to make Helene in love with London and Englishness, Frank
smitten with American zest. Both dream of elsewhere – but they never
meet. It's a sad moment in book and film when news comes that Frank
has died. The atmosphere has been so charmed, death makes its entrance
prickingly. Thou interuptest our merriment. 'He was rushed to hospital
on the 15th of December ... and he died seven days later. He had been
with the firm for over forty years ... Do you still wish us to try and
obtain the Austens for you?' Like a true hero's, the death of a salesman has
occurred offstage.

'As far as I know, this part hasn't been based on anybody,' said
Hopkins. 'I played it as myself. To make myself look younger, I tried to
Brylcreem back my hair, as I do for Lambert Le Roux, but I had to have a
wig. I refused to see any pictures of Frank Doel, because I didn't want to
be trapped by any image of the man. Nor did I want him to be a meek,
pathetic little clerk. He was a good man, a kindly man.'

But by playing Doel as himself, Hopkins opened himself up to his
other recent characters – and hence the suggestion of Hooper's haunted
courtesy. Hooper and Doel both have darkish hollows in the face; each
has an intensity; each yearns for a fantasy of far-away – Hooper where he
can be self-sufficient, Doel where he can be fulfilled. Hooper's a romantic
rebel and reactionary; Doel's in a tale of medieval romance, with Helene
his flighty lady, inscrutable and coquettish – an itchy paragon. Hooper's a
narcissistic Galahad; Doel's a diligent Lancelot, collecting the fine-bound
trophies his Belle Dame demands. In dreary London he looks to the
heights of New York as a disconsolate troubadour left out in the snow.
Helene's his white goddess, his muse, his diva. Hooper finds his princess,
Mary, an artist living in a loft, and she bores him. Having found the grail,
what does he do with it?

By no means is it a shame Helene and Doel didn't meet. The relationship was sustained by the mystery of the mails. They were able to imagine
versions of one another. It's always fatal for such pen-pals to meet: they're
the intimately known strangers, and there's a hint of a tarnished ideal
when Nora calls Helene Helen, 'because that's how we've always thought
of you.' *Helen* has mythical resonance; her remote eyrie in the land across
the sea was as distant as a tower in Troy.

Written by Hugh Whitemore (who caught the ghost in Turing's
machine) and directed by David Jones (who's responsible for Pinter's

crabwise analysis of infidelity, *Betrayal*), the film of *84 Charing Cross Road* is the most clandestine and self-deprecating study of adultery ever made. Good and kindly Doel's wistful dream of the exotic is a cinematic equivalent of Bloom writing to Martha Clifford (as Henry Flower); or a much-muted *Les Liaisons Dangereuses*.

Director and scenarist constructed lives for hero and heroine, imagining the biographies beyond the letters. Doel spends hours searching for books, at no financial profit, intent upon serving a brave new world; Helene sits in her brownstone, scissoring open the offerings. When the film begins, the goddess is flying up in the air: the aged American lady finally voyaging to England – 'the England of English literature' is what she hopes to find, happily oblivious of the fact that English literature, like her idea of Doel, belongs only in the geography of fancy and paper moons. She then takes a cab through London, gasps at the postcard sights, and ends up in that cave of nostalgia – the Charing Cross Road bookshop, now a gutted commercial property. Helene mumbles a prayer, and we flashback to the beginning.

To a great extent *84 Charing Cross Road* can be dismissed as an illustrated voice-over. The camera insists we appreciate the authentically reproduced interiors, the props, objects, junk of the Forties and Fifties. Helene's apartment, in a crumbling walk-up, is a museum of period grocery packets, newsprint, kettles, milk bottles and a coffee percolator. The *Saturday Review* is on the street vending booths; fresh copies of *The Naked and the Dead* pile high in stores. Art Deco limos with whitewalls purr along the highways. Helene visits the dentist: she's probed with historically accurate steel prongs.

There being little actual dialogue, the camera chats to us. What are we to make of the mess on Helene's desk – the photos and book-matches; or of her embroidered cushions? And who is the framed sailor, his portrait signed 'Dearest Heart. How like you this?' A lost love is signalled. Helene's the American Lieutenant's woman. And like Fowles's Mrs Woodruff, she's monumentally lonely.

Intercutting with New York, where we hear a jaunty jazz soundtrack, is England's old curiosity shop, where we hear trams and buses chugging past, plus the plonking of a plangent piano, oboe and strings. 84 Charing Cross Road is a carefully crafted antique; musty, dusty, cluttered with donnish assistants: Maurice Denham witters about cups of tea; Ian McNeice (with his cascading chins, he looks as if his head is being pushed through a blancmange) files maps and prints like any Bodleian curator. These custodians of literature are wonderfully boring – and chief dud and office-overseer is Doel himself, who keeps himself apart in a glass office.

On both sides of the Atlantic postmen come and go. The camera dwells on authentic frankings and sealing-wax. Helene gets her *Virginibus Pueris-*

que★; the booksellers get their food parcels. But beyond the decor, in the film's undergrowth, the director encourages an idealized philandering. Hopkins's character, gazing into the middle-distance, is thinking of an invisible darling. We discover he's been married twice; he has attractive secretaries, and he keeps mentioning miniskirts. When this unlikely libertine travels by coach to a stately-home sale, and buys a gold-embossed volume of Elizabethan Love Lyrics for Helene, it's like he's crept to the country for an illicit weekend. The sensation is not lessened when the book is despatched as a gift from all the staff. And when Connie Booth manifests herself in the shop, as a lady from Delaware after an Orwell edition, and Hopkins rushes from the office, rashly thinking this vision of feminine beauty is Helene – his flush of mingled embarrassment and hope is the expression of a self-chastening knight, and he recites from Yeats's *The Wind Among The Reeds*:

> Had I the heavens' embroidered cloths,
> Enwrought with golden and silver light,
> The blue and the dim and the dark cloths
> Of night and light and the half-light,
> I would spread the cloths under your feet:
> But I, being poor, have only my dreams;
> I have spread my dreams under your feet;
> Tread softly because you tread on my dreams.

Doel's Calypso never does come down to earth (the running joke of the film is a thwarted brief encounter, like a parody of Celia Johnson and Trevor Howard); she arranges for silk stockings, beautifully wrapped, to be left as if by magic in the shop. Doel finds them, and is deliciously affrighted. It's as if Hippolyta's girdle has fallen from the firmament.

After the occultation of a calling-card, the characters are momentarily conjoined by the Coronation of 1952. The Doels watch a smudgy monochrome television set, a crackling box of tricks; Helene rises at night to listen to the wireless. Richard Dimbleby intones across the planet. A queen is crowned – and Helene, having promised faithfully to visit England for the event, calls off the trip at the last moment. Coitus interruptus, of a kind.

Though the juxtapositioning of letters on the voice-overs is like a telepathic conversation (and Hopkins's talking to himself is reminiscent of the lawyer in *Guilty Conscience*), the apartness of the lovers is their sweet sorrow. Helene refuses a request for a photograph: 'For the first time in my life I'm a woman of mystery.' And the irony is that la belle Helene is no trim coiff'd goddess. She's a tweedy, bespectacled drab – Anne Bancroft, the most glazed of actresses, rather failing to play Hanff's

---

★ Amongst other things, a repudiation of marriage.

insatiable wit and assurance. This was necessary for the film, which had
to make her out to be melancholy and lonely: a counterpart to Doel's
scholarly withdrawnness. But where Hopkins's acting is multilayered,
Anne Bancroft's is direct and dead. She has, I always feel, no sense of
humour; Mel Brooks laughs for two.

Helene's isolation is marked by her being a babysitter and bridesmaid,
never a mother or wife; she enjoys marginalia in texts, and secondhand
books generally, for the comradely feel, and she's emotionally on the
margin. Her way of being intimate is to finger paper. When Nora and
Frank stiffly dance at the Festival of Britain, their shuffle cross-cuts with
Helene throwing confetti. The Doels are like the couple she's blessing,
and the implication is that Frank is embracing the wrong woman.

The Doel homelife is a cycle of tedium: the same meals come out of the
kitchen, the same rain falls outside the window. Nothing happens except
that the family grows older; folk become fatter, with thicker spectacle
lenses. London is polluted with pop music. Hopkins's plod is heavier and
he takes his ease on a bench in Soho Square – one of those indeterminately
middle-aged men, innocuous and weary. But by casting Judi Dench as
Nora, ordinariness resonated. Her tremors of intonation collude with the
performance Hopkins gives – so that the wife's flicker of jealousy comes
across. Hopkins is tender and dutiful; Judi Dench, busy and diligent – yet
inside the routine, in their silences and responses, they had the phantom
of Helene intervene. Nora knows Helene's the absent fancywoman; and
as the second wife, there are intimacies of her husband's she'll never know
about. Absent, Helene's present in her gifts and as a disembodied voice.

She's Frank's Kundry, but it's Nora's tears which end the film. Judi
Dench put all her warmth into the widow's note to the other woman,
each commonplace glowing with feeling, each light-hearted comment
wriggling with suggestion: 'Thank you for your letter, nothing about it
at all offends me . . . At times I don't mind telling you I was very jealous of
you, as Frank so enjoyed your letters and they or some were so like his
sense of humour . . . Frank and I were so very much opposites, he so kind
and gentle and me with my Irish background always fighting for my
rights. I miss him so . . . Please excuse my scrawl.'

'Judi Dench plays my wife, Nora. She is so giggly. A constant stream
of humour. We'd go through a scene, and she'd look at me and say,
"Now, I mean, you aren't intending really doing it like that, are you? Of
course not. You are? Look, I'm sorry, Tony, but this is my first time
acting with amateurs. I usually act with professionals." We're doing
Antony and Cleopatra together. We were like schoolchildren about it. I'd
never even read it – you'll be surprised at how many actors have yet to
read the whole of Shakespeare: we are an ignorant profession – though
ignorance can be very useful. I'm very ignorant! Anyway, I'd never even
read it – and I confessed this to Judi one day: "I'm afraid I've not read

Antony and Cleopatra ... Have you ... studied it much?" And do you know, Judi Dench had not read *Antony and Cleopatra* either? She seldom reads anything. It's all instinct, intuition.'

In *84 Charing Cross Road*, though the crucial mythical relationship is between Hopkins's Doel and Anne Bancroft's Helene, the relationship which extended the limits of what acting can accomplish was that of the bookseller and his wife – the little digressions that make domesticity epic. And that's how they played Antony and Cleopatra. Judi Dench, who has an Irish background, was like Irish Nora 'always fighting for my rights'; and Hopkins was besotted – like Doel dissolving. Antony was a grizzled warlock, rotund in his armour, and constituted Hopkins's most licentious performance – as if his Bligh had let go.

A near-sybarite, Antony, as Guy Burgess would've done, drunkenly groped and straddled at Pompey's stag party, hypnotized by his own dilapidated dignity. And we never had the impression that he was close, emotionally, to Cleopatra – rather, as with Frank and Nora Doel, they are people who have started to grow old together. He hangs around the enchanting queen out of habit. And Octavia he never even looked in the eye. He's married her to consolidate power (with Cleopatra, too, he's thinking of private gain in the East.) Hence, perhaps, Cleopatra's insistent fantasy of Antony: the real Antony she's not had, not fully. Nor shall she. To her, he's as Helene to Frank.

Any self-preservation he may have had she's massively corrupted. Cleopatra aids the melting of discipline, releasing Antony into potentialities beyond anyone's control. As Octavius says:

> If he fill'd
> His vacancy with his voluptuousness,
> Full surfeits, and the dryness of his bones
> Call on him for't.

Alongside Hopkins's molten Mars, Peter Hall's production cast Michael Bryant as Enobarbus, who assumed the poise of a Gloucester excused an aristocratic tinge. Remembering the chair Cleopatra sat in, and how like a burnished throne it was, he recovered a sense, as the speech went on, of how much he himself was in love with her when she put on a show – like Garbo or Monroe, making men drunk with female beauty. Bryant *acted* his lines: he didn't recite them, and Enobarbus functioned like a sober Fool – for he has, like Feste or Lear's crony, the confidence of Cleopatra and of Antony, who has to remind him that 'Thou art a soldier only, speak no more'; and he wanders at liberty in and out of the courts of Alexandria and Rome – where Tim Piggott-Smith made Octavius the play's school-sneak, and John Bluthal (a graduate of Spike Milligan shows) made Lepidus the Empire's first Hebrew consul.

David Scofield's Pompey, a military nuisance like Hotspur, like Hotspur was rather personable. Hall had him waft around in a thin black cloak, and his fidgets exactly duplicated Judi Dench's Cleopatra in her gold cape. Pompey is the son of her former lover – and the same imagery is used of the two characters. Pompey's on a barge, as Cleopatra was. Pompey 'doth this day laugh away his fortune'; Cleopatra laughs Antony in and out of patience. (Is he her lost baby?)

Emerging from the billows and flares of coloured smoke, with trumpets tooting from the loudspeakers, Hopkins's Antony, in gold armour and red fashion accessories (Eros, his dresser or squire, dolls him up in front of us), was like Othello sailing out of the storm, having put the Turks to rout. Antony, indeed, had been summoned back to help Rome as Othello's needed by the Venetians. And like Othello, he's a hero falling apart, his alliances with other people miscarrying. Married to Octavia, he doesn't speak; the marriage is a symptom of being bonded to Octavius, with whom he later goes to war and offers personal combat. Emotionally he's bonded to Cleopatra, and fails to break loose; temperamentally he's drawn to Pompey, an official friend, whose house he commandeers and whom he has an officer go out and kill. His best friend, Enobarbus, walks out on him, as do his attendants, whom he'd thought 'married to your good service, stay till death' (another connubial image).

Antony's the loneliest character in Shakespeare next to Macbeth. He's divorced from all company. Not having any Scottish estate to yield up, he's a man who forfeits, as labours to be lost, his own nature. He dies an empty space ('all-disgraced'), an egoist with no ego.

Hopkins converted the character's degradation into a theatrical resuscitation. He played Antony's demolition like a civilization being sacked, or the last phase in the extinction of a primitive beast. Octavius describes him as an animal who'd live in the wilderness like a stag off bark and moss; no water to be had, he'd sip 'the stale of horses'. When he dies, his body is lugged like a side of beef. This was Hopkins's Antony: an atavistic lumberer – as his Lear was a moon-man, and Le Roux a dinosaur.

With Hopkins, more than any other actor, the thing he himself is shall make his characters live: their fate comes from his nature, which is bloody, bold and resolute. Hopkins is devoted to acting and its meaning – a quality he recognized in Ian Richardson, who for Hopkins's muscle and movement has gesture and grace: 'The instinct of an actor. Ian's an utter actor, and so precise. He has perfect recall of moves, of inflection, of what he's done, take after take. What the sound-man did, what the lighting cameraman did, take after take. I love that. He loves acting, fully and completely and totally – and so do I. When he was pacing about, going through his part, completely absorbed, I thought, "I know how you are loving every second of this, boy. How it is your life. And it's mine, too ..." It is mine too. I hate actors who slouch around, being bored, being sullen. GET OUT, I want to say? FUCK OFF! Don't bring your bad moods and atmospheres with you. Take your atmosphere somewhere else. If you are ill, and don't feel like acting, go away, go home, GO BACK TO BED!

'Some actors – and Americans are the worst, though some English ones as well – they think the thing to do is to be temperamental. So, we all wait until they've got through their tempers and doldrums and fannying around, and I get very, very angry, sitting there snapping come on, *come on* . . .

'This is what I mean when I say acting is a job you work, work, work at. No point waiting for the gods to look down kindly at you. You've got to be alert and earn their attention. I ask a lot of other people. So what? I ask a lot of myself.

'I say, when people ask, acting isn't everything. There are more important things. But that's a lie. It's the only thing in the world that matters to me. It's the only world that matters to me.'

Character is fate.

Remember the *Wilhelm Meister* quotation? Hopkins, who requires the confidence of rubrics, devices wrought on the figurative shield of his craft, like the mottoes on Achilles's armour, or the epic motifs on Othello's stomacher in the Miller production, wrote to say that 'another part belonging somewhere in it is *"Whatever you can do, or dream you can, begin it: courage has genius, power and magic in it."* '

Genius, power, magic – terms pertinent to Hopkins. His nature is, as another Hopkins (Gerard Manley) would put it, a Heraclitean fire. A heart's clarion! Away grief's gasping! Hopkins (Anthony) is an exemplar of Heraclitus's aphorism, come down to us through Friedrich von Hardenberg (the novelist known as Novalis): *die Persönlichkeit ist Schicksal*. Character is fate.

SEVEN

The Reptile Joys of the Bee: Antony Sher

Character may be fate for Hopkins; not necessarily for Antony Sher – for whom character is gymnastics, a disciplined routine of trimming, sleeking, improving. Joan Bakewell once interviewed him in a locker-room, and in a colour-supplement feature on fitness, amongst the executive joggers and the wheelchair-bound bruisers – the style of the article that of a body-building advertisement, exhorting the puny to become incredible hulks like Steve Reeves or Arnold Schwarzenegger or the littler-known Rock Stevens, star of cult-classic *Hercules and the Tyrants of Babylon* – there's 'Antony Sher, 37, actor . . . he goes to a gym at least three times a week for an hour's circuit training'. Accompanying the caption is a large photograph of the actor himself, puffing astride a pec-deck, a tubular-steel apparatus with pulleys and weights. Sher, in sweat-stained white singlet and black shorts, glistening from chest to shins, glowers. Heavily bearded, half his face in shadow, he's a grim-visaged beef: the bellhop from *Superman II* (who smirks 'Everything's complimentary until you get the bill') transforming his body into Clark Kent's.

Richard III and *Pravda* overlapping in the London season, the former opening on 14 June 1984, the latter on 2 May 1985, Sher and Hopkins provoke comparison and analysis – for they were in the same play, Brenton and Hare merely replacing a Plantagenet with a Press Baron. Richard is Shakespeare's Lambert Le Roux. Antony and Anthony overmastered their respective productions, making pageants one-man shows; the productions also lived long in the repertoires, earnests of the central performances.

Elsewhere, Antony and Anthony are alike: they are without equal at playing megalomaniacs or spirited underdogs; they are demanding and ambitious, seizing and pulverizing audiences – we *know* when they are acting; they are stars. To discriminate further:

(i) Hopkins is an epic actor. Epic because acting is for him a generous disburdening of personality – so that Lambert Le Roux released temper brewed by a bad *King Lear* rehearsal. The characters he plays are induced and stimulated by his own nature.

Sher's characters are tracked down and absorbed from external stimulation, like muscles from a bull-worker rather than muscles from natural endowment. But to say his acting is showy, external, is too simple. His talent is to donate an inner life to surface elements; psychology is something worn on the outside – like a building designed by Richard Rogers, where architectural innards, pipes, flues, air-vents, electrical circuitry, are not concealed but flaunted as part of the design. Like a theatrical crustacean, Sher carries the house of fiction on his back.

(ii) Hopkins's acting, like the art of Michelangelo and the career of Napoleon (as determined by Hazlitt and Carlyle), is an emblem of power. As an actor he's an icon of man made mighty. A force of destiny: ' 'Twas *in* him, and it comed out all times and shapes,' as Kipling says of a hero in *Rewards and Fairies*. Though both Hopkins and Sher are virtuosic and spectacular, Sher has a higher level of self-consciousness, Hopkins emanating a rage Sher breathtakingly contrives. Hopkins is in touch with the heavens on fire; a man of myth who can call spirits from the vasty deep. Sher's a history-man, though not quite in the same kind of way as Howard Kirk in Malcolm Bradbury's novel *The History Man* – whom he played in a television adaptation. But Kirk's life is a prestidigitation; he magicked himself and his wife Barbara from graduate-student indigence in Leeds to academic glamour at the University of Watermouth (variously East Anglia, Sussex and St Catherine's College, Oxford): 'the old Kirks faded from sight and the new Kirks came into being . . . For, let us remember, here were two people who had grown up . . . in two different Northern towns, one in Yorkshire and one in Lancashire . . .' Howard and Barbara, between them, represent a modern War of the Roses, the world against which Richard III was raised.

(iii) Hopkins is an actor of the tribe – and I don't mean Hopkins's ligatures of Welshness; rather, his acting, powerful and commonly about power, raises the issue of leadership and tribal responsibility: Lear's Britain simultaneously a tribe atavistic and futuristic; Le Roux's territorial imperatives, absorbing journals into his paper universe, over which he presides, a volatile chieftain; Frank Doel, snug in his acreage of books, communicating with the remainder of the world by polite typed letter; Burgess, in *Blunt*, a traitor to his tribe; Treves, in *The Elephant Man*, rehabilitating a freak in xenophobic Edwardian society; St Paul praying alone in the Kingdom of the wicked; Corky, in *Magic*, withdrawing to a lakeside motel, killing interlopers, protecting a tribe of two members: himself and a mannequin double; Hooper, in *The Good Father*, enthroned on a deckchair in his stockaded pocket garden – the tribe diminished to an single survivor; Donald Campbell, the last hero in the world, clamped into the cockpit of Blue Bird and atomizing over Lake Coniston (in *Across the Lake*).

Where Hopkins is the epic hero, his characters needing a community to dominate or aid or betray or shun, Sher's preferred characters are urgent solipsists, who want to eradicate their communities, leaving room for the nurturing of private idiosyncrasy and the happy populating of their environments with zany thoughts and actions. How distinct, for example, from Hopkins's Hooper, who sulks and does not exult – his entrenchment being like Achilles's retreat to his tent: an emanation of stubborn anger and pride, of Coriolanus's tantrum: 'I banish *you*.' A claustrophobic nightmare: bounded into a nutshell.

Sher's Tartuffe, played as a con-man Californian guru tele-transported to a seventeenth century Parisian dining room, was a hypocrite intent on becoming a king of infinite space. He schemes to appropriate Orgon's estate and dispense with all its inhabitants, quite happy to see his former patron wander away destitute:

> As you're no doubt aware, there is no question
> that at the present moment this house here
> belongs to our revered Monsieur Tartuffe.
> From now on he is lord and master of
> your possessions . . .

With the house about to become exclusively his to bustle in, Sher materialized to supervise the eviction of Orgon (Christopher Benjamin, his expression that of a perpetually perplexed old Labrador) dressed as an excessive beau, his clerical subfusc discarded for weeds dripping with lace and jewels. Tartuffe's face was heavily made up with rouge, lip gloss, mascara and studded with beauty spots, the whole apparition trailing face powder and scent, hissing and spitting like a demonic sphinx whose secret has been found out. Here was Molière's creature suggestive of lurid decadence and spangled cross-dressing; his new residence, perhaps, to be converted into a costumier's catwalk for personal delectation.

Arnold, the wisecracking transvestite in *Torch Song Trilogy*, was a reformed Tartuffe in Manhattan; Oliver Shadey was a junior Tartuffe in London. Philip Saville's film was determinedly oddball. Sher played a garage mechanic who, to earn money for a sex-change operation, sells his sci-fi talent – the ability to transfer his mind-reading on to celluloid. (The film is full of surveillance cameras, videos, projectors, television screens, photo albums and the fever of cinema.) Shadey is meant to be credulous and innocent; he dresses in a stripy blazer a size too small, a boater and bow tie – like Pee Wee Herman. But with Sher operating the idea of harmlessness, filaments of its opposite quickly registered, and the film became a devil-doll *Tootsie*. Shadey has the evil eye, despatching Lady Landau (Katherine Helmond) deeper into madness. He sits in her sink, taunting her about incest, a cackling Puck, unrolling his tongue, making obscene finger movements, a hobgoblin that frights the maidens of the villagery, and so she sinks a carving knife deep in his crotch. We're not spared his orgasmic smile of terrible satisfaction, nor the blood pumping from his crotch.

With Shadey's balls off, the films strapped to his brain are black. He's a testosterone Samson. We see him shaving off chest hair, putting on suspenders and bra and make-up, and then getting stuck in an elevator, which whizzes up and down the shaft, as if bouncing from heaven to hell, Shadey an insane angelic demon – and the elevator finally bursts through the roof, flying off in a shower of sparks: a kinky space pod.

The History Man was about more than an urgent solipsist: it discovered a Machiavel. Kirk, the sociology lecturer, creates insurrection amongst the students and dissension among the dons. He's a prince of picket line and boardroom; a celebrated radical in tank-top and Zapata moustache, he has resolutions ratified entirely to his own advantage. Pupils and masters believe they own his loyalty – but he is true only to himself; he wins and keeps the university for personal advantages – his kingdom being an asphalt excrescence in the grounds of an Elizabethan mansion. And Renaissance learning has evolved, over the centuries – through history – from the enlightenment and telescopes to social studies degrees, modules, interdisciplinary happenings and videos of group dynamics. Watermouth's gowns are by Mary Quant, the impractical cutlery by a Dane named Jop Kaakinen. (St Catherine's implements are by Arne Jacobsen, another Dane.)

A product of history (grammar-school swot making it to a redbrick on a scholarship in 1957), Kirk becomes history-in-action. Emboldened by the new spirit of a new decade – the Beatles, David Hockney, Joe Orton, Vietnam, *Lady Chatterley*, astrology, Terence Conran – he drinks, he chats, he writes a book called *The Coming of the New Sex*. Kirk's days are deliberated; spontaneity is rehearsed. Marriage he describes as 'society's technique for permanentizing the inherent contingency of relationships.' His wife knows how he is, in fact, sustained by the very society he appears to rail against: 'You've substituted trends for morals and commitments' – but then, trends are his area of expertise, he being a sociologist. Kirk revolts into style, his termly parties being seigneurial banquets for the Age of Aquarius, with pot-smoking and groping sessions in the oiled-pine kitchen.

Casualty of Kirk's stage-managed casualness is his Lady Anne: Barbara smashes her hand through glass in mute, brute rage. Otherwise, it's an existence of campus swiving, disturbed only by easily demolished efforts to question his preferential essay-grading system, and heightened by pre-arranged coups. 'When he has the chance,' we read in *Principe* (1513), 'an able prince should cunningly foster some opposition to himself so that by overcoming it he can enhance his own stature.' Kirk's stature – in Sher's portrayal – represented Niccolò Machiavelli in the guise of a modish academic.

The Italian political theorist composed a brochure for Shakespeare's Richard III; but first, what of Lear's Fool, Lear's prattling, half-regarded conscience, whom Sher played at Stratford in 1982? How did the know-all comedian, who dies off-stage and forgotten, fit into Sher's company of up-stagers? In Sher's personification, the eejit predominated over the emir. A hyperactive clown, sinister and wily with his pathos, his voice an asthmatic gurgle, like a baby being smothered, Sher appeared even before the play began, in a bizarre tableau: the Fool and Cordelia entwined on a throne, throttled by a rope of pearls; a horror-comic image, instantly animated into a children's game of cat's-cradle, with much giggles, when Kent and Gloucester trundle on, agreeing that the King had more regard for the Duke of Albany than Cornwall. And having appeared before the play'd begun, Sher had bitten into the audience's imagination; he reigned henceforward.

Dressed in a wreck of an Edwardian morning suit – foreshortened pinstripes and elongated buskins – and hunched inside the frock coat and clamped into a dicky; carrying a tiny violin case and wearing white gloves, Lear's Fool ventured out of a Fellini film. *Satyricon* Sher has seen upward of a dozen times; he appreciates the flickering and grotesque frescos the director re-created, and the Fool's make-up (smudgy white face with blurred gashes of red, topped with a tangled top-knot of hair) resembled a mouldering Italian carnival mask.

Sher painted a picture of himself in the role. Called *Antony Sher as the Fool in King Lear*, it hangs in the gallery at Stratford. The self-portrait shows a crippled vaudevillian, feet splayed at an odd angle, shoulders narrow and crookbacked, jigging and sweeping off his hat. There are three top-knots, the hair tied by coloured ribbon. The Fool's trousers are red and blue stripe. He jigs on a tiny stage with a tinier window set into the puce wall. It looks like the prison where Cordelia goes to sing like a caged bird.

In Adrian Noble's production, the Fool used the court as a vaudeville hall, and the heath as an even bigger vaudeville hall. He stomped, sang, yelped and caroused, Michael Gambon's Lear dwindling into his straight man – or, at best, his light-comedian support – during abrasive routines.

> *Fool*: Dost thou know the difference, my boy, between a bitter
>   Fool and a sweet one?
> *Lear*: No, lad; teach me.
> *Fool*: That lord that counsell'd thee
>   To give away thy land,
>   Come place him here by me,
>   Do thou for him stand:

> The sweet and bitter fool
>   Will presently appear;
> The one in motley here,
>   The other found out there

With bulbous red nose throbbing like a galvanic gob-stopper (written up as a play in itself – *Red Noses* by Peter Barnes was Sher's vehicle at the Barbican), Sher was a lucky-dip of Keaton, Chaplin, Norman Wisdom, Beckett's tramps and the morose Tony Hancock. The audience began to await the clearing out of the noble tragedians for the arrival of the coarse comic; all we wanted were Sher's eruptions and coruscations. *King Lear* seemed to exist, not as an essay on old age centred upon a dispossessed pensioner, but as a demonstration in clowning. Lear was the Fool's shadow.

Turning cartwheels, goose-stepping, crouching at the King's feet or climbing onto his back, balancing on a wobbling pole high above the storm, or hiding in a wooden barrel, Sher's was a ceaselessly physical performance. Singlehanded, he commandeered and revamped the play. Poetry was left behind by restiveness and the tragedy flagged once the comedy departed – for the Fool, eventually, did depart, luridly, and on stage. The scene in Tom O'Bedlam's hut grew riotous. A trio of Karnos: real lunatic (Lear), pretend lunative (Edgar), professional lunatic (Fool). Beginning as slapstick humour – rushing, bumping, falling, shouting – the imbroglio ended with a murder. Lear stabbed the Fool through a cushion, his pantomine of a judge and executioner out of control.

What the action actually signified was that the tragedian was obliged to kill the comedian if he had any intention of getting on with the drama of being more sinned against than sinning, etc. etc. The next time we see Lear, he tries to *be* the Fool – dressing in wild flowers, trying out gags about mice and toasted cheese. But it was to no avail. Sher closed *King Lear* at Act III, scene vi, line 88: 'And I'll go to bed at noon.' A typically topsy-turvy sentiment. He spluttered blood, wheezed, sank into the barrel (a barrel out of *Fin de Partie* – the sort of death which, in a circus, would be instantly revoked with jets of water and brass horn squawks. To counterfeit dying. Whoop, Jug, I love thee.

From Lear's Fool to Richard III, for Sher, was a logical step. Comedians to the grotesque, both; figures on the margin, observers, both; sweet and bitter, both. At the time, however, it was a literally misplaced step which set off a personal history of cause and effect. Slamming his legs in a funny walk in *King Lear*, for the soliloquy after the storm:

> Then comes the time, who lives to see't,
> That going shall be us'd with feet.
> This prophecy Merlin shall make; for I live before his time

– Sher snapped his Achilles tendon. He squirmed in agony, and the audience thought it part of the show, like when Tommy Cooper died doing conjuring tricks.

There began half a year of convalescence, and locomotion on crutches. The humiliation of being gazed at and condescended towards, the daily lot of a cripple, Sher would utilize for crippled Richard – whose cruelty was seen to come from his life-long resentment of the healthy. *Richard III* is the revenge of the malformed and mistreated ('I, that am rudely stamped, and want love's majesty . . .'). To cure his own disability, Sher attended the Remedial Dance Clinic in Harley Street, the rehabilitation centre for pranged theatricals, and he began a fitness programme at the City Gym and Body Control Studio, pumping iron – hence his acting becoming increasingly gymnastic. His body was henceforward his instrument – which allows another point of contrast with Anthony Hopkins, in addition to their distinct kinds of hegemony. Hopkins leads with the voice, which he modulates from a bellow to a flute. Had he failed as an actor, he'd like to have been a musician – he likes to toy with piano and electronic synthesizers. Music is his recreation.

Sher, whose voice manages a small range of different hoots – silky, verging on a slow chuckle; convulsive, tending towards a pant – leads with the physique. He's never still. The Fool and Richard were generously agile; Tartuffe would as soon run about on top of a table as around it. In *Superman II*, Sher appears as a non-stop bellhop, checking Lois Lane and Clark Kent into the Honeymoon Hotel (a place of dreadful gilt mirrors and purple lamp-shades) with snickering innuendo. 'Happy . . whatevers,' he wishes the couple, eyeing the undulating waterbed. Eyebrows dancing, his jaw chewing gum, with serious abandon, Sher's was a perfect cameo of itchy prurience. A cousin of Tartuffe. Or the uncredited walk-on in Alan Bennett's *One Fine Day* – as a bubble-blowing midget wearing mirrored goggles who buzzes about the office block Robert Stephens and Dave Allen want to sell. His burly minders ask him for an opinion. Only when he turns to camera and announces, '*It's shit!*' do we know for sure the magnificently unimpressed client is Sher.

Hopkins is stocky and strong, of course, but he's the bull versus Sher's terrier or fox (or fox-terrier). Or, to proliferate the fauna, they are illustrative of Fuseli's wonderful query, 'Can the reptile joys of the bee rival the lion's colossal pleasures?' A single play awaits to unite them: they are born to play Iago and the Moor together. Othello music plus the infernal gesturing of the ensign.

Had Sher failed as an actor, he'd like to have been a painter. As it happens, he's a successful painter as well as being a great actor, and he can also write. A trinity of agents handle the separate talents. But are they separate skills? Acting and painting are certainly connected. A version of easel and sketch-pad, Sher's performances are visual, as opposed to vocal, flourishes. Pictures at an exhibition. Tartuffe's maquillage has been mentioned; also there's the Ringo Starr clone in *John, Paul, George, Ringo and Bert*; the Enoch Powell clone in *Tarzan's Last Stand*; the trans-sexual in *Shadey*, who in his feminine demeanour is a clone of Lady Agatha D'Ascoyne from *Kind Hearts and Coronets* (suffragette's hat tethered by loose scarf). A book of Alec Guinness photographs was a hierograph to Sher the South African schoolboy. And Arnold in *Torch Song Trilogy*, scrubbed and clear of complexion at the beginning of the play, was an opportunity for Sher to illustrate himself in full view of the audience – a palpable canvas, physiognomical decoration. A practical demonstration, like Tom Keating squirting the oils about. By the end, Arnold was an archetype of a drag queen's overladen look; the depilated integument.

Painting and the aspects of the eye also percolate Sher's prose. *Year of the King* stirs with visual, and cinematic, imagery. Of *Red Noses* Sher says, 'it glows with colours you've never dreamed of'; Snoo Wilson's work is a 'brightly coloured turd'; Neil Kinnock radiates an orangey glow; *Camille* 'moves . . . as effortlessly as a film'; and when acting to music, it's 'like you're in a film'. The Cotswolds, where Sher makes his home when at Stratford, tax his sensibility: the silver light, the harvest moon, the iridescent oil-seed rape carpeting the fields.

Returning to South Africa – the first return journey, we are made to feel, for many years – Sher found his parents' house full of posters and pictures of the prodigal son, 'as if I've died and this is the shrine'. His moma has made a MOMA, crammed with 'Antony Sher' exhibits. His mother and Katie, the black maid, dote upon him – one of his drawings shows a stocky Negress, with a careworn smile, looking down shyly, standing behind a thin affluent woman, whose smile is a bit hard, and whose hair is expensively highlighted. It's like a still from *Gone with the Wind*. Vivien Leigh and Hattie McDaniel. And as for Sher's father, he's described as José Ferrer (Lautrec) or Anthony Quinn (Gauguin). A grainy home-movie from 1957 is discovered, transposed on video (the 'bleached colours and hazy outlines' make it like an ancient newsreel), and Sher is aghast to notice what an eight-year-old exhibitionist he was; his father looms into frame, a lugubrious Groucho Marx.

Satyricon is an abiding inspiration: 'A sense of decadence' in the colours Fellini uses, 'the colours of illness, milky blues and yellows, watery greens and purples, the colour of runny eggs, of mould.' This is the visual environment Sher wants for *Richard III*; and for the feel of menace, he wants the corrida – the pouncing, swirling black sheen of the bulls, pierced by the picadors, bleeding 'like someone's thrown paint at them'.

Year of the King is a twelve-month journal, August to August, from the author's casting as Richard III to the opening night; a diary, but with the tone of an epistolary novel: meditative notes about the character's taking shape, jotted from day to day, mailed by Sher to himself. The plot, how to find and portray Richard, the process of a performance, is the progress of an obsession. The search infected the actor's life; a combination of chanced-upon inspiration and purposeful study, of the random (a gargoyle flying off York Minster in a storm) and the researched (reading a medical text about hunchbacks) – Richard is the dyer's hand: Sher's nature was subdued to what it worked in.

Year of the King is sure that the character *exists*, and the actor is bound to capture it, for the rose, as Ezra Pound would say, is in the steel dust – informing on the whereabouts of a magnet; or like a sculptor, who releases the statue already latent in the marble. 'Richard III is in here somewhere,' says Sher of the Lion's Head Mountain, an extinct volcano in South Africa. The crag, lit by the sun from different angles, different heights, fascinates him; he draws its planes and crevices, rumps and curves; the feminine cracks and masculine hardness; its wrinkled, plated, humped transformations. A geomorphological mummer. Sher sketches his way, doodling his ideas down. The first thoughts are for a Richard of laden disguise, an accumulation of make-up and disfigurement, like Charles Laughton in *The Hunchback of Notre Dame*, with 'collapsed pudding features'. Sher's drawing is of a monster Humpty Dumpty; a second attempt makes Richard an alloy of the heavy Quasimodo, a harelip from Coetzee's *Life and Times of Michael K*, Klaus Kinski's mad eye from *Fitzcarraldo*, a hint of Brando's Don, and the creases and folds of that Lion's Head Mountain, Johannesburg. Quite a cocktail.

Richard was first suggested when Trevor Nunn made himself manifest beside Sher's table at Joe Allen's restaurant. 'He smiles politely, a touch of enigma.' Throughout *Year of the King*, the management of the Royal Shakespeare Company is portrayed as loftily enigmatic; a group of Olympian directors conducting mystifying planning meetings, toying with the destinies of the actors; and such aloof power becomes useful for Richard, who diverts himself by keeping Hastings and Buckingham in partial ignorance of his will. Terry Hands, for instance, 'smiling slightly and knowingly from hooded eyes' – serene, a touch cold, capable of a deadly glance: 'It's rumoured that politics was his second choice of career.'

Politics is power. Neil Kinnock comes to see *Maydays* and then goes backstage to meet the cast. His instant charm makes everybody suspicious. 'You can't want to lead any party,' an actor remarks later, 'without desiring power, which actually makes you unsuitable for the job.' A flaw is required for the ambition, paradoxically, to succeed. 'Richard III?' murmers Sher to himself, his mind coiling to the character. And he's no mean politician himself. He tries to act a slackening of enthusiasm about doing a Stratford season – a season intended for 'the next generation of leading Shakespearean players' – so as to tempt improved offers of parts.

Lunching with Ron Daniels (the two of them reminisce about being raised by servants), Sher is a shrewd negotiator. He will not allow *ifs* and *promises* to blind him to realities and hard bargains.

Generating the character meant Sher metamorphosed into a specialized antenna, detecting Richard everywhere. Concurrently, the Denis Nilsen case was in the news: the vapid clerk who parboiled severed human heads at home on his range. 'The sick, black humour seems to have a flavour of *Richard III*.' Sher tries to draw Nilsen: to try and draw from that ordinary face its capacity for extraordinary deeds. He's also fascinated by Peter Sutcliffe, the 'Yorkshire Ripper', and those evil mobsters, the Krays. And, at least initially, he wants his Richard to have an extraordinary shape ('Perhaps a whole false body could be built, not just the hump') and his plan is to connect personality with deformity; a warped mind with a warped body.

How, the question arises, may deformity be acted convincingly and practically? The answer was to use the crutches, relics of the *King Lear* accident. Crutches, to an habitual invalid, are extensions of his body, advantages rather than impediments – dangerous prongs. Thinking about disability, Sher finds that 'I keep crossing paths with the disabled'. A man with a palsied leg, like a fibrous stalk, at the City Gym; a limper flailing in the street; the landlord of a Moreton-in-Marsh pub having a scoliotic spine (a side hump). Purposeful field trips are made to the Central Middlesex Works Centre and to King Edward's School, Hampstead. These venues are intensively Felliniesque: the blind, the mentally ill, the physically handicapped, the drooling and the mewling, all busy playing games and sports, a carnival of cripples, rooms of cheery hideosities.

At the Marylebone Medical Library, Sher studies 'many useful photographs' of kyphotic (central hump) and scoliotic spines. He also watches a television documentary about polio victims. The designer of *Richard III*, Bill Dudley, wants the actor to sport a naked twisted back in the coronation scene; the beast next to the beauty of Lady Anne. So Chris Tucker, a special-effects expert who constructed John Merrick's deformities for John Hurt in *The Elephant Man*, who made the vulpine heads in *The Company of Wolves*, and who moulded Derek Jacobi's Cyrano de Bergerac nose, was commissioned to make a model that would be strapped to Sher's back. Sher wanted a central hump; Tucker makes a side hump (overriding the actor's orthopaedic research) which is too small to be visible much further away than the central Stratford stalls. To save what could have been a catastrophe, padding is thrust into the costume. Richard's chest and shoulders bulk out, his legs get made to look spindly with black tights – and long tapering sleeves, plus the crutches, get the King insectile: a 'bottled spider', with the strength of an ape.

Animals and creepy-crawlies lurk in the foliage of *Richard III*. The king is a boar, hedgehog, toad, dog, 'any . . . envenomed thing that lives!' Sher thinks about the great white shark in *Jaws*, the murderousness of a fox in a chicken coop, lions dozing ('great strength resting'), death in the afternoon at a bullfight, a dove crushed by a tyre – animals killing or being killed. He is anxious, for all Richard's ugliness, to be true to nature red in tooth and claw – the unnatural brutality of nature: Richard's 'inner ugliness'. Beneath the physical shape, there's warped mental space – of a Nilsen, of a Sutcliffe – which Sher finds everywhere in abundance: the macabre comedy of the electric chair, for example, where the eyeballs of the executed explode and the brain boils; or the politics of South Africa: 'I gotta think of me first,' a coloured manager tells the actor, 'get me sorted out first then I can start worrying about my neighbours'; or the plumage of Nazis and dictators, Goebbels and Mussolini; or the fierce resentment and bad fortune of PC Olds; or, on a possibly lighter note, the menacing pauses with which a distinguished playwright ventilates his conversation.

Inspirational cramming accrued; inquiry proceeded apace. Sher drew his own face changing into Richard's: 'I cannot perform with a face less good than I myself have sketched.' He scribbles his own image from mirrors – like Rembrandt – portraits of the artist as a questing beast; the artist his own intimate subject-matter. And this is where, after all the research, Richard's appearance was to be located. Sher remembers a conversation with David Hare, about artists copying and plundering reality – and how friends and strangers can be offended by this, and how actors then feel guilty. 'We all feel that,' responded the co-author of *Pravda*, 'and yet we take what we need.' As a consequence, Sher resolved to look and listen and to store information 'with a new unsentimental vigour and ruthlessness' – like Richard, single-minded.

As opening night approached, Sher began to concentrate on the text rather than on what the text, syncopatedly, suggested to his imagination. 'Must trust language more,' he advises himself – because his instructive priority is visual; how a play will look, not sound. Shakespeare's Richard grows congenial ('He *is* funny') because he is congenital; he is Sher's shadow: 'We have agreed to use my own face. Richard is coming up from within now, not painted on top . . . The monster to strike pity and terror has gone; the new man has become funny and even a bit sexy.' The phantom of the opera replaced with Raoul.

In *Year of the King*, Sher is candid about his ambitiousness and arrogance ('I've discovered I have something in common with Richard; neither of us can afford to indulge in self-doubt or fear'); but despite the advocations, at the end of the book, at the end of rehearsals, that *Richard III* would be a journey into hyper-reality ('Richard . . . looks and sounds very much like me. I'm rather pleased'), Sher remains a pictorial actor and an actorial painter, holding a pose in his voluptuous parts – he demonstrates 'the mysterious, secretive, orphic nature of the theatre', which is how Giulio Carlo Argan described the work of Henry Fuseli. Sher, in fact, his stage people creatures of gingered chiaroscuro, his art and acting meaning to scintillate, is a modern Fuseli.

Johann Heinrich Füssli was born in February 1741, and translated himself into John Henry when he moved from Zürich to London in 1779: a writer, a painter, a scholar of Winckelmann (he adapted his treatise about muscle-bound antiquity, *Reflections on the Painting and Sculptures of the Greeks*), his best-known work is *The Nightmare* (1781). A woman, clad in silks, is collapsed across an ottoman; a malevolent smirking gnome squats on her stomach – like a monstrous external foetus, or a monstrous rapist, or a monstrous ape (or a dwarfish King Kong); and the pop-eyed head of a stallion lunges through the curtains beyond the couch. What it adds up to is an oil portrait of rapture.

Curtains, fabrics, drapes, are big in Fuseli's pictures, making for the swathes and festoons of the stage. Silks, velvets, golden tassels, set in a shimmering murk – 'a sort of vivid green,' said Leigh Hunt, 'like brass diseased.' An atmosphere apt for the diableries. Fuseli depicts the underworld of his subject's drama – so that in *The Nightmare*, horse and hellhound are emanations of the woman's fantasy; an imagination of horror which is queasily sensual, evilly erotic. (Visiting a gaol, during his intensive research for *Richard III*, Sher fell into a discussion with the inmates about the attractions of wickedness. 'Evil,' said a prisoner, 'is erotic.')

Fuseli's theatricality is his fondness for weird display: the theatre as public arena of private emotion. (Freud had a print of *The Nightmare* in his consulting rooms.) And Fuseli's theatricality is also his representation of actual theatre. *Richard III Visited by Ghosts* (1777) is the picture Sher's monarch might have stepped from; it more than illustrates Shakespeare, it illuminates him.★ Shakespeare provides the script; Fuseli, like an actor, performs it. The pen and ink wash delineates memory and conscience; Richard's nightmare before Bosworth, when he's encircled by apparitions of his victims:

> Let us be lead within thy bosom, Richard,
> And weigh thee down to ruin, shame and death!

★ I derive my ideas here from Maurice Sendak's comments on Randolph Caldecott and illustration: 'Words taking on unobvious meanings, colors and dramatic qualities. He *reads* into things, and this, of course, is what the illustrator's job is really about – to interpret the text much as a musical conductor interprets a score'. Sendak also says, later on: 'Fuseli *does* create bizarre images, but he knew what he was doing' (*Victorian Color Picture Books*, edited by Jonathan Cott, 1984).

Fuseli has a procession of cowled figures emerging from the floor, or a trap, and making their exit through a flap in the tent – or through a half-pulled pair of curtains. The bivouac is a set.

Richard is not tormented; nor is he a bunch-backed toad. He is a lithe, reclining anatomical model, with his sinews and brawn exposed; he sprawls in pride; he does not squirm in fear. So less, then, Act V, scene iii, lines 152–153, (above), than the soliloquy following the ghosts's vanishing, lines 183–187

> Richard loves Richard; that is, I am I.
> Is there a murderer here? No; – yes; I am:
> Then fly. What, from myself?
> Alack, I love myself.

This is Sher's Richard: the solipsist who is a narcissist, fascinated by his own skill at plots and deadly gambits; and Fuseli's Richard is one who upon lines 152–153 superimposes lines 183–187 – so that the latter is what the king thinks whilst the spooks speak the former.

Richard III Visited by Ghosts a picture of thought? Compare the picture with *Garrick as Richard III* (1746) by Hogarth. Here we have the same scene – Richard's nightmare – but the artist declines to make his work a commentary; it is a representation. Garrick is elaborately costumed in ermine and ruff, and elaborately startled – holding out an upspread palm. The tent is grandiose with gold braid, scattered armour, a discarded letter and, in the shadow, a portrait of Christ crucified – which all imply the reverse of Fuseli: here Richard is panic-stricken, clinging to ritual and religion. Fuseli draws Richard's dream-vision of himself; he draws the slumbering subtext of the play – which says that Richard in Richard's own mind's-eye is beautiful. He fantasizes away deformity. *His* dream-vision, but a nightmare for the other characters.★

Acting Richard as Fuseli sketched him, Sher played a lissom athlete. The crutches were useful improvements on the body – as though the body, animal but buddingly metallurgical, was metamorphosing into an invincible machine, a marriage of flesh and iron. A thorny, prickly, yet paradoxically streamlined cybernant, unnatural nature, the king was a one-man species evolved to endure, to survive, like hawk with his claw, a murderous trigger, in Ted Hughes's poem 'Hawk Roosting':

★ Like Sher, Garrick had a pictorial imagination. In *An Essay on Acting* (1744), he talks of positioning his body and face exactly; he's concerned with posture and pose – like an artist's model. Of putting together a villain, 'it finishes the compleatest low picture of grotesque terror than can be imagined by a Dutch painter'; and of his Macbeth – 'a moving statue, or indeed a petrify'd man.'

It took the whole of Creation
To produce my foot, my each feather:
Now I hold Creation in my foot . . .

The foot, the crutches: hawk and Sher's Richard have had Darwin's
science make them eldrich windhovers; angels of darkness.

Richard III permitted the apotheosis of Sher's acting style – his stage
people's gymnastics, camouflage and solipsism. Tartuffe got the house to
himself; Richard intended having Plantagenet England to himself. He
murders those who trespass onto William Dudley's white cathedral set – a
perpendicular limestone stadium; he's a cacodemon, wanting to be alone
in the crypt:

Clarence hath not another day to live;
Which done, God take King Edward to his mercy.
And leave the world for me to bustle in!

And leave the world for him to bustle in: 'I kill where I please,' says
Hawk, 'because it is all mine.' Richard effected the removal of Brian
Blessed's Long-John-Silver Hastings; Malcolm Storry's shaggy blond
Buckingham; the wee princes (who fatally bantered with their uncle,
getting him to cavort as Don Corleone cavorts in the vine plot as a
gorilla); Penny Downie's Lady Anne, surrounded by slayings and slowly
swaying with poison; Edward IV, played by Harold Innocent as a gouty
old hen; Roger Allam's scholarly Clarence; and assorted other of his
cousins and his sisters and his aunts, plus their retinues.

The note of Bill Alexander's production was gargoyle and devil-ridden
religiosity. Housing Richard in a sepulchre emphasized his petulant
hypocrisy – for he even refers to killing as his 'holy work'. He's a madder
Tartuffe. To be the only man in the house, you evict; to be the last man in
the world, you essay genocide. The tombs, apse and nave for knavery
served to highlight references to God, to superstition, to the heavens – an
apparently deserted and echoing vault. There was a great deal of oath-
making, fumbling with rosaries and spilling of incense. *Tartuffe* (also
directed by Bill Alexander) commenced with a long Latin incantation;
there was even a silver altar in the dining room. *Richard III*, for actor and
director, was massively dilated Molière.

Sher's Richard leapt from the sarcophagus, making aeronautical feats;
he raced from upstage to downstage; he rubbed the crutches like mand-
ibles, he used them as spears, pistons, even as a double-barrelled shoot-
ing-stick. Lambent in black tunics and head-dresses with fluffy plumes,
like flaps of skin or hide residue, pouring with sweat, it was a bravura
performance, no question. But how did it square with *Year of the King*, the
actor's manifesto?

The first divergence concerned cripples. Examination in the field and in libraries showed that the disabled move tentatively, with exasperating slowness. Sher's Richard, a peppy paraplegic, ignored this. He moved fast. He was agile.

Secondly, the intention had been to bypass easy black comedy and act Richard's wit as coming from a sense of hurt; to find his rage in his self-pity. Sher's Richard, however, gagged, rolled his eyes, lolled his tongue, hopped, skipped, winked.

So Sher succumbed, majestically, to exaggeration – but that's consistently his manner. His acting is a chemical reaction of diligent solus preparation and the fact of theatre – that it's a place for inversion, invention, surprise, wonder-working, conjury. From Howard Kirk to Richard, from Enoch Powell in *Tarzan's Last Stand* to Arnold in *Torch Song Trilogy*, Sher has laboured towards a lively inflation – detectable also in his drawings which, like Fuseli's, break out as caricature. The drawing of Molière, for example, from Bulgakov's play, shows a frizzy-haired actor-author who resembles prints of Shakespeare, but who is really a portrait of Sher in the role. Or the sketches of Tartuffe – monkish, with a pert arse, which was indeed flashed liberally in performance. Fuseli ogled musculature; Sher often delineates his bottom – as in Sher-as-Richard-in-Australia, where a salivating set of fangs belonging to an angry sea-lion is about to sink into the fleeing, quivering globe. The cover for *Year of the King* is a nightmarish oil, with Richard's long face, crowned, slumped beneath the undulating shoulders. The bracelets of the crutches gleam; the crown gleams – the rest is heavy shadow and sickly ochre. Though, like the Bulgakov Molière, a portrait of the artist-as-actor, the effect is of a transfigured portrait: acting seems absent. It *is* Molière; it *is* Richard. Only the crazy subject-matter (a hump-backed king? A false-nosed, pancake Molière?) alerts us to performance, to theatricality.

His drawings, then, inclining to cartoonery, his acting grasping an arch kind of fine art, Sher's hyperbole needs to be distinguished from camp – which it may appear to court – yet which is hyperbolic in a different way.* His performances are gleeful, but free from camp's deep frivolity, its studied, self-regarding imposture. Sher's is an intense merriment; his excesses are somehow contained – earnests of passion where camp, by contrast, means a dawdling evasion of passion in favour of caprice. Sher's rants imply no parody – and camp is itself a brand of parody, where content (the actor) detaches itself from form (the role; the play), to fill the fissure thus opened up with gestures signalling to the audience a mood of relentless, though languid, insouciance. With camp, the medium is a massage, a titivation; with Sher, the medium is a provocation. Sher, contrary to camp, is frantically sincere – hence the paradox of this actor.

* For a lengthier discussion of camp see chapter 8; also Susan Sontag's essay in *Against Interpretation* (1966).

He forces us to witness the errant unreality of his characters; we appreciate the truth of, and are happy with, cartoons; we see the sensibility of surface or showy acting. And because of all these qualifications, Sher gets away with what would otherwise be blatant over-acting.

Crowned with *Drama* magazine's Best Actor Award, the *City Limits* Best Stage Actor Award, the *London Standard* Best Stage Actor Award and the Laurence Olivier Best Actor Award, Sher, in 1986, took *Richard III* on a lap of honour to Australia – as Laurence Olivier had taken his own production of *Richard III* (plus Sheridan's *The School for Scandal* and Thornton Wilder's *The Skin of Our Teeth*) to Australia and New Zealand in 1948, when Sher himself was still a babe lisping words.

Sher's tour began triumphantly in Adelaide, contended with Barry Humphries in Melbourne, and ended with the star deeply bored by Brisbane. A drizzle of folk in the auditorium; the Australians either tediously respectful of culture or, in conversation, xenophobically colonial. 'Can this really be the same show that had people queuing overnight at the Barbican?' the actor wrote in *The Times*. Sher also contributed to the newspaper three drawings of Richard on holiday in the Antipodes: Richard and that sea-lion; Richard, unshaven, working at an easel, his model Dame Edna Everage – she's like a Rubens sketch of Marie dè Medici, flaunting a gladiolus; Richard on the beach, a paperback and bottle of suntan lotion beside his towel, his crutches sticking from the sand like crutches in Salvador Dalí – the king, wearing Sher's tinted specs, peers at the surf; a film crew peers at his browning hump.

In retrospect, the revival of *Richard III* was retrogressive. Sher needed to move on, not repeat – though Olivier's *Richard* recurred from September 1944 until the film of 1956; recurred, that is to say, from the year of D-Day to the year Mies van der Rohe's Seagram Building began construction in New York. But before moving on, Sher was scheduled to undergo a Platform Performance at the institution invented by Olivier, the National Theatre. A question-and-answer session with a paying pack of fans who, it was hoped, would pay later for autographed copies of *Year of the King*. 31 July 1986, the day of paperback publication.

'Come to the Platform Performance,' the actor suggested, 'and if there's anything else you want to know, find me afterwards and we can have a chat.'

Let the citizens of London catechize; I'll listen. So:

AN AUDIENCE WITH ANTONY SHER

I saw Sher sneak towards the Lyttelton bar, where the Platform Performance was preceded by Peter Hall, the fat controller, publicly thanking

British Rail for underwriting the appearance of the actor. Chubbier, chummier than I expected, Sher, abashed, stared into his mineral water, apprehensive; even, it seemed, embarrassed.

We all went into the auditorium. Sher walked on to the stage in the company of Sue MacGregor, quondam the hostess on BBC-Radio 4's gynaeceum, *Woman's Hour*.

'Tony Sher acts well enough to win many awards,' she told us. 'Now, Richard III seemed physically very demanding . . . ?'

'Yes,' replied Sher, his olive tan and scrabbity beard offset with a powder-blue suit, white shirt, no tie. 'Yes, the part is famous for crippling the actors who play it. You can do yourself some serious damage. I broke my tendon in *King Lear*. Acting is a physical and dangerous business. I've had personal experience of disability – and so I could use it for Richard, my experience of disablement. So it could be said, owing to the notoriety of the production's crutches, that my own disaster turned out rather well.'

'I like your sketches, Mr Sher,' said an old lady with clicking pearls, 'Especially your Dame Edna in *The Times*, which I thought was absolutely marvellous. Do you get inspiration from your sketches?'

'Drawing helps me to capture a character, it's true. The bottled spider in the play, mentioned by Queen Margaret, was very suggestive. I tried to sketch and doodle a response to that.'

('Why strew'st thou sugar on that bottled spider . . .' Queen Margaret also calls Richard, amongst other animals, an 'elvish-mark'd, abortive, rooting hog'.)

'I heard you'd cut Queen Margaret for Australia?'

By now, the audience was hoping to interrogate freely. Confident public speakers, these Londoners. Sue MacGregor, in a black dress streaked with tinsel, a Christmas tree in mourning, apt for a production of *Richard III* directed by Noël Coward, had a hard time chairing the inquisitive. 'You. Not you! You! You!' she pointed. 'You in the red jersey. Yes, madam?' And, at one frightful juncture, 'Sorry. Yes, *Sir*?'

'Actually,' responded Sher, 'it was the director's decision, not mine, about old Queen Margaret. Though I'm not against altering Shakespeare. We alter other writers to accommodate original interpretations. Olivier cut Queen Margaret out of his film. She belongs to the *Henry VI* cycle of plays – and she is a problem to audiences who don't know those plays. Anyway,' Sher added, covering up a fumbling implication that Australians are ignorant of the *Henry VI* cycle's existence, their most tremendous import since the Spanish merino being *Cats*, which had lately opened in Sydney's sole theatre – 'Anyway, Pat Routledge was unavailable.'

Patricia Routledge, attired in a smock tailored from a Lancastrian flag, was Sher's equal, in the original production, in bravura; a cackling pre-incarnation of an Alan Bennett harpy. Her removal, or absence, weakened the play, flattening its perspectives, which should recede to Henry V's death after Agincourt, and proceed to herald the grandchild, Gloriana herself.

'Our *Richard III*,' said Sher, 'was a black comedy-thriller. We lost Richard's most formidable opponent, when Queen Margaret went; but the play, I think, was faster and brisker without her.'

(More like a cartoon.)

'You don't mind cutting?'

'I'm not a purist. It's good and healthy to fiddle around with Shakespeare and make him more accessible; more accessible to a modern audience. I'm partial to experimentation, and the plays can take it.'

'Your crutches, Mr Sher?' Inevitably.

'I really was convinced they were my absolutely original contribution to acting the part. Then I discovered that when, in the 1940s, Olivier was on tour with *Richard III*, he sprained his ankle, and played some performances on crutches! So the bugger even did that first!'

The tour was the British Council expedition to Australia. Vivien Leigh was Lady Anne. Olivier already had gout, and tapped his way through Sir Peter Teazle's part with a walking stick; at a matinée of *Richard III* in Sydney, he damaged his right knee cartilage in the fight with Richmond. A crutch was located, writes Garry O'Connor, chronicler of the trip (and the man Ralph Richardson wanted to murder), which Olivier 'put to brilliant use, integrating it into his performance just as if Shakespeare had written the part for an actor using a crutch . . .' The crutch 'revitalized' Richard for Olivier; newspapers ran cartoons of the actor, as the king, with his new prop. The crutch was the talk of the town.

Sher's calling Olivier a bugger earned a big laugh, and not only because it was a cheeky expletive to level in the baron's direction. Rather, the comic exasperation betrayed a rich underworld of feeling: the concealed theme of *Year of the King*, which makes the book more than a rehearsal diary for *Richard III*: it makes it an embodiment of the meaning of *Richard III*. The struggle for power; Gloucester versus Richmond, the hero from across the sea. Further back, the struggle gets mythological: Oedipus versus Laius. Sons against fathers; sons striking the father dead. Sher's Oedipal battle with Olivier transmutes parricide to regicide: the younger actor wanting to become pre-eminent, and Olivier outwitting the attempt.

That's what *Year of the King* is about: warring in the interstices of a diary against heaven's matchless king ('fuck off snapping tendons and Laurence Olivier'). Searching for his own interpretation, Sher implies that all other Richards have failed. Ian Holm's squat gnome (like the Fuseli incubus),

Ian Richardson's warped dandy (an afflicted Edinburgh boulevardier), Alan Howard's claudicated leather-boy, Norman Rodway's tusky brute, John Wood's walnut-shell Moriarty: none have eclipsed the clipped, mannered vocal delivery and ostentatious limp of Olivier's Richard, that prompter of impersonations: a Peter Sellers Richard; Crookback is the staple of every third-rate mimic. Sher does not want to be a clone of this creature – whom both Peter Postlethwaite and Mike Gambon ape when they hear their colleague has been cast in the play. 'Has Olivier done the part definitively? Surely not . . . The trouble is, Olivier put it *on film.*'

It is precisely an Oedipal moment when, at the gala opening of the Barbican in March 1982, Sher jostled with a white-haired elder; the knock was 'as soft and cushioned', recalls the actor who was Kirk the history man, 'as befits a collision with Destiny.' Startled, the white-haired elder, his demeanour that of the old Harold in Kipling's 'The Tree of Justice', turns upon his clumsy assailant and mutters, 'Are you trying to kill me?' Laurence Olivier, of course. He was steered to safety by Joan Plowright, whom Sher recognized before he identified her husband. *Rex cedidit Laium, rex cecidit regem.*★ 'I had just brushed shoulders with Richard III.'

Throughout his preparations for the role, Sher's good ideas were anticipated. The crutches, a nuisance in battle: perhaps Richard could be winched on to his horse at Bosworth? But armoured hulks are levered aloft in Olivier's *Henry V* ('The unmentionable'). Bill Dudley's cathedral set: perhaps Richard could appear to fly by swinging on a bell-rope? But Olivier did that ('I drop the idea like a hot brick and will never bring it up again').

If Olivier obsesses as much as Richard himself obsesses, it's because the two have conflated in Sher's imagination: 'this fully formed, famously formed, infamous child murderer leaning over the cradle'. A giant to conquer; a spectre to exorcize. Even Tartuffe becomes goblinized. The make-up box is haunted: 'he's here again: the long black wig together with my own pointed nose have turned me into a first cousin of that famous Crookback.' The light and shade staining the Stratford brick-work are haunted: 'Suddenly I spy my shadow on the wall . . . Even though we've gone for a different shape, a different costume, different hair, the crutches, twisted knees, I looked at my shadow tonight and saw Laurence Olivier in the part.'

Death seems to have no dominion over an interpretation forty years old. Olivier obtrudes into Sher's life, leaving call-cards. Journeying to Chris Tucker's laboratory, to have his back cast in wax, Sher espies a shelf of plaster heads – like hunting trophies. They're heads of Olivier, cast at different ages, before and after different illnesses. The junior actor makes

★ A King slew Laius, a King slew the King.

towards a blanched and disembodied relic of the senior actor: 'I instinctively reach out for it,' recalls Sher, '. . . strange to hold this face in my
hands. The expression rather grim . . . You can't help thinking of a death
mask.' A charged moment; a symbolic confrontation, almost religious;
Hamlet and the skull. And, as intensification of the laboratory's spookiness, Tucker makes the scoliotic spine, though a kyphotic spine was
ordered. Olivier's Richard was scoliotic.

But it's in Sher's own drawings that Olivier's famous performance
looms, menacing and in-waiting, a once and future king. If on a winter's
night he attempts a self-portrait, the sketch edges into being somebody
else: Sher's long face, long nose, black frizzy hair and thinnish lips
become alien – 'the lips I have drawn are not my own, but Olivier's.' A
scribbly, unfinished eye looks sinister and glaucous. Returning from a
dinner, where Olivier's thraldom over Kenneth Branagh's Henry V was
mentioned, Sher takes up his drawing. 'The lips,' he is now convinced,
'don't look even remotely like Laurence Olivier's.' As in M. R. James's
The Mezzotint, the content of the picture appears to alter of its own accord
and tell its own story.

The thin sneer dominates in a drawing Sher makes of a nightmare. He
dreamt of 'Olivier's face in extreme close-up . . . Circling the giant.
Closer and closer it comes . . .' The picture is of that wicked eye, the ski-
slope nose and the lank wig: Olivier the Big Bad Wolf. Sher himself is in
the drawing, a wee figurine, hands clutching its crotch, a tiny nude
Pinocchio (Collodi's boy desperate to have no strings to hold him down)
– or, more tellingly, the waif springing from Sher's haunted crayons,
casting a disproportionate and substantial shadow, is the Boy Oedipus,
maker of the bad dreams which endanger Sher's self-confidence ('Olivier's interpretation is definitive'); and yet which also galvanize resolve.
For what Olivier's Richard represents is an eminence. He's the personality to obliterate if Sher shall shine as *the* late twentieth-century actor.
When he won the Laurence Olivier Award in 1985, Laurence Olivier
presided, silently, invisibly, from a darkened private box, absent in
presence, like the hologram in *Time*. Sher waved the statuette towards
where the old man presumably sat, and thanked the judges for an award
to both a King (*Richard III*) and a queen (*Torch Song Trilogy*). That's one
monarch more than Olivier managed in a season. After the Barbican
collision, this was the second direct confrontation. And they faced each
other a third time at *Happy Birthday, Sir Larry*, a revue organized by John
Mortimer, in which great actors through the ages strutted, to culminate
in Olivier. Ben Kingsley was Edmund Kean doing Richard III; Sher was
Henry Irving doing *The Bells* – acting over-acting. From his seat, the
baron smiled wanly down.

Yet it is in Sher's contribution to *Olivier in Celebration*, an essay-
collection for the eightieth birthday, published in 1987, that Oedipus can

most teasingly be detected challenging Laius – and, to be true to the myth, Oedipus must perform his action entirely unawares; by which is meant, he must be unaware of its significance.

Sher provided the painting for the cover. Olivier, in all his famous guises, forms a frantic collage (drawn in the main from Angus McBean stills); a multiplication of Oliviers; a storm-cloud of Oliviers, with which Sher must contend, like aversion therapy. As in Goya's *El sueño de la razon produce monstruos*★ (1796–8), where bats flap from a man's brain, these Oliviers bustle from, and have been arranged by, Sher's imagination.

The actor bursts from the frame. Swooping Hamlet's forearms, the upturned torso of falling Coriolanus, Othello's thumb, the brim of Clifford Mortimer's hat, Baron Brighton's nose, Olivier's own Oedipus's bloodied hand – all these bits of body or costume press, nudge, bulge beyond their official contour: art cracking its way into life.

What story does the picture tell?

At the centre Sher has placed Archie Rice, raffish and past it, from Osborne's *The Entertainer*. The seedy vaudevillian who has hung around too long. Done over in blue, with ruddy cheeks, gap-toothed Archie is a waxwork, or corpse. Leering over his shoulder, his evil eye on the reader, is Richard III. Charcoal black, with mouse-thin legs, heavy shoulders, nose like the prong of an isosceles triangle, Richard *stalks* Archie, and his sword pierces the back of cadaverous Clifford Mortimer's neck. He also steps on dying Hotspur.

Hamlet, his skinny legs in black tights the equal of Richard's, flies like Peter Pan from the curly pampas of Othello's hair; James Tyrone, from O'Neill's *Long Day's Journey into Night*, hands him a ball, or catches from him a globe. Tyrone balances on Richard's shoulder. Lear, a snarling Ben Gunn, pops his head under Hamlet's oxter, his scowl on the prince.

Henry V, both rosy and blank, evinces the higher doltishness of the patriot. Olivier's film (1944) was a contribution to the war effort and quite overlooked the king's hypocrisy. Here, he's mocked by the askance eye of Mr. Puff – Mr. Puff from *The Critic*; Sheridan's play constituted half of the double bill with *Oedipus Rex*.

Olivier's Oedipus nearly, but not quite, joins his pallid hand with the outspread palm of Othello, who pads like a panther with drooping eyelids. Edgar, from Strindberg's *The Dance of Death*, is about to strut and kick his way towards Oedipus, and he does manage to prick the heel of the Moor with the tip of his boot.

From between Archie Rice's legs, Shylock glides – the nineteenth-century usurer, with rounded gob and clerk's pince-nez; a humourless gentleman merchant, Strindberg's Edgar's grimace aimed in his direction.

★ The Sleep of Reason produces Monsters,' (*Capricho* 43)

Also about the picture, partially obscured heads, are Romeo (a white skull cap to match Shylock's black one); big browed Maxim de Winter ('That's not the northern lights! That's Manderley!'); a kiss-curl Macbeth and, rising from the bottom, like Jaws from the deep, Dr Szell, the wicked fang-bandit from *Marathon Man*.

The cover celebrates Olivier, but arraigns him. The figures, from Archie Rice's stick nearing Othello's eye, to Hamlet diving sword in hand, hinder, gird and cunningly defame each other: not a harmonious family group but a pack of solipsists – apt for Sher, who in this picture *performs* Olivier as Fuseli *performed* Shakespeare. 'I wanted to draw Olivier from life,' he told me, 'but the family absolutely forbade it. So I worked on the images he's most famous for.' The picture is Sher's ingestion of Olivier; he has converted Olivier into a gathering of icons – which is itself a cryptograph, a sphinx's riddle. Unriddled, it means that Sher has articulated a fantasy, where Olivier's creations kill themselves off; and so, for the time being, Sher has won. *Sphynga solvi carmen*.

Meantime, back at the Lyttelton, a student with wireframe spectacles and a collarless shirt was asking whether the Australians appreciated *Richard III*.

'Audience reaction,' explained Sher, 'changed alarmingly from state to state. It was as if we were playing in entirely different nations. Brisbane was appalling. Shakespeare's just a boring pom in Queensland! And we couldn't get to Sydney, the obvious city, because the only suitable theatre housed *Cats*. It'll probably be housing *Cats* for the next hundred years . . . !'

'Hello. Mr Sher . . .' This from a man in a green tweed jacket with elbow patches.

'Hello.'

'You have a question?' asked Sue MacGregor.

'Yes. D'you think Shakespeare should be taught in schools? I wondered what you'd think about this?'

'If he can be made interesting, sure. But he next-to-never is. Shakespeare's taught very badly, and audiences are far too respectable and respectful. He's almost a national liability!'

Sue MacGregor steered the discussion elsewhere; she asked about the Arab in Mike Leigh's *Goose-Pimples*, a comedy about the fleecing of a supposed potentate. Sher had ninety-two lines, all of them in Arabic. 'Wallah hadhola fitna. Fi kill mukan. Sufal Yemen wal' Araq u Eran.' (By Allah. They are a nuisance. Everywhere. Look at Yemen and Iraq and Iran.) Sher researched Mohammed, his character, with characteristic scrupulousness. He loitered in Park Lane hotels, listening hard to the yapping sheiks, ordering their drinks, ordering their wives about, advertising their Cartier watches and snakeskin shoes, which slid from under flapping robes.

So convincing was Sher's impersonation, he once hoodwinked a cab driver into thinking him the real thing. The cab driver intended to take his passenger's money and run. 'Let's take him to the West End and dump him . . .', Sher's more obviously white consort was told.

Mohammed didn't speak English; the other characters, Vernon, Jackie, Irving and Frankie, didn't speak Arabic. Sher's character could thus chatter away oblivious (a chirpy linguistic solipsist) and, transformed into the foreigner, his was a compact portrayal of cross-purpose, misunderstanding and blithe racial superiority.

'With Mike Leigh,' said Sher, 'there's a long incubation period for the play. He works for several weeks with each actor in isolation, improvising. I was quite alone with the director. Then, gradually we were brought together, the actors with their parts.'

Goose-Pimples, which opened in 1981, involved Jim Broadbent, Marion Bailey, Paul Jesson and Jill Baker.

'Then gradually, the story evolves. The play itself evolves. Sometimes it doesn't. Mike Leigh has had to abandon several projects. But, anyway, after the improvising, there is a normal period of rehearsal, as for any other kind of play. There's now a script. In performance, there's no improvisation – none at all. People don't really realize this. They don't realize the script has been fixed, and that improvisation only belonged to early rehearsal.'

(But that's successful acting: when the rehearsed and preordained appear improvisatory night after night.)

'Regarding *Goose-Pimples*, Mohammed was controversial. Arabs don't like any portrayal of themselves that's not heroic.'

A member of the audience picked up a theme of heroes and antiheroes. 'In *The History Man*, in the book, Kirk is laughable; he's ridiculed, *then* he becomes evil. *Your* portrayal was of a man nasty from the start . . .'

(A good point: how to act Bradbury's irony?)

'I thought,' replied Sher, bridling a trace, 'that the television version was a very faithful adaptation. Christopher Hampton left whole chunks of Bradbury's dialogue intact, actually. But Howard and Barbara's background was left out. On television we didn't see how the character formed; his early years. We didn't do those flashbacks. He was already formed as a monster – if it's a monster you reckon he was!'

'Another question?' said Sue brightly.

'Your make-up for Arnold in *Torch Song Trilogy* was superb. Did you practise at home?'

'Well, thank you! I do think, yes, that my drawing and painting helped me to do the make-up. But I didn't doll myself up in the privacy of my own home, if that's what you mean! I always enjoyed those hours in the show, where Arnold gets ready. I enjoyed that immensely. Lots of white on the face to hide the stubble, then the foundation . . . A little tip . . . for any would-be transvestites here this evening!'

(There was a titter at that.)

'*Mr Sher*,' boomed a man near to me in a Fair Isle jumper and with lenses thick enough to halt a bullet. '*Mr Sher!* I am very sorry that nobody has yet mentioned your life-enhancing performance in *Red Noses* . . .'

Down he sat, nodding to his wife for support, like a villager at a temperamental hustings. He'd worked himself up; now he was spent. There was even a jerk of clapping for his sentiment.

'*Red Noses*,' Sue MacGregor said, shuffling her cards, '*Red Noses*, Tony? By Peter Barnes, was it?'

'Yes. Peter Barnes,' assisted Sher.

'*Red Noses* was about a clown who entertained people whilst they were dying from the plague . . .'

'Dying from the plague, yes. I responded to the play, rather than to my part. A terrific play, written in a language conveying disease and rancid pestilence. Wonderful! I enjoyed doing it, but it was not enormously stretching.'

Sher had avoided a troubling implication. The sell-out success of *Richard III* and *Tartuffe* implied the public's enjoyment of the actor's enjoyment of acting. *Red Noses* was produced as another window box for Sher to cavort in. But the play did bad business – implying that Sher alone could not yet quite fill a theatre. Real stardom abhors a vacuum and works alchemy on unpromising material. Michael J. Fox and *Teen Wolf*, for example, or the Dirty Harry pictures of Clint Eastwood, or, on the stage, anything with Maggie Smith in it.

'Simon Callow,' said a girl from the stalls I couldn't see, mercifully changing the subject, 'has cited you as an actor who uses make-up to the best advantage.'

So the issue of make-up had arisen again. Hardly surprising, for Sher's fame rests on his ability to metamorphose – though like Orson Welles, and unlike Alec Guinness, he doesn't hide himself with disguise: he's more evidently the monstrous presence. He'd do the police in different disguises. Vulpine Kirk; crazied Stan Laurel (*King Lear*); flower-power Tartuffe; wild-eyed Molière (smeared with white paint and wearing a clown's nose); Martin Glass (*Maydays*), the CND Trot who evolves into a Tory gent, portrayed in a blond flaxen wig; and Richard – that opera of mannerisms and prosthesis, gnarled crutches, thick shoulders, black curls falling to a knotted trail, bulging gauntlets, Mickey Mouse legs duplicated by thin sleeves . . .

'Simon compliments me on my make-up,' said Sher neatly, 'I compliment him on his writing. Neither of us mentions the others' acting. Ringo, in *John, Paul, George, Ringo and Bert*, about the Beatles, took four hours to apply, which rather bit into the day. For Richard, I was weaned off the idea of cauliflower ears and broken noses. I'm *not* as obsessed by make-up as I once was.'

'Mr Sher! What about the hump!'

'Not that many parts are called for with a hump. So the hump must be part of what the actor is doing – for so much of Richard's problem is his hump. So I had to make it look as though the hump was something *I'd* grown – so we showed it naked in the coronation scene.'

'Have you always been able to draw?' asked a friend of the lady who admired the Dame Edna cartoon.

'Yes. It's something I've always done, since the age of about four. Drawing came naturally to me. I wanted to go to Art School – in Italy, for some reason. I think I knew there were galleries there, though I'd not have understood the teacher's language. I was a shy child. Drawing and painting are solitary pursuits.

'Then I started going to Elocution class, and I realized I needed acting more than I needed drawing. I came to England to attend drama school, and I very consciously lost my South African accent in case I got thumped. But there was no need. South Africans have never been really resented in this country.'

Luckily, South African political issues were not broached by any of the audience so far. What people wanted to know about was *Richard III*.

'Did you do any research into the real Richard?'

'Historical research into Richard III is a total dead end – because the historical Richard was nothing like Shakespeare's. To play him kindly and wise, to play him historically accurate, wouldn't make sense. There's a Richard III Society, maybe you've heard of it? Well . . . you know . . . it happened so very . . . long . . . ago. I don't understand how they get so worked up about it. I received green-ink letters, accusing me of writing the play! I thought to myself: there are a lot of very peculiar people out there in the world.'

'What did you make of Richard?'

'That, especially towards the end, he's psychologically complex – after the nightmare of the ghosts. He realizes he's never understood himself. He sees himself in a new way.'

Richard, before Bosworth, has a dawning conscience; his personality sunders into judge and accused (though Fuseli drew praiser and praised);

> Is there a murderer here? No – yes, I am.
> Then fly. What, from myself? Great reason why –
> Lest I revenge. What, myself upon myself!

Myself upon myself: ultimate solipsism. Richard is another instance of the haunting spirit and the haunted man. Jonas Chuzzlewit.

The session moved towards its climax with a series of snappy answers to preponderant questions, Sher growing aphoristic with seeming ease. It was a little like the end of an act in Meyerbeer, where the chorus barks and the principal's voice weaves its own theme amidst the clamour. When Sue piped up, it was like Selika in *L' Africaine*.

'Does undergoing psychoanalysis help you as an actor?'

'I've found it beneficial to everything. I'm a great supporter of psychotherapy. Looking at the workings of the mind and what it reveals, and all that.'

'What is success like?'

'Good reviews aren't helpful to people in a production, because they've got to stay and perform night after night, duplicating the success, maintaining the success. I don't read my own reviews, though I avidly read about other people's performances, their successes and failures.'

'Tony,' said Sue, 'you take risks as an actor. A sense of danger about what you do.'

'I don't consciously take risks. The parts I get are sometimes dangerous men, so I have to engender and portray a sense of unpredictability. If you've a good rapport with the other actors, it's possible to change things each night. This'll create a certain frisson, which the audience picks up immediately. As for a sense of danger, as you put it, that's panic! Or just the parts themselves. You mustn't confuse the actor with the parts he plays.'

'Would you ever perform in South Africa?'

'No. I wouldn't even go back there if it wasn't for my family. Equity shouldn't ban actors from going out there, though. Actors must choose for themselves.'

'What other classical parts, especially in Shakespeare, would you like to play?'

'Not saying!'

'Well, what are you going to do next?'

'I'm going to write a book. I'm taking time off acting to return to civilian life. To civilized life. I've had enough of eating at midnight.'

'Well, perhaps it's time we brought things to an end now,' said Sue, beaming. 'Tell me, Tony, you're giving up acting for a while to write. Do you ever think of giving up for good?'

'Actors think of giving up all the time. After every bad performance or every bad audience, we think, *that's it*. Acting is tough on every level – your confidence, your body. We all want to give it up.'

There was big applause while the duo made their exit. They'd been sitting before the set for a John Mills play called *The Petition*. Half a gentleman's mahogany library; half a chintzy Home-Counties lounge. Sher sat in the lounge part, Sue MacGregor in the library. 'I'd wanted,' Sher told me afterwards, 'to make a funny comment about it, but the opportunity never arose.'

Sher was next disclosed at a trestle adjacent to an exhibition of wood furniture. A long queue curled past the plywood chairs and the kindling beds. Like Anthony Hopkins's landscape in *King Lear*, the arboretum was both archaic and ultra-modern – designer rusticity. Large photo-portraits of Lord Linley presided over the sylvan discomfort.

Within the grotto, flunkeys from Sher's publisher spilled out crates of *Year of the King*. Copies were being sold as quickly as they could be signed. Briar Silich and Nick Hern, from Methuen, looked at the line of patient fans.

'This is more than we had for Arthur Miller.'

'Now, you're seeing Tony afterwards, right? Great. We can hand him over to you. When we introduce you, he'll be your responsibility.'

Introduction to the actor was being discussed as if we were master-minding the swop of contraband, the lifting of a secret document, the fencing of swag.

Sher was giving a smile and a few words to every votary, inscribing and dedicating his book for a thousand birthday presents. The queue took two solid hours to shift. Eventually the last person scurried off, and Sher was left, leaning heavily on the trestle, shining with sweat, surrounded by empty boxes and smudged wine glasses.

Anna and myself were formally made acquainted with the actor; Briar Silich and Nick Hern scarpered. It was just me, Anna, a lot of wood, and Sher. Having only ever seen Sher leaping and screaming, devising whirli-gigs of revenges or being, as Huck Finn said of kings, most a rapscallion, I was justifiably trepidatious. Even the talk show with Sue MacGregor was a poised and calculated performance; the charm ready to trigger a wither-ing retort, if necessary – which it wasn't. It was a talk show of a man who had no intention of giving intimacies away; and who had no intention of being messed about.

We decided to go and have dinner. Sher borrowed a coin and made a reservation at an Islington eatery. The proprietor evidently knew who was making the call. Sher identified himself merely as 'Tony'.

'Can I have a lift with you?' he asked on returning from the booth. A perfectly reasonable request, but that we had arrived in a yellow MG Midget. A Noddy car, hardly designed for passengers.

'Never mind. I'll get a taxi and see you there.'

'What's the address?'

'The address? God, I don't remember. I can picture it, but I don't actually know the actual name of the street.'

'We could follow your taxi,' I said, brightly.

'Not through London traffic,' said my wife, reprovingly. She is my chauffeuse.

'Are you sure I can't fit into your car?'

'Well, let's try. Why don't we take the hood down and' – this by the chauffeuse to me – 'you can perch on the boot.'

We descended to the car park, passing laughing lost patrons, and after only a short delay the Midget was found crouched between two family saloons.

'How,' said Sher, surveying, 'are three persons going to ride in that? How,' he then added, 'does one person ride in that?'

Anna and I unclipped and folded the roof in unison, like a quilt, rolling the perspex windows and dissassembling the metal frame.

'I still don't see where we're going to fit,' commented Sher.

To ride shotgun, I clambered up with my bag. But there was no room for my legs, plus bag; or bag, plus legs.

'No. Impossible, quite impossible,' said Sher, making a circle around us.

'Pull the seats forward,' I requested.

Anna pulled the seats forward, and I clambered back again, smiling. Sher handed me my Gladstone. I was cramped, obviously, but snug. Now, however, there wasn't room for the driver and passenger. Seats touched the dashboard.

'No. That's not right,' remarked Sher.

I was disentangled and hopped out. My bag was to go in the boot; but the spare tyre filled the boot.

'What if,' I said, 'I dangle the Gladstone over the side?'

The seats were adjusted; Anna and Sher stepped aboard – yet despite the adjustment, the pregnant chauffeuse failed to fit behind the wheel. The bump prodded the horn. The driver's seat was pushed back; I yelped and dropped the bag. Sher got out and handed me my bag; he then got back in again.

Somehow Sher had acquired oil on his hands – I think from surreptitious seat adjustment. His knees were by his ears. Anna got out and fetched a cloth from the boot. Anna out; boot open, boot closed; Anna in.

Driver and passenger clutched for their seat-belts, which wouldn't budge because I was squatting on the inertia drums. I fed the straps gingerly through my buttocks; a chorus of 'Just a little bit more', and 'Slowly does it', and 'here it comes', and polite 'Thanks, thanks, thank you'.

Settled, if not comfortable, we were at last on our regal way. Following the EXIT signs we found ourselves back by the entrance to the lift – the EXIT signs were for pedestrians.

'I'm sorry,' said Sher, considerably more distorted than he'd been as Richard III, 'but I can't help us escape. I spent several months working here, but I'm still none the wiser.'

Concrete balustrades filtered us away from any place of egress. Daylight flickered in the distance, from time to time, but arrows and iron fences kept us going round and round.

'Journey to the centre of the earth,' said Sher.

'Orpheus in the underworld,' said Anna.

339

'Dante's dear old inferno,' I think I added.

'They designed this place,' Sher added, quite enjoying the calamity, 'to keep people in. The ghosts of audiences past. All this flickering sodium light and distant thunder: it portends that any second we'll stray onto the secret route to Peter Hall's office . . .'

Round and round. The cheery Negro in the pay-booth waving at the yellow auto full of silly buggers.

'We'll find the secret passage, and find ourselves running the company.'

'Having fun?' asked the cheery attendant, satirically. After pausing only to find some money from a purse in the boot, and pausing only a little longer, for us all to readjust seats, legs, a bulging womb and the dangling Gladstone, we were up the ramp and steaming over Waterloo Bridge, our limbs and legs protruding in all directions. Fares looked from taxi windows at a pregnant blonde, a bewhiskered actor and a crushed Welshman, plus bag, accommodated in a speeding dodgem. Dom Bell, Marty Eggs and Mel Funn, liberated from the celluloid of *Silent Movie*.

We even got as far as the Aldwych before it started to rain.

DUNKEY FITLOW'S, N1

Assailed by the wails of pandas and Hondas, by the electronic jangles billowing from casinos and late-night boutiques, by the tintinnabulation of the town, conversation was impossible during the journey; we grew damp and waved back to the curious.

Sher did a dumb-show for the navigation. Eventually we arrived at the restaurant.

'Mike Leigh,' he said, 'would have spent two years perfecting our trip here tonight.'

I was helped from my nest, buckled over and twisted. 'You know what I need?'

'Tell us,' said Anna.

'Don't tell us!' said Sher, 'Crutches!'

The hood of the Midget was reconstructed. We went into the darkened chop-shop, were handed outsize menus, like the wings on Leonardo's ornithopter, and we plunged down into the ground by way of a metal spiral stairs.

It was our wedding anniversary; Sher ordered champagne.

'If,' I said, 'you could get rid of Queen Margaret with impunity, what other characters of Shakespeare's could be jettisoned?'

'Hamlet! Long pauses where the soliloquies would normally be! *Hamlet* without the prince. All the characters talk about him, so why not take him out! We'd concentrate on other people's reaction to him.'

'Short pauses instead of soliloquies. Then we'd have the rest of the evening free.'

Sher was once in a radio play by Malcolm Bradbury, where the central character – a professor who became the hero of *Rates of Exchange* – never said a word. A silent space. What we heard were other characters talking to him. Sher played several parts at an academic foreign conference; he provided many different Slav voices.

'Bill Alexander and I,' he said, 'wanted to do a rehearsal where we cut out Richard's asides, smirks, monologues, and just left the public Richard – so we'd see how it is he looks and speaks to all the other characters in the play. The outgoing, gregarious Richard. What's he like? A complete charmer? Still a villain? Or is the villainy subdued and unapparent?'

'His nature is never disguised,' I said. 'Look at the Lady Anne seduction. He's a monster, but a charming monster. Brilliant, brittle banter, like restoration drama.'

'Yes. A comedy of bad manners, like Congreve with blood.'

'If Richard is so evil,' said Anna, 'why is he the only character in the whole play we actually care about?'

'Because, I think,' answered Sher, 'he becomes Macbeth – he has a conscience. Or maybe he becomes Hamlet – especially as Roger Rees played Hamlet, that season I was in Stratford. Hamlet's as in love with exploring his mind, sportively, intellectual and scheming . . .'

'Sportive tricks . . .'

'. . . as Richard is. They love just being themselves.'

'He's as ugly as hell: but he's a narcissist.'

'Lady Anne sees Richard's visage in his mind, and so to his valiant parts does she her fortunes consecrate.'

'It's the rape fantasy: the big black man; the incredible hulk. King Kong and Fay Wray.'

'Would you join me in the adventure of a Robert Mondavi?' I said pretending to be William Boot's friend Baldwin on the Blue Train, the sommelier having been roused.

'I don't drink red wine. I'll stay with this,' Sher raised his flute.

'And I can't drink at all,' said the mother-to-be.

The food was arriving. Discs of lamb accompanied by microscopic carrots and potatoes cheated of feature, unfinished, sent before their time. Nouvelle imposture. Islington, first and last bastion of the slivered kiwi fruit; portions so prettily arranged, it's a sin to muck up the patterns.

'Whatever happened,' asked Sher, prodding a wee pea, 'to John Wood?'

'I heard he'd been reincarnated as Edward Everett Horton. I think I saw him last in *The Purple Rose of Cairo*, in the monochrome picture with Milo O'Shea that Mia Farrow watches.'

'There was a brilliant actor. I don't think I know of any other actor quite so capable of presenting icy intelligence, cold brilliance, and making it mesmerizing. Yet,' said Sher, 'his Richard III was meant to be a disappointment.'

(At the National, about six years ago, directed by Christopher Morahan.)

'It opened the same week as the Rustaveli Company', I remembered, 'with that big Russian fellow as the King – the character you drew like a grey toad with a spiky crown growing out of his skull; and little paddle hands and obscene gash of a gob.'

'Ramaz Chkhivadze was the name of that actor. I saw the Rustaveli *Richard*. They rehearse for years.'

'They performed at the Round House in Russian?' asked Anna.

'Yes,' said Sher, 'they do it in Russian. But it's so infinitely thought through and the actors have so absorbed the story and themes – it's absorbing for the audience, regardless of the language.'

'So you can't understand what they're speaking; but you understand what they mean?' I said.

'Like opera,' said Anna, 'it communicates in a different way. Mood tone, suggestion, stylization – which is why we make sense of Janáček.'

'And *Boris Godunov*,' mentioned Sher, 'Russian.'

'*Richard III* is operatic,' I suggested, 'colourful and over-the-top. There was a very operatic interpolation in your production, with the coronation.'

'I loved that! The ghosts coming out of the tombs, the fanfares, the chorus. Being carried aloft on the throne, flashing the naked hump!'

'*The Naked Hump* – now there's a title.'

'*The Naked and the Dead* – another.'

'*The Naked City*.'

'*The Naked Truth*, with Peter Sellers.'

'*The Naked Maja*.'

'*The Naked Maja*?' asked Sher and Anna in unison.

'With Ava Gardner, about Goya.'

Francisco de Goya y Lucientes: Sher's distant artistic predecessor, out of Fuseli. His impressionistic browns and flesh tints; the winged demons; gryphons; bats and nighthawks; creatures of cruelty.

'That audience earlier loved your drawings,' I said, 'especially Dame Edna's portrait.'

'I'm an enormous admirer of Barry Humphries; he fits seamlessly into his characters. There's no half-hearted, ragged, joking distance between himself and Edna, when he's dressed up as Edna; or Sir Les, if he's Sir Les.'

'Like demonic possession.'

'He is a bit creepy, in what he does. I went to see a show in Australia. I was terrified the Dame would weave me into her mockeries. Humphries does that: he'll spot a member of the audience, and he'll give them hell all night.'

'I hate audience participation,' I said. 'I'd never even go to a Humphries show.★ I'm a terrible coward like that. I dreaded pantomimes as a child. But other children couldn't wait to get up there with Ted Rogers and Jack Douglas to be made fools of.'

'Are they the ones who grow up to be actors?' asked Anna. 'How did you like playing yourself with Sue MacGregor?'

'I was absolutely dreading it. It was the first thing I've done of that kind. Playing myself! A real launch into the unknown.'

'Weren't you acting?' persisted Anna.

'When does anyone ever actually stop acting – whether they are professional actors, or not? Those people on that table: they're conducting a ritual. It's all a suite of performances. We put on performances of different kinds with everyone we meet.'

'Acting is adaptation?'

'Yes, I suppose so. But the worry with this talk-thing at the Lyttleton was no rehearsal or preparation of any kind – yet it took place on stage.'

'If you'd practised with Sue MacGregor, would you have been more or less the real Antony Sher? Are rehearsals a way of working away from your true self, rather than focusing in on it?'

'Rehearsals are about getting into a character; and there's no more a real me, a really real me, than there is a really real you, or Roger, or anybody.'

'You like Barry Humphries,' I said, 'and Edna and Sir Les don't seem to bear much similarity to the urbane wit, whom Humphries reverts to when the make-up and frocks come off; and I read that you like Alec Guinness. Where's their real reality? Their performances are consummate – they don't travesty the art of acting; neither do they tarnish their own privacy. What we get to see is extravagantly artificial.'

'Dame Edna and Sir Les are extravagant, vulgar creations – caricatures of Australians. But they're still sincere creations, in their mad way. And Alec Guinness. I loved his Fagin. I couldn't believe the before-and-after photographs of the make-up procedure. *Kind Hearts and Coronets*, I've seen it dozens of times, is the best quick-change multi-role film ever.'

'Smiley?' said Anna.

'Smiley,' I said, 'he's the reverse of disguise and quick-change routines. He couldn't be blanker. And people say it's the best thing he's done.'

'They do. *Tinker, Tailor*, with Alec Guinness polishing his glasses for twenty episodes, is reckoned to be his triumph – but to me its a triumph of

---

★ Actually, I've now been to many, though on two occasions I swapped my tickets to get away from the combat zone of the front stalls. And Humphries told me that though Dame Edna did a *Richard III* show, the RSC pathetically didn't reciprocate with gladioli in any of their productions.

non-acting. For instance: what would have happened if some worn-out old nonentity had shuffled through the part in exactly the same way?'

'So there's a difference between a minor and diffident actor being unassuming, and Sir Alec Guinness's portrayal of modesty and quiet – even though the performances could be identical.'

'Yes, I think something strange happens. Subconsciously,' argued Sher, 'when you see Guinness do something, however ordinary, whatever it is, you *know* about his fame, his knighthood, his past triumphs: "That's Sir Alec Guinness, so it must be good" – we all think along those lines.'

'Sounds like what Walter Benjamin called an aura: the breeze of celebrity, the halo of special status, attendant upon the unique.'

This is important and needs brief exposition.

The term *aura* was discussed in 'The Work of Art in the Age of Mechanical Reproduction', first published in *Zeitschrift für Sozialforschung* (V,i, 1936); and collected in *Schriften* (1955); *Illuminations* (1968). Benjamin, a German Jew born in 1892, who fled to Paris in 1933, and who killed himself in 1940 on being denied sanctuary in Spain, believed that the invention of photography was obliterating the sacred power of painting; cinema was, in its turn, making redundant actors having to appear live on stage – 'Changes in the medium of contemporary perception,' he wrote, 'can be comprehended as decay of the aura.' A work of art's privilege of originality was being eradicated by shutterbugging and printing; theatre was being eradicated by celluloid. Scientific advance would make art henceforward freely *available*.

Thus, copies of La Gioconda should weaken the exceptional attraction of the canvas in the Louvre; anybody could buy a poster. Thus, the cult of theatre would diminish; anybody could see a film, which could be replayed endlessly – mechanically. And of course, none of this happened. Benjamin's vision of a Marxist utopia achieved its opposite; his vision has been replaced by new cults, different kinds of auras. The easy duplicating of paintings has made the originals the more precious and revered – £25 million paid for the Van Gogh *Sunflowers* we all had in our student rooms. Available and happy fakes and facsimiles refocillate the desire for authenticity; for possession of the real thing.

The cinema, meantime, has revived the cult of pagans. Hollywood is a modern Olympus (also the name of a camera brand): actors and actresses on film, instead of becoming, as Benjamin prophesied, familiar, convivial – and thereby ordinary – have ended up as gods and goddesses. Their very familiarity has enhanced their aura, which becomes a kind of halo. They are divinities. And flickering their way onto every fleapit screen or, latterly, beaming themselves into every home on television, these obedient talking ghosts (Cocteau's phrase) are, paradoxically, the more remote and unreachable – *unavailable*.

Ubiquitous, actors and actresses lose the common touch; ubiquitous, they flaunt being a race apart. Mechanical reproduction means they individually multiply – so that a new film opens simultaneously in a hundred cinemas. They are everywhere, and nowhere. Fabulously wealthy; fabulously charmed, distant from the depredations afflicting the rest of us, stars are tricks of money and light, filtered by projection equipment and cathode rays; disembodied presences. And they are also immortal. Marion Michael Morrison may have died from cancer in 1979, but John Wayne will live for ever, fighting his holy wars.

Likewise, on some television channel, in some art-house, at some late night screening, Sam will still be playing it again and Ingrid Bergman, from all the bars in all the world will be electing to walk into Bogart's; and Rathbone will be telling Bruce to pack his revolver; and Chaplin will be heading off down that dusty road with Paulette Goddard . . . Mechanical reproduction hasn't decayed auras; it has been their liberation, strength and opportunity for polyphiloprogenitiveness.

And at what cost? Original works merely get more expensive, tokens of stock-market caprice and corporate boasting; and the Olympians of cinema and television, behind the gates of their Bel Air palazzos, exist in a world of recrimination, divorce, madness, hubris, plastic surgery and the diamanté rag trade. Auras are kept up with strenuous effort; they're willed. Performance can usurp private lives – Marilyn Monroe is the prime-cut example; or Richard Burton.

But, even so, Guinness, a star even if he refuses to flaunt his star-quality; a professional, who in *Star Wars* becomes Merlin/Wotan, a stately English actor amidst American frenzy and hardware, a symbol of dignity – he rises to meet us: a celebrity, part of our movie-going, theatre-going, shared recollection. In our unconscious we know that behind Obi-Wan Kenobi's tutoring Luke Skywalker there is Fagin supervising Oliver's welfare. And when Arthur Lowe, as editor of *Titbits*, awaits answer from Dennis Price about the serialization of the Duke of D'Ascoyne's memoirs – the previous dukes and heirs having been wiped out rapidly and serially, Guinness recurring as members of the doomed dynasty – we see the actor as unkillable, re-emerging in different clothes and different voices to be the snob, the banker, the snapshooter, the suffragette, the captain, the vicar. Guinness, in a single film, is reborn over and over, just as in each film – and each time each film is shown – the actor is reborn. So the Lavender Hill mobster rises from the table hand-cuffed; the colonel at the conclusion of *The Bridge on the River Kwai* rolls his eyes in a death-throe, and throws himself on the dynamite plunger; Fagin sits in his condemned cell; the fanged professor is brained by the railway signal in *The Ladykillers* – all of them do these things, for eternity. Thus, when Smiley grunts and gestures to Haydon for the return of his fountain pen, there is a long history of Sir Alec Guinness in the public's minds-eye. He has an aura, which has accrued. Sher, for the moment, has no aura – and the cinema awaits him – but he has a history. Generation of an aura, or its acquisition, quite naturally, is his intention.

'Guinness comes with great expectations, which we subliminally fulfill for him, as Smiley. People praised his new minimalism – but, you know, was it acting, or was it breathing? Smiley was a blank, and yet so universally congratulated.'

'Acting or breathing: I like that distinction,' I said. 'Samuel Beckett wrote a play called *Breath*, offered for inclusion in Kenneth Tynan's *Oh! Calcutta!*'

'Sexual panting?'

'I expect that's what Tynan had in mind; but I've always imagined the squawk of the new born babe.'

'Or a death-rattle,' said Anna.

'To Beckett, one and the same, I'm sure,' said Sher.

'There was no actor – just lights coming up on a rubbish dump; the breath breathed, and that was it. That's pretty blank; pretty minimalist. A George Smiley reduction. And I remember Salvador Dalí wanting to make one of Edward James's rooms have red rubber walls, which would reverberate like the lung-linings of a dying dog. But that's not minimalist; it's cartoon-pleurisy.'

'That idea of aura does affect,' said Sher, 'any performance or gesture of the famous. Because it's Beckett who had dreamt up wheezing over a tower of trash – it's art!'

'And Dalí's art?' said Anna. 'Doesn't he seem to be famous for parodying his aura? We expect him to be outrageous. He's trapped into being crazier and crazier.'

'He's the Liberace of Figueras. Parodying his aura, he's its prisoner; compelled to be bizarre, he has to stage-manage his death – that recent immolation. His latest notion, I think, is to sign blank paper, for the later imprint of a lithograph. Lovely! Imprimatur on blankness, empty space – like laden Alec Guinness of *Kind Hearts and Coronets* ending up as Smiley; from overplaying to underplaying, and both being the same.'

'They're not the same!' responded Sher. 'They're contradictions.'

'Oscar Wilde reckoned a truth in art is that whose contradiction is also true.'

'Wilde's aphorisms were clever ways of silencing opposition; snapping shut debate,' said Anna.

'Yes,' said Sher, 'but it's true that an aura can be an impediment, I suppose. Fame will follow you around.'

'People are always bad at trying to explain their own auras, if they have one; the secrets of their success. Stars don't quite know why they shine.'

'Ah yes,' said Sher. 'You can't originate a performance in extraneous parts of the body – like Olivier's nose or Alec Guinness's shoes. Yet Olivier'd have you believe he can't conceive of a part until the false nose is on; Alec Guinness says he feels nothing until a character's shoes fit, and then he works from the socks up.'

'They're just stalling.'

'Stalling and being pat. Complete nonsense. Shoes! The nose! You have to have some sort of mental excitement, an inkling, a half-acknowledged image, way, way before you get to noses and shoes. But people like to believe this stuff about disguise and costume. Noses! Shoes! If only it was as easy! Part of the legend, of the aura, is to make it sound easy and mundane. And this enhances their reputation, rather than the reverse. Bigger magic because apparently commonplace.'

'Extraordinary from the ordinary.'

'I don't know about stardom,' said Anna, 'because stars may be world-famous yet can't act for the life of them – like all the soap-opera divinities – and great acting doesn't have to mean extraordinary extravagance and elegance, no matter how mundane in motive (noses and shoes); great acting can be messy and ragged. Nor does any aura, so called, necessarily mean a long and assiduous stockpiling of achievements.'

'True, you can slog for years, and be good, but not be great. And stardom can happen by chance,' Sher answered.

'So what's greatness?' I asked.

'Sex-appeal?' said Anna rhetorically.

'Brando in *On the Waterfront* or Travolta in *Saturday Night Fever* had immediate presence; Garbo in *Anna Christie* similarly smouldered. Marilyn Monroe, whose technique is to make us embarrassed at her struggle to try and act – embarrassed for her, we feel protective towards her.'

'Sexiness contributes to the aura, but it's not enough in its own right, otherwise every guy and doll would be part of the folk-memory, and very few are. Mere beauty is expendable.'

'Guinness, Gielgud and Ralph Richardson were never sexy; Olivier was a bit of a matinée idol.'

'Gielgud fancied himself as a matinée idol, surely. His Hamlet, for instance.'

'But photographs of his Hamlet look winsome and effeminate. Brando and Garbo are attractive now. Monroe and Jimmy Dean.'

'Gielgud's lanky poise has dated.'

'They keep themselves private – that's a lot to do with it; or they die young. Manic privacy – like not accepting Oscars. Being invisible. Everywhere and nowhere like Zeus.'

We referred to the topic often; contradicting ourselves in the Whitman way; succeeding only in demonstrating that definitions were fated to fail.

That an actor builds up his reputation, his aura, as he goes; that eminence is the accruing of triumphs – such diligence is scoffed at by the instant idol. But then instant idols need to keep themselves before an audience, or else they'll become yesterday's men, yesterday's women. Even Brando knows when to appear in a *Superman*; Garbo knows when to lurch into the street behind her sunglasses, a living ghost.

Sher is a combination of both approaches. His Richard, Howard Kirk, Tartuffe were immediately lauded; his energy was prodigious; his performances, in their way, luxuriated in the art of acting. They've come and they've gone. On the other hand, he has cannily husbanded remembrance of his roles – *Year of the King* is an exercise in personal myth-making, refreshingly free from false modesty. That even the paperback was a bestseller means the production memoir is lodged in many a home library. Those who never even saw the RSC *Richard III* know of the RSC *Richard III*. It's the beginning of folk-memory; of an aura. For Sher, the process of self-invention is long – but it is constituted from short bursts of fame. Perhaps it is commonly thus.

'The hardest thing,' he said, 'is to be new and to be trying to make a mark. An indelible mark. It's hard when you start, and you're trying to beg an Equity Card; it's hard when you've made it, because you've got to keep being an original. You cannot afford to flag.'

'What did you do before the RSC and *The History Man* and your known famous parts?'

'I did the usual thing.'

'The usual thing?'

'I worked at the Liverpool Everyman and at Nottingham, with Richard Eyre. I worked in reps. There was great work being done in the reps – there probably still is; but you never get to hear about it, not really. Liverpool bristled with talent. Julie Walters, Bernard Hill, Willy Russell, Pete Postlethwaite. Do you know Liverpool?'

'No.'

'No, I don't.'

'I know Stanley Reynolds, its eulogist and elegist.'

'Stanley Reynolds! I know that name! He was theatre critic for the *Guardian*, and it was so important to us that a new play, *Andorra* by Max Frisch, had a good notice. We were all vaguely socialist in those days, and the opinion of the *Guardian* mattered. And Stanley Reynolds shouted at the stage, caused a disruption, and was asked to leave. If you see him, tell him he nearly caused a young actor to give up his career!'

'I can't imagine much deflecting you from your vocation.'

'When you're just starting, you can be vulnerable. You're *always* vulnerable; but when you're young you're prone to much more severe humiliation.'

(And I did, as a matter of fact, have leisure to mention Sher to Stanley Reynolds, the ex-*Punch* columnist, at the Randolph Hotel, Oxford.

'Antony Sher? Yes, I recall Antony Sher. Liverpool Everyman. It was my birthday, and I came in late – covering Max Frisch's *Andorra* for the *Guardian*, which was a newspaper then. Anyway, I came in late, and there was Sher on the stage saying something like "I think I have to go to the bathroom," so I stood up and said, "What a good idea!" and went back out to the gents – followed by the director, who put me on the street . . .')

'Is the extended-family atmosphere of the RSC or the National any kind of comfort or protection?'

'I liked the family feeling at the RSC, but that might be because I was playing large parts.'

'Head of the family.'

'In a sense; but there was always the sense of the company being a big institution, with bigger, more powerful fathers lurking in the hierarchy who'd look after you. I was at the National, too, but I didn't feel much family cohesiveness there. I was there for six months in a play called *True West*, and I never *saw* Peter Hall, let alone received a summons to meet him. He must have a secret lift, in which he is whooshed up each day. A secret tower.'

'Like Howard Hughes.'

'Everybody has a cavil about Peter Hall, but I've great admiration for him – especially after reading the *Diaries*.'

'I thought they were like St Augustine's *Confessions*.'

'Whilst I was in *True West*, I discovered from the *Diaries*, Hall was running that arts programme, *Aquarius*; he was directing in London and America; he may even have been at Glyndebourne. He was doing all the office chores at the National – plus he had a very hectic private life, which the published diary only skims. I've great admiration for Hall: how does the man find enough hours in the day?'

'Is time vexing to you?' asked Anna.

'The timing of a career is crucial. There are certain moments when certain parts must be played – and those moments will never come again and mustn't be squandered. When you're young, you play young parts; then there are the middle-aged parts; the old parts. I know of a brilliant actor, the best of his generation, who should be playing Romeo right now. He's the perfect age, but he turned it down!

'It is so important that you do the right parts at the right time – as you become emotionally ready. That's what's so absurd about drama schools. Pimply adolescents thrown into doing parts they cannot possibly be ready for. They won't know enough about *life*.'

'So real-life experience affects the fantasy-life of the role?'

'Emotionally, yes. Which is why I don't see how you can be taught to be an actor at the age of eighteen. You haven't seen enough; done enough; observed and listened enough. You need to have experience to be an actor, to play parts fully.'

'Richard III?'

'An actor wrote to me to say, after seeing the show, that he enjoyed the energy, bravura I suppose you'd call it – but what about the wickedness? He said Richard's evil seemed pantomimic; why didn't I play the evil as innocence, as sweetness and light, unsuspected by anybody.'

'Sounds an interesting idea.'

'But it's not how its written. His evil can't be hidden entirely.'

'From what you were saying about real-life experience feeding acting, who'd want only to connect with wickedness?'

'I tried hard to think about evil – Sutcliffe, Nilsen, and so on, but they are incredibly undramatic men. And so the stage representation of evil is inevitably blacker, more obviously horrific. Even a bit pantomimic, now and again.

'But I'd not want to play Richard and keep my distance from his wickedness, by advertising my *own* goodness or innocence! I went to see *La Cage aux Folles*. The trouble with the musical is that the actors keep advertising their heterosexuality; they insist we're aware they're not *really* drag-queens. And it's like playing Othello white. The comedy is completely lost – a screaming drag-queen having to be tutored in masculinity; being taught how to be a man. What the drama's about is obliterated.

'This must have been put in, this *distancing*, to appease the British matinée crowds – utterly deadening. I wondered if, for New York, the production was as cowardly and disastrous. Have you seen the film? That showed how it ought to have been done.'

'Didn't *Torch Song's* Harvey Fierstein do the book?'

'I know. I'm curious. I think the musical was aimed at a different kind of coach-party audience. The actors, George Hearn and Denis Quilley, held back from the parts, as if to say, "I'm only acting. I'm not gay." Just as if I'd come down to the front of the stage before *Richard III* to announce "Well, actually, ladies and gentlemen, I'm not a mass murderer."'

'Those alienation tactics were best detailed by Peter Quince and his friends in the Athens wood. "Will not the ladies be afeared of the lion? That would hang us, every mother's son."'

'I don't believe in any mystical sense of theatre, or of roles. I didn't "become" Richard in order to play him, in order the better to leap about. I still injured myself.'

'So there's a crucial distinction between *La Cage aux Folles* "distancing" and the pragmatism of your own style.'

'I would say so. You mustn't send up acting, or succumb to it, swooning, hypnotized. That won't get you anywhere.'

'Would you ever want to do a one-man show – your characters are often the kind of men who think they're in such a show in any case?'

'A Kipling? A Siegfried Sassoon? The Bible? I can't see anything remotely interesting or challenging in the idea. A one-man show! I totally fail to see the attraction. The whole point of acting is interaction with other actors. The interacting of acting! Giving each other confidence in the wings. The gossip. Talking about the audience. Sharing ideas and impressions. The conviviality. To do a Kipling or a Sassoon you'd have none of that. Like being on a desert island. Richard is at his lowest when he realizes he's a complete solitary – he panics. Also his best scenes, incidentally: he realizes he's got a conscience. Thinking he was free of one, he never bothered to be worried, to show remorse. Suddenly, he's belittled by self-knowledge: other people matter – and they come at him as ghosts.'

'Would you ever like to direct?'

'I'd love to direct! I drove Bill Alexander mad with all my suggestions; with all my Richards! I can't believe how bad and lifeless so much Shakespeare, for example, is.'

'Especially on television.'

'So bad! So bad! They should wait for a good production in the theatre and adapt that. The BBC Shakespeare will kill off the plays for generations. The trouble is, people in the future are going to see these fustian Cedric Messina attempts – wrinkly tights, cardboard sets and what-ho! forsooths! – and they'll think, so that's how it was all done in the 1970s and 1980s, Christ, how pathetic! There's a dead-hand institutional flavour all over it – as if to bring imagination to Shakespearean production is taboo.'

'You spoke with Sue MacGregor about cutting Shakespeare – making him our contemporary. Are there any works which are sacrosanct?'

'Two come to mind. Billy Wilder's *Some Like it Hot*. You can't change a frame of it without spoiling it in some way. And *The Importance of Being Earnest*. You can't change a word of it without spoiling it in some way.'

'Wilde's language is so deliciously artificial – Auden said it was like a verbal opera: "The characters have no existence apart from what they say . . . the greatest composer on earth could have nothing to add to it." '

'I'd like to see the play shifted about in time and space. There's no reason to keep John Worthing and Algernon Moncrieff in the 1890s. They could be high-tech media persons or marketing wizards or designer yuppies from the 1990s.'

'And who's Lady Bracknell?'

'The Prime Minister of England?'

'You know,' said Sher, 'there are other films I'd not want altered. Those Ealing comedies, which were quite subversive in their gentle way. Though contemporary then, they are period-pieces now. They're instrumental in my image of what England was like in the Forties and Fifties.'

'Yes. I always think that life before I was born took place in monochrome. I once saw colour footage of Hitler, and the war was suddenly sunny and pretty. My imagination of it was grainy, blotchy, sooty, all the colour drained out and realistically murky. A newsreel.'

'Ealing had an idiosyncratic attitude to colour,' said Sher. 'Look at *The Ladykillers*. Those blues shimmer oddly. Stylized and mannered. And the films work well on television – they become little and cosy.'

'Writing and painting,' said Anna, 'must be solitary pursuits – after acting. You work at home.'

'I've turned to writing, yes. I've three years to write a book for Andrew Motion★. I'm not indoors the whole time. I like to walk from place to place; I like pacing ideas out. Lonely rambles around London. I'd love the peace of the countryside. In Australia, I was fascinated by the way landscape meant so much to the Aborigines. Kids would make portraits of themselves in terms of rocks, rivers and trees.'

'Is the walking prevarication?'

'No. I've no difficulty getting down to work. You get enwrapped in a project, in creativity. When I'm writing or painting, I play music constantly. Time passes without my knowing it. I know I shouldn't want time to speed by; I know I shouldn't want to use time up – but those inspired, ferociously creative days are so exciting, whether I'm writing or painting.

'Time can speed up; it can slow down. Whole days go by when I'm working. I don't eat or do domestic chores. Then there are other days, when a day goes on forever. I was in Stratford once for a whole season, just waiting to go on as Lear's Fool. And during a bad rehearsal, it's very hard to abolish the clock – with other people having claims upon you, or if they're fidgeting.'

'That's an advantage of a one-man show,' said Anna.

'But I still don't think it's enough of an advantage or attraction!'

'*Nicholas Nickleby*, ten hours of it,' I ventured, 'can go by in a twinkling. But I've known some single acts drag and the shortest of poems sag.'

'Time is completely subjective, personal,' said Sher. 'We strive for an optimum balance – which is what the clock represents – but time is an inner conception and can't quite be regulated.'

'Did you have time on your hands only playing Richard? In your book you lobby for other parts.'

'No. I realize now it would have been impossible to rehearse them all. Richard makes such demands.'

★ *Middlepost*: see page 357ff.

'I enjoy the timing of farce,' I said. 'Farce is about men in thraldom to the clock – the precision, the mechanical perfection of the plot; the idiocy of the characters, who want to glide and fit with time, but who can only fail and collide: they're slapstick, when they want to impress and be graceful. The more precise the form, the more the characters collapse.'

'The plots,' said Anna, 'are so often about people wanting sex, but failing to get it.'

'That's the mechanical in-and-out aspect; but the characters flop and fall-over, bendy and wilting and impotently frenetic.'

'I saw *Clockwise* on the plane coming back from Australia. I enjoy farce, when it's done brilliantly. The paradox is that to be so calamitous and slapstick – all that has to be rehearsed and rehearsed. And once it's right, it can't be changed – which must get very boring to be in. Rigid, by its very nature. Can't grow in performance.'

'What,' asked Anna, as the restaurant staff clattered signals about wanting to shut up shop, 'would be your ideal job, if you weren't an actor?'

'I'd love to be an Egon Ronay inspector. That must be bliss.'

The bill arrived, as did, for Sher, a fingerbowl.

First, the fingerbowl.

It was a white ceramic effort in the shape of a lotus, with ice-cubes floating and fast melting in hot water; slices of lemon bobbed and collided. The idea was that the ice should cool the hot water and reach the correct temperature for digit immersion – but it was a decadent gesture, exactly reminiscent of that moment in *Brideshead Revisited* when Charles Ryder has a whisky on the liner with Julia, and he is fetched a pair of silver jugs, one of iced water, the other of boiling water, which he mixes to the right tepidity. The steward smiles on: 'he was paid,' remarks Ryder, 'to fortify self-esteem.'

In Waugh's jeremiad, the eccentric dilution of the Scotch marks the moment when we turn away from Ryder in disgust; the besotted memoirist of Arcady switches into being a boring male gold-digger, who is brutish towards his wife and for whom Julia is a surrogate Sebastian.

Sher's reaction to this kinky *rince-doigts* was telling; it was, was it not, a kind of test? The actor was recognized at this restaurant; the little demonstration was for his amusement; to fortify his self-esteem.

He smiled sweetly (and I noticed he has very many small teeth), but he was faintly repulsed. 'This fingerbowl,' he said, 'is like the musical *La Cage aux Folles*, neither one thing nor the other.'

Sher passed the secret test; he was anything but gleeful when confronting the absurd and pretentious object. If the fingerbowl was to be an allegoric/symbolic decoction of personality, Sher's response betrayed no admiration of form without content; no love of sham for its own sake; no approval of camp. For the fingerbowl was the campest artefact. And the ice never did adequately cool the steamy infusion.

Second, the bill.

Sher insisted on paying for the Bollinger and his share of the food. The table became the desktop of a boffin; a wizard's office. Access cards, cheques, notes, coins, billets-doux – any moment the actor might fill the room with flags. I have the bill before me. It is covered with sums, tallies, reckonings, bits of algebra. None of the answers conform to current usages of mathematics. Painstaking and adroit arithmetic, but whackily wrong.

This may also be interpreted as a symbol/allegory of character. Sher works frantically hard, sinking himself into research and study, only to have two and two make five – the agile paraplegic Plantagenet; the pagan Venetian rabbi.

The pagan Venetian rabbi was at Stratford in 1987 – a year after our dinner. And Shylock encapsulates Sher's technique. Bill Alexander set the play in a bladder-red brick alley, the walls daubed with Byzantine icons and dribbly yellow-star graffiti. Gold smoke billowed as fumes from poisoned canals. The light – saffron and jaundiced hued – rippled up biliously from the water.

The Christians were an indistinct mob of bloods, spitting at the Jews, beating and mocking Shylock when his daughter leaves him and when Antonio defaults, torturing him into making the sign of the cross. Salerio, Solanio, Lorenzo, Gratiano and Bassanio coalesced to form a loose, baggy crimson-and-braid monster, intent on little except ugly self-preservation and financial gain. The flâneurs may be Christian officially, but in practice they're satanically corrupt.

All this didn't make Sher's Shylock the sentimental outsider: he was the robust outsider, and the only distinct individual in the play (Deborah Findlay's Portia was a colourless tib). Lounging on bright cushions and rugs, intensely studying his abacus and beads, with long fuzzy hair and oriental robes, the Jew was like a tribal chief in the heart of the city. Even his house, with awnings and carpets, was a pitched tent. Sher's voice was extravagantly foreign, Levantine. He swooshed and wheezed in purple kilts and orange shirts, hitting out with his hands in elaborate gesticulation. Jessica (Deborah Goodman) matched him in oddness – but whereas Sher can outmatch cartoon ructions, this actress flopped as wan caricature, a gypsy in green headscarf with coins dangling at her forehead. A dowry on display.

Sher, his walk a rolling, hobbling saunter propelled by a heaving right shoulder, and dressed in a black cloak sewn with the yellow-triangle stigmatum, smiling his lines as forced jokes to appease his tormentors, played Shylock's agony as Rigoletto's – another deformed mordant comedian with a clamorous daughter lost to a libertine. But, Jessica performed so boringly, there was no relationship to be had with any Gilda. Sher found emotion, therefore, in Shylock's memory of his late wife Leah. He is frenzied that he's had his daughter abducted, along with much money – and loss of the girl and loss of cash are equivalents. Nothing, though, can buy back the ring he hears Jessica has sold to buy a monkey: it was the ring her mother had given her father when he was a bachelor.

And if Sher's touching acting concerned a character who doesn't appear, his most startling speeches and utterances weren't in the text. Bill Alexander had the Venetians spit, kiss, hawk, shout, hiss, splutter, and Sher did all this too, plus pray and yell in Hebrew, Yiddish, Aramaic and Graeco-Latin. Shylock's legal entrapment of Antonio was the occasion for lurid benedictions. Dressed in charcoal robes and a scarlet belt inlaid with jewels, smoothing saliva on a knife blade and ostentatiously sharpening it, Shylock was back in the Old Testament desert, about to exact revenge. With much elaborate ritual, the court scene is turned into a sacrificial site – the dock is an altar. Sher hypnotically intoned interpolated spells – lavish speeches, giving the performance a baleful edge, raising a Shakespearean disquisition on justice into a black Mass.

Where did the invocations come from? What had Sher researched?

For the actor to use *The Merchant of Venice* as a chance for a lurid and brilliantly self-instructed cameo, an ethnic moneylender in his booth, a hated alien, Sher made Shylock a fierce exile who makes no attempt to merge into his adopted home. He's as exotic as Othello in the same city. And where the Moor is put up with for his strategist's skill, the Jew is countenanced for his cash. They are higher slaves.

Sher's Shylock is a solipsist, living by tribal laws in tribal dress. But where Othello has Desdemona and Iago for company, Shylock is friendless – Sher even playing down the acquaintanceship with Tubal. Thus, chanting and mumbling Judaic rites is his only comfort. He communes with his ancestors. As Shakespeare didn't think of this, the actor had to consult the Scriptures. Sher's Shylock is a proof of Holy Writ.

Judaism is governed by complex, strict and ancient rules; over the millennia, attempts have been made to organize and render systematic the oral law of Moses, the *Torah (Pentateuch)*. The *Aggadah* and *Haggadah* are Aramaic and Hebrew instructional forms. The *Mishna* classifies the ancient decrees into 'Nezikim' (damages to do with civil and criminal cases) and 'Nashim' (the obligations of family life). The commentary for all of this is the *Talmud*. And the breviary, *Shulchan Aruch*, of Joseph Caro (1480–1575) arranged the theology into prescriptions for daily conduct (*Orah Hayyim*), decisions of the scholar and teacher (*Yoreh Deah*) and family behaviour (*Eben-ha-Ezer*).

What's instantly clear is that the religion is much given to legal operations and pettifoggery. It's a litigious creed – apt for Shylock. In the ceremonies, honour is a paramount consideration – and Shylock is doubly dishonoured, by Jessica and by Portia's satire on the statute: her idea of mercy is his humiliation. Under Jewish law, daughters were mature at twelve – but the state of young womanhood (*Naarat*) required paternal authority for any marriage, and marriages were invalid without consent. So in a very technical sense, Jessica lives in sin, and will always do so with Lorenzo.

Shylock's abused as a patriarch; and when his devoutness is lampooned, so is his law-abiding integrity. To a Jew, fatherhood, piety and jurisprudential obedience are interlinked. *Haf ha-Asif*, for example, the Feast of the Ingathering, celebrates crops harvested, debts settled, children raised. The observance is designed upon two principal quotations: 'And the Feast of the Ingathering which is at the end of the year when thou hast gathered in thy labours out of the field' (Exodus, XXII, 16) and 'Give thanks to the Lord, for He is good because his mercy endureth forever'. (Psalms, CXVIII, 1). And, we might say, Shylock follows the first example, Portia the second.

Throughout the play, Sher yelped in supplication – the *Albinu Malkenu*, or forty-five ways of saying 'Our Father, Our God', and he wore a psychedelic *Tallith*, or prayer shawl, decorated with *zizith* – the fringes on formal garments, made of wool and dyed blue. Amongst Shylock's many vests was a *Tallith Katan* or *Arba Kanfot*, the cloth worn under the upper garment; and his bivouac, in accordance with Deuteronomy VI, 4–8 and XI, 13–21, had its *Mezuzah* on the doorpost – religious quotation and rubric. In that observance at the play's end, when Shylock was made to yodel a solemnity fit for incipient human sacrifice, the poetic prayer called the *Hoshanoth* could be heard (based on Psalms CXVIII, verse 25): '*Ana Adonai Hoshia na.*' Save, I beseech Thee, O Lord.

Characteristically, Sher took such lore, and adapted it to his own use. 'The ritual I use in the trial scene,' he explained, 'is an invented one (concocted from different real Jewish rituals) since there is, of course, no ritual in Jewish law for the taking of human life! The prayer is from the Passover Service – powerful Old Testament stuff calling on the Lord to unleash His wrath on the unbelievers. The idea for it all came from Shylock's repeated claim that he has "an oath in heaven" to take his pound of flesh. Since, as I say, there is no justification in the religion for this we reckoned he had simply flipped and created his own religious structure for the fanatical act that he embarks on.'

The ascription of madness for Shylock – as an excuse for the sorcery – underestimates the actor's real achievement. Lunacy was not apparent in performance; manic energy, yes, but not a breakdown. What is really going on is that Sher is so entirely a creature of creativity – painting, acting, writing, the desire to direct – he's now adding to a play's number of lines. His inspissations are verbal Fuseli: subtext brought to the surface, a hidden life revealed. (Imaginatively, he's collaborating with Shakespeare.)

The babbling Shylock, like that fingerbowl (attitude towards) and the bill (computation of), represents Sher's style. As an actor he wilfully miscalculates, and yet his gambles come off. His waywardness is an earnest of probity; his speculative exaggerations, caricatures daring to be called fine art; his vehement aggravations, consistent challenges to our presumption of preciosity – Sher's performances make for a vigour which is, for us, so mesmeric and, for him, so right.

ADDENDUM: OR, THE ELECTRIFICATION OF SOUTH AFRICA

What can reasonably be expected from a novel? I incline towards the convalescent-home theory of Sir Walter Scott, who in his Introductory Epistle to *The Fortunes of Nigel* (1822) said a story-book should attempt to 'amuse in one corner the pain of body; in another to relieve anxiety of mind; in a third place, to unwrinkle a brow bent with the furrows of daily toil; in another, to fill the place of bad thoughts, or to suggest better . . .' This is the house of fiction as a cottage hospital, though with as many nooks as Gormenghast – and Antony Sher's shrieky *Middlepost* resolutely provides no balm; his house of fiction is a house of horrors. The book's bogey-filled, replete with hawk-moths, jangly on the nerves. I took five months to read it. Why?

Because, whilst it gambols, it yet stays still; hallucinatory, it's yet inert; turbulent, it is somehow cramped; leering and brilliantly descriptive, the narrative force is at degree zero. But all this is part of Sher's purpose. With *Middlepost*, we're not to keep our usual assumptions about the novelistic art. Momentum is slack and plot absent because the book is a picture in prose – the action becalmed like a painting, where space is packed and time of no object. Smous, the hero, can't compute how long he's been in South Africa ('I think it's two years. Give or take . . . Maybe it's five, ten, one'), and having emigrated from Lithuania, the seasons and calendar are now upside down to his mind, with October readying the climate for Spring.

There's no clock in the veld; and when Sher wants to convey frenzy, the characters run full pelt and get nowhere: Buthlay's horse gallops off, returning with its master a skeleton tangled in the stirrup; Smous 'ran on, and on, for what seemed like miles', but he can't lose us, or we him; the ostrich runs from its enclosure, 'coming as close to flying as it ever would', but lingers as a symbol of all the novel's misfits. (The dustjacket shows long-necked creatures in an ochre swoon: our dramatis personae.) Characters scarper towards the horizon, wish to become dots, but Sher's perspective won't liberate them. They stay in the frame – like the view Smous gets when he trundles off in the cart with Garbett: 'the tiny figure of Naoksa tore out of another doorway and began to race down the road ..., screaming wildly, only to be intercepted by April who looped her neck with his umbrella, lifting her off the ground and overbalancing himself.'

We hardly read this: we watch it. A tableau. And a farcical tableau at that. Sher's writing, like his acting, is determinedly cartoonish. Iridescent and spectacular, his pen streams with rainbow ink. (Rousseau, de Chirico and Dali traverse his pages.) Naoksa, the bushgirl, has 'yellow thighs and a watery bloodstain that looked like orange dye'; Kottler wears a 'mustard-coloured hat'; the land is 'dusty yellowish brown, biscuit-coloured', the 'boulders ... scorched purple'; we're told of 'the great yellow-grey plains' and the 'yellow-green glow on the sand'; the 'glowing sky was lilac, the distant hills purple', and after the rains 'patches of colour began to seep into view; green, orange, blue, scarlet, white, gold ... the whorls and clusters of colour.' And amidst this effulgent fall-out, Smous, working as a trader, sells 'buttons, thimbles, sewing and knitting needles, cottons in every colour'.

Middlepost's chromatoscopy continues in the way characters behave; Sher peoples his novel with caricatures – and just as he acts like Fuseli sketched, he writes like James Gillray drew, his eye irresistibly exaggerative and satirical. South Africa, at the turn of the century, is a cartoon country packed with cripples, imbeciles and psychopaths; a Disneyfied thieves's kitchen. When Smous arrives, and hires a bearer, the 'dark-skinned man fled from underneath the trunk, which remained momentarily in the air before crashing to the floor.' The passport controller is a dwarf, his boss, turning up late, a giant – Smous wonders whether the stature of both men swells and diminishes in accordance with toil.

When Mommie Gommie eats, her face becomes 'a balloon of food'; Smous requests food, and a 'shoulder of mutton flew out of the darkness and thudded against his skull'. The donkey drops dead – the driver is 'catapulted from his seat'; to fall off a balcony means your imprint, including moustache, will be in the sand below; and even Smous's defloration is a strange fruit ('Naoksa reached up and took hold of what was more banana than grape now'), a comic scene in a slapstick venue, where buttons always whizz off the weskits of the stout and people's jaws look 'capable of working free and flying through the air, where they would continue to judder and chatter'.

But, like Gillray (an actor, incidentally, as well as a cartoonist), Sher's burlesque is seldom funny. His objective is an exposure of violence, exorbitant and magnified. Such as the personality of Breedt, the taciturn Boer, given to Popeye punches ('Smous was appalled; again and again, he saw Breedt's bunched fist slamming into April's face . . . Breedt's arm . . . was still raised in mid-air, hard and cold as metal'), and the hysterical sermons of Buthlay, who preaches with 'lips foaming, disgorging curses, threats and visions of damnation'. These are men metamorphosed into robotic brutes; maddened machines. Quinn, a fey British officer left over from the Boer War, remembers Breedt in battle, flesh ossifying into root and armour plate: 'His bulbous features seemed to draw in and close, so you couldn't see eyes, nostrils or mouth, but only the stump of a head.' He's an engine of war, like Gillray's snarling guillotine. Physique, vulcanized.

Colours are lurid, conduct cartoonish. Language, too, in *Middlepost*, boils and rallies out of a comic-book bubble: Ahh nhh ha newwh hehhah, Baashhh, . . . Phhhf . . . Nhhhh . . . Uhhhhh . . . Np . . . Naa! Naa! Naa! . . . Tschee . . . Skwish . . . Ag . . . Huhn . . . Waalaa! *waaaah*! . . . Ck-ck . . . AAAAAK! . . . Trrrr . . . *Zoop*! . . . uff-uff-uff . . . WHAAA-BUR-R-R-H-GAAAN, etc. Sher shows that much sound makes no sense; conversation is dogged with grunts and mumbles. The world is a noisy place, our ears constantly assailed by babble and discord – as much as by cadenced sentences and polite verbal exchange.

That the novel booms with dialects and inexplicable rant is part of its order-foisted-from-chaos theme. Smous, the Lithuanian emigrant, understands nothing bar Yiddish. (South Africa to him is a cacophonous opera of Chinese sailors, British Army lingo, parrot screeches, brays from dying donkeys, guttural Afrikaans, panic-stricken Italian, German, a Scottish burr – 'There is music in every language for all to hear.') And so, placed in a country he can't translate, forcibly falling into a silence, he seems, to his new acquaintances, either simple-minded, a Holy Fool, or supernatural, a Holy Innocent. (Luckily for us, Sher conveys the lot in English, otherwise we'd have *Finnegans Wake*. Smous, of course, sorting out the sonic confusion of the Cape, is exactly like a disorientated reader of late Joyce.)

Discriminating sense in clatter is the beginning of consciousness, and *Middlepost* opens deep in an apparent hallucination: Smous arrives in Johannesburg after a long voyage, feeling like Jonah spewed from the belly of the whale, and confronts a jabber of new languages, colours, smells, sights. Trying to make a life and home here; trying to settle the spinning globe; trying to get the eddying dust particles to form themselves into recognizable shapes – these'll be his tasks: 'Here I am in Southern Africa . . . , how different life will be from now on.'

Like a new-born infant Smous, who is in fact swarthy and middle-aged, has to figure out environmental laws of cause and effect. He makes progress, as a baby does, by clumsy trial and error. And his existential new birth is linked to many incidents of renaissance throughout the novel. Gommie, struck by a cart and presumed killed, later comes round – 'a man being dead then alive'; Smous yells to a dead Bushman in the gutter, 'Get up and make everything all right again'; the dead land burgeons with gaudy blooms after the cloudburst; Naoksa buries her still-living neonate – 'it must be their way to bury their young in the ground like seeds, and let them lie there, apparently dead, until the next rainfall, when they would burst through the surface like flowers.' Like Eliot's waste land, Sher's earth is plugged with mythical resonance. (Along the way we hear Lèvi-Strauss/James Frazer style tales about the moon beating a hare and creating the cleft palate, and much importance is given to circumcision rites and vanished foreskins – April's is buried in an ant hill.)

Myths are songs of the earth. Ancient lore which roots a people in a place and celebrate a cycle of rise and fall, decay and resurrection. *Middlepost* is about Smous's uprooting and transplantation; his re-settlement and quest for belonging – for otherwise, his life in limbo, he wakes 'trying to work out . . . whether he was dead or alive'. He needs to prove to himself that he exists. He needs to know he's not invisible. No easy task, even before he leaves home. The medievalesque Russia can't agree on its map. Smous's region of Lithuania assumes different guises as it travels in and out of dialects and different overlords; as its borders alter after a war. Plungyan, Plunge, Plunjani. His very name, too, is a matter for dispute. Zeev Zali, Zeev Immerman, Maurice Josif Brodnik. (*Smous* is an Afrikaner monnicker for pedlar. Pleonastically, he's Smous the smous.)

Before the departure for South Africa, Smous's father insists on the drawing up of a charter, stating his son's name and origin; an existential voucher, inscribed on parchment with a flourished quill. But the problem of a proliferating surname isn't solved, nor is the delicate diplomacy of what a Litvak's to be called on a quasi-legal document. 'How could the man have forgotten his own family name?' wonders the notary, as his clients argue over geneology. And Smous's mother is disgusted at the use of Russian over the local tongue; a betrayal.

These are all problems of 'true identity', and having disembarked at the Cape, Smous meets Queen Victoria's immigration officers too fagged to make sense of his contorted Yiddish, who spill water on his parchment, and who invent a history for him out of nothing – Maurice Josif Brodnik, of Poland, 'a new identity is already yours'. A new identity, a new century, a new sovereign, a new land, and the opportunity to become someone else.

'One reads of the astounding versatility of an actor who is stout and lean on the same evening,' writes J. M. Barrie in *Margaret Ogilvy*, 'but what is he to the novelist who is a dozen persons within the hour?' Sher, in *Middlepost*, joins J. D. Salinger, Beryl Bainbridge, Dickens, Golding, Arthur Machen and Hesketh Pearson as an actor who has become a novelist. The stage obsesses writers. Goethe managed a theatre; John Wilson ('Anthony Burgess') produced plays in Banbury; John Osborne was a distinguished actor, as was Harold Pinter; as is Alan Bennett. Successfully to create characters in stories and plays, you need a hyper-sensitivity to gesture and behaviour; you need to know how people move, what they do with themselves when they think they're unob-served; how they sound. On the prowl for mannerisms, you need all the actor's alertness and selectiveness. The economics and architecture of acting and novel-making are the same.

Sher brings to his book a theatrical skill – just as he acts in a painterly chiaroscuro. He notices light, shade, temperature (emotional and physi-cal); he watches what happens to droplets of sweat, discarded clothes, scattered buttons. He knows the measure of a dying donkey. He wit-nesses April's attempts to balance himself, 'going into a little tumbling run, as though on a steep slope'; he catches Smous filling 'his cheeks with air and puffing silently at an imaginary trombone'. Mostly, in *Middlepost*, Sher parades the acting up of the alphabet.

The name-changing is actorial, Smous's pedigree hiding out in ono-mastics; and the map is a mummer, quick-changing its spelling. (Smous wants to reach Kulvidya, but now they call it Calvinia.) Mevrou Breedt farts incessantly in our hero's company, 'a greeting, a code, yet another unintelligible language for him to decipher.' Naoksa chants in her 'ludi-crous chewing, clicking noise she called a language,' mystifying Smous for 'you know I can't understand a word you're saying'. Quinn, how-ever, takes advantage of the non-comprehension by muttering his fanta-sies out loud, daring an obscene proposition: 'You great walking piece of circumcised sausage, how I'd love to lower my naked nancy onto your oiled head and squirm about.' And the Italian singers and barbers can abuse each other openly and noisily – and it sounds like a libretto: 'You play sloppier than a dog's dong.'

The novel is constructed around conversations between people who don't know what's being said – so there are hundreds of soliloquies going on, the pivotal monologuist (in the privacy of his own head), the eye of the chattering hurricane, of course, Smous himself – who, as a displaced person, wishing to become rooted, floats on a cloud of unknowing similar to Muhammad's in Mike Leigh's *Goose-Pimples*, whom Sher played at the Garrick Theatre in 1981 – a part demanding paroxysms of misunder-standing, as he gets fleeced and mistakes Vernon's flat for a brothel.

And if Smous's nimbus of ignorance can be located in a Sher character, what other performances are in the novel? *Middlepost*, in fact, is a rich

entanglement of Sher's acting. Vernon says of the Arab-speaking innocent: 'You've got to be careful with these geezers. Can't trust them, can
you?' And the prejudice accorded Muhammad is matched by the anti-
semitism aimed at Smous – who suffers like Sher's Shylock. Lithuania is a
sacred wood, where the cabins and synagogues, packed with furs, goose-
grease, parchment and inks, ululate with Yiddish and piety. Smous is
fluent in the terminology – *shivah*, *Pesach*, *Rosh-Ha-Shanah* – and proud of
his curly beard. Suddenly, houses burn down in the night; bodies turn up
in gutters, sticky and black. Then a soldier, seemingly so gallant, spits in
Smous's face – like Sher's Shylock, he's a-drip with phlegm, which no
amount of washing can cleanse. He's defiled, stigmatized – and so underneath his diffidence and appeasement, as with Shylock, malice gestates.

The silent rage and ambition connect him to other Sher characters.
Particularly, Richard III. Smous loves to idle, sitting in the doorway,
sunning himself, watching the world – and waiting for it to end, like the
idling Gloucester at the start of the play, the oh-so-innocent cripple
wheeled outside the house, secretly plotting in the morning air. 'You
might think you're dealing with a weak little man, but take care. Take
great care.'

Smous crouches on a broken milking stool (the legs bandaged: they
could be extra limbs), and we eavesdrop on his brooding mantram; he's
eager to hear 'stories of disaster, of cataclysm, of mass annihilation'. His
placidity has Richard III depths. 'Rising through the stillness was . . . a
prickling of fear and anger, of hatred . . . hatred for everybody,
everything.'

He enjoyed summoning illness at his barmitzvah, ruining the solemn
ceremony with a tantrum: 'Me making or breaking, creating, destroying'; and at Middlepost, he enjoys watching the animals slaughtered
('feeding his secret appetite for these things') and itches for a massacre of
the innocents at the besieged school: 'There would be violence – real,
bloody violence. Smous feared it, and longed for it . . . a violence that he
could . . . feast off, secretly . . .'

Fortunately, nothing comes of these forces – the novel is no melodrama
– except that, dozing in the yard, filling his lungs 'with the smell of milk
and blood', Smous gradually gains local acceptance – 'This is the ugliest
place in all Creation,' he decides, 'and so I live here: the ugliest man.'

South Africa as a freak-show, with Smous in essence fitting in, elicits
from Sher a Jacobean relish for torture and depravity. Smous sublimates a
revenger's tragedy (Sher was Vindice in Tourneur's play at Stratford),
thinking he'd 'always expected his destiny to be filled with such things'
when he sees the brawling soldiery cruelly ripping their horses with
hooked spurs. Sher puts in the book a Jacobean fastidiousness – a recoiling
at odours, for example (Bok's distillery, Buthlay's decaying body, Antjie's medicine room), which is combined with enthralment: the decaying

donkey, ants crowding its eyes; Quinn's fresco of excrement, vomit and blood; Buthlay's tongue quivering with maggots. These are images from the seventeenth-century poisoned palaces, visions from 'a huge pit of flames, smoke and dust'. Quinn (whose room is 'an evil sore'), the dipso homo hopelessly looking for a goldfield, with Garbett his dilapidated batman, form a pair of ravaged courtiers, spying on the Boers – who play a fiendish trick on them, by serving up their pet lamb on a platter, which April drops – 'sending the lamb's head shooting off the plate and skidding across the table towards Quinn, its boiled eyes meeting his in equal surprise.'

Eyes, organs of vision and perception, bewitch Sher. When April sees Breedt copulating with Signora Scuteri, his eyes are gouged out as punishment. Breedt, who reckons himself 'forced to inflict' elaborate mutilations, once cut out the cook's tongue and can't even sight a frog without carefully aiming boot or wheel at its 'rippling back'. Nor can the native children keep themselves from taunting Garbett's bedraggled ostrich. Half snake, half mute, the loathsome bird is God's Jacobean joke; a patchwork creature, like badly assembled fancy-dress.

Cartoon horror reaches a Jacobean pitch with the attitude to children. April, the polyglot black, appears educated and enlightened, until he impales a boy on his umbrella; Breedt flays Klippie's feet with a slicing machine, rubbing the wounds with salt; the Boer farmers shoot the Thembu pupils who want to be taught the history of their tribes ('all the children lay scattered across the veld . . . within the rainbow gardens' – feasted on by the jackals and meercats). Klippie, April's son, is befuddled about folklore and Quinn mysteriously corrupts him; Breedt's daughter Antjie is disfigured with sores; worst of all, Naoksa kills her baby, smothering it in the red earth, its tiny fingers wiggling through the soil like snowdrops.

It is as if, in Sher's Jacobean landscape, the immaculacy of childhood can't survive. He depicts a world founded on corruption and deformation – the only childlike person, Smous, is a retarded adult. Vacant and knowing, an angel who'd like to be a devil, he is adopted by Breedt, the violent and Satanic Boer, as a 'new spiritual guide'. Breedt, whose farm was laid waste by the British, takes to religion as a cure for his anger; dispossessed, he's the novel's Lear, and Smous, scampering shadow to his blasted oak, is the Fool. ('With Smous at his side, Breedt could not remember when last he felt happier.')

Smous even looks like Sher's own make-up for the *King Lear* clown ('the skin around Smous's eyes was purple and his cheeks were two white blotches'), and when he and his protector stomp into the veld, driven out by Quinn, they are as Lear and the Fool on the heath, 'the sky filling with foaming white and purple masses,' like the cyclorama and tinted dry ice that enveloped Sher and Michael Gambon.

Smous and Breedt enter a whirlpool of lambent dust – 'Pebbles and small stones ... shooting, dancing and springing, advancing like living things' – which, as in Shakespeare, becomes a representation of interior states. The spouting cataracts and hurricanoes image Lear's mind; here in *Middlepost*, the black sky and forked lightning ('white spears of light') engender a mood of angry awe, emanating from the Boer – whose temper belongs with a language beyond words. He tears rents in space itself. Smous sees him biting at the rain, 'roaring and churning', with the thunder and merging into the pewtery night, hoarsely and insistently panting. Like Lear, he is at one with the elements; and, like in Adrian Noble's production of *King Lear*, where Lear and the Fool, having communed with the storm by rising to meet it, return to the ground on a wobbling plinth, Smous and Breedt slowly re-enter the sublunary plane. 'Breedt boomed with joy, shook himself down, then noticed the other man crouched at his feet.' The tempest scene, in *King Lear*, was a levitation; in Sher's novel, an hallucination.

Smous was known as 'the little family fool' – but imbecility is his defence; his expert disguise. And this expertise is coupled with the beneficial side of his name-changing (Smous can indeed hide out in onomastics) to end *Middlepost* with the hero accepting his lot as lucky. He gets around to interpreting his failures as advantages, his drawbacks as strengths, his weakness as a power. Smous eventually treks to Calvinia and discovers his uncle and cousin, the doctors – and though 'they'd always disliked him, always thought him a fool', it is now the fool's turn to see through his elders and betters. Nasty to their servants, bitter, disappointed, suppurating from a sense of failure and disaster: Smous walks out on them. They're far less integrated into South Africa than he is; they don't see, as Smous does, the newcomer's duty to 'shape this vast black mass' of a country: a black Mass to be moulded and sculpted, artistically; a black mass to be celebrated, ritualistically. The secret, in life as in art, is in the selection and handling of form.

Middlepost traces Sher responding to his homeland, his profession, his ancestry*: each is an opportunity for self-expression, and in Smous the

---

* Sher tempts us with autobiography. The novel is prefaced with an acknowledge-ment to the Lithuanian Library, which tracked down Plunge/Plungyan 'where three of my grandparents were born'. And Sher researched the real Middlepost district, 'where I had holidayed as a child'. He has also said, of his Henry Irving at the National for Olivier's birthday, 'I was identifying with my grandfather, who was a barely literate Lithuanian pedlar, and I suddenly saw the absurdity and wonder in the fact that two generations later here I was as part of British theatre's tribute to Laurence Olivier. I was thinking of the journey he had travelled and the journey I had travelled. I suddenly had a terrible sense of trespassing.' (*Sunday Times Magazine*, 20 November 1988. Interview by Mary Dunkin.) Sher himself, like Smous, has had to re-invent himself in a new country.

novelist/actor has his composite character: Shylock's persecution, Muhammad's isolation, Richard's energy and blackness, the Fool's spirituality, Tourneur's Jacobean dandyism. He makes, in his novel as a whole, a complex pattern out of the links between acting and exile, drawing and writing. Colour and language combine as tools, as substance, to examine the lot of outcasts; the fate of existential exiles. Smous seeks a past he can connect to – and finds it originating in his own nature. 'It was so easy to exert his strength, his choice, his judgement. It was so easy, why did he always resist it?' He surprises himself at being a good trader.★ He knows when to feign disdain and uninterest, to lower a price; he learns to glower and look reluctant to up value: 'pretence, he now discovered, was the key to good trading. He had always believed it to be a dull and uninspiring occupation, but how wrong he was.' Smous, the smous, is an actor.

Fitting in, at last, finding his role in society, Smous discovers he has a home where he'll belong – and the novel's vista opens out, to become transcendental, interplanetary, cosmic. Sanskrit-style chants are heard across the veld, 'Da da da da da,' as they are heard across Eliot's populous waste land when the prayed for rains are come. But the weird tribal music, stirring from a sound which formed our earliest ordered mutterings, is made by April and Klippie, the one blind, the other claudicated – whom the farmers ride off to murder.

Against Smous's sacred moments the origins of apartheid shimmer ('the smear-rags . . . the *savages* . . . don't feel pain like we do'; 'we must all face the fact that our scheme to school our labourers's offspring alongside our own has been a mistake'; 'their hearts are still dancing around their witchfires in the veld'). Evil isn't eclipsed by Smous's transfiguration. Sher won't let his novel get away sentimentally. So it is against cries and whispers, then, that Smous sinks into the starry-starry night, absorbing noises, smells, colours – he is part of it all: part of the *picture*. He's mutated from stranger to inhabitant. The planet spins and swooshes under him – he's connected to a floating, flying continent – and 'he opened his eyes to find the universe filled with treasures, scent and light, him at the centre and everything else within reach.' Smous, tranquil at, or tranquillized by, 'the pulse of a million tiny bodies breathing, chewing, copulating, crawling across the surface of the land', experiences, in his milky way, the Lightness of Being. A stellar mysticism he pronounces anything but Unbearable.

★ He overmasters Breedt at the store, and the Lear-figure – Smous's father-figure, too – is seen as humbled and weak, giving off 'a look of defeat'. What with April's blinding and Klippie's ruined feet – is there a subtext in the novel of Oedipal affliction?

EIGHT

Being There:
Simon Callow

Antony Sher and Simon Callow were both born in 1949 – and there any real resemblance between the two actors ends, except that they've both written books. *Year of the King* is a diary which came out once the production of *Richard III* was recognized as a success. In the final pages, Sher describes himself as dictating to a secretary in a Cotswold garden: emotions are recollected in tranquillity. The content (assembling Richard) encroaches upon the form (journal entries), so that the *Year of the King* is a twelvemonth of Sher's Kingly ambitions: *Richard III* raised him to pre-eminence in his generation.

Callow's *Being an Actor* also explains acting through eloquent partial autobiography, but the text is intended as a joint-stock combat manual rather than as a retrospective private account. Despite the present-tense diary-style, Sher is looking back; he looks forward only to posterity. Callow writes a manifesto, punchily contemporary though drawing on his own past experiences in the theatre. A war-cry, and his eye is fully on the future.

Sher's haunted by Olivier's Richard III, Callow by Charles Laughton's Quasimodo – and there the real difference between the actors begins. Sher's stage people are wily, frighteningly opportunistic, dazzlingly technical, hell-hounds: acting as fire-eating and confident bricolage; it's acting hard and watchful. Callow's creations, by contrast, quivering of belly, make for soft, oleaginous performances; purring and honking, their laugh deep and resonant, they boom like men lost in an underground cave. Despite his girth, Callow skitters nimbly, like the hunchback of Notre Dame on the parapets and buttresses – but his physicality is not Sher's gymnastics: it is Laughton's stout glide.

Even when the body is slimmed down, Callow's personality remains plenteous and rich. He is snug, as Auden would say, in the den of himself; the sort of celebrity hired by the *Sunday Times* to discuss a favourite restaurant – Veronica's Chez Franco, in London's Westbourne Grove, where trout mousse comes wrapped in smoked salmon. Callow confesses he's 'addicted . . . to haute cuisine, and accustomed to paying a great deal for it'. Epicureanism tends to find its way into performances: Molina in *Kiss of the Spider Woman* tucking into exotic hampers, improbably permitted by the prison authorities; Beefy, in J.P. Donleavy's *The Beastly Beatitudes of Balthazar B*, a kind of Buck Mulligan, arranging delivery of a Fortnum's hamper during a Soho strip show; Hugo, the inscrutable aristocrat, with ear-stud, in Howard Brenton's *Dead Head*, expertly preparing roast pheasant prior to being gunned down in his hunting pinks; the psychiatrist in David Edgar's *Mary Barnes*, compulsively scoffing chocolate biscuits; Verlaine in *Total Eclipse*, swarthy and sagging, a 'derelict carnal hulk' in Christopher Hampton's description. And this 'safe playing with the danger of excess' (Henry James's fine phrase) culminated in Goethe's Faust, a man of excessive intellectual appetites, who craves both sexual and brainy fulfilment.

Callow's characters are creatures of appetite; unashamedly fleshly and physiological – whereas Sher's are metallurgical or, with Shylock, megalithic, a rolling stone wrapped in blankets whom we indeed would be surprised to see bleed. For Sher (and Olivier), Richard III's deformity made him a mad Narcissus, the play his pool, who hired a dozen tailors to decorate and glorify his unique shape – a unique shape which has long provoked a sense of the body's black comedy, and hence his solipsism; Richard's cacklingly alone. There's nobody in his image – certainly not God.

Quasimodo, by contrast, in his ragged smock and flaccid cardboard crown, is appalled by his own ghastliness, hiding his face when talking to Esmeralda and chatting naturally only with the cathedral's gargoyles – his brothers. He's stone become living matter, a freak-show tragedy of the body, his appearance making for a loveless solitary confinement. *The Hunchback of Notre Dame* is about the craving of company, just as *Richard III* is about the obliteration of it. Quasimodo is initially frightened, but then happy to be made King of Fools. He jigs and waves that crown almost schoolgirlishly. He endures the lash, stoically, for at least he is being reacted against, instead of ignored. At his trial, he almost gaily answers questions – pleased to be talked to, if it is only by a deaf judge. And Esmeralda: his love for her is shouted to Paris by means of the pealing bells. His apotheosis comes when he saves her from the gallows: 'The crowd stamped their feet with enthusiasm,' writes Hugo, 'for at that moment Quasimodo had really a beauty of his own. Yes – that orphan, that foundling, that outcast, was fair to look upon.'

That's how Laughton plays the scene – and, in fact, most of the film: a sainted gargoyle whose convivial efforts, though for the most part thwarted, occasionally result in sublimity. Callow's characters are variously convivial, eager to engage in conversation rather than soliloquy. The great Micawber in a tea-time Dickens adaptation of *David Copper-*

field, is a clear example. Callow played the eternal optimist, bankrupt and polyphilo-progenitor as a shaven-headed buffoon – the benevolent music-hall turn which Laughton never managed, abandoning Cukor's film set so W.C. Fields could take over. And the genial Reverend Beebe in *A Room with a View*, beaming and bobbing through everybody's home and hotel, is *the* organizer of excursions; scrubbed and, we feel, smelling of too much soap, a fat-priest: 'It was one of Mr Beebe's chief pleasures,' says Forster, 'to provide people with happy memories.' The Merchant/Ivory film scrupulously avoided any ironies, and so Callow played the home-counties hedonist as a twinkling uncle rather than as a chuckling sponger, fully aware of Lucy's budding instincts. Callow was the highlight of the film's most famous episode: the skinnydip in the woodland pool with George Emerson (Julian Sands) and Freddy Honeychurch (Rupert Graves). A naked skinnydip in the novel, the intention is something mystical – an Arthurian pool, the water a lustration. The film settled for a frolic in a duck pond. The boys and Beebe splash and throw mud; they chase each other, genitalia a-dangle – pubes prudently covered with weeds and branches when the ladies and Cecil Vyse stroll by.

Callow's Beebe was revealed as an abashed scoutmaster, his unrelenting good cheer connecting with and toned down from the prancing ninny in *Amadeus* – Callow played Mozart as giggling and dirty-mouthed, a cheeky receptacle of genius; Beebe's naughty younger brother. The glowering Salieri was Paul Scofield. Shaffer's play charts an unholy marriage between the envious mediocrity and the Salzburg composer; a theological bickering. 'My quarrel wasn't with Mozart,' says Salieri, 'it was *through* him! Through him to God who loved him so.' Amadeus was a saint in a fright-wig and a fan of the scatophagous; a convivial shrieker, by cosmic accident the conduit for great music.

The love-hate relationship is retraversed in *Total Eclipse*. Verlaine's friendship with Rimbaud is a poetic, aesthetic collaboration: the large older man and the beautiful stripling: 'What I love in old, sad flesh is the youth which whispers around it. I love its memories of youth.' Verlaine, like a big Wendy, rhapsodizes about Peter Pan – Rimbaud's a vision of childhood; he's a refugee from paradise lost. The two men talk and do deeds of violence and part – Rimbaud for abroad and a gangrenous fate, Verlaine for a life of nostalgia. 'He's not dead, he's trapped and living inside me. As long as I live, he has some kind of flickering and limited life ... I remember him of an evening and he lives.' Just like Salieri prone to remembering Mozart – but instead of with jealous scorn, with lovesick falsification.

Rimbaud (played by Hilton McRae as lithe and dangerous) repudiated his artistic gift at the age of twenty; he didn't want it to accompany him into adulthood, when he becomes a soldier of fortune. A Peter Pan who does grow up – but not as fast as Verlaine, who laments his lost soulmate.

Callow, switching between sentimental reflection and cowardly lashing-out, played Verlaine as 'some Laughtonesque variant of my imagination' – so he tells us in *Being an Actor*. The performance, outrageously camped up, recurred in *Kiss of the Spider Woman* which, like *Total Eclipse*, is colloquy between the fat and the lean, the old and the young.

Conviviality came in Molina's lavish accounts of B-movies, his total recall of the charmed cinema of the Forties. For the two men in the gaol cell, Jacques Tourneur's *Cat People* is exquisite escape. Molina tells the plot (about a strain of sophisticates who turn into erotic panthers) in incredible detail to Valentin, a political prisoner – played at the Bush Theatre by Mark Rylance, the Royal Shakespeare Company's star of *Peter Pan*. Valentin's the boy-man, an ardent proponent of revolution and a student of Marx. A thin pragmatist, he ought to despise his companion's blatant effeminacy and frivolity. It's the dour realist versus the dreamy fantasist. What happens, however, is that forced intimacy evolves into friendship and ultimately love – a wacky and inevitable marriage, as in *Total Eclipse*.

There's the twist of treachery when the food-parcels are revealed as the gift of the captors – Molina's reward for drawing details about rebels out of his cellmate. And matching the twist of plot, there's a psychological development, gradual and authentically acted. Valentin's sternness is a front for tears and insecurities; Molina's queerness and flouncing comes out of exquisite self-possession. The characters turn into their apparent opposites.

The Bush Theatre is above a pub next to the studio on Shepherd's Bush Green where *Wogan* is recorded. We were pressed into the gaol with its inmates; we were up against the mud walls (actually fibre-glass), iron grill, palliasses and yellowing Buenos Aires newspapers (comically donated by the Committee of Human Rights in Argentina) – yet instead of being claustrophobic and depressing, the effect of the evening was quite joyous. *Kiss of the Spider Woman* is a discourse on compassion; though voice-overs inform of the nasty destinies awaiting the characters when they get out, the quasi-connubial relationship woven between them, and before us, was their epithalamium. Callow's Molina was elephantine and pink; and clad only in scanty shorts and a torn white chemise rolled up and knotted about a seemingly pregnant paunch, the actor minced as a high-pitched Earth Mother, gentle, competent, flagrant. 'And what's so bad about being soft like a woman?' he asks. 'Why is it men or whoever, some poor bastard, some queen, can't be sensitive, too, if he's got a mind to?' Molina shocks and teases Valentin – who frowns, clad in khaki drab and exhausted by political theory. With his flip yet fervid utterances, Callow's brass tones of voice sent up their own camp delivery. Of men he eventually swoons, 'They're brutes, but I need them!'

The antecedent fooled nobody: 'He pirouettes . . . in a way that recalls the elderly Charles Laughton as the youngest of Bottoms' (Giles Gordon); 'He combines grossness and delicacy to a degree you can only compare with Charles Laughton' (Irving Wardle); 'Like Charles Laughton ... Callow is splendidly unafraid of going too far on stage and the result is an over-the-top but unmissable tragi-comic creation' (Sheridan Morley). Molina was a Mae-West Quasimodo, with Valentin his captive-audience Esmeralda.

The Laughton connection is more than physique: it's the way Callow challenges, and is victorious over, embarrassment. Sher never courts embarrassment. The homosexual in *Torch Song Trilogy* was a portrayal of the intense little warrior on the other side of the make-up; we appreciated the man inside the drag-queen: we appreciated Arnold's efforts when acting. Molina, by contrast, was entirely feminine, Callow's body, like Laughton's, steatopygous – where Sher has recourse to arduous gimmicks and greasepaint.

The newspapers snapped Sher in a gym, Callow in a luncheon-room; Malvolio versus Sir Toby. Sher sweats away his fat, banishing excess from his frame; Callow nurses his embonpoint, his empire of the senses. And he plays pleasure-seekers and dopes in a way Sher never could: Micawber, for instance, commenting upon 'my lack of cranial embellishment', or Tom Chance, the speaking telegram in *Chance in a Million*.

Sher's Tartuffe, a student of depravity, was a disciplined dandy, like Malvolio gone mad. His Malvolio *was* mad. And Richard was a cogitating comedian. Sher's stage people suggest terrifying repression. They contain their immoderations. Callow, on the other hand, sprawls and overspills with a generosity of spirit; his performances create an impression of great bounty. What Callow's Richard would be like we can guess from his Arturo Ui: a maniac spitting feathers from a bird he'd eaten raw. A messy eater, like Laughton's Henry VIII.

Callow plays bloated, braggarty, excitable roles; or, at least, as I see it, that's what his acting converts them into. Sher's brand of excitement is zealous and absolute. For all their caricature, his characters are aggressive and sincere; they stalk universes of their own devising – a place quite like ours, but distinct. Sher's characters breathe different air, function under different rules. Entirely consistent on their own terms, they have a fearsome authority; and Sher can, like Alec Guinness, bring a glint of menace to innocents (Arnold, Shadey, Flote); a touch of terrible innocence to his villains (Richard, Kirk, Tartuffe).

The terrible innocence keeps out camp. Camp, with its diamanté tentacles from which Sher's work was extricated in the last chapter, cheerfully embraces Callow's artistry. And before we proceed any further, you must note well that I use the word not in its *Concise Oxford Dictionary* sense – 'affected effeminate homosexual over-acting' – but as a serious critical term, coined by Susan Sontag, to define a sensibility and an ineffable matter of taste. 'Camp,' said Sontag, 'is a vision of the world in terms of style – but a particular kind of style. It is the love of the exaggerated, the "off", of things-being-what-they-are-not ... To perceive camp in objects and persons is to understand Being-as-Playing-a-Role. It is the furthest extension ... of the metaphor of life as theatre.' 'Camp,' it is concluded, 'is the consistently aesthetic experience of the world' – or of what Henry James called *the tone of things*.

Camp, Callow's stage and screen people are deeply frivolous; they're seldom passionate, always capricious – anger, for instance, when Callow played Emanuel Schikaneder in the film of *Amadeus*, came over as high temper, rather than as wrath. Callow is fond of parody and a languid delivery, occasionally a drawl – many of his characters speak in the vocal equivalent of a limp-wrist. Raimondi, the forger in *Cariani and the Courtesans*, lewdly twittered: 'Don't get excited,' he tells a fellow artist who has been admiring a Bellini nude, 'it's only a fat little girl with a mirror, my dear.' And of novices with low-cut bodices he exclaims, 'Sacred tits, I swear it!'

Molina in *Kiss of the Spider Woman* is candidly camp; his idolatry of movie divas being particularly revealing. Conglomerations of cosmetics and couture, Marlene Dietrich, Joan Crawford and Claudette Colbert are what they are not: apparitions in some Art Deco heaven, like Simone Simon in *Cat People*, who is certainly not what she seems. At moments of sexual excitation she turns into a beast (shape changing as a goddess should). An ancient erotic dream, this: fangs in the fur, the pussy with talons. The cat woman is also the spider woman; the black widow who kills as she copulates, evil disguised as love.

Vamps, with their jewels and accessories, with their interchangeable wigs and gowns, approximate drag queens (which is how Callow had Maggie Smith play Jocasta in Cocteau's *The Infernal Machine*, when he directed her in 1986). Molina is a spider woman; and connected with gender-bending, an essence of camp is moral ambivalence. Molina, whilst sharing his abundant provender with Valentin, and all the time spying on him, is aware that some of the picnic is poisoned. But the spying produces the food in the first place – and keeps them from starving. Nursing Valentin back to health after the excruciating stomach-cramps – that's when love develops. Hence *Cat People*, ostensibly the escapist night-time story, is a commentary on the relationship in the cell: the pain of betrayal, the rightness of wrong, arsenic apples.

Flooding the action of the play was Maria Callas singing an aria from Gluck's *Orfeo ed Euridice*. The opera singer is another camp heroine. In movies, the woman is a vision – anything but palpable flesh; in opera, she's a voice; an intangible soundtrack. Camp, moreover, is the tone of *Amadeus* because Mozart's music is used as a fashion accessory to frill a sensational story: the Wolfgang Murder Mystery. Callow's Mozart skipped and jigged; an exquisite in peruke and brocade, 'the creature', according to Salieri, 'shit-talking Mozart and his botty-smacking wife.'

Shaffer's drama presents a world of mountebanks. Salieri, the wealthy court composer who succumbs to paranoia; Mozart, the impecunious genius, dead at thirty-five. Historical truths give way to the fiction of camp, where the characters are required to become an array of bright little star turns. The technique is also to be found in Micawber, who in any case *is* an array of little music-hall star turns – though he's meant to be behaving himself in a novel. Informed that Dickens made no mention of Micawber's juggling in *David Copperfield*, W.C. Fields replied, 'He probably forgot.' Callow included other tricks Dickens forgot, such as a weird jutting jaw and a pouting mouth that sucked speech into a musical line.

The bass to contralto and back again, allied with a conjuror's white-gloved eccentric hand movements, were absent from the barrister in *The Good Father*. But Mark Varda was equally as camp. He dawdled, he slouched, he exuded a sleek arrogance. The part required a brusque professional indifference: Varda is hired to argue that Roger Miles's wife, Cheryl (Frances Viner), is unfit for motherhood because she's a lesbian. A murky brief, accepted with nonchalance. Whether at a party (clad in red pullover), or languishing in chambers and idly talking about a yacht he's to invest in (clad in the archaic robes), or in conference with Miles (Jim Broadbent) and Hooper (Anthony Hopkins), Callow acted the fat-cat legal-eagle, comfortably. He has one magnificent, almost improvised, moment when he uses the piles of trash in Clapham streets to essay dance steps upon. A silky silk, prosperous to the point of insouciance, Varda was the comic foil in the film, eventually providing a chance for some of Hooper's invective: 'Does the name Shit-Bum mean anything to you?' (An ancient public-school nickname apparently.)

Beebe is a bit of a Shit-Bum ('You know Mr Beebe's funny way, when you never quite know what he means') and so is Cecil Vyse, impersonated in *A Room with a View* by Daniel Day Lewis, another mannerist actor – and Callow's rival. Whether he's Kafka in Alan Bennett's *The Insurance Man* or the homosexual yob Johnny in *My Beautiful Laundrette*, Day Lewis seems to be giving the audience a knowing wink. *Knowingness*, that's the mark of camp. A closed-circuit of artfulness and innuendo. This can make for a peculiar deadness – and camp is fond of the deceased monochrome stars or of the formerly famous who've been overtaken by their screen images (Greta Garbo, Lillian Gish, Shirley MacLaine in *Sweet Charity*); of the confected spookiness of James Whale horror pictures; of the strangulations of Art Nouveau; of Art Deco's ocean-liner shapes – and what it all implies is effect obliquely placed to substance; form riffing off from content; a paradoxical saturation and detachment. Callow's bad performances have been over-saturated or over-detached in precisely this manner (Beebe, Mozart, Schikaneder, Tony Perelli in *On the Spot* – a mafia hood who came across as a London rep for Chianti); blank or fussy areas on stage and screen. When Callow's successful, however, he vindicates mannerist acting (Molina, Beefy, Micawber) by bringing it, against the odds, to life.

To be or not to be: the six words of Shakespeare everybody knows have been considerably pondered by Callow. Being and non-being; the characters which live, the characters which stay as shadows of shadows. *Being an Actor* is the treatise published in 1984. Callow's book discusses 'what actors go through' by means of self-referring chit-chat.

Being an actor, acting and being: contrary dimensions? The author's purpose is to show how an actor can give blood to the ghosts. He explains how the zero of character finds the matter of performance. The solution seems psychoanalytic; a process of mental discovery and transformation. Acting, we are told, is 'being in another way'; every new character is an opportunity for a personal renaissance – the actor must 'fill his consciousness' with the part; the part must achieve a sense of 'simply BEING THERE'; 'If you don't love BEING him, you can't play him.'

The theory is redolent of the revered Lee Strasberg's practical-sounding Method – Strasberg, the former wig-maker, nicknamed The Rabbi, who was inspired by the Moscow Art Theatre and Stanislavsky, and who was taught by Richard Boleslavsky, himself a Stanislavsky pupil, at the American Laboratory Theatre. In 'The Actor and Himself' we read: 'The basic problem for the actor is . . . how he begins to make his material alive to himself . . . The actor is . . . a human being and can create out of himself . . . I mean employing the unconscious or subconscious knowledge that we have, the experiences that we have stored away but which we cannot easily or quickly put our hand on by means of the conscious mind.'

Basically, all the theoretical white-water means is that the actor needs to acquire the courage to excavate his personality. Alumni from the Strasberg Actors Studio include Marlon Brando, Geraldine Page, Ben Gazzara, James Dean and Marilyn Monroe. The results of the teaching on those last two may be surmised: Dean, a mumbling Peter Pan, delved into memories of a childhood he'd never really left; Monroe made an acting career out of the fact she was not an actress, yet her stumbling and embarrassment won our hearts.

Dean and Monroe were victims of the Method's reliance on self-reflexive shenanigans; actors are encouraged to wander their own interiors – interiors inevitably sick if Freud is anything to go by,* the affores-

---

* Lionel Trilling, Lit-Crit.'s Strasberg, in *The Liberal Imagination* (1968), quotes Freud as saying 'if you look at the matter from a theoretical point of view and ignore [the] question of degree, you can very well see that *we are all ill*, i.e. neurotic; for the conditions required for symptom-formation are demonstrable also in normal persons.'

tations of mind impacted with neurosis. But what if the beautiful room is empty? Woody Allen, in *Interiors*, provides an illumination of such a pained cloister. Set latterly in an opulent but austere beach house – a tomb of taste – the film concerns three sisters, their consorts, and their mother (Geraldine Page) who pick at each other with bored moodiness. The house, though light and airy, is a receptacle for recrimination; the sound of the surf throbbing and breaking like white sound on an empty air-wave frequency, hems the characters in, provoking yelling and sulks. It's as if they're marooned in rarefactive mental space. Eve, the mother, an interior designer, decorates the home in chilly ice-greys, dried flowers, pale wood floors, pewters, 'my beiges and my earth tones'. Mother Eve is also a manic-depressive who, as soon as she's finished a room, has it torn apart again ('You picked a sofa, then you hated it'); and she later kills herself by walking into the freezing sea. She even sellotapes up gaps in the window frames to keep her house a cordon sanitaire – like a sealed coffin.

Interiors is about an ill compound; each of the characters nurses a complaint; the failed writer, the disaffected political activist, the film-maker who feels he's sold his soul, the drunk. Eve subsumes them all. Joey (Marybeth Hurt) tries to sum up, and says to a darkened room, thinking her mother inside: 'The truth is ... there's been perverseness – and willfulness of attitude – in many of the things you've done. At the centre of – of a sick psyche, there is a sick spirit ...'

Being an actor involves confronting the sick psyche, the sick spirit ('Only in theatre do we have the emotions, soul, spirit, mind, and muscles of the artist as the material of art': Strasberg). Acting is overcoming the shades in the rubber room, and the process is explained by Callow. For him, however, acting must be let out of the asylum; he is no casualty of liberty: 'If I hadn't found acting, I might have gone mad, or else died inside.' He bursts out of cramped interiors.

Initially, Callow disregarded the integrity of a stage person's mental life; he rigged up a self-image as loud and opinionated: 'I held court permanently' – a Belfast boulevardier or a Waterloo Road box-office clerk, sprinkling his conversation with references to Larry, Johnny G, Maggie and Bob, even though he'd not met them; he helped dress Micheál MacLiammóir, whom Orson Welles had led a merry dance over the making of *Othello*, and listened to his gossip about Noël Coward and Moroccan boys. (MacLiammóir's conversation was as 'a headlong plunge into a bubble bath spiked with cinnamon') Callow was a perpetual performance – but his performances on stage, in his opinion, were dead. Callow needed to let go and find 'a pool of liberated energy which was nothing to do with how I presented myself in life'.

Being an actor, in Callow's terms, is coping with an identity crisis: 'Who was I? It was a question I often asked myself.' The answer involves immersion in memory and desire, 'intense concentration' and 'great emotional intensity'. But such demands Callow found impossible when a student at the Drama Centre, and his tutors lamented his neglect of the inner-self; his performances were, literally, incredible, colourfully stillborn.

The Stanislavsky and Strasberg classes 'didn't work for me'. And so he was punished and humiliated – which made him angry: 'And here I was, hurling people across the stage, and roaring like a wild animal.' He'd made the breakthrough; the requirement, subsequently, was 'to romp around in the adventure playground that I myself had become' – without losing control. This requirement Callow has entirely achieved – hence his bubbling, squelching performances; he does indeed romp, and his opposite of romping is to romp fastidiously (a movement Tynan observed and admired in Noël Coward).

Callow's dependence upon what I consider his camp mode may be an effort to explain his energy; he seems to imply that he's parodying his energy. The figurative language of *Being an Actor* is an important clue: it is strident and belligerent, suggesting a vivid and tirading style. Shouting on an empty stage for the first time, he's shocked by 'the physical, ... even the psychical, power momentarily released'; wanting to be an actor becomes 'my violent ambition'; with the possibilities of theatre 'I had become intoxicated'; when at Belfast University Drama Society 'I had a nuclear explosion of projects'; the troubles in Ireland are 'the Ulster holocaust'.

Callow arrived at the Drama Centre with 'boundless expectation and absolute commitment'; any housewives he meets are 'power-crazed housewives'; to be tired is to be 'plain punch-drunk with exhaustion'; Christopher Fettes's lectures are 'blazing accounts'; the student life, indeed, was 'obsessional, passionate, exultant, despairing, incestuous ...' When Callow tries to sing, he manages only 'screaming pitch ... I became hysterical.' Cecil Taylor's *Burgher Schippel* was rehearsed in 'a mood of hysterical abandon' and the audience were 'paralytic with laughter'.

We are told that Edinburgh's granite greyness is to be 'bitterly resented' and that the life of the understudy is 'hateful'. Experiments carried out by the Joint Stock Company are 'heckled as we had never been heckled before'; in Dublin, theatre is 'a form of unarmed combat, in which only the fittest survived'. David Hare, the director, 'was ruthless with us as actors' and John Dexter is simply 'an actor-eater', who patrols the rehearsal room in pumps and a tracksuit, barking and inculcating a 'gladiatorial' atmosphere. Callow's dealings with Edward Bond were likewise 'stormily enjoyable'.

With regard to the script-in-progress of *Amadeus*, Callow 'was feasting hungrily off the extraordinary riches' Shaffer was sending his way – 'any actor reading the scenes would salivate. I drooled.' *Mary Barnes* was 'screaming out for celluloid'; at the end of *Total Eclipse* 'I wept unreservedly'; and the whole point of going before an audience is to see 'whether those lumps of bleeding flesh were dragged out of your entrails in vain and whether the public will ever see your offering to them' – which implies that the bleeding entrails are invisible, the actor willing their manifestation?

Callow's diction, therefore, is hungry, clamorous, incendiary, full of images of gobbling (an audience in Belfast 'ate us up passionately') and pulverizing ('theatre contains an element of hostility . . . standing on the stage is an aggressive act'), and the intention is to create a feeling of power and appetite; of Callow as omnivorous and the processes of acting overmastering. The effect, however, is otherwise. Recurrent mentions of 'the vital anarchic energy' when the actor fuses with a text, and the 'energy flowing uninterrupted' of a good performance, are so insistent that Callow ends up with too much; the blasting-and-bombardiering metaphors start to suggest, seditiously, their opposite – as though Callow's mocking himself. 'A little sincerity is a dangerous thing,' said Disraeli, 'and a great deal is absolutely fatal.' The earnestness of the blushes, smacks, acid-burns and explosions in *Being an Actor*, ultimately, we can't take seriously. Callow has taken what he needs from Stanislavsky and Strasberg, and remade it as camp.

That acting is about the possibility of personality, experiment with alternative selves, is all very interesting and as may be, but Callow is equally aware that the actor needs work and an income. *Being an Actor* is a double bill. The second half is a survival manual, telling the fledgling mummer (whose 'brain is bursting with new insights') how to deal with unemployment, auditions, agents and, generally, what they don't teach you at the Royal Academy of Dramatic Art.

We are informed of the foozler '*longing* for a commercial, *craving* a two-line part', and we read that only the unknowns are put through the indignities of auditions. Callow describes rehearsals, where (ideally) shifty strangers gradually bond into an intimate family; and we are told of that first-night custom, buying separate gifts for the entire company. 'This can bring you to the brink of a nervous breakdown,' he says with his customary hyperbole. Callow speaks about enduring a long run, the audience, the critics, and most of all, directors.

Directors Callow has been forced to regard as the enemy; uppity brigadiers who train their swivel-guns on their own men. Their war crime is to interpose between the actor and audience, the actor and the part. A highly organized and detailed director can kill a performance, smothering the actor's own imagination and contribution. A lackadaisical director, by describing no limits, ensures nothing but a flabby free-for-all. The Joint Stock Company, run by Bill Gaskill, Max Stafford-Clark and David Hare, desired an intimacy between directors, writers and actors. *Fanshen* was an early project, which 'changed everybody's lives in almost every way'. The play explored the workings of a rural Chinese settlement – a play about a community which was being put on by a commune of actors, who were themselves, ironically, in and between rehearsals, analysing who depended upon whom; the social and economic psychology of their group.

Politics and theatre are strange bedfellows, most often making for a drama which is tendentious and pretentious. Callow's descriptions of rehearsals suggest dour sociological seminars with actresses and lady playwrights yapping about feminist theory. Politics 'assumed such monumental proportions' at Joint Stock because it tried to practise its preaching – a dismal failure because the directors, writers and actors each had differing reputations and charisma. And differing personalities. Callow found Gaskill and Hare coldly demanding. Rehearsals had a destructive tension as it became clear that 'Joint Stock stood for the taste of its directors' – an appetitive image.

Callow clashed with John Dexter when he played Orlando in *As You Like It* at the National Theatre. 'To John, all problems are technical problems. To me, a technical problem is always the symptom of another deeper one.' Callow's wanting to be mystical found little favour with a director whose idea of a drama is exactly preconceived and rigid. Perhaps because of his work at the New York Met, Dexter's work had an operatic abstraction; a stiffness, as if the wind in the forest had reduced the exiled lords into a chilled chorus, like *Der Freischütz*; and Orlando and Rosalind became a tenor and soprano bereft of music. Dexter emerged as a 'mixture of erudition and bullying', using the actors as shapes and ciphers to do his bidding. 'I never engaged with Orlando creatively. I gave John's performance, not my own.'

Callow reckons this a brand of burglary; the souls of characters are taken, the director leaving his own calling-card in their place, like Raffles's glove. Directors – the 'Manifesto' which ends the book argues – underestimate or wilfully crush 'the rich and vital processes of acting'. A director should be an arbitrator, not an inscrutable autocrat, merely telling people to do as they're told. Dexter's *As You Like It* failed to many minds, as Callow thought it would, and the disappointment of the production 'seems to put in question ... the propriety of so much standing or falling on one man's personal vision'.

And so we return to convivial Callow, the actor whose acting is frequently an inquest on fellowship. *Being an Actor* is militant: actors must unite and 're-discover the ways of independence'. Unless they possess their own performances, they are not being actors, or even in a state of being. They are bits of geometry and mechanical brides.

What directorial depredations was Callow committing in Hammersmith, during the fall of 1986? He was in charge of Cocteau's *La Machine Infernale*, in his own translation, and to the Lyric Theatre I went to find out. This was not the first time I'd seen him in what we might call the flesh, and I had a fair idea of the character I'd meet, for he's often to be glimpsed purring on television chats and quizzes, such as *Face The Music*, where he recognized tunes with ease, fiddled nervously with a pink tongue of a tie, and laughed good-naturedly at quizmaster Joseph Cooper's leaden stabs of humour – he was remarkably composed, considering the host's spectacular slip when making the introduction: 'We welcome Simon Callow, making her first appearance on the show.'

In my younger years I was a big admirer of the Goons. My godfather, a grounded pilot, sent me tickets for *The Plumber's Progress* at the Prince of Wales, starring Harry Secombe. I remember Harry being quenched by a pantomimic firecracker of a portly Hapsburg princeling – played by Simon Callow who screamed, hissed, howled, and made much play with a monocle. He wore cream breeches and shiny black boots (I was in the front stalls, with on-stage footwear at my eye-level), and there was no discipline about him at all.

Callow was a Kraut straight out of bad amateur operetta. *The Plumber's Progress* was ostentatiously dismal. Harry waved at the audience and lapsed into planned corpsing. He swaggered and lugged a canvas bag of clinking tools – instruments to unplug the jakes – which he dropped with a clunk on a central table. On and under that central table Callow sat and jumped. Harry wasn't funny, unless he departed from the script. Callow stuck to the script like a drowning man clinging to the wreckage. Yet the image of his fizz and extraordinary high spirits has remained with me; and I was interested to learn that that play was his West-End break.

Originally called *Burgher Schippel*, Carl Sternheim's satire of 1913 was adopted by Cecil Taylor for the Traverse Theatre, Edinburgh. There it was a success; Harry Secombe took a fancy to the production, and bought it as a vehicle. A big mistake. Taken to London, and inflated with rewrites, it died. And Harry was ill at ease trapped in a play where he couldn't clown and be himself. *That's* Callow's mitigating circumstance, anyhow – though what's Harry when he's being himself? Strolling in the rain down a busy street, belted in a macintosh, miming to hymns for *Highway*? The most goonish thing he's done in years.

My second exposure was after *Kiss of the Spider Woman*, when my wife and I were to dine with Mark Rylance in a Shepherd's Bush honky-tonk. We made our way through the departing audience, with their bleached and cropped hair, their chains and rhinestone brooches, to the dressing room, a modest chamber off the saloon bar, shared by the two actors. Callow was already clad in his civilian attire, and the belly was sleeked away under a suit. All vistiges of Molina had vanished. Callow was clutching a mug containing Soave from a screw-top jeroboam; hands were shaken, mugs were passed around, he filled the air with his man-stuck-down-Lascaux laugh, and I don't recall a single thing that he said.

Stately, plump Buck Callow came from the stairhead, bearing a bowl of salad and Stilton on which the cutlery lay crossed. A grey coat, ungirdled, was sustained gently behind him on the mild morning air. He held the bowl aloft and intoned:

'Il tuera son père. Il épousera sa mère.'

Unfortunately, the James Joyce dramatization of the actor/director's entrance is too confident; Callow was a disconsolate Mulligan, who had hastened to the Lyric vestibule in a flap, late, and he made for the lift a little ahead of his deputy. A man who'd been slumped in his duffel reading a Fifties Penguin gave chase, and was later unmasked as the producer of a BBC arts programme called *Saturday Review*.

'I met him,' explained Callow, 'when I recited a Peter Levi Pindaric Ode for the Olympic games.'

'I didn't know he was a poet. I thought it was recipes.'

'That's Paul Levy.'

'The Jesuit?'

Callow and I were sitting in the corner of the canteen, he with his salad and Stilton, me with cold smoked kippers, both of us with a glass of chalky plonk. Callow ate with speed, tearing at the food with his fingers – I thought of Laughton's Henry VIII.

'It's going badly at the moment. We've had to cancel some previews, so we'll now have less time before the public; and there's been a panic with one of the actresses. A few little scenes, a few tears. We're at that ghastly point-of-no-return, when tickets have been sold, and opening night is moments away – and is there a show to put on? Or a fucking mess, frankly? It will be nice to talk about something else . . .'

I put the obvious question, about directors. Is he now a turncoat?

'I'm not in favour of dispensing with directors. What I want is for the development and return of good ones. I'm trying to be the kind of director I'd approve of. Firstly, a director mustn't arrive with the play worked out in his head. John Dexter does this. He works amazingly hard, anticipating all the problems of a text and a production – then he's cantankerous if any of the actors want to try things differently. His conception of *As You Like It* was fundamentally wrong! He thought the play a harsh lesson about ingratitude; harmony and colour he cut out as so much romantic slosh.

'He didn't shout and scream at me, but he picked on others – and that's sickening to watch. Bullying. The bad director is the director with too much power; but I can understand how it has happened, how they've been given authority; how we've let them get away with it. As theatre has become more complicated and technically demanding, it has seemed necessary to have one man who makes all the decisions. A boss; a generalissimo.

'I want a tiny bit more democracy. I want to give some of the decision-making back to the actors. Some directors don't understand actors; some directors don't even want to understand actors – it's forgotten that they're capable of intelligence and discussion.'

Callow sees the ideal director as a fountain of knowledge. He'd placed on the table Steegmuller's biography of Cocteau.

'I see my job as providing the actors with information about Cocteau, if they want it; background material and incidental information which they can draw on. I never tell them what to do: I suggest; I steer; I persuade. The ideal director would manage a different temperament, bring a different approach, to each individual in the cast. In practice, this is hardly feasible. Here we go from Robert Eddison, who is in his seventies, to an actress who's twenty-two.'

Here Callow was interrupted by a frightened flunky with an olive complexion and olive clothes, who held on a chrome leash a salivating and liverish brown boxer dog. The director was pressed for fundamental decisions: where was a certain seat to be placed? A mirror? Did he know that some props couldn't be seen by half the audience? And the lighting was doing nasty things to the costumes. And how was Jocasta's first entrance going to work?

'What exactly constitutes what you've called "acting's rich and vital processes?"' I asked, when I recaptured Callow's attention.

'It's a fascinating sociological phenomenon: the need to act; to be able to assume a part. Sociology, psychology, the lot. Working with this company I've had the opportunity to witness Maggie Smith in operation. She and Robert Eddison are acting machines.'

'Infernal machines?'

Callow had intriguingly altered his metaphor. *Being an Actor* uses mechanical allusions pejoratively; the robot against the malleable mind.

'I make a suggestion to Maggie and it will course right through her; the idea will be absorbed from her head to her toes. It's not a case of her saying a line differently, or waving her hands differently. She simply *alters totally*. She seems to have the ability to readjust her brain; to reprogram the computer or whatever it is she's got in that cranium. An entire, and subtle, transformation.'

'Is that what great acting is? The ability instantly to alter?'

'Yes. To be able to rewire the brain in an instant. Great actors have great brains. They may not use them to have thoughts with; they use them to metamorphose with – like flicking a switch, and new mental pathways open up.'

This notion of actors as delicate and complicated Babbage Engines links with the suggestiveness of Derek Jacobi in *Breaking the Code*; acting as a simulation of the world and of the people in it – a simulation so exact, we are duped, as if by Alan Turing's sorcerous Universal Machine; or by HAL in Kubrick's *2001: A Space Odyssey*.

Callow was getting carried away now.

'Acting is inside! As though a film is unspooling, and the light, the brilliant light, must project up and out through the brain...'

'Carlyle talked of heroes and heroines as being living light-fountains.'

'And the light filters through the brain. If the words are spoken, and the mind is not engaged, there's no acting – only a play-reading. Yes, the degree of genius in an actor depends upon the power of the brain.'

'What you seem to be describing is instinct, a quality which can be enhanced, but if you're not born with it, you'll never make it – *being* an actor, rather than *making* an actor.'

'Some people, I'm one, need to act; a craving. Many people never have that craving.'

'They do – at second hand, by being in the audience. They need nights of illusion. Theatre, cinema, television; sitting in the dark. But what you say of Maggie Smith is anciently so. My professor in St Andrews, Peter Bayley, directed the first thing she ever did – *He Who Gets Slapped*, when she was still a pupil at the Oxford High School. He used to say that her giggles and showing-off were hopeless, and yet then she'd give the most moving performance – of a tightrope walker, I think. Sometimes she'd snigger with the audience and be awful; Peter would take her aside for a ticking-off, and she'd change miraculously. Peter even used that flow-from-head-to-toe image you used. He said even in those days, as a schoolgirl, there was genius.'

'For Jocasta, Maggie is having to use acting muscles which have been in storage for some time, but she isn't prevailed upon to walk a tightrope.'

'Robert Stephens was amusingly abrasive about his ex's Kenneth Williams mannerisms.'

'What did he say? I translated *The Infernal Machine* with Maggie Smith and Robert Eddison in mind. I did it quickly, and I've been able to adapt it and change it as we go along – which seems the most sensible thing to do.'

'You read French at university, I think?'

'I was meant to do so, but I left the course after three weeks because I didn't agree with the way they did it.'

'Tell me about Cocteau.'

'He was an elaborate poseur. A painter, a film-maker, an author, an actor – though not a very good one. He said, 'I always lie in order to tell the truth,' and I love puzzling out the meaning of that. What does he mean by *always*, for instance? I'm drawn to Cocteau the flamboyant and multifarious man of the theatre. *The Infernal Machine* he did in 1934. It starts as a comedy and ends as a genuflexion to the classics. He had an obsession with Greek mythology; myths which grew out of a civilization which may be regarded as the childhood of our own. The Greeks are the infancy of humanity.'

'An idea of his age, I think: Pound, Joyce and Picasso used antiquity to interpret modernity. *Ulysses* has the King of Ithaca living in Eccles Street, Dublin.'

'Myths spoke to them. Cocteau had already adapted *Antigone* and *Orpheus*, the one as a ferocious hour, the other as an eccentric experiment in Dada. What he enjoyed doing was to shock by bringing together the commonplace and the contemporary with the mysterious and the primordial.'

'In Cocteau's time, the commonplace *was* getting to be extraordinary. All those inventions and machines.'

'Exactly. He was fascinated by modern devices.'

'The miracles of everyday life – telephones, cars, electric light, record-players, typewriters.'*

I was seeing where Callow had derived his figurative speech about artificial intelligence. Having researched Cocteau, he'd know all about *Le Cap de Bonne-Espérance* (1919), where an aeroplane makes a poet a modern Daedalus; and he'd know about *Les Mariés de la Tour Eiffel* (1921), with its on-stage commentary from gramophones; and he'd know about *La Voix Humaine* (1930), about a woman's afternoon on the phone (music possibly by Debussy?†); and he'd know about *La Machine à Écrire* (1941), with its hero paying homage to Qwert Yuiop. What with Leopold Bloom's visit to the printer and Eliot's throbbing taxis, and Pound's transfixion with the process of minting money, we have an art busy with gadgetry; technology's provided new eyes, new ways of writing and thinking.

Callow, drinking down his purple wine before he continued, continued:

'Combined with Cocteau's interest in scientific invention was an interest in drugs. *The Infernal Machine* has a dream-like base, an hallucinatory quality, which is mirrored in the ornamental tracery of language – Cocteau's baroque sentences, which wind in on themselves, questioning themselves, questioning their own meaning.'

'Which is what?'

'How downfall comes in the guise of good luck.'

Oedipus the King (good luck), Oedipus the motherfucker (bad luck). What's infernal is that fate itself is a ballet mécanique.

Callow's production exulted in Cocteau's sensual corruption; the junky

---

* As in T. S. Eliot's *The Cocktail Party*.
† A pun of Anthony Burgess's – *L'après-midi d'un faune*

dreamworld, whereby Thebes comes to look like an Art Deco staircase crossed with a temple; neo-classical camp. Bruno Santini's set played erotic jokes. When Oedipus (Lambert Wilson as a strapping matelot) met the street-walker sphinx, the erectile columns twitched to reform themselves as a vaginal arch, complete with a membraneous flap.

A sexual wanton boy, Oedipus bantered with Tiresias who, in Robert Eddison's incarnation, was quite the old man with wrinkled dugs of Eliot's poem. (Robert Eddison, whom I've seen over the years as a fussy Peter Quince and as a pederastic Lafeu, using Parolles as a pick-up.) They sparred like Encolpius and Ascyltus in the *Satyricon*. And, amidst the furs and carpets, Oedipus caved in to his wife/mother's blandishments.

The evening was Maggie Smith's. Jocasta's hair was held high on her forehead, like a great hat, surrounding a chalk face, the eyes laden with mascara, the lips becomingly glossy. She ogled and flirted with the soldiers, swished in her robes, toyed and twisted with a scarf, in obvious imitation of Isadora Duncan, whose death – strangulation when her muffler got trapped in the spokes of a Lagonda – made her a martyr to her clothes; a tragi-comic throttling, with the beautiful auto as avenging angel. Another startling premonition of doom was her brooch: a huge pulsating optic, 'that makes everybody's eyes pop out'.

An embalmed voluptuary, she relished the tragedy even as it was disgusting her. 'Is there a couple more proud of themselves than a son and a young mother?' she asked, hinting at the dilemma in another of Cocteau's Oedipal examinations – the film *Les Parents Terribles* (1948), where a restrictive mother and father don't want their son to grow up and have a girlfriend; when he does make a date, they call the police.

Jocasta, clattering down the staircase as if alighting at a Broadway musical, ticking off Tiresias's outmoded methods of divination ('Personally, I find your chicken entrails ridiculous'), was astonishingly acted because – it was like female impersonation. Maggie Smith (a woman) played a woman (Jocasta) as though the part was being played by a man. The production was kissed by a spider woman, or Oscar Wilde's sphinx:

> Lift up your large black satin eyes
> which are like
> cushions whereon one sinks!

The Queen of Thebes was evidently a slave to costume, fabrics and turning out well farded. Cocteau's heroine, like Tennessee Williams's women or Terence Rattigan's, is a man by other means to demonstrate the truth of a mask; the authenticity of cosmetics. The illusion of femininity is a betterment; an *imagined* reality. As Truman Capote says in *Answered Prayers*, because 'truth is nonexistent, it can never be anything but illusion – but illusion, the by-product of revealing artifice, can reach the summits nearer the unobtainable peak of Perfect Truth. For example, female impersonators. The impersonator is in fact a man (truth), until he recreates himself as a woman (illusion) – and of the two, the illusion is the truer.' And we need only to quote Oscar Wilde's 'The Decay of Lying' – 'What Art really reveals to us is Nature's lack of design, her curious crudities, her extraordinary monotony' – to realize that, actually, the spider woman's kiss is a misogynistic peck.

Maggie Smith gave the screws of Capote, Wilde, even Cocteau, a further turn, of course, and triumphantly, by giving a female's imperson-ation of female impersonation – like Rosalind, in Elizabethan times, when life, as Mulligan says, ran very high indeed, being played by a boy; a boy who disguises himself as Ganymede, and who then acts being a girl again for Orlando's titillation. Maggie Smith did this transformation, in reverse.

The Infernal Machine attempts grandiose comparison, which Callow abetted. Laius on the battlements, for instance, is King Hamlet standing and unfolding himself on the Elsinore barbican; by extension, Jocasta is a Gertrude, with Oedipus the troubled Wittenberg student. And there's an insistent rousing of Richard Strauss. Laius locked in the rock is the Emperor turned to stone in *Die Frau ohne Schatten*; Jocasta's lament about her waning beauty is the Marschallin in *Der Rosenkavalier*; the revenge-drama about parents and children is *Elektra*; the oriental grotesquerie is *Salome*.

But the more Cocteau looks like grand opera, the more his play reveals itself as a boulevard entertainment; a café conceit, which, in fact, avoids the domestic horror and tragedy of the Oedipus tale in favour of sen-timentality and a capricious kind of melodrama, its descendent being *La Cage aux Folles*.

A boulevardier's sexual politics Callow readily conceded:
'It's enticing, the boulevard quality – the boulevard mythology, if you like: the older man trying to teach the younger arrogant boy, and he's too cocky to listen; the whiffs of opium.'
'*The Infernal Machine* is a portrait of Cocteau,' I said, 'because Oedipus was a self-image. He'd already reworked the legend for Stravinsky in 1925, nearly ten years before your play.'
'I know. I have a recording of *Oedipus Rex*, conducted by Stravinsky and with Cocteau narrating.'
'The text is in Latin, Cocteau's narration in French.'
'That's right.'
'Alec McCowen is the narrator for an English version, making the oratorio cheerful, like St Mark's gospel.'
'Christ!'
'Cocteau is Oedipus the Lost Boy who gets one over on his parents, who displaces them and subverts biological laws of heredity; he confuses

the generations, Oedipus – so does Cocteau by being mythological and modern at the same time. Oedipus is the master-rebel, ruining the family, shocking society,' I said.

'Cocteau only had one subject: himself. He saw a kinship with actors, who are also people who need to impose themselves on the world. Cocteau thought that actors were heroes: they gave their huge personalities to an audience for, say, three solid hours.'

'Strangely selfless in their self-centredness.'

'And he thought the same of models. He thought of them all, all sorts of performers, as heroically giving of themselves. They are people who pose. What's remarkable, what is the heroic thing, is holding the pose; keeping it up; sustaining the act. Think of Quentin Crisp, who refused to compromise, who refused to be anything other than an effeminate homosexual, for the whole of his life, despite constant mockery and muggings.'

'Having conquered England, he's now living his life a second time in New York,' I said.

'To hold the pose: this is what's transcendent.'

'But Crisp is hardly as omnicompetent as Cocteau, though they look alike.'

'Cocteau was an aesthete, a drug-addict, a homosexual. He made extreme demands upon himself; he exerted himself to live on the edge. That's heroic. That gives him an existential bravery. But let's not forget that at his heart there was a little boy in love with the glitter and glamour of the theatre, which makes me think that *The Infernal Machine*, despite its depravities, has an innocence.'

'Oedipus commits his crimes innocently. The original Lost Boy. The Peter Pan of Peter Pans.'

'All sorts of Freudian murk is involved.'

'If actors want to dominate and change people's opinions – which perhaps Quentin Crisp has managed – is the motive for this merely arrogance?' I asked.

'On the contrary. They don't want to show off. "This is me! Am I not wonderful!" No, no, no. They want to impose because, in reality, in real life, they are weak, or began weak. Actors are transformed runts – like the ones Malcolm Bradbury writes about in *The History Man*, for example, when Howard Kirk becomes a brilliant success. The academic world must be the same as in acting – or whatever: people desperate to make a mark on their profession, to change its rules, to enlarge its possibilities. You begin, however, from a position not of confidence, but from its opposite. You'll have a ferocious, ill-disciplined talent, perhaps, but to no purpose. Only experience licks the talent into shape; and with experience comes confidence. The more confident you are, the less of a runt.'

'Do actors change with the parts they play?'

'Inevitable – just as experience shapes people in real life,' said Callow.

'You don't see old friends for a while: you meet: they're strangers. The experienced actor perhaps wouldn't recognize his earlier self.'

'Acting is a rite of passage?'

'It can be a very painful business, as it was for Charles Laughton. Nobody who knew him liked him as a man – which wouldn't much matter, except that he didn't like himself either. To act, he dug up the fear, bile and unhappiness inside of himself. This was a monstrous sacrifice, because in real life he strove to build a shell in which he'd be comfortable, and from inside which he could trundle through the world. Within the shell – he was a true Cancerian – he was mushy and messy and a chaos of anxieties and embarrassments. This was the true personality that had to go on display in performance; the naked personality, stripped of its protective carapace.'

'Why did he ditch Micawber, a happy character? Laughton would've not been required to demonstrate his dark side.'

'In 1935, Laughton thought he only had a dark side. He was not ready for Micawber's cheerful optimism; he couldn't understand it, so left after three days, suggesting to Selznick that they give the part to Fields. Maybe towards the end of his life Laughton could've played Micawber; when he'd mellowed. But he was always crusty. He was never exactly lovable. He tried playing a busker once, in *St Martin's Lane*, which was the nearest he got to being a cheeky chappie. His monster in *Witness for the Prosecution* is almost a twinkling old card. But the dark side was his genius, and his masterpiece of darkness was Captain Bligh. You just don't play Bligh as Laughton played Bligh. It nearly killed him; he gave so much to the part, dredging deep into himself for anger and malice. He went on from that to do Claudius for Korda.'

'A heroic disaster – worse than Micawber.'

'He couldn't take any more self-seeking for feebleness and poison. That Josef von Sternberg was clinically insane didn't help matters – the director having a nervous breakdown. Nobody bothered to realize what acting was doing to Laughton. Just train a camera on him, they thought, and he'd look "a character". But to look a character, to be a character, he gave everything, *everything*.'

'He flaunted the embarrassing interior he otherwise laboured to disguise.'

'Like Quentin Crisp, he had a lot to face. He had much courage, like Crisp, in an area where it is less necessary to be brave today. Courage to go out and be abused and hit, and to keep a core of integrity; to hang on to a spirit that won't be broken.'

'Was Laughton ever broken?'

'You might say, he was broken and maddened by acting.'

Laughton (1899–1962) is Callow's idol; even his ideal self-image, as

Oedipus was Cocteau's. He's functioned, as I said at the beginning, in the shadow of Quasimodo. In *Being an Actor* we read, 'If acting wasn't about confronting oneself in the darkest alleys of one's life, what was it?' As Laughton's career unfolded to expose byways in his mentality, he's the actor whom Callow is being; he's the tutelary spirit of the book. A tutelary spirit only half-concealed. Joint Stock's *A Mad World My Masters* saw Callow devising a 'multiphobic royalist Angela Rippon-obsessed insurance magnate' by the name of Claughton.

His Laughton fixation, however, was mocked by Bill Gaskill and his cohorts – Laughton a representative of 'rampant individualism' at odds with Joint Stock's egalitarianism. Callow was punished by having to play a dull policeman. Claughton was snatched away and given to David Rintoul.

Callow kept Laughton near with Verlaine in *Total Eclipse* (as we have seen); with Molina in *Kiss of the Spider Woman*; by playing Fulgazio in *Galileo* – Laughton and Brecht's adaptation; by taking on Micawber. In a revival of Edgar Wallace's *On the Spot*, Callow played Laughton's success of 1930, the mobster Tony Perelli. The project to give a dramatic recitation of Shakespeare's sonnets, all of them, was a Laughtonesque enterprise – Laughton the orator expounding books of the Bible. Callow interpreted the poems, and the way they interlock to tell a story, as a mental adventure. Of their original composition he surmised, the 'mental ferment must have been unendurable; and emotionally exhausting' – an honest exhaustion which, it is claimed, was the mark of Laughton when he agitated his nerves and begat a performance. Laughton was a sort of Shakespeare. Both forces of nature which, the more we press in study of them, 'the more we shall see proofs of design and self-supporting arrangement where the careless eye had seen nothing but accident!' (The words are opium-eater Thomas De Quincey's, 1823.)

Callow makes his lofty case for Laughton's art of acting in three forms: radio, television, and a book. Taken together the work constitutes a major achievement, exceeding some of Callow's stage and screen performances – though all the work on Laughton is itself a performance, of course. For the radio documentary, *Shakespeare on his Lips*, Callow spoke in an orotund staccato with a little lisp now and then. For the television programme, *Callow's Laughton*, the acolyte set his jaw and jowls in Laughton alignment and sat in cinemas and theatres watching crumbling footage of 'that celebrated face'. The book, *Charles Laughton: A Difficult Actor*, is a rococo dilatation of *Being an Actor*, with its anatomy of 'Being Charles Laughton on Behalf of Humanity . . . Being Charles Laughton at deeper and deeper levels'; acting for Laughton 'was another way of being'; Laughton was an actor 'whose genius consisted of being'.

The radio show rehearsed the career at speed. The Yorkshire childhood; gassing during the Great War; the Bancroft Gold Medal at RADA, won in spite of 'the apparent physical disadvantages under which he laboured'; the intertexture of menace and charm. It being a disembodied medium, Callow used the radio to air Laughton's different voices. He'd found a disc of the Old Vic *Macbeth* where, amidst fuzz and crackle, Laughton could be heard huffing in a Scarborough accent about Birnam Wood. Another record was a message to Brecht concerning the *Galileo* adaptation. We heard Laughton giving a public reading from the Bible – the 'ancient ceremony', as he put it, of storytelling: the marriage of audience and actor.

Callow included in his survey the memories of past colleagues. Ian Holm, the Stratford Fool to Laughton's King of Albion, said, 'Lear was an ordeal he himself had to go through'. And Alec Guinness admitted, 'He was an artist – which few actors are.'

Artistry is one of Callow's principal deliberations: the actor as work of art; the actor as creator. In this, he follows Hugh Walpole, who as theatre critic in the *Weekend Review*, explained that Laughton 'works on his part as a novelist does on a novel or a painter on a picture'. And Walpole himself follows Henry James, who in 1915 said of Coquelin, the French actor, that his procedure 'resembles the method of the psychological novelist who . . . builds up a character . . . by touch added to touch'. The suggestion is of performances replete with recesses; with digressions and unknowable possibilities – with acting as something more than the representation of character and style. What we get with Laughton is the evolved force of a personality. His characters don't just speak – they think. They have, in Callow's estimation, souls – souls spawned from the actor's own private self: 'His every performance was an encounter with himself, a liberation of another . . . part of his psyche.' Henry VIII, Angelo, Bligh, Mr Barrett of Wimpole Street, Rembrandt, Claudius – 'Every squirm,' wrote Walpole, 'is part of the new personality of the part.'

So consummate was Laughton's acting, Walpole thought him 'a poet and creator of beauty'. His villains were never ungivingly wicked; nor were his heroes heroic. As in great novels or painting, nothing was ever simply one thing – rather, as Callow says, a performance was 'a thing constructed of a million nerves . . . a baroque tissue . . .' And nowhere was the pattern more on display than in *The Hunchback of Notre Dame*. What Callow calls 'Laughton's great expressive soul, throbbing with pain and longing for beauty' may stand as a description of Quasimodo.

William Dieterle's film of 1939 is the object of Callow's veneration; his exorbitance. Quasimodo is a symbol of 'some kind of world-pain, world-suffering that was sucking his soul out of him'. Laughton's achievement 'is acting at its greatest; it is Laughton at his greatest; it is a cornerstone of this century's dramatic achievement'.

Actually, *The Hunchback of Notre Dame* is gloriously tacky; Laughton is stabled in Hollywood's Ruritania, which is never Paris, always Zenda or a nursery-book vista of houses apt for elves and jolly shoemakers. Characters speak with slurry Californian accents; heralds and clergy are dressed in velvet bonnets and cotton-wool copes. Sir Cedric Hardwicke, as Frollo, is as stiff and jerky as any radio actor trying to make his name in pictures; Harry Davenport (who, born in 1866, would have been a young man of nineteen when Victor Hugo died) plays Louis IX as a fussy old codger, his enlightenment conveyed by means of a chuckle; his geniality by a wizardly stoop. George Zucco – Rathbone's Moriarty – emerges from the shade as a torturer, communicating in Latin, and wearing a helmet shaped like Louise Brooks's bob in *Rolled Stockings*.

Maureen O'Hara plays Esmeralda as a dazed beauty, communing with a statue of the Virgin Mary, which uncannily resembles Lady Diana Cooper. Quasimodo, at another moment in the film, hugs a statue of Christ; he's the suffering child asking for protection, as Esmeralda is a version of the scourged Magdalen, falling amongst thieves. They talk to the masonry for two reasons: so that soliloquies can have an ostensible on screen audience; so that they can be eavesdropped upon. The shadows and nooks of Notre Dame are as dangerous as any in Elsinore.

Notre Dame, in fact, is a major character. Quasimodo lives amongst the hippogriffs and bandersnatches, his tower a version of the phantom of the opera's cellar. Architecture as exoskeletons for animate gargoyles. The gargoyles and flying buttresses; the towers and pinnacles of the cathedral, exactly mirror Erik's domain – which is a cathedral underground, complete with pipe-organ. Christine is taken to the subterranean prison, Esmeralda to the aerial sanctuary. Quasimodo's lair in the sky, in addition, is a joke on evolution: up his stairway, the ascent of man is to meet the mooncalf.

But, though he's a mooncalf, he's the most sophisticated character in the film. Laughton's creature emerges from the strutting, fretting historical pageant – where the mob of extras, the pickpockets, balladeers, pranksters, hot-toddy vendors, fiddlers and acrobats, either pull faces to look downtrodden, or else yell like a playground of imbecilic children in fancy dress, and who always come fearfully close to breaking into song, as the steerage crowds do in the Marx Brothers' films to ruinous effect – as polyvalent. Hidden inside a smeared pig snout and behind a protruberant blind eye, his fangs snapping and slashing, a cornered boar, Quasimodo is yet eloquent and noble. As we grow accustomed to the make-up, more of Laughton's own lips and jowls emerge from the mask. When he hands over the caged bird – which he wants Esmeralda to be, like the phantom's Christine – he hides his face; the bits left unobscured by parted fingers are recognizably Laughton's. And when he accepts water from his beloved, the whole action of flinching and recovery forms a graceful and balletic arc; a choreographed curve.

Quasimodo enraptures us; he is a sophisticated character because of Laughton's economy: he distils the essence of the part, gives it an inner life – so that despite the layers of plasticine wrapped on his face, we can determine motives behind movements, thoughts behind gestures, dreams behind silence. Whether he's the abashed boy kicking the bells, or whether he's Lord Greystoke swinging on the ropes of a petrified forest, launching himself at the gibbet to save Esmeralda, he's consistently the film's hero – and not Alan Marshal, who plays a character called Phoebus, eliciting remarks about his being a sun-god.

Laughton's hunchback is a satirical aesthete; he has a love-hate relationship with his physique; a petroglyphic dandy re-enacting vanity fair; Caliban cast in a part expected of Errol Flynn, flying through the air and celebrating liberty. Love, represented by Esmeralda, makes Quasimodo an exhibitionist – yet what's on display is his heart. His ugliness evaporates; we see his soul. Laughton is as much a metaphysician of appearance as Cocteau – for what Quasimodo raises is the very issue of beauty and truth, appearance and reality. 'In the bell-ringing scene,' writes Callow, 'his laughter as he compares himself to the man in the moon stems from very deep indeed, and is sustained so long that it becomes a laugh at the whole idea of deformity, *at the idea of appearance at all.*' Quasimodo's laugh melts the solid flesh and resolves personality as the dew of spirit.

'That I was not, after all, Charles Laughton' initiated Callow's investigation into the art and craft of acting. As he said in the proprietorially entitled *Callow's Laughton*, the television documentary, *The Hunchback of Notre Dame*, which he saw as an unhappy adolescent, showed him how 'acting would be a way out of the trap of my own personality. Actors use their own difficulties, doubts and pain in an artistic way. Laughton's performance had the effect of a healthy revelation.'

Acting as the opportunity to assuage, and make use of, darker proofs; as the route to self-gratification – these were the issues of *Being an Actor*. Of Shakespeare, Callow surmised 'speaking to people, he must have struggled not to start imitating their accent, twisting his features into their face . . . And that's what it's like to be an actor.' Shakespeare as the blank and fertile shape-changer, the ovoid of the Droeshout engraving: it's an equivalent of Quasimodo's laughter obliterating the notion of form. Like Peter Sellers's Chance the gardener in *Being There*, the ideal actor is a blank space, absorbing and reproducing; an innocent – or a child. 'Actors are indeed children,' Callow has said. They do not cease from exploration; the world for them is a school of enquiry. They have the opportunity to get reborn brand-new with each new part.

Callow's Laughton teased us with Callow's own partial renaissance as

Laughton. The programme began with newsreel footage of a black coffin and a Forest Lawns interment; a Gothick funeral, the cortège emerging from a Hollywood mansion of battlements and overgrown shrubs. We cut back to the birthplace, Scarborough, and Callow popped up, like the resurrection! He spoke with a strange halting emphasis, with breaks and pauses coming at random. Sometimes, Callow's hair was short and curly, sometimes longer and flaxen; his weight also waxed and waned. Interviewing Rex Harrison, he wasn't manifest at all – we merely heard a disembodied baritone laugh.

Walking around the Surrey treehouse, built by Clough Williams-Ellis of Portmeirion, Callow appeared leaning on a window ledge; we mixed to Laughton snapped in exactly the same pose, in exactly the same window. He 'wanted to leave a poetic image of the characters he played on the public's mind.' But the image we received was of Laughton's metamorphosis into Callow's image.

Next, Callow materialized in Hollywood, where Laughton went in 1931; he walked a dusty sunlit road, bordered with palms and orange trees. It might have been Galilee. America set Laughton free from constraints about social class (he was a hotelier's son: not quite a gentleman); he liked the size and promise of the continent. The vastness matched his imagination, whether he was playing patrician Nero in *The Sign of the Cross* or the proletarian butler in *Ruggles of Red Gap* – an Englishman who shames the Yanks by knowing Lincoln's Gettysburg Address by heart.

As Callow inspected flickering monitors, it was as if a youngish man was spookily casting an eye over a previous incarnation – Tony Perelli in *On the Spot*, for instance, where Laughton assumed his gangster disguise, using false eyelashes and blackening his hair: 'he is transformed,' says Callow, transfixed. 'He had an absolute belief in the characters. He found real emotions in the parts he played.'

The real emotions of Claudius were all too openly in collapse. Outtakes from the doomed Sternberg film are testimony to an actor losing control – because he's meant to be *acting* losing control. Laughton fluffs, dries, fails in concentration. Like Quasimodo, he's physically handicapped, but there's now an extra burden. Claudius is also emotionally handicapped. Laughton deconstructed himself; he tried to fathom the abjuration of power by listening to the abdication speech of Edward VIII, learning how to be a sensitive weakling, overcoming obligations and hurts. But it was his own gifts Laughton gave up. He couldn't grasp that Claudius's strength emerged in his moments of vulnerability; the Emperor was most powerful when giving power away (unlike the maudlin Edward VIII).

Laughton never again, according to Callow, risked all for acting. He instead became a teacher, a translator, a collaborator, working with Brecht; in films he contributed cameos, but no more sacred monsters. 'To act he delved into the blackest, most unpleasant aspects of his personality; after a while he decided not to ransack his psyche any more . . . And we should be grateful he showed us the potentials of acting.' The programme ended with a blotchy clip from Laughton's Bottom in *A Midsummer Night's Dream*, a hairy, ginger swaggerer in a hempen homespun shirt and a big belt. 'Would I have liked him if I'd met him?' Callow asks himself. 'I'd have been sucked in by his goodness and contrariness; he was a monumentally large personality.'

If the radio documentary was a postcard and the television transmission a love-letter, *Charles Laughton: A Difficult Actor* is a hardcover deification. For all its faults, the book is one of the best depictions of an actor's career I've come across; it's also one of the best descriptions of the acting process ever written. Laughton's guilts and secrecies are explored with infinite sympathy and discrimination; his performances are reconstructed and anatomized with wondrous skill. The resurrection in *Callow's Laughton* was a tricksy heresy; here Laughton's reputation is truly brought back from the dead. The Laughton-on-Callow and the Callow-in-Laughton emerge to bolster each other; a joint biography, extending the issues of acting as a psychic plight and the problems of appearance and vanity.★ *Being an Actor* was Callow's ostensible autobiography; *A Difficult Actor* becomes him best. Laughton is now an image of acting itself, instead of being a grandiose preincarnation.

Acting is a process for which theological claims are made; the difficult art is a way of reading the world, and of transfiguring it. Laughton's psychoanalytic cures alter into a religious purgation. Though a lapsed Catholic, like Cocteau he never stopped circumvallating the church. Through acting he was his own confessor; acting was a sanctification of his flesh; acting enabled a shrivening. Seeking out his sins, being the first to flaunt them, he encouraged a hope of redemption.

Laughton's religiosity, however, was brilliantly blasphemous – like the experiments against nature of his Dr Moreau in *Island of Lost Souls*. The creative vivisectionist, coeval with Dr Frankenstein, tampers with the laws of creation ('Believe me, Frankenstein, I was benevolent; my soul glowed with love and humanity; but am I not alone, miserably alone?') – exactly like an actor. 'What was Laughton trying to do,' asks Callow rhetorically, 'if not to release the soul of his character!'

Vivifying souls, Laughton is all the sons of his father's house – and their father, too. In *Les Misérables* he 'evokes Javert's soul . . . with unforgettable power'; his Bligh was 'a soul trapped by itself'; acting allowed him

★ After I'd read the book in proof, during the summer of 1987, I wrote asking Callow about autobiography in connection with Laughton – and he said 'your insight about the autobiographical element . . . is acute . . . the Laughton in me, the me in Laughton, I hope thus illuminating something about acting.'

'to cleanse his soul'. Blasphemy comes from the demonology of theatre – playing roles so convincingly, it's like possession by devils. And traditionally Catholicism condemned acting because of what Camus calls 'the heretical mulitiplication of souls'. Excommunicated, says Callow, Laughton 'doesn't tell you what to think or feel . . . he brings you face to face with the thing itself.'

Facing up is symptomatic of the era Laughton comes at the end of. He's the last of the Decadents – as Cocteau, born in 1889, was the first of the Modernists. Born in 1899, Laughton's literally *fin de siècle* – and Callow acknowledges the importance of a nineteenth-century sensibility, though he does not pursue the line far enough. Wilde is mentioned, yet the comparison requires amplification. Both Laughton and Wilde were stout homosexuals living secret lives; both were preoccupied with beauty. In *The Picture of Dorian Gray*, ugliness and beauty, age and youth, virtue and evil camouflage each other, and exchange places; in *The Hunchback of Notre Dame*, Quasimodo is a source of goodness fixed in a repulsive body – an inversion Wilde would have appreciated; as he would have appreciated suburban poisoner William Marble in Jeffrey Dell's *Payment Deferred*, of whom Laughton said, 'They crucified him, and by the end of the play they know they did it in secret fear of their own hidden loves under the mask of virtue.' The Christ on Calvary image, and the suggestion of sin safe under manners, might be directly out of *De Profundis*.

Wilde and Laughton were both performers, and self-willed martyrs. The actor's best performances constitute his own *De Profundis*; the dramatist's time of it in the dock, cross-examined by Carson, was his *I Claudius*. Both men were essentially Falstaffs compelled to play Hamlet. Nimble, vain, haunted, solitary, they were decadent because they experimented with identity – not with the liberated energy of the Romantics, but with the vivid energy of Victorians prevailed upon to be repressed. 'To realize one's nature perfectly – that is what each of us is here for,' wrote Wilde. 'People are afraid of themselves nowadays' – a fear Coleridge, for example, would not have understood. What has supervened between the *Biographia Literaria* and *De Profundis* is a century of the work-ethic, parliamentary government and metropolitan good behaviour; the worry of citizenship.

To realize one's nature perfectly is a dangerous business – as Dorian Gray discovers. It necessitates giving in to criminality; to forbidden pleasures and pains. Laughton links with Wilde, and is a hero to Callow, precisely because of his brave self-confrontations; his relentless self-examination. 'He seemed to view his roles,' writes Callow, 'not as problems to be solved or hurdles to be cleared but as challenges to self-knowledge: could he unlock the part of himself that would give meaning and life to the character?' Acting is an alarming metaphysical inquiry.

Architecture and paintings are important in *A Difficult Actor*. Laughton is difficult, we're told, as art is difficult: meanings are yielded up only when the spectators are sharp and persevering; and he used painting 'to inform his acting, transform his acting'. Acting and painting? Both deal with representation; duplications of the world, yet not entirely of it.

Nero, for instance, in *The Sign of the Cross*, was derived from Beardsley's illustrations for *Salome* – in which the Tetrarch is recognizably Wilde himself, with sensual lips and sagging cheeks; oriental and erotic drawings of bubbles, buds, pools and peacocks. For *The Private Life of Henry VIII*, Laughton betook himself to Hampton Court and studied the Holbeins and the size of the apartments; the atmosphere of the interiors and Tudor space – 'getting my mind accustomed to the square, squat architecture of the rooms and the cloisters'.

Laughton absorbed inferences of domestic detail from pictures and buildings: how folk ate, sat, moved. For *Rembrandt*, he went with Korda to Holland and studied paintings, drawings, houses, furniture and ornaments. 'He bought every book written about Rembrandt, he saw every canvas painted by Rembrandt . . .' He grew familiar with utensils and period studio techniques – he wanted his performance to be so convincing in its details, we don't even notice them. Callow regards the performance as Laughton's idealized self-portrait; his version of the Dutch master's own series of self-portraits. Rembrandt gazed back at himself with an innocence impossible to post-Romantic art, before the gratifying of desires replaced happiness, before the bizarrerie of mental life replaced character and any faith in public composure.

Working on *Galileo*, Brecht and Laughton would 'rush off to the museums and art galleries for clues'. They learnt how to construct the play, how to arrange character-relationships, by investigating period artefacts; they looked at telescopes and early scientific equipment. Laughton taught himself optical physics – as, when preparing Cyrano de Bergerac, he frisked the world of musketeers and courtiers. He became an agile fencer, experimented with scores of false noses, and designed high-heeled shoes to enable a cocky strut. Contemplating the Italian philanderer in *They Knew What They Wanted*, Laughton absorbed Michelangelo, Vivaldi, Dante; for a mad German, he read *Mein Kampf*; for the aborted share in *David Copperfield*, he sought old editions and the illustrations by Phiz.

If Laughton was a decadent, he was an intensely disciplined one (he spent days loitering with pickpockets to learn their skills for *Liliom*; sleuthing Bligh, he discovered in Grieves of Bond street the original measurements and counterfoils from the Captain's uniform, 1789) – yet that's no contradiction. Wilde was industrious; he rehearsed his spontaneity and epigram-ridden table-talk. And Burne-Jones wrote to Beardsley, 'I know you are not afraid of the work . . . You must not waver . . . You must learn to master the grammar of your art, and if your exercises are stiff and prosaic, so much the better.' The artists of the Nineties were raised on an entirely Victorian sense of research and obligation to produce. 'Tis the utmost thou hast in thee: out with it, then! There is a verisimilitude about their work – which outdoes itself; the labour of excess. Victorian art seems naturalistic, evolving logically into photography, but actually the bright colours and figurative arrangement make it fervid and stage-managed; the realism is a heightened reality: Ford Madox Brown's reds and yellows, Frith's rubies and black, Millais's golds and greens.

Victorian painting is iridescent, as if lit by an inner light. The muddy purples, tangled straw and flashes of white in Delaroche's *The Execution of Lady Jane Grey*, for example. The blindfolded girl is assisted to the block by a bishop – as if she's a child-bride helped to an altar. The axeman frowns and waits like an abashed groom. There's a sense of horror and oppression; a monstrous parody of protectiveness. The picture, as Ruskin said, is a short story – as is the same artist's *Cromwell Gazing at the Body of Charles I*. Dressed in heavy brown leathery jerkins and huge boots, lined and grizzled Cromwell★ lifts the coffin lid to examine the severed head of his regal victim. Charles lies Christ-like, his skin a glowing paleness; Cromwell is a devil on duty, the lining of his leggings and his slumped plume being slashings of arterial crimson. It's a painting of victory and defeat; court and country; poetic fragility and brute reality; life and death. King Charles and Lady Jane are pale beauties killed by strong ugliness – the demons win.

The Civil War was a common subject for the Victorians; it enabled allegories of their own divided natures: the Cavaliers and the Roundheads, pleasure-seeking and repentance, indolence and industry. Their art had a fondness for interior subjects – murders, interrogations, smotherings, preachings; landscapes, too, were enclosed with suffocating foliage and skies busy with cloud. A mood of menace and sadism; of sexual desecration. Thus, Laughton. He laboured at his acting; his theatre was a rummaging 'among the capacious folds in his own personality,' as Callow puts it. '... As long as he could bear it, it enabled him to give performances that have the force of great paintings from which he drew such comfort and inspiration.' Laughton himself once said 'great acting is like painting' – and Callow even uses pictorial phrases: the 'epic canvas' of performances; there are 'no straight lines with him'.

Acting is like painting because a play of gesture, posture, light, shade. The best in this kind are but shadows. Laughton's roles flamed forth from his mind as 'the bright efflorescence latent in it', to use Henry James's

---

★ Cromwell is a part made famous by Ivan Spears, the Laughton double in Michael Blakemore's novel, *Next Season*. See Part One.

phrase from *The Awkward Age*; like the indwelling fires of art. And where *Being an Actor* was written out of inflammatory language; *A Difficult Actor* is composed from the terminology of aestheticism, as though the text is itself a pronunciamento from the Nineties; a yellow book. As with any gazette by Wilde, there are jaunty ambiguities. One moment we're told Laughton was 'secret with his work', taciturn at rehearsals, next that 'he was a genuine team-worker'. One moment Laughton is 'almost morbidly perfectionist' and 'Only on stage did he belong', next that he 'was certain of nothing, not even his acting'. One moment 'Laughton may have been a mess', the next, there was 'nothing messy or impressionistic' about him. Cross-referenced like this, the book appears muddled and inconsistent – but the tone at the time is of excitement and forthright generalization: the zeal of camp, which is Callow's own contribution to a literature of nineteenth-century Decadence. *A Difficult Actor* is coeval with Beardsley, Wilde, Sickert and company. Conceptions of soul and spirit; the overriding lesson of 'what a serious thing it was to be actor' – these are enquiries into the importance of being earnest; the truth of masks; the decay of lying; the critic as actor. The picture of Charles Laughton is the picture of Simon Callow; a portrait of the artist as much as of the sitter.

Laughton's mood of the Nineties is what contributed to his old-fashioned air – hamminess is the cheap word. He comes before us now as a Victorian exaggeration, almost preposterous – an anachronistic mood Callow often cultivates; a theatrical picturesqueness. On the *Ed Sullivan Show*, Laughton was confronted with Elvis Presley, and looked 'like the Victorian he always was'. The fustian dominie versus the hip-grinding rebel. Callow's equivalent was on *Wogan*. He was paired with the cock-sparrow actor Dexter Fletcher, and it was like Peter Pan flicking pellets at an embarrassed Mr Darling. Callow talked of Laughton and attempted a theory of acting; Fletcher, who'd recently worked with Al Pacino, playing his son in the messy *Revolution*, dissented from any serious talk and slumped in his seat, seemingly pouting for the screaming girls in the studio audience. Acting, he smiled, was just a case of turning up and learning lines.

Callow's prose is a Laughtonesque performance; his acting, however, is lighter and never mystical – which is why he found he couldn't do anything with Perelli in *On the Spot*, the role Laughton made to demonstrate 'real sexual aggression'. An aggression is missing, also, from the recent conjunctions of acting and painting. There ought to be a sensual overlap: the actor and his body; the painter and his model – like Picasso's mating with his nudes in the guise of a minotaur; nymphs and satyrs. Instead, we have Peter Greenaway's *The Draughtsman's Contract* where Anthony Higgins's artist tups Janet Suzman's chatelaine, in part-payment for sketches of her property; the commissioned pictures tell a murder-story – which the film failed to elucidate satisfactorily, muddled as it was with conceits about perspective, Restoration landscapes, perukes and the artist's eye. Or then there's Derek Jarman's *Caravaggio*, where the holy personages in the pictures are posed for by renters and tarts. Religious scenes are improved street-life. Again, the film had a sensational premiss: Caravaggio (Dexter Fletcher, later Nigel Terry) killing the thing he loves, by knifing Ranuccio – played as an anachronistic bike-boy by Sean Bean. *Caravaggio* was a homoerotic flirt. Callow's contribution to the sub-genre was *Cariani and the Courtesans*. Paul McGann was the hand-some dauber and eponym, Callow a chirpy forger. The film played games with artistic lies and real-life duplicity, and with those corners of reality where fiction and fact appear to intersect. Venice was the setting, a place of political murders and expedient prostitution; of the 'tec feel of Greenaway and the slummy sex of Jarman. Callow's character's studio was a factory, hung with dripping catchpenny Dürers. He claims the paper gets wet when the floods seep between the flagstones.

As a forger, Raimondi is a kind of an actor: a counterfeiter, analysing pictures and styles. 'Is not beauty the greatest deceiver of all?' he asks. And, anticipating Keats, 'You're beautiful, but are you true?' Like Laugh-ton as Rembrandt, Callow was convincingly competent with the con-traptions of a studio: the engraving plates, stiletto, platen, inks. Cariani was told to sign his work, if he wants to be remembered; Raimondi, financially astute, signs his work with the monikers of famous others – far more lucrative. Raimondi lazily prods his naked models, Cariani falls in love with his – specifically, the demure daughter of a strangled admiral. The mystery of the father's death involved a plot as detached and obscure as in *The Draughtsman's Contract*. And as in that film, a picture was a language without words. We were meant to read Cariani's portrait of the girl, her mother, their visitors, as a solution to a tale which was never quite clear in the first place. 'You're a painter,' Cariani is told, 'trust your eyes.' Is the portrait of a family reunion, or a brothel?

Tricksy, too supersubtle, the film was a salad of preciosity; Callow played for comedy, a fluster of mannerism and sincerity – a fluster perfect for Wilkins Micawber. And in taking on that role, he completed a circuit Laughton fled from; a pleasing intersection of destinies.

In *A Difficult Actor*, he exculpates his predecessor by arguing that Dickens is difficult to act: the characters in the novels are already outra-geous; the theatre can't add to them. They are all mannerism and have no subconscious life. What a slander! Callow underestimates Dickens's depravities and violent imagination. Laughton was Dickensian without having to act in Dickens. He therefore threw off Micawber because the improvident genius was too close a personal satire: 'a man of some experience in life, and – of some experience, in short, in difficulties, generally speaking . . . My advice is so far worth taking, that . . . I have never taken it myself, and am the . . . miserable wretch you behold.'

Year in, year out, the BBC has trivialized Dickens, happy for him to be made a tea-time accompaniment for log fires and buttery scones; a fancy-dress parade of bonnets and crepe whiskers. Shot on streaky videotape, with hastily decorated locations, so that the carriages swish along tarmac roads and past Forestry Commission spruces, the serials are cheap and etiolated. Lawns are evidently striped by motor mowers; milestones and signposts are pure cardboard. *David Copperfield*, transmitted in November 1986, contained blurry cuts between overlit interiors and an exterior with a different intensity of sun. Pauses between a character quitting a room and emerging to the open air were badly paced – the actors forgot a continuity of stride. And from this circumambient mediocrity, Callow stood out – bearing in mind that all Dickens's characters expect to stand out, his works being a democracy of deviants.

Misfits here included Thorley Walters as the pink-cheeked kite-flyer, Mr Dick; Brenda Bruce as the dynamic Aunt Betsey; Oliver Cotton as the evil Mr Murdstone. Callow dominated because he did not seek to be dominant; his personification owed nothing to W. C. Fields's knowing spice. The actor divined that the key to Micawber is his self-delighting theatricality; that he really rejoices in creeping penury and dispossession because they provide him with moments for melodrama; and for Callow, Dickens's prose provided moments for song. Micawber's speeches were arias; his conversation, a libretto. Despatching his chattels to the pawnbroker, he was a feckless monarch giving away his kingdom; sent to the debtors' prison, he sailed off as if in a state landau, his wife a queen – a willing accomplice in her spouse's mad optimism.

With gleaming pate (resembling Brando's Kurtz? Otto Preminger? Philip French?), Callow was the only Dickens character authentically Dickensian. With his rolling eyes; his voice vagrant over several octaves; with a pout and a lisp, we never knew what this Micawber would essay next; nor where he'd next turn up to assure us 'something is about to turn up'.

Animated Phiz, the character was a success. As an earnest of Callow's adaptation to the part, he actually did have his head shaved. 'I had to,' he told me, 'bald wigs hardly ever work. Frowning is impossible – they crinkle. Turning the head is impossible – you look like a marionette. So off came the locks.' The effect was to make Micawber a giant baby, and thus in appearance what another Callow character is in spirit – Tom Chance, the innocent idiot.

Chance in a Million, like Judi Dench's and Mike Williams's *A Fine Romance*, is cheerfully mindless; another example of a television tradition:

the comedy without laughs. In both cases, the plot is the same. Will the male and female leads get married? Tom Chance and Alison Little's courtship is prehistorical; they don't have the gumption to organize a wedding. Ostensible humour arises from their mental retardation. Brenda Blethyn plays one of her Ayckbourn dopes; Callow is Stan Laurel in the body of Oliver Hardy with the speech pattern of Charlie Chan, the personal pronouns and indefinite articles filtered out.

Tom's life is the rolling dice; the moron who finds, aleatorically, the correct combination of safes, and who muddies his innocence with the police. The imbecile who succeeds, but who fails to make use of his success; as with Micawber, Tom survives – against the odds – and becomes, with his tawny frizz, bowler and floppy black coat a size or so too small, a version of an archetype: the Holy Fool who, wearing himself, or his language, away to silence and blank self-absorption, distantly connects with the vagabonds and derelicts in Samuel Beckett.

'Yes. Sam's sit-com,' joked Callow. 'He mails the scripts from Paris.'

'Chance has made you famous.'

'He's the character who's made me recognized in the street. My barber was delighted when I went in to have my beard trimmed.'

Chance is a lampoon on Callow the contemplator. The character cogitates fiercely, sincerely, to little effect. He's the infant struggling to form letters and make himself articulate. He had a child's seriousness; the way a child lives in a world of his own – and Chance is private and sullen. Marriage is evaded because it would obliterate his exclusive realm – a place of bird-nesting and funeral jokes and mother-in-law quips. The character's other-worldliness is signified by his archaic diction, anachronistic clothes and codes of honour. Alison is very chivalrically treated; she'd rather she wasn't.

The series is ritualistically dire, as though bad jokes have a right to regular recitation; as though actors have a duty to parade them before us, sure of our approval and refusal to mourn. Nobody is in the least bit taken in that they're funny. Similarly, nobody was in the least bit taken in that *A Room with a View* had anything to do with E. M. Forster. The film was an exercise in the precious and the picturesque; our nostalgia for the afternoon of Edwardian England, which was lost in 1914, and which is regained on celluloid in every other 'classic' adaptation since *Brideshead Revisited*.

The importance of the James Ivory/Ruth Prawer Jhabvala film for Callow is the company he's seen to keep. He joins a charmed circle of theatricals, including Maggie Smith, contriving to be an incompetent governess; Denholm Elliott, mouthing the platitudes George and Lucy are borne towards marriage on; Judi Dench, all frowning and gossipy simpers; and Rosemary Leach, tugging herself into a copious corset. A cast which relaxed into nostalgia; the flannels and panamas; the bustles and barouches. Dame Kiri te Kanawa's singing of Puccini suffused the film with pure treacle. Callow smirked through the opus, never disrupting the tone by playing *Forster's* Beebe – *A Room with a View*, an indictment of English travellers, was chastened as a travelogue; its romanticism played out as romance; and yet he, and the film, were in receipt of critical raptures. Ditto Forman's *Amadeus*.

'I had an unhappy time – not because I wasn't to be Mozart, but because Miloš Forman wanted me to play Schikaneder as myself, with an American accent – which was just ridiculous! Acting, he maintained, was not required in films; what he hated most was acting non-acting.'

In Shaffer's play, as in Pushkin's, Mozart and Salieri are antagonists in a cosmic battle – '*Dio Inguisto*! You are the enemy! I hate Thee now – *Nemico Eterno*!' This allegorical level is kept out of the film, and diabolism is reduced to sublunary spite and envy. Not the Devil versus God, but Iago (F. Murray Abraham) mismatched with Peter Pan (Tom Hulce, from *Animal House*). We don't even get the play's biological energy: fecund Wolfgang versus impotent Salieri – 'Have you heard his music?' asks Mozart. 'That's the sound of someone who can't get it up' – suggesting that creativity is gonadic.

What is common, to stage and screen, is a Mozart of altitudinous pink periwigs, showy curtsies and firecracker coats. He makes all his speeches into a rash of exclamation points – and the cloacal coarseness is excessive. Shaffer's Amadeus is not the intense little genius of the letters, say, or of contemporary accounts. He's a rudesby Lost Boy persecuted by father-figures: Leopold in Salzburg who becomes the Commendatore in *Don Giovanni*; Salieri himself ('When I reproved him,' over *Figaro*, 'he said I reminded him of his father.') And these Captain Hooks creak in an atmosphere of glutinous pastry. The film, especially, is a mega-calorific sweetmeat (like the cakes Salieri keeps eating in the play). The colours are caramel; the tones those of brown eclairs, tangerine sorbets, brandied chestnuts and granulated sugar.

'What do you do when you receive a script and accept a part?'

'The first thing, when lines have been learned, is – to forget the lines! Forget them all. Concentrate, instead, on their meaning and the feeling they represent: the world in, and on, and under the lines; but not the words themselves. A script is the starting point; the very beginning. You have to convert it from a written thing into a performance – so that in performance the words seem to well up quite unconsciously.'

Callow's ideas were tested in a masterclass he held in 1987 on Sir John Vanbrugh's *The Relapse*. We saw him in action as a director. Whether because his three actors were uniquely diffident, or whether Callow was nervous – but he lectured ungivingly, his special audience only interjecting with sceptical queries ('Define sensuousness'; 'What do you mean, "We are all everything"?'); otherwise they were silent, hunched in layers of cardigan and fiddling with spectacles on strings.

The turncoat director was at a disadvantage; as a rehearsal, the hour was cold and artificial. Callow sat on a chair yards from his line of actors; a stiff atmosphere, nobody ever relaxed. His remarks on Restoration drama were interesting – but how could they be translated to theatrical effect? *The Relapse*, we learned, dealt with fortunes and the grubby, vulgar, material facts of money; the beauty spots and fans, the elevated language, need to be made accessible and realistic. *But how?*

Callow's solutions were too subtle and complicated. He made a speech about the period's pleasure in clothes and sexual liberation; he played Ravel's *Daphnis and Chloe* on a tinny gramophone; he made gnomic utterances such as 'Every play is a world of its own, and we must find what makes it different from other plays'; he quoted Gielgud to the effect that 'Style is knowing what kind of play you're in'; he played a record of Dame Edith Evans in *The Way of the World*: querulous, the voice hovering, the despatcher of kine from *Tom Jones*; he played a trumpet voluntary, and asked the actor playing Lord Foppington 'to be like that'; he got lost using a metaphor about balls and jets of water.

'In Restoration comedy,' Callow said, 'the actor needs constant mental and vocal energy to liberate the wit.' The trouble with his masterclass was that the director's own mental energies, the manner in which allusions and analogies stockpiled, confused rather than illuminated the issues for the actors, whose attempts at reading through Vanbrugh's lines were stilted, amateurish, self-conscious. The 'inner world of emotion' was never found – and yet how could it have been? Callow's directorial inquisitions trod the method of Laughton; acting as an instance of psychological honesty, provoked who knows how. If he looked foolish in the masterclass it was the foolhardiness of brave innovation.

In Hammersmith, while he was rehearsing *The Infernal Machine*, I asked how a script can be a mere instigation, the starting-point for an actor's self-invention, and yet also sacrosanct – the end-all in itself.

'What I want,' Callow said, 'is to be true to the style and intention of the original. We shouldn't forget the times and climates in which specific plays were written. I believe it's mistaken to bring drama from the past up to date. I'm not asking for archaelogical reconstructions, museum pieces; but let's allow other ages and writers to speak for themselves; let their own contexts emerge.'

'In *Being an Actor* that's a directional arrogance: to interpose between a play, a playwright, an actor – and thereby the audience.'

'Shakespeare's not our contemporary; he was only his own. A successful production ought to forget "relevance" and celebrate the fact that his plays are living things in their own right.'

'Plays shouldn't be deformed by the imposition of modernity?'

'With Cocteau I want to do something Cocteauesque; with Restoration comedy, I'd want fidelity to Vanbrugh's world, say. What would be the point of putting Lord Foppington in dark glasses and a punk's designer rags?'

'What is your attitude to plays without scripts – improvisation?'

'I was asked to be in Mike Leigh's *Rhubarb*, but I was too fearful and wouldn't dare. Leigh is a director who carries, in his own head, whole biographies of his casts's characters; what gets acted is a dramatic distillation of all this material he accumulates.'

'Rather like Laughton, who wrote mental histories for his characters; long novels behind their actions and speech.'

'And that's too much of a burden for anyone for long.'

'Leigh collaborates with his actors to a huge extent; plus all the improvisation. His approach seems a genuine joint stock. How would this compare with having no director at all?'

'I've come to appreciate that it's probably only possible to get away without a director with a highly experienced cast; when the cast aren't being stretched. Then the actors can coast along on their own. But people *ought* to be stretched. The experimental co-operatives I've seen are disasters – productions which didn't work because of bad acting.'

Directors, as we have seen, have their autocracy questioned in *Being an Actor*. Callow's focus of discussion with Laughton was commonly the relationship between actor and director: Sternberg for *I, Claudius*, Hitchcock for *Jamaica Inn*, William Dieterle for *The Hunchback of Notre Dame*, Alexander Korda for *The Private Life of Henry VIII*, and *Rembrandt*; Boleslavsky for *Les Misérables* – who once wrote 'the soul of the artist is the source of all art'; Jean Renoir for *This Land Is Mine*. With the exception of the final two, Laughton did not generally seem to get along with the directors. Sternberg issued orders from the London Hospital; Hitchcock thought Laughton's agonies over deciding Sir Humphrey Pengallan's walk a pretentious nonsense; Dieterle abetted the actor's agonies as Quasimodo, so that the acted suffering was barely acted at all; Korda thought his star wayward, and did not figure out the method in the waywardness, so cancelled *Cyrano*.

Boleslavsky, contrariwise, had written a treatise called *Acting: the First Six Lessons* ('still one of the most useful and accessible things ever written about acting,' assures Callow), holding that the artistic temperament has to be attuned to the rhythms of seasons and seas. Laughton appreciated that. Against such pantheism was Renoir, who indulged Laughton's hunt for subtext. 'He wanted to know,' the director recalled, 'why he was being asked to do things.'

What do Callow's actor/director explications portend? Why is he so fascinated by the relationship? On an altruistic and public level, he's wanting to goad fellow actors into becoming their own champions, vigilant in the defence of their own interests; he wants deliverance from a dictatorship. On a less yielding level, however, motivations are deeply private. Directors are emblems of authority, father-figures. (As Alec McCowen says in *Double Bill*, the director is as necessary to an actor 'as a father in the upbringing of a child'.) And Callow never knew his own father. Subconsciously, he's excavating the myth of Oedipus, hero of *The Infernal Machine*. '*Il tuera son père* . . .' By either arguing away the importance of a director, or at best arguing for a parity between director and actor, he's rigging up a system for himself, I think, where overlords have diminished power. He wants them not to be remote gods; fathers who shall have no dominion, sons surviving without sires: performances resenting directorial influence, and wanting to be independent things. The actor as onlie begetter.

That we know an Oedipal theme lurks in Callow is hinted at in *Being an Actor*. While he is working in Scotland, a call comes through from Africa saying his father has died. As 'I barely knew him', Callow is unmoved – until he sees *Hamlet*, that same night: 'Then something primitive stirred inside me.' Shakespeare's play is rife with fathers and guilty sons: Hamlet and the ghost; Hamlet and Claudius; Laertes and Polonius. Sons making atonement with parental spirits; sons avenging their fathers. *Being an Actor*, its attitude to directors, perseveres (as Claudius would put it) in obstinate condolement; the son shrugging away patrimony, ostentatiously.

A Difficult Actor implies a different course: in filial obligation for some term Callow makkes obsequious sorrow – Laughton is a father substitute, and the son, instead of striking the father dead, wants to be consubstantial with him. The power of Callow's work on Laughton comes from this quality of apparentation. We see Callow generating himself out of a past master; we track a pedigree of styles. Laughton is co-opted kin.

> But you must know your father lost a father,
> That father lost, lost his . . .

Cocteau's *The Infernal Machine* makes the destiny of Oedipus as ineluctable as the operations of an engine; fate is no game, its deployment of love and chance is a paradise of mechanics. Fate, in fact, is camp in its insouciance. Free will is only a little free.

Thus, theatre as a form. Nineteenth-century stagecraft, derived from Diderot, expected the stage to be an insulated box; the tableaux; every element predetermined and awaiting the audience's attention. We'd have read the set as we'd read the epic pictures in galleries; drama would have unfolded with all the power of historical inevitability. And the duty of the actor is still to sustain energy and conviction each night; they have to re-live what they know to be laid down in advance. This is the paradox of acting, and why it is in itself an infernal machine. Actors are only a little free.

Diderot made a metaphysical sport out of the conundrum in *Jacques le fataliste et son maître*, a celebration of freewheeling conversation; the forks and flourishes of chat. The art was to make the polished opus seem improvisatory; to make fiction snap like fact. His novel is therefore highly theatrical. The characters, overspilling with anecdote, are self-dramatists; inveterate inventors. As a young man, Diderot thought of becoming an actor ('the theatre for which I had some inclination') but instead he ended up editing the *Encyclopédie*. Mostly impecunious, he survived on the proceeds of selling his library to Catherine the Great.

Diderot exalted the trivial, the digressive; he enjoyed the war between mind and body; he pondered the breach between freedom and constraint. Reality, he maintained, was a compound of contradiction – and he wanted acting to embody such disorder, with the difference that muddle is planned in advance. He advocated overlapped dialogue and scenes; he expected the actor to be an infernal machine of passion, bringing 'confusion and fear into an audience's souls'.

Appreciative of flux and the generously circuitous, Diderot seems perfect for Callow, and they do indeed coincide in the 1986 translation *Jacques and His Master*, made from Milan Kundera's play *Jacques et son Maître*. Kundera turned to Diderot in 1968, wanting a high-spirited author to palliate contemporary politics in Prague. *Jacques le Fataliste*, its dialogues and stories-within-stories, was convoluted and loud and shut out the trundle of tanks: 'The whole novel is nothing but a vast, very loud, conversation,' Kundera claimed.

He also found in the book a brutal honesty which seemed appropriate; the action, or the talk, uncoils in a no-man's-land. Diderot 'creates a space never before glimpsed in the history of the novel: a stage without scenery: where do they come from? We don't know. What are their names? None of our business.' Which is rather to read baroque Diderot as though he's bleak Brecht (*Mother Courage*) or a precursor of Beckett's depopulated plains – where Didi and Gogo do nothing but talk.

Kundera's Diderot represents irrepressible human spirits in the face of a wanton threat – that is, in 1968, the wicked Russians. Callow, remaking both Diderot and Kundera by the alchemy of translation, adapts *Jacques et son Maître* to his own particular ends: the issues of theatricality; the relationship between a director and an actor.

Jacques and his master, the servant and his sovereign, are the actor and the director, with the servant/actor ever the more resourceful. When the master explains his attitude ('As a master, it is my absolute right to interrupt my servant whenever I wish'), we are back with the manifesto against directorial suzerainty of *Being an Actor*, with the associated Oedipal undercurrent – best seen in Diderot's own writings as *Le neveu de Rameau* (translated by Goethe in 1805), where the dispute is displaced avuncularly: the nephew resents his own talents being stifled by the greater fame of his uncle. His bitterness and envy caught the eye of Freud, who noted this: 'If your little savage were left to himself and to his native blindness, joining the infant's reasoning to the grown man's violent passions, he would strangle his father and go to bed with his mother.'*

Master and servant genially invade each other's anecdotes and speechifying, but the covert battle for psychological leadership is very real. The innkeeper eventually remarks of their squabbles, 'It is written up there that you can't get along without each other' – the up-above referring to a theatrical heaven of predestination, where such issues as this are resolved: 'Are you a rat because it was written up above? Or is it written up above because they knew you would be a rat?'

Talk, and its dramatization, is entirely about sex. Interruptions of chat come like a series of *coitus interrupti*; anecdotes about mislaying virginity and provoking cuckoldry entangle and overlap – a conversational orgy. Jacques cuckolds his friend Bigre in the loft with Justine ('You first-class shit,' says the master admiringly. 'And then what did you do?'). The master, in his turn, is betrayed by Saint-Ouen and Agathe. Tales interact and juxtapose almost musically.

The characters then start to wonder whether they've been well constructed; they are conscious of owing their existence to a trio of masters: Diderot, Kundera, Callow. And beyond the scriptwriters, they've also had to filter through the sensibility of actors. 'What I want to know is: is it well written?' The play plays with the idea that it's a paper chase. When the heroes halt at an inn, they are reminded, 'It was written that you would have duck, spuds and a bottle of wine.'

Callow translates with salty liveliness, with many idiomatic sprinklings of pissing, arses, fuck, bugger, etc. Kundera much admired the adaptation, and Callow had first come to his notice in *Amadeus*, the director, Miloš Forman, being a fellow Czech. He was sent a copy of *Being an Actor* and especially appreciated the diatribe against directors, his equivalent being translators, who distort and impose and expropriate. Callow's *Jacques and His Master*, for Kundera, is the exception proving the rule.

'Why did you elect to translate Milan Kundera's *Jacques et son Maître*?'

'Blatant sycophancy! I made the translation so that I could meet the

---

* Quoted in Introductory Lectures (1917), XXI.

author. I adore Kundera, and *Jacques and His Master* was a homage to catch his eye . . .'

The novel particularly lofty in Callow's esteem is *The Unbearable Lightness of Being* – a title pregnant with association. The plot deals with a hypersensitive doctor called Tomas, who tries to make a philosophic dissection of his emotions. He's a cold, calculating Don Juan, for whom Tereza is a flirtatious Elvira. Is he in love with her, or is love just his own selfish fantasy by another name? A hysteria? Or spermatorrhoea?

Somewhere in the background is a wife divorced a decade ago (Tomas 'could be fully himself only as a bachelor'), and a dispossessed son.

'For the film,' said Callow, 'Daniel Day Lewis is to be Tomas. In my opinion he's too young; and references to the son and a long past have been cut, which seems to me rather important. Kundera is so fussy about his work, but he's approved the script.'*

The long past is rather important because Tomas, as Don Juan, has won and discarded dozens of ancient lovers. Why does Tereza obsess him? Exactly like the haggard libertine in Byron and Mozart, his womanizing signified 'a fear of women'. She's the innocent only gradually made aware of her squire's nature, his constant infidelities and lies.

Prague is subjugated to Moscow, as Tereza is to Tomas; they escape to Geneva, but Tereza opts for a return: 'She was weighing him down and would do so no longer.' Tomas is glad she goes: 'He was enjoying the sweet lightness of being.' Later, he's remorseful, heavy with a sense of destiny and responsibility.

Kundera's symbolism (light/dark, light/heavy) is what stops the novel from reading like a novelette. Wrought into the text are many references either to lightness as weight, mass, solidity, fragility; or lightness as illumination, harmony, spirituality; blood. Lightness is a synonym of irresponsibility and froth; heaviness is associated with the call of duty and accountability and judgment.

Tomas sees sex as light, love as heavy. Reconciling himself to a life as a

---

* Callow was correct to have misgivings. The film, directed by Philip Kaufman, could do nothing with what Kundera calls the *architecture* of his novels – their ability to be 'poetry, fantasy, philosophy, aphorism, and essay all rolled into one'. Metaphysics was out (what can actors do with *ideas*?), and so instead we had an interminable triangulated sex romp, slowed down to legato speed, the *Carry on Doctor* and *Confessions of a Window Cleaner* elements atomized by Sven Nykvist's misted-up camera lens.

What was needed, to obliterate the romancing and inject a vicious and allusive comedy of manners, was the genius of Luis Buñuel. Somebody obviously twigged this, because Buñuel's co-writer, Jean-Claude Carrière, did the script. The only diversion was the running theme of voyeurism: windows, photo-reportage, modelling, rolling on a new film like fitting a condom, the click of the shutter a little death – *Lightness* being a camera's apprehension of dark and shade.

being of light, however, he gets to feel weightless: an actor, a shadow whose character has no substance. Solidity can only occur for him in the repetition of performance; his insistent copulativeness. And adding to his monotonous sterility, his refusal to extend allegiance beyond a moment's gratification, Tomas's favourite part of a woman's body is her arse – 'the anus, the spot he loved most'. This is against nature, and so is his mythical self-image – Oedipus. 'How many ancient myths begin with the rescue of an abandoned child,' Tomas remarks, expounding on Sophocles's drama of the adventitious.

He'd hoped to live a life as a being of the light: carefree; his own master. Events, however, make him a being of weight: '*Muss es sein? Es muss sein! Es muss sein!*' he murmurs, picking up a motif from a Beethoven quartet. (Must it be? It must be! It must be!) Only the real actor, on stage, knows the paradoxical bliss of Oedipus: functioning in a drama, its origins and conclusions ordered in advance, speaking words perfected by somebody else – a weightiness disguised as the unbearable lightness of being: 'The main issue is whether a man is innocent because he didn't know.' An actor acting has control of his destiny, for the duration of the performance. 'And blest are those,' says Hamlet, 'Whose blood and judgement are so well commingled/That they are not a pipe for Fortune's finger/To sound what stop she please.'

The control is manufactured through terminal camp – known as Kitsch. Kitsch is theatre's errant fakery. If camp is a very serious frivolity, Kitsch is camp about its own campness; it's spoiled, corrupted, exhibitionistic. The extremity of self-consciousness. 'Kitsch causes two tears to flow in quick succession,' says Kundera. 'The first tear says: "How nice to see the children running on the grass!" The second tear says: "How nice to be moved, together with all mankind, by children running on the grass!" It is the second tear that makes Kitsch Kitsch.' (The most perfect example known to me is Cocteau's seeing an old lady weep at *La Belle Helene* – and he's told it's Cosima Wagner.)

Kitsch is the actor's fatal knowingness; his knowledge that his art lies in repetition, 'the stopover between being and oblivion'. Callow's Laughton, Callow himself, forming the conception of his stage people, demonstrate the second tear: actors acting on behalf of us all. Actors as reactors. Callow's extremest example of this is his Faust, who flies through space and time, conquering both. He's holy and he's blasphemous, Mephistopheles (Peter Lindford) also Christlike (perching on a pentangle like the crucified messiah) and diabolic. Light/heavy becomes the transcendental opposition to mind/body, beauty/ugliness, fire/water. 'Two souls in me,' says Faust, 'struggle for possession.' The glandular, physiological aspects versus a pure and disinterested intelligence.

Perhaps he achieves a balance. The aged, crabbed Faust is doused in a furnace and reborn youthful and full of promise; he's allowed a renaissance as sensual and serene, fulfilling a dream of Laughton's. Faust experiences, as Cocteau wanted, mental and physical ecstasies; and he's a parent of sorts, creating the stretch-bubble Homunculus. Like Christopher Isherwood's Frankenstein, he creates a monster which is beautiful, and which grows ugly as it learns the ways of men – adding to the oppositions angel/demon, innocence/experience.

Faust works out his salvation with public works: he reclaims land from the sea, and this is a powerful metaphor of making the light weighty – like making the shifty, churning experiences of life a safe and certain thing of art. Kundera's novel – in which Tomas is, as a doctor, a sort of Faust – is fond of argument about free will and determinism; singular events and their semi-camouflaged resurrection; random and planned existences – just like Diderot and Goethe; just like Callow, for the notions subtend his career, and, indeed, the whole art of acting itself, which is the subject of this book. Acting reveals a strategy for combatting the Unbearable Lightness of Being. Only by fixedly assuming a part is there weight – and this is a lesson for us all. As we assemble our personalities, choosing clothes for the day, gesture, phrases, we are tugged to the earth; the words we speak, actions we perform, fill out flimsy reality. We stop being invisible, we take on colour. Acting holds us back from oblivion. Lightness means the fleeting and unique; heaviness the substantial and the recurrent. The Unbearable Lightness of Being a professional actor, however, is that being-there, on stage or film or tube, dreaming in the dark, giving the spirit expression, is, contrariwise, to make the fleeting seem substantial and the recurrent unique.

Index